CW00518046

THE COMPLETE RESULTS & LINE-UPS OF THE INTERTOTO CUP 2002-2008

Dirk Karsdorp

The Author

Dirk Karsdorp was born on 5th October 1946 in Molenaarsgraaf, the Netherlands.

After high school, he spent several years working as a clerk at a large steel company before switching to IT and he then worked in that business for many years.

Working with computers became a hobby as well as a profession and, after taking early retirement, Dirk continued to use computers along with his iPad. Of course, the internet has now become an almost inexhaustible source of information when it comes to gathering statistical information about soccer.

Dirk's interest in football statistics began in the 1960s when he first collated seasonal summaries of results and began to document team line-ups. As there were no personal computers available in the sixties, all this data was recorded on paper, using a typewriter.

The first information Dirk collated was for the European Champions Clubs' Cup (now the UEFA Champions League) and the European Cup Winners' Cup, soon followed by the Inter-Cities Fairs Cup (which later became the UEFA Cup and is now the UEFA Europa League), as well as the International Football Cup (later called the UEFA Intertoto Cup). After this, other Cups followed including the Mitropa Cup, Latin Cup, Alpen Cup and the Balkan Cup. Dirk also took an interest in the club tournaments of South America and similar club tournaments from Africa, Asia, North and Central America, Arabia and Oceania.

In the era before the internet, most of the data was collected through correspondence with the various football associations and participating clubs. With the arrival of the internet, a new world of information opened up. Furthermore, the contacts Dirk has made with fellow statisticians at home and abroad have made an important contribution both to this book and also to the wide range of other football statistics which he has collated.

The extensive database Dirk has built over the years has been used in several publications by other statisticians. Until now, publishing this data has never been a high priority.

British Library Cataloguing in Publication Data
A catalogue record for this book is available from the British Library

ISBN: 978-1-86223-246-4

Copyright © 2012, SOCCER BOOKS LIMITED (01472 696226)
72 St. Peter's Avenue, Cleethorpes, N.E. Lincolnshire, DN35 8HU, England
Web site www.soccer-books.co.uk   e-mail   info@soccer-books.co.uk

All rights are reserved. No part of this publication may be reproduced, stored in a retrieval system or transmitted, in any form or by any means, electronic, mechanical, photocopying, recording, or otherwise, without the prior written permission of Soccer Books Limited.

Printed in the UK by 4Edge Ltd.

FOREWORD

The *UEFA Intertoto Cup* was a European club tournament played during the summer months which was the idea Ernst B. Thommen (later FIFA vice-president and founder of the Inter-Cities Fairs Cup) and the Austrian coach Karl Rappan. The concept behind the competition was partly as a "Cup for the Cupless" to allow less successful teams to play some European games before their national Leagues had started, but more importantly, to provide some meaningful games to support football betting pools during the summertime. Thommen had set up the football pools in Switzerland in 1932 so it is not surprising that he was so keen to get such a competition up and running!

The first game in the competition was played in 1961 and, as UEFA were not inclined to support the tournament due to its betting background, the competition was named the *International Football Cup*. Initially, teams entering the competition played in a group stage with the winners of each group qualifying for a knock-out tournament leading to a final game. However, by 1967 it had become increasingly difficult to organise many of the games, so it was decided that the knock-out stages and final should be scrapped with the winners of each group instead receiving prize money.

By the time that the 1995 competition began, UEFA had taken the decision to change their stance and therefore officially took over the running of the tournament, changing the format and renaming it the *UEFA Intertoto Cup*. As an incentive for clubs to enter the Intertoto Cup, two winners from the competition were awarded places in the more prestigious UEFA Cup, the number of places available increasing to three the following year.

The UEFA Intertoto Cup continued until 2008 when it was abolished following the major reorganisation of the UEFA club competitions which saw the creation of the Champions League and Europa League from the European Cup and UEFA Cup respectively. Clubs which would formerly have entered the UEFA Intertoto Cup now directly enter the qualifying stages of the UEFA Europa League.

The tournament was open any top-division club who wished to participate, but each had to actively apply for entry. The highest placed club in their domestic league at the end of the season (beneath the clubs who had qualified for the European Cup or UEFA Cup) could enter the competition. However, if the club which was in that position did not apply for the Intertoto Cup, they would not be eligible to compete, the place instead is going to the nearest club below them which did apply.

The 1995 tournament commenced with a group stage of 60 clubs which were divided in 12 groups of 5 clubs each. Much as with other UEFA tournaments, countries were allocated places according to their UEFA coefficients with countries with more successful teams being awarded more entrants. In each group the clubs played two home matches and two away matches and the 12 group-winners and four best runners-up qualified for a knock-out round of 16 teams. In a single knock-out match, the winners qualified for a round of 8 which was also decided by a single match. The final 4 teams played home and away legs against a single opponent in much the same style as a semi-final but the victors of the ties were the joint-winners. In 1995 two clubs from France, FC Girondins de Bordeaux and Racing Club de Strasbourg, became the winners of first UEFA Intertoto Cup and qualified for the UEFA Cup 1995- 96.

As previously mentioned, the success of one of the first winners, FC Girondins de Bordeaux, in reaching the final of the UEFA Cup 1995/96 encouraged the UEFA to add a third UEFA Cup place for competitors in the 1996 UEFA Intertoto Cup.

Many clubs disliked the Intertoto Cup as they saw it as too disruptive in their preparation for the new season and did not nominate themselves for participation even if entitled to do so. In particular, following its 1995 relaunch, English clubs were very sceptical about the competition. After initially being offered three places in the UEFA Intertoto Cup, all the top division English clubs rejected the chance to take part but, following the threat of bans of English clubs from all UEFA tournaments, the situation was eventually resolved with three English clubs entering weakened teams, none of which qualified.

In following years, UEFA made it possible for nations to forfeit Intertoto places. For example, in 1998, Scotland, San Marino and Moldova forfeited all their places and England, Portugal and Greece forfeited one of their two. Crystal Palace FC was the sole English entrant despite finishing bottom of the Premiership. Other clubs built upon their success in the UEFA Intertoto Cup and followed it up with great campaigns in the UEFA Cup tournament.

The format of the 1996 and 1997 tournaments was changed slightly as just the 12 group-winners qualified for a semi-final stage. The 6 ties were decided by a home and an away match with the winners of each qualifying for one of three finals. The three finals were also decided by the aggregate score of home and away legs and the three winners qualified for the UEFA Cup tournament.

The competition continued in this format until 1998 when the group stages were cancelled and it became a straight knock-out tournament, with clubs from more successful countries entering at a later stage. As before, the winners of the three finals qualified for the UEFA Cup tournament, an arrangement which lasted until 2005.

I have endeavoured to make the contents of this book as accurate as possible but often, checking with different sources leads to different information for the same match. In case such as this, I have used what I consider to be the most trustworthy information which I could find.

Dirk Karsdorp

2002

FIRST ROUND

22-06-2002   The Showgrounds, Coleraine: Coleraine FC – UE Sant Julià   5-0 (2-0)
Coleraine FC: David O'HARE, Gerald FLYNN, Stuart CLANACHAN (YC13), Paul
GASTON, Joseph GRAY, Stephen BEATTY (80' Stephen MAGUIRE), Rory HAMILL (75'
Barry CURRAN), Ian McCOOSH, Patrick McALLISTER, Jody TOLAN, Michael McHUGH
(IRL) (70' Sean ARMSTRONG).
UE Sant Julià: Ivan PERIANES (ESP), Francesco Xavier RAMÍREZ Paloma (YC58), Josep
Maria MATAMALA (ESP), Manuel Garcia "TXEMA GARCIA", Santiago BARRANCO,
Oscar SONEJEE Masan, Alex GODOY, Mañuel Jimenez SORIA (YC,YC53), Jordi PUJOL
(ESP) (63' Nuno DE ALMEIDA (POR)), David CODINA (46' Sergio Patricio ROCA Moraga
(CHI)), Armand GODOY.
Goals: Coleraine FC: 1-0 Paul GASTON (17'), 2-0 Michael McHUGH (23'), 3-0 Sean
ARMSTRONG (75'), 4-0 Francesco Xavier RAMÍREZ Paloma (90' own goal), 5-0 Barry
CURRAN (90+').
Referee: Imankhan SULTANI (AZE)

22-06-2002   Gradski Stadion, Skopje: FK Cementarnica 55 – F.H. Hafnarfjördur   1-3 (0-1)
FK Cementarnica 55: Ljupco KMETOVSKI, Dejan DIMITROVSKI, Goran HRISTOVSKI
(66' Borce JAKIMOVSKI (RC90)), Igor MILEVSKI (YC65), Dejan CVETKOVSKI, Dragi
STEFANOVSKI, Vlatko GROZDANOVSKI, Feim BEGANOVIC (YC33), Aleksandar
TOLESKI (46' Goran TRPKOVSKI), Toni JAKIMOVSKI (RC42), Riste NAUMOV.
F.H. Hafnarfjördur: Dadi LÁRUSSON, Magnús Ingi EINARSSON (YC90), Hilmar
BJÖRNSSON, Róbert MAGNÚSSON, Emil HALLFREDSSON (66' Gudmundur
SÆVARSSON), Jóhann Georg MÖLLER, Benedikt Egill ÁRNASON, Baldur BETT, Vaidas
TRAKYS (LIT) (YC60) (75' Sigmundur Pétur ÁSTTHÓRSSON), Heimir GUDJÓNSSON
(82' Vidir LEIFSSON), Jon Thorgrímur STEFÁNSSON.
Goals: FK Cementarnica 55: 1-2 Feim BEGANOVIC (77').
F.H. Hafnarfjördur: 0-1 Vaidas TRAKYS (32'), 0-2 Vaidas TRAKYS (64'), 1-3 Gudmundur
SÆVARSSON (80').
Referee: Alan KELLY (IRL)

22-06-2002   Estádio Municipal "Dr. Magalhães Pessoa", Leiria:
                Uniao Desportiva Leiria – FC Levadia Maardu   1-0 (0-0)
Uniao Desportiva Leiria: Paulo Rebelo COSTINHA Melo Castro (YC41), Luís Miguel BILRO
Pereira, Micael Simão Pedrosa "MICAS" (FRA) (35' Frederico de Castro Roque dos Santos
"FREDDY" (ANG)), RENATO Jorge M.Dias Assunção, TIAGO César Moreira Pereira (68'
António José Ramos Ribeiro "TÓZÉ" (ANG)), Jorge Manuel Rebelo Fernandes "SILAS",
JOÃO MANUEL Loureiro dos Santos (YC44), Augusto Duarte Pinto Maia "LEÃO" (88'
PEDRO Miguel Santos REGUEIRA), JOÃO PAULO Andrade, MACIEL Lima Barbosa da
Cunha (BRA), Roudolphe DOUALA M'Bele (CMR).
FC Levadia Maardu: Artur KOTENKO, Sergei HOHLOV-SIMSON, Andrei KALIMULLIN,
Eduard VINOGRADOV, Dmitri KULIKOV (YC71), Martin MAASING (65' Vladimir
DOLININ), Mark SHVETS (YC30), Maksim RÕTSHKOV, Eduard RATNIKOV (80' Sergiy
CHOPIK (UKR)), Vitali LEITAN, Vladimir TSELNOKOV.
Goal: Uniao Desportiva Leiria: 1-0 Jorge Manuel Rebelo Fernandes "SILAS" (77').
Referee: Sergo KVARATSKHELIA (GEO)
*After it was discovered that Uniao Desportiva Leiria had fielded an ineligible player
(Roudolphe DOUALA M'Bele), UEFA awarded the match to FC Levadia with a 3-0 scoreline.*

7

22-06-2002   Paralimni Municipal Stadium, Paralimni:
Enosis Neon Paralimni FC – SW Bregenz   0-2 (0-1)
Enosis Neon Paralimni FC: Georgios MERTAKKAS, Demosthenis GOUMENOS, Georgios
ALONEFTIS (61' Iacovos ROUSSOS), Costas LOIZOU, Andonis KEZOS (86' Andonis
MOUSHIS), Angelos MISOS, Marios KARAS, Andonis MERTAKKAS (YC73) (75' Nicos
NICOLAOU), Georgios KOLANIS, Goran PETKOFSKI (YUG) (YC47), Georgios
NICOLAOU.
SW Bregenz: Almir TOLJA (BOS), Patrick PIRCHER, Asmir IKANOVIC (BOS) (81' Florian
KARASEK), Lars UNGER (GER), Jirí ROSICKY (CZE), SERKAN Aslan (TUR) (YC72),
Oliver MATTLE (81' Michael MEHLEM), Thomas ELLER (YC73), Peter HLINKA (SVK),
Axel LAWARÉE (BEL) (86' Mario KONRAD), László KLAUSZ (HUN) (YC86).
Goals: SW Bregenz: 0-1 Jirí ROSICKY (24'), 0-2 Axel LAWARÉE (55').
Referee: Nikolai IVANOV (RUS)

22-06-2002   Stadionul Municipal, Tiraspol:
FC Constructorul Cioburciu – 1.FC Synot Staré Mêsto   0-0
FC Constructorul Cioburciu: Alexandru MELENCIUC, Ivan ZABOLOTNII (68' Vladimir
DRAGAN), Alexandru BUDANOV, Radu TALPA, Yuriy BUKEL (UKR), Andriy
PARKHOMENKO (UKR), Eugen CARABULEA, Viorel DINU (ROM), Victor BARÎSEV,
Roman RADCENCO (56' Serghei DADLI), Oleksandr BYCHROV (UKR) (65' Joshua
ONYEACHONAM (NGR)).
1.FC Synot Staré Mêsto: Petr DROBISZ, Pavel NEMCICKY, Velice SUMULIKOSKI
(MCD), Ján PALINEK (YC10), Roman VESELY, Radim KRUPNÍK (63' Tomas MICA),
Alexander HOMER (SVK), Petr SLONCÍK (79' Martin ABRAHAM), Tomas VAJDA, Jiri
KOWALIK (75' Dalibor SLEZÁK), Michal MEDUNA.
Referee: Dimitar DIMITROV (BUL)   Attendance: 1.000

22-06-2002   József Bozsik Stadium, Budapest:
Kispest Honvéd FC – FK Zalgiris Vilnius   0-1 (0-0)
Kispest Honvéd FC: József TÓTH, István TÉGER (ROM), Florin Cornelas Ionel BATRÂNU
(ROM) (YC63), Adám BABOS, Cristian DULCA (ROM) (YC21) (62' Mátyás LÁZÁR),
Antal LÖRINCZ, Norbert NÉMETH (46' Zoltán HERCEGFALVI), Krisztián FÜZI, Jánosz
DUBECZ, Sándor TORGHELLE, Marius SASU (ROM) (72' BORGULYA).
FK Zalgiris Vilnius: Mindaugas MAKSVYTIS, Yauhen ZHUK (BLS), Darius
ARTIOMOVAS (53' Tomas MIKUCKIS), Aliaksandr DAVIDOVICH (BLS), Audrius TOLIS
(YC8), Giedrius BAREVICIUS, Andzej MAKSIMOVIC, Arturas STESKO, Igorius STESKO,
Andrius BRAZAUSKAS (46' Marius KIZYS), Dainius SAULENAS.
Goal: FK Zalgiris Vilnius: 0-1 Dainius SAULENAS (83').
Referee: Sead KULOVIC (BOS)

8

22-06-2002   Espenmoos Stadium, St.Gallen: FC St.Gallen – B68 Toftir   5-1 (2-0)
FC St.Gallen: Oliver STÖCKLI, Carlos CHALLE (ARG), Stefan WOLF, Patrick WINKLER, Daniel IMHOF (CND), Nicola COLACINO (ITA) (73' Jerren NIXON (TRI)), Ivan DAL SANTO, Sascha MÜLLER (YC10) (64' Tranquillo BARNETTA), Pascal JENNY, Ionel Tersinio GANE (ROM) (YC40) (81' Luiz Filho JAIRO (BRA)), Alexander (Alex) TACHIE-MENSAH (GHA).
B68 Toftir: Michal KOKOSZANEK (POL), Øssur HANSEN (YC90), Messias FERREIRA (BRA) (YC29), Oleif JOENSEN (78' Jan PETERSEN), Fródi BENJAMINSEN (YC61), Jann Ingi PETERSEN, Fridin ZISKASSON, Marlon Christiano JORGE (BRA), John Heri DAM (YC68), Arnold JOENSEN, Marcelo MARCOLINO (BRA) (YC32),
Goals: FC St.Gallen: 1-0 Alexander (Alex) TACHIE-MENSAH (9'), 2-0 Ionel Tersinio GANE (42' penalty), 3-0 Daniel IMHOF (56'), 4-1 Alexander (Alex) TACHIE-MENSAH (82' penalty), 5-1 Alexander (Alex) TACHIE-MENSAH (90+').
B68 Toftir: 3-1 Jann Ingi PETERSEN (76').
Referee: Sokol JARECI (ALB)

22-06-2002   Gorodskoj Stadion, Borisov: FC BATE Borisov – Akademisk BK   1-0 (1-0)
FC BATE Borisov: Yuriy ZHEVNOV, Vladimir NIAVINSKI, Gennadiy MARDAS, Alexei BAGA, Dmitri MOLASH, Aleksandr KOBETS, Dmitry LIKHTAROVICH, Ihor CHUMACHENKO (56' Vyacheslav GRYGOROV), Vadim SKRIPCHENKO, Pavel SHMIHERA (63' Aleh STRAKHANOVICH), Artem KONTSEV (49' Yevgeniy LOSHANKOV).
Akademisk BK: Peter LARSEN, Martin "ZAPPA" FROST, Thomas GULPBORG CHRISTENSEN, Klaus LYKKE, Casper "STRUDS" ANDERSEN (YC31), Paymann ALEI, Rasmus GREEN, Jesper SØRENSEN, Mohammed NABATE (84' Thomas KRISTENSEN), Morten Hobel ANDERSSON (59' Allan Krover LARSEN), Andreas POURKAMALI (89' Kim Rory WOOLSEY).
Goal: FC BATE Borisov: 1-0 Artem KONTSEV (10').
Referee: Meir LEVI (ISR)

22-06-2002   Bonchuk Stadium, Dupnitsa: FC Marek Dupnitsa – Caersws FC   2-0 (0-0)
FC Marek Dupnitsa: Armen AMBARZUMYAN, Emil PETKOV, Nikolai ALEXANDROV, Hristo ARANGELOV, Stefan LULCHEV, Veselin VELIKOV (46' Angel STOIKOV), Vladimir YONKOV, Krasimir DIMITROV, Anton EVTIMOV (54' Vladislav VLADOV (YC72)), Ivaylo KIRILOV, Lyubomir LYUBENOV (31' Rumen SHANKULOV).
Caersws FC: Matthew Christian GRIFFITHS, Andrew James Calvin THOMAS, Sean JEHU, Anthony GRIFFITHS (YC43), Hugh David CLARKE, David Rhys WILLIAMS (75' Martyn Roger GRIFFITHS), Mark Ryan HOWELLS (46' Colin REYNOLDS), Derek Robert HAMER, Graham Paul EVANS (84' Andrew MARFELL (ENG)), Graham JONES (YC23), James Andrew DAVIES.
Goals: FC Marek Dupnitsa: 1-0 VladislavVLADOV (65'), 2-0 Vladislav VLADOV (80').
Referee: Luc WILMES (LUX)   Attendance: 3.000

22-06-2002   Hibernians Ground, Paola: Valletta FC – KS Teuta Durrës   1-2 (0-1)
Valletta FC: Ernest BARRY, Nicholas SALIBA, Daniel THEUMA, Rennie FORACE, Jonathan BONDIN (84' Sharlon PACE), Kamil DVORAK (CZE) (YC70,YC90), Karl BONNICI (60' Malzerob OKORO (NGR)), Edward AZZOPARDI (39' Antoine SACCO), Christian LAFERLA, Christopher ORETAN (NGR), Gilbert AGIUS.
KS Teuta Durrës: Orges SHEHI (YC84), Markelian XHA, Arjan ZËRE, Shpetim IMERAJ (YC59), Ervin KOTOMELO (55' Habib REXHEPI (YC63)), Olgerd MUKA, Admir TOSHKALLARI (YC27), Migen MEMELLI (30' Vasjan BALICO), Gentian BEGEJA (70' Justin BESPALLA (YC77)), Armando CUNGU, Dritan BABAMUSTA (YC51,YC79).
Goals: Valletta FC: 1-2 Gilbert AGIUS (82').
KS Teuta Durrës: 0-1 Gentian BEGEJA (10'), 0-2 Shpetim IMERAJ (72').
Referee: José Luís MENGUAL PRADES (AND)

22-06-2002   Stadion Kantrida, Rijeka: NK Rijeka – St.Patrick's Athletic FC   3-2 (0-1)
NK Rijeka: Doni TAFRA, Miroslav WEISS (MCD), Stjepan SKOCIBUSIC, Mladen IVANCIC, Goran VINCETIC, Goran BRAJKOVIC, Mario MESTROVIC (71' Sandro KLIC), Kristijan CAVAL, Blendi SHKEMBI (ALB), Natko RACKI (90' Josip MODRIC), Mate BRAJKOVIC (90' Marin MIKAC).
St.Patrick's Athletic FC: Seamus KELLY, Trevor CROLY, Colm FOLEY, Darragh MAGUIRE, Willie BURKE, Paul OSAM, Paul MARNEY (ENG) (86' Michael HOLT (ENG)), Charles Livingstone MBABAZI (UGA) (54' Paul DONNELLY), Martin RUSSELL, Ger McCARTHY, Robert GRIFFIN.
Goals: NK Rijeka: 1-1 Goran VINCETIC (53'), 2-2 Sandro KLIC (89'), 3-2 Sandro KLIC (90').
St.Patrick's Athletic FC: 0-1 Paul OSAM (44'), 1-2 Ger McCARTHY (77').
Referee: Loizos LOIZOU (CYP)

22-06-2002   Mestský Stadión na Sihoti, Trencin:
              FK Ozeta Dukla Trencin – NK Slaven Belupo   3-1 (2-0)
FK Ozeta Dukla Trencin: Frantisek SMAK, Jan NECAS (CZE) (50' Michal PARASKA), Martin KONECNY, Milan MICENEC (YC60), Ondrej SMELKO, Peter DURIS (83' Tomas MARTAUS), Pavol KOPACKA, Róbert HANKO, Marcel SVRCEK (YC85), Martin FABUS, Marian STAS (51' Milan IVANA).
NK Slaven Belupo: Ivica SOLOMUN, Zdravko MEDJIMOREC, Petar BOSNJAK (YC23), Igor GAL, Dario BRGLES, Roy FERENCINA, Srebrenko POSAVEC (72' Marko JURIC), Danijel RADICEK, Dalibor TUKSER, Miljenko KOVACIC (89' Tomislav FILIPOVIC), Mario DODIK (YC68).
Goals: FK Ozeta Dukla Trencin: 1-0 Martin FABUS (23' penalty), 2-0 Peter DURIS (42'), 3-0 Martin FABUS (74').
NK Slaven Belupo: 3-1 Mario DODIK (76').
Referee: Delce JAKIMOVSKI (MCD)   Attendance: 1.700

22-06-2002   Stadion Letzigrund, Zürich: FC Zürich – NK Brotnjo Citluk   7-0 (2-0)
FC Zürich: Miroslav KÖNIG (SVK), Alain NEF, Wilco HELLINGA (HOL), Stephan
KELLER, Urs FISCHER, Yvan QUENTIN (31' Marc SCHNEIDER), David PALLAS REY
(ESP), Luca JODICE (ITA) (65' Mario RAIMONDI), Ursal YASAR (57' Daniel GYGAX),
Kanga Gauthier AKALE (CIV), Alhassane KEITA (GUI).
NK Brotnjo Citluk: Vladimir MARKOTIC, Mato DADIC, Ante MILICEVIC (48' Josip
CUTUK), Danijel KRIVIC, Kazimir RAGUZ, Andrija SUSAC, Mario RIMAC (26' Dario
GAGRO), Milenko SEVEL (YC63), CVIJANOVIC (65' Rino MEDIC), Milan PECEL, Elvis
CORIC.
Goals: FC Zürich: 1-0 Alhassane KEITA (5'), 2-0 Alhassane KEITA (33'), 3-0 Kanga
Gauthier AKALE (63'), 4-0 Daniel GYGAX (67'), 5-0 Kanga Gauthier AKALE (70'), 6-0
Kanga Gauthier AKALE (72'), 7-0 Kanga Gauthier AKALE (90').
Referee: Augustus Viorel CONSTANTIN (ROM)

22-06-2002   Daknamstadion, Lokeren: KSC Lokeren – FC WIT Georgia Tbilisi   3-1 (2-1)
KSC Lokeren: Sven VAN DER JEUGT, Suvad KATANA, Soley SEYFO (GAM), Mamadou
COULIBALY (CIV), Ibrahima Sory CONTÉ (GUI), Arnar GRÉTARSSON (ISL), Rúnar
KRISTINSSON (ISL), Davy DE BEULE, Alain SYLLA (GUI) (75' Michael VAN HOEY),
Camille MUZINGA, Patrick ZOUNDI BONSDAWENDE (BKF) (46' Okitanyi KIMOTO
(DRC) (YC68)).
FC WIT Georgia Tbilisi: Mirza MERLANI, George KVAKHADZE, Aleksandr
INTSKRIVELI (YC29), Tengiz KOBIASHVILI, Levan MEREBASHVILI (34' Giorgi
PEIKRISHVILI (YC,YC64)), Lasha NOZADZE, David DIGMELASHVILI, David
DOLIDZE, Vladimir GOCHASHVILI (YC44), Giorgi KIPIANI (63' Besik TEPORADZE),
Giorgi ADAMIA (84' Kakhaber TSITSUNAVA).
Goals: KSC Lokeren: 1-0 Patrick ZOUNDI BONSDAWENDE (22'), 2-1 Arnar
GRÉTARSSON (45' penalty), 3-1 Rúnar KRISTINSSON (86').
FC WIT Georgia Tbilisi: 1-1 David DOLIDZE (30' penalty).
Referee: Sinisa ZRNIC (BOS)

22-06-2002   Estádio de São Miguel, Ponta Delgada:
                      CD Santa Clara – FC Shirak Gyumri   2-0 (0-0)
CD Santa Clara: JORGE Soares da SILVA, Carlos Manuel G.Alonso "KALI" (ANG), PEDRO
Ricardo Quintela HENRIQUES , SÉRGIO Manuel Ferreira NUNES, Ivan CortesGarcia
"MINER" (ESP), Marco Paulo PAIVA Rocha, VÍTOR Sérgio C.Barbosa VIEIRA (46'
BRUNO Miguel Fernandes RIBEIRO), Paulo José Lopes FIGUEIREDO (ANG) (46'
GLAEDSON Batista Campos (BRA)), JOÃO PEDRO Fernandes (FRA), Luis Miguel Silva
Tavares "LUIS VOUZELA" (80' LUÍS Miguel Borges SOARES), Ildebrando Dalsoto
"BRANDÃO" (BRA).
FC Shirak Gyumri: Raymond ZADURYAN, MARGARYAN (YC43), Artaches ANTONYAN
(81' Artyom HAKOBYAN), Arman TONOYAN (77' Henrik BADIKYAN (YC90)), Ararat
HARUTYUNYAN, Hovhannes TAHMAZYAN, DAVTYAN, Vardan BICHAKHCHYAN
(66' HAKOBYAN), GRIGORYAN, Karen ALEKSANYAN (YC13), KHACHATRYAN
(YC71).
Goals: CD Santa Clara: 1-0 JOÃO PEDRO Fernandes (57'), 2-0 Ildebrando Dalsoto
"BRANDÃO" (83').
Referee: Anthony ZAMMIT (MLT)

11

23-06-2002   Olympiastadion, Helsingborg: Helsingborgs IF – NK Koper   1-0 (0-0)
Helsingborgs IF: Conny ROSÉN, Mikael GUSTAVSSON, Ola NILSSON (YC45), Marcus
LINDBERG, Christian JÄRDLER, Christoffer ANDERSSON, Ulrik JANSSON, Lars
BAKKERUD (NOR), Martin FRIBROCK, Hans EKLUND (72' Marcus EKENBERG),
ÁLVARO Márcio dos SANTOS (BRA).
NK Koper: Ermin HASIC, Matjaz LUNDER, KAPIC, Andrej POLJSAK, Manuel PERSIC,
Alfred JERMANIS, Nebojsa KOVACEVIC, Vili BECAJ (83' Igor BENEDEJCIC), Mirko
BUNJEVCEVIC (YUG), Romano OBILINOVIC (CRO), Patrik IPAVEC (79' Andrej
TASIC).
Goal: Helsingborgs IF: 1-0 Marcus EKENBERG (84').
Referee: Egill Mar MARKUSSON (ISL)   Attendance: 1.874

23-06-2002   Stadion Zaglebia, Lubin:
              MKS Zaglebie Lubin – FC Dinaburg Daugavpils   1-1 (1-1)
MKS Zaglebie Lubin: Jedrzej KEDZIORA, Nerijus RADZIUS (LIT), Piotr PRZERYWACZ,
Tomasz ROMANIUK (67' Boguslaw LIZAK), Jaroslaw KRZYZANOWSKI, Grzegorz
NICINSKI, Jacek MANUSZEWSKI (84' Robert BUBNOWICZ (YC86)), Ireneusz
KOWALSKI, Krzysztof KAZIMIERCZAK, Zbigniew GRZYBOWSKI, Enkelejd DOBI
(ALB) (76' Alexandr OSIPOVICH (BLS) (YC78)).
FC Dinaburg Daugavpils: Vadim FYODOROV, Vadim LOGINS (46' Yury MOLOTKOV
(YC72)), Yurgis PUCHINSKY, Orest DOROSH (UKR) (YC60), Andrey ZHUROMSKY
(YC72), Dmitry NALIVAIKO, Hennadiy PRIKHODKO (UKR), Andriy CHERNOV (UKR),
Mikhail ZIZILEV, Pavel KOLTSOV (61' Vitaly RYABININ), Erik PELCIS (86' Igor
STASYUK (UKR)).
Goals: MKS Zaglebie Lubin: 1-1 Zbigniew GRZYBOWSKI (31').
FC Dinaburg Daugavpils: 0-1 Erik PELCIS (28').
Referee: Brian LAWLOR (WAL)   Attendance: 300

23-06-2002   Stadion Obilica na Vracaru, Beograd:
              FK Obilic Beograd – FC Haka Valkeakosken   1-2 (0-1)
FK Obilic Beograd: Igor DIMITRIJEVIC, Miroslav SAVIC, Nenad DJORDJEVIC, Ede
VISINKA, Predrag OCOKOLJIC, Bojan ZAJIC, Mirko ALEKSIC (56' Ivan PEJCIC), Sasa
ZIMONJIC, Nenad MLADENOVIC (YC49) (70' Mirko TEODOROVIC), Bojan FILIPOVIC,
Nikola VUJOSEVIC.
FC Haka Valkeakosken: Michal SLAWUTA (POL) (YC60), Lasse KARJALAINEN, Jaakko
PASANEN (54' Jukka KOSKINEN), Jarkko OKKONEN, Juha PASOJA, Harri YLÖNEN,
Juuso KANGASKORPI, Mikko INNANEN, Jukka RUHANEN (59' Tarmo KOIVURANTA),
Jukka RANTALA (YC41), Péter KOVÁCS (HUN) (86' Iiro AALTO).
Goals: FK Obilic Beograd: 1-1 Bojan FILIPOVIC (62' penalty).
FC Haka Valkeakosken: 0-1 Péter KOVÁCS (12'), 1-2 Juuso KANGASKORPI (70').
Referee: Duarte Nuno PEREIRA GOMES (POR)   Attendance: 1.000

12

23-06-2002   Stadionul Gloria, Bistrita: FC Gloria Bistrita – U.S. Luxembourg   2-0 (2-0)
FC Gloria Bistrita: Eugen Catalin ANGHEL (YC81), Sergiu Sebastian MÂNDREAN, Alin
Valer RUS (YC27), Lucian Iulian SANMARTEAN (YC18,RC62), Sergiu Ioan Viorel
COSTIN, Dorin Gheorghe TUTURAS, Adrian Valentin VELCEA (YC44), Christian Florin
DAN, Cristian TURCU (82' Razvan RADU), Sorin Ciprian BUCUROAIA (89' Dinu Daniel
SANMARTEAN), Constantin BÂRSAN (69' Alin Nicu CHIBULCUTEAN). (Coach: Remus
VLAD).
U.S. Luxembourg: Alija BESIC, Laurent PELLEGRINO (FRA) (YC27), Luciano CRAPA
(BEL), Enver KELMENDI (ALB), Fernando GUTIÉRREZ (BEL) (YC71), Mourad LAZAAR
(MAR), Mabrouk DOUSEN (FRA), Enver SABOTIC (YUG) (YC14) (75' Alen MILAK
(YUG)), Rida BOUKHAROUBA (ALG), Carlos TEIXEIRA, Ousmane DERRA (BKF) (46'
Pasquale ANTONICELLI). (Coach: Rachid BELHOUT (ALG)).
Goals: FC Gloria Bistrita: 1-0 Enver SABOTIC (15' own goal), 2-0 Constantin BÂRSAN
(24').
Referee: Paulius MALZINSKAS (LIT)   Attendance: 1.000

23-06-2002   Mestský Stadion na Srbské, Brno:
                    FC Stavo Artikel Brno – FC Ashdod   0-5 (0-2)
FC Stavo Artikel Brno: Lubos PRIBYL (RC34), Ales SCHUSTER, Petr KRIVANEK (YC90),
Roman DRGA, Milos KRSKO (SVK), Martin ZIVNY (61' Michal BELEJ), Petr MUSIL (38'
Peter BREZOVAN goalkeeper), Marek ZUBEK, Milan PACANDA, Libor DOSEK, Marcel
CUPAK (73' Tomas ABRAHAM).
FC Ashdod: Yaniv BEN ISHAY, Yair AZULAY, Blagoje MILEVSKI (MCD), Sharon AMAR
(YC90), Adir TUBUL, Oshri ELFASI, Moshe OHAYON, Alon HAZAN (78' David BITON),
Yaniv AZRAN (71' Yosef OFIR), David REVIVO, Hanan FADIDA (YC42) (75' Hanan
PERETS).
Goals: FC Ashdod: 0-1 Hanan FADIDA (23'), 0-2 Alon HAZAN (38'), 0-3 David REVIVO
(57'), 0-4 Alon HAZAN (68'), 0-5 Moshe OHAYON (90').
Referee: Robert KRAJNC (SLO)   Attendance: 750

29-06-2002   Park Avenue Ground, Aberystwyth:
                    Caersws FC – FC Marek Dupnitsa   1-1 (1-0)
Caersws FC: Matthew Christian GRIFFITHS, Andrew James Calvin THOMAS, Sean JEHU,
Anthony GRIFFITHS, Hugh David CLARKE (YC90), David Rhys WILLIAMS (73' Martyn
Roger GRIFFITHS), Mark Ryan HOWELLS, Andrew MARFELL (ENG) (31' Colin
REYNOLDS), Graham Paul EVANS, Graham JONES (87' Alexandre FLETCHER), Derek
Robert HAMER.
FC Marek Dupnitsa: Armen AMBARZUMYAN, Emil KREMENLIEV, Nikolai
ALEXANDROV (14' Amiran MUDJIRI (GEO)), Hristo ARANGELOV, Stefan LULCHEV,
Veselin VELIKOV (YC42), Krasimir DIMITROV, Todor STOIKOV, Vladimir YONKOV,
Ivaylo KIRILOV (84' Vladislav VLADOV), Rumen SHANKULOV (78' Zhivko
IROBALIEV).
Goals: Caersws FC: 1-0 Graham Paul EVANS (19').
FC Marek Dupnitsa: 1-1 Rumen SHANKULOV (49').
Referee: Ghenadie ORLIC (MOL)   Attendance: 300

13

29-06-2002   Laugardalsvöllur, Reykjavik:
                    F.H. Hafnarfjördur – FK Cementarnica 55   1-2 (1-1)
F.H. Hafnarfjördur: Dadi LÁRUSSON, Magnús Ingi EINARSSON, Hilmar BJÖRNSSON,
Róbert MAGNÚSSON, Benedikt Egill ÁRNASON, Jóhann Georg MÖLLER (64' Jónas Grani
GARDARSSON), Gudmundur SÆVARSSON, Baldur BETT, Vaidas TRAKYS (LIT) (74'
Atli Vidar BJORNSSON), Heimir GUDJÓNSSON (YC30), Jon Thorgrímur STEFÁNSSON
(YC32) (76' Emil SIGURDSSON). (Coach: Sigurdur JÓNSSON).
FK Cementarnica 55: Ljupco KMETOVSKI, Igor MILEVSKI (YC10) (36' Riste NAUMOV),
Goran HRISTOVSKI, Dejan CVETKOVSKI, Dragi STEFANOVSKI, Stole DORDIEV,
Vlatko GROZDANOVSKI, Feim BEGANOVIC, Zanko SAVOV, Esad COLAKOVIC,
Aleksandar TOLESKI (68' Goran TRPKOVSKI).
Goals: F.H. Hafnarfjördur: 1-0 Gudmundur SÆVARSSON (10').
FK Cementarnica 55: 1-1 Aleksandar TOLESKI (24'), 1-2 Riste NAUMOV (52').
Referee: Oleg TIMOFEYEV (EST)

29-06-2002   Stade Achille Hammerel, Luxembourg:
                    U.S. Luxembourg – FC Gloria Bistrita   0-0
U.S. Luxembourg: Alija BESIC, Laurent PELLEGRINO (FRA), Luciano CRAPA (BEL)
(YC50), Enver KELMENDI (ALB), Fernando GUTIÉRREZ (BEL), Mourad LAZAAR
(MAR), Mabrouk DOUSEN (FRA) (11' Pasquale ANTONICELLI (YC44), 75' Laurent
AQUISTAPACE (FRA)), Enver SABOTIC (YUG), Rida BOUKHAROUBA (ALG), Carlos
TEIXEIRA (67' Ousmane DERRA (BKF)), Alen MILAK (YUG). (Coach: Rachid BELHOUT
(ALG)).
FC Gloria Bistrita: Costel CÂMPEANU (YC64), Sergiu Sebastian MÂNDREAN, Sergiu Ioan
Viorel COSTIN, Vasile Nicolae POPA, Alin Valer RUS, Dorin Gheorghe TUTURAS, Alin
Ilie MINTEUAN (YC32) (74' Christian Florin DAN), Cristian Ambrozie COROIAN (83'
Razvan RADU), Adrian Valentin VELCEA (YC62), Sorin Ciprian BUCUROAIA (67'
Constantin BÂRSAN), Cristian TURCU (RC63). (Coach: Remus VLAD).
Referee: Khagani MAMMEDOV (AZE)   Attendance: 350

29-06-2002   Gradski Stadion, Koprivnica:
                    NK Slaven Belupo – FK Ozeta Dukla Trencin   5-0 (3-0)
NK Slaven Belupo: Ivica SOLOMUN, Petar BOSNJAK (YC25), Stipe BOSNJAK, Igor GAL,
Dalibor BOZAC (YC75), Roy FERENCINA, Srebrenko POSAVEC, Domagoj KOSIC (56'
Mario KOVACEVIC), Davor BAJSIC (46' Danijel RADICEK), Miljenko KOVACIC (77'
Goran GERSAK), Mario DODIK.
FK Ozeta Dukla Trencin: Frantisek SMAK, Jan NECAS (CZE), Milan MICENEC (64' Michal
PARASKA (YC86)), Ondrej SMELKO (YC64), Martin KONECNY, Peter DURIS, Pavol
KOPACKA (YC70), Róbert HANKO, Marcel SVRCEK (59' Tomas MARTAUS), Martin
FABUS, Milan IVANA (69' Jozef PLACEK).
Goals: NK Slaven Belupo: 1-0 Domagoj KOSIC (24'), 2-0 Mario DODIK (26'), 3-0 Miljenko
KOVACIC (33'), 4-0 Miljenko KOVACIC (53'), 5-0 Mario DODIK (90').
Referee: Ceri RICHARDS (WAL)   Attendance: 2.500

14

29-06-2002   Stadion Bare, Citluk: NK Brotnjo Citluk – FC Zürich   2-1 (0-0)
NK Brotnjo Citluk: Vladimir MARKOTIC, Danijel KRIVIC, Kazimir RAGUZ, Andrija
SUSAC, Josip CUTUK (YC42) (46' Slaven KORAC), Mario RIMAC (YC34), Igor
IVANKOVIC (46' Mato DADIC), CVIJANOVIC, Milenko SEVEL (YC45), Milan PECEL,
Elvis CORIC (68' Dario KARACIC).
FC Zürich: Miroslav KÖNIG (SVK), Marc SCHNEIDER, Alain NEF, Sébastien
JEANNERET, Wilco HELLINGA (HOL) (59' Kanga Gauthier AKALE (CIV)), Stephan
KELLER, Mario RAIMONDI, Adnan JASARI (46' David PALLAS REY (ESP)), Luca
JODICE (ITA), Daniel GYGAX, Alhassane KEITA (GUI) (57' Ursal YASAR).
Goals: NK Brotnjo Citluk: 1-1 Elvis CORIC (67'), 2-1 Danijel KRIVIC (77').
FC Zürich: 0-1 Alhassane KEITA (50').
Referee: Costas THEODOTOU (CYP)

29-06-2002   Svangaskard, Toftír: B68 Toftir – FC St.Gallen   0-6 (0-3)
B68 Toftir: Michal KOKOSZANEK (POL), Hans Fródi HANSEN, Jan PETERSEN, Messias
FERREIRA (BRA), Oleif JOENSEN (Øssur JACOBSEN), Jann Ingi PETERSEN, Fridin
ZISKASSON (YC46), Marlon Christiano JORGE (BRA) (Bogi PETERSEN), John Heri
DAM, Fródi BENJAMINSEN, Marcelo MARCOLINO (BRA) (61' Arnold JOENSEN).
FC St.Gallen: Oliver STÖCKLI, Stefan WOLF, Patrick WINKLER (YC46), Daniel IMHOF
(CND) (46' Carlos CHALLE (ARG)), Ivan DAL SANTO, Sascha MÜLLER, Jerren NIXON
(TRI), Pascal JENNY (69' Tranquillo BARNETTA), Luiz Filho JAIRO (BRA), Ionel Tersinio
GANE (ROM), Alexander (Alex) TACHIE-MENSAH (GHA) (58' Rainer BIELI).
Goals: FC St.Gallen: 0-1 Alexander TACHIE-MENSAH (5'), 0-2 Ionel Tersinio GANE (14'),
0-3 Daniel IMHOF (40'), 0-4 Rainer BIELI (61'), 0-5 Ionel Tersinio GANE (73'), 0-6 Ionel
Tersinio GANE (85').
Referee: Darius MIEZELIS (LIT)

29-06-2002   Estadi Comunal d'Andorra la Vella, Andorra la Vella:
              UE Sant Julià – Coleraine FC   2-2 (1-1)
UE Sant Julià: Ivan PERIANES (ESP), Francesco Xavier RAMIREZ Paloma (49' Alex
GODOY), Josep Maria MATAMALA (ESP), Manuel Garcia "TXEMA GARCIA" (YC12),
Josep A.MARTINEZ (ESP), Santiago BARRANCO, Oscar SONEJEE Masan, Bertand PETIT
(FRA), Sergio Patricio ROCA Moraga (CHI), Richard IMBERNON RIOS (89' Igansi
LASHERAS), Jordi PUJOL (ESP) (75' Nuno DE ALMEIDA (POR)).
Coleraine FC: David O'HARE, Gerald FLYNN, Stuart CLANACHAN, Paul GASTON,
Gareth McAULEY, Rory HAMILL (YC45) (46' Joseph GRAY (YC63)), Barry CURRAN
(67' Stephen MAGUIRE), Ian McCOOSH, Patrick McALLISTER, Jody TOLAN (70' Sean
ARMSTRONG), Michael McHUGH (IRL).
Goals: UE Sant Julià: 1-1 Bertand PETIT (19' penalty), 2-1 Santiago BARRANCO (65').
Coleraine FC: 0-1 Michael McHUGH (8'), 2-2 Gareth McAULEY (85').
Referee: Levan PANIASHVILI (GEO)

29-06-2002   SRC Bonifika Stadion, Koper: NK Koper – Helsingborgs IF   0-0
NK Koper: Ermin HASIC, Matjaz LUNDER, KAPIC, Andrej POLJSAK, Nebojsa
KOVACEVIC, Mirko BUNJEVCEVIC (YUG), Manuel PERSIC (YC), Vili BECAJ (76' Jaka
STROMAJER), Alfred JERMANIS, Romano OBILINOVIC (CRO), Patrik IPAVEC (67'
Andrej TASIC).
Helsingborgs IF: Conny ROSÉN, Mikael GUSTAVSSON, Marcus LINDBERG, Jozo
MATOVAC, Christian JÄRDLER (YC), Marcus EKENBERG (66' Christoffer
ANDERSSON), Lars BAKKERUD (NOR), Andreas DAHL (66' Ulrik JANSSON), Martin
FRIBROCK (YC), Hans EKLUND (77' John PELU), ÁLVARO Márcio dos SANTOS (BRA).
Referee: Saso LAZAREVSKI (MCD)   Attendance: 2.500

15

29-06-2002   Mestský Futbalový Stadión, Dunajská Streda (SVK):
FC Ashdod – FC Stavo Artikel Brno   1-1 (0-0)
FC Ashdod: Yaniv BEN ISHAY, Yair AZULAY, Blagoje MILEVSKI (MCD), Sharon
AMAR, Adir TUBUL (YC15), Oshri ELFASI, Moshe OHAYON, Alon HAZAN, Yaniv
AZRAN (60' Hanan PERETS (YC77)), David REVIVO, Hanan FADIDA (53' Yosef OFIR).
FC Stavo Artikel Brno: Peter BREZOVAN, Martin KOTÜLEK (YC30), Ales SCHUSTER,
Tomas ABRAHAM (84' Pavel SUSTR), Milos KRSKO (SVK), Petr KRIVANEK, Martin
ZIVNY, Marek ZUBEK, Petr MUSIL (79' Zdenek VALNOHA), Milan PACANDA, Libor
DOSEK (YC85).
Goals: FC Ashdod: 1-0 Hanan PERETS (81').
FC Stavo Artikel Brno: 1-1 Milan PACANDA (88').
Referee: Spiridon PAPADAKOS (GRE)

29-06-2002   Gladsaxe Idrætspark, Søborg: Akademisk BK – FC BATE Borisov   0-2 (0-2)
Akademisk BK: Jan HOFFMANN, Rasmus DAUGAARD HANSEN (YC83), Steen
TRÄGER, Thomas GULPBORG CHRISTENSEN, Casper "STRUDS" ANDERSEN (50'
Nicolai MELCHIORSEN), Andreas POURKAMALI (YC57) (83' David LEDSTRUP),
Rasmus GREEN, Klaus LYKKE (YC85), Mohammed NABATE, Heine FERNANDEZ (68'
Morten Hobel ANDERSSON), Simon Azoulay PEDERSEN.
FC BATE Borisov: Yuriy ZHEVNOV, Alexei BAGA, Gennadiy MARDAS, Valery
TARASENKA, Dmitri MOLASH, Aleksandr KOBETS, Dmitry LIKHTAROVICH (YC84),
Alexandr YERMAKOVICH (48' Yevgeniy LOSHANKOV), Vadim SKRIPCHENKO, Artem
KONTSEV (60' Aleh STRAKHANOVICH), Pavel BIAHANSKI (YC67) (72' Artem
GONCHARUK).
Goals: FC BATE Borisov: 0-1 Artem KONTSEV (34'), 0-2 Pavel BIAHANSKI (42').
Referee: Dejan STANISIC (YUG)   Attendance: 309

29-06-2002   Kadrioru Stadium, Tallinn:
FC Levadia Maardu – Uniao Desportiva Leiria   1-2 (0-0)
FC Levadia Maardu: Artur KOTENKO, Sergei HOHLOV-SIMSON, Andrei KALIMULLIN,
Eduard VINOGRADOV, Dmitri KULIKOV, Eduard RATNIKOV, Maksim RÕTSHKOV
(YC32), Mark SHVETS (78' Vladimir DOLININ), Martin MAASING, Vitali LEITAN,
Vladimir TSELNOKOV (83' Sergiy CHOPIK (UKR)).
Uniao Desportiva Leiria: Paulo Rebelo COSTINHA Melo Castro, Luís Miguel BILRO Pereira,
JOÃO PAULO Andrade, PAULO Jorge Rebelo DUARTE, TIAGO César Moreira Pereira
(YC27), Jorge Manuel Rebelo Fernandes "SILAS", JOÃO MANUEL Loureiro dos Santos,
RENATO Jorge M.Dias Assunção (46' António José Ramos Ribeiro "TÓZÉ" (ANG)),
MACIEL Lima Barbosa da Cunha (BRA) (YC87), Frederico de Castro Roque dos Santos
"FREDDY" (ANG) (85' Micael Simão Pedrosa "MICAS" (FRA)), Roudolphe DOUALA
M'Bele (CMR).
Goals: FC Levadia Maardu: 1-0 Vitali LEITAN (52').
Uniao Desportiva Leiria: 1-1 Roudolphe DOUALA M'Bele (80'), 1-2 Roudolphe DOUALA
M'Bele (82').
Referee: Jari MAISONLAHTI (FIN)

29-06-2002   Casino-Stadion, Bregenz : SW Bregenz – Enosis Neon Paralimni FC   3-1 (1-1)
SW Bregenz: Almir TOLJA (BOS), Patrick PIRCHER (66' Ralph GEIGER), Asmir
IKANOVIC (BOS), Lars UNGER (GER), Jirí ROSICKY (CZE), Oliver MATTLE, Thomas
ELLER, Peter HLINKA (SVK), Enrico KULOVITS (81' SERKAN Aslan (TUR)), Axel
LAWARÉE (BEL), László KLAUSZ (HUN) (28' Mario KONRAD).
Enosis Neon Paralimni FC: Pavel KAMESCH (SVK), Costas LOIZOU, Marios KARAS
(YC21) (89' Andonis MOUSHIS), Angelos MISOS (YC83), Andonis MERTAKKAS (78'
Georgios KARAS), Iacovos ROUSSOS, Georgios ALONEFTIS (YC41) (55' Andonis
KEZOS), Georgios KOLANIS, Demosthenis GOUMENOS, Goran PETKOFSKI (YUG),
Georgios NICOLAOU (YC75).
Goals: SW Bregenz: 1-1 Jirí ROSICKY (22'), 2-1 Axel LAWARÉE (49'), 3-1 Peter HLINKA
(80').
Enosis Neon Paralimni FC: 0-1 Demosthenis GOUMENOS (18').
Referee: Anton GUENOV (BUL)

29-06-2002   Mikheil Meskhi Stadium, Tbilisi:
                FC WIT Georgia Tbilisi – KSC Lokeren   3-2 (1-1)
FC WIT Georgia Tbilisi: Mirza MERLANI, George KVAKHADZE (61' Levan
MEREBASHVILI), Aleksandr INTSKRIVELI (69' Kakhaber TSUTSUNAVA), Tengiz
KOBIASHVILI, Besik TEBORADZE, David DOLIDZE, Giorgi ADAMIA, Lasha
NOZADZE, Giorgi KIPIANI, Vladimir GOCHASHVILI (83' Erekle MEREBASHVILI),
Levan MELKADZE.
KSC Lokeren: Sven VAN DER JEUGT, Ibrahima Sory CONTÉ (GUI), Suvad KATANA,
Patrice ZERE (CIV), Soley SEYFO (GAM), Arnar VIDARSSON (ISL), Alain SYLLA (GUI),
Arnar GRÉTARSSON (ISL) (YC77), Patrick ZOUNDI BONSDAWENDE (BKF) (87'
Michael VAN HOEY (YC90)), Rúnar KRISTINSSON (ISL) (46' Okitanyi KIMOTO (DRC)),
Davy DE BEULE.
Goals: FC WIT Georgia Tbilisi: 1-1 Vladimir GOCHASHVILI (44'), 2-2 Giorgi KIPIANI
(61'), 3-2 Kakhaber TSUTSUNAVA (90').
KSC Lokeren: 0-1 Alain SYLLA (14'), 1-2 Okitanyi KIMOTO (53').
Referee: Michael Thomas ROSS (NIR)   Attendance: 3.000

29-06-2002   Vilniaus Zalgirio Stadionas, Vilnius:
                FK Zalgiris Vilnius – Kispest Honvéd FC   0-0
FK Zalgiris Vilnius: Mindaugas MAKSVYTIS, Yauhen ZHUK (BLS), Darius
ARTIOMOVAS (YC32), Aliaksandr DAVIDOVICH (BLS), Audrius TOLIS, Giedrius
BAREVICIUS, Andzej MAKSIMOVIC, Arturas STESKO, Igorius STESKO (YC79),
Mindaugas GRIGALEVICIUS (26' Gordon OSUSU (NIG), 65' Marius KIZYS), Dainius
SAULENAS (YC83).
Kispest Honvéd FC: József TÓTH, Attila MESZAROS, István TÉGER (ROM) (46' Mátyás
LÁZÁR), Florin Cornelas Ionel BATRÂNU (ROM) (YC16), Adám BABOS (YC72), Antal
LÖRINCZ, Norbert NÉMETH (74' BORGULYA (YC87)), Krisztián FÜZI (YC82), Sándor
TORGHELLE, Marius SASU (ROM) (YC82), Jánosz DUBECZ (YC31).
Referee: Lassin ISAKSEN (FAR)

17

29-06-2002   Qemal Stafa Stadium, Tiranë: KS Teuta Durrës – Valletta FC   0-0
KS Teuta Durrës: Orges SHEHI, Markelian XHA, Arjan ZËRE, Shpetim IMERAJ, Oerd
KOTJA (60' Elidon DEMIRAJ), Ervin KOTOMELO (YC57), Admir TOSHKALLARI (82'
Vasjan BALICO), Olgerd MUKA (YC33), Armando CUNGU, Gentian BEGEJA, Bledar
MANCAKU (85' Justin BESPALLA).
Valletta FC: Sean SULLIVAN, Daniel THEUMA, Darren DEBONO (YC45), Jeffrey
CHETCUTI (YC50), Jonathan BONDIN (80' Jerryton AGIUS), Karl BONNICI (72' Lee
GRIMA), Christian LAFERLA, Rennie FORACE (YC67), Christopher ORETAN (NGR),
Antoine SACCO (56' Sharlon PACE), Gilbert AGIUS.
Referee: Robert JOHNSDORF (LUX)

30-06-2002   Richmond Park, Dublin: St.Patrick's Athletic FC – NK Rijeka   1-0 (1-0)
St.Patrick's Athletic FC: Seamus KELLY, Trevor CROLY, Darragh MAGUIRE, Colm
FOLEY, Willie BURKE, Paul DONNELLY, Paul OSAM, Robert GRIFFIN (52' Anthony
BIRD (WAL)), Martin RUSSELL, Charles Livingstone MBABAZI (UGA) (88' Philip
HUGHES), Ger McCARTHY.
NK Rijeka: Matko KALINIC, Stjepan SKOCIBUSIC, Andre MIJATOVIC, Mladen
IVANCIC, Goran VINCETIC, Goran BRAJKOVIC, Blendi SHKEMBI (ALB) (71' Marin
MIKAC), Mario MESTROVIC (79' Mate BRAJKOVIC), Kristijan CAVAL, Natko RACKI,
Sandro KLIC.
Goal: St.Patrick's Athletic FC: 1-0 Charles Livingstone MBABAZI (22').
Referee: Gevorg HOVHANNISYAN (ARM)

30-06-2002   Stadion Siruch, Staré Mêsto:
                1.FC Synot Staré Mêsto – FC Constructorul Cioburciu   4-0 (0-0)
1.FC Synot Staré Mêsto: Petr DROBISZ, Pavel NEMCICKY, Velice SUMULIKOSKI
(MCD), Ján PALINEK (YC71), Roman VESELY, Alexander HOMER (SVK), Václav
CINCALA (81' Martin ABRAHAM), Radim KRUPNÍK, Tomas VAJDA, Jiri KOWALIK
(61' Dalibor SLEZÁK), Michal MEDUNA (YC35) (75' Tomas MICA).
FC Constructorul Cioburciu: Alexandru MELENCIUC, Radu TALPA, Vladimir DRAGAN,
Alexandru BUDANOV (YC66), Yuriy BUKEL (UKR), Andriy PARKHOMENKO (UKR)
(58' Cristian Mihal IONESCU (ROM)), Eugen CARABULEA, Viorel DINU (ROM) (73'
Serghei DADLI), Victor BARÎSEV, Oleksandr BYCHROV (UKR) (73' Roman
RADCENCO), Joshua ONYEACHONAM (NGR).
Goals: 1.FC Synot Staré Mêsto: 1-0 Michal MEDUNA (46'), 2-0 Ján PALINEK (49'), 3-0
Michal MEDUNA (55'), 4-0 Tomas MICA (86').
Referee: Alojzije SUPRAHA (CRO)   Attendance: 1.529

18

30-06-2002   Municipal Stadium, Gyumri: FC Shirak Gyumri – CD Santa Clara   3-3 (1-3)
FC Shirak Gyumri: Raymond ZADURYAN, MARGARYAN, Arman TONOYAN, Ararat
HARUTYUNYAN, Hovhannes TAHMAZYAN, DAVTYAN, Vardan BICHAKHCHYAN
(75' Andranik BARIKYAN), GRIGORYAN, Karen ALEKSANYAN, Henrik BADIKYAN
(55' HAKOBYAN), KHACHATRYAN (YC44) (55' Artyom HAKOBYAN).
CD Santa Clara: JORGE Soares da SILVA, Carlos Manuel G.Alonso "KALI" (ANG), PEDRO
Ricardo Quintela HENRIQUES, SERGIO Manuel Ferreira NUNES, SANDRO da Cunha
BARBOSA (BRA), Ivan Cortes Garcia "MINER" (ESP), Marco Paulo PAIVA Rocha, VITOR
Sérgio C.Barbosa VIEIRA (46' GEORGE Dos Santos Paladini (BRA), 87' NUNO Alexandre
T.SOCIEDADE), Paulo José Lopes FIGUEIREDO (ANG), JOÃO PEDRO Fernandes (FRA),
Luis Miguel Silva Tavares "LUIS VOUZELA" (YC50) (60' BRUNO Miguel Fernandes
RIBEIRO).
Goals: FC Shirak Gyumri: 1-2 Ararat HARUTYUNYAN (37'), 2-3 Ararat HARUTYUNYAN
(75' penalty), 3-3 Karen ALEKSANYAN (89').
CD Santa Clara: 0-1 JOÃO PEDRO Fernandes (30'), 0-2 JOÃO PEDRO Fernandes (35'), 1-3
JOÃO PEDRO Fernandes (45').
Referee: Oleg CHIKUN (BLS)

30-06-2002   Celtnieks Stadium, Daugavpils:
                     FC Dinaburg Daugavpils – MKS Zaglebie Lubin   1-0 (1-0)
FC Dinaburg Daugavpils: Vadim FYODOROV, Vadim LOGINS (YC17), Yurgis
PUCHINSKY (7' Andriy CHERNOV (UKR)), Orest DOROSH (UKR) (YC56), Andrey
ZHUROMSKY, Dmitry NALIVAIKO, Volodymyr MELNYK (UKR) (70' Pavel KOLTSOV),
Yury MOLOTKOV (YC53), Mikhail ZIZILEV, Zans DERJUGINS, Erik PELCIS (81' Vitaly
RYABININ).
MKS Zaglebie Lubin: Jedrzej KEDZIORA, Robert BUBNOWICZ (69' Nerijus RADZIUS
(LIT)), Piotr PRZERYWACZ, Tomasz ROMANIUK (YC45) (46' Alexandr OSIPOVICH
(BLS)), Jacek MANUSZEWSKI, Grzegorz NICINSKI (YC71), Jaroslaw KRZYZANOWSKI,
Krzysztof KAZIMIERCZAK, Ireneusz KOWALSKI, Enkelejd DOBI (ALB) (78' Boguslaw
LIZAK), Zbigniew GRZYBOWSKI (YC75).
Goal: FC Dinaburg Daugavpils: 1-0 Zans DERJUGINS (9').
Referee: Jaromir HLAVAC (CZE)

30-06-2002   Tehtaan kenttä, Valkeakoski:
                     FC Haka Valkeakosken – FK Obilic Beograd   1-1 (0-1)
FC Haka Valkeakosken: Michal SLAWUTA (POL), Jukka KOSKINEN (58' Iiro AALTO),
Juha PASOJA, Harri YLÖNEN (YC90), Jarkko OKKONEN, Tarmo KOIVURANTA (YC53),
Jukka RUHANEN (59' Péter KOVÁCS (HUN)), Juuso KANGASKORPI (80' Jaakko
PASANEN), Mikko INNANEN, Jukka RANTALA, Valeri POPOVICH (RUS).
FK Obilic Beograd: Igor DIMITRIJEVIC, Nenad DJORDJEVIC, Miroslav SAVIC (65'
Branislav KARIC), Ede VISINKA, Predrag OCOKOLJIC (YC88), Dragan
LJUBISAVLJEVIC (83' Bojan ZAJIC), Mirko ALEKSIC (89' Marko TEPAVCEVIC), Sasa
ZIMONJIC, Mirko TEODOROVIC, Nikola VUJOSEVIC (YC90), Nenad MLADENOVIC.
Goals: FC Haka Valkeakosken: 1-1 Péter KOVÁCS (78').
FK Obilic Beograd: 0-1 Nenad MLADENOVIC (44').
Referee: Roland BECK (LIE)

19

SECOND ROUND

06-07-2002   The Showgrounds, Coleraine: Coleraine FC – ES Troyes AC   1-2 (0-1)
Coleraine FC: David O'HARE, John NEILL, Gerald FLYNN, Stuart CLANACHAN, Paul
GASTON, Gareth McAULEY, Rory HAMILL, Ian McCOOSH, Jody TOLAN, Patrick
McALLISTER (YC52) (85' Stephen MAGUIRE), Michael McHUGH (IRL) (74' Sean
ARMSTRONG).
ES Troyes AC: Tony HEURTEBIS, David HAMED, Sékou BERTHÉ (MLI), Mohamed
BRADJA, Frédéric DANJOU, Gharib AMZINE, Carl TOURENNE, Nick CARLE (AUS) (80'
Nicolas FLORENTIN), Nassim AKROUR (46' Rafik SAÏFI (ALG)), Nicolas GOUSSÉ,
Mamadou NIANG (SEN) (65' Farid GHAZI (ALG)).
Goals: Coleraine FC: 1-1 Ian McCOOSH (49' penalty).
ES Troyes AC: 0-1 Mamadou NIANG (45+'), 1-2 Nicolas GOUSSÉ (69').
Referee: Joseph ATTARD (MLT)

06-07-2002   Craven Cottage, London: Fulham FC – FC Haka Valkeakosken   0-0
Fulham FC: Maik TAYLOR (NIR), Abdeslam OUADDOU (MAR), Andy MELVILLE
(WAL), Alain GOMA (FRA), Jon HARLEY, Sean DAVIS, John COLLINS (SCO), Steed
MALBRANQUE (FRA) (YC61) (79' Bjarne GOLDBÆK (DEN)), Steve MARLET (FRA)
(70' Luís BOA MORTE (POR)), Louis SAHA (FRA), Facundo SAVA (ARG) (69' Barrington
Edward HAYLES (JAM)).
FC Haka Valkeakosken: Michal SLAWUTA (POL), Lasse KARJALAINEN, Juha PASOJA,
Harri YLÖNEN (YC64), Jarkko OKKONEN (YC53), Jukka RUHANEN (69' Tarmo
KOIVURANTA), Mikko INNANEN (78' Ville VÄISÄNEN), Jukka RANTALA (YC30),
Sami Antero RISTILÄ (63' Iiro AALTO), Juuso KANGASKORPI, Péter KOVÁCS (HUN).
Referee: Ladislav GADOSI (SVK)   Attendance: 7.908

06-07-2002   Gradski Stadion, Koprivnica:
               NK Slaven Belupo – CF Os Belenenses   2-0 (1-0)
NK Slaven Belupo: Ivica SOLOMUN, Petar BOSNJAK (YC34,YC90), Stipe BOSNJAK (46'
Pavo CRNAC (YC46)), Igor GAL, Dalibor BOZAC, Davor BAJSIC (79' Zdravko
MEDJIMOREC), Roy FERENCINA (YC71), Danijel RADICEK (YC56) (61' Mario
KOVACEVIC), Domagoj KOSIC, Miljenko KOVACIC, Mario DODIK.
CF Os Belenenses: MARCO AURÉLIO Siqueira (BRA), MARCO PAULO Faria De Lemos,
Luís Carlos FILGUEIRA (BRA), WILSON Constantino Novo Estrela (ANG) (YC90),
CARLOS Miguel Brandão FERNANDES (YC80), ROGERIO Paulo Felisberto Brito, João
Carlos Novo Araújo Gonçalves "TUCK", RUI Pedro Viegas E. Silva Gomes DUARTE (59'
RUI Fernando Nascimento BORGES), Meirival Bezerra "VERONA" (BRA), João Alexandre
Duarte Fernandes "NECA" (75' FRANKLIN Luis Manuel (ANG)), DJALMIR Vieira de
Andrade (BRA) (70' ELISEU Pereira dos Santos).
Goals: NK Slaven Belupo: 1-0 Mario DODIK (25'), 2-0 Miljenko KOVACIC (77').
Referee: Vasily MELNICHUK (UKR)   Attendance: 3.000

06-07-2002   Stadionul Gloria, Bistrita: FC Gloria Bistrita – KS Teuta Durrës   3-0 (2-0)
FC Gloria Bistrita: Costel CÂMPEANU, Sergiu Sebastian MÂNDREAN, Alin Valer RUS, Vasile Nicolae POPA, Sergiu Ioan Viorel COSTIN, Dorin Gheorghe TUTURAS, Alin Ilie MINTEUAN, Cristian Ambrozie COROIAN (YC48) (87' Ioan MISZTI), Horatiu Daniel CIOLOBOC, Sorin Ciprian BUCUROAIA (67' Sandu NEGREAN), Constantin BÂRSAN (76' Ioan Vasile OANA). (Coach: Remus VLAD).
KS Teuta Durrës: Orges SHEHI, Markelian XHA, Arjan ZËRE, Shpetim IMERAJ, Ervin KOTOMELO (78' Elidon DEMIRAJ), Olgerd MUKA, Admir TOSHKALLARI (YC7), Bledar MANCAKU (46' Migen MEMELLI), Gentian BEGEJA, Armando CUNGU, Dritan BABAMUSTA (78' Oerd KOTJA). (Coach: Hasan LIKA).
Goals: FC Gloria Bistrita: 1-0 Cristian Ambrozie COROIAN (6'), 2-0 Constantin BÂRSAN (36'), 3-0 Cristian Ambrozie COROIAN (77' penalty).
Referee: Haim YAACOV (ISR)   Attendance: 800

06-07-2002   Mestský Futbalový Stadión, Dunajská Streda (SVK):
                    FC Ashdod – FC Marek Dupnitsa   1-1 (1-0)
FC Ashdod: Yaniv BEN ISHAY, Amir ELKARIF, Sharon AMAR, Adir TUBUL, Blagoje MILEVSKI (MCD) (YC73), Alon HAZAN (38' Yaniv AZRAN), Oshri ELFASI, David REVIVO, Moshe OHAYON, Hanan FADIDA (65' Andrzej KUBICA (POL)), István PISONT (HUN) (58' Yosef OFIR).
FC Marek Dupnitsa: Armen AMBARZUMYAN, Emil KREMENLIEV, Tsvetelin SHISHKOV (YC66), Hristo ARANGELOV, Stefan LULCHEV, Veselin VELIKOV, Krassimir DIMITROV, Todor STOIKOV, Vladimir YONKOV, Ivaylo KIRILOV (83' Lyubomir LYUBENOV), Rumen SHANKULOV (87' Zhivko IROBALIEV (YC90)).
Goals: FC Ashdod: 1-0 Yaniv AZRAN (42').
FC Marek Dupnitsa: 1-1 Vladimir YONKOV (70').
Referee: Vladimir ANTONOV (MOL)   Attendance: 100

06-07-2002   Metallurg Stadium, Samara:
                    FC Krylya Sovetov Samara – FC Dinaburg Daugavpils   3-0 (1-0)
FC Krylya Sovetov Samara: Olexandr LAVRENTSOV (UKR), Karen DOKHOYAN (ARM), Vladimir SUNEIKO (BLS), Evgeny BUSHMANOV, Patrick OVIE (NGR), Andriy KARYAKA (UKR) (YC71), Vladislav RADIMOV, Denis KOUBA (BLS) (YC9) (73' ROGÉRIO GAÚCHO Márcio Botelho (BRA)), Anton BOBER (73' Robertas RINGYS (LIT)), Serguei VINOGRADOV (46' Viktor BULATOV), Robertas POSKUS (LIT) (YC78).
FC Dinaburg Daugavpils: Vadim FYODOROV, Vadim LOGINS (62' Alexey BORUN), Orest DOROSH (UKR) (YC58), Dmitrijs CUGUNOVS, Andrey ZHUROMSKY, Dmitry NALIVAIKO (YC8), Volodymyr MELNYK (UKR), Yury MOLOTKOV (YC45), Mikhail ZIZILEV, Zans DERJUGINS (40' Pavel KOLTSOV), Erik PELCIS (80' Jurijs SOKOLOVS).
Goals: FC Krylya Sovetov Samara: 1-0 Andriy KARYAKA (38'), 2-0 Robertas POSKUS (72'), 3-0 ROGÉRIO GAÚCHO Márcio Botelho (74').
Referee: Jonas ERIKSSON (SWE)

21

06-07-2002   Willem II Stadion, Tilburg: Willem II Tilburg – FC St.Gallen   1-0 (1-0)
Willem II Tilburg: Geert DE VLIEGER (BEL), Kew JALIENS, Jos VAN NIEUWSTADT, Christiaan JANSSENS (BEL), Joris MATHIJSEN, Denny LANDZAAT, Tom CALUWÉ (BEL) (YC49) (81' Regilio SIMONS), Youssef MARIANA (MAR), Jatto CEESAY (GAM) (62' James Stephen QUINN (NIR)), Tarik SEKTIOUI (MAR) (YC54), Dmitriy SHUKOV (RUS) (66' Raymond VICTORIA).
FC St.Gallen: Oliver STÖCKLI, Carlos CHALLE (ARG), Stefan WOLF, Patrick WINKLER (YC51), Daniel IMHOF (CND) (YC35), Jan BERGER (CZE) (81' Nicola COLACINO (ITA)), Sascha MÜLLER, Pascal JENNY, Tranquillo BARNETTA, Ionel Tersinio GANE (ROM) (64' Luiz Filho JAIRO (BRA)), Alexander TACHIE-MENSAH (GHA) (77' Rainer BIELI).
Goal: Willem II Tilburg: 1-0 Tom CALUWÉ (14').
Referee: Romans LAJUKS (LAT)   Attendance: 2.900

06-07-2002   Stadion Letzigrund, Zürich: FC Zürich – FC Levadia Maardu   1-0 (0-0)
FC Zürich: Miroslav KÖNIG (SVK), Alain NEF (46' Daniel GYGAX, 65' Mario RAIMONDI), Wilco HELLINGA (HOL), Stephan KELLER, Yvan QUENTIN (YC87), Daniel TARONE, Urs FISCHER, Ursal YASAR, Kanga Gauthier AKALE (CIV), David PALLAS REY (ESP), Alhassane KEITA (GUI).
FC Levadia Maardu: Artur KOTENKO, Sergei HOHLOV-SIMSON, Andrei KALIMULLIN, Eduard VINOGRADOV (YC86), Dmitri KULIKOV, Eduard RATNIKOV (61' Arjo ARBEITER (YC68)), Maksim RÕTSHKOV, Mark SHVETS, Martin MAASING, Vladimir TSELNOKOV (75' Sergiy CHOPIK (UKR)), Vitali LEITAN (YC23).
Goal: FC Zürich: 1-0 Daniel TARONE (86' penalty).
Referee: Karen NALBANDYAN (ARM)

06-07-2002   Stade Auguste-Bonal, Montbéliard:
                       FC Sochaux Montbéliard – FK Zalgiris Vilnius   2-0 (1-0)
FC Sochaux Montbéliard: Teddy RICHERT, Maxence FLACHEZ, Nisa SAVELJIC (YUG), Philippe RASCHKE, Sylvain MONSOREAU, Yohann LONFAT (SUI) (69' Fabien BOUDARENE), Adel CHEDLI, Benoît PEDRETTI, Jérémy MATHIEU, Pierre-Alain FRAU (80' Jaouad ZAIRI (MAR)), Basile DE CARVALHO (SEN) (60' Mickaël ISABEY).
FK Zalgiris Vilnius: Mindaugas MAKSVYTIS, Sergejus NOVIKOVAS, Yauhen ZHUK (BLS), Darius ARTIOMOVAS, Aliaksandr DAVIDOVICH (BLS), Arturas SOBOLIS, Giedrius BAREVICIUS, Andzej MAKSIMOVIC, Arturas STESKO, Igorius STESKO, Dainius SAULENAS (83' Marius KIZYS).
Goals: FC Sochaux Montbéliard: 1-0 Sylvain MONSOREAU (24'), 2-0 Pierre-Alain FRAU (55').
Referee: Andrejs SIPAILO (LAT)   Attendance: 7.576

22

06-07-2002   Jules Ottenstadion, Gentbrugge-Gent:
KAA Gent – St.Patrick's Athletic FC   2-0 (1-0)
KAA Gent: Olivier VAN IMPE, Mladen KRIZANOVIC (CRO) (YC15) (46' Ahmed Salah
HOSNY (EGY)), Nenad VANIC (YUG), Morten PEDERSEN (NOR), Ibrahima FAYÉ (SEN),
Günther SCHEPENS, Jimmy HEMPTE, Wim DE DECKER, Nasrédine KRAOUCHE (FRA)
(87' Brecht VERBRUGGHE), Djima OYAWOLÉ (FRA), Alexandros KAKLAMANOS
(GRE).
St.Patrick's Athletic FC: Seamus KELLY, Trevor CROLY, Darragh MAGUIRE, Colm
FOLEY, Willie BURKE, Paul DONNELLY, Paul OSAM, Charles Livingstone MBABAZI
(UGA) (77' Philip HUGHES), Martin RUSSELL, Anthony BIRD (WAL), Ger McCARTHY.
Goals: KAA Gent: 1-0 Alexandros KAKLAMANOS (1'), 2-0 Alexandros KAKLAMANOS
(66').
Referee: Jaroslav JARA (CZE)   Attendance: 2.937

06-07-2002   Estadio El Madrigal, Villarreal: Villarreal CF – F.H. Hafnarfjördur   2-0 (1-0)
Villarreal CF: Javier LÓPEZ VALLEJO, Jesús GALVÁN Carrillo (YC22) (84' Javier "JAVI"
Rodríguez VENTA), UNAI Vergara Diaz Caballero, Enrique "QUIQUE" ÁLVAREZ San
Juan, Rodolfo Martín ARRUABARRENA (ARG) (YC44), JORGE LÓPEZ Montaña,
Constantin GÂLCA (ROM), Antonio GUAYRE Betancur Perdomo (75' Héctor FONT
Romero (YC84)), VÍCTOR Manuel Fernández Gutiérrez, Javier CALLEJA Revilla (68' Carlos
Reina ARANDA), Martín PALERMO (ARG). (Coach: Víctor MUÑOZ Manrique).
F.H. Hafnarfjördur: Dadi LÁRUSSON, Magnús Ingi EINARSSON, Hilmar BJÖRNSSON,
Róbert MAGNÚSSON, Benedikt Egill ÁRNASON, Ásgeir Gunnar ÁSGEIRSSON,
Gudmundur SÆVARSSON, Calum Thór BETT, Vaidas TRAKYS (LIT) (78' Jóhann Georg
MÖLLER), Heimir GUDJÓNSSON (YC24), Jon Thorgrímur STEFÁNSSON. (Coach:
Sigurdur JÓNSSON).
Goals: Villarreal CF: 1-0 VICTOR Manuel Fernández Gutiérrez (31'), 2-0 Jesús GALVÁN
Carrillo (64').
Referee: Edgar Sorin ALTMAYER (ROM)   Attendance: 7.000

07-07-2002   Stadion Siruch, Staré Mêsto:
1.FC Synot Staré Mêsto – Helsingborgs IF   4-0 (2-0)
1.FC Synot Staré Mêsto: Petr DROBISZ, Velice SUMULIKOSKI (MCD), Ján PALINEK,
Roman VESELY, Martin ABRAHAM (75' Tomas MICA), Václav CINCALA (82' Tomas
POLACH), Petr SLONCÏK (YC63), Marek SEMAN (SVK), Tomas VAJDA, Jiri KOWALÍK ,
Michal MEDUNA (68' Dalibor SLEZÁK).
Helsingborgs IF: Conny ROSÉN, Mikael GUSTAVSSON, Ola NILSSON, Marcus
LINDBERG, Christian JÄRDLER (YC7), Christoffer ANDERSSON, Andreas DAHL (65'
Eldin KARISIK), Lars BAKKERUD (NOR) (46' Jesper JANSSON), Mattias LINDSTRÖM,
Marcus EKENBERG (70' Hans EKLUND), ÁLVARO Márcio dos SANTOS (BRA).
Goals: 1.FC Synot Staré Mêsto: 1-0 Jiri KOWALÍK (3'), 2-0 Michal MEDUNA (13'), 3-0 Jiri
KOWALÍK (78'), 4-0 Václav CINCALA (80').
Referee: Miroslav RYSZKA (POL)   Attendance: 2.037

23

07-07-2002   Mestský Stadion, Litomerice: FK Teplice – CD Santa Clara 5-1 (1-0)
FK Teplice: Radomir HAVEL, Vladimir LEITNER (SVK) (73' Martin SIGMUND), Zdenko
FRTALA (SVK), Patrik GROSS, Roman LENGYEL, Pavel HORVÁTH, Dusan TESARIK,
Petr VORISEK (YC62), Michal DOLEZAL, Ludek ZELENKA (60' Pavel VERBÍR), Radek
DIVECKY (86' Jan REZEK).
CD Santa Clara: JORGE Soares da SILVA, Carlos Manuel G.Alonso "KALI" (ANG), PEDRO
Ricardo Quintela HENRIQUES, SÉRGIO Manuel Ferreira NUNES (YC77), SANDRO da
Cunha BARBOSA (BRA), Ivan Cortes Garcia "MINER" (ESP), Marco Paulo PAIVA Rocha,
Paulo José Lopes FIGUEIREDO (ANG), BRUNO Miguel Fernandes RIBEIRO (71'
Ildebrando Dalsoto "BRANDÃO" (BRA)), JOÃO PEDRO Fernandes (FRA), Luis Miguel
Silva Tavares "LUIS VOUZELA" (46' Gábor VAYER (HUN)).
Goals: FK Teplice: 1-0 Patrik GROSS (10'), 2-0 Radek DIVECKY (65'), 3-0 Radek
DIVECKY (67'), 4-0 Vladimir LEITNER (71'), 5-1 Pavel VERBÍR (87').
CD Santa Clara: 4-1 JOÃO PEDRO Fernandes (82').
Referee: Attila ABRAHAM (HUN)   Attendance: 2.219

07-07-2002   Stadio delle Alpi, Torino: AC Torino – SW Bregenz 1-0 (1-0)
AC Torino: Luca BUCCI, Luigi GARZYA (18' Vincenzo SOMMESE (YC59), 81' José María
FRANCO RAMALLO (URU)), Fabio GALANTE (YC57), Paolo CASTELLINI, Stefano
FATTORI (YC84), Daniele DELLI CARRI, Alessio SCARCHILLI (71' Luca MEZZANO),
Simone VERGASSOLA, Diego DE ASCENTIS, Cristiano LUCARELLI, Marco FERRANTE.
SW Bregenz: Almir TOLJA (BOS), Patrick PIRCHER, Asmir IKANOVIC (BOS), Lars
UNGER (GER) (34' Ralph GEIGER (YC61)), Jirí ROSICKY (CZE), Oliver MATTLE (77'
Michael MEHLEM), Thomas ELLER (61' Oliver NZUZI POLO (CON)), Jan Ové
PEDERSEN (NOR), Peter HLINKA (SVK), Enrico KULOVITS, Axel LAWARÉE (BEL).
Goal: AC Torino: 1-0 Marco FERRANTE (19').
Referee: Espen BERNTSEN (NOR)

07-07-2002   Grünwalder Stadion, München:
                  TSV 1860 München – FC BATE Borisov 0-1 (0-0)
TSV 1860 München: Simon JENTZSCH, Martin STRANZL (AUT) (YC63), Remo MEYER
(SUI), Marco KURZ (53' Daniel BORIMIROV (BUL)), Harald CERNY (AUT) (46' Michael
WIESINGER), Rodrigo COSTA (BRA) (YC61), Markus WEISSENBERGER (AUT), Danny
SCHWARZ, Roman TYCE (CZE), Martin MAX, Paul AGOSTINO (ITA) (71' Markus
SCHROTH).
FC BATE Borisov: Yuriy ZHEVNOV, Gennadiy MARDAS, Alexei BAGA, Valery
TARASENKA, Dmitri MOLASH (YC76), Aleksandr KOBETS, Alexandr YERMAKOVICH,
Dmitry LIKHTAROVICH (YC67), Vadim SKRIPCHENKO, Yevgeniy LOSHANKOV (72'
Pavel SHMIHERA), Pavel BIAHANSKI (7' Artem KONTSEV, 84' Sergei MIRONCHYUK).
Goal: FC BATE Borisov: 0-1 Artem KONTSEV (74').
Referee: Ali AYDIN (TUR)   Attendance: 13.500

24

07-07-2002   Gottlieb-Daimler-Stadion, Stuttgart: VfB Stuttgart – KSC Lokeren   2-0 (1-0)
VfB Stuttgart: Timo HILDEBRAND, RUI Manuel MARQUES (POR), Fernando MEIRA
(POR), Marcelo José BORDON (BRA), Heiko GERBER, Aleksandr HLEB (BLS) (46' Jens
TODT), Silvio MEIßNER, Ioannis AMANATIDIS (GRE) (46' Christian TIFFERT, 68'
Ferreira de Camargo Neto ADHEMAR (BRA)), Krasimir Guenchev BALAKOV (BUL),
Jochen SEITZ, Sean DUNDEE.
KSC Lokeren: Sven VAN DER JEUGT, Ibrahima Sory CONTÉ (GUI), Suvad KATANA,
Soley SEYFO (GAM), Arnar VIDARSSON (ISL), Alain SYLLA (GUI) (60' Okitanyi
KIMOTO (DRC)), Camille MUZINGA, Arnar GRÉTARSSON (ISL), Dany DE BEULE,
Patrick ZOUNDI BONSDAWENDE (BKF) (85' Bureima MAIGA (BKF)), Rúnar
KRISTINSSON (ISL).
Goals: VfB Stuttgart: 1-0 Jochen SEITZ (8'), 2-0 Sean DUNDEE (54').
Referee: Carlo BERTOLINI (SUI)   Attendance: 5.500

13-07-2002   Kaplakrikavöllur, Hafnarfjördur: F.H. Hafnarfjördur – Villarreal CF   2-2 (1-1)
F.H. Hafnarfjördur: Dadi LÁRUSSON, Magnús Ingi EINARSSON, Hilmar BJÖRNSSON,
Freyr BJARNASON, Gudmundur SÆVARSSON, Ásgeir Gunnar ÁSGEIRSSON (YC32),
Benedikt ARNASON, Baldur BETT, Vaidas TRAKYS (LIT) (YC7) (80' Sigmundur Pétur
ÁSTTHORSSON), Jónas Grani GARDARSSON (89' Vidir LEIFSSON (YC90)), Jon
Thorgrímur STEFÁNSSON (86' Emil SIGURDSSON). (Coach: Sigurdur JÓNSSON).
Villarreal CF: José Manuel REINA Paez, Jesús GALVÁN Carrillo (YC39) (73' Javier "JAVI"
Rodríguez VENTA), Enrique "QUIQUE" ÁLVAREZ San Juan, UNAI Vergara Diaz Caballero
(YC81), Rodolfo Martín ARRUABARRENA (ARG), Antonio GUAYRE Betancur perdomo,
Constantin GÂLCA (ROM), JORGE LÓPEZ Montaña (YC45) (62' Francisco Xavier "XAVI"
GRACIA Carlos), Javier CALLEJA Revilla, VÍCTOR Manuel Fernández Gutiérrez (62'
Carlos Reina ARANDA), Martín PALERMO (ARG). (Coach: Víctor MUÑOZ Manrique).
Goals: F.H. Hafnarfjördur: 1-0 Benedikt ARNASON (11'), 2-1 Baldur BETT (67').
Villarreal CF: 1-1 JORGE LÓPEZ Montaña (28'), 2-2 Constantin GÂLCA (81').
Referee: Gerald LEHNER (AUT)   Attendance: 500

13-07-2002   Bonchuk Stadium, Dupnitsa: FC Marek Dupnitsa – FC Ashdod   1-0 (1-0)
FC Marek Dupnitsa: Armen AMBARZUMYAN, Emil KREMENLIEV, Vladimir YONKOV
(YC71), Hristo ARANGELOV, Stefan LULCHEV, Veselin VELIKOV (YC87), Krasimir
DIMITROV, Angel STOIKOV (YC52) (85' Nikolai ALEXANDROV), Ivaylo KIRILOV (63'
Tsvetelin SHISHKOV), Amiran MUDJIRI (GEO), Rumen SHANKULOV (YC74) (89'
Vladislav VLADOV).
FC Ashdod: Yaniv BEN ISHAY, Amir ELKARIF (YC47), Adir TUBUL, Sharon AMAR,
Blagoje MILEVSKI (MCD) (YC70), Yosef OFIR (YC32), David REVIVO (79' Yair
AZULAY (YC88)), Oshri ELFASI (46' David BITON (YC78)), Moshe OHAYON (73' Yaniv
OFIR (YC86)), Hanan FADIDA, István PISONT (HUN).
Goal: FC Marek Dupnitsa: 1-0 Rumen SHANKULOV (10').
Referee: Muhittin BOSAT (TUR)   Attendance: 3.000

25

13-07-2002   Estádio de São Miguel, Ponta Delgada:
CD Santa Clara – FK Teplice   1-4 (0-2)
CD Santa Clara: JORGE Soares da SILVA, Carlos Manuel G.Alonso "KALI" (ANG) (28'
LUÍS Miguel Borges SOARES), PEDRO Ricardo Quintela HENRIQUES, SÉRGIO Manuel
Ferreira NUNES, SANDRO da Cunha BARBOSA (BRA), Marco Paulo PAIVA Rocha, Paulo
Jose L.FIGUEIREDO (46' Ivan Cortes Garcia "MINER" (ESP)), BRUNO Miguel Fernandes
RIBEIRO, GEORGE Dos Santos Paladini (BRA) (46' Gábor VAYER (HUN)), JOÃO PEDRO
Fernandes (FRA), Luis Miguel Silva Tavares "LUIS VOUZELA".
FK Teplice: Radomir HAVEL, Zdenko FRTALA (SVK), Patrik GROSS, Roman LENGYEL,
Pavel HORVÁTH, Dusan TESARIK (YC51), Jirí SKÁLA (70' Vlastimil RYSKA), Petr
VORISEK, Michal DOLEZAL, Ludek ZELENKA (76' Martin SIGMUND), Radek
DIVECKY (79' Pavel VERBÏR).
Goals: CD Santa Clara: 1-2 JOÃO PEDRO Fernandes (48').
FK Teplice: 0-1 Ludek ZELENKA (27'), 0-2 Michal DOLEZAL (29'), 1-3 Pavel HORVÁTH
(72' penalty), 1-4 Vlastimil RYSKA (81').
Referee: Ben H.HAVERKORT (HOL)   Attendance: 700

13-07-2002   Kadrioru Stadium, Tallinn: FC Levadia Maardu – FC Zürich   0-0
FC Levadia Maardu: Artur KOTENKO, Andrei KALIMULLIN, Eduard VINOGRADOV (87'
Sergiy CHOPIK (UKR)), Sergei HOHLOV-SIMSON, Martin MAASING (61' Arjo
ARBEITER), Dmitri KULIKOV, Oleg GORJATSHOV (73' Vladimir TSELNOKOV),
NAHK, Maksim RÕTSHKOV, Mark SHVETS, Vitali LEITAN.
FC Zürich: Miroslav KÖNIG (SVK), Tariq CHIHAB (MAR) (YC53), Alain NEF (65' Daniel
TARONE), Wilco HELLINGA (HOL), Stephan KELLER (YC38), Urs FISCHER, Yvan
QUENTIN, Luca JODICE (ITA), Ursal YASAR (46' Mario RAIMONDI), Kanga Gauthier
AKALE (CIV) (84' Marc SCHNEIDER), Alhassane KEITA (GUI).
Referee: Drago KOS (SLO)

13-07-2002   Espenmoos Stadium, St.Gallen: FC St.Gallen – Willem II Tilburg   1-1 (0-0)
FC St.Gallen: Oliver STÖCKLI, Stefan WOLF, Oscar TATO (ESP), Patrick WINKLER,
Sascha MÜLLER (15' Nicola COLACINO (ITA)), Pascal JENNY, Jan BERGER (CZE), Luiz
Filho JAIRO (BRA) (55' GUIDO Alves Neto (BRA) (YC85)), Tranquillo BARNETTA,
Rainer BIELI (70' Jerren NIXON (TRI)), Alexander TACHIE-MENSAH (GHA).
Willem II Tilburg: Geert DE VLIEGER (BEL), Kew JALIENS (YC84), Jos VAN
NIEUWSTADT, Christiaan JANSSENS (BEL), Joris MATHIJSEN, Denny LANDZAAT,
Tom CALUWÉ (BEL) (46' Regilio SIMONS), Youssef MARIANA (MAR) (YC61), Jatto
CEESAY (GAM) (66' Raymond VICTORIA (YC75)), Tarik SEKTIOUI (MAR), Dmitriy
SHUKOV (RUS) (82' James Stephen QUINN (NIR) (YC98)).
Goals: FC St.Gallen: 1-0 Jerren NIXON (90+').
Willem II Tilburg: 1-1 Youssef MARIANA (112').
Referee: Martin HANSSON (SWE)   Attendance: 2.400
(After extra time)

13-07-2002   Stade de l'Abbé Deschamps, Auxerre:
ES Troyes AC – Coleraine FC   2-1 (0-0)
ES Troyes AC: Tony HEURTEBIS, David HAMED, Sékou BERTHÉ (MLI), Mohamed
BRADJA, Frédéric DANJOU, Gharib AMZINE (56' Benjamin NIVET), Carl TOURENNE
(YC90), Mehdi LEROY, Rafik SAÏFI (ALG) (76' Ibrahima BANGOURA (GUI)), Nicolas
GOUSSÉ, Mamadou NIANG (SEN) (56' Farid GHAZI (ALG) (YC59)).
Coleraine FC: David O'HARE, John NEILL (YC59), Gerald FLYNN, Stuart CLANACHAN
(YC90), Paul GASTON, Gareth McAULEY, Rory HAMILL (38' Barry CURRAN), Ian
McCOOSH (YC63), Jody TOLAN (YC27) (79' Stephen MAGUIRE), Patrick McALLISTER
(YC73), Michael McHUGH (IRL) (84' Sean ARMSTRONG).
Goals: ES Troyes AC: 1-1 Nicolas GOUSSÉ (62'), 2-1 Farid GHAZI (64').
Coleraine FC: 0-1 Jody TOLAN (53').
Referee: Yuri KLIUCHNIKOV (RUS)

13-07-2002   Casino-Stadion, Bregenz : SW Bregenz – AC Torino   1-1 (1-0)
SW Bregenz: Almir TOLJA (BOS), Patrick PIRCHER, Asmir IKANOVIC (BOS), Jirí
ROSICKY (CZE), Oliver MATTLE, Michael MEHLEM, Oliver NZUZI POLO (CON) (66'
Alexander HAUSER), Jan Ové PEDERSEN (NOR), Peter HLINKA (SVK) (72' SERKAN
Aslan (TUR)), Axel LAWARÉE (BEL) (46' Mario KONRAD), László KLAUSZ (HUN).
AC Torino: Luca BUCCI, Fabio GALANTE, Paolo CASTELLINI, Stefano FATTORI,
Gianluca COMOTTO (82' Luca MEZZANO), Daniele DELLI CARRI (YC16), Alessio
SCARCHILLI (75' Vincenzo SOMMESE), Simone VERGASSOLA, Diego DE ASCENTIS,
Cristiano LUCARELLI, Marco FERRANTE (88' Yksel OSMANOVSKI (SWE)).
Goals: SW Bregenz: 1-0 László KLAUSZ (6').
AC Torino: 1-1 Cristiano LUCARELLI (47').
Referee: Igorj ISHCHENKO (UKR)

13-07-2002   Qemal Stafa Stadium, Tiranë: KS Teuta Durrës – FC Gloria Bistrita 1-0 (0-0)
KS Teuta Durrës: Orges SHEHI, Markelian XHA, Arjan ZËRE, Shpetim IMERAJ, Ervin
KOTOMELO, Olgerd MUKA (82' Vasjan BALLCO), Migen MEMELLI, Bledar MANCAKU
(73' Justin BESPALLA (YC80)), Gentian BEGEJA (YC65), Armando CUNGU, Aritan
BABAMUSTA (68' Oerd KOTJA). (Coach: Hasan LIKA).
FC Gloria Bistrita: Costel CÂMPEANU, Ioan MISZTI (79' Ioan LUCA), Sergiu Ioan Viorel
COSTIN, Vasile Nicolae POPA, Alin Valer RUS, Sorin Ciprian BUCUROAIA, Alin Ilie
MINTEUAN, Cristian Ambrozie COROIAN (74' Adrian Valentin VELCEA), Lucian Iulian
SÂNMARTEAN (27' Sandu NEGREAN), Horatiu Daniel CIOLOBOC, Constantin BÂRSAN.
(Coach: Remus VLAD).
Goal: KS Teuta Durrës: 1-0 Gentian BEGEJA (53').
Referee: Zbigniew MARCZYK (POL)

13-07-2002   Celtnieks Stadium, Daugavpils:
FC Dinaburg Daugavpils – FC Krylya Sovetov Samara   0-1 (0-1)
FC Dinaburg Daugavpils: Vadim FYODOROV, Vadim LOGINS, Jurijs SOKOLOVS (74'
Milan STRELEC (SVK)), Dmitrijs CUGUNOVS, Andrey ZHUROMSKY, Dmitry
NALIVAIKO, Volodymyr MELNYK (UKR) (86' Aleksandrs SUMILOVS), Mikhail
ZIZILEV, Pavel KOLTSOV (88' Dmitry KOHAN), Zans DERJUGINS, Erik PELCIS.
FC Krylya Sovetov Samara: Olexandr LAVRENTSOV (UKR), Karen DOKHOYAN (ARM),
Vladimir SUNEIKO (BLS), Evgeny BUSHMANOV, Patrick OVIE (NGR), Andriy
KARYAKA (UKR), Vladislav RADIMOV, Denis KOUBA (BLS) (27' ROGÉRIO GAÚCHO
Márcio Botelho (BRA)), Anton BOBER (46' Robertas RINGYS (LIT)), Viktor BULATOV,
Robertas POSKUS (LIT) (57' Serguei VINOGRADOV).
Goal: FC Krylya Sovetov Samra: 0-1 Anton BOBER (24').
Referee: Gylfi Thor ORRASON (ISL)

13-07-2002   Richmond Park, Dublin: St.Patrick's Athletic FC – KAA Gent   3-1 (0-0)
St.Patrick's Athletic FC: Seamus KELLY, Trevor CROLY, Willie BURKE (80' Michael
HOLT (ENG)), Paul DONNELLY, Darragh MAGUIRE (YC), Colm FOLEY, Paul OSAM,
Martin RUSSELL (88' Jamie HARRIS (WAL)), Ger McCARTHY, Charles Livingstone
MBABAZI (UGA) (YC), Anthony BIRD (WAL) (77' Philip HUGHES).
KAA Gent: Olivier VAN IMPE, Dries BERNAERT (90' David VAN HOYWEGHEN),
Ibrahima FAYÉ (SEN), Jimmy HEMPTE, Ahmed Salah HOSNY (EGY), Nasrédine
KRAOUCHE (FRA) (73' Mladen KRIZANOVIC (CRO) (YC15)), Djima OYAWOLÉ (FRA),
Morten PEDERSEN (NOR), Nenad VANIC (YUG), Brecht VERBRUGGHE (73' Patrick
DIMBALA), Wim DE DECKER.
Goals: St.Patrick's Athletic FC: 1-0 Ger McCARTHY (48'), 2-0 Charles Livingstone
MBABAZI (59'), 3-1 Paul OSAM (89').
KAA Gent: 2-1 Ahmed Salah HOSNY (76').
Referee: Josef KACENGA (SVK)   Attendance: 3.500

13-07-2002   Daknamstadion, Lokeren: KSC Lokeren – VfB Stuttgart   0-1 (0-0)
KSC Lokeren: Mladen DABANOVIC (SLO), Ibrahima Sory CONTÉ (GUI), Soley SEYFO
(GAM), Suvad KATANA, Arnar VIDARSSON (ISL) (YC84), Alain SYLLA (GUI), Rúnar
KRISTINSSON (ISL) (YC44), Arnar GRÉTARSSON (ISL), Davy DE BEULE, Patrick
ZOUNDI BONSDAWENDE (BKF) (40' Okitanyi KIMOTO (DRC)), Sambegon
BANGOURA (GUI).
VfB Stuttgart: Timo HILDEBRAND, RUI Manuel MARQUES (POR) (84' Timo WENZEL),
Fernando MEIRA (POR) (YC35), Marcelo José BORDON (BRA), Heiko GERBER, Andreas
HINKEL (65' Christian TIFFERT), Jochen SEITZ (YC44), Aleksandr HLEB (BLS) (YC68),
Krasimir Guenchev BALAKOV (BUL), Silvio MEIßNER (46' Jens TODT), Ioan Viorel
GANEA (ROM) (YC71).
Goal: VfB Stuttgart: 0-1 Aleksandr HLEB (88').
Referee: Zsolt SZABO (HUN)   Attendance: 2.500

14-07-2002   Estádio José Alvalade, Lisboa:
CF Os Belenenses – NK Slaven Belupo   0-1 (0-0)
CF Os Belenenses: MARCO AURÉLIO Siqueira (BRA), MARCO PAULO Faria de Lemos, Luís Carlos FILGUEIRA (BRA) (YC79), WILSON Constantino Novo Estrela (ANG), CARLOS Miguel Brandão FERNANDES, ROGERIO Paulo Felisberto Brito (73' FRANKLIN Luis Manuel (ANG)), João Carlos Novo Araújo Gonçalves "TUCK", RUI Pedro Viegas E. Silva Gomes DUARTE (46' RUI Fernando Nascimento BORGES), Meirival Bezerra "VERONA" (BRA), João Alexandre Duarte Fernandes "NECA" (61' Hélio Armando Pereira NETO), DJALMIR Vieira de Andrade (BRA).
NK Slaven Belupo: Ivica SOLOMUN, Pavo CRNAC, Dalibor BOZAC, Danijel RADICEK, Domagoj KOSIC (67' Marko JURIC), Davor BAJSIC (46' Srebrenko POSAVEC), Igor GAL (RC75), Roy FERENCINA (YC49), Miljenko KOVACIC, Mario KOVACEVIC (YC11) (54' Zdravko MEDJIMOREC), Mario DODIK.
Goal: NK Slaven Belupo: 0-1 Mario DODIK (52').
Referee: Hubert BYRNE (IRL)

14-07-2002   Olympiastadion, Helsingborg:
Helsingborgs IF – 1.FC Synot Staré Mêsto   2-0 (1-0)
Helsingborgs IF: Conny ROSÉN, Mikael GUSTAVSSON, Ola NILSSON, Marcus LINDBERG (YC66), Fredrik ELGSTRÖM, Christoffer ANDERSSON (56' Christian JÄRDLER), Andreas DAHL, Mattias LINDSTRÖM, Martin FRIBROCK (YC41) (69' Eldin KARISIK), Hans EKLUND (YC16) (60' Marcus EKENBERG), ÁLVARO Márcio dos SANTOS (BRA).
1.FC Synot Staré Mêsto: Petr DROBISZ (YC72), Velice SUMULIKOSKI (MCD), Ján PALINEK (46' Rastislav KOSTKA (SVK)), Roman VESELY, Martin ABRAHAM, Václav CINCALA (80' Tomas POLACH (YC81)), Petr SLONCÏK, Marek SEMAN (SVK) (YC28), Tomas VAJDA (YC25), Jiri KOWALIK (87' Dalibor SLEZÁK), Michal MEDUNA (YC90).
Goals: Helsingborgs IF: 1-0 Andreas DAHL (45+'), 2-0 Christian JÄRDLER (66').
Referee: Sten KALDMA (EST)   Attendance: 997

14-07-2002   Gorodskoj Stadion, Borisov:
FC BATE Borisov – TSV 1860 München   4-0 (2-0)
FC BATE Borisov: Yuriy ZHEVNOV, Gennadiy MARDAS, Alexei BAGA, Dmitri MOLASH (YC65), Valery TARASENKA, Aleksandr KOBETS (69' Yevgeniy LOSHANKOV), Alexandr YERMAKOVICH, Dmitry LIKHTAROVICH (74' Aleh STRAKHANOVICH), Vadim SKRIPCHENKO (YC8), Sergei MIRONCHYUK, Artem KONTSEV (58' Pavel SHMIHERA).
TSV 1860 München: Simon JENTZSCH, Rodrigo COSTA (BRA), Remo MEYER (SUI), Marco KURZ, Michael WIESINGER (46' Markus SCHROTH), Harald CERNY (AUT), Vidar RISETH (NOR) (46' Paul AGOSTINO (ITA)), Markus WEISSENBERGER (AUT) (YC75), Roman TYCE (CZE) (YC89), Martin MAX, Benjamin LAUTH (54' Daniel BORIMIROV (BUL)).
Goals: FC BATE Borisov: 1-0 Dmitri MOLASH (16'), 2-0 Sergei MIRONCHYUK (35'), 3-0 Pavel SHMIHERA (66'), 4-0 Aleh STRAKHANOVICH (80').
Referee: David MALCOLM (NIR)   Attendance: 5.000

29

14-07-2002   Vilniaus Zalgirio Stadionas, Vilnius:
FK Zalgiris Vilnius – FC Sochaux Montbéliard   1-2 (0-1)
FK Zalgiris Vilnius: Mindaugas MAKSVYTIS, Sergejus NOVIKOVAS, Yauhen ZHUK
(BLS), Darius ARTIOMOVAS, Aliaksandr DAVIDOVICH (BLS), Audrius TOLIS
(YC42,YC67), Giedrius BAREVICIUS, Andzej MAKSIMOVIC, Arturas STESKO, Igorius
STESKO, Dainius SAULENAS (42' John Kingsley MADUBUGWU (NIG), 83' Marius
KIZYS).
FC Sochaux Montbéliard: Teddy RICHERT, Maxence FLACHEZ, Nisa SAVELJIC (YUG)
(YC52), Philippe RASCHKE (85' Jean-Jacques DOMORAUD (CIV)), Sylvain
MONSOREAU, Yohann LONFAT (SUI) (61' Mickaël ISABEY), Adel CHEDLI, Fabien
BOUDARÉNE, Jérémy MATHIEU, Pierre-Alain FRAU (72' Marcelo TRAPASSO (ARG)),
Basile DE CARVALHO (SEN).
Goals: FK Zalgiris Vilnius: 1-1 Arturas STESKO (47').
FC Sochaux Montbéliard: 0-1 Sylvain MONSOREAU (30'), 1-2 Jérémy MATHIEU (66').
Referee: Goran MARIC (CRO)   Attendance: 1.000

14-07-2002   Tehtaan kenttä, Valkeakoski: FC Haka Valkeakosken – Fulham FC   1-1 (0-0)
FC Haka Valkeakosken: Michal SLAWUTA (POL), Lasse KARJALAINEN, Jukka
KOSKINEN (55' Iiro AALTO), Juha PASOJA (75' Ville VÄISÄNEN), Harri YLÖNEN
(YC86), Jarkko OKKONEN, Mikko INNANEN, Jukka RANTALA, Sami Antero RISTILÄ
(YC65), Juuso KANGASKORPI (83' Tommi TORKKELI), Valeri POPOVICH (RUS).
Fulham FC: Maik TAYLOR (NIR), Abdeslam OUADDOU (MAR), Andy MELVILLE
(WAL), Alain GOMA (FRA) (YC70), Jon HARLEY, Sylvain LEGWINSKI (FRA) (57' Luís
BOA MORTE (POR) (YC60)), Sean DAVIS, Steed MALBRANQUE (FRA) (90' Bjarne
GOLDBÆK (DEN)), John COLLINS (SCO) (79' Zat KNIGHT), Louis SAHA (FRA), Steve
MARLET (FRA).
Goals: FC Haka Valkeakosken: 1-1 Sami Antero RISTILÄ (66').
Fulham FC: 0-1 Steve MARLET (47').
Referee: Emil LAURSEN (DEN)   Attendance: 3.500

THIRD ROUND

20-07-2002   Craven Cottage, London: Fulham FC – Egaleo FC Athens   1-0 (0-0)
Fulham FC: Edwin VAN DER SAR (HOL), Abdeslam OUADDOU (MAR) (46' Sylvain
LEGWINSKI (FRA)), Jon HARLEY, Zat KNIGHT, Alain GOMA (FRA), Steed
MALBRANQUE (FRA) (66' Barrington Edward HAYLES (JAM)), Steve MARLET (FRA),
Sean DAVIS, Facundo SAVA (ARG) (46' Louis SAHA (FRA)), John COLLINS (SCO), Luís
BOA MORTE (POR).
Egaleo FC Athens: Mohamadou SIDIBE (MLI), Konstantinos PAPOUTSIS, Dimitrios
MEIDANIS (YC24), Giorgios ALEXOPOULOS (YC21), Michael CHATZIS (68' Jean-Pierre
ANTONETTI (FRA)), Daniel EDUSEI (MLI), Dejan STEFANOV (YUG) (52' Jean-Denis
WANGA ENDINGUE (CMR) (Y85)), John SKOPELITIS, Ioannis CHRISTOU, Georgios
FOTAKIS, John CHLOROS (61' Anastasios AGRITIS).
Goal: Fulham FC: 1-0 Louis SAHA (77').
Referee: Johny VER EECKE (BEL)   Attendance: 5.199

30

20-07-2002   Bonchuk Stadium, Dupnitsa:
FC Marek Dupnitsa – NK Slaven Belupo 0-3 (0-1)
FC Marek Dupnitsa: Armen AMBARZUMYAN (RC49), Emil KREMENLIEV (YC63),
Nikolai ALEXANDROV, Hristo ARANGELOV (50' Emil OVCHAROV *goalkeeper*), Stefan
LULCHEV (YC55), Veselin VELIKOV, Krasimir DIMITROV (YC38), Angel STOIKOV
(46' Anton EVTIMOV), Vladimir YONKOV, Amiran MUDJIRI (GEO) (YC19,YC52),
Rumen SHANKULOV (YC32) (70' Ivaylo KIRILOV).
NK Slaven Belupo: Ivica SOLOMUN (YC51), Pavo CRNAC, Petar BOSNJAK, Stipe
BOSNJAK (22' Mario KOVACEVIC), Dalibor BOZAC, Roy FERENCINA (YC54) (88'
Marko JURIC (YC88)), Danijel RADICEK (YC43), Domagoj KOSIC, Davor BAJSIC, Mario
DODIK, Miljenko KOVACIC (75' Goran GERSAK).
Goals: NK Slaven Belupo: 0-1 Pavo CRNAC (21'), 0-2 Domagoj KOSIC (76'), 0-3 Dalibor
BOZAC (90').
Referee: Damien LEDENTU (FRA)   Attendance: 4.000

20-07-2002   Stadionul Gloria, Bistrita: FC Gloria Bistrita – Lille Olympique SC 0-2 (0-0)
FC Gloria Bistrita: Costel CÂMPEANU, Dan Marius MATEI (YC59) (69' Ioan MISZTI),
Alin Valer RUS, Vasile Nicolae POPA, Sergiu Ioan Viorel COSTIN, Sorin Ciprian
BUCUROAIA, Alin Ilie MINTEUAN, Adrian Valentin VELCEA (YC27), Horatiu Daniel
CIOLOBOC (77' Constantin BÂRSAN), Cristian Ambrozie COROIAN (YC78), Ioan Vasile
OANA (57' Sandu NEGREAN). (Coach: Remus VLAD).
Lille Olympique SC: Grégory WIMBÉE, Stéphane PICHOT, Mathieu CHALMÉ (56'
Christophe LANDRIN), Abdelilah FAHMI (MAR) (YC69), Mathieu DELPIERRE, Fernando
D'AMICO (ARG), Rafaël SCHMITZ (BRA), Nicolas BONNAL (YC71), Philippe BRUNEL
(YC41), Djezon BOUTOILLE (89' Sylvain N'DIAYE (SEN)), Héctor Santiago TAPIA Urdile
(CHI) (73' Matt MOUSSILOU). (Coach: Claude PUEL).
Goals: Lille Olympique SC: 0-1 Djezon BOUTOILLE (63'), 0-2 Philippe BRUNEL (85').
Referee: Petteri KARI (FIN)   Attendance: 10.000

20-07-2002   FUJIFILM-Stadion, Breda: N.A.C. Breda – ES Troyes AC 1-1 (0-0)
N.A.C. Breda: Gábor BABOS (HUN), Delvic MENSAH, Júrgen COLIN (YC84), Rob
PENDERS, Nebojsa GUDELJ (YUG), Tamás PETÖ (HUN) (84' Rob HAEMHOLMS (BEL)),
Arne SLOT, Alfred SCHREUDER (70' Orlando ENGELAAR), Ali BOUSSABOUN (88'
Anouar HAMDI), Bart VAN DEN EEDE (BEL), Kevin BOBSON.
ES Troyes AC: Tony HEURTEBIS, David HAMED, Sékou BERTHÉ (MLI), Mohamed
BRADJA, Frédéric DANJOU, Carl TOURENNE, Benjamin NIVET, Mehdi LEROY, Rafik
SAÏFI (ALG) (75' Gharib AMZINE), Nicolas GOUSSÉ (84' Nassim AKROUR), Mamadou
NIANG (SEN) (67' Nicolas FLORENTIN),
Goals: N.A.C. Breda: 1-1 Arne SLOT (73').
ES Troyes AC: 0-1 Frédéric DANJOU (51').
Referee: Markus NOBS (SUI)   Attendance: 5.434

20-07-2002   Gottlieb-Daimler-Stadion, Stuttgart: VfB Stuttgart – AC Perugia   3-1 (0-1)
VfB Stuttgart: Timo HILDEBRAND, Thomas SCHNEIDER (YC58), Fernando MEIRA
(POR), Marcelo José BORDON (BRA), Silvio MEIßNER, Jochen SEITZ, Aleksandr HLEB
(BLS), Krasimir Guenchev BALAKOV (BUL) (34' Christian TIFFERT), Heiko GERBER
(87' Timo WENZEL), Ioan Viorel GANEA (ROM), Ionnis AMANATIDIS (GRE) (46' Sean
DUNDEE).
AC Perugia: Zeljko KALAC (AUS), Marco DI LORETO (YC90), William VIALI, Mauro
MILANESE (YC27), José Ferreira ZÉ MARIA (BRA), Giovanni TEDESCO, Manuele
BLASI, Fabio GROSSO, Fabrizio MICCOLI, Nicola AMORUSO, Zisis VRYZAS (GRE)
(YC25) (56' Fabio GATTI).
Goals: VfB Stuttgart: 1-1 Marcelo José BORDON (66'), 2-1 Ioan Viorel GANEA (71'), 3-1
Jochen SEITZ (90').
AC Perugia: 0-1 Fabrizio MICCOLI (14').
Referee: Robert STYLES (ENG)   Attendance: 7.000

20-07-2002   Stadio Renato dall'Ara, Bologna: FC Bologna – FC BATE Borisov   2-0 (1-0)
FC Bologna: Gianluca PAGLIUCA, Cristian ZACCARDO, Giulio FALCONE, Marcello
CASTELLINI, Carlo NERVO (63' Alessandro GAMBERINI), Alessandro FRARA, Renato
OLIVE (YC61), Leonardo COLUCCI (YC56), Vlado SMIT (YUG), Julio Ricardo CRUZ
(ARG) (89' Mourad MEGHNI (FRA)), Giuseppe SIGNORI (73' Claudio BELLUCCI).
FC BATE Borisov: Yuri ZHAUNOV, Aleksei BAGA, Gennadi MARDAS, Dmitri MOLASH,
Aleksandr KOBETS, Dmitry LIKHTAROVICH (YC24), Valery TARASENKA (YC26),
Aleksandr YERMAKOVICH (78' Pavel SHMIHERA), Vadim SKRYPCHENKO (YC63),
Aleh STRAKHANOVICH (46' Yevgeni LASHANKOV), Artem KONTSEV.
Goals: FCBologna: 1-0 Julio Ricardo CRUZ (44'), 2-0 Claudio BELLUCCI (80').
Referee: Athanassios BRIAKOS (GRE)

20-07-2002   Estadio La Rosaleda, Málaga: Málaga CF – KAA Gent   3-0 (2-0)
Málaga CF: Pedro CONTRERAS González, José Miguel "JOSEMI" González Rey (YC69)
(85' Roberto ROJAS González), FERNANDO SANZ Durán, Mikel ROTETA Lopetegui,
Vicente VALCÁRCE Cano, GERARDO García Leon Moreno (YC75), Carlos Alejandro
"SANDRO" Sierra Fumero, EDGAR Patricio de Carvalho Pacheco (POR) (67' Antonio
Manuel "MANU" SÁNCHEZ Gómez), Kizito "KIKI" MUSAMPA (HOL), Julio César DELY
VALDÉS (PAN), Manuel CANABAL Fiestras (67' Ivan LEKO (CRO)). (Coach: Joaquín
PEIRÓ Lucas).
KAA Gent: Frédéric HERPOEL, Spencer VERBIEST (71' Gaby MUDINGAYI (DRC)
(YC87)), Jacky PEETERS, Morten PEDERSEN (NOR), Ibrahima FAYÉ (SEN) (RC52),
Nasrédine KRAOUCHE (FRA), Alexandros KAKLAMANOS (GRE), Nenad VANIC (YUG)
(YC28) (46' Brecht VERBRUGGHE), Jimmy HEMPTE, Djima OYAWOLÉ (FRA) (60'
Patrick DIMBALA), Ahmed Salah HOSNY (EGY). (Coach: Jan OLDE RIEKERINK (HOL).
Goals: Málaga CF: 1-0 Julio César DELY VALDÉS (18'), 2-0 Manuel CANABAL Fiestras
(32'), 3-0 Julio César DELY VALDÉS (82').
Referee: Bertrand LAYEC (FRA)   Attendance: 10.000

21-07-2002   Fritz-Walter-Stadion, Kaiserslautern:
                    1.FC Kaiserslautern – FK Teplice   2-1 (2-0)
1.FC Kaiserslautern: Georg KOCH, Aleksander KNAVS (SLO), Hany RAMZY (EGY), Petr
GABRIEL (CZE), Thomas RIEDL, Markus ANFANG, Stefan MALZ, Mario BASLER (74'
Thorsten REUTER), Cássio Souza Soares LINCOLN (BRA), Marian HRISTOV (BUL) (61'
Selim TEBER), Vratislav LOKVENC (CZE).
FK Teplice: Tomás POSTULKA, Roman LENGYEL, Zdenko FRTALA (SVK) (YC48),
Patrik GROSS (72' Jirí SKÁLA), Michal DOLEZAL, Petr VORISEK, Pavel HORVÁTH,
Vladimir LEITNER (YC66), Dusan TESARIK (81' Pavel VERBÍR), Radek DIVECKY,
Ludek ZELENKA (89' Martin SIGMUND).
Goals: 1.FC Kaiserslautern: 1-0 Mario BASLER (4'), 2-0 Mario BASLER (38').
FK Teplice: 2-1 Pavel HORVÁTH (89' penalty).
Referee: John UNDERHILL (SCO)   Attendance: 15.000

21-07-2002   Stadio delle Alpi, Torino: AC Torino – Villarreal CF   2-0 (1-0)
AC Torino: Luca BUCCI, Fabio GALANTE, Paolo CASTELLINI, Stefano FATTORI,
Gianluca COMOTTO (YC,YC60), Daniele DELLI CARRI (YC82), Alessio SCARCHILLI
(71' Luca MEZZANO), Simone VERGASSOLA, Diego DE ASCENTIS (60' Luigi
GARZYA), Cristiano LUCARELLI (YC36) (46' Vincenzo SOMMESE (YC85)), Marco
FERRANTE. (Coach: Giancarlo CAMOLESE).
Villarreal CF: Javier LÓPEZ VALLEJO, Javier "JAVI" Rodríguez VENTA (46' Juliano Haus
BELLETTI (BRA)), UNAI Vergara Diaz Caballero (YC63), Enrique "QUIQUE" ÁLVAREZ
San Juan, Rodolfo Martín ARRUABARRENA (ARG), Constantin GÂLCA (ROM), JORGE
LÓPEZ Montaña (66' Carlos Reina ARANDA), Antonio GUAYRE Betancur Perdomo (87'
Francisco Xavier "XAVI" GRACIA Carlos), VÍCTOR Manuel Fernández Gutiérrez, Javier
CALLEJA Revilla, Martín PALERMO (ARG). (Coach: Víctor MUÑOZ Manrique).
Goals: AC Torino: 1-0 Gianluca COMOTTO (44'), 2-0 Marco FERRANTE (48').
Referee: Michael WEINER (GER)   Attendance: 14.353

21-07-2002   Stadion Siruch, Staré Mêsto:
                    1.FC Synot Staré Mêsto – FC Sochaux Montbéliard   0-3 (0-1)
1.FC Synot Staré Mêsto: Petr DROBISZ, Velice SUMULIKOSKI (MCD), Rastislav KOSTKA
(SVK), Martin ABRAHAM (75' Petr VESELY (YC79)), Pavel NEMCICKY, Václav
CINCALA, Petr SLONCÍK, Marek SEMAN (SVK) (46' Tomas POLACH), Tomas VAJDA,
Jiri KOWALIK, Michal MEDUNA (78' Dalibor SLEZÁK).
FC Sochaux Montbéliard: Teddy RICHERT, Maxence FLACHEZ, Nisa SAVELJIC (YUG),
Philippe RASCHKE, Sylvain MONSOREAU, Yohann LONFAT (SUI), Fabien
BOUDARENE, Benoît PEDRETTI, Jérémy MATHIEU (69' Mickaël ISABEY (YC88)),
Pierre-Alain FRAU (80' Basile DE CARVALHO (SEN)), Francilendo DOS SANTOS (BRA)
(69' Ibrahim TALL).
Goals: FC Sochaux Montbéliard: 0-1 Pierre-Alain FRAU (21'), 0-2 Pierre-Alain FRAU (49'),
0-3 Yohann LONFAT (83').
Referee: Sergey SHMOLIK (BLS)   Attendance: 2.100

33

21-07-2002   Hardturm, Zürich: FC Zürich – Aston Villa FC   2-0 (1-0)
FC Zürich: Miroslav KÖNIG (SVK), Alain NEF, David PALLAS Rey (ESP) (77' Tariq
CHIHAB (MAR)), Wilco HELLINGA (HOL), Stephan KELLER (YC38), Daniel TARONE
(58' Luca JODICE (ITA)), Urs FISCHER, Yvan QUENTIN, Ursal YASAR (YC,YC83),
Kanga Gauthier AKALE (CIV), Alhassane KEITA (GUI) (47' Daniel GYGAX).
Aston Villa FC: Peter ENCKELMAN (FIN), Mark DELANEY (WAL) (YC45), Alan
WRIGHT, Gareth BARRY (81' Hassan KACHLOUL (MAR)), Jay Lloyd SAMUEL (TRI)
(YC,YC84), George BOATENG (HOL), Steve STONE, Thomas HITZLSPERGER (GER)
(73' Lee HENDRIE), Dion DUBLIN, Peter CROUCH, Michael BOULDING (58' Mustapha
HADJI (MAR)).
Goals: FC Zürich: 1-0 Alhassane KEITA (32'), 2-0 Ursal YASAR (83').
Referee: Florian MEYER (GER)

21-07-2002   Metallurg Stadium, Samara:
                FC Krylya Sovetov Samara – Willem II Tilburg   3-1 (2-1)
FC Krylya Sovetov Samara: Olexandr LAVRENTSOV (UKR), Karen DOKHOYAN (ARM),
Vladimir SUNEIKO (BLS), Evgeny BUSHMANOV, Patrick OVIE (NGR) (63' Nerijus
BARASA (LIT)), Andriy KARYAKA (UKR), Vladislav RADIMOV (YC,YC87), Denis
KOUBA (BLS), Viktor BULATOV (27' ROGÉRIO GAÚCHO Márcio Botelho (BRA)
(YC68)), Anton BOBER (78' Robertas RINGYS (LIT)), Robertas POSKUS (LIT).
Willem II Tilburg: Geert DE VLIEGER (BEL), Kew JALIENS, Jos VAN NIEUWSTADT,
Christiaan JANSSENS (BEL) (YC43), Joris MATHIJSEN, Denny LANDZAAT, Tom
CALUWÉ (BEL), Youssef MARIANA (MAR), Jatto CEESAY (GAM) (YC75), Tarik
SEKTIOUI (MAR) (88' James Stephen QUINN (NIR)), Dmitriy SHUKOV (RUS) (62'
Regilio SIMONS).
Goals: FC Krylya Sovetov Samara: 1-0 Denis KOUBA (33'), 2-1 Vladislav RADIMOV (44'),
3-1 ROGÉRIO GAÚCHO Márcio Botelho (70').
Willem II Tilburg: 1-1 Denny LANDZAAT (37' penalty).
Referee: Johan VERBIST (BEL)   Attendance: 25.000

27-07-2002   Villa Park, Birmingham: Aston Villa FC – FC Zürich   3-0 (1-0)
Aston Villa FC: Peter ENCKELMAN (FIN), Mark DELANEY (WAL), Gareth BARRY, Steve
STAUNTON (IRL) (YC74), Olof MELLBERG (SWE), Lee HENDRIE, Ian TAYLOR,
Thomas HITZLSPERGER (GER), Michael BOULDING (46' Paul MERSON), Marcus
ALLBÄCK (SWE) (71' Stefan MOORE), Peter CROUCH.
FC Zürich: Miroslav KÖNIG (SVK), Tariq CHIHAB (MAR) (63' David PALLAS Rey
(ESP)), Marc SCHNEIDER, Alain NEF, Wilco HELLINGA (HOL), Urs FISCHER, Yvan
QUENTIN, Mario RAIMONDI (YC74) (74' Daniel TARONE), Luca JODICE (ITA), Kanga
Gauthier AKALE (CIV), Alhassane KEITA (GUI) (46' Daniel GYGAX),
Goals: Aston Villa FC: 1-0 Michael BOULDING (32'), 2-0 Marcus ALLBÄCK (48'), 3-0
Steve STAUNTON (77').
Referee: Roberto ROSETTI (ITA)

27-07-2002   Městský Stadion na Stínadlech, Teplice:
FK Teplice – 1.FC Kaiserslautern   4-0 (0-0)
FK Teplice: Tomáš POSTULKA, Roman LENGYEL, Karel RADA, Patrik GROSS, Michal
DOLEŽAL, Petr VORISEK (89' Jiří SKÁLA), Pavel HORVÁTH, Vladimir LEITNER,
Tomas KUKOL (YC,YC51), Pavel VERBÍR (90' Zdenko FRTALA (SVK)), Radek
DIVECKY (83' Ludek ZELENKA).
1.FC Kaiserslautern: Georg KOCH, Petr GABRIEL (CZE), Aleksander KNAVS (SLO) (31'
Nzelo LEMBI (BEL)), Hany RAMZY (EGY), Thomas RIEDL, Markus ANFANG (YC60),
Stefan MALZ (YC29,YC44), Mario BASLER, Thorsten REUTER, Cássio Souza Soares
LINCOLN (BRA) (22' Michael MIFSUD (MLT) (YC26)), Vratislav LOKVENC (CZE).
Goals: FK Teplice: 1-0 Pavel HORVÁTH (47'), 2-0 Petr VORISEK (66'), 3-0 Ludek
ZELENKA (86'), 4-0 Pavel VERBÍR (90').
Referee: Stefano FARINA (ITA)   Attendance: 10.128

27-07-2002   Gradski Stadion, Koprivnica:
NK Slaven Belupo – FC Marek Dupnitsa   3-1 (1-1)
NK Slaven Belupo: Ivica SOLOMUN, Pavo CRNAC, Petar BOSNJAK, Danijel RADICEK,
Dalibor BOZAC, Igor GAL, Srebrenko POSAVEC (56' Davor BAJSIC), Domagoj KOSIC
(YC34), Mario KOVACEVIC (80' Zdravko MEDJIMOREC), Miljenko KOVACIC, Goran
GERSAK (56' Tomislav FILIPOVIC).
FC Marek Dupnitsa: Emil OVCHAROV, Dimitar KOEMDZHIEV (57' Veselin VELIKOV),
Nikolai ALEXANDROV, Stefan LULCHEV (YC86), Hristo ARANGELOV, Krasimir
DIMITROV, Vladimir YONKOV (YC44), Angel STOIKOV, Ivaylo KIRILOV (YC28) (60'
Vladislav VLADOV), Rumen SHANKULOV (63' Lyubomir LYUBENOV), Anton
EVTIMOV.
Goals: NK Slavan Belupo: 1-0 Miljenko KOVACIC (27'), 2-1 Miljenko KOVACIC (66'), 3-1
Dalibor BOZAC (87').
FC Marek Dupnitsa: 1-1 Krasimir DIMITROV (32' penalty).
Referee: Tonny Kolbech POULSEN (DEN)   Attendance: 3.000

27-07-2002   Stadio Druso, Bolzano: AC Perugia – VfB Stuttgart   2-1 (0-0)
AC Perugia: Zeljko KALAC (AUS), Marco DI LORETO, William VIALI (RC72), Mauro
MILANESE (YC71), José Ferreira ZÉ MARIA (BRA), Giovanni TEDESCO (77'
Massimillano FUSANI), Manuele BLASI, Fabio GROSSO (YC86), Zisis VRYZAS (GRE)
(55' Antonio CRITINI), Nicola AMORUSO (79' Emanuele BERRETTONI), Fabrizio
MICCOLI.
VfB Stuttgart: Timo HILDEBRAND, Thomas SCHNEIDER (46' RUI Manuel MARQUES
(POR)), Fernando MEIRA (POR) (RC68), Marcelo José BORDON (BRA), Timo WENZEL
(YC36), Christian TIFFERT, Zvonimir SOLDO (CRO) (YC30) (46' Jens TODT), Aleksandr
HLEB (BLS), Silvio MEIßNER, Ioan Viorel GANEA (ROM) (69' Heiko GERBER), Sean
DUNDEE.
Goals: AC Perugia: 1-1 Fabrizio MICCOLI (73'), 2-1 Emanuele BERRETTONI (90').
VfB Stuttgart: 0-1 Ioan Viorel GANEA (52').
Referee: Alfonso PEREZ BURRULL (ESP)   Attendance: 3.000

27-07-2002   Gorodskoj Stadion, Borisov: FC BATE Borisov – FC Bologna   0-0
FC BATE Borisov: Yuri ZHAUNOV, Aleksei BAGA (YC29), Gennadi MARDAS, Dmitri
MOLASH, Aleksandr KOBETS, Valery TARASENKA, Aleksandr YERMAKOVICH, Vadim
SKRYPCHENKO (YC70) (72' Aleh STRAKHANOVICH), Yevgeni LASHANKOV, Pavel
BIAHANSKI (44' Sergei MIRONCHYUK), Artem KONTSEV (65' Pavel SHMIHERA).
FC Bologna: Gianluca PAGLIUCA, Cristian ZACCARDO, Giulio FALCONE, Marcello
CASTELLINI (YC6), Carlo NERVO (69' Alessandro GAMBERINI), Renato OLIVE,
Leonardo COLUCCI, Vlado SMIT (YUG), Roberto GORETTI (77' Andrea ARDITO),
Claudio BELLUCCI, Julio Ricardo CRUZ (ARG) (89' Mourad MEGHNI (FRA)).
Referee: Luis MEDINA CANTALEJO (ESP)

27-07-2002   Stade de l'Abbé Deschamps, Auxerre: ES Troyes AC – N.A.C. Breda   0-0
ES Troyes AC: Tony HEURTEBIS, David HAMED, Sékou BERTHÉ (MLI), Mohamed
BRADJA, Frédéric DANJOU, Carl TOURENNE, Benjamin NIVET, Mehdi LEROY (YC35),
Rafik SAÏFI (ALG) (67' Gharib AMZINE), Nicolas GOUSSÉ (46' Nicolas FLORENTIN),
Mamadou NIANG (SEN) (83' Nassim AKROUR),
N.A.C. Breda: Gábor BABOS (HUN), Rob PENDERS, Júrgen COLIN, Mark SCHENNING
(YC45) (70' Orlando ENGELAAR), Nebojsa GUDELJ (YUG), Csaba FEHÉR (HUN)
(YC45), Arne SLOT (YC58), Alfred SCHREUDER (43' Delvic MENSAH), Kevin BOBSON,
Bart VAN DEN EEDE (BEL) (YC17), Ali BOUSSABOUN.
Referee: Alan FREELAND (SCO)   Attendance: 3.133

27-07-2002   Willem II Stadion, Tilburg:
              Willem II Tilburg – FC Krylya Sovetov Samara   2-0 (1-0)
Willem II Tilburg: Geert DE VLIEGER (BEL), Kew JALIENS (YC38), Jos VAN
NIEUWSTADT (67' Danny MATHIJSSEN), Christiaan JANSSENS (BEL), Joris
MATHIJSEN, Denny LANDZAAT, Tom CALUWÉ (BEL) (YC88), Youssef MARIANA
(MAR), Jatto CEESAY (GAM), Regilio SIMONS (YC61) (72' James Stephen QUINN
(NIR)), Dmitriy SHUKOV (RUS) (46' Tarik SEKTIOUI (MAR)).
FC Krylya Sovetov Samara: Olexandr LAVRENTSOV (UKR), Karen DOKHOYAN (ARM),
Vladimir SUNEIKO (BLS), Evgeny BUSHMANOV, Patrick OVIE (NGR) (YC22) (67'
Nerijus BARASA (LIT)), Andriy KARYAKA (UKR), Gustavo Alejandro LILLO (ARG),
Denis KOUBA (BLS), ROGÉRIO GAÚCHO Márcio Botelho (BRA) (YC53) (53' Viktor
BULATOV), Anton BOBER, Robertas POSKUS (LIT).
Goals: Willem II Tilburg: 1-0 Christiaan JANSSENS (37'), 2-0 Tarik SEKTIOUI (83').
Referee: Kjell ALSETH (NOR)   Attendance: 2.721

27-07-2002   Stade Auguste-Bonal, Montbéliard:
              FC Sochaux Montbéliard – 1.FC Synot Staré Mêsto   0-0
FC Sochaux Montbéliard: Teddy RICHERT, Maxence FLACHEZ, Nisa SAVELJIC (YUG),
Ibrahim TALL (YC81), Jérémy MATHIEU, Adel CHEDLI (YC26), Wilson ORUMA (NGR),
Michaël ISABEY, Omar DAF (SEN) (46' Sylvain MONSOREAU), Pierre-Alain FRAU (46'
Francilendo DOS SANTOS (BRA)), Basile DE CARVALHO (SEN).
1.FC Synot Staré Mêsto: Petr DROBISZ, Pavel NEMCICKY, Velice SUMULIKOSKI
(MCD), Marek SEMAN (SVK) (YC75), Rastislav KOSTKA (SVK) (YC36) (81' Alexander
HOMER (SVK)), Tomas VAJDA, Petr SLONCÏK (YC78), Václav CINCALA (73' Tomas
POLACH), Martin ABRAHAM, Jiri KOWALIK (55' Michal MEDUNA), Dalibor SLEZÁK.
Referee: Uriah RENNIE (ENG)   Attendance: 8.843

36

27-07-2002   Stade Grimonprez-Jooris, Lille:
Lille Olympique SC – FC Gloria Bistrita   1-0 (0-0)
Lille Olympique SC: Grégory WIMBÉE, Stéphane PICHOT, Abdelilah FAHMI (MAR),
Mathieu DELPIERRE, Rafaël SCHMITZ (BRA), Nicolas BONNAL, Sylvain N'DIAYE
(SEN), Fernando D'AMICO (ARG) (66' Christophe LANDRIN), Philippe BRUNEL, Djezon
BOUTOILLE (70' Mile STERJOVSKI (AUS)), Héctor Santiago TAPIA Urdile (CHI) (66'
Matt MOUSSILOU). (Coach: Claude PUEL).
FC Gloria Bistrita: Costel CÂMPEANU, Dorel Ioan ZEGREAN (YC80), Sergiu Ioan Viorel
COSTIN, Vasile Nicolae POPA, Alin Valer RUS, Sorin Ciprian BUCUROAIA (81' Sandu
NEGREAN), Alin Ilie MINTEUAN, Horatiu Daniel CIOLOBOC (81' Sorin Vasile SABAU),
Ion Romica CEAUSU (YC48) (74' Ioan MISZTI), Lucian Iulian SÂNMARTEAN
(YC37,YC55)), Cristian Ambrozie COROIAN. (Coach: Remus VLAD).
Goal: Lille Olympique SC: 1-0 Fernando D'AMICO (52').
Referee: Miroslav RADOMAN (YUG)   Attendance: 9.906

27-07-2002   Jules Ottenstadion, Gentbrugge-Gent: KAA Gent – Málaga CF   1-1 (1-0)
KAA Gent: Frédéric HERPOEL, Morten PEDERSEN (NOR) (46' Patrick DIMBALA), David
VAN HOYWEGHEN, Jacky PEETERS, Gaby MUDINGAYI (DRC) (46' Wim DE
DECKER), Jimmy HEMPTE, Brecht VERBRUGGHE, Nasrédine KRAOUCHE (FRA)
(YC36), Dries BERNAERT, Alexandros KAKLAMANOS (GRE), Ahmed Salah HOSNY
(EGY). (Coach: Jan OLDE RIEKERINK (HOL)).
Málaga CF: Pedro CONTRERAS González, José Miguel "JOSEMI" González Rey,
FERNANDO SANZ Durán (YC70), Mikel ROTETA Lopetegui, Vicente VALCÁRCE Cano,
GERARDO García Leon Moreno, Carlos Alejandro "SANDRO" Sierra Fumero (YC76) (76'
MIGUEL ÁNGEL Lozano Ayala), EDGAR Patricio de Carvalho Pacheco (POR) (68' Antonio
Manuel "MANU" SÁNCHEZ Gómez), Kizito "KIKI" MUSAMPA (HOL) (YC47), Julio César
DELY VALDÉS (PAN), Manuel CANABAL Fiestras (YC39) (54' Ivan LEKO (CRO)).
(Coach: Joaquín PEIRÓ Lucas).
Goals: KAA Gent: 1-0 Alexandros KAKLAMANOS (41').
Málaga CF: 1-1 Julio César DELY VALDÉS (90+').
Referee: Wolfgang SOWA (AUT)   Attandence: 5.000

27-07-2002   Stadio Apóstolos Nikolaidis, Athens:
Egaleo FC Athens – Fulham FC   1-1 (1-1)
Egaleo FC Athens: Nenad BIKIC (YUG), Konstantinos PAPOUTSIS, Giorgios
ALEXOPOULOS, Dimitrios MEIDANIS, Nikolaos NIKOLOPOULOS (46' Anastasios
AGRITIS), Daniel EDUSEI (MLI), Ioannis CHRISTOU, John SKOPELITIS, Jean-Denis
WANGA ENDINGUE (CMR) (60' Michael CHATZIS), Georgios FOTAKIS, John
CHLOROS.
Fulham FC: Edwin VAN DER SAR (HOL), Abdeslam OUADDOU (MAR), Jon HARLEY,
Andy MELVILLE (WAL), Alain GOMA (FRA), Sylvain LEGWINSKI (FRA) (71' Bjarne
GOLDBÆK (DEN)), Steve MARLET (FRA) (71' Barrington Edward HAYLES (JAM)),
Steed MALBRANQUE (FRA) (85' Andrejs STOLCERS (LAT)), Louis SAHA (FRA), Sean
DAVIS, Luís BOA MORTE (POR).
Goals: Egaleo FC Athens: 1-0 John CHLOROS (24').
Fulham FC: 1-1 Steve MARLET (34').
Referee: Ruud BOSSEN (HOL)

27-07-2002   Estadio El Madrigal, Villarreal: Villarreal CF – AC Torino   2-0 (0-0)
Villarreal CF: José Maunel REINA Paez, Jesús GALVÁN Carrillo (46' Juliano Haus
BELLETTI (BRA)), Enrique "QUIQUE" ÁLVAREZ San Juan (YC,YC117), Enrique
"QUIQUE" MEDINA Ortega, Rodolfo Martín ARRUABARRENA (ARG) (100' RUBÉN
REYES Diaz), Constantin GÂLCA (ROM), JORGE LÓPEZ Montaña, Antonio GUAYRE
Betancur Perdomo (72' Carlos Reina ARANDA), VÍCTOR Manuel Fernández Gutiérrez,
Javier CALLEJA Revilla, Martín PALERMO (ARG). (Coach: Víctor MUÑOZ Manrique).
AC Torino: Luca BUCCI, Fabio GALANTE (YC60), Paolo CASTELLINI (YC37), Stefano
FATTORI, Daniele DELLI CARRI, Alessio SCARCHILLI (66' Vincenzo SOMMESE
(YC90)), Simone VERGASSOLA, Diego DE ASCENTIS (61' Luca MEZZANO), Cristiano
LUCARELLI (YC,YC103), Marco FERRANTE, Gennaro SCARLATO. (Coach: Giancarlo
CAMOLESE).
Goals: Villarreal CF: 1-0 Antonio GUAYRE Betancur Perdomo (46'), 2-0 Rodolfo Martín
ARRUABARRENA (61').
Referee: Antonio Manuel ALMEIDA COSTA (POR)   Attendance: 11.000
Penalties: * Marco FERRANTE   * Constantin GÂLCA
                1 Luca MEZZANO   1 Juliano Haus BELLETTI
                2 Paolo CASTELLINI   2 Martín PALERMO
                * Daniele DELLI CARRI   3 JORGE LÓPEZ Montaña
                3 Vincenzo SOMMESE   4 Carlos Reina ARANDA
(After extra time)

SEMI-FINALS

31-07-2002   Loftus Road, London: Fulham FC – FC Sochaux Montbéliard   1-0 (0-0)
Fulham FC: Edwin VAN DER SAR (HOL), Abdeslam OUADDOU (MAR) (63' Zat
KNIGHT), Rufus Emanuel BREVETT, Andy MELVILLE (WAL), Alain GOMA (FRA),
Sylvain LEGWINSKI (FRA) (46' Junichi INAMOTO (JPN)), Steve MARLET (FRA) (YC21),
Steed MALBRANQUE (FRA) (68' Barrington Edward HAYLES (JAM)), Louis SAHA
(FRA), Sean DAVIS (YC26), Luís BOA MORTE (POR).
FC Sochaux Montbéliard: Teddy RICHERT (YC78), Maxence FLACHEZ, Nisa SAVELJIC
(YUG) (YC37), Philippe RASCHKE, Sylvain MONSOREAU, Yohann LONFAT (SUI) (88'
Adel CHEDLI), Fabien BOUDARENE, Benoît PEDRETTI, Jérémy MATHIEU, Pierre-Alain
FRAU (12' Jaouad ZAIRI (MAR)), Francilendo DOS SANTOS (BRA) (77' Basile DE
CARVALHO (SEN)).
Goal: Fulham FC: 1-0 Sean DAVIS (90').
Referee: Sorin CORPODEAN (ROM)   Attendance: 4.717

31-07-2002   Stade Grimonprez-Jooris, Lille:
              Lille Olympique SC – Aston Villa FC   1-1 (0-0)
Lille Olympique SC: Grégory WIMBÉE, Stéphane PICHOT, Abdelilah FAHMI (MAR),
Mathieu DELPIERRE, Grégory TAFFOREAU, Mathieu CHALMÉ (71' Djezon
BOUTOILLE), Sylvain N'DIAYE (SEN), Fernando D'AMICO (ARG) (YC67), Phlippe
BRUNEL (61' Nicolas BONNAL), Matt MOUSSILOU (71' Hector Santiago TAPIA Urdile
(CHI)), Mile STERJOVSKI (AUS).
Aston Villa FC: Stefan POSTMA (HOL), Mark DELANEY (WAL), Lloyd SAMUEL (YC46),
Steve STAUNTON (IRL) (YC83), Olof MELLBERG (SWE), Mustapha HADJI (MAR) (69
Darius VASSELL), Thomas HITZLSPERGER (GER), Ian TAYLOR, Gareth BARRY,
Marcus ALLBÄCK (SWE) (81' Steve STONE), Peter CROUCH.
Goals: Lille Olympique SC: 1-1 Fernando D'AMICO (90'+3').
Aston Villa FC: 0-1 Ian TAYLOR (76').
Referee: Zeljko SIRIC (CRO)   Attendance: 14.437

31-07-2002   Gottlieb-Daimler-Stadion, Stuttgart:
VfB Stuttgart – NK Slaven Belupo   2-1 (1-0)
VfB Stuttgart: Timo HILDEBRAND, Andreas HINKEL, Thomas SCHNEIDER, Marcelo José BORDON (BRA), Timo WENZEL, Aleksandr HLEB (BLS), Zvonimir SOLDO (CRO) (46' Christian TIFFERT (YC86)), Silvio MEIßNER, Jochen SEITZ, Ioannis AMANATIDIS (GRE) (54' Sean DUNDEE), Ioan Viorel GANEA (ROM).
NK Slaven Belupo: Ivica SOLOMUN, Stipe BOSNJAK (67' Zdravko MEDJIMOREC), Pavo CRNAC, Igor GAL (YC30), Dalibor BOZAC (YC46), Mario KOVACEVIC (46' Srebrenko POSAVEC), Roy FERENCINA (YC75), Danijel RADICEK (YC51), Miljenko KOVACIC, Domagoj KOSIC (YC90), Goran GERSAK (71' Davor BAJSIC).
Goals: VfB Stuttgart: 1-0 Thomas SCHNEIDER (9'), 2-0 Thomas SCHNEIDER (61').
NK Slaven Belupo: 2-1 Davor BAJSIC (84').
Referee: Joaquim Paulo GOMES Ferreira PARATY DA SILVA (POR) Attendance: 5.120

31-07-2002   Stadio Renato dall'Ara, Bologna: FC Bologna – FK Teplice   5-1 (3-0)
FC Bologna: Gianluca PAGLIUCA, Cristian ZACCARDO (YC25), Giulio FALCONE, Marcello CASTELLINI, Carlo NERVO (YC41) (69' Claudio BELLUCCI), Leonardo COLUCCI, Renato OLIVE (YC61), Roberto GORETTI (79' Tomas LOCATELLI), Vlado SMIT (YUG), Julio Ricardo CRUZ (ARG), Giuseppe SIGNORI (69' Alessandro GAMBERINI).
FK Teplice: Tomás POSTULKA, Roman LENGYEL, Zdenko FRTALA (SVK) (YC60) (78' Vlastimil RYSKA), Patrik GROSS, Michal DOLEZAL, Petr VORISEK, Pavel HORVÁTH, Vladimir LEITNER, Jirí SKÁLA, Pavel VERBÏR (74' Martin SIGMUND), Radek DIVECKY (YC19) (46' Ludek ZELENKA).
Goals: FC Bologna: 1-0 Carlo NERVO (3'), 2-0 Giuseppe SIGNORI (31'), 3-0 Giuseppe SIGNORI (37' penalty), 4-1 Cristian ZACCARDO (67'), 5-1 Renato OLIVE (75').
FK Teplice: 3-1 Ludek ZELENKA (64').
Referee: Dani KOREN (ISR)   Attendance: 15.174

31-07-2002   Estadio La Rosaleda, Málaga: Málaga CF – Willem II Tilburg   2-1 (1-0)
Málaga CF: Pedro CONTRERAS González, José Miguel "JOSEMI" González Rey, FERNANDO SANZ Durán, Mikel ROTETA Lopetegui, Vicente VALCÁRCE Cano (YC48), GERARDO García Leon Moreno, Carlos Alejandro "SANDRO" Sierra Fumero (81' Sérgio Paulo Barbosa Valente "DUDA" (POR)), EDGAR Patricio de Carvalho Pacheco (POR) (72' Antonio Manuel "MANU" SÁNCHEZ Gómez), Kizito "KIKI" MUSAMPA (HOL), Sergio Contreras Pardo "KOKE" (65' Ivan LEKO (CRO)), Julio César DELY VALDÉS (PAN). (Coach: Joaquín PEIRÓ Lucas).
Willem II Tilburg: Geert DE VLIEGER (BEL), Nuelson WAU, Kew JALIENS (YC64), Christiaan (Chris) JANSSENS (BEL), Joris MATHIJSEN, Denny LANDZAAT, Tom CALUWÉ (BEL), Youssef MARIANA (MAR), Jatto CEESAY (GAM) (62' James Stephen QUINN (NIR)), Tarik SEKTIOUI (MAR) (57' Regilio SIMONS), Dmitriy SHUKOV (RUS) (64' Danny MATHIJSSEN). (Coach: Mark WOTTE).
Goals: Málaga CF: 1-0 Sergio Contreras Pardo "KOKE" (34'), 2-1 Julio César DELY VALDÉS (64' penalty).
Willem II Tilburg: 1-1 Kew JALIENS (61').
Referee: Ivan DOBRINOV (BUL)   Attendance: 12.000

39

31-07-2002   Estadio El Madrigal, Villarreal: Villarreal CF – ES Troyes AC   0-0
Villarreal CF: Javier LOPEZ VALLEJO, Juliano Haus BELLETTI (BRA) (85' Jesús
GALVÁN Carrillo), Enrique "QUIQUE" MEDINA Ortega, Iñaki BERRUET Michelena,
Rodolfo Martín ARRUABARRENA (ARG) (YC77), Constantin GÂLCA (ROM) (YC37) (85'
José Joaquín Moreno Verdu "JOSICO"), JORGE LÓPEZ Montaña, Antonio GUAYRE
Betancur Perdomo (60' Carlos Reina ARANDA), VÍCTOR Manuel Fernández Gutiérrez,
Javier CALLEJA Revilla, Martín PALERMO (ARG). (Coach: Víctor MUÑOZ Manrique).
ES Troyes AC: Tony HEURTEBIS, David HAMED, Sékou BERTHÉ (MLI) (YC75),
Mohamed BRADJA, Frédéric DANJOU, Gharib AMZINE, Carl TOURENNE (YC43), Mehdi
LEROY (70' Badile LUBAMBA (SUI) (YC85)), Nicolas FLORENTIN, Benjamin NIVET
(65' Rafik SAÏFI (ALG)), Nassim AKROUR (46' Nicolas GOUSSÉ). (Coach: Jacques (Jacky)
BONNEVAY).
Referee: Erol ERSOY (TUR)   Attendance: 7.000

07-08-2002   Gradski Stadion, Koprivnica: NK Slaven Belupo – VfB Stuttgart   0-1 (0-1)
NK Slaven Belupo: Ivica SOLOMUN, Petar BOSNJAK, Pavo CRNAC (YC58), Igor GAL,
Dalibor BOZAC, Roy FERENCINA, Zdravko MEDJIMOREC (55' Mario KOVACEVIC),
Davor BAJSIC (73' Goran GERSAK), Srebrenko POSAVEC (46' Tomislav FILIPOVIC),
Domagoj KOSIC, Miljenko KOVACIC.
VfB Stuttgart: Timo HILDEBRAND, RUI Manuel MARQUES (POR), Thomas SCHNEIDER,
Marcelo José BORDON (BRA), Heiko GERBER, Silvio MEIßNER (YC34), Jens TODT,
Aleksandr HLEB (BLS) (40' Ioannis AMANATIDIS (GRE)), Krasimir Guenchev BALAKOV
(BUL) (84' Michael MUTZEL), Jochen SEITZ, Sean DUNDEE (90' Ioan Viorel GANEA
(ROM)).
Goal: VfB Stuttgart: 0-1 Sean DUNDEE (39').
Referee: Vladimir HRINAK (SVK)   Attendance: 4.000

07-08-2002   Mestský Stadion na Stínadlech, Teplice: FK Teplice – FC Bologna   1-3 (0-3)
FK Teplice: Tomás POSTULKA, Zdenko FRTALA (SVK) (46' Roman LENGYEL),
Vlastimil RYSKA, Damir GRLIC, Jirí SKÁLA, Pavel VORISEK (46' Vladimir LEITNER),
Martin SIGMUND, Miroslav JIRKA, Dusan TESARIK, Jan REZEK, Radek DIVECKY (61'
Pavel VERBÍR).
FC Bologna: Gianluca PAGLIUCA, Cristian ZACCARDO, Giulio FALCONE (46'
Alessandro GAMBERINI (YC48)), Marcello CASTELLINI, Carlo NERVO, Roberto
GORETTI, Renato OLIVE (59' Tomas LOCATELLI), Leonardo COLUCCI, Vlado SMIT
(YUG), Julio Ricardo CRUZ (ARG) (59' Mourad MEGHNI (FRA)), Claudio BELLUCCI.
Goals: FK Teplice: 1-3 Damir GRLIC (90').
FC Bologna: 0-1 Carlo NERVO (15'), 0-2 Leonardo COLUCCI (19'), 0-3 Leonardo
COLUCCI (38').
Referee: Tom Henning OVREBO (NOR)   Attendance: 2.780

07-08-2002   Stade de l'Aube, Troyes: ES Troyes AC – Villarreal CF   2-1 (1-1)
ES Troyes AC: Tony HEURTEBIS, David HAMED (YC54), Sékou BERTHÉ (MLI) (YC48),
Mohamed BRADJA, Mehdi MENIRI (ALG) (YC34), Carl TOURENNE, Gharib AMZINE
(YC37,YC44), Medhi LEROY (YC83) (83' David VAIRELLES), Nicolas FLORENTIN (62'
Mamadou NIANG (SEN)), Nicolas GOUSSÉ, Farid GHAZI (ALG) (74' Benjamin NIVET).
(Coach: Jacques (Jacky) BONNEVAY).
Villarreal CF: José Manuel REINA Paez, Juliano Haus BELLETTI (BRA), Enrique
"QUIQUE" MEDINA Ortega (YC52), Enrique "QUIQUE" ÁLVAREZ San Juan (YC17),
Jesús GALVÁN Carrillo (68' Antonio GUAYRE Betancur Perdomo), Constantin GÂLCA
(ROM) (YC62), José Joaquín Moreno Verdu "JOSICO" (72' Carlos Reina ARANDA),
JORGE LÓPEZ Montaña, VÍCTOR Manuel Fernández Gutiérrez, Javier CALLEJA Revilla,
Martín PALERMO (ARG) (YC23). (Coach: Víctor MUÑOZ Manrique).
Goals: ES Troyes AC: 1-1 Sékou BERTHÉ (41'), 2-1 Nicolas GOUSSÉ (52' penalty).
Villarreal CF: 0-1 Javier CALLEJA Revilla (14').
Referee: Fritz STUCHLIK (AUT)   Attendance: 5.624
*After it was discovered that ES Troyes AC had fielded an ineligible player (David Vairelles),
UEFA awarded the match to Villarreal CF with a 3-0 scoreline.*

07-08-2002   Stade Auguste-Bonal, Montbéliard:
              FC Sochaux Montbéliard – Fulham FC   0-2 (0-0)
FC Sochaux Montbéliard: Jean-Baptiste DAGUET, Ibrahim TALL, Nisa SAVELJIC (YUG),
Maxence FLACHEZ, Sylvain MONSOREAU, Wilson ORUMA (NGR) (55' Benoît
PEDRETTI (YC71,YC80)), Fabien BOUDARENE (YC21) (55' Michaël PAGIS), Adel
CHEDLI (YC63), Jérémy MATHIEU, Mickaël ISABEY, Jaouad ZAIRI (MAR) (55'
Francilendo DOS SANTOS (BRA)).
Fulham FC: Edwin VAN DER SAR (HOL), Abdeslam OUADDOU (MAR), Andy
MELVILLE (WAL), Alain GOMA (FRA), Rufus Emanuel BREVETT (YC59), Sylvain
LEGWINSKI (FRA), Steed MALBRANQUE (59' Junichi INAMOTO (JPN)), Sean
DAVIS (YC26), Luís BOA MORTE (POR) (77' John COLLINS (SCO)), Louis SAHA (FRA)
(77' Barrington Edward HAYLES (JAM)), Steve MARLET (FRA).
Goals: Fulham FC: 0-1 Sylvain LEGWINSKI (63'), 0-2 Barrington Edward HAYLES (77').
Referee: Franz-Xaver WACK (GER)   Attendance: 9.130

07-08-2002   Villa Park, Birmingham: Aston Villa FC – Lille Olympique SC   0-2 (0-1)
Aston Villa FC: Peter ENCKELMAN (FIN), Mark DELANEY (WAL), Gareth BARRY, Steve
STAUNTON (IRL) (YC90), Olof MELLBERG (SWE), Thomas HITZLSPERGER (GER), Ian
TAYLOR (YC34) (57' Mustapha HADJI (MAR)), Darius VASSELL, Dion DUBLIN (46' Lee
HENDRIE), Peter CROUCH (80' Stefan MOORE (YC90)), Marcus ALLBÄCK (SWE).
Lille Olympique SC: Grégory WIMBÉE, Matthieu CHALMÉ (YC48), Mathieu DELPIERRE,
Abdelilah FAHMI (MAR), Rafaël SCHMITZ (BRA), Grégory TAFFOREAU, Christophe
LANDRIN, Sylvain N'DIAYE (SEN) (YC44,YC89), Nicolas BONNAL (69' Djezon
BOUTOILLE), Philippe BRUNEL (62' Benoît CHEYROU), Matt MOUSSILOU (81' Mile
STERJOVSKI (AUS) (YC86)).
Goals: Lille Olympique SC: 0-1 Abdelilah FAHMI (45'), 0-2 Nicolas BONNAL (47').
Referee: Paulo Manuel GOMES COSTA (POR)   Attendance: 26.192

41

07-08-2002   Willem II Stadion, Tilburg: Willem II Tilburg – Málaga CF   0-1 (0-0)
Willem II Tilburg: Geert DE VLIEGER (BEL), Nuelson WAU, Danny MATHIJSSEN,
Christiaan (Chris) JANSSENS (BEL) (69' Raymond VICTORIA (YC78)), Joris MATHIJSEN
(YC44), Denny LANDZAAT, Tom CALUWÉ (BEL) (YC64), Youssef MARIANA (MAR)
(24' Tarik SEKTIOUI (MAR)), Jatto CEESAY (GAM), Regilio SIMONS (61' James Stephen
QUINN (NIR)), Dmitriy SHUKOV (RUS). (Coach: Mark WOTTE).
Málaga CF: Pedro CONTRERAS González (YC74), José Miguel "JOSEMI" González Rey,
FERNANDO SANZ Durán, Mikel ROTETA Lopetegui, Vicente VALCÁRCE Cano,
GERARDO García Leon Moreno (83' Juan Jesús "JUANITO" Gutiérrez Robles), Carlos
Alejandro "SANDRO" Sierra Fumero (YC56) (60' Clever Marcelo "GATO" ROMERO Silva
(URU)), EDGAR Patricio de Carvalho Pacheco (POR) (YC37), Kizito "KIKI" MUSAMPA
(HOL), Ivan LEKO (CRO) (60' DARÍO de Bray SILVA (URU) (YC65)), Julio César DELY
VALDÉS (PAN). (Coach: Joaquín PEIRÓ Lucas).
Goal: Málaga CF: 0-1 Julio César DELY VALDÉS (67').
Referee: Thomas Michael McCURRY (SCO)   Attendance: 8.200

FINALS

13-08-2002   Stade Grimonprez-Jooris, Lille: Lille Olympique SC – VfB Stuttgart   1-0 (1-0)
Lille Olympique SC: Grégory WIMBÉE, Stéphane PICHOT, Mathieu DELPIERRE, Abdelilah
FAHMI (MAR) (YC35) (42' Rafaël SCHMITZ (BRA)), Matthieu CHALMÉ, Nicolas
BONNAL, Fernando D'AMICO (ARG), Christophe LANDRIN, Philippe BRUNEL (YC16),
Matt MOUSSILOU (86' Djezon BOUTOILLE), Mile STERJOVSKI (AUS) (64' Benoît
CHEYROU).
VfB Stuttgart: Timo HILDEBRAND, Andreas HINKEL, Marcelo José BORDON (BRA),
Fernando MEIRA (POR) (YC74), Timo WENZEL, Aleksandr HLEB (BLS), Zvonimir
SOLDO (CRO) (46' Jens TODT (YC81)), Krasimir Guenchev BALAKOV (BUL) (YC44),
Silvio MEIßNER (YC39) (67' Ioan Viorel GANEA (ROM)), Sean DUNDEE, Christian
TIFFERT (46' Michael MUTZEL).
Goal: Lille Olympique SC: 1-0 Nicolas BONNAL (19').
Referee: Jacek GRANAT (POL)   Attendance: 10.695

13-08-2002   Stadio Renato dall'Ara, Bologna: FC Bologna – Fulham FC   2-2 (0-0)
FC Bologna: Gianluca PAGLIUCA, Cristian ZACCARDO, Giulio FALCONE, Marcello
CASTELLINI, Carlo NERVO (YC77) (82' Emanuele BRIOSCHI), Roberto GORETTI
(YC67) (69' Tomas LOCATELLI), Renato OLIVE, Leonardo COLUCCI (YC58), Vlado
SMIT (YUG), Giuseppe SIGNORI (86' Claudio BELLUCCI), Julio Ricardo CRUZ (ARG).
Fulham FC: Edwin VAN DER SAR (HOL), Abdeslam OUADDOU (MAR) (YC75), Andy
MELVILLE (WAL), Alain GOMA (FRA), Rufus Emanuel BREVETT, Sylvain LEGWINSKI
(FRA) (YC52), Sean DAVIS (YC51), Steed MALBRANQUE (FRA) (61' Junichi INAMOTO
(JPN)), Luís BOA MORTE (POR) (YC60), Barrington Edward HAYLES (JAM) (61' Louis
SAHA (FRA) (YC71)), Steve MARLET (FRA).
Goals: FC Bologna: 1-0 Giuseppe SIGNORI (53' penalty), 2-1 Giuseppe SIGNORI (76'
penalty).
Fulham FC: 1-1 Junichi INAMOTO (62'), 2-2 Sylvain LEGWINSKI (88').
Referee: Eduardo ITURRALDE GONZÁLEZ (ESP)   Attendance: 23.620

42

13-08-2002   Estadio El Madrigal, Villarreal: Villarreal CF – Málaga CF   0-1 (0-1)
Villarreal CF: Javier LÓPEZ VALLEJO, Juliano Haus BELLETTI (BRA), UNAI Vergara
Diaz Caballero (YC84), Enrique "QUIQUE" ÁLVAREZ San Juan (YC15), Rodolfo Martín
ARRUABARRENA (ARG) (YC62), Constantin GÂLCA (ROM), José Joaquín Moreno Verdu
"JOSICO" (56' Carlos Reina ARANDA), JORGE LÓPEZ Montaña (85' Francisco Xavier
"XAVI" GRACIA Carlos), VÍCTOR Manuel Fernández Gutiérrez (YC35), Javier CALLEJA
Revilla (YC45) (46' José Antonio GUAYRE Betancur Perdomo), Martín PALERMO (ARG).
(Coach: Víctor MUÑOZ Manrique).
Málaga CF: Pedro CONTRERAS González, José Miguel "JOSEMI" González Rey,
FERNANDO SANZ Durán, Mikel ROTETA Lopetegui (YC54), Vicente VALCÁRCE Cano,
GERARDO García Leon Moreno, Clever Marcelo "GATO" ROMERO Silva (URU) (YC26)
(65' Carlos Alejandro "SANDRO" Sierra Fumero), Juan Jesús "JUANITO" Gutiérrez Robles
(YC14), Raúl IZNATA Zabala (YC22) (79' Sérgio Paulo Barbosa Valente "DUDA" (POR)
(YC90+)), DARÍO de Bray SILVA (URU) (65' Ivan LEKO (CRO)), Julio César DELY
VALDÉS (PAN). (Coach: Joaquín PEIRÓ Lucas).
Goal: Málaga CF: 0-1 GERARDO García Leon Moreno (8').
Referee: Michael RILEY (ENG)   Attendance: 16.000

27-08-2002   Gottlieb-Daimler-Stadion, Stuttgart:
              VfB Stuttgart – Lille Olympique SC   2-0 (0-0)
VfB Stuttgart: Timo HILDEBRAND, RUI Manuel MARQUES (POR), Andreas HINKEL (54'
Christian TIFFERT), Marcelo José BORDON (BRA), Fernando MEIRA (POR) (YC27), Timo
WENZEL, Aleksandr HLEB (BLS), Krasimir Guenchev BALAKOV (BUL), Ioan Viorel
GANEA (ROM) (YC90), Ioannis AMANATIDIS (GRE), Jochen SEITZ (YC53) (70' Kevin
KURÁNYI).
Lille Olympique SC: Grégory WIMBÉE, Stéphane PICHOT (RC48), Mathieu DELPIERRE,
Abdelilah FAHMI (MAR), Rafaël SCHMITZ (BRA), Nicolas BONNAL (YC58), Grégory
TAFFOREAU, Benoît CHEYROU (YC44) (70' Marc FORTUNÉ), Christophe LANDRIN,
Sylvain N'DIAYE (SEN) (YC24) (90' Philippe BRUNEL), Matt MOUSSILOU (YC56) (59'
Fernando D'AMICO (ARG)).
Goals: VfB Stuttgart: 1-0 Krasimir Guenchev BALAKOV (81'), 2-0 Kevin KURÁNYI (88').
Referee: Knud Erik FISKER (DEN)   Attendance: 16.000

27-08-2002   Loftus Road, London: Fulham FC – FC Bologna   3-1 (1-1)
Fulham FC: Edwin VAN DER SAR (HOL), Steve FINNAN (IRL) (YC45), Rufus Emanuel
BREVETT, Zat KNIGHT, Alain GOMA (FRA), Junichi INAMOTO (JPN) (72' Steed
MALBRANQUE (FRA)), Steve MARLET (FRA) (72' Louis SAHA (FRA)), Sylvain
LEGWINSKI (FRA) (YC16), Facundo SAVA (ARG), Sean DAVIS (74' John COLLINS
(SCO)), Luís BOA MORTE (POR).
FC Bologna: Gianluca PAGLIUCA, Cristian ZACCARDO, Giulio FALCONE, Marcello
CASTELLINI, Michele PARAMATTI (YC67) (78' Vlado SMIT (YUG)), Carlo NERVO
(YC42), Tomas LOCATELLI (87' Alessandro FRARA), Renato OLIVE (YC36), Leonardo
COLUCCI (YC58), Giuseppe SIGNORI (61' Claudio BELLUCCI), Julio Ricardo CRUZ
(ARG).
Goals: Fulham FC: 1-0 Junichi INAMOTO (12'), 2-1 Junichi INAMOTO (47'), 3-1 Junichi
INAMOTO (50').
FC Bologna: 1-1 Tomas LOCATELLI (34').
Referee: Massimo BUSACCA (SUI)   Attendance: 13.756

43

27-08-2002   Estadio La Rosaleda, Málaga: Málaga CF – Villarreal CF   1-1 (1-0)
Málaga CF: Pedro CONTRERAS González, José Miguel "JOSEMI" González Rey (RC90+),
FERNANDO SANZ Durán, Mikel ROTETA Lopetegui (81' Carlos Manuel de Oliveira
Magalhães "LITOS" (POR)), Vicente VALCÁRCE Cano, GERARDO García Leon Moreno,
Clever Marcelo "GATO" ROMERO Silva (URU), MIGUEL ÁNGEL Lozano Ayala (YC90+),
Kizito "KIKI" MUSAMPA (HOL), Carlos Alejandro "SANDRO" Sierra Fumero (YC58) (60'
Julio César DELY VALDÉS (PAN)), DARÍO de Bray SILVA (URU) (YC70) (68' Ivan
LEKO (CRO)). (Coach: Joaquín PEIRÓ Lucas).
Villarreal CF: José Manuel REINA Paez, Sergio Martínez BALLESTEROS, Enrique
"QUIQUE" ÁLVAREZ San Juan, Iñaki BERRUET Michelena (YC49) (60' VÍCTOR Manuel
Fernández Gutiérrez), Juliano Haus BELLETTI (BRA), Constantin GÂLCA (ROM) (YC52),
José Joaquín Moreno Verdu "JOSICO" (YC61), Javier CALLEJA Revilla, José Antonio
GUAYRE Betancur Perdomo, Carlos Reina ARANDA (YC90+,YC90+), Martín PALERMO
(ARG) (YC70,RC90+).(Coach: Víctor MUÑOZ Manrique).
Goals: Málaga CF: 1-0 Mikel ROTETA Lopetegui (32').
Villarreal CF: 1-1 Carlos Reina ARANDA (65').
Referee: Helmut FLEISCHER (GER)   Attendance: 19.000

Málaga CF, Fulham FC and VfB Stuttgart all qualified for the UEFA Cup competition.

2003

FIRST ROUND

21-06-2003   Belle Vue, Rhyl: Bangor City FC – FC Gloria Bistrita   0-1 (0-0)
Bangor City FC: Philip (Phil) PRIESTLEY, Alan GOODALL, Eifion JONES, Aled
ROWLANDS, Chris SHORT, Peter HOY (ENG), Richard (Ricky) EVANS (67' Gareth
WILLIAMS), Owain JONES, Kenny BURGESS, Gary REAY (ENG) (61' Lee HUNT), Gary
ROBERTS (77' Ross JEFFERIES (YC89)). (Coach: Keith HARRIS).
FC Gloria Bistrita: Costel CÂMPEANU, Sergiu Sebastian MÂNDREAN, Sergiu Viorel Ioan
COSTIN, Vasile Nicolae POPA, Vasile Ilie JULA, Alin Valer RUS, Dorian Constantin
ARBANAS (88' Dinu Daniel SÂNMARTEAN), Adrian Valentin VELCEA, Ciprian
VASILACHE (79' Danut SABAU), Cristian Ambrozie COROIAN, Sandu NEGREAN (75'
Vasile PRODAN (YC,YC90)). (Coach: Remus VLAD).
Goal: FC Gloria Bistrita: 0-1 Cristian Ambrozie COROIAN (71').
Referee: Brage SANDMOEN (NOR)   Attendance: 1.032

21-06-2003   Omladinski Stadium, Beograd: O.F.K. Beograd – JK Trans Narva   6-1 (1-0)
O.F.K. Beograd: Sasa STEVANOVIC, Ivan CVETKOVIC, Dorae JOKIC, Marko BASA, Igor
RADOVIC (YC42) (46' Aleksandar SIMIC), Srdan STANIC, Dragan STANCIC, LEANDRO
Netto de Macedo (BRA) (YC49) (62' Branko BAKOVIC), Zoran STOINOVIC (GRE) (46'
Dusko TOSIC), Vanja GRUBAC, Milos KOLAKOVIC.
JK Trans Narva: Vitas MALISHAUSKAS, Andrei PRUSS, Oleg KOLOTSEI, Oleg
KUROCHKIN (46' Ilya DJORD (RUS), 76' Anton SEREDA), Sergei KAZAKOV, Nikolai
LYSANOV, Konstantin KARIN (YC57), Stanislav KITTO (YC86), Sergei ZAMORSKI (54'
Siksten KAZIMIR (YC74)), Dmitri LIPARTOV (RUS), Maksim GRUZNOV.
Goals: O.F.K. Beograd: 1-0 Srdan STANIC (25'), 2-1 Vanja GRUBAC (66'), 3-1 Branko
BAKOVIC (72'), 4-1 Aleksandar SIMIC (81'), 5-1 Srdan STANIC (86'), 6-1 Aleksandar SIMIC
(88').
JK Trans Narva: 1-1 Oleg KOLOTSEI (59').
Referee: Iain Robertson BRINES (SCO)

UEFA awarded the game to JK Trans Narva with a 3-0 scoreline following an 80-minute
interruption caused by smoke and C.S. gas drifting onto the pitch. O.F.K. Beograd
subsequently won an appeal against this punishment and the result was declared null and void.
Progress to the next round therefore rested entirely on the result of the second match.

21-06-2003   Mestský futbalový stadión, Dubnica nad Váhom:
                    FK ZTS Dubnica – Olympiakos FC Nicosia   3-0 (1-0)
FK ZTS Dubnica: Pavol KOVÁC (YC76), Martin SEVELA, Martin SVESTKA, Branislav
MRÁZ, Marian ZIMEN (90' Andrej SUPKA), Juraj DOVICOVIC (YC63) (69' Roman
GREGUSKA), Igor DRZIK, Peter KISKA, Anton SUCHÝ, Pavol STRAKA (YC88), Marian
BELLAK (57' Ján SVIKRUHA).
Olympiakos FC Nicosia: Spiros NEOFYTIDES, Loucas STYLIANOU (YC86), Kyriakos
KYRIAKOU, Georgios PELAGIA, Michalis PATOUNAS, Nicolaos NICOLAOU, Christos
IOANNOU (90' Andreas TSIAKLES), Evangelos CHRYSTODOULOU, Marios ADAMOU
(70' Georgios GEORGIADES), Konstantinos ZORPAS (64' Kostas KONSTANTINOU),
Michalis CHRISTOFI.
Goals: FK ZTS Dubnica: 1-0 Martin SVESTKA (20'), 2-0 Ján SVIKRUHA (71'), 3-0 Martin
SEVELA (81').
Referee: Miroslav RADOMAN (SBM)   Attendance: 2.750

45

21-06-2003   Qemal Stafa Stadium, Tiranë:
KS Partizani Tiranë – Maccabi Nethanya FC   2-0 (2-0)
KS Partizani Tiranë: Blendi NALLBANI, Ardian BEHARI, Ardit BEQIRI (83' Elis BAKAJ
(YC89)), Henri NDREKA, Perparim DAIU, Rahman HALLACI, Igli ALLMUÇA, Bekim
KULI (79' Matios METAJ), Viana Alexander Antonio CARIOCA (BRA) (67' Romeo
HAMZA), Gjergj MUZAKA, Alket KRUJA.
Maccabi Nethanya FC: Ido LANGER, Lior GENISH (YC42), Alon PETITO (28' Assaf BEN
DAVID), Yariv MULI, Yaakov HASAN, Ran KOZUCH, Asaf BRUNSTEIN (70' Guy
ALMOG), Roy Yehoshua Vili SHMIDEL, Amos NEHAISI, David HADAD (57' Udi Dudu
POLTIGER), Maher GABARIN.
Goals: KS Partizani Tiranë: 1-0 Viana Alexander Antonio CARIOCA (15'), 2-0 Bekim KULI
(21').
Referee: Panayiotis GERASIMOU (CYP)

21-06-2003   Stadion Lesní ulice, Breclav: 1.FC Brno – FC Kotayk Abovyan 1-0 (1-0)
1.FC Brno: Tomas BELIC (SVK), Martin ZIVNY (75' Petr MUSIL), Petr KRIVANEK,
Martin KOTÜLEK, Patrik KRAP, Tomás ABRAHAM, Milan PACANDA, Marek ZUBEK,
Roman DRGA (63' Milos KRSKO (SVK)), Libor DOSEK, Pavel SUSTR.
FC Kotayk Abovyan: Eduard YERITSYAN, Valeri ALEKSANYAN, Gevork
MIRIDZHANYAN, Arsen MELOYAN, Albert AFYAN, Vadim GHAHRAMANOV (87'
Hrachya VARDAZARYAN), Gor MIRZAKHANYAN, Sarkis NAZARYAN (83' Armen
BABAYAN), Arshak AMIRYAN, Artur KOCHARYAN, Tigran DAVITYAN (YC83) (90'
Arman POGHOSYAN).
Goal: 1.FC Brno: 1-0 Libor DOSEK (4').
Referee: Valery VIALICHKA (BLS)   Attendance: 1.321

21-06-2003   Traktor Stadion, Minsk: FC Shakhter Soligorsk – Omagh Town FC 1-0 (1-0)
FC Shakhter Soligorsk: Alexandr MARTESHKIN, Andrei SIAROHIN, Alexandr YUREVICH
(YC9), Aliaksei BELAVUSAV, Tsimafei KALACHOV, Andrei LEONCHIK (YC86),
Dzmitry BESPANSKI (RC90), Vadim SKRIPCHENKO (53' Roman TREPACHKIN), Sergei
NIKIFORENKO, Vazdim BOIKA (70' Dmitriy PODREZ), Anatoliy TIKHONCHIK (56' Igor
SLESARCUK (LAT)).
Omagh Town FC: Gavin James CULLEN (IRL), Michael KELLY, Eamon KAVANAGH,
Saemus FANTHORPE (YC4), John McELROY, Patrick McLAUGHLIN, Andrew Patrick
CRAWFORD (75' Sean Austin FRIEL), Martin McCANN, Dermot Paul DOHERTY (IRL)
(89' Frankie WILSON), Ivan SPROULE (90' Noel Patrick JOHNSTON), Glen Philip
BOVAIRD (IRL).
Goal: FC Shakhter Soligorsk: 1-0 Anatoliy TIKHONCHIK (22').
Referee: Ivan NOVAK (CRO)

21-06-2003   Stadionul Republican, Chisinau: FC Dacia Chisinau – GÍ Gøtu 4-1 (1-0)
FC Dacia Chisinau: Alexander MEREUTA, Vitaly MARDARI (YC41), Cornel POPOV, Liviu
ANDRIUTA, Serghey POTRIMBA (78' Lilian CODA), Vitalie GLUHENKI, Andrei
MARTIN, Sergiu JAPALAU (87' Alexander GOROBET), Grigory BADEA, Alexandru
GOLBAN, Vladimir JAPULAU (63' Gennady ORBU).
GÍ Gøtu: Jacek PRZYBYLSKI (POL), Poul Andrias JACOBSEN, Áslakkur PETERSEN (69'
Jónreid DALHEIM), Leivur HANSEN, Poul ENNIGARD, Bárdur á LAKJUNI (77' Magnus
SKORALID), Simun Louis JACOBSEN, Krysztof POPCZYNSKI (POL), Zdzislaw JANIK
(POL) (YC47), Hogni MADSEN (88' Anton SKORADAL), Simun SAMUELSEN.
Goals: FC Dacia Chisinau: 1-0 Sergiu JAPALAU (33'), 2-0 Alexandru GOLBAN (47'), 3-1
Alexandru GOLBAN (85'), 4-1 Andrei MARTIN (90'+2').
GÍ Gøtu: 2-1 Krysztof POPCZYNSKI (55').
Referee: Stefano PODESCHI (SMR)   Attendance: 2.000

21-06-2003   Stadion Tusanj, Tuzla: FK Sloboda Tuzla – K.A. Akureyri 1-1 (0-0)
FK Sloboda Tuzla: Romeo MITROVIC, Muhamed JUSUFOVIC (84' Nedzad BAJROVIC),
Nusret MUSLIMOVIC (YC29), Gradimir CRNOGORAC, Samir KUDUZOYIC (YC31),
Senad HADZIC (YC13), Stanisa NIKOLIC, Adnan SARAJLIC (YC,YC69), Tarik
OKANOVIC (70' Admir BRDZANOVIC), Admir JOLDIC, Alen MESANOVIC.
K.A. Akureyri: Soren BYSKOV, Jon Orvar ERIKSSON, Thorvaldur Sveinn
GUDBJÖRNSSON, Dean MARTIN (60' Steingrimur EIDSSON), Slobodan MILISIC (SBM)
(YC10), Ronnie HARTVIG, Steinn Vidar GUNNARSSON (YC59), Steinar TENDEN (75'
Orlygur Por HELGASON), Thorvaldur Maka SIGBJÖRNSSON, Bjarni PALMASON, Ol
Thor SIRGISSON.
Goals: FK Sloboda Tuzla: 1-0 Nusret MUSLIMOVIC (80' penalty).
K.A. Akureyri: 1-1 Orlygur Por HELGASON (81').
Referee: Sergiy BEREZKA (UKR)

21-06-2003   Celtnieks Stadion, Daugavpils:
                FC Dinaburg Daugavpils – FC Wil 1900 1-0 (1-0)
FC Dinaburg Daugavpils: Sergey DIGULYOV, Yurgis PUCHINSKY (YC79) (82' Andrey
MARKOV (RUS)), Alexander SHUMILOV, Vadim LOGINS, Dmitrij CUGUNOV, Jurij
SOKOLOV, Alexey BORUN, Dmitry KOKHAN (71' Olexandr KRIKLIVY (UKR)),
Christian SAGNA (SLO) (26' Pavel KOLTSOV), Alexey KOSTENKO (RUS), Orest
DOROSH (UKR).
FC Wil 1900: Nicolas BENEY, Alessandro MANGIARRATTI, Philippe MONTANDON,
Michael RENGGLI, Dilaver SATILMIS, Umberto ROMANO, FABIO de Souza (BRA),
Davide CALLA (ITA) (77' Peter EUGSTER), Stefan BLUNSCHI, Mauro LUSTRINELLI,
Markus GSELL (59' Marco HÄMMERLI).
Goal: FC Dinaburg Daugavpils: 1-0 Dmitrij CUGUNOV (28').
Referee: Zbigniew MARCZYK (POL)

47

21-06-2003   Stadion Odry Wodzislaw, Wodzislaw Slaski:
MKS Odra Wodzislaw – Shamrock Rovers FC   1-2 (0-0)
MKS Odra Wodzislaw: Marius PAWELEK, Wojciech MYSZOR, Jan CIOS, Blazej
JANKOWSKI (YC52), Wojciech GRZYB (77' Wojciech SALEK), Dariusz KLUS (58'
Roman MADEJ), Wojciech GORSKI, Rafal JAROSZ, Marcin NOWACKI, Bartlomiej
SOCHA, Jacek ZIARKOWSKI (31' Michal CHALBINSKI).
Shamrock Rovers FC: Barry Paul RYAN, James Michael KEDDY, Richard Philip BYRNE,
Terry PALMER, Stephen James GOUGH, Stephen GRANT, Alan REYNOLDS, Jason John
COLWELL (YC13), Shane ROBINSON (YC18), Glen Paul FITZPATRICK (YC55) (78'
Trevor MOLLOY), Anthony James GRANT.
Goals: MKS Odra Wodzislaw: 1-0 Marcin NOWACKI (73').
Shamrock Rovers FC: 1-1 Stephen GRANT (76'), 1-2 Anthony James GRANT (83').
Referee: Sead KULOVIC (BOS)

21-06-2003   Györi ETO Stadion, Györ: Györi ETO FC – Ethnikós Áchnas FC   1-1 (0-1)
Györi ETO FC: Zsolt SEBÖK, Csaba REGEDEI, Atilla BÖJTE, Goran JOVANOVIC (SBM)
(YC69), Miklos SALAMON (55' Norbert NÉMETH), Antal JAKL, Tamas GERI, Darko
PERIC (CRO) (58' Zoltán VARGA (YC61)), Daniel DJOSEVSKI (MCD), Márton OROSS,
Aleksandar BAJEVSKI (MCD) (36' Miklós HERCZEG (YC37)).
Ethnikós Áchnas FC: Marios KYRIAKOU, Panayiotis DIONYSIOU (90' Costantinos
MARINOU), Loizos KAKOYIANNIS, Petros HATZIAROS, Dimitris SIMOU (YC1),
Kyriakos APOSTOLOU (YC2), Christakis POYIATZIS, Elipidoforos ILIA (90' Andreas
APOSTOLOU), Nicos SOFOCLEOUS (YC86), Chrysafis CHRYSAFIS, Kyriakos
CHATZIAROS (82' Marios NICOLA).
Goals: Györi ETO FC: 1-1 Márton OROSS (58').
Ethnikós Áchnas FC: 0-1 Chrysafis CHRYSAFIS (45').
Referee: Delce JAKIMOVSKI (MCD)   Attendance: 1.000

22-06-2003   Estadi Comunal d'Andorra la Vella, Andorra la Vella:
FC Encamp Dicoansa – K.Lierse SK   0-3 (0-2)
FC Encamp Dicoansa: Ricardo FERNÁNDEZ LIZARTE (ESP), Emanuel GOLDSCHMIDT
(ARG), Josep PORTAS (ESP), Federico Alfonso COTO ARAGONES (ESP) (88 Rui Jorge
CABOT JACINTO (ESP)), Oscar ALFONSO DA CUNHA (POR), Christian XINOS (GRE),
Carlos CONGIL (ESP) (80' Claudio ROMERO (ARG)), Laureano MIRAGLIA (ITA),
Alejandro ROMERO (ARG), Leonardo MIRAGLIA (ITAL), Luis Maria VERIZ (ARG) (65'
Miguel Angel BELDA (ESP)).
K.Lierse SK: Yannick DIERICK, Nicolas TIMMERMANS, Toon GLASSEE, Stéphane
RONGE (YC59), Timothy HEYLEN, Maxence COVELIERS, Timothy DREESEN, Archie
THOMPSON (AUS) (57' Kenny RUCQUOY), Kevin DIJCK (72' Cédric MEDARD), Stijn
JANSSENS, Issame CHARAI (46' Jurgen RAEYMAECKERS).
Goals: K.Lierse SK: 0-1 Nicolas TIMMERMANS (8'), 0-2 Styn JANSSENS (22'), 0-3 Jurgen
RAEYMAECKERS (76').
Referee: Richard HAVRILLA (SVK)

22-06-2003   Zalgirio Stadionas, Vilnius: FK Zalgiris Vilnius – Örgryte IS 1-1 (0-0)
FK Zalgiris Vilnius: Pavelas LEUSAS, Mindaugas PUODZIUNAS (79' Darius
ARTIOMOVAS), Sergejus NOVIKOVAS, Andrejus SOROKINAS, Tomas MIKUCKIS,
Elman SULTANOV (AZE), Andrei SHILO (BLS), Virmantas LEMEZIS, Andrius
MILISKEVICIUS (YC46) (46' Erik PELCIS (LAT)), Mindaugas GRIGALEVICIUS (86'
Marius KIZYS), Dainius SAULENAS.
Örgryte IS: Tommy NAURIN, Atli THÓRARINSSON (ISL), Anders PRYTZ, Edwin PHIRI
(ZAM), Patrik HELLBERG (YC55), Eric GUSTAFSSON, RICARDO SALVES Alves dos
Santos (BRA) (62' Mentor ZHUBI), Daniel LOHM, Robin GANEMYR (84' Marcus
JOHANNESSON), Patrik FREDHOLM, Christian HEMBERG (69' Boyo MWILA (ZAM)).
Goals: FK Zalgiris Vilnius: 1-0 Andrei SHYLA (55' penalty).
Örgryte IS: 1-1 Boyo MWILA (84').
Referee: PEDRO PROENÇA Oliveira Alves Garcia (POR)

22-06-2003   SRC Bonifika Stadium, Koper: NK Koper – NK Zagreb 1-0 (0-0)
NK Koper: Ermin HASIC, Edmond GUNJAC, Andrej POLJSAK, Andrej RASTOVAC, Alen
SCULAC, Darko KREMENOVIC, Igor BENEDEJCIC, Sasa BOZICIC (YC70), Nebojsa
KOVACEVIC, Sasa JAKOMIN, Oliver BOGATINOV.
NK Zagreb: Tomislav PELIN, Josip BARISIC (YC9) (46' Erion RIZVANOLLI (ALB)), Emir
SPAHIC (BOS), Igor NOVAKOVIC, Tonci ZILIC, Luko BISKUP (YC26), Mensur
MUJDZA, Mario BRKLJACA, Josip FUCEK (64' Antonio MAMIC), Radomir DALOVIC
(SBM), Ivan BABIC.
Goal: NK Koper: 1-0 Sasa JAKOMIN (59').
Referee: Dietmar DRABEK (AUT)

22-06-2003   Stadion kraj Bistrice, Niksic:
                     FK Sutjeska Niksic – U.S. Luxembourg 3-0 (0-0)
FK Sutjeska Niksic: Zoran BANOVIC, Srdjan DAMJANOVIC, Darko KRSTESKI (MCD),
Kristijan TUCAKOVIC, Vladan KOSTIC, Milenko MILOSEVIC, Goran BOSKOVIC, Drazen
MEDJEDOVIC (55' Anzor NAFAS), Novica MIKOVIC, Nikola NIKEZIC, Ivan BOSKOVIC
(89' Vlado JEKNIC).
U.S. Luxembourg: Jimmy GILLANDER, Claude REITER, Tom SCHNELL, Pasquale
ANTONICELLI, Yannick LOOSE, Marc BAUM, Luciano CRAPA (BEL) (79' Assim
ALLOMEROVIC (YC90)), Enver SABOTIC (SBM), Amédé SUZZI (73' Laurent
AQUISTAPACE (FRA)), Alen MILAK (SBM) (84' Paul ENGEL), Jeff FELLER.
Goals: FK Sutjeska Niksic: 1-0 Novica MIKOVIC (47'), 2-0 Darko KRSTESKI (84' penalty),
3-0 Ivan BOSKOVIC (87').
Referee: Knud STADSGAARD (DEN)

22-06-2003   Stadión Antona Malatinského, Trnava:
FC Spartak Trnava – FK Pobeda Prilep   1-5 (1-3)
FC Spartak Trnava: Ilizi LUBOS, Souleymane de Sagana FALL (SEN), Peter HLUSKO,
Martin POLJOVKA, Jaroslav HRABAL (YC63), Milos JUHASZ (37' Michal GASPARIK),
Marek UJLAKY, Andrej FILIP (37' Marián HOLNÁR), Pavol STAŇO, Miroslav KRISS (71'
Tomás BARTOS), Vladimir KOZUCH.
FK Pobeda Prilep: Tome PANCEV, Marjan NACEV, Saso ZDRAVEVSKI, Cedomir
MIJANOVIC (SBM), Pance CHUMBEV, GILSON de Jesus da Silva (BRA), Nikolce
ZDRAVESKI (84' Marijanco MAIEV), Toni MEGLENSKI, Dimitar KAPINKOVSKI,
Draganco DIMITROVSKI (79' Aleksandar POPOVSKI), Blagoja GESOSKI (74' Goran
SEAD (SBM)).
Goals: FC Spartak Trnava: 1-1 Souleymane de Sagana FALL (9').
FK Pobeda Prilep: 0-1 Dimitar KAPINKOVSKI (5'), 1-2 Blagoja GESOSKI (15'), 1-3
Blagoja GESOSKI (28'), 1-4 Draganco DIMITROVSKI (75'), 1-5 GILSON de Jesus da Silva
(90').
Referee: Oleh ORIEKHOV (UKR)   Attendance: 2.198

22-06-2003   Schwan-Stadion, Schwanenstadt:
SV Pasching – FC WIT Georgia Tbilisi   1-0 (0-0)
SV Pasching: Josef SCHICKLGRUBER, Hakki Tolunay KAFKAS (TUR), Tomasz WISIO
(POL), Manfred ROTHBAUER (77' Metin ASLAN), Markus KIESENEBNER (70' Bozo
KOVACEVIC), Michael HORVATH, Edi GLIEDER, Helmut RIEGLER, George Martin
DATORU (61' Christian MAYRLEB), Torsten KNABEL, Wolfgang MAIR.
FC WIT Georgia Tbilisi: Mirza MERLANI, Aleksandre INTSKIRVELI, Jaba MUJIRI, Levan
MEREBASHVILI (90' David BOLKVADZE), Oleg GVELESIANI, Giorgi KVAKHADZE,
David DIGMELASHVILI (79' Otar MARTSVALADZE), Lasha NOZADZE, David
DOLIDZE, Vladimer GOCHASHVILI, Levan MELKADZE (86' Pawel DATUNAISHVILI).
Goal: SV Pasching: 1-0 Edi GLIEDER (66' penalty).
Referee: Sokol JARECI (ALB)   Attendance: 700

22-06-2003   Stadion Eszperantó Út, Dunaújváros:
Videoton FC – FC Marek Dupnitsa   2-2 (2-0)
Videoton FC: Árpád MILINTE, Krisztián TIMÁR, Ivan RISTIC (SBM), Gabriel VOCHIN
(ROM), Zoltán VASAS, Tamás SZALAI (YC21), Balázs TÓTH (46' MONYE Precious
Onyeabor (NGR)), Zsolt DVÉRI, Ferenc KÓCZIÁN (YC70), Gábor FÖLDES (76' Tibor
SZABÓ (SBM)), Attila KORSÓS (59' Lajos TERJÉK).
FC Marek Dupnitsa: Ivaylo IVANOV, Dimitar KOEMDZHIEV, Saso LAZAREVSKI (MCD),
Georgi VAZHAROV, Alexei DIONISIEV, Ianek KIUTCHUKOV (YC75), Angel STOIKOV
(YC43), Ivo PARGOV (84' Kroum BIBISHKOV), Liubomir LIUBENOV (78' Toni
PITOSKA (MCD)), Anzhelo KIUCHUKOV (90' Emil PETKOV), Vassil KIROV.
Goals: Videoton FC: 1-0 Ferenc KÓCZIÁN (1'), 2-0 , Gábor FÖLDES (36').
FC Marek Dupnitsa: 2-1 Angel STOIKOV (58' penalty), 2-2 Ivo PARGOV (60').
Referee: Sergo KVARATSKHELIA (GEO)   Attendance: 500

22-06-2003   Stadion Polonii Warszawa, Warszawa:
KF Polonia Warszawa – FK Tobol Kostanay   0-3 (0-1)
FK Polonia Warszawa: Mindaugas MAKSVYTIS (LIT), Marcin KUS, Vlado DANILOV
(MCD), Rafal SZWED, Andrei SINITSYN (BLS), Igor GOLASZEWSKI, Lukasz
JAROSIEWICZ, Pawel HAJDUCZEK (YC88), Piotr KOSIOROWSKI, Patryk
ALEKSANDROWICZ (46' Sebastian KESKA (YC90)), Maciej NUCKOWSKI.
FK Tobol Kostanay: Valeri SHANTALOSOV (BLS), Petr BADLO (YC60) (87' Sergey
MASLENOV), Oleg LOTOV, Andrey SHKURIN, Sergey ANDREEV (RUS), Oleg
GOLOVAN (RUS) (89' Sergey KAPUTIN), Konstantin KOTOV, Alexey KOSOLAPOV
(RUS), Nurbol ZHUMASKALIYEV (YC18), Daniar MUHANOV (YC90), Nurken
MAZBAYEV (82' Valeriy GARKUSHA).
Goals: FK Tobol Kostanay: 0-1 Nurken MAZBAYEV (23'), 0-2 Andrey SHKURIN (49'), 0-3
Nurken MAZBAYEV (72').
Referee: Mark Steven WHITBY (WAL)   Attendance: 600

22-06-2003   Pohjola Stadion, Vantaa: AC Allianssi – Hibernians FC Malta   1-0 (0-0)
AC Allianssi: Alexander MISHCHUK (RUS), Ari-Pekka ROIKO, Janne MOILANEN, Jarno
TUUNAINEN, Harri HAAPANIEMI, Timo MARJAMAA, Rami RANTANEN, Mikko
SIMULA, Markus PAATELAINEN (65' Mikko PAATELAINEN), Petteri KAIJASILTA (82'
John AHLBERG), ADRIANO Munoz (BRA).
Hibernians FC Malta: Mario MUSCAT, Branko NISEVIC (SBM) (YC1), Adrian PULIS,
Aaron XUEREB, Cesar Oscar PAIBER (ARG), Essien MBONG (NGR), Adrian MIFSUD
(86' Udochukwu NWOKO (NGR)), Ndubisi CHUKUNYERE (NGR) (72' Antoine ZAHRA),
Edmond LUFI (ALB) (46' Adrian CIANTAR), Peter PULLICINO, Roderick
BALDACCHINO.
Goal: AC Allianssi: 1-0 ADRIANO Munoz (90').
Referee: Mark COURTNEY (NIR)

22-06-2003   Ratina Stadium, Tampere:
Tampere United FC – FC Ceahlaul Piatra Neamt   1-0 (1-0)
Tampere United FC: Mikko KAVEN, Pasi SALMELA, Mikko SALO, Vasile MARCHIS
(ROM) (YC66) (88' Antti OJANPERÄ), Jussi KUOPPALA, Heikki AHO, Janne RÄSÄNEN,
Kari SAINIO, Tero KOSKELA, Sakari SAARINEN (YC6) (79' Mika LAHTINEN), Henri
SCHEWELEFF (85' Antti HYNYNEN). (Coach: Ari Juhani HJELM).
FC Ceahlaul Piatra Neamt: Radu Gabriel LEFTER, Angelo Dumitru ALISTAR (YC86), Vasile
Valentin AVADANEI, Nicolae Dorin GOIAN (YC75), Constantin Ionut ILIE, Dumitru
BOTEZ, Tiberiu SERBAN, Sergiu BRUJAN, Lucian BURDUJAN (69' Constantin
ENACHE), Mihai NEMTANU (57' Cristian Ciprian LUPUT), Shenif FEIZULLAH (77'
Adrian Constantin SOLOMON). (Coach: Viorel HIZO).
Goal: Tampere United FC: 1-0 Kari SAINIO (26').
Referee: Eduard CICHY (SVK)   Attendance: 4.300
(Constantin Ionut ILIE missed a penalty in the 66th minute)

28-06-2003   Nya Ullevi, Göteborg: Örgryte IS – FK Zalgiris Vilnius   3-0 (0-0)
Örgryte IS: Tommy NAURIN, Atli THÓRARINSSON (ISL), Anders PRYTZ, Edwin PHIRI
(ZAM), David MAREK, Marcus DAHLIN, Mentor ZHUBI (77' RICARDO SALVES Alves
dos Santos (BRA)), Daniel LOHM (YC62), Patrik FREDHOLM (62' Christian HEMBERG),
Alfonso ALVES Martins Júnior (BRA) (63' Walter TOMAZ Jr (BRA)), Paulo Roberto
Chamon de Castillo "PAULINHO" (BRA).
FK Zalgiris Vilnius: Audrius DILYS, Mindaugas PUODZIUNAS, Sergejus NOVIKOVAS,
Andrejus SOROKINAS, Tomas MIKUCKIS (YC,YC86), Andrei SHILO (BLS), Elman
SULTANOV (AZE), Virmantas LEMEZIS (54' Marius KIZYS), Mindaugas
GRIGALEVICIUS, Erik PELCIS (LAT) (71' Remigijus POCIUS), Dainius SAULENAS.
Goals: Örgryte IS: 1-0 Alfonso ALVES Martins Júnior (52'), 2-0 Paulo Roberto Chamon de
Castillo "PAULINHO" (75'), 3-0 Paulo Roberto Chamon de Castillo "PAULINHO" (90').
Referee: Lassin ISAKSEN (FAR)

28-06-2003   Akureyrarvöllur, Akureyri: K.A. Akureyri – FK Sloboda Tuzla   1-1 (0-1)
K.A. Akureyri: Soren BYSKOV, Jon Orvar ERIKSSON (55' Hreinn HRINGSSON),
Thorvaldur Sveinn GUDBJÖRNSSON, Dean MARTIN, Slobodan MILISIC (SBM) (YC37),
Thorvaldur ÖRLYGSSON, Steinn Vidar GUNNARSSON, Steinar TENDEN (55' Elmar Dan
SIGTHÓRSSON (YC89)), Thorvaldur Maka SIGBJÖRNSSON, Bjarni PALMASON (91'
Steingrimur EIDSSON), Ronnie HARTVIG.
FK Sloboda Tuzla: Mirsad DEDIC, Nusret MUSLIMOVIC, Gradimir CRNOGORAC, Samir
KUDUZOYIC, Nedzad BAJROVIC (YC102), Admir JOLDIC (79' Armin DELIC), Zvjezdan
KRESIC (59' Muhamed JUSUFOVIC), Tarik OKANOVIC, Stanisa NIKOLIC (YC66), Senad
HADZIC (YC100), Alen MESANOVIC.
Goals: K.A. Akureyri: 1-1 Thorvaldur Maka SIGBJÖRNSSON (55').
FK Sloboda Tuzla: 0-1 Gradimir CRNOGORAC (19').
Referee: Brian LAWLOR (WAL)
Penalties: * Hreinn HRINGSSON   1 Tarik OKANOVIC
                  1 Steinn Vidar GUNNARSSON   * Gradimir CRNOGORAC
                  * Elmar Dan SIGTHÓRSSON   2 Stanisa NIKOLIC
                  2 Steingrimur EIDSSON   * Nedzad BAJROVIC
                  * Thorvaldur Sveinn GUDBJÖRNSSON   3 Nusret MUSLIMOVIC
(After extra time)

28-06-2003   Brandywell Stadium, Derry:
              Omagh Town FC – FC Shakhter Soligorsk   1-7 (1-4)
Omagh Town FC: Gavin James CULLEN (IRL), Michael KELLY, Eamon KAVANAGH,
Saemus FANTHORPE, Noel Patrick JOHNSTON (46' Coim Joseph McCULLASH), Patrick
McLAUGHLIN, Andrew Patrick CRAWFORD, Martin McCANN (60' Frankie WILSON),
Dermot Paul DOHERTY (IRL) (68' Sean Austin FRIEL), Ivan SPROULE, Glen Philip
BOVAIRD (IRL).
FC Shakhter Soligorsk: Alexandr MARTESHKIN, Anatoliy BUDAYEV, Andrei SIAROHIN
(YC65), Alexandr YUREVICH, Aliaksei BELAVUSAV, Tsimafei KALACHOV (61' Vazdim
BOIKA), Andrei LEONCHIK, Vadim SKRIPCHENKO (46' Alexandr NOVIK), Roman
TREPACHKIN, Sergei NIKIFORENKO (60' Dmitriy PODREZ), Anatoliy TIKHONCHIK.
Goals: Omagh Town FC: 1-4 Ivan SPROULE (41').
FC Shakhter Soligorsk: 0-1 Andrei LEONCHIK (2'), 0-2 Tsimafei KALACHOV (4'), 0-3
Tsimafei KALACHOV (25'), 0-4 Anatoliy TIKHONCHIK (28'), 1-5 Alexandr NOVIK (52'),
1-6 Andrei SIAROHIN (57'), 1-7 Alexandr NOVIK (68').
Referee: Bragi BERGMANN (ISL)

28-06-2003   Stadionul Gloria, Bistrita: FC Gloria Bistrita – Bangor City FC 5-2 (1-1)
FC Gloria Bistrita: Costel CÂMPEANU, Sergiu Sebastian MÂNDREAN (RC90), Sergiu
Viorel Ioan COSTIN, Vasile Nicolae POPA, Vasile Ilie JULA (RC90), Alin Valer RUS,
Ciprian VASILACHE (69' Sorin Ciprian BUCUROAIA), Lucian Iulian SÂNMARTEAN,
Alin Ilie MINTEUAN (YC9), Cristian Ambrozie COROIAN (78' Razvan RADU), Adrian
ANCA (YC34) (64' Sandu NEGREAN). (Coach: Remus VLAD).
Bangor City FC: Philip (Phil) PRIESTLEY, Alan GOODALL (RC80), Eifion JONES, Aled
ROWLANDS, Chris SHORT (YC68), Peter HOY (ENG) (74' Gary REAY (ENG)), Clayton
BLACKMORE (60' Kenny BURGESS), Richard (Ricky) EVANS (YC27), Owain JONES,
Gary ROBERTS (66' Gareth WILLIAMS), Ross JEFFERIES (RC90). (Coach: Keith
HARRIS).
Goals: FC Gloria Bistrita: 1-1 Adrian ANCA (26'), 2-1 Lucian Iulian SÂNMARTEAN (56'),
3-1 Sergiu Sebastian MÂNDREAN (64'), 4-1 Lucian Iulian SÂNMARTEAN (85'), 5-1 Sorin
Cirpian BUCUROAIA (90').
Bangor City FC: 0-1 Richard (Ricky) EVANS (19'), 5-2 Richard (Ricky) EVANS (90'+1'
penalty).
Referee: Adrian D.CASHA (MLT)

28-06-2003   Neo GSZ Stadium, Larnaca: Ethnikós Áchnas FC – Györi ETO FC 2-2 (2-1)
Ethnikós Áchnas FC: Marios KYRIAKOU, Panayiotis DIONYSIOU, Loizos
KAKOYIANNIS, Petros HATZIAROS (YC46), Dimitris SIMOU, Kyriakos APOSTOLOU
(YC87), Christakis POYIATZIS, Elipidoforos ILIA, Nicos SOFOCLEOUS, Chrysafis
CHRYSAFIS, Kyriakos CHATZIAROS. (used sub: Marios NICOLA (YC90)).
Györi ETO FC: Zsolt SEBÖK, Goran JOVANOVIC (SBM) (YC73), Atilla BÖJTE, Antal
JAKL (YC25), Csaba REGEDEI, Elek NYILAS (YC43), Zoltán VARGA, Norbert NÉMETH,
Tamas GERI (YC90), Márton OROSS, Tibor KALINA. (used sub: Marko KARTELO (CRO)).
Goals: Ethnikós Áchnas FC: 1-0 Kyriakos CHATZIAROS (6'), 2-0 Kyriakos CHATZIAROS
(10)'.
Györi ETO FC: 2-1 Zoltán VARGA (45'), 2-2 Marko KARTELO (57').
Referee: Novo PANIC (BOS)

28-06-2003   Goce Delcev Stadium, Prilep:
              FK Pobeda Prilep – FC Spartak Trnava 2-1 (1-0)
FK Pobeda Prilep: Tome PANCEV, Dimitar KAPINKOVSKI, Marjan NACEV (75'
Marijanco MAIEV), Cedomir MIJANOVIC (SBM), Saso ZDRAVEVSKI, Pance CHUMBEV
(YC20) (59' Aleksandar POPOVSKI), Toni MEGLENSKI, GILSON de Jesus da Silva (BRA),
Nikolce ZDRAVESKI, Draganco DIMITROVSKI (64' Goran SEAD (SBM)), Blagoja
GESOSKI.
FC Spartak Trnava: Ilizi LUBOS, Souleymane de Sagana FALL (SEN), Martin POLJOVKA,
Dusan BESTVINA, Roman KONECNY (YC25) (61' Milos JUHASZ (YC89)), Michal
GASPARIK (70' Peter HODÙR), Marek UJLAKY, Andrej FILIP, Marián HOLNÁR,
Miroslav KRISS, Ivan LIETAVA (81' Kamil KOPÙNEK).
Goals: FK Pobeda Prilep: 1-0 GILSON de Jesus da Silva (39'), 2-0 Dimitar KAPINKOVSKI
(58').
FC Spartak Trnava: 2-1 Miroslav KRISS (83').
Referee: Kuddusi MÜFTÜOGLU (TUR)

53

28-06-2003   Stadion u Kranjcevicevoj, Zagreb: NK Zagreb – NK Koper 2-2 (0-1)
NK Zagreb: Tomislav PELIN, Igor NOVAKOVIC (YC44) (46' Antonio MAMIC), Josip
BARISIC (YC66), Luko BISKUP (YC61) (68' Ivan MILAS), Tonci ZILIC, Vedran JESE,
Mensur MUJDZA, Emir SPAHIC (BOS) (YC64), Ivan BABIC (68' Sead BRUNCEVIC
(SBM)), Kruno LOVREK, Radomir DALOVIC (SBM).
NK Koper: Ermin HASIC, Alen SCULAC, Andrej RASTOVAC, Edmond GUNJAC (YC58),
Igor BENEDEJCIC (YC42) (83' Brne BORUT), Sasa BOZICIC, Darko KREMENOVIC (90'
Marko GRIZONIC), Nebojsa KOVACEVIC, Andrej POLJSAK (YC33), Sasa JAKOMIN
(YC18) (80' Oliver BOGATINOV), Viktor TRENEVSKI (MCD).
Goals: NK Zagreb: 1-1 Radomir DALOVIC (66'), 2-2 Sead BRUNCEVIC (81').
NK Koper: 0-1 Viktor TRENEVSKI (27'), 1-2 Viktor TRENEVSKI (71' penalty).
Referee: Andriy SHANDOR (UKR)

28-06-2003   Hibernians Ground, Paola: Hibernians FC Malta – AC Allianssi 1-1 (1-0)
Hibernians FC Malta: Mario MUSCAT, Branko NISEVIC (SBM), Adrian PULIS, Aaron
XUEREB, Cesar Oscar PAIBER (ARG), Essien MBONG (NGR) (YC54), Adrian MIFSUD,
Ndubisi CHUKUNYERE (NGR), Antoine ZAHRA (57' Miguel MIFSUD (YC90)), Peter
PULLICINO (87' Andrew COHEN), Roderick BALDACCHINO (67' Terence SCERRI).
AC Allianssi: Alexander MISHCHUK (RUS), Harri HAAPANIEMI, Jarno TUUNAINEN,
Janne MOILANEN (YC87), Ari-Pekka ROIKO (YC73), Timo MARJAMAA, Rami
RANTANEN, Peter SAMPO (88' Heikki PULKKINEN), Mikko SIMULA (YC67) (84'
Mikko PAATELAINEN), ADRIANO Munoz (BRA), Petteri KAIJASILTA (72' Justus
VAJANNE).
Goals: Hibernians FC Malta: 1-0 Adrian MIFSUD (30').
AC Allianssi: 1-1 Mikko SIMULA (50').
Referee: Pavel Cristian BALAJ (ROM)

28-06-2003   Stadion Albena-1, Albena (BUL):
            Maccabi Nethanya FC – KS Partizani Tiranë 3-1 (1-1)
Maccabi Nethanya FC: Ido LANGER, Lior GENISH, Assaf BEN DAVID, Yariv MULI,
Yaakov HASAN, Ran KOZUCH, Asaf BRUNSTEIN (60' David HADAD), Roy Yehoshua
Vili SHMIDEL, Amos NEHAISI (72' Elad YOSSEF), Udi Dudu POLTIGER (51' Kfirzvi
NAHMANI), Maher GABARIN (YC11).
KS Partizani Tiranë: Blendi NALLBANI (YC85), Ardian BEHARI (YC43), Ardit BEQIRI,
Henri NDREKA (YC15), Perparim DAIU, Rahman HALLACI, Igli ALLMUÇA, Bekim
KULI (74' Romeo HAMZA), Viana Alexander Antonio CARIOCA (BRA) (90' Robert
GRIZHA), Gjergj MUZAKA (RC41), Alket KRUJA (83' Fatjon TAFAJ).
Goals: Maccabi Nethanya FC: 1-1 Lior GENISH (38'), 2-1 Yaakov HASAN (64'), 3-1 David
HADAD (80').
KS Partizani Tiranë: 0-1 Gjergj MUZAKA (16').
Referee: Per Ivar STABERG (NOR)

54

28-06-2003   Boris Paichadze Stadium, Tbilisi:
FC WIT Georgia Tbilisi – SV Pasching   2-1 (0-0)
FC WIT Georgia Tbilisi: Mirza MERLANI, Jaba MUJIRI, Aleksandre INTSKIRVELI, Levan MEREBASHVILI, Oleg GVELESIANI, David DIGMELASHVILI, Lasha NOZADZE (YC75), David DOLIDZE, Vladimer GOCHASHVILI, Levan MELKADZE, Otar MARTSVALADZE. (Used subs: Pawel DATUNAISHVILI (YC73)).
SV Pasching: Josef SCHICKLGRUBER, Hakki Tolunay KAFKAS (TUR), Bozo KOVACEVIC, Tomasz WISIO (POL), Manfred ROTHBAUER, Markus KIESENEBNER, Michael HORVATH, Patrick PIRCHER, Helmut RIEGLER, George Martin DATORU, Christian MAYRLEB.
Goals: FC WIT Georgia Tbilisi: 1-0 Levan MELKADZE (53'), 2-1 Levan MEREBASHVILI (90+').
SV Pasching: 1-1 Michael HORVATH (62').
Referee: Robert MALEK (POL)

28-06-2003   Republican Stadium, Yerevan: FC Kotayk Abovyan – 1.FC Brno   3-2 (1-0)
FC Kotayk Abovyan: Eduard YERITSYAN, Gevork MIRIDZHANYAN, Valeri ALEKSANYAN, Arsen MELOYAN, Albert AFYAN (66' Hrachya VARDAZARYAN), Gor MIRZAKHANYAN (64' Vadim GHAHRAMANOV), Artur KOCHARYAN, Sarkis NAZARYAN (85' Armen BABAYAN), Arshak AMIRYAN, Artur VOSKANYAN, Tigran DAVITYAN (RC90).
1.FC Brno: Tomas BELIC (SVK), Martin ZIVNY (YC..), Ales SCHUSTER, Martin KOTÜLEK, Milos KRSKO (SVK) (90' Petr KRIVANEK), Petr MUSIL (62' Radek MEZLIK), Tomás ABRAHAM, Marek ZUBEK (YC..), Roman DRGA (65' Pavel SIMR), Milan PACANDA, Libor DOSEK.
Goals: FC Kotayk Abovyan: 1-0 Artur VOSKANYAN (45'+1'), 2-0 Artur KOCHARYAN (52'), 3-1 Artur VOSKANYAN (89' penalty).
1.FC Brno: 2-1 Milan PACANDA (83'), 3-2 Pavel SIMR (90'+4').
Referee: José Luis MENGUAL PRADES (AND)   Attendance: 4.500

28-06-2003   Tórsvøllur, Tórshavn: GÍ Gøtu – FC Dacia Chisinau   0-1 (0-0)
GÍ Gøtu: Hallur HANSEN (52' Jacek PRZYBYLSKI (POL)), Áslakkur PETERSEN, Anton SKORADAL, Poul Andrias JACOBSEN (46' Poul ENNIGARD), Bárdur á LAKJUNI, Súni OLSEN, Zdzislaw JANIK (POL), Hans Pauli PETERSEN (YC59) (75' Jónreid DALHEIM), Simun SAMUELSEN, Krysztof POPCZYNSKI (POL), Simun Louis JACOBSEN.
FC Dacia Chisinau: Alexandre MEREUTA, Vitaly MARDARI, Cornel POPOV, Liviu ANDRIUTA, Serghey POTRIMBA, Vitalie GLUHENKI (87' Igor NEGRESCU), Andrei MARTIN, Sergiu JAPALAU (75' Alexander GOROBET), Grigory BADEA, Alexandru GOLBAN, Vladimir JAPULAU (46' Gennady ORBU).
Goal: FC Dacia Chisinau: 0-1 Grigory BADEA (46').
Referee: Luc WILMES (LUX)   Attendance: 500

28-06-2003   Néo GSP Stadium, Nicosia:
Olympiakos FC Nicosia – FK ZTS Dubnica   1-4 (0-3)
Olympiakos FC Nicosia: Demetris STYLIANOU, Iakovos APOSTOLOU, Georgios
PELAGIA, Loucas STYLIANOU, Michalis PATOUNAS, Nicolaos NICOLAOU (YC52),
Christos IOANNOU (62' Marios ADAMOU), Panyiotis PANAYIOTOU (46' Georgios
GEORGIADES), Evangelos CHRYSTODOULOU, Constantinos ELIA, Michalis CHRISTOFI
(53' Konstantinos ZORPAS).
FK ZTS Dubnica: Pavol KOVÁC (62' Marian POSTRK), Martin SEVELA, Martin
SVESTKA, Branislav MRÁZ, Marian ZIMEN, Juraj DOVICOVIC, Igor DRZIK, Ján
SVIKRUHA (72' Marian BELLAK), Anton SUCHÝ (46' Michal FILO), Andrej PORAZIK
(YC24), Peter KISKA.
Goals: Olympiakos FC Nicosia: 1-4 Constantinos ELIA (75').
FK ZTS Dubnica: 0-1 Martin SEVELA (21'), 0-2 Peter KISKA (31'), 0-3 Juraj DOVICOVIC
(37'), 0-4 Peter KISKA (66').
Referee: Craig Alexander THOMSON (SCO)

29-06-2003   Richmond Park, Dublin:
Shamrock Rovers FC – MKS Odra Wodzislaw   1-0 (0-0)
Shamrock Rovers FC: Barry Paul RYAN, Stephen James GOUGH (YC73), James Michael
KEDDY, Richard Philip BYRNE, Terry PALMER, Stephen GRANT (73' Glenn LACEY),
Alan REYNOLDS, Jason John COLWELL, Shane ROBINSON (87' Derek TREACY
(YC90)), Glen Paul FITZPATRICK, Anthony James GRANT (82' Trevor MOLLOY).
MKS Odra Wodzislaw: Marcin BEBEN, Wojciech GRZYB (70' Blazej JANKOWSKI), Jan
CIOS, Piotr SZYMICZEK (YC52), Robert GORGKI, Rafal JAROSZ, Wojciech GORSKI
(YC88), Aleksander KWIEK, Marcin NOWACKI (70' Wojciech SALEK), Bartlomiej
SOCHA (YC45) (46' Wojciech MYSZOR), Jacek ZIARKOWSKI.
Goal: Shamrock Rovers FC: 1-0 Glen Paul FITZPATRICK (66').
Referee: Veaceslav BANARI (MOL)

29-06-2003   Stade Josy Barthel, Luxembourg:
U.S. Luxembourg – FK Sutjeska Niksic   1-1 (0-1)
U.S. Luxembourg: Alija BESIC, Tom SCHNELL, Paul ENGEL, TRIEM, Claude REITER,
Luciano CRAPA (BEL), Marc BAUM (78' Pasquale ANTONICELLI), Reda
BOUKHAROUBA (BEL) (86' Assim ALLOMEROVIC), Enver SABOTIC (SBM), Amédé
SUZZI (46' Laurent AQUISTAPACE (FRA)), Jeff FELLER.
FK Sutjeska Niksic: Zoran BANOVIC, Srdjan DAMJANOVIC, Darko KRSTESKI (MCD),
Kristijan TUCAKOVIC, Bojan COSIC (YC17) (46' Drazen MEDJEDOVIC), Milenko
MILOSEVIC, Novica MIKOVIC, Goran BOSKOVIC, Anzor NAFAS (62' Vlado JEKNIC),
Nikola NIKEZIC (81' Aleksandar CADJENOVIC), Ivan BOSKOVIC (YC68).
Goals: U.S. Luxembourg: 1-1 Marc BAUM (46').
FK Sutjeska Niksic: 0-1 Kristijan TUCAKOVIC (37').
Referee: Sergey TSAREGRADSKIY (KAZ)

29-06-2003   A. Le Coq Arena, Tallinn: JK Trans Narva – O.F.K. Beograd   3-5 (3-2)
JK Trans Narva: Vitas MALISHAUSKAS, Andrei PRUSS, Oleg KOLOTSEI, Oleg
KUROCHKIN, Sergei KAZAKOV, Nikolai LYSANOV, Konstantin KARIN (YC13),
Stanislav KITTO, Sergei ZAMORSKI (67' Siksten KAZIMIR), Dmitri LIPARTOV (RUS)
(73' Anton SEREDA), Maksim GRUZNOV.
O.F.K. Beograd: Sasa STEVANOVIC, Igor RADOVIC, Marko BASA, Milos BAJALICA
(YC43), Dusko TOSIC, Aleksandar SIMIC, Dragan STANCIC, Zoran STOINOVIC (GRE)
(88' Ivan CVETKOVIC), LEANDRO Netto de Macedo (BRA) (73' Eristijan KIROVSKI),
Milos KOLAKOVIC, Vanja GRUBAC (46' Filip DESPOTVSKI (MCD)).
Goals: JK Trans Narva: 1-0 Maksim GRUZNOV (5'), 2-2 Dmitri LIPARTOV (38'), 3-2
Maksim GRUZNOV (44').
O.F.K. Beograd: 1-1 Dusko TOSIC (7'), 1-2 Milos KOLAKOVIC (11'), 3-3 Eristijan
KIROVSKI (75'), 3-4 Eristijan KIROVSKI (95'), 3-5 Milos KOLAKOVIC (105').
Referee: Peter VER EECKEN (BEL)
*After the match played on 21-06-2003 was declared void, qualification was decided by the
result of this single game. O.F.K. Beograd qualified after the first period of extra-time by the
silver goal rule.*

29-06-2003   Stadion Bonchuk, Dupnitsa: FC Marek Dupnitsa – Videoton FC   3-2 (2-0)
FC Marek Dupnitsa: Ivaylo IVANOV, Dimitar KOEMDZHIEV, Saso LAZAREVSKI (MCD),
Alexei DIONISIEV, Ianek KIUTCHUKOV (YC98), Angel STOIKOV (YC57), Amiran
MUJIRI (GEO) (YC25), Ivo PARGOV (65' Kroum BIBISHKOV (YC94)), Liubomir
LIUBENOV (77' Toni PITOSKA (MCD)), Anzhelo KIUCHUKOV, Vassil KIROV (48' Emil
PETKOV).
Videoton FC: Géza TURI, Dejan VILOTIC (SBM) (46' Ivan RISTIC (SBM)), Gabriel
VOCHIN (ROM), Tamás SZALAI (98' Péter TEREÁNSZKI TÓTH), KOLLER, SWARCZ,
Balázs TÓTH, Ferenc KÓCZIÁN, Tibor SZABÓ (SBM), József MAGASFÖLDI (46' Gábor
FÖLDES), Lajos TERJÉK (YC18).
Goals: FC Marek Dupnitsa: 1-0 Liubomir LIUBENOV (29'), 2-0 Alexei DIONISIEV (42'),
3-2 Amiran MUJIRI (93').
Videoton FC: 2-1 Gábor FÖLDES (48'), 2-2 Gábor FÖLDES (60').
Referee: Tony ASUMAA (FIN)
FC Marek Dupnitsa qualified after the first period of extra-time by the silver goal rule.

29-06-2003   Stadionul Ceahlaul, Piatra Neamt:
                   FC Ceahlaul Piatra Nemat – Tampere United FC   2-1 (1-0)
FC Ceahlaul Piatra Neamt: Radu Gabriel LEFTER, Cristian Ciprian LUPUT (15' Vasile
Valentin AVADANEI (YC83)), Dumitru BOTEZ, Angelo Dumitru ALISTAR, Nicolae Dorin
GOIAN, Constantin Ionut ILIE (YC69), Tiberiu SERBAN, Sergiu BRUJAN, Constantin
ENACHE (63' Adrian Constantin SOLOMON (YC82)), Shenif FEIZULLAH (57' Mihai
NEMTANU), Lucian BURDUJAN (YC53).
Tampere United FC: Mikko KAVEN, Pasi SALMELA, Mikko SALO, Jussi KUOPPALA
(YC79), Sakari SAARINEN, Kari SAINIO (YC57), Tero KOSKELA, Heikki AHO (YC63),
Henri SCHEWELEFF (72' Antti HYNYNEN), Janne RÄSÄNEN, Noah HICKEY (NZL) (85'
Antti OJANPERÄ).
Goals: FC Ceahlaul Piatra Neamt: 1-0 Nicolae Dorin GOIAN (29'), 2-1 Angelo Dumitru
ALISTAR (71').
Tampere United FC: 1-1 Henri SCHEWELEFF (59').
Referee: Damir SKOMINA (SLO)

57

29-06-2003   Herman Vanderpoortenstadion, Lier:
K.Lierse SK – FC Encamp Dicoansa 4-1 (2-1)
K.Lierse SK: Yannick DIERICK, Steve LAEREMANS (YC43), Toon GLASSEE, Stéphane
RONGE, Timothy HEYLEN, Pieter GEENS, Timothy DREESEN (68' Cédric MEDARD),
Kevin DIJCK (82' Tom KERMANS), Jurgen RAEYMAECKERS, Stijn JANSSENS (46'
Issame CHARAI), Kenny RUCQUOY.
FC Encamp Dicoansa: Ricardo FERNÁNDEZ LIZARTE (ESP),), Emanuel GOLDSCHMIDT
(ARG) (85' Luciano NASTRI (ITA)), Federico Alfonso COTO ARAGONES (ESP), Josep
PORTAS (ESP), Oscar ALFONSO DA CUNHA (POR), Christian XINOS (GRE), Carlos
CONGIL (ESP) (YC80) (82' Juan Carlos CALZADO), Laureano MIRAGLIA (ITA) (60' Luis
Maria VERIZ (ARG)), Alejandro ROMERO (ARG), Leonardo MIRAGLIA (ITAL), Miguel
Angel BELDA (ESP).
Goals: K.Lierse SK: 1-0 Steve LAEREMANS (7'), 2-0 Jurgen RAEYMAECKERS (11'), 3-1
Pieter GEENS (65'), 4-1 Cédric MEDARD (87').
FC Encamp Dicoansa: 2-1 Carlos CONGIL (19').
Referee: Raivo LATTIK (EST)

29-06-2003   Stadion Bergholz, Wil: FC Wil 1900 – FC Dinaburg Daugavpils 2-0 (2-0)
FC Wil 1900: Nicolas BENEY, Philippe MONTANDON (88' Alessandro MANGIARRATTI),
Patrick WINKLER (YC16), Michael RENGGLI, Dilaver SATILMIS, Umberto ROMANO,
FABIO de Souza (BRA), Davide CALLA (ITA) (81' Massimo RIZZO (YC82)), Kristian
MUSHI (SBM), Stefan BLUNSCHI, Mauro LUSTRINELLI (78' Elsra ZVEROTIC (SBM)).
FC Dinaburg Daugavpils: Sergey DIGULYOV, Vadim LOGINS, Dmitrij CUGUNOV, Alexey
BORUN, Jurij SOKOLOV (71' Andrey ZHUROMSKY), Alexander SHUMILOV
(YC,YC90), Dmitry KOKHAN (55' Olexandr KRIKLIVY (UKR)), Pavel KOLTSOV, Yurgis
PUCHINSKY (YC,YC89), Alexey KOSTENKO (RUS) (57' Aleksander IVANOV), Orest
DOROSH (UKR) (YC67).
Goals: FC Wil 1900: 1-0 Davide CALLA (22'), 2-0 Mauro LUSTRINELLI (45').
Referee: Goran MIHALJEVIC (SBM)

29-06-2003   Stadion Centralny, Kostanay:
FC Tobol Kostanay – KP Polonia Warszawa 2-1 (0-1)
FK Tobol Kostanay: Valeri SHANTALOSOV (BLS), Andrey SHKURIN, Petr BADLO, Oleg
LOTOV, Sergey ANDREEV (RUS), Oleg GOLOVAN (RUS) (YC..,YC83), Konstantin
KOTOV (81' Valeriy GARKUSHA), Alexey KOSOLAPOV (RUS) (YC32), Daniar
MUHANOV, Nurbol ZHUMASKALIYEV, Nurken MAZBAYEV.
FK Polonia Warszawa: Mindaugas MAKSVYTIS (LIT), Igor GOLASZEWSKI (YC36),
Mariusz MOWLIK (YC32), Wojciech SZYMANEK (YC79), Marcin DRAJER (YC83),
Dariusz DZWIGALA (87' Patryk ALEKSANDROWICZ), Piotr KOSIOROWSKI (64'
Krzystof BAK), Lukasz JAROSIEWICZ (71' Pawel HAJDUCZEK), Emiel NOWAKOWSKI
(YC35), Jaroslaw MAZURKIEWICZ, Maciej NUCKOWSKI.
Goals: FC Tobol Kostanay: 1-1 Daniar MUHANOV (74'), 2-1 Nurbol ZHUMASKALIYEV
(90'+3').
KP Polonia Warszawa: 0-1 Lukasz JAROSIEWICZ (21').
Referee: Alexey TIUMIN (RUS)   Attendance: 6.500

SECOND ROUND

05-07-2003   Nya Ullevi, Göteborg: Örgryte IS – O.G.C. Nice 3-2 (1-1)
Örgryte IS: Dick LAST, David MAREK (68' Alfonso ALVES Martins Júnior (BRA)), Atli
THÓRARINSSON (ISL), Marcus DAHLIN, Robert BENGTSSON-BÄRKROTH, Mentor
ZHUBI, Daniel LOHM (YC81), Eric GUSTAFSSON (23' Edwin PHIRI (ZAM)), Jeffrey
AUBYNN (74' Walter TOMAZ Jr (BRA)), Christian HEMBERG, Paulo Roberto Chamon de
Castillo "PAULINHO" (BRA).
O.G.C. Nice: Damien GRÉGORINI, Noé PAMAROT, José COBOS, Cedric VARRAULT,
Thibault SCOTTO Di Porfirio (77' Sebastien GIMENEZ), Romain PITAU, Yoann BIGNÉ
(60' Oumar BAKARI), Eric ROY, EVERSON Pereira da Silva (BRA), Abdelmalek
CHERRAD (ALG), Cédric MIONNET 86' Diakite BAKARY (GER)).
Goals: Örgryte IS: 1-0 Paulo Roberto Chamon de Castillo "PAULINHO" (8' penalty), 2-1
Paulo Roberto Chamon de Castillo "PAULINHO" (51'), 3-2 Alfonso ALVES Martins Júnior
(90').
O.G.C. Nice: 1-1 Abdelmalek CHERRAD (26'), 2-2 Abdelmalek CHERRAD (68').
Referee: Jaromir HLAVAC (CZE)   Attendance: 1.500

05-07-2003   Goce Delcev Stadium, Prilep: FK Pobeda Prilep – SV Pasching 1-1 (1-0)
FK Pobeda Prilep: Tome PANCEV, Saso ZDRAVEVSKI (YC39), Marjan NACEV (YC88),
Pance CHUMBEV, Dimitar KAPINKOVSKI, Cedomir MIJANOVIC (SBM), GILSON de
Jesus da Silva (BRA), Toni MEGLENSKI, Nikolce ZDRAVESKI, Draganco DIMITROVSKI
(66' Blaze GEORGIESKI), Blagoja GESOSKI.
SV Pasching: Josef SCHICKLGRUBER (YC88), Hakki Tolunay KAFKAS (TUR) (YC44)
(63' Patrick PIRCHER), Michael BAUR, Tomasz WISIO (POL), Markus KIESENEBNER
(YC,YC87), Michael HORVATH, Bozo KOVACEVIC, Helmut RIEGLER, Manfred
ROTHBAUER (YC81), Christian MAYRLEB (68' Faruk ATALAY (TUR)), Edi GLIEDER
(76' George Martin DATORU).
Goals: FK Pobeda Prilep: 1-0 Blagoja GESOSKI (44').
SV Pasching: 1-1 Bozo KOVACEVIC (59').
Referee: Oleg CHIKUN (BLS)   Attendance: 4.000

05-07-2003   SRC Bonifika Stadium, Koper: NK Koper – FK ZTS Dubnica 1-0 (0-0)
NK Koper: Ermin HASIC, Edmond GUNJAC, Alen SCULAC (YC63), Andrej POLJSAK,
Elvis RIBARIC, Darko KREMENOVIC (46' Viktor TRENEVSKI (MCD)), Nebojsa
KOVACEVIC (82' Marko BOZIC), Igor BENEDEJCIC, Sasa BOZICIC, Oliver
BOGATINOV (62' Jaka STROMAJER), Sasa JAKOMIN.
FK ZTS Dubnica: Pavol KOVÁC (RC24), Martin SEVELA, Martin SVESTKA, Branislav
MRÁZ, Marian ZIMEN (YC34), Andrej SUPKA (25' Marian POSTRK goalkeeper), Juraj
DOVICOVIC, Igor DRZIK, Peter KISKA, Pavol STRAKA (90' Roman GREGUSKA),
Andrej PORAZIK (71' Alexander HOMER).
Goal: NK Koper: 1-0 Viktor TRENEVSKI (90').
Referee: Alexander GVARDIS (RUS)   Attendance: 1.800

05-07-2003 Traktor Stadion, Minsk:
FC Shakhter Soligorsk – HNK Cibalia Vinkovci 1-1 (1-0)
FC Shakhter Soligorsk: Alexandr MARTESHKIN, Alexandr YUREVICH, Aliaksei BELAVUSAV, Andrei SIAROHIN, Tsimafei KALACHOV, Andrei LEONCHIK, Roman TREPACHKIN, Vadim SKRIPCHENKO (YC59) (62' Alexandr NOVIK (YC84)), Sergei NIKIFORENKO, Igor SLESARCUK (LAT) (87' Anatoliy BUDAYEV), Anatoliy TIKHONCHIK (82' Dmitriy PODREZ).
HNK Cibalia Vinkovci: Ivica MARIC, Mario LUCIC, Boris LEUTAR, Ivan MAROSLAVAC, Mario JURIC (72' Darko JOZINOVIC), Zoran RATKOVIC (YC45) (46' Bosko PERAICA), Ivan ZGELA, Mladen BARTOLOVIC, Dejan PAVLICIC (46' Mladen KRIZANOVIC), Ivan LAJTMAN, Vedran IVANKOVIC.
Goals: FC Shakhter Soligorsk: 1-0 Andrei LEONCHIK (44').
HNK Cibalia Vinkovci: 1-1 Ivan LAJTMAN (79').
Referee: Attila ABRAHAM (HUN)

05-07-2003 Stadion Bonchuk, Dupnitsa: FC Marek Dupnitsa – VfL Wolfsburg 1-1 (0-1)
FC Marek Dupnitsa: Nikolay CHAVDAROV, Ianek KIUTCHUKOV, Veselin VELIKOV (YC17), Dimitar KOEMDZHIEV (16' Hristo ARANGUELOV), Emil PETKOV, Angel STOIKOV, Anzhelo KIUCHUKOV (YC61) (90' Bzagos DONEV (MCD)), Georgi VAZHAROV, Amiran MUJIRI (GEO), Kroum BIBISHKOV, Ivo PARGOV (46' Liubomir LIUBENOV).
VfL Wolfsburg: Simon JENTZSCH, Marino BILISKOV (CRO), Stefan SCHNOOR, Patrick WEISER (46' Miroslav KARHAN (SVK)), Thomas RYTTER (DEN), Sven MÜLLER, Pablo THIAM, Mirko HRGOVIC (BOS) (YC75), Martin PETROV (BUL) (72' Dorinel MUNTEANU (ROM)), Roy PRÄGER (81' Hans SARPEI), Diego Fernando KLIMOWICZ (ARG).
Goals: FC Marek Dupnitsa: 1-1 Kroum BIBISHKOV (58').
VfL Wolfsburg: 0-1 Diego Fernando KLIMOWICZ (24').
Referee: Carlos MEGÍA DÁVILA (ESP)   Attendance: 4.000

05-07-2003 Stadionul Republican, Chisinau:
FC Dacia Chisinau – KS Partizani Tiranë 2-0 (0-0)
FC Dacia Chisinau: Alexandre MEREOUTSA, Vitaly MARDARI, Corneliu POPOV, Liviu ANDRIUTA, Serghey POTRIMBA, Vitalie GLUHENCHI (85' Alexander GOROBET), Andrei MARTIN, Sergiu JAPALAU (YC26) (71' Ghenadie ORBU), Grigory BADEA (YC65), Alexandru GOLBAN (YC79), Vladimir JAPULAU (90' Lilian CODA).
KS Partizani Tiranë: Ervis AGOLLI, Fatjon TAFAJ (YC28), Ardit BEQIRI, Henri NDREKA (YC12), Rahman HALLACI, Igli ALLMUÇA, Bekim KULI (81' Elis BAKAJ (YC87)), Romeo HAMZA, Robert GRIZHA, Alket KRUJA, Viana Alexander Antonio CARIOCA (BRA) (YC75).
Goals: FC Dacia Chisinau: 1-0 Alexandru GOLBAN (61'), 2-0 Ghenadie ORBU (78').
Referee: Gerald LEHNER (AUT)

05-07-2003   Stadion Lachen, Thun: FC Thun – 1.FC Brno   2-3 (1-1)
FC Thun: Fabio COLTORTI, Andreas GERBER, Armanch DEUMI TCHANI (CMR), Ljubo
MILICEVIC (AUS), Marc SCHNEIDER, Nelson FERREIRA "NELO" (POR) (46' Reto
ZANNI), Silvan AEGERTER, Mario RAIMONDI (YC60) (80' Patrick BAUMANN),
ANTONIO dos Santos (BRA), Mallaim RAMA, Pascal RENFER (46' Adrian MOSER).
1.FC Brno: Tomas BELIC (SVK) (YC75), Patrik KRAP, Ales SCHUSTER, Martin
KOTÜLEK (90' Petr KRIVANEK), Milos KRSKO (SVK), Martin ZIVNY (YC60,YC90),
Tomás ABRAHAM, Marek ZUBEK, Roman DRGA (67' Radek MEZLIK), Milan
PACANDA (90' Pavel SIMR), Libor DOSEK.
Goals: FC Thun: 1-1 Silvan AEGERTER (42'), 2-1 Mallaim RAMA (75').
1.FC Brno: 0-1 Martin ZIVNY (10'), 2-2 Martin KOTÜLEK (76'), 2-3 Milan PACANDA
(83').
Referee: Kostadin KOSTADINOV (BUL)   Attendance: 3.000

05-07-2003   Willem II Stadion, Tilburg: Willem II Tilburg – FC Wil 1900   2-1 (1-1)
Willem II Tilburg: Peter ZOÏS (AUS), Nuelson WAU (73' Kew JALIENS), Emile VAN DE
MEERAKKER (YC53) (58' Öscar ÖZKAYA), Jos VAN NIEUWSTADT, Joris MATHIJSEN
(YC89), Denny LANDZAAT, Mourad MGHIZRAT (MAR) (46' Anouar HADOUIR),
Raymond VICTORIA, James QUINN (NIR), Tom CALUWÉ (BEL) (YC73), Tarik
SEKTIOUI (MAR).
FC Wil 1900: Nicolas BENEY, Alessandro MANGIARRATTI, Massimo RIZZO, Philippe
MONTANDON, Patrick WINKLER (YC76), Umberto ROMANO, Michael RENGGLI (78'
Marco HÄMMERLI), FABIO de Souza (BRA), Mauro LUSTRINELLI (64' Stefan
BLUNSCHI (YC89)), HELDER MIGUEL La Costa Vrea (POR) (87' Peter EUGSTER),
Davide CALLA (ITA).
Goals: Willem II Tilburg: 1-0 Tarik SEKTIOUI (9'), 2-1 Denny LANDZAAT (72' penalty).
FC Wil 1900: 1-1 Davide CALLA (32').
Referee: Levan PANIASHVILI (GEO)   Attendance: 2.797

05-07-2003   Stadion Tusanj, Tuzla: FK Sloboda Tuzla – K.Lierse SK   1-0 (0-0)
FK Sloboda Tuzla: Mirsad DEDIC, Muhamed JUSUFOVIC, Nusret MUSLIMOVIC, Gradimir
CRNOGORAC (YC60), Samir KUDUZOYIC, Nedzad BAJROVIC (YC7), Admir JOLDIC
(75' Zvjezdan KRESIC), Adnan SARAJLIC (82' Admir BRDZANOVIC), Senad HADZIC,
Tarik OKANOVIC (89' Iljko TOMIC (RC90)), Alen MESANOVIC.
K.Lierse SK: Yves VAN DER STRAETEN, Laurent FASSOTTE (56' Werry SELS), Stef
WILS, Jonas DE ROECK (YC90), Bertrand CRASSON (YC12) (56' Nicolas
TIMMERMANS), Hasan KACIC (CRO) (YC21), Marc SCHAESSENS (YC47) (68' Laurent
DELORGE), Kristof IMSCHOOT, Maxence COVELIERS (YC15), Geir FRIGÅRD (NOR)
(YC62), Stein HUYSEGEMS.
Goal: FK Sloboda Tuzla: 1-0 Samir KUDUZOYIC (90'+2').
Referee: Athanassios BRAIKOS (GRE)

61

05-07-2003   Stadio Mario Rigamonti, Brescia:
Brescia Calcio SpA – FC Gloria Bistrita   2-1 (1-1)
Brescia Caldio SpA: Tiziano RAMON, Marius STANKEVICIUS (LIT) (YC89), Victor Hugo
MARECO (PAR), Marco PISANO, Alejandro Adrián CORREA Rodríguez (URU), Ermanno
LEONI (YC16) (53' Simone DEL NERO), Roberto GUANA, Roberto CORTELLINI,
Abderrazzak JADID (MAR) (73' Raúl Alberto GONZALEZ (ARG)), Mario Antonio
SALGADO Jimenez (CHI) (YC9) (73' Marc NYGAARD (DEN)), Andrea CARACCIOLI.
(Coach: Giovanni DE BIASI).
FC Gloria Bistrita: Costel CÂMPEANU, Adrian Valentin VELCEA, Sergiu Viorel Ioan
COSTIN, Vasile Nicolae POPA, Dorian Constantin ARBANAS, Alin Valer RUS, Alin
MINTEUAN, Ciprian VASILACHE (YC67) (90' Sorin Ciprian BUCUROAIA), Lucian Iulian
SÂNMARTEAN (86' Razvan RADU), Cristian Ambrozie COROIAN (YC30), Sandu
NEGREAN (68' Adrian ANCA). (Coach: Remus VLAD).
Goals : Brescia Calcio SpA: 1-0 Roberto CORTELLINI (4'), 2-1 Simone DEL NERO (85'
penalty).
FC Gloria Bistrita: 1-1 Adrian Valentin VELCEA (10').
Referee: Nikolay IVANOV (RUS)   Attendance: 6.000

06-07-2003   Bergéstadion, Tienen: K.Sint Truidense VV – FK Tobol Kostanay   0-2 (0-1)
K.Sint Truidense VV: Bram CASTRO, Wouter VRANCKEN (46' Frank GERAERTS), Nicky
HAYEN (RC35), Peter VOETS, Stijn VANGEFFELEN, Tom VAN IMSCHOOT, Kris
BUVENS, Thomas CAERS (20' Robbie DELLO, 46' Benjamin DE CEULAER), Peter
DELORGE (YC73), Timmy BROUX, Danny BOFFIN.
FK Tobol Kostanay: Valeri SHANTALOSOV (BLS), Sergey ANDREEV (RUS), Oleg
LOTOV, Petr BADLO, Konstantin KOTOV, Alexey KOSOLAPOV (RUS), Nurbol
ZHUMASKALIYEV, Andrey SHKURIN, Sergey KAPUTIN, Daniar MUHANOV (30'
Valeriy GARKUSHA (YC71)), Nurken MAZBAYEV (86' Serguei BOGDANOV (RUS)).
Goals: FK Tobol Kostanay: 0-1 Nurken MAZBAYEV (35' penalty), 0-2 Valeriy GARKUSHA
(81').
Referee: Dragomir TANOVIC (SBM)   Attendance: 2.000

06-07-2003   Stadion Siruch, Staré Mêsto:
1.FC Synot Staré Mêsto – O.F.K. Boegrad   1-0 (0-0)
1.FC Synot Staré Mêsto: Petr DROBISZ, Pavel NEMCICKY, Rastislav KOSTKA (SVK), Ján
PALINEK, Marek SEMAN (SVK), Václav CINCALA (YC20,RC26), Tomas POLACH (81'
Velice SUMULIKOSKI (MCD)), Martin ABRAHAM, Josef LUKASTIK (YC61) (87' Ivan
DVORÁK),Jiri KOWALIK (68' Michal MEDUNA), Vladimir MALAR (YC5).
O.F.K. Beograd: Sasa STEVANOVIC, Ivan CVETKOVIC, Igor RADOVIC (46' Branko
BAKOVIC), Marko BASA, Dorae JOKIC, Aleksandar TRISOVIC (YC16), Aleksandar
SIMIC, Dragan STANCIC (YC81), Zoran STOINOVIC (GRE) (74' Filip DESPOTVSKI
(MCD)), Milos KOLAKOVIC, Miljan MRDAKOVIC (68' Eristijan KIROVSKI).
Goal: 1.FC Synot Staré Mêsto: 1-0 Aleksandar TRISOVIC (53' own goal).
Referee: Selçuk DERELI (TUR)   Attendance: 2.112

06-07-2003   Stadion u Nisy, Liberec: FC Slovan Liberec – FC Shamrock Rovers 2-0 (2-0)
FC Slovan Liberec: Antonín KINSKY, Tomás ZÁPOTOCNY, Miroslav HOLENÁK, Petr
LUKÁS, Tomás JANU (YC35), Karol KISEL (SVK), David LANGER, Václav KOLOUSEK,
Juraj ANCIC (SVK), Filip HOLOSKO (SVK) (59' Jan NEZMAR), Michal POSPÍSIL (89'
Miroslav SLEPICKA).
Shamrock Rovers FC: Barry Paul RYAN, Stephen James GOUGH, James Michael KEDDY,
Jason John COLWELL (74' Keith John DOYLE), Terry PALMER, Richard Philip BYRNE,
Shane ROBINSON, Anthony James GRANT (82' Liam KELLY), Glen Paul FITZPATRICK
(46' Trevor MOLLOY), Alan REYNOLDS (YC20), Stephen GRANT.
Goals: FC Slovan Liberec: 1-0 Tomás ZÁPOTOCNY (12'), 2-0 David LANGER (21').
Referee: Karen NALBANDYAN (ARM)   Attendance: 5.100

06-07-2003   El Sardinero, Santander:
            Real Racing Club Santander – Györi ETO FC 1-0 (1-0)
Real Racing Club Santander: Francisco BORJA Lavín Vitorero, Claude GNAKPA (FRA),
David COROMINA Pararols, Ilan BAKHAR (ISR), José Manuel Suárez Rivas "SIETES"
(YC87), PABLO Ballesteros LAGO (64' Juan José COLLANTES), JUVENAL Edjogo
Owono Montalban, Eduardo "EDU" AGUILAR Leiva (78' RAÚL Martín Del Campo), Daniel
Rodríguez Pérez "TXIKI", Juan Ramón EPITIÉ Valle Trueba (59'
Fernando MORÁN Escudero). (Coach: Fernando Trío Zabala "NANDO YOSU").
Györi ETO FC: Zsolt SEBÖK, Atilla BÖJTE, Antal JÄKL, Elek NYILAS (YC57), Marko
KARTELO (CRO), Tamás GERI, Miklós HERCZEG (46' Tibor KALINA), Zoltán VARGA,
Norbert NÉMETH, Tamás NAGY (72' Daniel DJOSEVSKI (MCD)), Márton OROSS (YC47)
(52' Darko PERIC (CRO)). (Coach: Zoltán VARGA).
Goal: Real Racing Club Santander: 1-0 David COROMINA Pararols (42').
Referee: Anton GUENOV (BUL)   Attendance: 4.895
(PABLO Ballesteros LAGO missed a penalty in the 46th minute)

06-07-2003   Stadio Yiannis Pathiakakis, Athens: Akratitos FC – AC Allianssi 0-1 (0-0)
Akratitos FC: Giannis IOANNIDIS, Athanasios TSOUKIS, Fotios KOUTOLO, Achilleas
TSIAKALOS, Adrianos BALASKAS (YC46), Christos PIPINIS, Angelos PALLIS, Thomas
BIBIRIS (63' Spiridon REDOUMIS), Vassilios SKARLATOS, Konstandinos PAGONIS (78'
Adonios SCHIZAS), Efstathios STEFANIDIS (74' Panagiotis PAPADOPOULOS).
AC Allianssi: Alexander MISHCHUK (RUS), Ari-Pekka ROIKO, Jarno TUUNAINEN, Janne
MOILANEN, Harri HAAPANIEMI, Timo MARJAMAA, Rami RANTANEN, Peter SAMPO
(82' Heikki PULKKINEN), Mikko SIMULA, ADRIANO Munoz (BRA) (87' Mikko
PAATELAINEN), Justus VAJANNE (84' Petteri KAIJASILTA).
Goal: AC Allianssi: 0-1 ADRIANO Munoz (67').
Referee: Goran MARIC (CRO)   Attendance: 230

06-07-2003   Tammelan Stadion, Tampere: Tampere United FC – FK Sutjeska Niksic 0-0
Tampere United FC: Mikko KAVEN, Pasi SALMELA, Mikko SALO, Jussi KUOPPALA,
Sakari SAARINEN (74' Jaakko LAHTINEN), Kari SAINIO, Tero KOSKELA, Henri
SCHEWELEFF, Janne RÄSÄNEN, Noah HICKEY (NZL), Antti HYNYNEN (60' Antti
OJANPERÄ).
FK Sutjeska Niksic: Zoran BANOVIC, Srdjan DAMJANOVIC, Kristijan TUCAKOVIC,
Darko KRSTESKI (MCD) (YC27), Bojan COSIC, Vlado JEKNIC, Milenko MILOSEVIC,
Goran BOSKOVIC, Boban KRISANOVIC (79' Anzor NAFAS), Vladan KOSTIC (56' Novica
MIKOVIC (YC,YC90)), Ivan BOSKOVIC (YC81) (90' Drazen MEDJEDOVIC).
Referee: Krzysztof SLUPIK (POL)

63

12-07-2003   Stadionul Gloria, Bistrita: FC Gloria Bistrita – Brescia Calcio SpA   1-1 (0-0)
FC Gloria Bistrita: Costel CÂMPEANU, Sergiu Viorel Ioan COSTIN, Vasile Nicolae POPA
(YC75), Alin Valer RUS (YC61), Sergiu Sebastian MÂNDREAN, Adrian Valentin VELCEA,
Alin MINTEUAN, Ciprian VASILACHE (72' Sorin Ciprian BUCUROAIA (RC90+1)),
Lucian Iulian SÂNMARTEAN, Cristian Ambrozie COROIAN, Adrian ANCA (79' Razvan
RADU). (Coach: Remus VLAD).
Brescia Caldio SpA: Tiziano RAMON, Marius STANKEVICIUS (LIT), Victor Hugo
MARECO (PAR) (YC51) (73' Simone DEL NERO), Alessandro LUCARELLI, Marco
PISANO (RC86), Mattia TURETTA (67' Raúl Alberto GONZÁLEZ (ARG)), Alejandro
Adrián CORREA Rodríguez (URU) (YC30), Roberto GUANA, Roberto CORTELLINI (79'
Abderrazzak JADID (MAR)), Marc NYGAARD (DEN), Andrea CARACCIOLI (YC70).
(Coach: Giovanni DE BIASI).
Goals: FC Gloria Bistrita: 1-0 Lucian Iulian SÂNMARTEAN (59').
Brescia Calcio SpA: 1-1 Raúl Alberto GONZÁLEZ (90').
Referee: Meir LEVI (ISR)   Attendance: 8.000

12-07-2003   Omladinski Stadium, Beograd:
                    O.F.K. Beograd – 1.FC Synot Staré Mêsto   3-3 (1-1)
O.F.K. Beograd: Sasa STEVANOVIC, Milos BAJALICA, Marko BASA, Dorae JOKIC,
Aleksandar TRISOVIC (YC67) (72' Vanja GRUBAC), Aleksandar SIMIC, Dragan
STANCIC, Branko BAKOVIC (46' LEANDRO Netto De Macedo (BRA)), Zoran
STOINOVIC (GRE) (38' Filip DESPOTVSKI (MCD)), Milos KOLAKOVIC (YC57), Miljan
MRDAKOVIC.
1.FC Synot Staré Mêsto: Petr DROBISZ, Pavel NEMCICKY, Rastislav KOSTKA (SVK), Ján
PALINEK, Martin ABRAHÁM, Vladimir MALAR, Velice SUMULIKOSKI (MCD), Tomas
POLÁCH (68' Ivan DVORÁK), Josef LUKASTIK, Petr SLONCÍK (81' Michal MEDUNA),
Jiri KOWALIK (67' Tomas MICA).
Goals: O.F.K. Beograd: 1-0 Milos KOLAKOVIC (14'), 2-1 Aleksandar SIMIC (50'), 3-3
Vanja GRUBAC (90').
1.FC Synot Staré Mêsto: 1-1 Tomas POLÁCH (31'), 2-2 Rastislav KOSTKA (54'), 2-3
Martin ABRAHÁM (77').
Referee: Ferenc BEDE (HUN)   Attendance: 2.000

12-07-2003   Stadion Mladost, Vinkovci:
                    HNK Cibalia Vinkovci – FC Shakhter Soligorsk   4-2 (1-2)
HNK Cibalia Vinkovci: Ivica MARIC, Darko JOZINOVIC, Mario LUCIC, Boris LEUTAR,
Ivan MAROSLAVAC, Zoran RATKOVIC, Ivan ZGELA (46' Elvis CORIC (YC83)), Mladen
BARTOLOVIC, Dejan PAVLICIC (46' Mario JURIC (YC76)), Ivan LAJTMAN (YC64),
Vedran IVANKOVIC (YC43).
FC Shakhter Soligorsk: Alexandr MARTESHKIN, Alexandr YUREVICH, Aliaksei
BELAVUSAV, Andrei SIAROHIN, Tsimafei KALACHOV, Andrei LEONCHIK, Roman
TREPACHKIN, Vadim SKRIPCHENKO (YC40) (61' Dmitriy PODREZ), Sergei
NIKIFORENKO, Igor SLESARCUK (LAT) (78' Vadzim BOIKA), Anatoliy TIKHONCHIK
(65' Alexandr NOVIK).
Goals: HNK Cibalia Vinkovci: 1-1 Mladen BARTOLOVIC (43' penalty), 2-2 Elvis CORIC
(59'), 3-2 Zoran RATKOVIC (74'), 4-2 Ivan MAROSLAVAC (84').
FC Shakhter Soligorsk: 0-1 Vadim SKRIPCHENKO (13'), 1-2 Sergei NIKIFORENKO (45').
Referee: Loizos LOIZOU (CYP)

12-07-2003   Qemal Stafa Stadium, Tiranë:
FK Partizani Tiranë – FC Dacia Chisinau   0-3 (0-2)
KS Partizani Tiranë: Ervis AGOLLI, Ardit BEQIRI, Rahman HALLACI, Fatjon TAFAJ, Igli ALLMUÇA, Bekim KULI (65' Dorian LUSHI (YC73)), Geraldo do Karmo JUNIOR (BRA), Romeo HAMZA (65' Matos METAJ), Viana Alexander Antonio CARIOCA (BRA), Robert GRIZHA, Alket KRUJA (83' Emiljano CELA).
FC Dacia Chisinau: Alexandre MEREOUTSA, Vitaly MARDARI (63' Ghenadie ORBU), Corneliu POPOV, Liviu ANDRIUTA, Serghey POTRIMBA, Vitalie GLUHENCHI, Andrei MARTIN (YC51), Sergiu JAPALAU, Grigory BADEA (68' Alexander GOROBET), Alexandru GOLBAN, Vladimir JAPULAU (87' Igor NEGRESCU).
Goals: FC Dacia Chisinau: 0-1 Vladimir JAPULAU (4'), 0-2 Liviu ANDRIUTA (30'), 0-3 Ghenadie ORBU (67').
Referee: Roland BECK (LIE)   Attendance: 2.000

12-07-2003   Mestský futbalový stadión, Dubnica nad Váhom:
FK ZTS Dubnica – NK Koper   3-2 (1-2)
FK ZTS Dubnica: Marian POSTRK, Branislav MRÁZ (55' Anton SUCHÝ), Martin SEVELA, Martin SVESTKA, Marian ZIMEN, Jan SVIKRUHA, Igor DRZIK (66' Roman GREGUSKA), Andrej PORAZIK (YC88), Juraj DOVICOVIC, Peter KISKA, Micahl FILO (7' Marian BELLAK).
NK Koper: Ermin HASIC, Edmond GUNJAC, Alen SCULAC, Elvis RIBARIC, Andrej POLJSAK, Sasa BOZICIC (90' Andrej RASTOVAC), Igor BENEDEJCIC (YC88), Nebojsa KOVACEVIC (YC41), Juan Sebastian VITAGLIANO Cruz (ARG) (83' Marko BOZIC), Sasa JAKOMIN (82' Jaka STROMAJER), Viktor TRENEVSKI (MCD).
Goals: FK ZTS Dubnica: 1-0 Juraj DOVICOVIC (6'), 2-2 Anton SUCHÝ (80'), 3-2 Juraj DOVICOVIC (90+' penalty).
NK Koper: 1-1 Sasa BOZICIC (14'), 1-2 Viktor TRENEVSKI (45+').
Referee: Saso LAZAREVSKI (MCD)   Attendance: 1.346

12-07-2003   Stadion Lesní ulice, Breclav: 1.FC Brno – FC Thun 1-1 (1-0)
1.FC Brno: Tomas BELIC (SVK), Milos KRSKO (SVK), Ales SCHUSTER, Martin KOTÜLEK, Patrik KRAP, Radek MEZLIK (YC61) (68' Tomás MÁSA), Marek ZÚBEK, Tomás ABRAHAM, Michal BELEJ (84' Milan SVOBODA), Milan PACANDA (YC85), Karel KROUPA (74' Pavel SIMR).
FC Thun: Fabio COLTORTI, Andreas GERBER, Ljubo MILICEVIC (AUS), Marc SCHNEIDER, Pascal CERRONE, Reto ZANNI (46' Nelson FERREIRA "NELO" (POR)), Patrick BAUMANN, Silvan AEGERTER (YC87), ANTONIO dos Santos (BRA), Adrian MOSER (46' Pascal RENFER, 58' Mario RAIMONDI), Mallaim RAMA.
Goals: 1.FC Brno: 1-0 Karel KROUPA (11').
FC Thun: 1-1 Mario RAIMONDI (63').
Referee: Romans LAJUKS (LAT)   Attendance: 2.110

12-07-2003   Herman Vanderpoortenstadion, Lier:
K.Lierse SK – FK Sloboda Tuzla   5-1 (0-1)
K.Lierse SK: Yves VAN DER STRAETEN, Stef WILS, Jonas DE ROECK (YC42), Bertrand
CRASSON (YC19) (64' Nicolas TIMMERMANS), Hasan KACIC (CRO), Igor
NIKOLOVSKI (MCD) (64' Laurent FASSOTTE), Marc SCHAESSENS, Karel SNOECKX,
Werry SELS (55' Arouna KONÉ (CIV)), Laurent DELORGE, Stein HUYSEGEMS (YC81).
FK Sloboda Tuzla: Mirsad DEDIC, Velimir VIDIC, Nusret MUSLIMOVIC, Gradimir
CRNOGORAC, Samir KUDUZOYIC, Nedzad BAJROVIC (YC39), Admir JOLDIC, Adnan
SARAJLIC, Senad HADZIC (YC63) (81' Zvjezdan KRESIC), Tarik OKANOVIC (53' Admir
BRDZANOVIC), Alen MESANOVIC (YC26).
Goals: K.Lierse SK: 1-1 Karel SNOECKX (47'), 2-1 Stein HUYSEGEMS (54'), 3-1 Arouna
KONÉ (75'), 4-1 Marc SCHAESSENS (83' penalty), 5-1 Karel SNOECKX (89').
FK Sloboda Tuzla: 0-1 Admir JOLDIC (1').
Referee: Augustus Viorel CONSTANTIN (ROM)

12-07-2003   Stadion Centralny, Kostanay:
FC Tobol Kostanay – K.Sint-Truidense VV   1-0 (0-0)
FK Tobol Kostanay: Valeri SHANTALOSOV (BLS), Sergey ANDREEV (RUS), Oleg
LOTOV, Petr BADLO (YC28) (73' Sergey KAPUTIN), Konstantin KOTOV, Alexey
KOSOLAPOV (RUS), Nurbol ZHUMASKALIYEV, Nurken MAZBAYEV (67' Valeriy
GARKUSHA), Andrey SHKURIN, Oleg GOLOVAN (RUS), Daniar MUHANOV.
K.Sint Truidense VV: Dusan BELIC (SBM), Peter VOETS, Stijn VANGEFFELEN, Frank
GERAERTS, Tom VAN IMSCHOOT, Kris BUVENS (YC51), Desiré M'BONABUCYA
(YC61), Peter DELORGE, Claude KALISA (RWA), Robbie DELLO, Danny BOFFIN.
Goal: FK Tobol Kostanay: 1-0 Konstantin KOTOV (85').
Referee: Martin HANSSON (SWE)   Attendance: 6.000

12-07-2003   Stadion Bergholz, Wil: FC Wil 1900 – Willem II Tilburg   3-1 (1-0)
FC Wil 1900: Nicolas BENEY, Alessandro MANGIARRATTI, Massimo RIZZO, Philippe
MONTANDON, Patrick WINKLER (YC28) (78' Stefan BLUNSCHI (YC89)), Umberto
ROMANO, Michael RENGGLI, FABIO de Souza (BRA) (YC40), Mauro LUSTRINELLI,
HELDER MIGUEL La Costa Vrea (POR) (87' Stephan BALMER), Davide CALLA (ITA)
(72' Kristian MUSHI (SBM)).
Willem II Tilburg: Geert DE VLIEGER (BEL), Nuelson WAU, Joris MATHIJSEN, Jos VAN
NIEUWSTADT (60' Bart VAN DEN EEDE (BEL) (YC86)), Kew JALIENS, Denny
LANDZAAT, Mourad MGHIZRAT (MAR) (46' Anouar HADOUIR), Raymond VICTORIA
(YC45), James QUINN (NIR), Tom CALUWÉ (BEL), Dmitri SHOUKOV (RUS) (66' Danny
MATHIJSEN).
Goals: FC Wil 1900: 1-0 Mauro LUSTRINELLI (4'), 2-1 Mauro LUSTRINELLI (78'), 3-1
Umberto ROMANO (83' penalty).
Willem II Tilburg: 1-1 Tom CALUWÉ (61').
Referee: Espen BERNTSEN (NOR)   Attendance: 6.000

12-07-2003   Györi ETO Stadion, Györ:
Györi ETO FC – Real Racing Club Santander   2-1 (1-0)
Györi ETO FC: Zsolt SEBÖK, Atilla BÖJTE, Antal JÄKL, Marko KARTELO (CRO) (YC15),
Tamás GERI, Miklós HERCZEG, Zoltán VARGA (YC30), Norbert NÉMETH (46'
Aleksandar BAJEVSKI (MCD)), Goran JOVANOVIC (SBM) (YC44) (69' Csaba REGEDEI
(YC77)), Tamás NAGY, Márton OROSS (46' Tibor KALINA). (Coach: Zoltán VARGA).
Real Racing Club Santander: Alberto BESOY López "TREVI", Claude GNAKPA (FRA),
David COROMINA Pararols (YC70), Ilan BAKHAR (ISR) (YC48), José Manuel Suárez
Rivas "SIETES", PABLO Ballesteros LAGO (YC38) (73' JONATHÁN Valle Trueba),
JUVENAL Edjogo Owono Montalban (73' Ignacio "NACHO" Rodriguez Ortiz), Eduardo
"EDU" AGUILAR Leiva (48' Fernando MORÁN Escudero), Daniel Rodríguez Pérez
"TXIKI", Sergio MATABUENA Delgado, Juan Ramón EPITIÉ Dyowe Roig. (Coach:
Fernando Trío Zabala "NANDO YOSU").
Goals: Györi ETO FC: 1-0 Marko KARTELO (13'), 2-0 Aleksandar BAJEVSKI (64').
Real Racing Club Santander: 2-1 JONATHÁN Valle Trueba (84').
Referee: Carlo BERTOLINI (SUI)   Attendance: 2.000

12-07-2003   Waldstadion, Pasching: SV Pasching – FK Pobeda Prilep   2-1 (0-0)
SV Pasching: Josef SCHICKLGRUBER, Michael BAUR, Patrick PIRCHER, Tomasz WISIO
(POL), Manfred ROTHBAUER (YC63), Bozo KOVACEVIC, Helmut RIEGLER, Alexander
HÖRTNAGL (77' Faruk ATALAY (TUR)), Michael HORVATH (YC61), Edi GLIEDER,
George Martin DATORU (64' Christian MAYRLEB).
FK Pobeda Prilep: Tome PANCEV, Saso ZDRAVEVSKI, Marjan NACEV (90' Goran SEAD
(SBM)), Pance CHUMBEV (YC83), Dimitar KAPINKOVSKI, Cedomir MIJANOVIC (SBM)
(YC..,YC89), GILSON de Jesus da Silva (BRA), Toni MEGLENSKI (YC26), Nikolce
ZDRAVESKI (YC66) (78' Aleksandar POPOVSKI), Draganco DIMITROVSKI, Blagoja
GESOSKI.
Goals: SV Pasching: 1-0 Michael BAUR (51'), 2-1 Edi GLIEDER (75').
FK Pobeda Prilep: 1-1 Marjan NACEV (71').
Referee: Drazenko KOVACIC (CRO)   Attendance: 1.400

12-07-2003   Stade Municipal du Ray, Nice: O.G.C. Nice – Örgryte IS   2-1 (2-1)
O.G.C. Nice: Damien GRÉGORINI, Noé PAMAROT, José COBOS, Jacques
ABARDONADO, Cedric VARRAULT, Yoann BIGNÉ (73' Sammy TRAORÉ), Eric ROY
(YC87), Romain PITAU (YC63), EVERSON Pereira da Silva (BRA), Abdelmalek
CHERRAD (ALG) (89' Serge DIÉ (CIV)), Daniel MESLIN (55' Lilian LASLANDES
(YC58)).
Örgryte IS: Tommy NAURIN, Atli THÓRARINSSON (ISL), Anders PRYTZ, Robert
BENGTSSON-BÄRKROTH (YC79), Marcus JOHANNESSON, Daniel LOHM, Jeffrey
AUBYNN (YC51), Robin GANEMYR, Mentor ZHUBI, Patrik FREDHOLM, Christian
HEMBERG (60' Boyo MWILA (ZAM)).
Goals: O.G.C. Nice: 1-0 Noë PAMAROT (8'), 2-0 Daniel MESLIN (22').
Örgryte IS: 2-1 Jeffrey AUBYNN (42').
Referee: Ioakim EFTHIMIADIS (GRE)   Attendance: 10.000

67

12-07-2003   Volkswagen Arena, Wolfsburg:
VfL Wolfsburg – FC Marek Dupnitsa 2-0 (1-0)
VfL Wolfsburg: Simon JENTZSCH, Thomas RYTTER (DEN), Marino BILISKOV (CRO),
Stefan SCHNOOR, Mirko HRGOVIC (BOS), Sven MÜLLER (69' Hans SARPEI), Pablo
THIAM, Miroslav KARHAN (SVK), Roy PRÄGER (90' Christian RITTER), Diego Fernando
KLIMOWICZ (ARG), Martin PETROV (BUL) (82' Dorinel MUNTEANU (ROM)).
FC Marek Dupnitsa: Nikolay CHAVDAROV, Ianek KIUTCHUKOV, Alexei DIONISIEV
(YC52) (69' Hristo ARANGUELOV), Veselin VELIKOV, Emil PETKOV, Angel STOIKOV,
Georgi VAZHAROV, Anzhelo KIUCHUKOV (YC43) (77' Toni PITOSKA (MCD)), Amiran
MUJIRI (GEO) (YC55) (60' Vassil KIROV), Liubomir LIUBENOV, Kroum BIBISHKOV.
Goals: VfL Wolfsburg: 1-0 Martin PETROV (43'), 2-0 Dorinel MUNTEANU (90' penalty).
Referee: Gylfi Thor ORRASON (ISL)   Attendance: 6.337

13-07-2003   Richmond Park, Dublin: FC Shamrock Rovers – FC Slovan Liberec   0-2 (0-0)
Shamrock Rovers FC: Barry Paul RYAN, Stephen James GOUGH, James Michael KEDDY,
Jason John COLWELL, Terry PALMER, Richard Philip BYRNE, Trevor MOLLOY (59'
Shane ROBINSON (YC66)), Anthony James GRANT, Glen Paul FITZPATRICK, Alan
REYNOLDS, Stephen GRANT.
FC Slovan Liberec: Antonín KINSKY, Tomás ZÁPOTOCNY (YC37), Petr LUKÁS, Jozef
VALACHOVIC (SVK) (YC47), Tomás JANU, Karol KISEL (SVK), David LANGER (24'
Jan BROSCHINSKY), Václav KOLOUSEK (78' Jan NEZMAR), Jan POLÁK, Juraj ANCIC
(SVK), Michal POSPÍSIL (74' Filip HOLOSKO (SVK)).
Goals: FC Slovan Liberec: 0-1 Václav KOLOUSEK (76'), 0-2 Jan NEZMAR (86').
Referee: Jouni HYYTIÄ (FIN)   Attendance: 1.500

13-07-2003   Stadion kraj Bistrice, Niksic:
FK Sutjeska Niksic – Tampere United FC   0-1 (0-0)
FK Sutjeska Niksic: Zoran BANOVIC, Srdjan DAMJANOVIC (YC24) (67' Nikola
NIKEZIC), Darko KRSTESKI (MCD), Kristijan TUCAKOVIC (YC4), Bojan COSIC (87'
Anzor NAFAS), Goran BOSKOVIC, Milenko MILOSEVIC (YC72), Drazen MEDJEDOVIC
(77' Vlado JEKNIC), Boban KRISANOVIC, Vladan KOSTIC, Ivan BOSKOVIC (RC90).
Tampere United FC: Mikko KAVEN, Heikki AHO, Pasi SALMELA, Mikko SALO, Jussi
KUOPPALA, Sakari SAARINEN (63' Antti OJANPERÄ), Kari SAINIO (YC74), Tero
KOSKELA (YC24), Henri SCHEWELEFF (71' Antti HYNYNEN), Janne RÄSÄNEN, Noah
HICKEY (NZL) (90' Jaakko LAHTINEN).
Goal: Tampere United FC: 0-1 Tero KOSKELA (90').
Referee: Paulius MALZINSKAS (LIT)

13-07-2003   Pohjola Stadion, Vantaa: AC Allianssi – Akratitos FC   0-0
AC Allianssi: Alexander MISHCHUK (RUS), Ari-Pekka ROIKO, Jarno TUUNAINEN, Janne
MOILANEN, Harri HAAPANIEMI, Timo MARJAMAA, Rami RANTANEN, Mikko
SIMULA (85' Heikki PULKKINEN), Peter SAMPO (74' Petteri KAIJASILTA), ADRIANO
Munoz (BRA), Justus VAJANNE.
Akratitos FC: Grigoris ATHANASSIOU, Athanasios TSOUKIS, Achilleas TSIAKALOS,
Ioannis PARASIDIS (YC65), Christos PIPINIS, Konstandinos PAGONIS (86' Panagiotis
PAPADOPOULOS), Themis TZIMOPOULOS, Thomas BIBIRIS, Angelos PALLIS,
Efstathios STEFANIDIS (90' Loukas NIKOLAOU), Spiridon REDOUMIS (72' Fotios
KOSTOPOULOS).
Referee: Eric BLAREAU (BEL)   Attendance: 2.662

THIRD ROUND

19-07-2003   Stadion Siruch, Staré Mêsto:
1.FC Synot Staré Mêsto – VfL Wolfsburg 0-1 (0-0)
1.FC Synot Staré Mêsto: Petr DROBISZ, Pavel NEMCICKY, Rastislav KOSTKA (SVK)
(YC..), Ján PALINEK, Marek SEMAN (SVK), Vladimir MALAR, Velice SUMULIKOSKI
(MCD), Tomas POLACH (69' Jiri KOWALIK), Ivan DVORÁK (77' Ondrej VORISEK),
Martin ABRAHAM, Michal MEDUNA (64' Petr SLONCÍK).
VfL Wolfsburg: Simon JENTZSCH, Marino BILISKOV (CRO), Stefan SCHNOOR, Hans
SARPEI, Sven MÜLLER, Miroslav KARHAN (SVK) (63' Dorinel MUNTEANU (ROM)),
Pablo THIAM, Mirko HRGOVIC (BOS), Marko TOPIC (BOS) (79' Maik FRANZ), Diego
Fernando KLIMOWICZ (ARG), Martin PETROV (BUL).
Goal: VfL Wolfsburg: 0-1 Marko TOPIC (47').
Referee: Paolo BERTINI (ITA)   Attendance: 3.400

19-07-2003   Stadionul Republican, Chisinau: FC Dacia Chisinau – FC Schalke 04 0-1 (0-1)
FC Dacia Chisinau: Alexandre MEREOUTSA, Vitaly MARDARI (90' Igor NEGRESCU),
Corneliu POPOV, Liviu ANDRIUTA (YC8), Serghey POTRIMBA, Vitalie GLUHENCHI
(84' Alexander GOROBET), Andrei MARTIN, Sergiu JAPALAU (68' Ghenadie ORBU),
Grigory BADEA, Alexandru GOLBAN, Vladimir JAPULAU.
FC Schalke 04: Frank ROST, Aduardo ALCIDES (BRA), Tomasz HAJTO (POL) (YC70),
Aníbal Samuel MATELLÁN (ARG), Levan KOBIASHVILI (GEO), Gerald ASAMOAH (79'
Octavio Darío RODRÍGUEZ Peña (URU)), Hamit ALTINTOP (TUR), Christian POULSEN
(DEN) (YC31), Gustavo Antonio VARELA (URU), Simon CZIOMMER (90' Sven
VERMANT (BEL)), Victor AGALI (NGR).
Goal: FC Schalke 04: 0-1 Simon CZIOMMER (24').
Referee: Sten KALDMA (EST)   Attendance: 7.000

19-07-2003   Stadion Centralny, Kostanay: FK Tobol Kostanay – SV Pasching 0-1 (0-0)
FK Tobol Kostanay: Valeri SHANTALOSOV (BLS), Andrey SHKURIN, Sergey ANDREEV
(RUS), Oleg LOTOV, Sergey KAPUTIN, Oleg GOLOVAN (RUS), Alexey KOSOLAPOV
(RUS), Nurbol ZHUMASKALIYEV, Daniar MUHANOV, Konstantin KOTOV (46' Valeriy
GARKUSHA), Nurken MAZBAYEV.
SV Pasching: Josef SCHICKLGRUBER, Michael BAUR, Bozo KOVACEVIC, Tomasz
WISIO (POL), Torsten KNABEL, Alexander HÖRTNAGL, Faruk ATALAY (TUR) (65'
Michael HORVATH), Wolfgang BUBENIK (85' Manfred ROTHBAUER), Markus
KIESENEBNER, Edi GLIEDER, Christian MAYRLEB (68' George Martin DATORU).
Goal: SV Pasching: 0-1 Edi GLIEDER (79').
Referee: Emil LAURSEN (DEN)

19-07-2003   Stade René-Gaillard, Niort: FC Nantes Atlantique – FC Wil 1900 2-1 (0-1)
FC Nantes Atlantique: Willy GRONDIN, Sylvain ARMAND, Mathieu BERSON, Mauro
CETTO (ARG), Pascal DELHOMMEAU, Chiva Star N'ZIGOU (GAB) (83' Hassan
AHAMADA), Olivier QUINT, Nicolas SAVINAUD (YC72), Jérémy TOULALAN, Marama
VAHIRUA (65' Grégory PUJOL), Stéphane ZIANI (65' Frédéric DA ROCHA).
FC Wil 1900: Nicolas BENEY, Alessandro MANGIARRATTI, Philippe MONTANDON,
Umberto ROMANO, Michael RENGGLI, Mauro LUSTRINELLI (65' Stefan BLUNSCHI),
FABIO de Souza (BRA), ROGERIO Luiz da Silva (BRA) (87' Peter EUGSTER), Stephan
BALMER, HELDER MIGUEL La Costa Vera (POR), Davide CALLA (ITA).
Goals: FC Nantes Atlantique: 1-1 Chiva Star N'ZIGOU (50'), 2-1 Grégory PUJOL (86').
FC Wil 1900: 0-1 ROGERIO Luiz da Silva (23').
Referee: Michael Thomas ROSS (NIR)

69

19-07-2003   Abe Lenstra Stadion, Heerenveen: SC Heerenveen – K.Lierse SK   4-1 (3-1)
SC Heerenveen: Hans VONK (RSA), Marcel SEIP, Petter HANSSON (SWE), Tieme
KLOMPE (69' Paul DE LANGE), Erik EDMAN (SWE) (84' Said BAKKATI), Arek
RADOMSKI (POL), Richard KNOPPER, Mika VÄYRYNEN (FIN), Stefan SELAKOVIC
(SWE) (53' Georgios SAMARAS (GRE)), Gerald SIBON, Romano DENNEBOOM.
K.Lierse SK: Cliff MARDULIER, Bertrand CRASSON (58' Nicolas TIMMERMANS),
Laurent FASSOTTE (YC72), Igor NIKOLOVSKI (MCD), Adolph TOMOUA (CIV), Werry
SELS, Stef WILS, Marc SCHAESSENS (58' Laurent DELORGE), Karel SNOECKX, Stein
HUYSEGEMS (58' Arouna KONÉ (CIV)), Geir FRIGÅRD (NOR).
Goals: SC Heerenveen: 1-0 Gerald SIBON (1'), 2-1 Romano DENNEBOOM (29'), 3-1
Richard KNOPPER (35'), 4-1 Georgios SAMARAS (80').
K.Lierse SK: 1-1 Geir FRIGÅRD (22').
Referee: Gianluca PAPARESTA (ITA)   Attendance: 8.300

19-07-2003   Stade Municipal du Roudourou, Guingamp:
               En Avant Guingamp – 1.FC Brno   2-1 (0-1)
En Avant Guingamp: Ronan LE CROM, Nicolas LASPALLES, Blaise KOUASSI (CIV),
Milovan SIKIMIL (SBM), Romain FERRIER, Claude MICHEL (YC55), Stéphane CARNOT
(60' Hakim SACI (ALG)), Ricardo CABANAS (SUI), Christophe LE ROUX, Nicolas
GOUSSÉ, Pierre-Yves ANDRÉ.
1.FC Brno: Tomas BELIC (SVK), Patrik KRAP, Ales SCHUSTER (RC87), Martin
KOTÜLEK, Milos KRSKO (SVK), Martin ZIVNÝ (YC37), Marek ZÚBEK (YC16), Michal
BELEJ (71' Radek MEZLIK), Tomás ABRAHAM, Karel KROUPA (66' Petr SVANCARA),
Milan PACANDA (88' Petr KRIVÁNEK).
Goals: En Avant Guingamp: 1-1 Ricardo CABANAS (81'), 2-1 Christophe LE ROUX (87'
penalty).
1.FC Brno: 0-1 Milos KRSKO (19').
Referee: Jack C.D.VAN HULTEN (HOL)   Attendance: 4.970

19-07-2003   Stade Municipal du Ray, Nice: O.G.C. Nice – SV Werder Bremen   0-0
O.G.C. Nice: Damien GRÉGORINI, José COBOS (YC62), Noé PAMAROT, Jacques
ABARDONADO, Yoann BIGNÉ (69' Sammy TRAORÉ), Romain PITAU, Eric ROY, Cedric
VARRAULT (67' Serge DIÉ (CIV)), EVERSON Pereira da Silva (BRA), Lilian
LASLANDES, Daniel MESLIN (89' Cédric MIONNET).
SV Werder Bremen: Andreas REINKE, Valérien ISMAÉL (FRA), Mladen KRSTAJIC (SBM),
Frank BAUMANN (YC89), Johan MICOUD (FRA), Ludovic MAGNIN (SUI), Fabian
ERNST (72' Krisztián LISZTES (HUN)), Ivica BANOVIC (CRO), Paul STALTERI (CAN),
AILTON Goncalves da Silva (BRA), Ivan KLASNIC (CRO) (20' Marco REICH).
Referee: Muhittin BOSAT (TUR)   Attendance: 9.448

19-07-2003   Stadio Renato Curi, Perugia: AC Perugia – AC Allianssi   2-0 (2-0)
AC Perugia: Zeljko KALAC (AUS), Souleymane DIAMOUTENE (MLI) (YC69), Jamel
ALIOUI (FRA), Marco DI LORETO, Fabio GATTI (YC68), Fabio GROSSO, "ZÉ
MARIA"José Marcelo Ferreira (BRA), Giovanni TEDESCO, Jay BOTHROYD (ENG),
Massiniliano FUSANI, Zisis VRYZAS (GRE).
AC Allianssi: Alexander MISHCHUK (RUS), Heikki PULKKINEN, Jarno TUUNAINEN,
Janne MOILANEN, Ari-Pekka ROIKO, Timo MARJAMAA, Rami RANTANEN, Mikko
SIMULA (86' Mikko PAATELAINEN), Peter SAMPO, Justus VAJANNE, ADRIANO
Munoz (BRA).
Goals: AC Perugia: 1-0 Jay BOTHROYD (23'), 2-0 Massiniliano FUSANI (45').
Referee: Mark Richard HALSEY (ENG)

70

19-07-2003   Stadio Yiannis Pathiakakis, Athens: Egaleo FC Athens – NK Koper   2-3 (0-0)
Egaleo FC Athens: Srdan KLJAJEVIC (SBM), Konstantinos PAPOUTSIS, Christos MITSIS
(73' Ioannis CHRISTOU), Giorgios ALEXOPOULOS, Emmanuel PSOMAS, Theodoros
AGGOS, Michael CHATZIS, Georgios FOTAKIS, Nikolaos NIKOLOPOULOS (34' John
CHLOROS), Jean-Denis WANGA ENDINGUE (CMR) (55' Evgenios KITSAS), Anastasios
AGRITIS.
NK Koper: Ermin HASIC, Edmond GUNJAC, Andrej POLJSAK, Alen SCULAC, Darko
KREMENOVIC, Juan Sebastian VITAGLIANO Cruz (ARG) (74' Dalibor VUCKOVIC),
Elvis RIBARIC, Sasa BOZICIC, Nebojsa KOVACEVIC (YC43), Viktor TRENEVSKI
(MCD) (85' Andrej RASTOVAC), Sasa JAKOMIN (62' Jaka STROMAJER).
Goals: Egaleo FC Athens: 1-1 John CHLOROS (60'), 2-1 Michael CHATZIS (61').
NK Koper: 0-1 Viktor TRENEVSKI (48'), 2-2 Nebojsa KOVACEVIC (66'), 2-3 Viktor
TRENEVSKI (80').
Referee: Alfonso PÉREZ BURRULL (ESP)   Attendance: 266

19-07-2003   El Sardinero, Santander:
                     Real Racing Club Santander – FC Slovan Liberec   0-1 (0-1)
Real Racing Club Santander: Francisco BORJA Lavín Vitorero, Ilan BAKHAR (ISR), Claude
GNAKPA (FRA), David COROMINA Pararols, José Manuel Suárez Rivas "SIETES" (9' José
Moratón "MORA" Taeño), PABLO Ballesteros LAGO (30' RUBÉN GARCÍA Martínez),
Fernando MORÁN Escudero, Sergio Matabuena "MATA" Delgado, Daniel Rodríguez Pérez
"TXIKI", RAÚL Martín Del Campo, JONATHÁN Valle Trueba (64' Ignacio "NACHO"
Rodriguez Ortiz). (Coach: Fernando Trío Zabala "NANDO YOSU").
FC Slovan Liberec: Antonín KINSKY, Tomás ZÁPOTOCNY, Petr LUKÁS, Jozef
VALACHOVIC (SVK), Tomás JANU, Karol KISEL (SVK), Václav KOLOUSEK, Jan
POLÁK, Jan BROSCHINSKY (77' Ivan HODÚR (SVK)), Juraj ANCIC (SVK), Michal
POSPÍSIL (60' Filip HOLOSKO (SVK), 89' Jan NEZMAR). (Coach: Ladislav SKORPIL).
Goal: FC Slovan Liberec: 0-1 Michal POSPÍSIL (41').
Referee: Damien LEDENTU (FRA)   Attendance: 3.951

19-07-2003   Estadio El Madrigal, Villarreal: Villarreal CF – Brescia Calcio SpA   2-0 (1-0)
Villarreal CF: Javier LÓPEZ VALLEJO, Javier "JAVI" Rodríguez VENTA, Sergio Martínez
BALLESTEROS, Pedro MARTÍ Castello, Rodolfo Martín ARRUABARRENA (ARG),
Antonio GUAYRE Betancor Perdomo (69' CÉSAR ARZO Amposta), José Joaquín Moreno
Verdú "JOSICO", HÉCTOR FRONT Romero (YC83), Javier CALLEJA Revilla (YC29) (89'
David GALINDO Gallego), VÍCTOR Manuel Fernández Gutiérrez, "SONNY" ANDERSON
da Silva (BRA) (69' Francisco Sebastian "XISCO" NADAL Martorell). (Coach: Benito
FLORO Sanz).
Brescia Calcio SpA: Luca CASTELLAZZI, Marius STANKEVICIUS (LIT), Dario
DAINELLI (YC62), Víctor Hugo MARECO (PAR) (YC4) (46' Francelino MATUZALÉM da
Silva (BRA) (YC77)), Roberto CORTELLINI, Alejandro Adrián CORREA Rodríguez (URU),
Fabio PETRUZZI (YC57), Roberto GUANA (YC21) (66' Marc NYGAARD (DEN)), Markus
SCHOPP (AUT), Igli TARE (ALB), Raúl Alberto GONZÁLEZ (ARG) (YC34) (68' Simone
DEL NERO). (Coach: Giovanni DE BIASI).
Goals: Villarreal CF: 1-0 Javier CALLEJA Revilla (15'), 2-0 VÍCTOR Manuel Fernández
Gutiérrez (81').
Referee: Uriah Duddley RENNIE (ENG)   Attendance: 6.000

71

20-07-2003   Ratina Stadium, Tampere:
Tampere United FC – HNK Cibalia Vinkovci   0-2 (0-0)
Tampere United FC: Mikko KAVEN, Heikki AHO, Pasi SALMELA, Mikko SALO, Jussi
KUOPPALA, Sakari SAARINEN (YC56) (80' Jaakko LAHTINEN), Kari SAINIO, Tero
KOSKELA, Henri SCHEWELEFF (65' Antti HYNYNEN), Janne RÄSÄNEN, Noah
HICKEY (NZL) (73' Antti OJANPERÄ).
HNK Cibalia Vinkovci: Ivica MARIC, Mladen KRIZANOVIC, Darko JOZINOVIC (YC56),
Mario LUCIC, Boris LEUTAR (YC35), Ivan MAROSLAVAC, Mario JURIC, Zoran
RATKOVIC (68' Ivan ZGELA), Elvis CORIC (83' Dejan PAVLICIC), Ivan LAJTMAN (76'
Bosko PERAICA), Vedran IVANKOVIC.
Goals: HNK Cibalia Vinkovci: 0-1 Mario JURIC (78'), 0-2 Ivan ZGELA (88').
Referee: Antonio Manuel ALMEIDA COSTA (POR)

26-07-2003   Stadion Mladost, Vinkovci:
HNK Cibalia Vinkovci – Tampere United FC   0-1 (0-0)
HNK Cibalia Vinkovci: Ivica MARIC, Mladen KRIZANOVIC, Darko JOZINOVIC (YC38),
Mario LUCIC, Boris LEUTAR,Drazen PERNAR, Ivan MAROSLAVAC (58' Hrvoje
KOVACEVIC), Mario JURIC (YC47), Zoran RATKOVIC, Dejan PAVLICIC (46' Ivan
LAJTMAN), Elvis CORIC (71' Vedran IVANKOVIC).
Tampere United FC: Mikko KAVEN, Heikki AHO, Pasi SALMELA, Mikko SALO, Jussi
KUOPPALA, Sakari SAARINEN (YC38), Kari SAINIO (YC80), Tero KOSKELA, Henri
SCHEWELEFF (75' Jaakko LAHTINEN), Janne RÄSÄNEN, Antti OJANPERÄ (46' Antti
HYNYNEN).
Goal: Tampere United FC: 0-1 Janne RÄSÄNEN (65').
Referee: Markus NOBS (SUI)

26-07-2003   Herman Vanderpoortenstadion, Lier: K.Lierse SK – SC Heerenveen   0-1 (0-0)
K.Lierse SK: Yves VAN DER STRAETEN, Bertrand CRASSON (YC8) (74' Nicolas
TIMMERMANS), Hasan KACIC (CRO), Igor NIKOLOVSKI (MCD) (78' Werry SELS), Stef
WILS, Marc SCHAESSENS, Karel SNOECKX (YC68), Laurent DELORGE (74' Geir
FRIGÅRD (NOR)), Dan Marius MITU (ROM) (RC75), Stein HUYSEGEMS (YC45), Arouna
KONÉ (CIV).
SC Heerenveen: Hans VONK (RSA), Marcel SEIP (YC62), Petter HANSSON (SWE), Arek
RADOMSKI (POL), Erik EDMAN (SWE), Mika VÄYRYNEN (FIN) (YC68), Paul DE
LANGE, Richard KNOPPER (YC34), Jesper HÅKANSSON (DEN) (65' Said BAKKATI),
Georgios SAMARAS (GRE) (YC27) (84' Antonio CORREIA (ANG)), Romano
DENNEBOOM.
Goal: SC Heerenveen: 0-1 Mika VÄYRYNEN (90+').
Referee: Wolfgang SOWA (AUT)   Attendance: 3.000

26-07-2003   Volkswagen Arena, Wolfsburg:
VfL Wolfsburg – 1.FC Synot Staré Mêsto   2-0 (1-0)
VfL Wolfsburg: Simon JENTZSCH, Thomas RYTTER (DEN), Stefan SCHNOOR, Marino
BILISKOV (CRO), Hans SARPEI, Pablo THIAM, Mirko HRGOVIC (BOS), Andres
D'ALESSANDRO (ARG) (88' Dorinel MUNTEANU (ROM)), Marko TOPIC (BOS) (57'
Albert STREIT), Diego Fernando KLIMOWICZ (ARG), Martin PETROV (BUL) (83'
Miroslav KARHAN (SVK)).
1.FC Synot Staré Mêsto: Petr DROBISZ, Pavel NEMCICKY, Velice SUMULIKOSKI
(MCD), Ján PALINEK (46' Michal KADLEC), Marek SEMAN (SVK), Vladimir MALAR,
Petr SLONCÍK, Tomas POLACH (73' Michal MEDUNA), Ivan DVORÁK, Martin
ABRAHAM, Jiri KOWALIK (59' Josef LUKASTRIK).
Goals: VfL Wolfsburg: 1-0 Diego Fernando KLIMOWICZ (23'), 2-0 Martin PETROV (76').
Referee: Paul McKEON (IRL)   Attendance: 13.290

26-07-2003   Stadion u Nisy, Liberec:
FC Slovan Liberec – Real Racing Club Santander   2-1 (1-0)
FC Slovan Liberec: Antonín KINSKY, Tomás ZÁPOTOCNY, Jozef VALACHOVIC (SVK)
(YC72), Petr LUKÁS (77' Miroslav HOLENÁK), Tomás JANU, Karol KISEL (SVK), David
LANGER, Jan POLÁK (YC1), Václav KOLOUSEK (YC76) (86' Ivan HODÚR (SVK)), Juraj
ANCIC (SVK), Michal POSPÍSIL (64' Filip HOLOSKO (SVK)). (Coach: Ladislav
SKORPIL).
Real Racing Club Santander: Francisco BORJA Lavín Vitorero, Ilan BAKHAR (ISR) (79'
JONATHÁN Valle Trueba), José Moratón "MORA" Taeño, Juan María "JUANMA" Delgado
Moreno, David COROMINA Pararols (YC2), Sergio Matabuena "MATA" Delgado (RC76),
Diego MATEO Alustiza (ARG) (54' RUBÉN GARCÍA Martínez), Fernando MORÁN
Escudero (86' Juan José COLLANTES), Yossi Shai BENAYOUN (ISR), Daniel Rodríguez
Pérez "TXIKI" (YC74,YC85), Mario Ignacio REGUEIRO (URU). (Coach: Fernando Trío
Zabala "NANDO YOSU").
Goals: FC Slovan Liberec: 1-0 Václav KOLOUSEK (34'), 2-1 Tomás ZÁPOTOCNY (83').
Real Racing Club Santander: 1-1 Daniel Rodríguez Pérez "TXIKI" (53').
Referee: Igorj ISHCHENKO (UKR)   Attendance: 8.288

26-07-2003   Arena AufSchalke, Gelsenkirchen:
FC Schalke 04 – FC Dacia Chisinau   2-1 (0-0)
FC Schalke 04: Frank ROST, Aduardo ALCIDES (BRA), Tomasz HAJTO (POL), Aníbal
Samuel MATELLÁN (ARG), Levan KOBIASHVILI (GEO), Hamit ALTINTOP (TUR),
Christian POULSEN (DEN), Gerald ASAMOAH (83' Sergio PINTO), Simon CZIOMMER
(69' Mike HANKE), Gustavo Antonio VARELA (URU) (69' Jochen SEITZ), Ebbe SAND
(DEN).
FC Dacia Chisinau: Alexandre MEREOUTSA, Serghey POTRIMBA, Liviu ANDRIUTA,
Corneliu POPOV, Vitaly MARDARI, Vitalie GLUHENCHI, Vladimir JAPULAU (85' Igor
NEGRESCU), Grigory BADEA, Sergiu JAPALAU (19' Ghenadie ORBU), Andrei MARTIN
(YC80), Alexandru GOLBAN (90'+1' Alexander GOROBET).
Goals: FC Schalke 04: 1-0 Ebbe SAND (78'), 2-0 Mike HANKE (88').
FC Dacia Chisinau: 2-1 Ghenadie ORBU (90'+2')
Referee: Joseph ATTARD (MLT)   Attendance: 56.256

73

26-07-2003   Mestský fotbalový stadion Srbská, Brno:
1.FC Brno – En Avant Guingamp   4-2 (1-0)
1.FC Brno: Tomas BELIC (SVK), Milos KRSKO (SVK), Petr KRIVÁNEK, Martin
KOTÜLEK, Patrik KRAP (83' Karel KROUPA (YC90)), Tomás ABRAHÁM (YC16), Milan
PACANDA, Marek ZÚBEK, Michal BELEJ (76' Radek MEZLIK (YC118)), Libor DOSEK,
Petr SVANCARA (61' Milan SVOBODA (YC86)).
En Avant Guingamp: Ronan LE CROM, Nicolas LASPALLES, Blaise KOUASSI (CIV)
(YC35), Milovan SIKIMIL (SBM) (YC34), Romain FERRIER (50' Hakim SACI (ALG)
(YC67,RC118)), Alla Adrine YAHIA (TUN) (YC22) (77' Steeve Joseph REINETTE
(RC119)), Claude MICHEL, Ricardo CABANAS (SUI) (YC112), Stéphane CARNOT (63'
Yann YOUFFRE), Pierre-Yves ANDRÉ, Nicolas GOUSSÉ.
Goals: 1.FC Brno: 1-0 Tomás ABRAHÁM (15'), 2-1 Milan SVOBODA (88'), 3-1 Libor
DOSEK (107'), 4-1 Radek MEZLIK (111').
En Avant Guingamp: 1-1 Nicolas LASPALLES (74'), 4-2 Pierre-Yves ANDRÉ (116').
Referee: Martin INGVARSSON (SWE)   Attendance: 7.480
(After extra time)

26-07-2003   Stadio Mario Rigamonti, Brescia:
Brescia Calcio SpA – Villarreal CF   1-1 (0-0)
Brescia Calcio SpA: Tiziano RAMON, Dario DAINELLI, Fabio PETRUZZI (YC81),
Alessandro LUCARELLI, Markus SCHOPP (AUT), Antonio FILIPPINI (YC32), Francelino
MATUZALÉM da Silva (BRA), Roberto CORTELLINI (46' Jonathan BACHINI), Guiseppe
COLUCCI (78' Mario Antonio SALGADO Jimenez (CHI)), Andrea CARACCIOLI (69' Raúl
Alberto GONZÁLEZ (ARG)), Igli TARE (ALB). (Coach: Giovanni DE BIASI).
Villarreal CF: Javier LÓPEZ VALLEJO, Javier "JAVI" Rodríguez VENTA, Rodolfo Martín
ARRUABARRENA (ARG) (YC27), Sergio Martínez BALLESTEROS (YC58), Enrique
"QUIQUE" ÁLVAREZ Sanjuán, Pedro MARTÍ Castello, Antonio GUAYRE Betancor
Perdomo, JORGE LÓPEZ Montaña, "SONNY" ANDERSON da Silva (BRA) (46' JOSÉ
"MARI" María Romero Poyón), VÍCTOR Manuel Fernández Gutiérrez (79' HÉCTOR
FRONT Romero), Javier CALLEJA Revilla (YC51) (72' Juliano Haus BELLETTI (BRA)).
(Coach: Benito FLORO Sanz).
Goals: Brescia Calcio SpA: 1-1 Fabio PETRUZZI (88').
Villarreal CF: 0-1 Antonio GUAYRE Betancor Perdomo (52').
Referee: Stefan JOHANNESSON (SWE)   Attendance: 9.000

26-07-2003   Weserstadion, Bremen: SV Werder Bremen – O.G.C. Nice   1-0 (0-0)
SV Werder Bremen: Andreas REINKE, Paul STALTERI (CAN), Valérien ISMAÉL (FRA),
Mladen KRSTAJIC (SBM), Ludovic MAGNIN (SUI), Ivica BANOVIC (CRO) (61' Krisztián
LISZTES (HUN)), Frank BAUMANN (YC44), Fabian ERNST (YC59), Johan MICOUD
(FRA), Angelos CHARISTEAS (GRE), AILTON Goncalves da Silva (BRA).
O.G.C. Nice: Damien GRÉGORINI, Noé PAMAROT (YC90), José COBOS, Jacques
ABARDONADO (YC55), Cedric VARRAULT (79' Diakité BAKARY (GER)), Sammy
TRAORÉ (YC20), Romain PITAU, Eric ROY, EVERSON Pereira da Silva (BRA), Lilian
LASLANDES (YC83), Abdelmalek CHERRAD (ALG) (72' Daniel MESLIN).
Goal: SV Werder Bremen: 1-0 Johan MICOUD (75').
Referee: Zsolt SZABO (HUN)   Attendance: 24.300

26-07-2003   Stadion Bergholz, Wil: FC Wil 1900 – FC Nantes Atlantique   2-3 (2-2)
FC Wil 1900: Nicolas BENEY, Alessandro MANGIARRATTI, Philippe MONTANDON
(YC50) (56' Michael RENGGLI), Patrick WINKLER, Umberto ROMANO, Mauro
LUSTRINELLI (69' Stefan BLUNSCHI), FABIO de Souza (BRA) (YC5), Stephan BALMER,
Felix MONDEKU (GHA), Kristian MUSHI (SBM) (72' Massmo RIZZO), Davide CALLA
(ITA).
FC Nantes Atlantique: Mickaél LANDREAU, Sylvain ARMAND, Mathieu BERSON (YC41),
Pascal DELHOMMEAU, Emmers FAE (54' Fodil HADJADJ (ALG)), Grégory PUJOL,
Olivier QUINT (YC61) (61' Frédéric DA ROCHA), Nicolas SAVINAUD, Marama
VAHIRUA (72' Hassan AHAMADA), Mario YEPES (COL), Stéphane ZIANI.
Goals: FC Wil 1900: 1-0 Umberto ROMANO (10' penalty), 2-1 Felix MONDEKU (23').
FC Nantes Atlantique: 1-1 Mario YEPES (12'), 2-2 Marama VAHIRUA (43'), 2-3 Grégory
PUJOL (64').
Referee: Jörg KESSLER (GER)

26-07-2003   SRC Bonifika Stadium, Koper: NK Koper – Egaleo FC Athens   2-2 (1-1)
NK Koper: Ermin HASIC, Edmond GUNJAC, Andrej POLJSAK, Alen SCULAC, Elvis
RIBARIC, Darko KREMENOVIC (85' Dalibor VUCKOVIC), Juan Sebastian VITAGLIANO
Cruz (ARG), Andrej RASTOVAC, Sasa BOZICIC, Viktor TRENEVSKI (MCD), Sasa
JAKOMIN (75' Oliver BOGATINOV, 90'+2' Marko BOZIC).
Egaleo FC Athens: Andreas TRIANTAFILLOU, Apostolos GOUDELITSAS, Ioannis
CHRISTOU, Miltiades GOUGOULAKIS, Dimitrios MEIDANIS, Georgios FOTAKIS,
Theodoros AGGOS (60' Konstantinos PAPOUTSIS), Jean-Denis WANGA ENDINGUE
(CMR), Evgenios KITSAS, Abraam SIMEONIDIS, John CHLOROS (46' Anastasios
AGRITIS).
Goals: NK Koper: 1-0 Sasa JAKOMIN (9'), 2-1 Sasa BOZICIC (73').
Egaleo FC Athens: 1-1 John CHLOROS (11'), 2-2 Ioannis CHRISTOU (87').
Referee: Matthew David MESSIAS (ENG)   Attendance: 2.300

26-07-2003   Pohjola Stadion, Vantaa: AC Allianssi – AC Perugia   0-2 (0-1)
AC Allianssi: Alexander MISHCHUK (RUS), Ari-Pekka ROIKO, Jarno TUUNAINEN, Timo
MARJAMAA, Heikki PULKKINEN, Pasi SOLEHMAINEN, Rami RANTANEN (89' Ilpo
VERNO), Mikko SIMULA (YC76) (82' Harri HAAPANIEMI), Peter SAMPO, Justus
VAJANNE (46' Petteri KAIJASILTA), ADRIANO Munoz (BRA).
AC Perugia: Zeljko KALAC (AUS), Souleymane DIAMOUTENE (MLI), Jamel ALIOUI
(FRA) (75' Giovanni IGNOFFO), Marco DI LORETO, Fabio GATTI (59' Christian OBODO
(NGR)), Fabio GROSSO, "ZÉ MARIA"José Marcelo Ferreira (BRA), Giovanni TEDESCO,
Jay BOTHROYD (ENG) (YC37) (71' Emanuele BERRETTONI), Massiniliano FUSANI,
Zisis VRYZAS (GRE).
Goals: AC Perugia: 0-1 Fabio GATTI (21'), 0-2 "ZÉ MARIA"José Marcelo Ferreira (69').
Referee: Peter SIPPEL (GER)

75

26-07-2003   Waldstadion, Pasching: SV Pasching – FK Tobol Kostanay   3-0 (1-0)
SV Pasching: Josef SCHICKLGRUBER, Bozo KOVACEVIC (82' Hakki Tolunay KAFKAS
(TUR)), Tomasz WISIO (POL), Alexander HÖRTNAGL, Torsten KNABEL, Michael BAUR,
Patrick PIRCHER (YC53), Wolfgang BUBENIK, Faruk ATALAY (TUR) (69' Helmut
RIEGLER), Edi GLIEDER (78' Christian MAYRLEB), George Martin DATORU.
FK Tobol Kostanay: Valeri SHANTALOSOV (BLS), Sergey ANDREEV (RUS), Petr
BADLO (YC25), Oleg LOTOV (RC67), Andrey SHKURIN (YC45), Oleg GOLOVAN (RUS)
(YC52) (54' Konstantin KOTOV, 72' Sergey KAPUTIN), Nurbol ZHUMASKALIYEV,
Alexey KOSOLAPOV (RUS), Daniar MUHANOV, Valeriy GARKUSHA (YC76), Nurken
MAZBAYEV (31' TARASOV).
Goals: SV Pasching: 1-0 George Martin DATORU (3'), 2-0 Edi GLIEDER (61'), 3-0 Christian
MAYRLEB (88').
Referee: Kamen ALEXIEV (BUL)

SEMI-FINALS

30-07-2003   Stadion Mladost, Vinkovci:
              HNK Cibalia Vinkovci – VfL Wolfsburg   1-4 (1-2)
HNK Cibalia Vinkovci: Ivica MARIC, Mario LUCIC (YC16), Boris LEUTAR, Vedran
IVANKOVIC (46' Hrvoje KOVACEVIC), Mladen KRIZANOVIC, Ivan MAROSLAVAC
(YC36), Mario JURIC (46' Goran IVELJ (YC61)), Ivan LAJTMAN, Darko JOZINOVIC,
Elvis CORIC (61' Dejan PAVLICIC), Zoran RATKOVIC.
VfL Wolfsburg: Simon JENTZSCH, Thomas RYTTER (DEN), Stefan SCHNOOR, Marino
BILISKOV (CRO) (YC85), Sven MÜLLER, Pablo THIAM, Hans SARPEI, Andres
D'ALESSANDRO (ARG) (61' Patrick WEISER), Marko TOPIC (BOS), Diego Fernando
KLIMOWICZ (ARG) (71' Roy PRÄGER), Martin PETROV (BUL) (57' Mirko HRGOVIC
(BOS)).
Goals: HNK Cibalia Vinkovci: 1-1 Mario LUCIC (28').
VfL Wolfsburg: 0-1 Diego Fernando KLIMOWICZ (13'), 1-2 Martin PETROV (38'), 1-3
Diego Fernando KLIMOWICZ (53'), 1-4 Pablo THIAM (58').
Referee: Nicolai VOLLQUARTZ (DEN)   Attendance: 5.000

30-07-2003   Waldstadion, Pasching: SV Pasching – SV Werder Bremen   4-0 (3-0)
SV Pasching: Josef SCHICKLGRUBER, Manfred ROTHBAUER, Michael BAUR, Patrick
PIRCHER (YC54), Tomasz WISIO (POL) (YC34), Helmut RIEGLER, Bozo KOVACEVIC,
Markus KIESENEBNER (81' Wolfgang BUBENIK), Michael HORVATH, Edi GLIEDER
(YC62) (78' Christian MAYRLEB (YC85)), Faruk ATALAY (TUR) (63' Alexander
HÖRTNAGL).
SV Werder Bremen: Pascal BOREL, Paul STALTERI (CAN), Valérien ISMAÉL (FRA)
(YC34), Mladen KRSTAJIC (SBM), Ludovic MAGNIN (SUI), Fabian ERNST (YC59),
Krisztián LISZTES (HUN) (YC89), Tim BOROWSKI (46' Frank BAUMANN), Johan
MICOUD (FRA), Angelos CHARISTEAS (GRE), AILTON Goncalves da Silva (BRA) (70'
Marco REICH).
Goals: SV Pasching: 1-0 Michael HORVATH (36'), 2-0 Edi GLIEDER (40' penalty), 3-0 Edi
GLIEDER (41'), 4-0 Michael BAUR (83').
Referee: Grzegorz GILEWSKI (POL)   Attendance: 4.500

76

30-07-2003   Abe Lenstra Stadion, Heerenveen: SC Heerenveen – NK Koper   2-0 (2-0)
SC Heerenveen: Hans VONK (RSA), Ronnie VENEMA, Petter HANSSON (SWE), Tieme
KLOMPE (53' Jos HOOIVELD), Erik EDMAN (SWE), Arek RADOMSKI (POL) (46' Paul
DE LANGE), Richard KNOPPER (78' Santi KOLK), Mika VÄYRYNEN (FIN), Georgios
SAMARAS (GRE), Gerald SIBON, Romano DENNEBOOM.
NK Koper: Ermin HASIC, Edmond GUNJAC, Alen SCULAC, Andrej POLJSAK (YC41),
Elvis RIBARIC, Sasa BOZICIC, Juan Sebastian VITAGLIANO Cruz (ARG) (81' Andrej
RASTOVAC), Nebojsa KOVACEVIC, Darko KREMENOVIC (69' Dalibor VUCKOVIC),
Viktor TRENEVSKI (MCD), Sasa JAKOMIN (90' Oliver BOGATINOV).
Goals: SC Heerenveen: 1-0 Gerald SIBON (11'), 2-0 Richard KNOPPER (30').
Referee: Tommy SKJERVEN (NOR)   Attendance: 12.200

30-07-2003   Mestský fotbalový stadion Srbská, Brno: 1.FC Brno – Villarreal CF   1-1 (0-1)
1.FC Brno: Tomás BELIC (SVK), Milos KRSKO (SVK), Ales SCHUSTER (YC83), Martin
KOTULEK (YC63), Patrik KRAP, Martin ZIVNY (55' Pavel MEZLIK), Marek ZÚBEK,
Milan SVOBODA (55' Michal BELEJ), Tomás ABRAHÁM, Libor DOSEK, Milan
PACANDA (83' Karel KROUPA). (Coach: Karel VECERA).
Villarreal CF: Javier LÓPEZ VALLEJO, Javier "JAVI" Rodríguez VENTA, Sergio Martínez
BALLESTEROS, Enrique "QUIQUE" ÁLVAREZ Sanjuán, Rodolfo Martín
ARRUABARRENA (ARG), Antonio GUAYRE Betancor Perdomo, JORGE LÓPEZ Montaña,
Pedro MARTÍ Castello, Javier CALLEJA Revilla (61' Juliano Haus BELLETTI (BRA)
(YC66)), VÍCTOR Manuel Fernández Gutiérrez (46' "SONNY" ANDERSON da Silva
(BRA)), JOSÉ "MARI" María Romero Poyón (79' David GALINDO Gallego). (Coach: Benito
FLORO Sanz).
Goals: 1.FC Brno: 1-1 Libor DOSEK (53').
CF Villarreal: 0-1 JOSÉ "MARI" María Romero Poyón (45'+1').
Referee: Edo TRIVKOVIC (CRO)   Attendance: 10.506

30-07-2003   Stade René-Gaillard, Niort: FC Nantes Atlantique – AC Perugia   0-1 (0-0)
FC Nantes Atlantique: Willy GRONDIN, Jean-Hugues ATEBA BILAYI (CMR), Mauro
CETTO (ARG) (YC72), Pascal DELHOMMEAU, Mario YEPES (COL) (RC86), Mathieu
BERSON (76' Nicolas SAVINAUD), Frédéric DA ROCHA, Fodil HADJADJ (ALG), Olivier
QUINT (YC8) (69' Luigi GLOMBARD), Hassan AHAMADA, Chiva Star N'ZIGOU (GAB)
(69' Grégory PUJOL).
AC Perugia: Zeljko KALAC (AUS), Souleymane DIAMOUTENE (MLI), Jamel ALIOUI
(FRA), Marco DI LORETO (YC90), Fabio GATTI (81' Christian OBODO (NGR)), Fabio
GROSSO (YC60), "ZÉ MARIA"José Marcelo Ferreira (BRA), Giovanni TEDESCO (YC72),
Jay BOTHROYD (ENG) (86' Emanuele BERRETTONI (YC,YC90)), Massiniliano FUSANI
(89' Luigi PAGLIUCA), Zisis VRYZAS (GRE).
Goal: AC Perugia: 0-1 Marco DI LORETO (61').
Referee: Alon YEFET (ISR)

77

30-07-2003   Arena AufSchalke, Gelsenkirchen:
FC Schalke 04 – FC Slovan Liberec   2-1 (0-0)
FC Schalke 04: Frank ROST, Gustavo Antonio VARELA (URU), Tomasz WALDOCH (POL)
(YC26), Thomas KLÄSENER, Nico VAN KERCKHOVEN (BEL), Sergio PINTO (65' Gerald
ASAMOAH), Hamit ALTINTOP (TUR), Christian POULSEN (DEN) (YC90), Jochen SEITZ
(79' Filip TROJAN (CZE)), Mike HANKE (69' Simon CZIOMMER), Ebbe SAND (DEN).
FC Slovan Liberec: Antonín KINSKY, Tomás ZÁPOTOCNY, Jozef VALACHOVIC (SVK),
Miroslav HOLENÁK, Tomás JANU (YC71), Karol KISEL (SVK), Jan POLÁK (YC56) (89'
Ivan HODÚR (SVK)), Václav KOLOUSEK, Juraj ANCIC (SVK) (YC13) (85' David
LANGER), Michal POSPÍSIL (73' Filip HOLOSKO (SVK)), Jan NEZMAR.
Goals: FC Schalke 04: 1-1 Filip TROJAN (81'), 2-1 Gerald ASAMOAH (85').
FC Slovan Liberec: 0-1 Václav KOLOUSEK (79').
Referee: Pasquale RODOMONTI (ITA)   Attendance: 52.288
(Hamit ALTINTOP missed a penalty in the 14th minute)

06-08-2003   SRC Bonifika Stadium, Koper: NK Koper – SC Heerenveen   1-0 (1-0)
NK Koper: Ermin HASIC, Edmond GUNJAC, Alen SCULAC (YC64), Alfred JERMANIS,
Elvis RIBARIC, Dalibor VUCKOVIC, Nebojsa KOVACEVIC, Marko BOZIC (64' Darko
KREMENOVIC), Sasa BOZICIC (88' Jaka STROMAJER), Igor BENEDEJCIC (YC57) (76'
Oliver BOGATINOV), Sasa JAKOMIN (YC32).
SC Heerenveen: Hans VONK (RSA), Said BAKKATI, Petter HANSSON (SWE), Marcel
SEIP, Erik EDMAN (SWE), Arek RADOMSKI (POL), Mika VÄYRYNEN (FIN), Richard
KNOPPER, Georgios SAMARAS (GRE) (86' Mark Jan FLEDDERUS), Gerald SIBON
(YC80), Romano DENNEBOOM (46' Antonio CORREIA (ANG)).
Goal: NK Koper: 1-0 Sasa JAKOMIN (28').
Referee: Miroslav LIBA (CZE)   Attendance: 2.500

06-08-2003   Volkswagen Arena, Wolfsburg:
VfL Wolfsburg – HNK Cibalia Vinkovci   4-0 (1-0)
VfL Wolfsburg: Simon JENTZSCH, Maik FRANZ, Stefan SCHNOOR (63' Christian
RITTER), Marino BILISKOV (CRO), Sven MÜLLER, Miroslav KARHAN (SVK), Pablo
THIAM (51' Patrick WEISER), Dorinel MUNTEANU (ROM), Mirko HRGOVIC (BOS), Roy
PRÄGER, Diego Fernando KLIMOWICZ (ARG) (46' Marko TOPIC (BOS)).
HNK Cibalia Vinkovci: Ivica MARIC, Mario LUCIC, Goran IVELJ (YC59), Drazen
PERNAR, Mladen KRIZANOVIC, Mario ANDRICEVIC, Mario JURIC (46' Igor KIRIN),
Hrvoje KOVACEVIC, Vedran IVANKOVIC (63' Ivan BOSNJAK), Dejan PAVLICIC (77'
Petar TOMIC), Bosko PERAICA.
Goals: VfL Wolfsburg: 1-0 Diego Fernando KLIMOWICZ (31'), 2-0 Miroslav KARHAN
(49'), 3-0 Marko TOPIC (58'), 4-0 Dorinel MUNTEANU (74').
Referee: Laurent DUHAMEL (FRA)   Attendance: 6.114

06-08-2003   Stadion u Nisy, Liberec: FC Slovan Liberec – FC Schalke 04   0-0
FC Slovan Liberec: Antonín KINSKY, Tomás ZÁPOTOCNY, Jozef VALACHOVIC (SVK),
Miroslav HOLENÁK, Tomás JANU, Karol KISEL (SVK), David LANGER (78' Ivan
HODÚR (SVK)), Václav KOLOUSEK, Juraj ANCIC (SVK) (73' Petr PAPOUSEK), Jan
NEZMAR (61' Miroslav SLEPICKA), Michal POSPÍSIL.
FC Schalke 04: Frank ROST, Thomas KLÄSENER, Tomasz WALDOCH (POL) (YC0),
Aníbal Samuel MATELLÁN (ARG), Octavio Darío RODRÍGUEZ Peña (URU) (YC66),
Gerald ASAMOAH (77' Ebbe SAND (DEN)), Hamit ALTINTOP (TUR), Sven VERMANT
(BEL) (61' Levan KOBIASHVILI (GEO)), Jochen SEITZ (77' Filip TROJAN (CZE)), Simon
CZIOMMER, Victor AGALI (NGR).
Referee: Stefan MESSNER (AUT)   Attendance: 9.090

78

06-08-2003   Weserstadion, Bremen: SV Werder Bremen – SV Pasching 1-1 (1-0)
SV Werder Bremen: Andreas REINKE, Mladen KRSTAJIC (SBM) (YC64), Valérien
ISMAÉL (FRA) (YC58), Frank BAUMANN (70' Markus DAUN), Paul STALTERI (CAN),
Krisztián LISZTES (HUN), Ümit DAVALA (TUR) (46' Holger WEHLAGE), Marco REICH
(63' Ludovic MAGNIN (SUI)), Johan MICOUD (FRA), Angelos CHARISTEAS (GRE),
AILTON Goncalves da Silva (BRA).
SV Pasching: Josef SCHICKLGRUBER, Torsten KNABEL, Michael BAUR, Patrick
PIRCHER, Tomasz WISIO (POL), Helmut RIEGLER (65' Hakki Tolunay KAFKAS (TUR)),
Bozo KOVACEVIC, Markus KIESENEBNER (YC8), Alexander HÖRTNAGL, Edi
GLIEDER (YC85) (86' Christian MAYRLEB), Faruk ATALAY (TUR) (54' Michael
HORVATH (YC56)).
Goals: SV Werder Bremen: 1-0 Angelos CHARISTEAS (33').
SV Pasching: 1-1 Markus KIESENEBNER (89').
Referee: Anton STREDAK (SVK)   Attendance: 24.000

06-08-2003   Stadio Renato Curi, Perugia: AC Perugia – FC Nantes Atlantique 0-0
AC Perugia: Zeljko KALAC (AUS), Jamel ALIOUI (FRA) (YC52), Souleymane
DIAMOUTENE (MLI), Marco DI LORETO, Fabio GATTI (46' Christian OBODO (NGR)),
Fabio GROSSO, "ZÉ MARIA"José Marcelo Ferreira (BRA), Giovanni TEDESCO, Jay
BOTHROYD (ENG), Massiniliano FUSANI (71' Konstantinos LOUMPOUTIS (GRE)), Zisis
VRYZAS (GRE) (87' Sasa BJELANOVIC (CRO)).
FC Nantes Atlantique: Mickaël LANDREAU, Hassan AHAMADA (81' Luigi GLOMBARD),
Sylvain ARMAND, Mauro CETTO (ARG), Pascal DELHOMMEAU (YC..,YC63), Loïc
GUILLON, Fodil HADJADJ (ALG) (YC87), Chiva Star N'ZIGOU (GAB), Nicolas
SAVINAUD, Jérémy TOULALAN (75' Loïc PAILLÈRES), Stéphane ZIANI.
Referee: Julian RODRÍGUEZ SANTIAGO (ESP)

06-08-2003   Estadio El Madrigal, Villarreal: Villarreal CF – 1.FC Brno 2-0 (1-0)
Villarreal CF: José Manuel REINA Páez, Javier "JAVI" Rodríguez VENTA, Rodolfo Martín
ARRUABARRENA (ARG), Sergio Martínez BALLESTEROS (YC72), Enrique "QUIQUE"
ÁLVAREZ Sanjuán, Pedro MARTÍ Castello (YC52), Juliano Haus BELLETTI (BRA) (83'
Fabricio COLOCCINI (ARG), JORGE LÓPEZ Montaña, Antonio GUAYRE Betancor
Perdomo, VÍCTOR Manuel Fernández Gutiérrez (90' José Antonio García Rabasco
"VERZA"), Javier CALLEJA Revilla (63' "SONNY" ANDERSON da Silva (BRA)). (Coach:
Benito FLORO Sanz).
1.FC Brno: Tomás BELIC (SVK), Milos KRSKO (SVK) (56' Pavel MEZLIK), Ales
SCHUSTER (YC,YC76), Martin KOTULEK, Patrik KRAP (YC65), Martin ZIVNY, Tomás
ABRAHÁM (YC44) (67' Milan SVOBODA), Marek ZÚBEK, Michal BELEJ, Libor DOSEK,
Milan PACANDA (80' Petr KRIVÁNEK). (Coach: Karel VECERA).
Goals: Villarreal CF: 1-0 JORGE LÓPEZ Montaña (22'), 2-0 "SONNY" ANDERSON da
Silva (90+').
Referee: Michael WEINER (GER)   Attendance: 12.000

FINALS

12-08-2003   Waldstadion, Pasching: SV Pasching – FC Schalke 04   0-2 (0-1)
SV Pasching: Josef SCHICKLGRUBER, Manfred ROTHBAUER, Michael BAUR (YC40),
Patrick PIRCHER, Tomasz WISIO (POL), Bozo KOVACEVIC, Markus KIESENEBNER (73'
Michael HORVATH), Helmut RIEGLER, Faruk ATALAY (TUR) (58' Christian
MAYRLEB), Alexander HÖRTNAGL, Edi GLIEDER (80' George Martin DATORU).
FC Schalke 04: Frank ROST, Tomasz HAJTO (POL), Tomasz WALDOCH (POL), Aníbal
Samuel MATELLÁN (ARG) (YC54) (68' Thomas KLÄSENER), Nico VAN
KERCKHOVEN (BEL), Gerald ASAMOAH, Hamit ALTINTOP (TUR) (YC45), Christian
POULSEN (DEN), Levan KOBIASHVILI (GEO), Ebbe SAND (DEN) (76' Octavio Darío
RODRÍGUEZ Peña (URU)), Victor AGALI (NGR) (83' Jochen SEITZ).
Goals: FC Schalke 04: 0-1 Hamit ALTINTOP (19'), 0-2 Victor AGALI (47').
Referee: Cosimo BOLOGNINO (ITA)   Attendance: 6.000

12-08-2003   Abe Lenstra Stadion, Heerenveen: SC Heerenveen – Villarreal CF   1-2 (1-2)
SC Heerenveen: Hans VONK (RSA), Marcel SEIP, Petter HANSSON (SWE), Tieme
KLOMPE (69' Said BAKKATI), Erik EDMAN (SWE), Arek RADOMSKI (POL) (46' Paul
DE LANGE (YC57)), Richard KNOPPER, Mika VÄYRYNEN (FIN), Stefan SELAKOVIC
(SWE) (65' Georgios SAMARAS (GRE)), Gerald SIBON, Romano DENNEBOOM. (Coach:
Foppe DE HAAN).
Villarreal CF: José Manuel REINA Páez, Javier "JAVI" Rodríguez VENTA, Sergio Martínez
BALLESTEROS, Enrique "QUIQUE" ÁLVAREZ Sanjuán (YC28), Rodolfo Martín
ARRUABARRENA (ARG), Juliano Haus BELLETTI (BRA), Fabricio COLOCCINI (ARG),
Pedro MARTÍ Castello, Javier CALLEJA Revilla (64' Antonio GUAYRE Betancor Perdomo),
VÍCTOR Manuel Fernández Gutiérrez (87' MARCOS Antonio SENNA da Silva (BRA)),
JOSÉ "MARI" María Romero Poyón (YC41) (71' "SONNY" ANDERSON da Silva (BRA)).
(Coach: Benito FLORO Sanz).
Goals: SC Heerenveen: 1-1 Sergio Martínez BALLESTEROS (25' own goal).
Villarreal CF: 0-1 Javier CALLEJA Revilla (13'), 1-2 VÍCTOR Manuel Fernández Gutiérrez
(44').
Referee: Peter FRÖJDFELDT (SWE)   Attendance: 13.000

12-08-2003   Stadio Renato Curi, Perugia: AC Perugia – VfL Wolfsburg   1-0 (1-0)
AC Perugia: Zeljko KALAC (AUS), Souleymane DIAMOUTENE (MLI), Marco DI
LORETO, Jamel ALIOUI (FRA), "ZÉ MARIA"José Marcelo Ferreira (BRA), Giovanni
TEDESCO (46' Raymundo DO PRADO (BRA)), Christian OBODO (NGR), Massiniliano
FUSANI, Fabio GROSSO (88' Konstantinos LOUMPOUTIS (GRE)), Jay BOTHROYD
(ENG) (YC16), Zisis VRYZAS (GRE) (79' Emanuele BERRETTONI).
VfL Wolfsburg: Simon JENTZSCH, Marino BILISKOV (CRO), Stefan SCHNOOR (YC60),
Maik FRANZ, Sven MÜLLER, Pablo THIAM, Andres D'ALESSANDRO (ARG) (YC29),
Patrick WEISER (YC17), Martin PETROV (BUL), Marko TOPIC (BOS), Diego Fernando
KLIMOWICZ (ARG).
Goal: AC Perugia: 1-0 Jay BOTHROYD (38').
Referee: Paulo Manuel GOMES COSTA (POR)   Attendance: 14.473

80

26-08-2003   Arena AufSchalke, Gelsenkirchen: FC Schalke 04 – SV Pasching   0-0
FC Schalke 04: Frank ROST, Aduardo ALCIDES (BRA) (46' Tomasz HAJTO (POL)),
Tomasz WALDOCH (POL), Aníbal Samuel MATELLÁN (ARG), Octavio Darío
RODRÍGUEZ Peña (URU) (YC90), Gerald ASAMOAH (60' Levan KOBIASHVILI (GEO)),
Hamit ALTINTOP (TUR), Gustavo Antonio VARELA (URU) (YC34), Jochen SEITZ (80'
Sven VERMANT (BEL)), Simon CZIOMMER (YC51), Victor AGALI (NGR) (YC66).
SV Pasching: Josef SCHICKLGRUBER, Markus KIESENEBNER, Michael BAUR, Patrick
PIRCHER, Tomasz WISIO (POL) (YC82), Manfred ROTHBAUER, Helmut RIEGLER (89'
Wolfgang BUBENIK), Bozo KOVACEVIC (YC84), Faruk ATALAY (TUR) (61' George
Martin DATORU), Alexander HÖRTNAGL, Edi GLIEDER (YC72) (83' Christian
MAYRLEB).
Referee: Stephen Graham BENNETT (ENG)   Attendance: 56.067

26-08-2003   Volkswagen Arena, Wolfsburg: VfL Wolfsburg – AC Perugia   0-2 (0-1)
VfL Wolfsburg: Simon JENTZSCH, Thomas RYTTER (DEN), Maik FRANZ (YC78), Albert
STREIT (46' Mirko HRGOVIC (BOS) (YC55)), Pablo THIAM (RC42), Stefan SCHNOOR
(YC48), Patrick WEISER, Andres D'ALESSANDRO (ARG), Martin PETROV (BUL), Diego
Fernando KLIMOWICZ (ARG) (YC68,YC90), Marko TOPIC (BOS) (12' Sven MÜLLER,
60' Miroslav KARHAN (SVK)).
AC Perugia: Zeljko KALAC (AUS), Souleymane DIAMOUTENE (MLI), Marco DI
LORETO, Jamel ALIOUI (FRA), "ZÉ MARIA"José Marcelo Ferreira (BRA), Giovanni
TEDESCO, Christian OBODO (YC22), Massimiliano FUSANI, Fabio GROSSO (16'
Konstantinos LOUMPOUTIS (GRE)), Jay BOTHROYD (ENG) (YC33) (64' Emanuele
BERRETTONI), Zisis VRYZAS (GRE) (YC46) (90' Raymundo DO PRADO (BRA)).
Goals: AC Perugia: 0-1 Giovanni TEDESCO (17'), 0-2 Emanuele BERRETTONI (90+').
Referee: Dick J.H.VAN EGMOND (HOL)   Attendance: 12.496

26-08-2003   Estadio El Madrigal, Villarreal: Villarreal CF – SC Heerenveen   0-0
Villarreal CF: José Manuel REINA Páez, Javier "JAVI" Rodríguez VENTA, Enrique
"QUIQUE" ÁLVAREZ Sanjuán, Sergio Martínez BALLESTEROS, Rodolfo Martín
ARRUABARRENA (ARG), Juliano Haus BELLETTI (BRA) (70' Antonio GUAYRE
Betancor Perdomo), Fabricio COLOCCINI (ARG), Pedro MARTÍ Castello, Javier CALLEJA
Revilla, JOSÉ "MARI" María Romero Poyón (YC39) (60' "SONNY" ANDERSON da Silva
(BRA)), VÍCTOR Manuel Fernández Gutiérrez (88' José Joaquín Moreno Verdú "JOSICO").
(Coach: Benito FLORO Sanz).
SC Heerenveen: Hans VONK (RSA) (YC62), Marcel SEIP, Petter HANSSON (SWE), Said
BAKKATI (YC11), Erik EDMAN (SWE), Richard KNOPPER, Paul DE LANGE (88' Mark
Jan FLEDDERUS), Mika VÄYRYNEN (FIN) (88' Ronnie VENEMA), Stefan SELAKOVIC
(SWE) (58' Jos HOOIVELD), Georgios SAMARAS (GRE), Santi KOLK. (Coach: Foppe DE
HAAN).
Referee: Stuart DOUGAL (SCO)   Attendance: 15.000

**FC Schalke 04, AC Perugia and Villarreal CF all qualified for the UEFA Cup
competition.**

2004

FIRST ROUND

19-06-2004   Latham Park, Newtown:
Aberystwyth Town FC – FC Dinaburg Daugavpils   0-0
Aberystwyth Town FC: Dean WILLIAMS (ENG), David Clyne BURROWS (YC6), Andrew
LEE (ENG), Aneurin THOMAS, Gary FINLEY (ENG), Phillip BAKER (68' Glyndwr
HUGHES), Bari David Rees MORGAN (YC4), David BRIDGEWATER (ENG) (85' Gerrard
HENNIGAN (ENG)), Lee SPIKE, Gavin ALLEN (60' Marc LLOYD-WILLIAMS), John
LAWLESS.
FC Dinaburg Daugavpils: Vadim FYODOROV, Andrey ZHUROMSKY, Dmitriy
CHUGUNOV, Vadim LOGINS, Edgar BURLAKOV, Tamaz PERTIYA (GEO), Alexey
KOSTENKO (RUS) (70' Vitali PINIASKINE (RUS)), Andrey MARKOV (RUS) (YC59),
Yuri SOKOLOV (YC18), Pavel KOLCOV (YC90), Vladimir VOLKOV (72'
R.GRYGORCHUK).
Referee: Gylfi Thor ORRASON (ISL)   Attendance: 746

19-06-2004   Esbjerg Atletikstadion, Esbjerg: Esbjerg FB – NSÍ Runavík   3-1 (3-1)
Esbjerg FB: Lars WINDE, Martin JENSEN, Nikolai Jacobsen HØGH, Kjetil PEDERSEN
(NOR), Frank HANSEN, Jan KRISTIANSEN (46' Tommy LØVENKRANDS), Jakob
POULSEN, Jerry Ruben LUCENA, Søren BARSLUND (77' Henrik HANSEN), Fredrik
BERGLUND (SWE) (46' Morten FRIIS JENSEN), Jess Christian THORUP.
NSÍ Runavík: Jens Martin KNUDSEN, Brynjolvur NIELSEN, Dánjal HANSEN, Óli
HANSEN, Sjúrdur JACOBSEN (63' Andy OLSEN), Aleksandar JOVOVIC (SBM) (YC17)
(46' Kári HANSEN), Ian HØJGAARD (YC64), Jústinus R.HANSEN, Helgi L.PETERSEN
(YC50), Gert LANGGAARD (81' Eddie MIKKELSEN), Jónstein PETERSEN.
Goals: Esbjerg FB: 1-0 Jerry Ruben LUCENA (4'), 2-1 Søren BARSLUND (36'), 3-1 Jess
Christian THORUP (38').
NSÍ Runavík: 1-1 Ian HØJGAARD (30').
Referee: Adrian D.CASHA (MLT)   Attendance: 400

19-06-2004   Hibernians Stadium, Paola:
Hibernians FC Malta – NK Slaven Belupo Koprivnica   2-1 (1-1)
Hibernians FC Malta: Mario MUSCAT, Peter PULLICINO, Adrian PULIS, Aaron XUEREB,
Ryan MINTOFF, Andre SCHEMBRI (81' Kevin CASSAR), Essien MBONG (NGR), Adrian
MIFSUD, Antoine ZAHRA (45' Andrew COHEN), Terence SCERRI, Roderick
BALDACCHINO (58' Jonathan CARUANA).
NK Slaven Belupo Koprivnica: Robert LISJAK, Dalibor VISKOVIC, Igor GAL, Dalibor
BOZAC, Ognjen VUKOJEVIC (70' Ivica SERTIC), Srebrenko POSAVEC, Marko SURIC
(61' Dario BRGLES), Bojan VRUCINA, Pero PEJIC, Alen GUC, Mario MIJATOVIC (YC55)
(77' Nikica SRPAK).
Goals: Hibernians FC Malta: 1-0 Terence SCERRI (13'), 2-1 Andre SCHEMBRI (63').
NK Slaven Belupo Koprivnica: 1-1 Srebrenko POSAVEC (42' penalty).
Referee: Gabriele ROSSI (SMR)   Attendance: 500

19-06-2004　　Dasáki, Áchnas: Ethnikós Áchnas FC – FK Vardar Skopje 1-5 (0-0)
Ethnikós Áchnas FC: Andreas LAMPROU, Loizos KAKOYIANNIS, Dimitris SIMOU, Christofis PASHIALIS, Andreas KATZIS (YC66) (75' Elipidoforos ILIA), Nicos SOFOCLEOUS, Kyriakos APOSTOLOU, Christos POYIATZIS, Petros HATZIAROS, Kyriakos CHATZIAROS (75' Constantinos CONSTANTINOU), Georgios KOUNNOUSHI (70' Andreas KONTOU).
FK Vardar Skopje: Velimir ZDRAVKOVIC (SBM), Nikola DOSEVSKI, Aleksandar VASOSKI, Blessing Chinedu ANYANVIU (NGR), Bojan MARKOSKI, Vlatko GROZDANOVSKI (73' Danio MASEV), Jovica TRAJCEV (81' Dragan NACEVSKI), Zarko SERAFIMOVSKI, Darko TASEVSKI (73' Almir BAJRAMOVSKI), ROGÉRIO da Costa Oliveira (BRA), Oliveira WANDEIR Dos Santos (BRA).
Goals: Ethnikós Áchnas FC: 1-1 Kyriakos APOSTOLOU (56').
FK Vardar Skopje: 0-1 Oliveira WANDEIR Dos Santos (47'), 1-2 Andreas KATZIS (57' *own goal*), 1-3 Oliveira WANDEIR Dos Santos (71'), 1-4 Dragan NACEVSKI (89'), 1-5 Zarko SERAFIMOVSKI (90').
Referee: Richard HAVRILLA (SVK)

19-06-2004　　Turners Cross, Cork: Cork City FC – Malmö FF 3-1 (2-0)
Cork City FC: Michael DEVINE, Cillian LORDAN, Alan BENNETT (YC20), Daniel MURRAY, Danny MURPHY, Liam KEARNEY (YC90), Colin O'BRIEN, George O'CALLAGHAN, Kevin DOYLE, John O'FLYNN (YC11), Neale FENN (88' Brendan SWEENEY).
Malmö FF: Joel RINGSTRÖM, Olof PERSSON, Daniel MAJSTOROVIC, Thomas OLSSON, Hasse MATTISSON, Joseph ELANGA (CMR), Afonso ALVES Martins (BRA), Glenn HOLGERSSON, Tobias GRAHN (71' Louay CHANKO), Niklas SKOOG, Behrang SAFARI (64' Darko LUKANOVIC).
Goals: Cork City FC: 1-0 John O'FLYNN (10'), 2-0 Daniel MURRAY (35'), 3-0 Daniel MURRAY (61').
Malmö FF: 3-1 Darko LUKANOVIC (85').
Referee: Marijo STRAHONJA (CRO)　　　　Attendance: 5.500

19-06-2004　　Stadión Antona Malatinského, Trnava:
　　　　　　　　FC Spartak Trnava – Debreceni VSC 3-0 (1-0)
FC Spartak Trnava: Marek CECH, Souleymane FALL (SEN), Martin POLJOVKA, Roman KONECNY, Dusan BESTVINA, Marián MOLNÁR (57' Marcel GASPARIK), Andrej FILIP (35' Peter HODUR), Michal GASPARIK (YC29), Pavol STANO, Martin HUSÁR, Miroslav KRISS (71' Pavol MASARYK).
Debreceni VSC: Sandro TOMIC (CRO), Zsolt BALOG, László ÉGER (YC66), Gábor VINCZE (YC63), Balász NIKOLOV (YC54), Csaba BERNÁTH, Tamás SÁNDOR, Ronald HABI (SBM), Zoltán KISS, Igor BOGDANOVIC (SBM), Péter ANDORKA (59' Zoltán CSEHI).
Goals: FC Spartak Trnava: 1-0 Marián MOLNÁR (11'), 2-0 Miroslav KRISS (48'), 3-0 Pavol MASARYK (90'+3').
Referee: Raivo LATTIK (EST)　　　　Attendance: 1.178

19-06-2004   Stadion Városi, Sopron: Matáv FC Sopron – FK Teplice 1-0 (0-0)
Matáv FC Sopron: Árpád MILINTE, Lajos HORVÁTH, Andreás HORVÁTH, István SIRA
(YC60), Mladen LAMBULIC (SBM), Bojan LAZIC (SBM), Gábor BAGOLY (YC70), Viktor
HANÁK, Tamás SIFTER (83' Adrián VARGA), Iván BALASKÓ, Zoltán FEHÉR
(YC..,YC36).
FK Teplice: Tomás POSTULKA, Michal DOLEZAL, Karel RADA (RC77), Tomás HUNAL
(YC22), Jiri SKÁLA, Pavel VERBÍR (89' Martin KLEIN), Pavel KRMAS, Pavel HORVÁTH
(YC10), Dusan TESARIK (YC..,YC74), Jakub MASEK (73' Pavel VELEBA), Jiri
KOWALÍK (YC36) (58' Petr BENÁT).
Goal: Matáv FC Sopron: 1-0 Iván BALASKÓ (64' penalty).
Referee: Sokol JARECI (ALB)   Attendance: 850

19-06-2004   Sportni Park, Celje: NK Publikum Celje – FK Sloboda Tuzla 2-1 (1-0)
NK Publikum Celje: Aleksander SELIGA, Matej SNOFL, Dejan KELHAR, Marijan
BUDIMIR (CRO) (29' Dare VRSIC (YC32)), Primoz BRUMEN, Sebastjan GOBEC, Simon
SESLAR, Vladislav LUNGU (MOL), Dejan PLASTOVSKI (YC89), Zoran BALDOVALIEV
(MCD) (YC27) (81' Gregor HELBL), Andrej KVAS.
FK Sloboda Tuzla: Mirsad DEDIC, Stanisa NIKOLIC, Mario LAMESIC, Gradimir
CRNOGORAC (YC76), Samir KUDUZOVIC (YC50), Nedzad BAJROVIC, Adnan
SARAJLIC, Zoran NOVAKOVIC (62' Emir BORIC), Tarik OKANOVIC (88' Armin
DELIC), Darko VOJVODIC (90' Amir REKIC), Senad HADZIC (YC23).
Goals: NK Publikum Celje: 1-0 Zoran BALDOVALIEV (41'), 2-0 Dare VRSIC (57').
FK Sloboda Tuzla: 2-1 Darko VOJVODIV (58').
Referee: Valery VIALICHKA (BLS)

20-06-2004   Atletkstadion, Odense: Odense BK – Ballymena United FC 0-0
Odense BK: Arek ONYSZKO (POL), Steen NEDERGAARD, Fernando DERVELD (HOL),
Jan SØNKSEN, Jacob GREGERSEN, Thomas LINDRUP (46' Kenneth Møller PEDERSEN),
Andrew TEMBO (ZAM) (71' Carsten HEMMINGSEN), Esben HANSEN, Martin BORRE,
Mwape MITI (ZAM) (46' Steffen HØJER), Søren BERG ANDERSEN.
Ballymena United FC: Robert ROBINSON, Ciaran DONAGHY, Albert WATSON, Gareth
SCATES, Gary SMYTH, Gordon SIMMS, Oran KEARNEY, Ruari McCLEAN, Shea Paul
CAMPBELL (75' Eddie HILL), John O'LOUGHLIN, Justin McBRIDE (75' Gareth
McLAUGHLIN).
Referee: José Luis MENGUAL PRADES (AND)   Attendance: 1.197

20-06-2004   Jules Ottenstadion, Gentbrugge: KAA Gent – IF Fylkir 2-1 (0-0)
KAA Gent: Frédéric HERPOEL, Bart GOOSSENS, Jacky PEETERS, David VAN
HOYWEGHEN (YC31), Mustapha OUSSALAH (MAR), Matthieu VERSCHUERE (FRA),
Madjid ADJAOUD (ALG) (YC49), Steven RIBUS, Ivica JARAKOVIC (SBM) (62' Jonathan
CONSTANCIA (ANT)), Sandy MARTENS, Jurgen CAVENS.
IF Fylkir: Bjarni Th.HALLDÓRSSON (YC64), Gudni Rúnar HELGASON, Valur Fannar
GÍSLASON, Ólafur STÍGSSON, Helgi Valur DANÍELSSON, Finnur KOLBEINSSON (86'
Jón B.HERMANNSSON), Gunnar Thór PÉTURSSON (YC38), Thórhallur Dan
JÓHANNSSON, Sævar Thór GÍSLASON (76' Kjartan Ágúst BREIDDAL), Eyjólfur
HÉDINSSON, Kristján VALDIMARSSON (62' Björgólfur Hidiaki TAKEFUSA).
Goals: KAA Gent: 1-0 Steven RIBUS (66' penalty), 2-1 Steven RIBUS (90').
IF Fylkir: 1-1 Finnur KOLBEINSSON (75' penalty).
Referee: Andriy SHANDOR (UKR)   Attendance: 2.012

84

20-06-2004   Estadi Comunal d'Andorra la Vella, Andorra la Vella:
                    UE Sant Juliá – FK Sartid Smederevo   0-8 (0-2)
UE Sant Juliá: Ignacio Javier SAIZ GONZALEZ (ESP), Josep MARTINEZ (ESP), Alex
RODRIGUEZ, ROBERTO JONÁS, Cristian ROIG MAURI, Gerard RODRIGUEZ (ESP),
Alejandro GODOY VENTURI, Flavio NEVES PIMENTEL (POR) (58' Jorge Filipe DA
SILVA (POR) (YC64)), Laureano MIRAGLIA (ITA) (78' Richard IMBERNON Rios),
Armand GODOY (77' Nicolas NUEVO MARTINEZ), Mario NEVES PIMENTEL.
FK Sartid Smederevo: Dragan ZILIC, Ivan ZIVANOVIC (61' Demir RAMOVIC), Zeljko
KOVACEVIC (YC63) (65' Miroslav GEGIC), Marko SOCANAC, Nebojsa SAVIC, Sasa
ZORIC, Dejan KEKEZOVIC, Sasa KOCIC, Milorad ZECEVIC, Dragan RADOSAVLJEVIC
(61' Nikola JEVTIC), Nenad MIROSAVLJEVIC.
Goals: FK Sartid Smederevo: 0-1 Nenad MIROSAVLJEVIC (18' penalty), 0-2 Milorad
ZECEVIC (43'), 0-3 Dragan RADOSAVLJEVIC (53'), 0-4 Cristian ROIG MAURI (57' *own
goal*), 0-5 Milorad ZECEVIC (60'), 0-6 Nenad MIROSAVLJEVIC (67'), 0-7 Nenad
MIROSAVLJEVIC (71'), 0-8 Nikola JEVTIC (74').
Referee: Lawrence SAMMUT (MLT)   Attendance: 800

20-06-2004   Casino-Stadion, Bregenz:
                    SW Bregenz – FK Khazar Universiteti Baku   4-0 (4-0)
SW Bregenz: Almir TOLJA (BOS), Patrick PIRCHER, Asmir IKANOVIC (BOS), Mirko
DICKHAUT (GER) (YC35), Denis DASOUL (BEL), Thomas HÖLLER, Jan-Ove
PEDERSEN (NOR), Günther SCHEPENS (BEL), Tomas PEKALA (46' Ulrich WINKLER),
Vladimir VUK (CRO) (YC62) (65' Markus KRAUTBERGER), Olivier NZUZI Niati Polo
(CGO).
FK Khazar Universiteti Baku: Temuri CHLAIDZE (46' Ilkin BAGIYEV), Zavr HASHIMOV,
Goderdzi GOGOLADZE (GEO) (YC49), Vasif HAGVERDIYEV, Elbrus Kh.MAMEDOV
(71' Einur MAMMADOV), Rashad ABDULAEV (YC37), Elmar BAKHSHIEV (YC34),
Elshan MAMMADOV (YC12), David CHIGOSHVILI, Samir KHAIROV (YC44), David
DATVADZE (GEO) (25' Ramil SAYADOV (YC41)).
Goals: SW Bregenz: 1-0 Asmir IKANOVIC (13'), 2-0 Asmir IKANOVIC (23'), 3-0 Patrick
PIRCHER (33'), 4-0 Günther SCHEPENS (44' penalty).
Referee: Novo PANIC (BOS)
*The result was changed by UEFA to a 3-0 win for FK Khazar Universiteti Baku after it was
discovered that SW Bregenz had fielded an unregistered and ineligible U-17 player.*

20-06-2004   Stade Josy Barthel, Luxembourg:
                    CS Grevenmacher – Tampere United FC   1-1 (1-0)
CS Grevenmacher: Jonathan JOUBERT (FRA), Alexander ZIEHL (GER), Stephan KORDIAN
(GER), Markus KOSTER (GER), Manuel MOROCUTTI (64' Steve BIRTZ), Daniel HUSS,
Luc THIMMESCH (57' Ahmed ZERROUKI (FRA)), Márcio RODRIGUES da Cruz (BRA),
Karim GROUNE (FRA), Jérôme HENROT (FRA) (70' Alain THIMMESCH), Volker
SCHMITT (GER) (YC86).
Tampere United FC: Mikko KAVEN, Pasi SALMELA (YC68), Antti OJANPERÄ, Jussi
KUOPPALA, Antti POHJA, Sakari SAARINEN, Jarkko WISS, Petri HEINÄNEN (72' Antti
HYNYNEN), Kari SAINIO, Heikko AHO (61' Toni JUNNILA), Janne RÄSÄNEN.
Goals: CS Grevenmacher: 1-0 Volker SCHMITT (37').
Tampere United FC: 1-1 Jarkko WISS (65').
Referee: Pavel SALIY (KAZ)

20-06-2004   Luzhniki Stadium, Moskva:
FC Spartak Moskva – FK Atlantas Klaipeda   2-0 (2-0)
FC Spartak Moskva: Wojciech KOWALEWSKI (POL), Roman SHISHKIN, Dusan
PETKOVIC (SBM), Adrian IENCSI (ROM), Yuriy KOVTUN (YC63), Alexandr SAMEDOV
(AZE), Goran TROBOK (SBM), Vladimir LESHONOK (86' Ales URBÁNEK (CZE)), Florin
SOAVA (ROM) (67' Oleg IVANOV), Pavel POGREBNYAK (YC72), Tarmo KINK (EST)
(80' Maxim KALYNYCHENKO (UKR)).
FK Atlantas Klaipeda: Liudvikas VALIUS, Kestutis DEVEIKA (59' Mindaugas ZIGUTIS),
Dainius KUNEVICIUS, Vidas ALUNDERIS, Kestutis IVASKEVICIUS (83' Mantas
SERNIUS), Egidijus ZUKAUSKAS, Andrius PETREIKIS, Donatas NAVIKAS, Dainius
ZERNYS (YC47) (69' Andrius BARTKUS), Martynas KARALIUS, Andrius PUOTKALIS.
Goals: FC Spartak Moskva: 1-0 Pavel POGREBNYAK (6' penalty), 2-0 Valdimir
LESHONOK (34').
Referee: Michael SVENDSEN (DEN)   Attendance: 2.000

20-06-2004   Niko Dovana Stadium, Durrës: KS Teuta Durrës – FK ZTS Dubnica   0-0
KS Teuta Durrës: Alfred OSMANI, Ervin KOTOMELO (84' Arlind LOJA), Arjan ZERE,
Johan DRIZA, T.OSMANI, Admir TOSHKOLLARI (YC6), Orgert KOTJA, Dritan
BABAMUSTA, Dritan CUKO (37' Edlir TETOVA), Edar BERZEZI (70' Arjan VOJO),
Daniel XHAFAJ.
FK ZTS Dubnica: Marian POSTRK, Dalibor PLEVA, Marian ZIMEN, Pavol KOPACKA,
Martin SVESTKA (CZE) (YC13), Juraj DOVICOVIC, Igor DRZIK, Martin DOKTOR (71'
Ján SVIKRUHA), Matej IZVOLT (84' Marian BELÁK), Andrej PORÁZIK, Adam NEMEC
(YC19) (71' Peter KISKA).
Referee: Christoforos ZOGRAFOS (GRE)   Attendance: 2.000

20-06-2004   Stadion Lachen, Thun: FC Thun – FC Gloria Bistrita   2-0 (0-0)
FC Thun: Fabio COLTORTI, Nelson FERREIRA (POR), Selver HODZIC, Armand DEUMI
TCHAMI (CMR), Pascal CERRONE, Andreas GERBER (46' BAYKAL Kulaksizoglu
(TUR)), Michael RENGGLI, Silvan AEGERTER, Mario RAIMONDI, Mauro LUSTRINELLI
(85' Adrian MOSER), Antonio DOS SANTOS (BRA) (72' Patrick BAUMANN).
FC Gloria Bistrita: Eugen Catalin ANGHEL, Marius MARGARIT (81' Danut SABOU), Alin
Valer RUS, Sergiu Ioan Viorel COSTIN, Sorin Adrian IODI (YC31), Cornel Flaviu CORNEA
(76' Alin Nicu CHIBULCUTEAN), Dorian Constantin ARBANAS, Dinu Daniel
SANMARTEAN, Cristian Nicolae VLAD (57' Miroslav Matea GIUCHICI), Sandu
NEGREAN, Marius DRULE.
Goals: FC Thun: 1-0 Mauro LUSTRINELLI (63'), 2-0 Mario RAIMONDI (65').
Referee: Bruno Miguel DUARTE PAIXAO (POR)   Attendance: 1.050

20-06-2004   Loro Boriçi Stadium, Shkodër:
KS Vllaznia Shkodër – Hapoel Beer Sheva FC   1-2 (1-0)
KS Vllaznia Shkodër: Orges SHEHI, Luan ZMIJANI, Edmond DOCI (YC25) (46' Marin Glen
KAPAJ (YC86)), Admir TELI, Safet OSJA (69' Erjon HOTI), Armando CUNGU, Julian
BRAHJA, January ZYAMBO, ABILIO Neves Dos Reis (BRA) (YC20), Albert KAÇI (60'
Amarildo BELISHA), Hamdi SALIHI.
Hapoel Beer Sheva FC: Mordichay SCHWARTZ, Eyal ABED, Sharon LEVI (64' Oren
SAGRON), Enon BARDA (82' Itzik PERETZ), Kobi VAKNIN (YC65), Amir ABUTBUL,
Rotem MISHALI (10' Yoni TAPIERO), Zohar HOGEG, Tomer TADESA, Eliezer LAVI,
Eviatar ILLOUZ.
Goals: KS Vllaznia Shkodër: 1-0 Hamdi SALIHI (2').
Hapoel Beer Sheva FC: 1-1 Kobi VAKNIN (65'), 1-2 Oren SAGRON (90').
Referee: Drago KOS (SLO)

20-06-2004   Stadion MOSiR, Wodzislaw Slaski:
MKS Odra Wodzislaw Slaski – FC Dinamo Minsk   1-0 (1-0)
MKS Odra Wodzislaw Slaski: Marcin BEBEN, Piotr SZYMICZEK (49' Krzysztof BIZACKI),
Roman MADEJ (YC11), Blazej JANKOWSKI (YC64), Wojciech MYSZOR, Jan WOS (76'
Mieczyslaw SIKORA), Wojciech GRZYB, Aleksander KWIEK (YC83), Slawomir SZARY,
Marcin RADZIEWICZ, Marek KUBISZ (87' Marek SOKOLOWSKI).
FC Dinamo Minsk: Yuri TSYGALKO, Dmitri LENTSEVICH, Sergey PAVLYUKOVICH,
Jan TIGOREV, Kirill PAVLYUCHEK (YC29) (46' David ZOUBEK (CZE)), Igor
ROZHKOV (YC85), Andrey RAZIN, Yuri SHUKANOV, Vitali VOLODENKOV (66' Dmitri
CHALEI), Leonid KOVEL, Maksim TSYGALKO (YC5) (69' Vitali LEDZIANIOU).
Goal: MKS Odra Wodzislaw Slaski: 1-0 Marek KUBISZ (37').
Referee: Per Ivar STABERG (NOR)   Attendance: 600

20-06-2004   Zalgirio stadionas, Vilnius:
FK Vetra Rudiskes Vilnius – JK Trans Narva   3-0 (2-0)
FK Vetra Rudiskes Vilnius: Marius POSKUS, Zydrunas GRUDZINSKAS, Nerijus
SASNAUSKAS, Julius RALIUKONIS, Zilvinas ZUDYS, Clement BEAUD (CMR), Gintaras
RIMKUS, Darvydas SERNAS (85' Gediminas BUTRIMAVICIUS), Ramunas STONKUS
(62' Rolandas VAINEIKIS), Nerijus VASILIAUSKAS, Vytautas KARVELIS (76' Awenayeri
DOUGLAS (NGR)).
JK Trans Narva: Vitas MALISHAUSKAS, Andrej PRUSS, Ilya DJORD (RUS), Aleksej
JAGUDIN (RUS), Sergey KAZAKOV, Alexandr TARASSENKOV, Dmitri LIPARTOV
(RUS) (68' Dmitri POTSETSUJEV), Maksim GRUZNOV, Stanislav KITTO (YC63) (83'
Mikhail MASLENIKOV), Oleg KUROCHKIN, Dmitri SHELEHHOV (46' Aleksandr
ZAHHARENKOV).
Goals: FK Vetra Rudiskes Vilnius: 1-0 Nerijus VASILIAUSKAS (13'), 2-0 Vytautas
KARVELIS (17'), 3-0 Nerijus VASILIAUSKAS (75').
Referee: David McKEON (IRL)   Attendance: 550

20-06-2004   Bonchuk Stadium, Dupnitsa: FC Marek Dupnitsa – FC Dila Gori   0-0
FC Marek Dupnitsa: Nikolay CHAVDAROV, Dimitar KOEMDZHIEV (65' Kaloyan ILIEV),
Ianek KIUTCHUKOV, Georgi KARAKANOV, Ventsislav BONEV, Veselin VELIKOV
(YC82), Ilia ILIEV (RC83), Emil PETKOV (46' Toni PITOSHKA (MCD)), Ivo PARGOV,
Vassil KIROV (YC84), Saso LAZAREVSKI (MCD) (61' Kroum BIBISHKOV).
FC Dila Gori: Ramaz SOGOLASHVILI, Georgi BELASHVILI, Giorgi LOMIDZE, Zaza
LATSABIDZE, Akvsenti GILAURI, Roin ONIANI, Kristepore SHATAKISHVILI (90'
Guram SAMADASHVILI), Zurab MUSHKUDIANI (61' Beka CHITAIA), Georgi
MASURASHVILI (74' Albert SAKVARELIDZE), Luka RAZMADZE, Levan
GOCHASHVILI.
Referee: Janos MEGYEBIRO (HUN)

20-06-2004   Anjalankosken Jalkapallostadion, Anjalankoski:
Myllykosken Pallo-47 – FK Tescoma Zlín   1-1 (0-0)
Myllykosken Pallo-47: Janne KORHONEN, Tero KARHU, Sampsa TIMOSKA, Tuomo
KÖNÖNEN (73' Tero TAIPALE), Tuomas KUPARINEN, Niki HELENIUS, Saku
PUHAKAINEN, Tuomas HAAPALA (64' Niklas TARVAJÄRVI), Toni HUTTUNEN,
Tuomas AHO, Tuomas KANSIKAS.
FK Tescoma Zlín: Vít BARÁNEK (YC89), Vlastimil VIDLICKA, Zdenik KROCA, Jiri
KOUBSKÝ, David HUBÁCEK, Bronislav CERVENKA, Vít VRTILKA, Roman DOBES,
Tomás DUJKA (76' Petr NOVOSAD), Edvard LASOTA, Fábio Luis GOMES (BRA) (86'
Marcel LICKA).
Goals: Myllykosken Pallo-47: 1-1 Saku PUHAKAINEN (79').
FK Tescoma Zlín: 0-1 Fábio Luis GOMES (65').
Referee: Siarhei SHMOLIK (BLS)   Attendance: 1.500

26-06-2004   Laugardalsvöllur, Reykjavik: IF Fylkir – KAA Gent   0-1 (0-1)
IF Fylkir: Bjarni Th.HALLDÓRSSON, Thórhallur Dan JÓHANNSSON, Valur Fannar
GÍSLASON, Ólafur STÍGSSON, Helgi Valur DANÍELSSON, Ólafur Páll SNORRASON,
Ragnar SIGURDSSON (46' Eyjólfur HÉDINSSON), Kristján VALDIMARSSON, Jón
B.HERMANNSSON (55' Albert B.INGASON), Thorbjörn Atli SVEINSSON (65' Kristinn
TÓMASSON), Thorlákur Árnason JOHANNSSON (YC58).
KAA Gent: Frédéric HERPOEL, Jacky PEETERS, David VAN HOYWEGHEN, Hamad
NDIKUMANA (RWA), Matthieu VERSCHUERE (FRA), Steven RIBUS, Madjid ADJAOUD
(ALG), Bart GOOSSENS (YC33), Mustapha OUSSALAH (MAR) (79' Jonathan
CONSTANCIA (ANT)), Sandy MARTENS, Jurgen CAVENS (90' Ivica JARAKOVIC
(SBM)).
Goal: KAA Gent: 0-1 Sandy MARTENS (26').
Referee: Emil LAURSEN (DEN)   Attendance: 500

26-06-2004   Ballymena Showgrounds, Ballymena:
Ballymena United FC – Odense BK   0-7 (0-2)
Ballymena United FC: Robert ROBINSON, John O'LOUGHLIN (60' Joseph GRAY), Ciaran
DONAGHY, Gordon SIMMS (61' Nigel BOYD), Albert WATSON, Gary SMYTH, Gareth
SCATES, Oran KEARNEY, Shea Paul CAMPBELL (YC85), Ruari McCLEAN (80' Jonathan
MONTGOMERY), Gareth McLAUGHLIN.
Odense BK: Arek ONYSZKO (POL), Steen NEDERGAARD, Fernando DERVELD (HOL)
(68' Chris SØRENSEN), Jan SØNKSEN, Jacob GREGERSEN (46' Ulrich VINZENTS),
Andrew TEMBO (ZAM), Esben HANSEN, Martin BORRE, Mwape MITI (ZAM), Søren
BERG ANDERSEN (68' Kenneth Møller PEDERSEN), Steffen HØJER.
Goals: Odense BK: 0-1 Mwape MITI (25'), 0-2 Steffen HØJER (33'), 0-3 Steffen HØJER
(58'), 0-4 Mwape MITI (62'), 0-5 Kenneth Møller PEDERSEN (80'), 0-6 Martin BORRE
(82'), 0-7 Mwape MITI (88').
Referee: Egill Mar MARKUSSON (ISL)   Attendance: 2.107

26-06-2004   Svangaskard, Toftír: NSÍ Runavík – Esbjerg FB   0-4 (0-2)
NSÍ Runavík: Jens Martin KNUDSEN, Brynjolvur NIELSEN, Óli HANSEN (YC56), Dánjal
HANSEN, Sjúrdur JACOBSEN (71' Áki L.HANSEN), Gert LANGGAARD (68' Jústinus
R.HANSEN), Ian HØJGAARD (YC14), Kári HANSEN, Helgi L.PETERSEN (71' Andy
OLSEN), Súni Fridi BARBÁ, Jónstein PETERSEN.
Esbjerg FB: Lars WINDE, Jerry Ruben LUCENA, Kjetil PEDERSEN (NOR) (YC31), Anders
EGHOLM, Martin JENSEN (66' Tommy LØVENKRANDS), Søren BARSLUND (68' Lasse
KRYGGER JØRGENSEN), Hans Henrik ANDREASEN, Jakob POULSEN, Jan
KRISTIANSEN, Fredrik BERGLUND (SWE) (83' Jesper JØRGENSEN), Jess Christian
THORUP.
Goals: Esbjerg FB: 0-1 Jan KRISTIANSEN (26'), 0-2 Anders EGHOLM (28'), 0-3 Jakob
POULSEN (69'), 0-4 Jan KRISTIANSEN (73').
Referee: Mark COURTNEY (NIR)

26-06-2004   Stadion Sartid, Smederevo: FK Sartid Smederevo – UE Sant Juliá   3-0 (3-0)
FK Sartid Smederevo: Dejan RANKOVIC, Ivan ZIVANOVIC, Zeljko KOVACEVIC, Marko
SOCANAC, Nebojsa SAVIC, Sasa ZORIC, Dejan KEKEZOVIC (67' Miroslav GEGIC), Sasa
KOCIC, Milorad ZECEVIC (56' Nikola JEVTIC), Dragan RADOSAVLJEVIC (49' Demir
RAMOVIC), Nenad MIROSAVLJEVIC.
UE Sant Juliá: Ignacio Javier SAIZ GONZALEZ (ESP) (82' Guillermo BURGOS (CHI)),
ROBERTO JONÁS, Cristian ROIG MAURI, Alejandro GODOY VENTURI, Flavio NEVES
PIMENTEL (POR), Laureano MIRAGLIA (ITA), Jorge Filipe DA SILVA (POR) (76' Sergio
ROCA MORAGA (CHI)), Mario NEVES PIMENTEL (POR) (YC47), Christian XINOS
(GRE) (85' Sergi GIRIBET), Luis Maria VERIZ (ARG), Luciano NASTRI (ITA).
Goals: FK Sartid Smederevo: 1-0 Milorad ZECEVIC (5'), 2-0 Nenad MIROSAVLJEVIC
(27'), 3-0 Milorad ZECEVIC (42').
Referee: Brian LAWLOR (WAL)   Attendance: 2.000

26-06-2004   Gradski Stadion, Koprivnica:
              NK Slaven Belupo Koprivnica – Hibernians FC Malta   3-0 (1-0)
NK Slaven Belupo Koprivnica: Robert LISJAK, Petar BOSNJAK, Pavo CRNAC, Igor GAL,
Dalibor VISKOVIC (YC32), Domagoj KOSIC (59' Ivica SERTIC), Roy FERENCINA
(YC24), Ognjen VUKOJEVIC (YC45) (52' Danijel RADICEK), Alen GUC (71' Mario
MIJATOVIC), Pero PEJIC, Bojan VRUCINA (YC16).
Hibernians FC Malta: Mario MUSCAT, Adrian PULIS, Ryan MINTOFF, Aaron XUEREB
(YC81), Antoine ZAHRA, Peter PULLICINO, Essien MBONG (NGR) (90' Kenneth
SPITERI), Andre SCHEMBRI, Roderick BALDACCHINO, Terence SCERRI, Adrian
MIFSUD (83' Kevin CASSAR).
Goals: NK Slaven Belupo Koprivnica: 1-0 Bojan VRUCINA (15'), 2-0 Dalibor VISKOVIC
(82' penalty), 3-0 Mario MIJATOVIC (88').
Referee: Delce JAKIMOVSKI (MCD)   Attendance: 800

26-06-2004   A. Le Coq Arena, Tallinn:
JK Trans Narva – FK Vetra Rudiskes Vilnius   0-1 (0-0)
JK Trans Narva: Vitas MALISHAUSKAS, Ilya DJORD (RUS) (63' Andrej PRUSS), Aleksej
JAGUDIN (RUS), Sergei KAZAKOV (68' Sergei LEONTOVICH (RUS) (YC87)), Alexandr
TARASSENKOV (38' Dmitri SHELEHHOV), Dmitri LIPARTOV (RUS), Maksim
GRUZNOV, Stanislav KITTO, Mikhail MASLENIKOV, Oleg KUROCHKIN, Aleksandr
ZAHHARENKOV.
FK Vetra Rudiskes Vilnius: Marius POSKUS, Zydrunas GRUDZINSKAS, Julius
RALIUKONIS, Zilvinas ZUDYS, Gintaras RIMKUS, Darvydas SERNAS, Gediminas
BUTRIMAVICIUS (75' Gediminas KONTAUTAS), Ramunas STONKUS, Rolandas
VAINEIKIS (81' Saulius KIJANSKAS), Nerijus VASILIAUSKAS, Vytautas KARVELIS
(YC42) (61' Sarunas LITVINAS).
Goal: FK Vetra Rudiskes Vilnius: 0-1 Sarunas LITVINAS (87').
Referee: Brage SANDMOEN (NOR)   Attendance: 130

26-06-2004   Gradski Stadion, Skopje: FK Vardar Skopje – Ethnikós Áchnas FC   5-1 (4-1)
FK Vardar Skopje: Velimir ZDRAVKOVIC (SBM), Nikola DOSEVSKI, Aleksandar
VASOSKI, Blessing Chinedu ANYANVIU (NGR) (59' Zlatko TANEVSKI (YC62)), Bojan
MARKOSKI, Vlatko GROZDANOVSKI, Jovica TRAJCEV, Zarko SERAFIMOVSKI
(YC23) (65' Nikola GLIGOROV), Darko TASEVSKI (59' Danio MASEV), ROGÉRIO da
Costa Oliveira (BRA), Oliveira WANDEIR Dos Santos (BRA).
Ethnikós Áchnas FC: Andreas LAMPROU, Loizos KAKOYIANNIS, Dimitris SIMOU,
Christofis PASHIALIS, Andreas KATZIS, Nicos SOFOCLEOUS, Kyriakos APOSTOLOU,
Christos POYIATZIS (46' Elipidoforos ILIA), Petros HATZIAROS (78' Emil SIMOV),
Kyriakos CHATZIAROS (69' Giovanis SHEPIS), Georgios KOUNNOUSHI.
Goals: FK Vardar Skopje: 1-0 Oliveira WANDEIR Dos Santos (3' penalty), 2-0 Nikola
DOSEVSKI (16'), 3-0 Oliveira WANDEIR Dos Santos (21'), 4-1 Oliveira WANDEIR Dos
Santos (30'), 5-1 Oliveira WANDEIR Dos Santos (66').
Ethnikós Áchnas FC: 3-1 Georgios KOUNNOUSHI (25').
Referee: Augustus Viorel CONSTANTIN (ROM)

26-06-2004   Municipal Stadium, Rishon LeZion:
Hapoel Beer Sheva FC – KS Vllaznia Shkodër   0-1 (0-1)
Hapoel Beer Sheva FC: Mordichay SCHWARTZ, Oz David YIFRAH (YC26), Eyal ABED,
Zohar HOGEG, Sharon LEVI (YC37) (56' Oren SAGRON), Kobi VAKNIN, Eliezer LAVI,
Enon BARDA (80' Tomer TADESA), Rotem MISHALI, Eviatar ILLOUZ (YC88), Amir
ABUTBUL.
KS Vllaznia Shkodër: Orges SHEHI, Luan ZMIJANI, Marin Glen KAPAJ, Admir TELI, Safet
OSJA, Armando CUNGU (71' Erjon HOTI (YC90)), Amarildo BELISHA, January ZYAMBO
(80' Edmond DOCI), ABILIO Neves Dos Reis (BRA), Albert KAÇI (YC21) (88' Franc AHI),
Hamdi SALIHI.
Goal: KS Vllaznia Shkodër: 0-1 Hamdi SALIHI (40').
Referee: Costas THEODOTOU (CYP)

*After it was discovered that Hapoel Beer Sheva FC had fielded an ineligible player (Tomer
Haliba), UEFA awarded the game to KS Vllaznia Shkodër with a 3-0 scoreline.*

26-06-2004   Shafa Stadium, Baku: FK Khazar Universiteti Baku – SW Bregenz   2-1 (1-0)
FK Khazar Universiteti Baku: Ilkin BAGIYEV (YC54), Zavr HASHIMOV, Goderdzi
GOGOLADZE (GEO), Elbrus Kh.MAMEDOV (YC87), Rashad ABDULAEV, Elmar
BAKHSHIEV, Elshan MAMMADOV (58' Ramil SAYADOV), David CHIGOSHVILI, Samir
KHAIROV, Zahir ASGAROV (YC13) (72' Orkhan RAJABOV), Robert ZIRAKISHVILI
(GEO) (77' Archil SOKHADZE (YC90)).
SW Bregenz: Almir TOLJA (BOS), Denis DASOUL (BEL) (RC61), Patrick PIRCHER,
Markus KRAUTBERGER, Thomas HÖLLER (YC65), Asmir IKANOVIC (BOS) (46' Jasmin
KLAPIJA (SWE)), Jan-Ove PEDERSEN (NOR), Mirko DICKHAUT (GER) (46' Dejan
GRABIC (SLO)), Jürgen KAUZ (YC72), Günther SCHEPENS (BEL), Olivier NZUZI Niati
Polo (CGO).
Goals: FK Khazar Universiteti Baku: 1-0 Markus KRAUTBERGER (29' *own goal*), 2-1
Rashad ABDULAEV (68').
SW Bregenz: 1-1 Günther SCHEPENS (51' penalty).
Referee: Bülent DEMIRLEK (TUR)   Attendance: 2.000

26-06-2004   Celtnieks Stadion, Daugavpils:
                    FC Dinaburg Daugavpils – Aberystwyth Town FC   4-0 (1-0)
FC Dinaburg Daugavpils: Vadim FYODOROV, Sergey VALYUSHKIN (YC77), Dmitriy
CHUGUNOV, Vadim LOGINS, Andrey MARKOV (RUS), Edgar BURLAKOV, Yury
SOKOLOV, Vitali PINIASKINE (RUS) (60' Alexey KOSTENKO (RUS)), Tamaz PERTIYA
(GEO), Pavel RYZHEVSKI (BLS) (71' Andrey SEMYONOV), Aleksandr MUSAJEV (65'
Vladimir VOLKOV).
Aberystwyth Town FC: Dean WILLIAMS (ENG), David Clyne BURROWS, Andy LEE
(ENG), Aneurin THOMAS (YC25), Gary FINLEY (ENG), Phillip BAKER, Marc LLOYD-
WILLIAMS, Bari David Rees MORGAN (YC61), Lee SPIKE, John LAWLESS (..' Gavin
ALLEN), David BRIDGEWATER (ENG).
Goals: FC Dinaburg Daugavpils: 1-0 Pavel RYZHEVSKI (17'), 2-0 Aleksandr MUSAJEV
(53'), 3-0 Aleksandr MUSAJEV (57'), 4-0 Vadim LOGINS (76').
Referee: Karel VIDLAK (CZE)   Attendance: 500

27-06-2004   Mestský Stadion na Stínadlech, Teplice:
                    FK Teplice – Matáv FC Sopron   3-1 (3-1)
FK Teplice: Tomás POSTULKA, Martin KLEIN, Tomás HUNAL, Vlastimil RYSKA, Michal
DOLEZAL, Pavel KRMAS, Petr BENÁT, Pavel HORVÁTH, Martin FENIN (70' Jiri
KOWALÍK (YC90)), Pavel VERBÍR (90' Jaroslav FÜRBACH), Pavel VELEBA (90'
Vitizslav BROZIK).
Matáv FC Sopron: Árpád MILINTE, Lajos HORVÁTH (YC54), István SIRA, Mladen
LAMBULIC (SBM), Bojan LAZIC (SBM), Gábor BAGOLY (YC69), Viktor HANÁK, Iván
BALASKÓ, Henrik KOVÁCS, Péter NAGY, Sándor TÖRÖK.
Goals: FK Teplice: 1-1 Pavel VELEBA (29'), 2-1 Mladen LAMBULIC (34' *own goal*), 3-1
Pavel VELEBA (40').
Matáv FC Sopron: 0-1 István SIRA (19').
Referee: Serge GUMIENNY (BEL)   Attendance: 1.610

27-06-2004   Stadion SK Hanácká Slavia Kromeriz, Kromeriz:
FK Tescoma Zlín – Myllykosken Pallo-47   3-2 (2-0)
FK Tescoma Zlín: Otakar NOVÁK, Vlastimil VIDLICKA, Zdenik KROCA, Jiri KOUBSKÝ, David HUBÁCEK, Petr NOVOSAD (73' Václav ZAPLETAL), Vít VRTILKA, Edvard LASOTA, Bronislav CERVENKA, Marcel LICKA (87' Tomás DUJKA), Fábio Luis GOMES (BRA) (76' Roman DOBES).
Myllykosken Pallo-47: Aapo KILJUNEN, Sampsa TIMOSKA, Tuomo KÖNÖNEN (69' Eetu MUINONEN), Tuomas KUPARINEN, Niki HELENIUS, Saku PUHAKAINEN, Tuomas HAAPALA (58' Niklas TARVAJÄRVI), Tero TAIPALE, Mika HERNESNIEMI (19' Tero KARHU), Toni HUTTUNEN, Tuomas AHO.
Goals: FK Tescoma Zlín: 1-0 Marcel LICKA (2'), 2-0 Bronislav CERVENKA (3'), 3-0 Fábio Luis GOMES (57').
Myllykosken Pallo-47: 3-1 Tero TAIPALE (67'), 3-2 Niklas TARVAJÄRVI (71').
Referee: Ghenadie ORLIC (MOL)   Attendance: 1.350

27-06-2004   Stadionul Gloria, Bistrita: FC Gloria Bistrita – FC Thun   0-0
FC Gloria Bistrita: Costel CAMPEANU, Sorin Adrian IODI (YC12), Alin Valer RUS, Alin Nicu CHIBULCUTEAN, Eusebiu Iulian TUDOR, Alin MINTEUAN, Marius MARGARIT (57' Florin MAGER), Marius DRULE (46' Dinu Daniel SANMARTEAN (YC88)), Cornel Flaviu CORNEA (YC58) (71' Miroslav Matea GIUCHICI), Cristian Ambrozie COROIAN, Sandu NEGREAN,
FC Thun: Fabio COLTORTI, Nelson FERREIRA (POR), Selver HODZIC, Armand DEUMI TCHAMI (CMR), Pascal CERRONE, Andreas GERBER, Michael RENGGLI, Mario RAIMONDI, Silvan AEGERTER, Antonio DOS SANTOS (BRA) (87' Adrian MOSER), Mauro LUSTRINELLI (69' Israel Rodrigo RODRIGUEZ Colman (PAR)).
Referee: Ivan BEBEK (CRO)   Attendance: 300

27-06-2004   Mestský futbalový Stadión, Dubnica Nad Vahom:
FK ZTS Dubnica – KS Teuta Durrës   4-0 (1-0)
FK ZTS Dubnica: Marian POSTRK, Marian ZIMEN, Cyril SPENDLA, Martin SVESTKA (CZE), Dalibor PLEVA, Juraj DOVICOVIC (61' Ján SVIKRUHA (YC89)), Pavol KOPACKA (76' Branislav MRÁZ), Igor DRZIK (68' Jan SOKOL), Martin DOKTOR, Matej IZVOLT, Andrej PORÁZIK.
KS Teuta Durrës: Alfred OSMANI, Ervin KOTOMELO (YC52) (70' Xhenald RADA), Arjan ZERE, T.OSMANI, Johan DRIZA, Edlir TETOVA (81' Bledar SHIMA), Dritan BABAMUSTA, Orgert KOTJA, Arjan VOJO (70' Edar BERZEZI), Daniel XHAFAJ, Admir TOSHKOLLARI.
Goals: FK ZTS Dubnica: 1-0 Matej IZVOLT (2'), 2-0 Martin SVESTKA (47'), 3-0 Matej IZVOLT (65'), 4-0 Andrej PORÁZIK (68').
Referee: Lassin ISAKSEN (FAR)   Attendance: 2.250

92

27-06-2004   Stadion Oláh Gábor Út, Debrecen:
Debreceni VSC – FC Spartak Trnava 4-1 (2-1)
Debreceni VSC: János BALOGH, Balász NIKOLOV, László ÉGER (YC38), Csaba
SZATMÁRI (65' Péter ANDORKA), Csaba BERNÁTH, Tamás SÁNDOR (YC86), Ronald
HABI (SBM), Zoltán KISS, Csaba MADAR, Péter BAJZÁT, Igor BOGDANOVIC (SBM).
FC Spartak Trnava: Marek CECH, Souleymane FALL (SEN), Martin POLJOVKA, Pavol
STANO (YC53), Dusan BESTVINA (YC73), Peter HODÙR (82' Marcel GASPARIK), Peter
DURIS, Andrej FILIP (56' Kamil KOPÙNEK), Marek UJLAKY, Martin HUSÁR (62' Michal
GASPARIK (YC64)), Miroslav KRISS (YC61).
Goals: Debreceni VSC: 1-0 Péter BAJZÁT (23'), 2-0 László ÉGER (34'), 3-1 Csaba MADAR
(77'), 4-1 Igor BOGDANOVIC (84').
FC Spartak Trnava: 2-1 Miroslav KRISS (44').
Referee: Robert JOHNSDORF (LUX)   Attendance: 2.000

27-06-2004   Novi Gradski Stadion, Ugljevik:
FK Sloboda Tuzla – NK Publikum Celje 1-0 (1-0)
FK Sloboda Tuzla: Mirsad DEDIC, Stanisa NIKOLIC (79' Samir KUDUZOVIC), Mario
LAMESIC, Gradimir CRNOGORAC (RC90), Covic MEHMEDALIDA, Nedzad BAJROVIC,
Adnan SARAJLIC, Zoran NOVAKOVIC (46' Armin DELIC), Tarik OKANOVIC, Darko
VOJVODIC (71' Emir BORIC (YC71)), Senad HADZIC.
NK Publikum Celje: Aleksander SELIGA, Matej SNOFL, Dejan KELHAR, Primoz BRUMEN
(YC22), Gregor HELBL (72' Jaka STROMAJER), Sebastjan GOBEC (YC31), Simon
SESLAR (RC90), Vladislav LUNGU (MOL), Dejan PLASTOVSKI (72' Dejan URBANC),
Dare VRSIC, Andrej KVAS (78' Dejan ROBNIK).
Goal: FK Sloboda Tuzla: 1-0 Adnan SARAJLIC (3').
Referee: Marek MIKOLAJEWSKI (POL)

27-06-2004   Dinamo Stadion, Minsk:
FC Dinamo Minsk – MKS Odra Wodzislaw Slaski 2-0 (1-0)
FC Dinamo Minsk: Yuri TSYGALKO, Dmitri LENTSEVICH, Sergey PAVLYUKOVICH,
Dmitri CHALEI, Andrey RAZIN, David ZOUBEK (CZE) (46' Igor ROZHKOV), Petar
ZLATINOV (BUL) (YC64) (81' Anton PUTILO), Kirill PAVLYUCHEK, Vitali
VOLODENKOV (YC60), Maksim TSYGALKO, Vitali LEDZIANIOU (56' Leonid KOVEL
(YC90)).
MKS Odra Wodzislaw Slaski: Marcin BEBEN, Wojciech MYSZOR, Roman MADEJ (77'
Krzysztof BIZACKI), Blazej JANKOWSKI, Slawomir SZARY, Jan WOS (YC45), Wojciech
GRZYB, Aleksander KWIEK (YC..,YC90), Marek SOKOLOWSKI (21' Rafal JAROSZ, 76'
Mariusz NOSAL), Marek KUBISZ, Marcin RADZIEWICZ.
Goals: FC Dinamo Minsk: 1-0 Maksim TSYGALKO (43'), 2-0 Vitali VOLODENKOV (75').
Referee: Iain Robertson BRINES (SCO)   Attendance: 3.000

27-06-2004   Malmö Stadion, Malmö: Malmö FF – Cork City FC 0-1 (0-0)
Malmö FF: Mattias ASPER, Daniel MAJSTOROVIC, Patrik ANDERSSON (46' Glenn
HOLGERSSON), Olof PERSSON, Jon Inge HØILAND (NOR), Hasse MATTISSON (71'
Tobias GRAHN), Thomas OLSSON, Joseph ELANGA (CMR) (71' Jon JÖNSSON
(YC90+2)), Afonso ALVES Martins (BRA) (YC43), Niklas SKOOG, Darko LUKANOVIC.
Cork City FC: Michael DEVINE (YC54), Cillian LORDAN (YC90), Alan BENNETT
(YC20), Daniel MURRAY, Danny MURPHY, Kevin DOYLE (90'+2 Denis BEHAN), Colin
O'BRIEN (YC76), George O'CALLAGHAN, Liam KEARNEY, Neale FENN, John
O'FLYNN (81' Darragh William WOODS).
Goal: Cork City FC: 0-1 Liam KEARNEY (56').
Referee: Alexander GVARDIS (RUS)   Attendance: 2.258

93

27-06-2004   Mikheil Meskhi Stadium, Tbilisi:
FC Dila Gori – FC Marek Dupnitsa   0-2 (0-1)
FC Dila Gori: Ramaz SOGOLASHVILI, Georgi BELASHVILI, Giorgi LOMIDZE, Zaza
LATSABIDZE, Akvsenti GILAURI, Albert SAKVARELIDZE (46' Beka CHITAIA), Roin
ONIANI, Kristepore SHATAKISHVILI (YC60) (65' Guram SAMADASHVILI), Zurab
MUSHKUDIANI, Luka RAZMADZE, Levan GOCHASHVILI.
FC Marek Dupnitsa: Nikolay CHAVDAROV, Ianek KIUTCHUKOV, Hristo
ARANGUELOV, Galin IVANOV, Ventsislav BONEV, Veselin VELIKOV, Emil PETKOV,
Georgi KARAKANOV (78' Stanislav ROUMENOV (YC82)), Ivo PARGOV, Vassil KIROV
(YC42) (60' Ilia ILIEV), Kroum BIBISHKOV (85' Ivan VALKOV).
Goals: FC Marek Dupnitsa: 0-1 Ivo PARGOV (42'), 0-2 Ivo PARGOV (90').
Referee: Radek MATEJEK (CZE)

27-06-2004   Klaipedos Miesto Centrinis Stadionas, Klaipeda:
FK Atlantas Klaipéda – FC Spartak Moskva   1-0 (0-0)
FK Atlantas Klaipeda: Liudvikas VALIUS, Kestutis DEVEIKA (63' Mindaugas ZIGUTIS),
Dainius KUNEVICIUS, Vidas ALUNDERIS (YC62), Kestutis IVASKEVICIUS, Egidijus
ZUKAUSKAS (YC90), Andrius PETREIKIS, Donatas NAVIKAS, Dainius ZERNYS (YC36)
(60' Mantas SERNIUS), Martynas KARALIUS (74' Andrius BARTKUS), Andrius
PUOTKALIS.
FC Spartak Moskva: Wojciech KOWALEWSKI (POL), Roman SHISHKIN (76' Gabriel
Sebastian TAMAS (ROM) (YC82)), Dusan PETKOVIC (SBM), Adrian IENCSI (ROM),
Yuriy KOVTUN (YC38), Alexandr SAMEDOV (AZE), Goran TROBOK (SBM) (YC40),
Aleksandr PAVLENKO (86' Florin SOAVA (ROM)), Maxim KALYNYCHENKO (UKR)
(46' Ales URBÁNEK (CZE)), Pavel POGREBNYAK, Roman PAVLYUCHENKO.
Goal: FK Atlantas Klaipeda: 1-0 Donatas NAVIKAS (80').
Referee: Dejan STANISIC (SBM)   Attendance: 3.200

27-06-2004   Ratina Stadium, Tampere: Tampere United FC – CS Grevenmacher   0-0
Tampere United FC: Mikko KAVEN, Pasi SALMELA, Antti OJANPERÄ, Mika LAHTINEN
(YC73) (82' Antti HYNYNEN), Antti POHJA (90'+1' Jussi-Pekka SAVOLAINEN), Sakari
SAARINEN (YC68), Jarkko WISS, Kari SAINIO, Toni JUNNILA (57' Petri HEINÄNEN),
Heikko AHO, Janne RÄSÄNEN.
CS Grevenmacher: Marc OBERWEIS, Alexander ZIEHL (GER) (71' Nino HELBIG (GER)),
Stephan KORDIAN (GER), Markus KOSTER (GER), Christian ALBRECHT (GER), Manuel
MOROCUTTI, Daniel HUSS, Luc THIMMESCH (76' Ahmed ZERROUKI (FRA)), Márcio
RODRIGUES da Cruz (BRA), Karim GROUNE (FRA), Volker SCHMITT (GER).
Referee: Zohrab GADIYEV (AZE)   Attendance: 3.022

SECOND ROUND

03-07-2004   Easter Road, Edinburgh:
Hibernian FC Edinburgh – FK Vetra Rudiskes Vilnius   1-1 (0-0)
Hibernian FC Edinburgh: Alistair BROWN, Steven WHITTAKER, Alan REID (76' Stephen
DOBBIE), Gary CALDWELL, Colin MURDOCK (NIR), Kevin NICOL, Thomas McMANUS
(YC7) (60' Samuel MORROW (NIR)), Grant BREBNER (YC17), Garry O'CONNOR, Scott
BROWN, Alen ORMAN (AUT) (60' Stephen GLASS).
FK Vetra Rudiskes Vilnius: Marius POSKUS, Zydrunas GRUDZINSKAS (YC66), Nerijus
SASNAUSKAS (YC64), Julius RALIUKONIS, Zilvinas ZUDYS, Gintaras RIMKUS,
Darvydas SERNAS, Gediminas BUTRIMAVICIUS (85' Awenayeri DOUGLAS (NGR)),
Rolandas VAINEIKIS (64' Ramunas STONKUS), Nerijus VASILIAUSKAS, Vytautas
KARVELIS (YC25) (72' Saulius KIJANSKAS).
Goals: Hibernian FC Edinburgh: 1-1 Gary O'CONNOR (77').
FK Vetra Rudiskes Vilnius: 0-1 Nerijus SASNAUSKAS (63').
Referee: Tony ASUMAA (FIN)   Attendance: 8.630

03-07-2004   Volkswagen Arena, Wolfsburg: VfL Wolfsburg – FC Thun   2-3 (0-1)
VfL Wolfsburg: Simon JENTZSCH, Thomas RYTTER (DEN), Maik FRANZ, Kevin
HOFLAND (HOL), Patrick WEISER, Miroslav KARHAN (SVK), Oscar AHUMADA (ARG),
Stefan SCHNOOR (90'+1' Hans SARPEI), Cedric MAKIADI (55' Roy PRÄGER (YC90)),
Marko TOPIC (BOS), Juan Carlos MENSEGUEZ (ARG) (86' Bartosz ROMANCZUK
(POL)).
FC Thun: Fabio COLTORTI, Nelson FERREIRA (POR), Armand DEUMI TCHAMI (CMR)
(YC39), Selver HODZIC (YC90), Pascal CERRONE, Andreas GERBER, Michael RENGGLI
(YC52), BAYKAL Kulaksizoglu (TUR) (80' Mathias FAHMI), Silvan AEGERTER, Mauro
LUSTRINELLI (56' Samuel OJONG (CMR)), Mario RAIMONDI.
Goals: VfL Wolfsburg: 1-3 Stefan SCHNOOR (75'), 2-3 Roy PRÄGER (88').
FC Thun: 0-1 BAYKAL Kulaksizoglu (14'), 0-2 Samuel OJONG (59'), 0-3 Mario
RAIMONDI (70').
Referee: Anton STREDAK (SVK)   Attendance: 5.087

03-07-2004   Stadion ved Messecenter, Herning: Esbjerg FB – O.G.C. Nice   1-0 (1-0)
Esbjerg FB: Lars WINDE, Kolja AFRIYIE (GER), Anders Møller CHRISTIANSEN, Kjetil
PEDERSEN (NOR) (46' Martin JENSEN), Tommy LØVENKRANDS, Jakob POULSEN,
Hans Henrik ANDREASEN (YC39), Jerry Ruben LUCENA, Jan KRISTIANSEN (70' Søren
BARSLUND), Fredrik BERGLUND (SWE), Jess Christian THORUP.
O.G.C. Nice: Damian GRÉGORINI, Noë PAMAROT, José COBOS, Jacques
ABARDONADO, Cédric VARRAULT, Yoann BIGNÉ, Olivier ECHOUAFNI, Romain
PITAU, Sébastien ROUDET (YC83), Roland LINZ (AUT), Christophe MESLIN (73' Olivier
FAUCONNIER).
Goal: Esbjerg FB: 1-0 Fredrik BERGLUND (2').
Referee: Damir SKOMINA (SLO)   Attendance: 966

03-07-2004   Luzhniki Stadium, Moskva:
FC Spartak Moskva – NK Kamen Ingrad Velika   4-1 (1-0)
FC Spartak Moskva: Wojciech KOWALEWSKI (POL), Yuriy KOVTUN, Dusan PETKOVIC (SBM) (YC67), Igor MITREVSKI (MCD), Kamaloutdin AKHMEDOV, Florin SOAVA (ROM), Maxim KALYNYCHENKO (UKR) (90' Ales URBÁNEK (CZE)), Aleksandr PAVLENKO (71' Roman SHISHKIN), Alexandr SAMEDOV (AZE) (88' Vladimir LESHONOK), Roman PAVLYUCHENKO, Pavel POGREBNYAK.
NK Kamen Ingrad Velika: Silvije CAVLINA, Antonio KOVAC (YC75), Sime KURILIC, Edin SARANOVIC (BOS), Davor BAJSIC, Valerio BALASKOVIC (76' Vasko BOZINOVSKI (MCD)), Mario CIZMEK (46' Mario KRALJ), Aleksandar KOPUNOVIC (CRO) (64' Jusuf DAJIC (BOS)), Krunoslav RENDULIC, Ivo SMOJE, Damir VUICA.
Goals: FC Spartak Moskva: 1-0 Alexandr SAMEDOV (34'), 2-0 Pavel POGREBNYAK (77'), 3-0 Dusan PETKOVIC (82'), 4-1 Roman PAVLYUCHENKO (86' penalty).
NK Kamen Ingrad Velika: 3-1Edin SARANOVIC (83').
Referee: Haim JAKOV (ISR)

03-07-2004   Gradski Stadion, Koprivnica:
NK Slaven Belupo Koprivnica – KS Vllaznia Shkodër   2-0 (1-0)
NK Slaven Belupo Koprivnica: Robert LISJAK, Petar BOSNJAK (81' Dario BRGLES), Pavo CRNAC, Dalibor BOZAC, Dalibor VISKOVIC (46' Marko JURIC), Ivica SERTIC (YC11), Ognjen VUKOJEVIC, Roy FERENCINA, Nikica SRPAK (67' Alen GUC), Marijo DODIK, Bojan VRUCINA.
KS Vllaznia Shkodër: Orges SHEHI, Julian BRAHJA (39' Erjon HOTI), Admir TELI, Marin Glen KAPAJ (53' Edmond DOCI), Safet OSJA, Armando CUNGU (65' Franc AHI), Amarildo BELISHA, Albert KAÇI, Hamdi SALIHI, January ZYAMBO, ABILIO Neves Dos Reis (BRA).
Goals: NK Slaven Belupo Koprivnica: 1-0 Marijo DODIK (26'), 2-0 Nikica SRPAK (51').
Referee: Brian LAWLOR (WAL)   Attendance: 1.000

03-07-2004   Mestský Stadion na Stínadlech, Teplice:
FK Teplice – FC Shinnik Yaroslavl   1-2 (1-2)
FK Teplice: Patrik KOLÁR, Josef KAUFMAN, Martin KLEIN, Tomás HUNAL (YC34), Vlastimil RYSKA (YC..,YC78), Michal DOLEZAL, Pavel KRMAS (56' Jakub MASEK), Pavel HORVÁTH (YC84), Petr BENÁT (76' Martin FENIN), Pavel VELEBA (56' Radek DIVECKY (YC65)), Pavel VERBÍR.
FC Shinnik Yaroslavl: Yevgeniy SAFONOV (UZB), Pavel KRYLOV, Iliya TKACHEV, Krzysztof LAGIEWKA (POL), Yevgeniy KAREV (YC30), Alexander TUMENKO (86' Dmitry GOLUBEV), Artiem ZASYADVOVK (UKR) (YC27), Igor SHTUKIN, Emzar ROZOMASHVILI (76' Girts KARLSONS (LAT)), Anton ARKHIPOV (YC49), Dmitry VASILYEV (58' Martin KOUCHEV (BUL)).
Goals: FK Teplice: 1-0 Pavel VERBÍR (28' penalty).
FC Shinnik Yaroslavl: 1-1 Anton ARKHIPOV (32'), 1-2 Alexander TUMENKO (45').
Referee: René ROGALLA (SUI)   Attendance: 1.320

03-07-2004   Mestský futbalový Stadión, Dubnica Nad Vahom:
FK ZTS Dubnica – FC Slovan Liberec 1-2 (0-1)
FK ZTS Dubnica: Marian POSTRK, Dalibor PLEVA (YC41), Martin SVESTKA (CZE) (57'
Branislav MRÁZ), Marian ZIMEN, Cyril SPENDLA, Igor DRZIK (YC73), Pavol KOPACKA
(YC23) (36' Juraj DOVICOVIC), Matej IZVOLT, Martin DOKTOR, Andrej PORAZÍK,
Pavol STRAKA (70' Ján SVIKRUHA).
FC Slovan Liberec: Zbynék HAUZR, Peter SINGLÁR (SVK), Petr LUKÁS (85' Pavel
KOSTÁL), Jozef VALACHOVIC (SVK), Josef HAMOUZ (YC78), Miroslav SLEPIÈKA,
David LANGER, Jan POLÁK (81' Jan BROSCHINSKY), Petr PAPOUSEK, Filip HOLOSKO
(SVK), Michal POSPISIL (71' Juraj ANCIC (SVK)).
Goals: FK ZTS Dubnica: 1-2 Juraj DOVICOVIC (73').
FC Slovan Liberec: 0-1 Filip HOLOSKO (32'), 0-2 Cyril SPENDLA (66' own goal).
Referee: Asaf KENAN (ISR)   Attendance: 2.742

03-07-2004   Gradski Stadion, Skopje: FK Vardar Skopje – KAA Gent 1-0 (0-0)
FK Vardar Skopje: Velimir ZDRAVKOVIC (SBM), Bojan MARKOSKI, Blessing Chinedu
ANYANVIU (NGR), Aleksandar VASOSKI, Nikola DOSEVSKI, Jovica TRAJCEV, Darko
TASEVSKI (YC15) (60' Nikola GLIGOROV), Vlatko GROZDANOVSKI (75' Almir
BAJRAMOVSKI), Zarko SERAFIMOVSKI, ROGÉRIO da Costa Oliveira (BRA) (63' Danio
MASEV), Oliveira WANDEIR Dos Santos (BRA) (YC90).
KAA Gent: Frédéric HERPOEL, Jacky PEETERS, Stephen LAYBUTT (AUS) (YC12),
Matthieu VERSCHUERE (FRA) (82' Ersin MEHMEDOVIC (SBM) (YC89)), Steven RIBUS,
Sandy MARTENS, David VAN HOYWEGHEN, Madjid ADJAOUD (ALG), Steve
COOREMAN, Nordin JBARI, Wouter VRANCKEN.
Goal: FK Vardar Skopje: 1-0 Oliveira WANDEIR Dos Santos (90').
Referee: Kostadin KOSTADINOV (BUL)

03-07-2004   Stadión Antona Malatinského, Trnava:
FC Spartak Trnava – FK Sloboda Tuzla 2-1 (0-0)
FC Spartak Trnava: Marek CECH, Souleymane FALL (SEN), Martin POLJOVKA, Pavol
STANO (YC90), Roman SIMKO (YC42), Peter HODÙR, Marek UJLAKY, Kamil
KOPÙNEK (78' Jaroslav HRABAL), Peter DURIS, Martin HUSÁR (YC58) (62' Tomás
BARTOS), Miroslav KRISS (78' Pavol MASARYK).
FK Sloboda Tuzla: Mirsad DEDIC, Samir KUDUZOVIC (YC48), Nedzad BAJROVIC, Covic
MEHMEDALIDA (YC29), Stanisa NIKOLIC (YC70), Senad HADZIC, Tarik OKANOVIC
(87' Armin DELIC), Adnan SARAJLIC, Mario LAMESIC, Darko VOJVODIC, Zoran
NOVAKOVIC (70' Emir BORIC).
Goals: FC Spartak Trnava: 1-0 Kamil KOPÙNEK (46'), 2-1 Souleymane FALL (79').
FK Sloboda Tuzla: 1-1 Mario LAMESIC (77').
Referee: Karen NALBANDYAN (ARM)   Attendance: 988

03-07-2004   De Goffert, Nijmegen: N.E.C. Nijmegen – Cork City FC 0-0
N.E.C. Nijmegen: Dennis GENTENAAR, Peter WISGERHOF (55' Romano DENNEBOOM),
Rob WIELAERT, Arjan EBBINGE, José VALENCIA Murillo (ECU), Björn VAN DER
DOELEN (YC49), Pascal HEIJE, Jarda SIMR (CZE), Saïd BOUTAHAR, Ronildo Pereira de
Freitas "TININHO" (BRA), Frank DEMOUGE (YC44).
Cork City FC: Michael DEVINE, Cillian LORDAN, Alan BENNETT, Daniel MURRAY,
Danny MURPHY (YC75), Darragh William WOODS (85' Joe GAMBLE), Colin O'BRIEN,
George O'CALLAGHAN, Liam KEARNEY, Neale FENN, Kevin DOYLE.
Referee: Damien LEDENTU (FRA)   Attendance: 7.500

03-07-2004   Het Kuipje, Westerlo: KVC Westerlo – FK Tescoma Zlín   0-0
KVC Westerlo: Jonathan BOURDON, Marc WAGEMAKERS, Wim MENNES, Christiaan
JANSSENS (YC34), Bobsam ELEJIKO, Stijn VANGEFFELEN (66' Sadio BA), Tosin
S.DOSUNMU (NGR) (66' Jo KEENAN (ENG)), Zdenek SVOBODA (CZE) (66' Simphiwe
Boy-Boy MOSIA), David PAAS, Knut Henry HARALDSEN (NOR), Jef DELEN.
FK Tescoma Zlín: Otakar NOVÁK, Vlastimil VIDLICKA, Zdenik KROCA, David
HUBÁCEK, Tomás DUJKA (YC61), Bronislav CERVENKA, Edvard LASOTA, Vít
VRTILKA, Josef LUKASTIK (80' Roman DOBES), Václav CINCALA (80' Fabio Luis
GOMES (BRA)), Vladimir MALÁR (70' Jaroslav SVACH).
Referee: Dragomir TANOVIC (SBM)   Attendance: 1.000

03-07-2004   Atletion, Aarhus: Odense BK – Villarreal CF   0-3 (0-0)
Odense BK: Arek ONYSZKO (POL), Steen NEDERGAARD, Jan SØNKSEN, Jacob
GREGERSEN (YC77), Fernando DERVELD (HOL), Martin BORRE (52' Søren BERG
ANDERSEN), Esben HANSEN (67' Ulrich VINZENTS), Andrew TEMBO (ZAM), Kenneth
Møller PEDERSEN (52' Thomas LINDRUP), Mwape MITI (ZAM), Steffen HØJER. (Coach:
Klavs RASMUSSEN).
Villarreal CF: José Manuel REINA Páez, ARMANDO Miguel Correia de SÁ (BRA), Sergio
Martínez BALLESTEROS, Enrique "QUIQUE" ÁLVAREZ Sanjuán, Rodolfo Martín
ARRUABARRENA (ARG), HÉCTOR FONT Romero (60' Santiago "SANTI" CAZORLA
González), Sebastián BATTAGLIA (ARG), José Joaquín Moreno Verdú "JOSICO", Javier
CALLEJA Revilla, JOSÉ "MARI" María Romero Poyón (85' José Antonio GUAYRE
Betancor Perdomo), "SONNY" ANDERSON da Silva (BRA) (70' VÍCTOR Manuel
Fernández Gutiérrez). (Coach: Manuel Luis PELLEGRINI Ripamonti (CHI)).
Goals: Villarreal CF: 0-1"SONNY" ANDERSON da Silva (66'), 0-2 Santiago "SANTI"
CAZORLA González (69'), 0-3 José Antonio GUAYRE Bentacort Perdomo (87').
Referee: Michael Leslie DEAN (ENG)   Attendance: 523

04-07-2004   Omladinski Stadion, Beograd:
               O.F.K. Beograd – FC Dinaburg Daugavpils   3-1 (2-1)
O.F.K. Beograd: Nikola DAMJANAC, Branislav IVANOVIC, Marko BASA (YC41), Djordje
JOKIC, Dusko TOSIC, Aleksandar SIMIC (88' Filip ARSENIJEVIC), Branko BAKOVIC,
Boris VASKOVIC, Igor MATIC (63' Dusan MIHAJLOVIC), Milos KOLAKOVIC, Rade
VUKOTIC.
FC Dinaburg Daugavpils: Vadim FYODOROV, Dmitriy CHUGUNOV, Vadim LOGINS,
Andrey ZHUROMSKY, Edgar BURLAKOV, Yury SOKOLOV (81' Sergey VALYUSHKIN),
Andrey MARKOV (RUS), Alexey KOSTENKO (RUS) (63' Vitali PINIASKINE (RUS)
(YC76)), Aleksandr MUSAJEV, Tamaz PERTIYA (GEO) (84' Pavel KOLCOV), Pavel
RYZHEVSKI (BLS).
Goals: O.F.K. Beograd: 1-0 Milos KOLAKOVIC (3'), 2-0 Milos KOLAKOVIC (18' penalty),
3-1 Dusko TOSIC (54').
FC Dinaburg Daugavpils: 2-1 Yury SOKOLOV (35').
Referee: Levan PANIASHVILI (GEO)

04-07-2004   Fenix Stadion, Genk: KRC Genk – FC Marek Dupnitsa 2-1 (1-0)
KRC Genk: Jan MOONS, Indridi SIGURDSSON (ISL), Eric MATOUKOU (CMR), Gert
CLAESSENS (YC62), Kevin VANDENBERGH (62' Igor DE CAMARGO (BRA)), Thomas
CHATELLE (78' Mirsad BESLIJA (BOS)), Dimitri DE CONDÉ (87' Cedric ROUSSEL),
Daan VAESEN, Paul KPAKA (SLE), Koen DAERDEN, Justice WAMFOR (CMR).
FC Marek Dupnitsa: Nikolay CHAVDAROV, Galin IVANOV, Ianek KIUTCHUKOV
(YC20), Hristo ARANGUELOV, Veselin VELIKOV, Emil PETKOV (82' Stanislav
ROUMENOV), Georgi KARAKANOV (YC90) (90' Kaloyan ILIEV), Ivo PARGOV, Vassil
KIROV, Ilia ILIEV, Kroum BIBISHKOV.
Goals: KRC Genk: 1-0 Paul KPAKA (26'), 2-1 Koen DAERDEN (67').
FC Marek Dupnitsa: 1-1 Georgi KARAKANOV (65').
Referee: Pavel Cristian BALAJ (ROM)   Attendance: 7.853

04-07-2004   Traktor Stadium, Minsk: FC Dinamo Minsk – FK Sartid Smederevo 1-2 (0-1)
FC Dinamo Minsk: Yuri TSYGALKO, Dmitri LENTSEVICH (YC32), Sergey KONTSEV
(46' Jan TIGOREV), Aleksey DOBROVOLSKI, Yuri SHUKANOV (YC70), Sergey
PAVLYUKOVICH, Andrey RAZIN (53' Dmitri CHALEI), David ZOUBEK (CZE), Anton
PUTILO, Vitali VOLODENKOV (57' Maksim TSYGALKO), Vitali LEDZIANIOU.
FK Sartid Smederevo: Dragan JILIC, Ivan ZIVANOVIC (46' Dragan PAUNOVIC), Zeljko
KOVACEVIC, Marko SOCANAC, Nebojsa SAVIC, Sasa ZORIC, Dejan KEKEZOVIC, Sasa
KOCIC (YC86), Milorad ZECEVIC (90' Nikola JEVTIC), Dragan RADOSAVLJEVIC,
Nenad MIROSAVLJEVIC.
Goals: FC Dinamo Minsk: 1-1 Andrey RAZIN (49').
FK Sartid Smederevo: 0-1 Nenad MIROSAVLJEVIC (12'), 1-2 Nenad MIROSAVLJEVIC
(62').
Referee: Attila JUHOS (HUN)

04-07-2004   Ratina Stadium, Tampere:
                  Tampere United FC – FK Khazar Universiteti Baku 3-0 (1-0)
Tampere United FC: Mikko KAVEN, Jussi KUOPPALA, Mika LAHTINEN (46' Antti
OJANPERÄ), Antti POHJA, Sakari SAARINEN (79' Toni JUNNILA), Jarkko WISS, Petri
HEINÄNEN, Kari SAINIO (YC67), Heikko AHO, Henri SCHEWELEFF (66' Antti
HYNYNEN), Janne RÄSÄNEN.
FK Khazar Universiteti Baku: Ilkin BAGIYEV, Zavr HASHIMOV (YC47), Goderdzi
GOGOLADZE (GEO), Elbrus Kh.MAMEDOV, Rashad ABDULAEV, Elmar BAKHSHIEV,
David CHIGOSHVILI, Archil SOKHADZE (52' Elshan MAMMADOV), Samir KHAIROV,
Orkhan RAJABOV (49' Ramil SAYADOV), Ruslan GAFITULIN.
Goals: Tampere United FC: 1-0 Henri SCHEWELEFF (18'), 2-0 Antti POHJA (54'), 3-0
Jarkko WISS (85').
Referee: Stanislav SUKHINA (RUS)   Attendance: 1.415

99

10-07-2004   Zalgirio stadionas, Vilnius:
FK Vetra Rudiskes Vilnius – Hibernian FC Edinburgh   1-0 (0-0)
FK Vetra Rudiskes Vilnius: Marius POSKUS, Zydrunas GRUDZINSKAS (YC30), Nerijus
SASNAUSKAS, Julius RALIUKONIS (YC20), Zilvinas ZUDYS, Clement BEAUD (CMR),
Gintaras RIMKUS, Darvydas SERNAS, Gediminas BUTRIMAVICIUS (46' Ramunas
STONKUS), Nerijus VASILIAUSKAS (90' Rolandas VAINEIKIS), Vytautas KARVELIS
(71' Saulius KIJANSKAS).
Hibernian FC Edinburgh: Alistair BROWN, Steven WHITTAKER, Alan REID, Gary
CALDWELL, Colin MURDOCK (NIR), Kevin NICOL, Scott BROWN (YC77) (78' Thomas
McMANUS), Grant BREBNER (70' Stephen DOBBIE), Gary O'CONNOR (YC65), Samuel
MORROW (NIR), Alen ORMAN (AUT) (YC50) (62' Stephen GLASS).
Goal: FK Vetra Rudiskes Vilnius: 1-0 Nerijus VASILIAUSKAS (62').
Referee: Krzysztof SLUPIK (POL)   Attendance: 800

10-07-2004   Bonchuk Stadium, Dupnitsa: FC Marek Dupnitsa – KRC Genk   0-0
FC Marek Dupnitsa: Nikolay CHAVDAROV, Galin IVANOV, Ianek KIUTCHUKOV, Hristo
ARANGUELOV, Veselin VELIKOV (53' Enyo KRASTOVCHEV), Ilia ILIEV, Georgi
KARAKANOV (YC20), Vassil KIROV (62' Ivo PARGOV), Stanislav ROUMENOV (78'
Ivan VALKOV), Kroum BIBISHKOV (YC11), Emil PETKOV.
KRC Genk: Jan MOONS, Indridi SIGURDSSON (ISL) (YC65), Gert CLAESSENS (YC47),
Eric MATOUKOU (CMR) (YC11), Daan VAESEN, Koen DAERDEN (YC88), Justice
WAMFOR (CMR), Dimitri DE CONDÉ, Mirsad BESLIJA (BOS) (61' Thomas CHATELLE),
Cedric ROUSSEL (46' Paul KPAKA (SLE)), Igor DE CAMARGO (BRA) (84' Kenneth VAN
GOETHEM).
Referee: Georgios BOROVILOS (GRE)   Attendance: 2.000

10-07-2004   Celtnieks Stadion, Daugavpils:
FC Dinaburg Daugavpils – O.F.K. Beograd   0-2 (0-0)
FC Dinaburg Daugavpils: Vadim FYODOROV, Dmitriy CHUGUNOV, Vadim LOGINS
(YC55), Andrey ZHUROMSKY, Edgar BURLAKOV, Yury SOKOLOV (YC44) (46' Sergey
VALYUSHKIN), Andrey MARKOV (RUS) (YC15) (72' Alexey KOSTENKO (RUS)), Vitali
PINIASKINE (RUS), Tamaz PERTIYA (GEO), Aleksandr MUSAJEV (74' Pavel KOLCOV,
Pavel RYZHEVSKI (BLS) (YC8).
O.F.K. Beograd: Nikola DAMJANAC, Branislav IVANOVIC, Marko BASA, Milos
BAJALICA, Dusko TOSIC, Aleksandar SIMIC (72' Miljan MRDAKOVIC), Djordje
KAMBER, Boris VASKOVIC, Igor MATIC (46' Vladimir BOZOVIC), Branko BAKOVIC,
Rade VUKOTIC (78' Ivan CVETKOVIC).
Goals: O.F.K. Beograd: 0-1 Rade VUKOTIC (61'), 0-2 Miljan MRDAKOVIC (89').
Referee: Ismet ARZUMAN (TUR)   Attendance: 600

10-07-2004   Novi Gradski Stadion, Ugljevik:
FK Sloboda Tuzla – FC Spartak Trnava   0-1 (0-0)
FK Sloboda Tuzla: Mirsad DEDIC, Stanisa NIKOLIC, Mario LAMESIC (YC28), Covic
MEHMEDALIDA (77' Adnan COKIC), Samir KUDUZOVIC, Nedzad BAJROVIC, Zoran
NOVAKOVIC (50' Emir BORIC), Adnan SARAJLIC, Tarik OKANOVIC (29' Amir
REKIC), Senad HADZIC, Jashinko BRCINOVIC.
FC Spartak Trnava: Marek CECH, Souleymane FALL (SEN), Jaroslav HRABAL, Pavol
STANO, Roman SIMKO (YC45), Peter HODÙR (81' Martin HUSÁR), Marek UJLAKY,
Kamil KOPÙNEK, Peter DURIS, Miroslav KRISS (89' Pavol MASARYK), Michal
GASPARIK.
Goal: FC Spartak Trnava: 0-1 Roman SIMKO (74').
Referee: David MALCOLM (NIR)   Attendance: 1.000

10-07-2004   SRC Kamen Ingrad Stadium, Velika:
NK Kamen Ingrad Velika – FC Spartak Moskva   0-1 (0-1)
NK Kamen Ingrad Velika: Silvije CAVLINA, Antonio KOVAC, Vasko BOZINOVSKI
(MCD), Sime KURILIC (YC36), Davor BAJSIC (46' Valerio BALASKOVIC), Jusuf DAJIC
(BOS), Krunoslav RENDULIC, Josko POPOVIC (46' Ivan LISNIC), Mario KRALJ (71'
Mario CIZMEK), Ivo SMOJE, Damir VUICA.
FC Spartak Moskva: Wojciech KOWALEWSKI (POL), Igor MITREVSKI (MCD),
Kamaloutdin AKHMEDOV, Roman SHISHKIN (YC55), Florin SOAVA (ROM), Adrian
IENCSI (ROM), Maxim KALYNYCHENKO (UKR), Gabriel Sebastian TAMAS (ROM),
Aleksandr PAVLENKO (YC33) (57' Vladimir LESHONOK), Roman PAVLYUCHENKO
(YC34) (46' Ales URBÁNEK (CZE)), Pavel POGREBNYAK (74' Aleksei REBKO).
Goal: FC Spartak Moskva: 0-1 Pavel POGREBNYAK (37').
Referee: Loizos LOIZOU (CYP)

10-07-2004   Shafa Stadium, Baku:
FK Khazar Universiteti Baku – Tampere United FC   1-0 (0-0)
FK Khazar Universiteti Baku: Ilkin BAGIYEV, Zavr HASHIMOV, Goderdzi GOGOLADZE
(GEO), Elbrus Kh.MAMEDOV, Rashad ABDULAEV (86' Ruslan GAFITULIN), Elmar
BAKHSHIEV, Elshan MAMMADOV (55' Archil SOKHADZE (YC90)), David
CHIGOSHVILI (YC67), Elnur MAMMADOV (77' Rahir ASKEROV), Samir KHAIROV,
Robert ZIZAKSVILI (GEO).
Tampere United FC: Mikko KAVEN, Antti OJANPERÄ (YC72), Jussi KUOPPALA, Antti
HYNYNEN (63' Mika LAHTINEN), Antti POHJA, Sakari SAARINEN (75' Toni JUNNILA),
Petri HEINÄNEN, Jarkko WISS (YC17), Kari SAINIO, Heikko AHO, Janne RÄSÄNEN.
Goal: FK Khazar Universiteti Baku: 1-0 Elmar BAKHSHIEV (85').
Referee: Andrejs SIPAILO (LAT)   Attendance: 3.000

10-07-2004   Shinnik Stadium, Yaroslavl: FC Shinnik Yaroslavl – FK Teplice   2-0 (1-0)
FC Shinnik Yaroslavl: Alexander MALYSHEV, Yevgeniy KAREV, Pavel KRYLOV, Wilians
Rodriges ILSON (BRA), Renat DUBINSKLIY (KAZ), Anton ARKHIPOV (YC9), Artiem
ZASYADVOVK (UKR) (72' Girts KARLSONS (LAT)), Viktor KARPENKO (UZB) (46'
Evgen LUTSENKO (UKR)), Alexander TUMENKO, Dmitry VASILYEV (64' Igor
SHTUKIN), Martin KOUCHEV (BUL).
FK Teplice: Tomás POSTULKA, Michal DOLEZAL, Tomás HUNAL (46' Pavel VELEBA),
Martin KLEIN (RC44), Josef KAUFMAN, Martin FENIN (58' Patrik GROSS), Pavel
HORVÁTH, Petr BENÁT (78' Jiri KOWALIK), Jakub MASEK, Pavel VERBÍR, Radek
DIVECKY.
Goals: FC Shinnik Yaroslavl: 1-0 Martin KOUCHEV (44' penalty), 2-0 Anton ARKHIPOV
(86').
Referee: Charles Joseph RICHMOND (SCO)   Attendance: 6.000

101

10-07-2004   Stadion u Nisy, Liberec: FC Slovan Liberec – FK ZTS Dubnica 5-0 (3-0)
FC Slovan Liberec: Zbynék HAUZR, Peter SINGLÁR (SVK), Petr LUKÁS, Pavel KOSTÁL
(67' Tomás ZÁPOTOCNY), Josef HAMOUZ, Juraj ANCIC (SVK) (61' Daniel PUDIL), Jan
POLÁK, Ivan HODÚR (SVK), Petr PAPOUSEK, Michal POSPISIL, Filip HOLOSKO (SVK)
(64' Lubomir BLAHA).
FK ZTS Dubnica: Marian POSTRK, Branislav MRÁZ, Marian ZIMEN, Cyril SPENDLA
(YC39), Ján SVIKRUHA (84' Jan SOKOL), Igor DRZIK (55' Michal FILO), Pavol
KOPACKA (YC43), Matej IZVOLT, Martin DOKTOR, Pavol STRAKA (80' Marian
BELLAK), Andrej PORAZÍK.
Goals: FC Slovan Liberec: 1-0 Pavel KOSTÁL (6'), 2-0 Juraj ANCIC (21'), 3-0 Filip
HOLOSKO (34'), 4-0 Michal POSPISIL (56'), 5-0 Petr PAPOUSEK (59').
Referee: Paulius MALZINSKAS (LIT)   Attendance: 3.150

10-07-2004   Letná Stadium, Zlín: FK Tescoma Zlín – KVC Westerlo 3-0 (2-0)
FK Tescoma Zlín: Vít BARÁNEK, Vlastimil VIDLICKA, Zdenik KROCA, Jiri KOUBSKY,
David HUBÁCEK, Petr NOVOSAD (61' Bronislav CERVENKA), Jaroslav SVACH (70'
Roman DOBES), Edvard LASOTA, Josef LUKASTIK (81' Vít VRTILKA), Vladimir
MALÁR, Václav CINCALA.
KVC Westerlo: Bart DEELKENS, Sadio BA, Knut Henry HARALDSEN (NOR), Bobsam
ELEJIKO (55' Stijn VANGEFFELEN), Jo KEENAN (ENG), Pule Jeffrey NTUKA (46' Marc
WAGEMAKERS), Christiaan JANSSENS, Zdenek SVOBODA (CZE) (75' Simphiwe Boy-
Boy MOSIA), Jef DELEN, David PAAS, Tosin S.DOSUNMU (NGR).
Goals: FK Tescoma Zlín: 1-0 Václav CINCALA (12'0, 2-0 Josef LUKASTIK (25'), 3-0 Stijn
VANGEFFELEN (87' own goal).
Referee: Dietmar DRABEK (AUT)   Attendance: 2.350

10-07-2004   Jules Ottenstadion, Gentbrugge: KAA Gent – FK Vardar Skopje 1-0 (0-0)
KAA Gent: Frédéric HERPOEL, Jacky PEETERS (YC102), Stephen LAYBUTT (AUS)
(YC53), David VAN HOYWEGHEN, Björn DE CONINCK, Matthieu VERSCHUERE (FRA)
(86' Ersin MEHMEDOVIC (SBM)), Steve COOREMAN (74' Steven RIBUS (YC115)),
Mamar MAMOUNI (FRA), Wouter VRANCKEN (87' Ivica JARACOVIC (SBM)), Sandy
MARTENS, Nordin JBARI (YC42).
FK Vardar Skopje: Velimir ZDRAVKOVIC (SBM), Nikola DOSEVSKI (YC27), Aleksandar
VASOSKI (YC82), Blessing Chinedu ANYANVIU (NGR), Vlatko GROZDANOVSKI,
Jovica TRAJCEV, ROGÉRIO da Costa Oliveira (BRA) (61' Danio MASEV), Zarko
SERAFIMOVSKI (69' Srdjan ZAHARIEVSKI), Oliveira WANDEIR Dos Santos (BRA),
Darko TASEVSKI (111' Almir BAJRAMOVSKI (YC115)), Bojan MARKOSKI.
Goal: KAA Gent: 1-0 Nikola DOSEVSKI (90' own goal).
Referee: Sinisa ZRNIC (BOS)   Attendance: 2.500
Penalties: 1 Mamar MAMOUNI   1 Oliveira WANDEIR Dos Santos
                 2 Steven RIBUS   * Nikola DOSEVSKI
                 3 Frédéric HERPOEL   2 Bojan MARKOSKI
                 * Björn DE CONINCK   3 Jovica TRAJCEV
                 * Ivica JARACOVIC   4 Danio MASEV

102

10-07-2004   Estadio El Madrigal, Villarreal: Villarreal CF – Odense BK   2-0 (2-0)
Villarreal CF: José Manuel REINA Páez, ARMANDO Miguel Correia de SÁ (BRA) (78'
Javier "JAVI" Rodríguez VENTA), Rodolfo Martín ARRUABARRENA (ARG) (YC66),
Sergio Martínez BALLESTEROS (68' GONZALO Javier RODRÍGUEZ (ARG)), Enrique
"QUIQUE" ÁLVAREZ Sanjuán, José Joaquín Moreno Verdú "JOSICO", Sebastián
BATTAGLIA (ARG), "SONNY" ANDERSON da Silva (BRA), HÉCTOR FONT Romero,
JOSÉ "MARI" María Romero Poyón (46' José Antonio GUAYRE Betancor Perdomo), Javier
CALLEJA Revilla. (Coach: Manuel Luis PELLEGRINI Ripamonti (CHI)).
Odense BK: Martin Sejer JENSEN, Steen NEDERGAARD, Jan SØNKSEN, Ulrich
VINZENTS, Chris SØRENSEN (81' Kenneth Møller PEDERSEN), Martin BORRE, Esben
HANSEN, Andrew TEMBO (ZAM), Thomas LINDRUP (67' Fernando DERVELD (HOL)),
Mwape MITI (ZAM) (46' Søren BERG ANDERSEN), Steffen HØJER. (Coach: Klavs
RASMUSSEN).
Goals: Villarreal CF: 1-0 JOSÉ "MARI" María Romero Poyón (23'), 2-0 HÉCTOR FONT
Romero (39').
Referee: Wolfgang SOWA (AUT)   Attendance: 4.000

11-07-2004   Turners Cross, Cork: Cork City FC – N.E.C. Nijmegen   1-0 (0-0)
Cork City FC: Michael DEVINE, Cillian LORDAN (YC90), Alan BENNETT, Daniel
MURRAY, Danny MURPHY, Kevin DOYLE, Colin O'BRIEN, George O'CALLAGHAN,
Liam KEARNEY, Neale FENN (89' Kevin MURRAY), John O'FLYNN.
N.E.C. Nijmegen: Dennis GENTENAAR, Pascal HEIJE (YC20) (81' Jarda SIMR (CZE)),
Patrick POTHUIZEN (YC6) (64' Peter WISGERHOF), Arjan EBBINGE, José VALENCIA
Murillo (ECU) (64' Alexander PRENT), Björn VAN DER DOELEN, Rob WIELAERT, Saïd
BOUTAHAR, Ronildo Pereira de Freitas "TININHO" (BRA), Frank DEMOUGE (YC38),
Romano DENNEBOOM.
Goal: Cork City FC: 1-0 Kevin DOYLE (47').
Referee: Sergiy BEREZKA (UKR)   Attendance: 7.500

11-07-2004   Stadion Sartid, Smederevo:
                FK Sartid Smederevo – FC Dinamo Minsk   1-3 (0-1)
FK Sartid Smederevo: Dragan JILIC, Ivan ZIVANOVIC (46' Nikola JEVTIC), Zeljko
KOVACEVIC, Marko SOCANAC, Nebojsa SAVIC, Sasa ZORIC (YC64), Dejan
KEKEZOVIC (YC45) (71' Miroslav GEGIC), Milorad ZECEVIC, Dragan
RADOSAVLJEVIC (64' Demir RAMOVIC), Nenad MIROSAVLJEVIC (YC89), Dragan
PAUNOVIC.
FC Dinamo Minsk: Yuri TSYGALKO, Dmitri CHALEI, Jan TIGOREV (YC88), Kirill
PAVLYUCHEK (RC57), Igor ROZHKOV (YC109), Vitali VOLODENKOV, Andrey RAZIN
(YC55), Sergey PAVLYUKOVICH (YC32), Aleksey DOBROVOLSKI (79' Anton PUTILO),
Yuri SHUKANOV, Leonid KOVEL (57' Dmitri LENTSEVICH).
Goals: FK Sartid Smederevo: 1-1 Nenad MIROSAVLJEVIC (89' penalty).
FC Dinamo Minsk: 0-1 Andrey RAZIN (45+' penalty), 0-2 Dmitri LENTSEVICH (74'), 1-2
Yuri SHUKANOV (94').
Referee: Johny VER EECKE (BEL)
(After extra time)

103

11-07-2004   Stadion Lachen, Thun: FC Thun – VfL Wolfsburg   4-1 (4-0)
FC Thun: Fabio COLTORTI, Nelson FERREIRA (POR), Armand DEUMI TCHAMI (CMR),
Selver HODZIC, Pascal CERRONE, Andreas GERBER, Michael RENGGLI, Mario
RAIMONDI (88' Samuel OJONG (CMR)), Silvan AEGERTER, Mauro LUSTRINELLI (56'
Adrian MOSER), Antonio DOS SANTOS (BRA) (57' BAYKAL Kulaksizoglu (TUR)).
VfL Wolfsburg: Simon JENTZSCH (YC), Thomas RYTTER (DEN) (20' Maik FRANZ),
Stefan SCHNOOR, Kevin HOFLAND (HOL), Patrick WEISER (75' Bartosz ROMANCZUK
(POL)), Miroslav KARHAN (SVK), Oscar AHUMADA (ARG) (YC), Hans SARPEI, Roy
PRÄGER (46' Cedric MAKIADI), Marko TOPIC (BOS), Juan Carlos MENSEGUEZ (ARG).
Goals: FC Thun: 1-0 Mauro LUSTRINELLI (21'), 2-0 Michael RENGGLI (35'), 3-0 Antonio
DOS SANTOS (42'), 4-0 Mario RAIMONDI (45'+2' penalty).
VfL Wolfsburg: 4-1 Hans SARPEI (78').
Referee: Ben H.HAVERKORT (HOL)   Attendance: 2.870

11-07-2004   Stade Municipal du Ray, Nice: O.G.C. Nice – Esbjerg FB   1-1 (1-0)
O.G.C. Nice: Damian GRÉGORINI, Noë PAMAROT, José COBOS (YC40), Jacques
ABARDONADO, Cédric VARRAULT (YC24) (81' Thibault SCOTTO Di Porfirio), Yoann
BIGNÉ, Romain PITAU (YC51), Olivier ECHOUAFNI, Sébastien ROUDET, Roland LINZ
(AUT), Christophe MESLIN.
Esbjerg FB: Lars WINDE, Kolja AFRIYIE (GER), Anders Møller CHRISTIANSEN, Martin
JENSEN, Nikolaj Jacobsen HØGH, Jan KRISTIANSEN (89' Kjetil PEDERSEN (NOR)),
Jerry Ruben LUCENA, Søren BARSLUND (73' Jakob POULSEN), Hans Henrik
ANDREASEN, Fredrik BERGLUND (SWE), Jess Christian THORUP.
Goals: O.G.C. Nice: 1-0 Cédric VARRAULT (45'+1').
Esbjerg FB: 1-1 Jerry Ruben LUCENA (89').
Referee: Alan KELLY (IRL)   Attendance: 8.665

11-07-2004   Loro Boriçi Stadium, Shkodër:
              KS Vllaznia Shkodër – NK Slaven Belupo Koprivnica   1-0 (1-0)
KS Vllaznia Shkodër: Orges SHEHI, Admir TELI, Ervis KRAJA, Edmond DOCI, Franc AHI
(69' Arsen BEQIRI), Erjon HOTI, Hamdi SALIHI, Amarildo BELISHA, Albert KAÇI,
January ZYAMBO (77' Senad MASHI), ABILIO Neves Dos Reis (BRA).
NK Slaven Belupo Koprivnica: Robert LISJAK, Petar BOSNJAK (YC6), Pavo CRNAC (61'
Mario MJATOVIC), Igor GAL (YC89), Dalibor BOZAC, Pero PEJIC (35' Danijel RADICEK,
54' Dalibor VISKOVIC), Ognjen VUKOJEVIC, Roy FERENCINA, Nikica SRPAK, Ivica
SERTIC, Bojan VRUCINA.
Goal: KS Vllaznia Shkodër: 1-0 ABILIO Neves Dos Reis (7').
Referee: Igorj ISHCHENKO (UKR)   Attendance: 8.000

THIRD ROUND

17-07-2004   Fenix Stadion, Genk: KRC Genk – Borussia Dortmund   0-1 (0-1)
KRC Genk: Jan MOONS, Indridi SIGURDSSON (ISL), Eric MATOUKOU (CMR) (YC33),
Gert CLAESSENS, Daan VAESEN, Koen DAERDEN, Justice WAMFOR (CMR), Kenneth
VAN GOETHEM (46' Igor DE CAMARGO (BRA)), Dimitri DE CONDÉ (70' Kevin
VANDENBERGH), Thomas CHATELLE (82' Mirsad BESLIJA (BOS)), Paul KPAKA
(SLE).
Borussia Dortmund: Guillaume WARMUZ (FRA), Aparecido EVANILSON (BRA), Florian
KRINGE, EWERTHON Henrique de Souza (BRA) (90'+1' Mehmet AKGÜN), Sunday
OLISEH (NGR), Leonardo de Deus Santos "DÉDÉ" (BRA), Lars RICKEN (78' Sebastian
KEHL), Ahmed MADOUNI (FRA), David ODONKOR (YC44), Saher SENESIE (74' Mahir
SAGLIK (TUR)), André BERGDØLMO (NOR).
Goal: Borussia Dortmund: 0-1 David ODONKOR (42').
Referee: Duarte Nuno PEREIRA GOMES (POR)   Attendance: 16.832

17-07-2004   Stadion Lachen, Thun: FC Thun – Hamburger SV   2-2 (2-0)
FC Thun: Fabio COLTORTI, Nelson FERREIRA (POR) (YC70) Armand DEUMI TCHAMI
(CMR), Selver HODZIC, Pascal CERRONE, Andreas GERBER, Michael RENGGLI, Mario
RAIMONDI, Silvan AEGERTER, Mauro LUSTRINELLI (60' Samuel OJONG (CMR)),
Antonio DOS SANTOS (BRA) (46' BAYKAL Kulaksizoglu (TUR)).
Hamburger SV: Stefan WÄCHTER, Björn SCHLICKE, Daniel VAN BUYTEN (BEL),
Raphael WICKY (SUI), Collin BENJAMIN (NAM), David JAROLIM (CZE), Stefan
BEINLICH, Stephan KLING, Sergej BARBAREZ (BOS) (YC65), Emile MPENZA (BEL),
Bernardo Daniel ROMEO (ARG).
Goals: FC Thun: 1-0 Antonio DOS SANTOS (28'), 2-0 Mario RAIMONDI (31' penalty).
Hamburger SV: 2-1Bernardo Daniel ROMEO (50'), 2-2 Bernardo Daniel ROMEO (85').
Referee: Selçuk DERELI (TUR)   Attendance: 4.150

17-07-2004   Shinnik Stadium, Yaroslavl:
              FC Shinnik Yaroslavl – União Desportiva Leiria   1-4 (1-1)
FC Shinnik Yaroslavl: Alexander MALYSHEV, Yevgeniy KAREV, Wilians Rodriges ILSON
(BRA), Rahmatullo FUZAILOV (UZB), Viacheslav SHEVCHUK (UKR), Yaroslav
KHARITONSKI, Evgen LUTSENKO (UKR) (46' Igor SHTUKIN), Artiem ZASYADVOVK
(UKR), Alexander TUMENKO, Anton ARKHIPOV (YC26,YC61), Martin KOUCHEV
(BUL) (56' Dmitry VASILYEV).
União Desportiva Leiria: HELTON da Silva Arruda (BRA), JOÃO PAULO Andrade,
RENATO Jorge Magalhães Dias Assunção (74' HUGO Filipe Silva CUNHA), GABRIEL
Fernando Atz (BRA), Luís Miguel da Assunção Joaquim "ALHANDRA", PAULO Jorge de
Sousa GOMES, Nuno Filipe Rodrigues LARANJEIRO, EDSON Luíz da Silva (BRA),
MÁRIO Jorge Costa CARLOS (59' Carlos Manuel FANGUEIRO Soares), FÁBIO Alexandre
Duarte FELÍCIO (YC28), Petar KRPAN (CRO) (9' Frederico de Costa Roque dos Santos
"FREDDY" (ANG)).
Goals: FC Shinnik Yaroslavl: 1-0 Yaroslav KHARITONSKI (16').
União Desportiva Leiria: 1-1 Nuno Filipe Rodrigues LARANJEIRO (42'), 1-2 FÁBIO
Alexandre Duarte FELÍCIO (73'), 1-3 Carlos Manuel FANGUEIRO Soares (76'), 1-4 EDSON
Luíz da Silva (90+').
Referee: Jonas ERIKSSON (SWE)   Attendance: 2.000

17-07-2004   Arena AufSchalke, Gelsenkirchen:
FC Schalke 04 – FK Vardar Skopje 5-0 (2-0)
FC Schalke 04: Frank ROST, Niels OUDE KAMPHUIS (HOL) (85' Tim HOOGLAND),
Tomasz WALDOCH (POL), Mladen KRSTAJIC (SBM), Christian PANDER, Hamit
ALTINTOP (TUR), Sven VERMANT (BEL) (74' Thomas KLÄSENER), Levan
KOBIASHVILI (GEO), Jörg BÖHME, Gerald ASAMOAH (85' Mike HANKE), Gonçalves
da Silva AILTON (BRA).
FK Vardar Skopje: Velimir ZDRAVKOVIC (SBM), Bojan MARKOSKI, Blessing Chinedu
ANYANVIU (NGR), Aleksandar VASOSKI, Nikola DOSEVSKI, Jovica TRAJCEV (46'
Zlatko TANEVSKI), Vlatko GROZDANOVSKI (52' Almir BAJRAMOVSKI (YC79)), Darko
TASEVSKI, ROGÉRIO da Costa Oliveira (BRA), Zarko SERAFIMOVSKI (46' Danio
MASEV), Oliveira WANDEIR Dos Santos (BRA).
Goals: FC Schalke 04: 1-0 Mladen KRSTAJIC (19'), 2-0 Hamit ALTINTOP (41'), 3-0
Gonçalves da Silva AILTON (49'), 4-0 Thomas KLÄSENER (81'), 5-0 Zlatko TANEVSKI
(90'+4' *own goal*).
Referee: Milan SEDIVY (CZE)   Attendance: 56.054

17-07-2004   Stadion u Nisy, Liberec: FC Slovan Liberec – SV Roda JC 1-0 (1-0)
FC Slovan Liberec: Zbyněk HAUZR, Peter SINGLÁR (SVK), Petr LUKÁS, Jozef
VALACHOVIC (SVK), Josef HAMOUZ, Miroslav SLEPICKA (80' Juraj ANCIC (SVK)),
Jan POLÁK (62' Jan BROSCHINSKY), Ivan HODÚR (SVK) (46' David LANGER), Petr
PAPOUSEK, Michal POSPISIL, Filip HOLOSKO (SVK).
SV Roda JC: Vladan KUJOVIC (SBM), Ger SENDEN, Roel BROUWERS (YC8), Mark
LUIJPERS, Boldiszár BODOR (HUN), Predrag FILIPOVIC (SBM), Gregoor VAN DIJK,
SERGIO Pacheco de Oliveira (BRA) (46' Ivan VICELICH (NZL)), Kevin VAN DESSEL
(BEL), Arouna KONÉ (CIV), CRISTIANO Dos Santos Rodrigues (BRA).
Goal: FC Slovan Liberec: 1-0 Petr PAPOUSEK (19').
Referee: Viktor KASSAI (HUN)   Attendance: 4.580

17-07-2004   Stadium Nord Lille Métropole, Villeneuve d'Ascq:
Lille Olympique SC – FC Dinamo Minsk 2-1 (2-1)
Lille Olympique SC: Yohann LACROIX, Grégory TAFFOREAU, Stéphane DUMONT,
DANTÉ Bonfim Costa Santos (BRA), Nicolas PLESTAN, Christophe LANDRIN (46'
Geoffrey DERNIS), Mathieu CHALMÉ, Mathieu BODMER, Matt MOUSSILOU (77' Nicolas
FAUVERGUE), Philippe BRUNEL, Milenko ACIMOVIC (SLO) (60' Mathieu DEBUCHY).
FC Dinamo Minsk: Yuri TSYGALKO, Dmitri CHALEI, Sergey PAVLYUKOVICH, Jan
TIGOREV (YC61), Andrey RAZIN, Aleksey DOBROVOLSKI (75' Dmitri LENTSEVICH),
Igor ROZHKOV, Petar ZLATINOV (BUL) (56' Viktor SOKOL), Vitali VOLODENKOV
(YC84), Leonid KOVEL, Yuri SHUKANOV (67' Vitali LEDENEV).
Goals: Lille Olympique SC: 1-0 Nicolas PLESTAN (23'), 2-1 Matt MOUSSILOU (29').
FC Dinamo Minsk: 1-1 Leonid KOVEL (26').
Referee: Pieter VINK (HOL)   Attendance: 7.330

106

17-07-2004   Gradski Stadion, Kopricnica:
NK Slaven Belupo Koprivnica – FC Spartak Trnava   0-0
NK Slaven Belupo Koprivnica: Robert LISJAK, Dario BRGLES, Igor GAL (YC53), Marko
JURIC, Davor RADIC, Krunoslav JAMBRUSIC (64' Mario MJATOVIC), Ante SARLIJA,
Dean SOMOCI, Dario BODRUSIC, Pero PEJIC (81' Petar BOSNJAK), Alen GUC (YC36)
(65' Ivica SERTIC).
FC Spartak Trnava: Lubos KAMENAR, Jaroslav HRABAL, Martin POLJOVKA, Pavol
STANO, Roman SIMKO (YC84), Souleymane FALL (SEN) (62' Peter HODÙR), Kamil
KOPÙNEK, Peter DURIS, Martin HUSÁR (77' Vladimir KOZUCH), Miroslav KRISS (90'
Pavol MASARYK), Marek UJLAKY.
Referee: Jari MAISONLAHTI (FIN)   Attendance: 1.000

17-07-2004   Letná Stadium, Zlín: FK Tescoma Zlín – Club Atlético Madrid   2-4 (0-1)
FK Tescoma Zlín: Otakar NOVÁK, Vlastimil VIDLICKA, Zdenik KROCA, Jaroslav SVACH,
David HUBÁCEK (YC38), Bronislav CERVENKA (77' Petr NOVOSAD), Roman DOBES
(88' Marcel LICKA), Edvard LASOTA, Josef LUKASTIK, Václav CINCALA (46' Vít
VRTELKA), Vladimir MALÁR. (Coach: Vlastimil PALICKA).
Club Atlético Madrid: Leonardo "LEO" Neoren FRANCO (ARG), Luis Amaranto PEREA
Mosquera (COL), José Antonio GARCÍA CALVO, PABLO Ibáñez Tebar, SERGI Barjuán
Esclusa, Diego Pablo SIMEONE (ARG) (YC79), Gabriel "GABI" Fernández Arenas (YC56)
(86' Santiago "SANTI" Denía Sánchez), Álvaro NOVO Ramírez (58' Carlos AGUILERA
Martin), Ariel Miguel Santiago IBAGAZA, Kizito "Kiki" MUSAMPA (HOL), Javíer "JAVI"
MORENO Varela (63' Veljko PAUNOVIC (SBM)). (Coach: César FERRANDO).
Goals: FK Tescoma Tlín: 1-1 Jaroslav SVACH (51'), 2-4 Jaroslav SVACH (88').
Club Atlético Madrid: 0-1 Álvaro NOVO Ramirez (1'), 1-2 Veljko PAUNOVIC (71'), 1-3
Kizito "Kiki" MUSAMPA (82'), 1-4 Veljko PAUNOVIC (85').
Referee: Pasquale RODOMONTI (ITA)   Attendance: 4.500

17-07-2004   Estadio El Madrigal, Villarreal: Villarreal CF – FC Spartak Moskva   1-0 (0-0)
Villarreal CF: José Manuel REINA Páez (46' Javier LÓPEZ VALLEJO), ARMANDO Miguel
Correia de SÁ (BRA), Enrique "QUIQUE" ÁLVAREZ Sanjuán, Sergio Martínez
BALLESTEROS, Rodolfo Martín ARRUABARRENA (ARG), HÉCTOR FONT Romero,
Sebastián BATTAGLIA (ARG) (YC12), José Joaquín Moreno Verdú "JOSICO", ROGER
García Junyent (68' Santiago "SANTI" CAZORLA González (YC85)), JOSÉ "MARI" María
Romero Poyón (79' VÍCTOR Manuel Fernández Gutiérrez (YC86)), "SONNY" ANDERSON
da Silva (BRA). (Coach: Manuel Luis PELLEGRINI Ripamonti (CHI)).
FC Spartak Moskva: Wojciech KOWALEWSKI (POL), Yuriy KOVTUN (YC38), Florin
SOAVA (ROM), Adrian IENCSI (ROM), Igor MITREVSKI (MCD) (YC39), Kamaloutdin
AKHMEDOV, Goran TROBOK (SBM), Aleksandr PAVLENKO, Alexandr SAMEDOV
(AZE) (YC29) (78' Vladimir LESHONOK), Maxim KALYNYCHENKO (UKR) (56' Pavel
POGREBNYAK), Roman PAVLYUCHENKO. (Coach: Nevio SCALA (ITA)).
Goal: Villarreal CF: 1-0 "SONNY" ANDERSON da Silva (51').
Referee: Matteo TREFOLONI (ITA)   Attendance: 7.000

107

18-07-2004   Vetros Stadionas, Vilnius: FK Vetra Rudiskes Vilnius – Esbjerg FB   1-1 (0-1)
FK Vetra Rudiskes Vilnius: Marius POSKUS, Zydrunas GRUDZINSKAS, Nerijus
SASNAUSKAS, Julius RALIUKONIS (YC30), Zilvinas ZUDYS, Clement BEAUD (CMR),
Gintaras RIMKUS, Darvydas SERNAS (76' Awenayeri DOUGLAS (NGR)), Ramunas
STONKUS (46' Rolandas VAINEIKIS), Nerijus VASILIAUSKAS (46' Saulius
KIJANSKAS), Vytautas KARVELIS.
Esbjerg FB: Lars WINDE, Anders Møller CHRISTIANSEN, Kolja AFRIYIE (GER) (YC28),
Martin JENSEN, Nikolaj Jacobsen HØGH (46' Kjetil PEDERSEN (NOR)), Jan
KRISTIANSEN (65' Tommy LØVENKRANDS), Hans Henrik ANDREASEN, Jerry Ruben
LUCENA, Søren BARSLUND (46' Jakob POULSEN), Fredrik BERGLUND (SWE), Jess
Christian THORUP.
Goals: FK Vetra Rudiskes Vilnius: 1-1 Vytautas KARVELIS (69').
Esbjerg FB: 0-1 Jess Christian THORUP (41').
Referee: Daniel STALHAMMAR (SWE)   Attendance: 2.200

18-07-2004   Stade de la Beaujoire, Nantes: FC Nantes Atlantique – Cork City FC   3-1 (2-0)
FC Nantes Atlantique: Willy GRONDIN, Loïc GUILLON, Stéphen DROUIN, Frédéric DA
ROCHA, Nicolas SAVINAUD, Aurélien CAPOUE, Olivier QUINT, Jérémy TOULALAN,
Emerse FAÉ (57' David LERAY), Loïc PAILLÈRES, Hassan AHAMADA (68' Luigi
GLOMBARD).
Cork City FC: Michael DEVINE, Cillian LORDAN, Alan BENNETT, Daniel MURRAY,
Danny MURPHY (YC26), Kevin DOYLE (YC65), Colin O'BRIEN (YC13), George
O'CALLAGHAN, Liam KEARNEY, Neale FENN, John O'FLYNN.
Goals: FC Nantes Atlantique: 1-0 Olivier QUINT (11'), 2-0 Hassan AHAMADA (22'), 3-0
Frédéric DA ROCHA (65').
Cork City FC: 3-1 Neale FENN (79').
Referee: Joao Francisco LOPES FERREIRA (POR)   Attendance: 11.056

18-07-2004   Ratina Stadium, Tampere: Tampere United FC – O.F.K. Beograd   0-0
Tampere United FC: Mikko KAVEN, Antti OJANPERÄ (46' Toni JUNNILA), Jussi
KUOPPALA, Antti HYNYNEN (62' Mika LAHTINEN), Antti POHJA, Sakari SAARINEN,
Jarkko WISS, Petri HEINÄNEN, Kari SAINIO, Heikko AHO, Janne RÄSÄNEN.
O.F.K. Beograd: Nikola DAMJANAC, Branislav IVANOVIC, Marko BASA, Djordje JOKIC,
Aleksandar SIMIC (66' Ivan CVETKOVIC), Boris VASKOVIC, Branko BAKOVIC, Dusko
TOSIC, Vladimir BOZOVIC, Igor MATIC, Milos KOLAKOVIC.
Referee: Joeri VAN DER VELDE (BEL)

24-07-2004   Westfalenstadion, Dortmund: Borussia Dortmund – KRC Genk   1-2 (0-1)
Borussia Dortmund: Guillaume WARMUZ (FRA), Aparecido EVANILSON (BRA), Ahmed
MADOUNI (FRA) (RC90), André BERGDØLMO (NOR), Leonardo de Deus Santos "DÉDÉ"
(BRA), Sunday OLISEH (NGR) (73' Guy DEMEL (FRA)), Lars RICKEN (46' Sebastian
KEHL), Florian KRINGE, David ODONKOR, Saher SENESIE (46' Mahir SAGLIK (TUR)),
EWERTHON Henrique de Souza (BRA).
KRC Genk: Jan MOONS, Brian PRISKE (DEN), Eric MATOUKOU (CMR) (YC60), Gert
CLAESSENS, Indridi SIGURDSSON (ISL), Mirsad BESLIJA (BOS) (85' Dimitri DE
CONDÉ), Justice WAMFOR (CMR), Soley SEYFO (GAM) (67' Faris HAROUN), Thomas
CHATELLE (35' Paul KPAKA (SLE)), Kevin VANDENBERGH, Igor DE CAMARGO
(BRA).
Goals: Borussia Dortmund: 1-1 Leonardo de Deus Santos "DÉDÉ" (55').
KRC Genk: 0-1 Igor DE CAMARGO (13'), 1-2 Igor DE CAMARGO (86').
Referee: Alberto UNDIANO MALLENCO (ESP)   Attendance: 47.800

108

24-07-2004   Stadion ved Messecenter, Herning:
Esbjerg FB – FK Vetra Rudiskes Vilnius   4-0 (3-0)
Esbjerg FB: Lars WINDE, Kolja AFRIYIE (GER), Anders Møller CHRISTIANSEN, Nikolaj
Jacobsen HØGH, Martin JENSEN, Søren BARSLUND (55' Jakob POULSEN), Hans Henrik
ANDREASEN (55' Henrik HANSEN), Jerry Ruben LUCENA, Jan KRISTIANSEN, Fredrik
BERGLUND (SWE), Jess Christian THORUP (55' Lass KRYGER JØRGENSEN).
FK Vetra Rudiskes Vilnius: Marius POSKUS, Zydrunas GRUDZINSKAS (36' Awenayeri
DOUGLAS (NGR)), Nerijus SASNAUSKAS, Julius RALIUKONIS, Zilvinas ZUDYS,
Clement BEAUD (CMR) (YC23), Gintaras RIMKUS (77' Ramunas STONKUS), Darvydas
SERNAS, Saulius KIJANSKAS (YC21), Rolandas VAINEIKIS (56' Gediminas
BUTRIMAVICIUS), Vytautas KARVELIS.
Goals: Esbjerg FB: 1-0 Fredrik BERGLUND (3'), 2-0 Fredrik BERGLUND (8'), 3-0 Fredrik
BERGLUND (36'), 4-0 Jess Christian THORUP (47' penalty).
Referee: Knut KIRCHER (GER)   Attendance: 982

24-07-2004   Parkstad Limburg Stadion, Kerkrade:
SV Roda JC – FC Slovan Liberec   1-1 (1-0)
SV Roda JC: Vladan KUJOVIC (SBM), Ger SENDEN, Roel BROUWERS, Mark LUIJPERS
(YC24) (109' Mohammed ELBERKANI (MAR)), Boldiszár BODOR (HUN) (97' Edrissa
SONKO (GAM)), Predrag FILIPOVIC (SBM), Gregoor VAN DIJK (YC32), Ivan VICELICH
(NZL), Kevin VAN DESSEL (BEL) (75' SERGIO Pacheco de Oliveira (BRA)), Arouna
KONÉ (CIV), CRISTIANO Dos Santos Rodrigues (BRA).
FC Slovan Liberec: Zbynék HAUZR, Petr LUKÁS, Jozef VALACHOVIC (SVK), Pavel
KOSTAL (YC53), Josef HAMOUZ, Peter SINGLÁR (SVK) (106' Juraj ANCIC (SVK)), Ivan
HODÚR (SVK) (YC44) (71' Jan BROSCHINSKY), Jan POLÁK (YC89), Petr PAPOUSEK,
Michal POSPISIL (98' Miroslav SLEPICKA), Filip HOLOSKO (SVK).
Goals: SV Roda JC: 1-0 CRISTIANO Dos Santos Rodrigues (15').
FC Slovan Liberec: 1-1 Filip HOLOSKO (109').
Referee: Alfonso PÉREZ BURRULL (ESP)   Attendance: 6.850
(After extra time)

24-07-2004   Dinamo Stadium, Minsk: FC Dinamo Minsk – Lille Olympique SC   2-2 (1-1)
FC Dinamo Minsk: Yuri TSYGALKO, Dmitri CHALEI, Sergey PAVLYUKOVICH, Jan
TIGOREV, Andrey RAZIN, Dmitri LENTSEVICH (86' Sergey KONTSEV), Igor
ROZHKOV, David ZOUBEK (CZE) (73' Anton PUTILO), Viktor SOKOL (YC40) (58'
Aleksey DOBROVOLSKI), Vitali VOLODENKOV, Leonid KOVEL.
Lille Olympique SC: Tony SYLVA (SEN), Grégory TAFFOREAU, DANTÉ Bonfim Costa
Santos (BRA), Nicolas PLESTAN, Philippe BRUNEL (YC40), Christophe LANDRIN,
Mathieu CHALMÉ, Stéphane DUMONT (52' Jean II MAKOUN (CMR)), Mathieu BODMER
(71' Mathieu DEBUCHY), Milenko ACIMOVIC (SLO), Matt MOUSSILOU (75' Nicolas
RAYNIER).
Goals: FC Dinamo Minsk: 1-0 Andrey RAZIN (33'), 2-1 Leonid KOVEL (50').
Lille Olympique SC: 1-1 Matt MOUSSILOU (41'), 2-2 Matt MOUSSILOU (66').
Referee: Mikko VUORELA (FIN)   Attendance: 3.000

24-07-2004   Gradski Stadion, Skopje: FK Vardar Skopje – FC Schalke 04   1-2 (0-2)
FK Vardar Skopje: Velimir ZDRAVKOVIC (SBM), Nikola DOSEVSKI, Aleksandar
VASOSKI (YC25), Blessing Chinedu ANYANVIU (NGR) (65' Nikola GLIGOROV), Bojan
MARKOSKI, Vlatko GROZDANOVSKI, Jovica TRAJCEV (65' Almir BAJRAMOVSKI
(YC80)), Zarko SERAFIMOVSKI (YC17) (87' Danio MASEV), Darko TASEVSKI, Oliveira
WANDEIR Dos Santos (BRA), Jovan KOSTOVSKI.
FC Schalke 04: Frank ROST, Thomas KLÄSENER, Mladen KRSTAJIC (SBM), Levan
KOBIASHVILI (GEO), Hamit ALTINTOP (TUR) (77' Mike HANKE), Jörg BÖHME (YC50)
(59' Michael DELURA), Cassio de Souza Soares LINCOLN (BRA), Sven VERMANT (BEL)
(YC36), Christian PANDER, Gonçalves da Silva AILTON (BRA), Ebbe SAND (DEN) (71'
Gerald ASAMOAH).
Goals: FK Vardar Skopje: 1-2 Oliveira WANDEIR Dos Santos (84').
FC Schalke 04: 0-1 Christian PANDER (4'), 0-2 Ebbe SAND (15').
Referee: Carlo BERTOLINI (SUI)   Attendance: 3.000

24-07-2004   Omladinski Stadion, Beograd:
              O.F.K. Beograd – Tampere United FC   1-0 (0-0)
O.F.K. Beograd: Nikola DAMJANAC, Branislav IVANOVIC (68' Ivan CVETKOVIC),
Marko BASA, Djordje JOKIC, Dusko TOSIC, Aleksandar SIMIC, Boris VASKOVIC, Branko
BAKOVIC (YC17), Igor MATIC (87' Vladimir BOZOVIC), Milan MRDAKOVIC (80' Rade
VUKOTIC), Milos KOLAKOVIC (YC90+2).
Tampere United FC: Mikko KAVEN, Heikki AHO, Jussi KUOPPALA, Janne RÄSÄNEN
(YC90+2), Petri HEINÄNEN (YC64), Jarkko WISS (YC36), Kari SAINIO, Sakari
SAARINEN (YC38), Antti POHJA, Mika LAHTINEN (77' Antti OJANPERÄ), Toni
JUNNILA (58' Antti HYNYNEN).
Goal: O.F.K. Beograd: 1-0 Marko BASA (76').
Referee: Marian Mircea SALOMIR (ROM)   Attendance: 2.000

24-07-2004   Stadión Antona Malatinského, Trnava:
              FC Spartak Trnava – NK Slaven Belupo Koprivnica   2-2 (0-2)
FC Spartak Trnava: Lubos KAMENAR, Jaroslav HRABAL (70' Souleymane FALL (SEN)),
Martin POLJOVKA, Pavol STANO, Andrej FILIP (38' Vladimir KOZUCH), Peter HODÚR,
Kamil KOPÙNEK, Peter DURIS (YC12), Michal GASPARIK (78' Tomás BARTOS), Marek
UJLAKY, Miroslav KRISS (YC27).
NK Slaven Belupo Koprivnica: Robert LISJAK, Petar BOSNJAK (YC..,YC86), Jurica
KARABATIC, Igor GAL (YC20), Dalibor VISKOVIC, Pero PEJIC (YC41) (70' Tomoslav
KELEMEN), Ognjen VUKOJEVIC, Roy FERENCINA (YC59), Dario BODRUSIC, Alen
GUC (46' Ivica SERTIC), Ivica KARABOGDAN (88' Marko JURIC).
Goals: FC Spartak Trnava: 1-2 Vladimir KOZUCH (49'), 2-2 Marek UJLAKY (58').
NK Slaven Bepulo Koprivnica: 0-1 Roy FERENCINA (16'), 0-2 Alen GUC (29').
Referee: Alexander GVARDIS (RUS)   Attendance: 2.098

110

24-07-2004   Luzhniki Stadium, Moskva: FC Spartak Moskva – Villarreal CF   2-2 (2-1)
FC Spartak Moskva: Wojciech KOWALEWSKI (POL), Kamaloutdin AKHMEDOV (YC87),
Florin SOAVA (ROM) (63' Roman SHISHKIN (YC69)), Dusan PETKOVIC (SBM), Igor
MITREVSKI (MCD), Gabriel Sebastian TAMAS (ROM), Goran TROBOK (SBM) (66'
Tarmo KINK (EST)), Aleksandr PAVLENKO, Alexandr SAMEDOV (AZE) (YC25) (71'
Vladimir LESHONOK), Sergej KOVALCHUK, Roman PAVLYUCHENKO. (Coach: Nevio
SCALA (ITA)).
Villarreal CF: José Manuel REINA Páez, ARMANDO Miguel Correia de SÁ (BRA), Enrique
"QUIQUE" ÁLVAREZ Sanjuán, Sergio Martínez BALLESTEROS (YC72), Rodolfo Martín
ARRUABARRENA (ARG) (YC78), Santiago "SANTI" CAZORLA González, Sebastián
BATTAGLIA (ARG), José Joaquín Moreno Verdú "JOSICO", ROGER García Junyent (84'
HÉCTOR FONT Romero), JOSÉ "MARI" María Romero Poyón, "SONNY" ANDERSON da
Silva (BRA) (58' VÍCTOR Manuel Fernández Gutiérrez). (Coach: Manuel Luis PELLEGRINI
Ripamonti (CHI)).
Goals: FC Spartak Moskva: 1-0 Roman PAVLYUCHENKO (11'), 2-1 Roman
PAVLYUCHENKO (36').
Villarreal CF: 1-1"SONNY" ANDERSON da Silva (32'), 2-2 ROGER García Junyent (52').
Referee: Craig Alexander THOMSON (SCO)   Attendance: 12.000
(This game was played on synthetic turf)

24-07-2004   AOL Arena, Hamburg: Hamburger SV – FC Thun   3-1 (1-0)
Hamburger SV: Martin PIECKENHAGEN, Björn SCHLICKE (71' Bastian REINHARDT),
Daniel VAN BUYTEN (BEL), Stephan KLING, Raphael WICKY (SUI), David JAROLIM
(CZE), Stefan BEINLICH (75' Oliver HAMPEL), Collin BENJAMIN (NAM), Bernardo
Daniel ROMEO (ARG), Sergej BARBAREZ (BOS) (20' Christian RAHN), Emile MPENZA
(BEL).
FC Thun: Fabio COLTORTI, Selver HODZIC, Michael RENGGLI, Pascal CERRONE,
Andreas GERBER, Armand DEUMI TCHAMI (CMR), Silvan AEGERTER, Antonio DOS
SANTOS (BRA) (78' Adrian MOSER), BAYKAL Kulaksizoglu (TUR), Mauro
LUSTRINELLI (65' Samuel OJONG (CMR)), Nelson FERREIRA (POR).
Goals: Hamburger SV: 1-0 Bernardo Daniel ROMEO (2'), 2-0 Emile MPENZA (66'), 3-0
Bernardo Daniel ROMEO (72').
FC Thun: 3-1 Adrian MOSER (81').
Referee: Pascal GARIBIAN (FRA)   Attendance: 27.117

24-07-2004   Turners Cross, Cork: Cork City FC – FC Nantes   1-1 (1-0)
Cork City FC: Michael DEVINE, Cillian LORDAN (81' Jamie NOLAN), Alan BENNETT,
Daniel MURRAY (YC47) (90'+3' Darragh William WOODS), Danny MURPHY, Kevin
DOYLE, George O'CALLAGHAN, Colin O'BRIEN (YC77), Liam KEARNEY, John
O'FLYNN, Neale FENN (81' Michael NWANKWO (NGR)).
FC Nantes: Willy GRONDIN, Julio César CÁCERES López (PAR), Loïc GUILLON, Frédéric
DA ROCHA, Nicolas SAVINAUD, Aurélien CAPOUE (YC23), Olivier QUINT (90'+1'
Stéphen DROUIN), Mathieu BERSON (74' Fodil HADJADJ (ALG)), Jérémy TOULALAN,
Mamadou BAGAYOKO (MLI) (64' Grégory PUYOL), Hassan AHAMADA (YC34,YC76).
Goals: Cork City FC: 1-0 Kevin DOYLE (6').
FC Nantes: 1-1 Grégory PUYOL (73').
Referee: Uriah Duddley RENNIE (ENG)   Attendance: 7.500

111

24-07-2004   Estádio Dr. Magalhães Pessoa, Leiria:
União Desportiva Leiria – FC Shinnik Yaroslavl   2-1 (1-0)
União Desportiva Leiria: HELTON da Silva Arruda (BRA), JOÃO PAULO Andrade,
RENATO Jorge Magalhães Dias Assunção (YC56), GABRIEL Fernando Atz (BRA), Nuno
Filipe Rodrigues LARANJEIRO, PAULO Jorge de Sousa GOMES (YC24) (63' Pedro Miguel
Ferreira Silva TORRÃO), EDSON Luíz da Silva (BRA) (75' Aírton Graciliano dos Santos
"CAÍCO" (BRA)), Luís Miguel da Assunção Joaquim "ALHANDRA" (YC29), Carlos Manuel
FANGUEIRO Soares (58' MÁRIO Jorge Costa CARLOS), Frederico de Costa Roque dos
Santos "FREDDY" (ANG), FÁBIO Alexandre Duarte FELÍCIO.
FC Shinnik Yaroslavl: Alexander MALYSHEV, Mihail Vladimirovich STAROSTYAK
(UKR) (YC72), Krzysztof LAGIEWKA (POL), Rahmatullo FUZAILOV (UZB), Emir
SPAHIC (BOS), Alexander TUMENKO, Artiem ZASYADVOVK (UKR), Viktor
KARPENKO (UZB) (58' Evgen LUTSENKO (UKR) (YC81)), Sergey GRISHIN (46'
Viacheslav SHEVCHENKO (UKR)), Aleksandr SHIRKO (70' Martin KOUCHEV (BUL)),
Andrej RUBINS (LAT).
Goals: União Desportiva Leiria: 1-0 Frederico de Costa Roque dos Santos "FREDDY" (36'),
2-0 FÁBIO Alexandre Duarte FELÍCIO (54').
FC Shinnik Yaroslavl: 2-1 Evgen LUTSENKO (61').
Referee: Alojzije SUPRAHA (CRO)   Attendance: 1.269

24-07-2004   Estadio Vicente Calderón, Madrid:
Club Atlético Madrid – FK Tescoma Zlín   0-2 (0-1)
Club Atlético Madrid: Leonardo "LEO" Neoren FRANCO (ARG), Luis Amaranto PEREA
Mosquera (COL), José Antonio GARCÍA CALVO (YC84), PABLO Ibáñez Tebar, Antonio
LÓPEZ Guerrero, Diego Pablo SIMEONE (ARG), Álvaro NOVO Ramirez (YC36) (53'
Carlos AGUILERA Martin (YC61)), JORGE Larena Avellaneda Roig (55' FERNANDO José
TORRES Sanz), Ariel Miguel Santiago IBAGAZA, Fernando "NANO" Macedo Da Silva
Rodilla (8' Kizito "Kiki" MUSAMPA (HOL)), Veljko PAUNOVIC (SBM). (Coach: César
FERRANDO).
FK Tescoma Zlín: Vít BARÁNEK, Tomás JANÍCEK (YC24), Zdenik KROCA, Jaroslav
SVACH (YC7), David HUBÁCEK, Tomás DUJKA (83' Roman DOBES), Václav CINCALA
(53' Marcel LICKA), Edvard LASOTA, Vít VRTELKA, Bronislav CERVENKA, Vladimír
MALÁR (73' Josef LUKASTIK). (Coach: Vlastimil PALICKA).
Goals: FK Tescoma Zlín: 0-1 Vladimir MALÁR (11'), 0-2 Zdenik KROCA (70').
Referee: Jörg KESSLER (GER)   Attendance: 15.000

SEMI-FINALS

28-07-2004   Omladinski Stadion, Beograd:
               O.F.K. Beograd – Club Atlético Madrid   1-3 (0-2)
O.F.K. Beograd: Nikola DAMJANAC, Branislav IVANOVIC (69' Ivan CVETKOVIC),
Marko BASA, Djordje JOKIC, Dusko TOSIC, Aleksandar SIMIC, Boris VASKOVIC, Branko
BAKOVIC, Igor MATIC (46' Vladimir BOZOVIC), Miljan MRDAKOVIC, Milos
KOLAKOVIC. (Coach: Branko BABIC).
Club Atlético Madrid: Leonardo "LEO" Neoren FRANCO (ARG), Cosmin Marius CONTRA
(ROM) (YC37), Luis Amaranto PEREA Mosquera (COL), PABLO Ibáñez Tebar, SERGI
Barjuán Esclusa (YC38), Diego Pablo SIMEONE (ARG), Gonzalo COLSA Abendea (80'
Gabriel "GABI" Fernández Arenas), Carlos AGUILERA Martin, Ariel Miguel Santiago
IBAGAZA (74' Ángel Javier ARIZMENDI de Lucas), Kizito "Kiki" MUSAMPA (HOL),
FERNANDO José TORRES Sanz (67' Veljko PAUNOVIC (SBM)). (Coach: César
FERRANDO).
Goals: O.F.K. Beograd: 1-2 Aleksandar SIMIC (53').
Club Atlético Madrid: 0-1 Ariel Miguel Santiago IBAGAZA (20'), 0-2 FERNANDO José
TORRES Sanz (40' penalty), 1-3 Diego Pablo SIMEONE (66').
Referee: Nikolay IVANOV (RUS)   Attendance: 7.000

28-07-2004   Fenix Stadion, Genk: KRC Genk – União Desportiva Leiria   0-0
KRC Genk: Jan MOONS, Brian PRISKE (DEN), Eric MATOUKOU (CMR), Aaron
MOKOENA (RSA) (YC86), Indridi SIGURDSSON (ISL), Mirsad BESLIJA (BOS), Dimitri
DE CONDÉ (78' Koen DAERDEN), Justice WAMFOR (CMR) (YC46), Soley SEYFO
(GAM) (84' Faris HAROUN), Paul KPAKA (SLE) (62' Kevin VANDENBERGH), Igor DE
CAMARGO (BRA).
União Desportiva Leiria: HELTON da Silva Arruda (BRA), JOÃO PAULO Andrade,
RENATO Jorge Magalhães Dias Assunção (YC54), GABRIEL Fernando Atz (BRA), Nuno
Filipe Rodrigues LARANJEIRO, PAULO Jorge de Sousa GOMES (78' HUGO Miguel
Magalhães FARIA), Aírton Graciliano dos Santos "CAÍCO" (BRA) (85' Pedro Miguel Ferreira
Silva TORRÃO), Luís Miguel da Assunção Joaquim "ALHANDRA", EDSON Luíz da Silva
(BRA), Frederico de Costa Roque dos Santos "FREDDY" (ANG) (YC87), FÁBIO Alexandre
Duarte FELÍCIO (69' Carlos Manuel FANGUEIRO Soares).
Referee: Gianluca PAPARESTA (ITA)   Attendance: 7.513

28-07-2004   Stadium Nord Lille Métropole, Villeneuve d'Ascq:
               Lille Olympique SC – NK Slaven Belupo Koprivnica   3-0 (2-0)
Lille Olympique SC: Tony SYLVA (SEN), Rafael SCHMITZ (BRA), Grégory TAFFOREAU,
Nicolas PLESTAN, Philippe BRUNEL (62' Vladimir MANCHEV (BUL)), Christophe
LANDRIN, Mathieu CHALMÉ, Jean II MAKOUN (CMR), Mathieu BODMER, Milenko
ACIMOVIC (SLO) (YC35) (81' Mathieu DEBUCHY), Matt MOUSSILOU (62' Geoffrey
DERNIS).
NK Slaven Belupo Koprivnica: Robert LISJAK, Dalibor VISKOVIC, Dalibor BOZAC, Roy
FERENCINA, Ognjen VUKOJEVIC, Marko JURIC (52' Bojan VRUCINA), Pero PEJIC (64'
Dario BRGLES), Alen GUC, Dario BODRUSIC (59' Tomislav KELEMEN), Jurica
KARABATIC, Ivica KARABOGDAN.
Goals: Lille Olympique SC: 1-0 Christophe LANDRIN (7'), 2-0 Matt MOUSSILOU (28'), 3-0
Milenko ACIMOVIC (47').
Referee: Olegario Manuel BARTOLO FAUSTINO BENQUERENÇA (POR)
Attendance: 6.969

28-07-2004   Stadion u Nisy, Liberec: FC Slovan Liberec – FC Nantes Atlantique 1-0 (1-0)
FC Slovan Liberec: Zbynék HAUZR, Peter SINGLÁR (SVK), Petr LUKÁS, Jozef
VALACHOVIC (SVK), Miroslav SLEPICKA, Petr PAPOUSEK (46' Karol KISEL (SVK)),
Jan POLÁK, Ivan HODÚR (SVK) (89' Jan BROSCHINSKY), Josef HAMOUZ (YC49) (73'
Juraj ANCIC (SVK)), Michal POSPÍSIL (YC65), Filip HOLOSKO (SVK).
FC Nantes Atlantique: Willy GRONDIN, Julio César CÁCERES López (PAR), Loïc
GUILLON, Frédéric DA ROCHA (YC43,RC70), Nicolas SAVINAUD, Olivier QUINT
(YC13) (81' Aurélien CAPOUE), Stéphen DROUIN, Mathieu BERSON, Jérémy
TOULALAN, Mamadou BAGAYOKO (MLI) (72' Luigi GLOMBARD), Grégory PUYOL
(72' Florin BRATU (ROM)).
Goal: FC Slovan Liberec: 1-0 Michal POSPÍSIL (27').
Referee: Stefan MESSNER (AUT)   Attendance: 4.750

28-07-2004   Stadion ved Messecenter, Herning: Esbjerg FB – FC Schalke 04 1-3 (1-1)
Esbjerg FB: Lars WINDE, Anders Møller CHRISTIANSEN (82' Tommy LØVENKRANDS),
Kolja AFRIYIE (GER), Martin JENSEN, Nikolaj Jacobsen HØGH, Jan KRISTIANSEN, Hans
Henrik ANDREASEN, Jerry Ruben LUCENA, Søren BARSLUND (61' Jesper
JØRGENSEN), Jess Christian THORUP (61' Lass KRYGER JØRGENSEN), Fredrik
BERGLUND (SWE).
FC Schalke 04: Frank ROST, Tomasz WALDOCH (POL), Mladen KRSTAJIC (SBM), Levan
KOBIASHVILI (GEO), Hamit ALTINTOP (TUR) (90' Gerald ASAMOAH), Jörg BÖHME
(61' Cassio de Souza Soares LINCOLN (BRA)), Sven VERMANT (BEL), Niels OUDE
KAMPHUIS (HOL), Christian PANDER, Gonçalves da Silva AILTON (BRA), Ebbe SAND
(DEN) (61' Mike HANKE).
Goals: Esbjerg FB: 1-0 Jerry Ruben LUCENA (8').
FC Schalke 04: 1-1 Gonçalves da Silva AILTON (40'), 1-2 Mike HANKE (71'), 1-3 Hamit
ALTINTOP (87').
Referee: Mark Richard HALSEY (ENG)   Attendance: 8.000

28-07-2004   Estadio El Madrigal, Villarreal: Villarreal CF – Hamburger SV 1-0 (0-0)
Villarreal CF: José Manuel REINA Páez, ARMANDO Miguel Correia de SÁ (BRA) (81'
GONZALO Javier RODRÍGUEZ (ARG) (YC85)), Sergio Martínez BALLESTEROS, Enrique
"QUIQUE" ÁLVAREZ Sanjuán, Rodolfo Martín ARRUABARRENA (ARG), Sebastián
BATTAGLIA (ARG), José Joaquín Moreno Verdú "JOSICO", ROGER García Junyent (77'
HÉCTOR FONT Romero), Santiago "SANTI" CAZORLA González, JOSÉ "MARI" María
Romero Poyón, "SONNY" ANDERSON da Silva (BRA) (70' VÍCTOR Manuel Fernández
Gutiérrez). (Coach: Manuel Luis PELLEGRINI Ripamonti (CHI)).
Hamburger SV: Martin PIECKENHAGEN, Björn SCHLICKE (YC24) (54' Christian RAHN),
Bastian REINHARDT, Daniel VAN BUYTEN (BEL), Stephan KLING (YC68), Raphael
WICKY (SUI) (83' Oliver HAMPEL), David JAROLÍM (CZE), Stefan BEINLICH, Collin
BENJAMIN (NAM), Bernardo Daniel ROMEO (ARG), Emile MPENZA (BEL). (Coach:
Klaus TOPPMÖLLER).
Goal: Villarreal CF: 1-0 "SONNY" ANDERSON da Silva (51' penalty).
Referee: Johan VERBIST (BEL)   Attendance: 7.000

114

03-08-2004   Arean AufSchalke, Gelsenkirchen: FC Schalke 04 – Esbjerg FB   3-0 (1-0)
FC Schalke 04: Frank ROST, Niels OUDE KAMPHUIS (HOL), Tomasz WALDOCH (POL), Mladen KRSTAJIC (SBM), Levan KOBIASHVILI (GEO), Gerald ASAMOAH, Christian POULSEN (DEN), Hamit ALTINTOP (TUR) (71' Gustavo Antonio VARELA Rodríguez (URU)), Jörg BÖHME (64' Sven VERMANT (BEL)), Mike HANKE (64' Cassio de Souza Soares LINCOLN (BRA)), Gonçalves da Silva AILTON (BRA).
Esbjerg FB: Lars WINDE, Kolja AFRIYIE (GER) (61' Jesper JØRGENSEN), Anders Møller CHRISTIANSEN, Nikolaj Jacobsen HØGH, Martin JENSEN (YC16) (61' Tommy LØVENKRANDS), Jacob POULSEN, Jerry Ruben LUCENA, Hans Henrik ANDREASEN, Jan KRISTIANSEN, Fredrik BERGLUND (SWE), Jess Christian THORUP (76' Lass KRYGER JØRGENSEN).
Goals: FC Schalke 04: 1-0 Mike HANKE (11'), 2-0 Hamit ALTINTOP (54'), 3-0 Gerald ASAMOAH (63').
Referee: Carlos MEGIA DAVILA (ESP)   Attendance: 56.320

04-08-2004   Gradski Stadion, Koprivnica:
                NK Slaven Belupo Koprivnica – Lille Olympique SC   1-1 (1-0)
NK Slaven Belupo Koprivnica: Tomislav PELIN, Dalibor BOZAC, Marijo DODIK (56' Bojan VRUCINA), Dario BRGLES (46' Krunoslav JAMBRUSIC), Marko JURIC, SOMOCI, Pero PEJIC, Nikica SRPAK, Ante SARLIJA, Jurica KARABATIC, Tomislav KELEMEN (71' Davor RADIC (YC81)).
Lille Olympique SC: Tony SYLVA (SEN), DANTÉ Bonfim Costa Santos (BRA), Nicolas PLESTAN (76' Grégory TAFFOREAU), Rafael SCHMITZ (BRA), Christophe LANDRIN (63' Geoffrey DERNIS (YC85)), Mathieu CHALMÉ, Jean II MAKOUN (CMR) (63' Mathieu BODMER), Stéphane DUMONT, Milenko ACIMOVIC (SLO), Vladimir MANCHEV (BUL), Johan AUDEL.
Goals: NK Slavan Belupo Koprivnica: 1-0 Pero PEJIC (4').
Lille Olympique SC: 1-1 Vladimir MANCHEV (52').
Referee: Peter SIPPEL (GER)   Attendance: 2.000

04-08-2004   Stade de la Beaujoire, Nantes:
                FC Nantes Atlantique – FC Slovan Liberec   2-1 (2-1)
FC Nantes Atlantique: Mickaël LANDREAU, Julio César CÁCERES López (PAR), Loïc GUILLON, Nicolas SAVINAUD, Aurélien CAPOUE, Jérémy TOULALAN (YC40) (54' Stéphen DROUIN), Emerse FAE, Loïc PAILLÈRES, Gilles YAPI-YAPO (CIV), Mamadou BAGAYOKO (MLI) (86' Luigi GLOMBARD), Grégory PUYOL (71' Florin BRATU (ROM)).
FC Slovan Liberec: Zbynék HAUZR, Jozef VALACHOVIC (SVK), Petr LUKÁS, Pavel KOSTÁL, Peter SINGLÁR (SVK), Ivan HODÚR (SVK) (77' Karol KISEL (SVK)), Jan POLÁK (YC76), Petr PAPOUSEK, Josef HAMOUZ (YC71), Michal POSPISIL, Filip HOLOSKO (SVK) (37' Juraj ANCIC (SVK), 68' Miroslav SLEPICKA).
Goals: FC Nantes Atlantique: 1-0 Gilles YAPI-YAPO (5'), 2-1 Gilles YAPI-YAPO (44').
FC Slovan Liberec: 1-1 Filip HOLOSKO (20').
Referee: Martin INGVARSSON (SWE)   Attendance: 21.857

04-08-2004   AOL Arena, Hamburg: Hamburger SV – Villarreal CF   0-1 (0-0)
Hamburger SV: Stefan WÄCHTER, Raphael WICKY (SUI) (73' Collin BENJAMIN (NAM)),
Daniel VAN BUYTEN (BEL), Bastian REINHARDT, Stephan KLING, Björn SCHLICKE
(YC17), David JAROLÍM (CZE) (YC75) (79' Oliver HAMPEL), Christian RAHN (YC66),
Sergej BARBAREZ (BOS) (73' Naohiro TAKAHARA (JPN)), Bernardo Daniel ROMEO
(ARG) (YC32), Emile MPENZA (BEL). (Coach: Klaus TOPPMÖLLER).
Villarreal CF: José Manuel REINA Páez, ARMANDO Miguel Correia de SÁ (BRA), Enrique
"QUIQUE" ÁLVAREZ Sanjuán, GONZALO Javier RODRÍGUEZ (ARG), Rodolfo Martín
ARRUABARRENA (ARG), José Joaquín Moreno Verdú "JOSICO", MARCOS António
SENNA da Silva (BRA), Santiago "SANTI" CAZORLA González (88' HÉCTOR FONT
Romero), ROGER García Junyent (YC55) (85' César ARZO Amposta), JOSÉ "MARI" María
Romero Poyón, VÍCTOR Manuel Fernández Gutiérrez (68' José Antonio GUAYRE Betancor
Perdomo (YC76)). (Coach: Manuel Luis PELLEGRINI Ripamonti (CHI)).
Goal: Villarreal CF: 0-1 JOSÉ "MARI" María Romero Poyón (69').
Referee: Ruud BOSSEN (HOL)   Attendance: 35.296

04-08-2004   Estádio Dr. Magalhães Pessoa, Leiria:
               União Desportiva Leiria – KRC Genk   2-0 (2-0)
União Desportiva Leiria: HELTON da Silva Arruda (BRA), JOÃO PAULO Andrade,
RENATO Jorge Magalhães Dias Assunção, GABRIEL Fernando Atz (BRA), Nuno Filipe
Rodrigues LARANJEIRO, PAULO Jorge de Sousa GOMES (YC21) (59' OTACILIO José
Gomes Lima (BRA), Aírton Graciliano dos Santos "CAÍCO" (BRA), Luís Miguel da
Assunção Joaquim "ALHANDRA", EDSON Luíz da Silva (BRA) (YC46) (88' Pedro Miguel
Ferreira Silva TORRÃO), Frederico de Costa Roque dos Santos "FREDDY" (ANG), FÁBIO
Alexandre Duarte FELÍCIO (79' Carlos Manuel FANGUEIRO Soares).
KRC Genk: Sem FRANSSEN, Brian PRISKE (DEN) (YC89'), Aaron MOKOENA (RSA)
(YC37), Gert CLAESSENS (YC83), Mirsad BESLIJA (BOS), Koen DAERDEN, Soley
SEYFO (GAM) (YC42) (67' Justice WAMFOR (CMR)), Faris HAROUN (67' Igor DE
CAMARGO (BRA)), Daan VAESEN (46' Indridi SIGURDSSON (ISL)), Paul KPAKA
(SLE), Kevin VANDENBERGH (YC56).
Goals: União Desportiva Leiria: 1-0 FÁBIO Alexandre Duarte FELÍCIO (23'), 2-0 EDSON
Luíz da Silva (45').
Referee: Pascal GARIBIAN (FRA)

04-08-2004   Estadio Vicente Calderón, Madrid:
               Club Atlético Madrid – O.F.K. Beograd   2-0 (1-0)
Club Atlético Madrid: SERGIO ARAGONÉS Almeida Sánchez, Cosmin Marius CONTRA
(ROM) (YC38), Luis Amaranto PEREA Mosquera (COL), José Antonio GARCÍA CALVO,
ANTONIO LÓPEZ Guerrero, Carlos AGUILERA Martin (74' Álvaro NOVO Ramírez), Diego
Pablo SIMEONE (ARG) (58' Veljko PAUNOVIC (SBM)), Gonzalo COLSA Abendea (84'
Gabriel "GABI" Fernández Arenas), Ariel Miguel Santiago IBAGAZA, Kizito "Kiki"
MUSAMPA (HOL), FERNANDO José TORRES Sanz. (Coach: César FERRANDO).
O.F.K. Beograd: Nikola DAMJANAC, Branislav IVANOVIC, Marko BASA, Djordje JOKIC,
Dusko TOSIC (YC21), Djordje KAMBER (YC15), Boris VASKOVIC (YC43), Aleksandar
SIMIC (73' Ivan CVETKOVIC), Igor MATIC, Vladimir BOZOVIC (86' Filip
ARSENIJEVIC), Branko BAKOVIC. (Coach: Branko BABIC).
Goals: Club Atlético Madrid: 1-0 FERNANDO José TORRES Sanz (10'), 2-0 Carlos
AGUILERA Martin (51').
Referee: Philippe LEUBA (SUI)   Attendance: 25.000

116

FINALS

10-08-2004   Stadium Nord Lille Métropole, Villeneuve d'Ascq:
             Lille Olympique SC – União Desportiva Leiria   0-0
Lille Olympique SC: Tony SYLVA (SEN), Mathieu CHALMÉ, Nicolas PLESTAN, Rafael
SCHMITZ (BRA), Grégory TAFFOREAU (YC86), Christophe LANDRIN (YC31) (72'
Nicolas FAUVERGUE), Stéphane DUMONT, Jean II MAKOUN (CMR), Geoffrey DERNIS
(59' Adekanmi OLUFADÉ (TOG)), Philippe BRUNEL, Vladimir MANCHEV (BUL) (76'
Mathieu DEBUCHY).
União Desportiva Leiria: HÉLTON da Silva Arruda (BRA), Nuno Filipe Rodrigues
LARANJEIRO, RENATO Jorge Magalhães Dias Assunção, GABRIEL Fernando Atz (BRA),
Luís Miguel da Assunção Joaquim "ALHANDRA", Aírton Graciliano dos Santos "CAÍCO"
(BRA), OTACILIO José Gomes Lima (BRA) (YC44) (59' Pedro Miguel Ferreira Silva
TORRÃO), PAULO Jorge de Sousa GOMES, ÉDSON Luíz da Silva (BRA) (YC90+),
Frederico de Costa Roque dos Santos "FREDDY" (ANG) (66' Petar KRPAN (CRO)), FÁBIO
Alexandre Duarte FELÍCIO (YC63) (73' BERNARDO Lino Castro Paes VASCONCELOS).
Referee: Paul ALLAERTS (BEL)   Attendance: 10.177

10-08-2004   Arena AufSchalke, Gelsenkirchen:
             FC Schalke 04 – FC Slovan Liberec   2-1 (2-0)
FC Schalke 04: Frank ROST, Thomas KLÄSENER, Marcelo José BORDON (BRA), Mladen
KRSTAJIC (SBM), Niels OUDE KAMPHUIS (HOL), Sven VERMANT (BEL), Cassio de
Souza Soares LINCOLN (BRA), Levan KOBIASHVILI (GEO), Christian PANDER (68'
Hamit ALTINTOP (TUR)), Gerald ASAMOAH (YC64) (73' Mike HANKE), Gonçalves da
Silva AILTON (BRA).
FC Slovan Liberec: Zbynék HAUZR, Jozef VALACHOVIC (SVK), Petr LUKÁS (YC51),
Pavel KOSTÁL, Peter SINGLÁR (SVK), Ivan HODÚR (SVK), Jan POLÁK (41' David
LANGER), Petr PAPOUSEK, Tomás ZÁPOTOCNY (77' Jan BROSCHINSKY (YC80)),
Michal POSPÍSIL, Miroslav SLEPICKA (62' Lubomir BLAHA).
Goals: FC Schalke 04: 1-0 Gonçalves da Silva AILTON (25'), 2-0 Gerald ASAMOAH (41').
FC Slovan Liberec: 2-1 Tomás ZÁPOTOCNY (74').
Referee: Roberto ROSETTI (ITA)   Attendance: 54.136

10-08-2004   Estadio El Madrigal, Villarreal:
             Villarreal CF – Club Atlético Madrid   2-0 (0-0)
Villarreal CF: José Manuel REINA Páez, ARMANDO Miguel Correia de SÁ (BRA) (YC90),
Enrique "QUIQUE" ÁLVAREZ Sanjuán, GONZALO Javier RODRÍGUEZ (ARG), Rodolfo
Martín ARRUABARRENA (ARG), Santiago "SANTI" CAZORLA González (67' Juan
Ramón RIQUELME (ARG)), José Joaquín Moreno Verdú "JOSICO", MARCOS António
SENNA da Silva (BRA), ROGER García Junyent (YC27) (81' HÉCTOR FONT Romero),
JOSÉ "MARI" María Romero Poyón, "SONNY" ANDERSON da Silva (BRA) (89' VÍCTOR
Manuel Fernández Gutiérrez). (Coach: Manuel Luis PELLEGRINI Ripamonti (CHI)).
Club Atlético Madrid: Leonardo "LEO" Neoren FRANCO (ARG), Cosmin Marius CONTRA
(ROM) (YC57), Luis Amaranto PEREA Mosquera (COL) (YC64), PABLO Ibáñez Tebar,
SERGI Barjuan Esclusa, Carlos AGUILERA Martin (87' JORGE Larena Avellaneda Roig),
Diego Pablo SIMEONE (ARG) (66' Veljko PAUNOVIC (SBM)), Gonzalo COLSA Abendea,
Ariel Miguel Santiago IBAGAZA (YC90+), Kizito "Kiki" MUSAMPA (HOL) (78' Fernando
"NANO" Macedo da Silva Rodilla), FERNANDO José TORRES Sanz (YC55). (Coach: César
FERRANDO).
Goals: Villarreal CF: 1-0 ROGER García Junyent (56'), 2-0 GONZALO Javier RODRÍGUEZ
(77').
Referee: Bertrand LAYEC (FRA)   Attendance: 15.000

24-08-2004   Stadion u Nisy, Liberec: FC Slovan Liberec – FC Schalke 04   0-1 (0-0)
FC Slovan Liberec: Zbynék HAUZR, Peter SINGLÁR (SVK) (77' Tomás ZÁPOTOCNY),
Jozef VALACHOVIC (SVK), Petr LUKÁS (YC50), Josef HAMOUZ, Jan POLÁK, Karol
KISEL (SVK), Ivan HODÚR (SVK) (82' David LANGER), Petr PAPOUSEK, Juraj ANCIC
(SVK), Michal POSPÍSIL (69' Miroslav SLEPICKA).
FC Schalke 04: Frank ROST, Tomasz WALDOCH (POL), Marcelo José BORDON (BRA),
Mladen KRSTAJIC (SBM), Niels OUDE KAMPHUIS (HOL), Sven VERMANT (BEL)
(YC77), Christian POULSEN (DEN), Octavio Dario RODRÍGUEZ Peña (URU) (YC64), (81'
Thomas KLÄSENER), Hamit ALTINTOP (TUR), Gerald ASAMOAH (80' Mike HANKE),
Gonçalves da Silva AILTON (BRA) (90'+3' Michael DELURA).
Goal: FC Schalke 04: 0-1 Gonçalves da Silva AILTON (87').
Referee: Yuri BASKAKOV (RUS)   Attendance: 7.880

24-08-2004   Estádio Dr. Magalhães Pessoa, Leiria:
              União Deportiva Leiria – Lille Olympique SC   0-2 (0-0)
União Desportiva Leiria: HÉLTON da Silva Arruda (BRA), Nuno Filipe Rodrigues
LARANJEIRO, RENATO Jorge Magalhaes Dias Assunção, GABRIEL Fernando Atz (BRA)
(YC119), Luís Miguel da Assunção Joaquim "ALHANDRA" (107' BERNARDO Lino Castro
Paes VASCONCELOS), OTACILIO José Gomes Lima (BRA), PAULO Jorge de Sousa
GOMES (YC23), Aírton Graciliano dos Santos "CAÍCO" (BRA) (84' Carlos Manuel
FANGUEIRO Soares), ÉDSON Luíz da Silva (BRA), Frederico de Costa Roque dos Santos
"FREDDY" (ANG), FÁBIO Alexandre Duarte FELÍCIO (67' Petar KRPAN (CRO)).
Lille Olympique SC: Tony SYLVA (SEN), Grégory TAFFOREAU (YC19) (79' DANTÉ
Bonfim Costa Santos (BRA)), Efstathios TAVLARIDIS (GRE) (YC87), Rafael SCHMITZ
(BRA), Christophe LANDRIN (YC120), Mathieu CHALMÉ, Jean II MAKOUN (CMR),
Mathieu BODMER (YC19), Milenko ACIMOVIC (SLO) (119' Nicolas PLESTAN), Johan
AUDEL (59' Philippe BRUNEL), Matt MOUSSILOU.
Goals: Lille Olympique SC: 0-1 Matt MOUSSILOU (105'), 0-2 Milenko ACIMOVIC (117').
Referee: Georgios KASNAFERIS (GRE)   Attendance: 12.048
(After extra time)

24-08-2004   Estadio Vicente Calderón, Madrid:
              Club Atlético Madrid – Villarreal CF   2-0 (0-0)
Club Atlético Madrid: Leonardo "LEO" Noeren FRANCO (ARG), Luis Amaranto PEREA
Mosquera (COL), José Antonio GARCÍA CALVO, PABLO Ibáñez Tebar, SERGI Barjuán
Esclusa, Diego Pablo SIMEONE (ARG), Gonzalo COLSA Abendea, Ariel Miguel Santiago
IBAGAZA (YC48) (98' Ángel Javier ARIZMENDI de Lucas), JORGE Larena Avellaneda
Roig (77' Carlos AGUILERA Martin), Kizito "Kiki" MUSAMPA (HOL) (75' Fernando
"NANO" Macedo da Silva Rodilla), FERNANDO José TORRES Sanz. (Coach: César
FERRANDO).
Villarreal CF: José Manuel REINA Páez, ARMANDO Miguel Correia de SÁ (BRA), Enrique
"QUIQUE" ÁLVAREZ Sanjuán (YC68), GONZALO Javier RODRÍGUEZ (ARG) (YC6),
Rodolfo Martín ARRUABARRENA (ARG), Santiago "SANTI" CAZORLA González (62'
HÉCTOR FONT Romero), Juan Ramón RIQUELME (ARG), José Joaquín Moreno Verdú
"JOSICO" (62' Sebastián BATTAGLIA (ARG)), MARCOS António SENNA da Silva (BRA),
JOSÉ "MARI" María Romero Poyón (110' VÍCTOR Manuel Fernández Gutiérrez), "SONNY"
ANDERSON da Silva (BRA). (Coach: Manuel Luis PELLEGRINI Ripamonti (CHI)).
Goals: Club Atlético Madrid: 1-0 Ariel Miguel Santiago IBAGAZA (47'), 2-0 José Antonio
GARCÍA CALVO (58').
Referee: Vladimir HRINÁK (SVK)   Attendance: 45.000

118

Penalties:
* José Antonio GARCÍA CALVO   1 "SONNY" ANDERSON da Silva
1 SERGI Barjuán Esclusa   2 VÍCTOR Manuel Fernández Gutiérrez
* Fernando "NANO" Macedo da Silva Rodilla 3 Juan Ramón RIQUELME
* Ángel Javier ARIZMENDI de Lucas

(JORGE Larena Avellaneda Roig missed a penalty in the 67th minute)

Lille Olympique SC, FC Schalke 04 and Villarreal CF all qualified for the UEFA Cup competition.

2005

FIRST ROUND

18-06-2005   Bloomfield Stadium, Tel-Aviv:
Beitar Jerusalem FC – FK Sileks Kratova   4-3 (1-2)
Beitar Jerusalem FC: Guy SALOMON, Shemoel KOZOKIN, Eli SASON, Yoni KIM, Eliran
DANIN, Mor EFRAIM, Maor MELIKSON (YC25), Aviram BROCHYAN (YC61), Ophir
AZO, Eliav YONI, Amit BEN SHOSHAN (YC73). (Coach: Azon GUY).
FK Sileks Kratova: Vukmir MIJANOVIC (SBM), Nikola TRIPUMOVSKI (58' Gjoksen
LIMANOV), Blagoja TODOROVSKI, Sasko PANDEV (68' Eftim AKSENTIEV), Marjan
MICKOV (82' Igor SAVEVSKI), Sinisa JOVANOVSKI, Dalibor STOJKOVIC, Daniel
IVANOVSKI, Stevica RISTIC (SBM), Aleksandar KONJANOVSKI, Igor ARSOVSKI
(YC86). (Coach: Nebojsa PETROVIC).
Goals: Beitar Jerusalem FC: 1-1 Amit BEN SHOSHAN (17'), 2-2 Amit BEN SHOSHAN
(48'), 3-2 Aviram BROCHYAN (61'), 4-3 Amit BEN SHOSHAN (80').
FK Sileks Kratova: 0-1 Sinisa JOVANOVSKI (2'), 1-2 Stevica RISTIC (28'), 3-3 Igor
ARSOVSKI (71').
Referee: Luc WILMES (LUX)

18-06-2005   Stade Josy Barthel, Luxembourg:
FC Victoria Rosport – I.F.K. Göteborg   1-2 (0-0)
FC Victoria Rosport: Sascha APITZ, Frank BUSCHMANN (YC86), Alexander PAULOS,
Mike WEBER, Asmeron HABTE, Denis GIESE (GER) (YC81), Markus HUWER, Werner
HEINZEN (YC50) (64' Thomas BERENS), Patrick ZÖLLNER, Fabio MORAIS (56' Marc
GÖRRES (GER)), David SCHMIDT (73' Laurent SCHILTZ). (Coach: Reiner BRINSA
(GER)).
I.F.K. Göteborg: John ALVBÅGE, Martin SMEDBERG, Mattias BJÄRSMYR, Dennis
JONSSON, Bastian ANDERSSON (88' Gustaf SVENSSON), Tommy LYCÉN, Håkan MILD,
Pontus WERNBLOM (YC35), Andres VASQUES, Marcus BERG, Jonathan BERG. (Coach:
Arne ERLANDSEN (NOR)).
Goals: FC Victoria Rosport: 1-1 Marc GÖRRES (70').
I.F.K. Göteborg: 0-1 Marcus BERG (59'), 1-2 Jonathan BERG (80').
Referee: Ghenadie ORLIC (MOL)   Attendance: 1.000

18-06-2005   Gradski Stadion, Koprivnica:
NK Slaven Belupo Koprivnica – NK Drava Ptuj   1-0 (0-0)
NK Slaven Belupo Koprivnica: Robert LISJAK, Pavo CRNAC, Jurica KARABATIC, Igor
GAL, Petar BOSNJAK (77' Krunoslav JAMBRUSIC), Dejan SOMOCI (YC63), Igor MUSA
(YC72) (74' Pero PEJIC (YC87)), Tomislav KELEMEN (YC44), Dalibor VISKOVIC, Bojan
VRUCINA (59' Marijo DODIK), Ivica KARABOGDAN. (Coach: Branko KARACIC).
NK Drava Ptuj: Mladen DABANOVIC, Matej MILJATOVIC, Emil STERBAL, Matjaz
LUNDER, Tomaz TOPLAK, Nedzad ALIBABIC (57' Ales CEH), Robert TEZACKI (CRO)
(YC72), Aljaz ZAJC, Majtaz KOREZ (57' Andrej PREJAC), Viktor TRENEVSKI (MCD),
Gorazd GORINSEK (79' Dragan LJUBANIC). (Coach: Srecko LUSIC (CRO)).
Goal: NK Slaven Belupo Koprivnica: 1-0 Marijo DODIK (83').
Referee: René ROGALLA (SUI)   Attendance: 1.200

18-06-2005   Makárion Athlitikó Kéntro, Nicosia:
Olympiakos FC Nicosia – FC Gloria Bistrita   0-5 (0-2)
Olympiakos FC Nicosia: Anastasios YIALLOURIS, Rodolfos POURGOURIDIS (46'
Odysseas STAVROU), Christodoulos CHRISTODOULOU, Giannis KYPRAIOS, Georgios
HADJIKYRIACOU, Joseph FRANGISKOS, Anoreas KAPSOS (57' Nicolas
THERAPONTOS), Fidias PANAYIOTOU, Loucas KARIPIS (64' Nicolas SAMPOURITS),
Giannis SERAPHIM, Christos EFTHYMIOU. (Coach: Costas SERAFIM).
FC Gloria Bistrita: Septimiu Calin ALBUT, Alin Valer RUS, Danut MATEI (62' Adrian
PREDICA), Daniel PAICA, Alin CHIBULCUTEAN, Marius DRULE, Adrian NALATI,
Sergiu Ioan COSTIN, Dinu Daniel SANMARTEAN (46' Florin PELECACI), Ionut Bogdan
PERES, Sandu NEGREAN (71' Catalin BUCUR). (Coach: Ion BALAUR).
Goals: FC Gloria Bistrita: 0-1 Ionut Bogdan PERES (23'), 0-2 Ionut Bogdan PERES (30'), 0-3
Ionut Bogdan PERES (59'), 0-4 Alin CHIBULCUTEAN (69'), 0-5 Catalin BUCUR (89').
Referee: Novo PANIC (BOS)

18-06-2005   Stadionul CFR Ecomax, Cluj-Napoca:
CFR Cluj – FK Vetra Rudiskes Vilnius   3-2 (3-1)
CFR Cluj: Petru TURCAS, Cristian Calin PANIN, Dorin TOMA (YC72), Sabin GOIA
(YC19), Csaba KISS, Florin Cristian DAN, Stefan Sorin ONCICA, Radu Leon
MARGINEAN, Cristian TURCU (67' Sead BRUNCEVIC (SBM), 89' Marius VINTILA),
Cosmin TILINCA (80' Laur Marian ASTILEAN), Adrian Gheorghe ANCA. (Coach: Aurel
SUNDA).
FK Vetra Rudiskes Vilnius: Ramunas MERKELIS, Zilvinas ZUDYS, Julius RALIUKONIS,
Igoris STESKO, Nerijus SASNAUSKAS (YC10), Darvydas SERNAS, Aidas PREIKSAITIS
(YC6), Gediminas BUTRIMAVICIUS (89' Andzejus SIVINSKIS), Janis RINKUS (LAT),
Rolandas VAINEIKIS (73' Arturas STESKO), Andrius KOCHANAUSKAS (YC21). (Coach:
Siarhei BAROUSKI (BLS)).
Goals: CFR Cluj: 1-0 Cosmin TILINCA (2'), 2-1 Adrian Gheorghe ANCA (11' penalty), 3-1
Cosmin TILINCA (12').
FK Vetra Rudiskes Vilnius: 1-1 Darvydas SERNAS (9'), 3-2 Arturas STESKO (85').
Referee: Christoforos ZOGRAFOS (GRE)   Attendance: 4.000

18-06-2005   Hibernians Stadium, Paola: Valletta FC – FK Buducnost Podgorica   0-5 (0-3)
Valletta FC: Sean SULLIVAN, Kevin CASSAR (YC35), Massimo GRIMA, Branko NISEVIC
(SBM), Rennie FORACE, Jonathan BONDIN (81' Stefano GRIMA), Keith FENECH, Milen
PENCHEV, Chris CAMILLERI (46' Anatole DEBONO), Ian ZAMMIT, Mark GALEA.
(Coach: John Joseph AQUILINA).
FK Buducnost Podgorica: Miroslav VUJADINOVIC, Risto LAKIC, Petar VUKCEVIC (76'
Milos LAKIC), Goran PERISIC, Ivan CARAPIC, Mirko RAICEVIC, Nikola VUJOVIC
(YC7), Nenad SOFRANAC (64' Goran BURZANOVIC), Radislav SEKULIC (YC16), Marco
MUGOSA, Bracan POPOVIC (46' Nebojsa DJORDJEVIC). (Coach: Branislav MILACIC).
Goals: FK Buducnost Podgorica: 0-1 Nikola VUJOVIC (8'), 0-2 Radislav SEKULIC (16'), 0-3
Nikola VUJOVIC (31'), 0-4 Radislav SEKULIC (70'), 0-5 Radislav SEKULIC (77').
Referee: Brian LAWLOR (WAL)

121

18-06-2005   Svangaskard, Toftír: Skála ÍF – Tampere United FC   0-2 (0-0)
Skála ÍF: Vlada FILIPOVIC (SBM), Paetur Dam JACOBSEN (62' Bárdur DANIELSEN),
Runi RASMUSSEN, Milic CURCIC (SBM), Iulian FLORESCU (ROM) (77' Arnhold BERG),
Bjarni JØRGENSEN, Nenad STANKOVIC (SBM), Pauli G.HANSEN (78' Sveinur
JUSTINUSSEN), Hanus THORLEIFSON (YC14), Bogi GREGERSEN, Jønhard
FREDERIKSBERG. (Coach: Jóhan NIELSEN).
Tampere United FC: Mikko KAVÉN, Jussi KUOPPALA, Jarkko WISS, Heikki AHO, Petri
HEINÄNEN, Kari SAINIO (YC49), Jussi KUJALA, Sakari SAARINEN, Henri
SCHEWELEFF (88' Antti OJANPERÄ), Mika LAHTINEN (59' Toni JUNNILA), Velibor
KOPUNOVIC (CRO) (46' Antti HYNYNEN). (Coach: Ari Juhani HJELM).
Goals: Tampere United FC: 0-1 Antti HYNYNEN (57'), 0-2 Antti HYNYNEN (67').
Referee: Aleh CHYKUN (BLS)   Attendance: 400

18-06-2005   Stadionul Republica, Chisinau:
               FC Tiligul Tiraspol – KS Pogon Szczecin   0-3 (0-1)
FC Tiligul Tiraspol: Evghenii MATIUGHIN, Serghei CUZNETOV, Eduard GROSU (YC80),
Serghei STROENCO, Yergen GOSTYEV (RC59), Olexandr DYNDIKOV (UKR) (YC87),
Serghei BUTELSCHI (YC16), Vitali PINIASKINE (RUS) (65' Igor DOBROVOLSKI), Victor
COMLEONOC, Vladimir TARANU, Dumitru POPOVICI. (Coach: Igor Ivanovich
DOBROVOLSKIY (UKR)).
KS Pogon Szczecin: Boris PESKOVIC (SVK), Krzysztof MICHALSKI (YC11), Pawel
MAGDON (YC26), JULCIMAR De Souza (BRA) (YC59), Mariusz MASTERNAK, Petr
KASPRAK (CZE) (YC48) (59' Tomasz PARZY), Przemyslaw KAZMIERCZAK (RC80),
Michal LABEDZKI (89' Lukasz TRALKA), Rafal GRZELAK, Radek DIVECKY (CZE)
(RC39), Roberto Claudio MILAR Decaudra (URU) (YC37). (Coach: Boguslaw PIETRZAK).
Goals: KS Pogon Szczecin: 0-1 Przemyslaw KAZMIERCZAK (45'), 0-2 Tomasz PARZY
(84'), 0-3 Krzysztof MICHALSKI (90+').
Referee: Kuddusi MÜFTÜOGLU (TUR)   Attendance: 300

18-06-2005   A. Le Coq Arena, Tallinn: JK Trans Narva – KSC Lokeren   0-2 (0-1)
JK Trans Narva: Sergei USSOLTSEV, Ilya DJORD (RUS), Aleksei GORSKOV, Sergei
KAZAKOV (63' Irfan AMETOV (UKR)), Aleksandr TARASSENKOV, Dmitri LIPARTOV
(RUS) (68' Aleksandr KULATSENKO), Maksim GRUZNOV, Dmytro DOBROVOLSKIY
(UKR), Stanislav KITTO, Sergei POPOV (80' Dmitri SELEHHOV), Aleksandr KULIK.
(Coach: Valeri BONDARENKO).
KSC Lokeren: Zvonko MILOJEVIC (SBM), JOÃO CARLOS Pinto Chaves (BRA), Ivan
VUKOMANOVIC (SBM), Arnar GRETARSSON (ISL), Runar KRISTINSSON (ISL) (69'
Killian OVERMEIRE), Marc HENDRIKX, Aboubacar M'BAYE CAMARA (GUI), José Ilson
dos Santos "TAILSON" (BRA) (77' Glen COPPENS), Lezou Hugues DOBA (CIV), Michael
VAN HOEY, Frederik DE WINNE (80' Xavier DESCHACHT). (Coach: Slavoljub MUSLIN
(SRB)).
Goals: KSC Lokeren: 0-1 Arnar GRETARSSON (2'), 0-2 Ivan VUKOMANOVIC (68').
Referee: Emil LAURSEN (DEN)

122

18-06-2005   Republican Stadium, Yerevan:
FC Lernagorts Ararat – Neuchâtel-Xamax FC   1-3 (1-2)
FC Lernagorts Ararat: Garik BOYAKHCHYAN, Vakhtang HAKOBYAN (GEO) (79' Gagik
AVAGYAN), Karen GRIGORYAN, Arkadi CHILINGARYAN, Hayk NARIMANYAN,
Karen NAVOYAN, Hayk MURADYAN (36' Gor ATABEKYAN (YC49)), Basden UZOHER
(40' Albert NERSISYAN), Vardan ABRAKHAMYAN, Paul Okwuchkwu BANNEY,
Irumenhay Musa IDOVU (NIG). (Coach: Sevada ARZUMANYAN).
Neuchâtel-Xamax FC: Florent DELAY, Kader MANGANE (SEN) (YC39), Eddy BAREA,
Mounir SOUFIANI (FRA), Pascal OPPLIGER, Bastien GEIGER, Christophe MARANINCHI
(FRA), Julien CORDONNIER (FRA) (75' Juan MUÑOZ JUAN (ESP)), Patrick BAUMANN
(88' Herve AKA'A (CMR)), Charles-André DOUDIN (70' Raphael NUZZOLO), Joel
GRIFFITHS (AUS). (Coach: Alain GEIGER).
Goals: FC Lernagorts Ararat: 1-1 Karen NAVOYAN (27').
Neuchâtel-Xamax FC: 0-1 Joel GRIFFITHS (2'), 1-2 Joel GRIFFITHS (32'), 1-3 Juan
MUÑOZ JUAN (90').
Referee: Ioannis TSAHEILIDS (GRE)

18-06-2005   Dalymount Park, Dublin: Bohemians FC – KAA Gent   1-0 (0-0)
Bohemians FC: Matthew GREGG (ENG), Stephen RICE, Ken OMAN, Desmond BYRNE,
James KEDDY, John KELLY (YC36) (73' Fergal HARKIN), Kevin HUNT (ENG), Gareth
FARRELLY, Stephen WARD, Anthony GRANT, Dominic FOLEY. (Coach: Patrick (Pat)
CLEARY).
KAA Gent: Zlatko RUNJE (CRO), Dario SMOJE (CRO), Stephen LAYBUTT (AUS), Nicolas
LOMBAERTS, Damir MIRVIC (BOS) (60' Tim MATTHIJS), Mamar MAMOUNI (ALG),
Yngvar HÅKONSEN (NOR), Steve COOREMAN, Wouter VRANCKEN, Nordin JBARI
(YC43), Moubarak (Mbark) BOUSSOUFA (HOL). (Coach: Georges LEEKENS).
Goal: Bohemians FC: 1-0 Anthony GRANT (49').
Referee: Saso LAZAREVSKI (MCD)

18-06-2005   Illovszky Rudolf Stadion, Budapest: Vasas SC – FK ZTS Dubnica   0-0
Vasas SC: Zsolt POSZA, Zoltán MOLNÁR, János GYÖRI, András TÓTH, György KISS,
Henrik RÓSA, Iván JANJIC (SBM) (83' Nobert HEGEDÜS), Zsolt BALOG (46' Ádám
WEITHER), László GAÁL (32' Levente SCHULTZ), Robert WALTNER (YC84), Péter
HORVÁTH. (Coach: Sándor EGERVÁRI).
FK ZTS Dubnica: Dusan PERNIS, Peter PEKÁRIK (YC70), Jozef ADAMÍK (38' Roman
SKULTÉTY), Martin SVESTKA (CZE) (YC35), Marián ZIMEN, Dalibor PLEVA, Juraj
DOVICOVIC (67' Matej IZVOLT), Pavol KOPACKA, Lukás TESÁK, Pavol STRAKA
(YC64) (86' Marián ADAM), Peter KISKA. (Coach: Lubomir NOSICKY).
Referee: Sinisa ZRNIC (BOS)   Attendance: 1.000

123

18-06-2005   Qemal Stafa Stadium, Tiranë:
KS Dinamo Tiranë – NK Varteks Varazdin   2-1 (2-0)
KS Dinamo Tiranë: Suat ZENDELI (MCD), Leandro ESCUDERO (ARG), Erion XHAFA,
Ibrahim KONI (MLI), Papa DIOP (SEN) (YC82), Juan Carlos MARIÑO Márquez (PER) (57'
Ligoraq TIKO), Ilir QORRI (46' Enkel ALIKAJ), Erald DELIALLISI, Masseye GAYE (SEN),
Paulin DHËMBI, Elhadji GOUDIABY (SEN) (75' Artion POÇI). (Coach: Ramón Armando
CABRERO (ARG)).
NK Varteks Varazdin: Miroslav KOPRIC, Nikola POKRIVAC, Mirko PLANTIC (YC53),
Goran MUJANOVIC, Kristijan IPSA (46' Enes NOVINIC), Zoran KASTEL, Dario JERTEC
(88' Ivan BEGOVIC), Nikola SAFARIC, Leon BENKO (83' Marko BASIC), Nikola
MELNJAK, Neven VUKMAN. (Coach: Zlatko DALIC).
Goals: KS Dinamo Tiranë: 1-0 Juan Carlos MARIÑO Márquez (6'), 2-0 Ilir QORRI (15').
NK Varteks Varazdin: 2-1 Enes NOVINIC (90'+2').
Referee: Anthony ZAMMIT (MLT)

19-06-2005   Estadi Comunal d'Andorra la Vella, Andorra la Vella:
FC Ranger's – SK Sturm Graz   1-1 (1-0)
FC Ranger's: Gregorio RODRIGUEZ (ESP), José PORTA (ESP), Francisco Javier MARTIN
SANCHEZ (ESP), Sergio ALBANELL (ESP), José ALVAREZ (ARG), Justo GONZALEZ
(ESP) (84' Carles BERGUES (ESP)), LEONARDO (88' Jorge Manuel MONTEIRO
CARVALHO (POR)), Manolo JIMÉNEZ (90'+2' Johnny CASAL (ESP)), Norberto URBANI
(ARG), Genis GARCÍA (YC72), Toni CAÇADOR (ESP). (Coach: Vicente MARQUES
Gonzalez).
SK Sturm Graz: Grzegorz SZAMOTULSKI (POL), Günther NEUKIRCHNER, Adam
LEDWON (POL), Franck SILVESTRE (FRA), Ronald GERCALIU, Johannes ERTL (46'
David MUJIRI (GEO)), Dragan SARAC (SBM), Jürgen SÄUMEL, Bojan FILIPOVIC (SBM),
Oliver NZUZI POLO (CGO), Amadou RABIHOU (CMR) (YC90+2). (Coach: Mihajlo
PETROVIC (SRB)).
Goals: FC Ranger's: 1-0 Norberto URBANI (35').
SK Sturm Graz: 1-1 Amadou RABIHOU (70').
Referee: Gabriele ROSSI (SMR)

19-06-2005   Belle Vue, Rhyl: Bangor City FC – FC Dinaburg Daugavpils   1-2 (1-1)
Bangor City FC: Andrew Oliver RALPH, Lee Francis ATHERTON (ENG), Clayton
BLACKMORE, Kevin SCOTT (YC61), Paul O'NEILL (ENG), Christopher PRIEST (ENG),
Owain JONES, Paul ROBERTS (YC15), Carl LAMB (ENG), Christopher McGINN (78' Tony
GRAY (ENG)), Gareth WILLIAMS (71' Leslie DAVIES). (Coach: Peter DAVENPORT
(ENG)).
FC Dinaburg Daugavpils: Maris ELTERMANIS, Deniss SOKOLSKIS, Andrejs
ZUROMSKIS, Sergey KHIMICH (RUS) (YC63), Jurijs SOKOLOVS, Edgars BURLAKOVS,
Nikita CHMYKOV (RUS), Pavels KOLCOVS, Olexandr KRIKLIVY (UKR) (84' Ritus
KRJAUKLIS), Mikhails ZIZILEVS, Sergejs VALUSKINS (81' Vladimir VOLKOVS).
(Coach: Roman Yosypovych GRYGORCHUK (UKR)).
Goals: Bangor City FC: 1-1 Maris ELTERMANIS (44' *own goal*).
FC Dinaburg Daugavpils: 0-1 Deniss SOKOLOVS (5'), 1-2 Sergejs VALUSKINS (67').
Referee: Svein Oddvar MOEN (NOR)   Attendance: 832

19-06-2005   Zalgirio stadionas, Vilnius:
FK Zalgiris Vilnius – Lisburn Distillery FC   1-0 (0-0)
FK Zalgiris Vilnius: Mindaugas MALINAUSKAS, Tomas MIKUCKIS (YC48), Andrejus
TERESKINAS (63' Karolis JASAITIS), Tadas GRAZIUNAS, Paulius PAKNYS, Marijan
CHORUZI (72' Andzey MAKSIMOVIC), Vadim PETRENKO, Virmantas LEMEZIS, Marius
BEZYKORNOVAS (24' Andrei SHYLO (BLS) (YC75)), Branislav JASUREK (SVK),
Aleksandr OSIPOVITCH (BLS) (YC80). (Coach: Saulius SIRMELIS).
Lisburn Distillery FC: Michael DOUGHERTY, Gareth McKEOWN, Michael FERGUSON
(YC45), Wayne BUCHANAN (YC62), Paul MUIR, Andy BARRON (USA), Andrew
KILMARTIN, Andrew DICKSON, Johm MARTIN (72' James WILLIS), Christopher
COFFEY, Darren ARMOUR (64' Sean ARMSTRONG). (Coach: Paul KIRK).
Goal: FK Zalgiris Vilnius: 1-0 Virmantas LEMEZIS (54').
Referee: Jöuni HIETALA (FIN)

19-06-2005   Torpedo Stadium, Minsk: FC Neman Grodno – FK Tescoma Zlín   0-1 (0-0)
FC Neman Grodno: Viatcheslav DOUSMANOV, Andrei KORZHUK (YC83), Artur
KRYVANOS, Gennadi MARDAS, Mikalai YASERSKI, Vitali NADZIYENSKI, Dzmitry
HINTAU (61' Ihor MALYSH (YC90+3)), Iouri LOUKACHOV, Vyacheslav GRYGORAV
(77' Dzmitry DOLIA), Nikoloz ZEDELASHVILI (GEO) (56' Andrei LIASIUK), Dzmitry
PARFIONAU. (Coach: Siarhei Vytalievych SOLODOVNIKOV).
FK Tescoma Zlín: Ales KORÍNEK (YC73), Tomás JANÍCEK, Jaroslav SVACH, Zdenik
KROCA (YC87), Bronislav CERVENKA (YC78), Václav ZAPLETAL (73' Jan JELÍNEK),
Edvard LASOTA (41' Vít VRTILKA (YC62)), Roman DOBES, Josef LUKASTÍK (YC51),
Tomás KLINKA (89' Martin BIELIK), Václav CINCALA. (Coach: Pavel HOFTYCH).
Goal: FK Tescoma Zlín: 0-1 Josef LUKASTÍK (49').
Referee: Milan KARADZIC (SBM)   Attendance: 550

19-06-2005   Stadion Sartid, Smederevo:
FK Sartid Smederevo – FK Pobeda Prilep   0-1 (0-0)
FK Sartid Smederevo: Dejan RANKOVIC, Dejan KEKEZOVIC, Nebojsa SAVIC, Zeljko
KOVACEVIC (YC86), Ivan ZIVANOVIC, Vladimir KRNJINAC, Milan NIKOLIC, Mario
GAVRILOVIC (46' Aleksandar JEVTIC), Aleksandar MILJKOVIC (YC10) (59' Vladen
CUKIC), Nicola JEVTIC, Petar DIVIC (59' Milorad ZECEVIC). (Coach: Tomislav SIVIC).
FK Pobeda Prilep: Darko TOFILOVSKI, Dejan CVETKOVSKI, Sulaimon OMO (NGR),
Aleksandar POPOVSKI (90'+3' Saso ZDRAVEVSKI), Blagojce DAMEVSKI (YC76), Toni
MEGLENSKI, Dimitar KAPINKOVSKI (YC59), Dejan RISTOVSKI (81' Pereira EMERSON
(BRA)), Vladimir VUJOVIC (SBM) (YC66), Marjan NACEV, Blagoja GESOSKI (70' Saso
KRSTEV). (Coach: Petar KURCUBIC (SRB)).
Goal: FK Pobeda Prilep: 0-1 Dejan RISTOVSKI (49').
Referee: Tomas CURIN (CZE)

19-06-2005   Perutz Stadion, Pápa: Lombard-Pápa TFC – FC WIT Georgia Tbilisi   2-1 (0-0)
Lombard-Pápa TFC: Anoras DOMBAI, Attila FARKAS, Viktor FARKAS, Dorel MUTICA
(ROM), Tamas GERI, Tibor SZABÓ, Zoltán SZABÓ (46' Péter KINCSES), Balász LÁSZKA,
Ákos KOVRIG (YC30), Miklós HERCZEG, Zoltán HERCEGFALVI (YC76) (79' Attila
CSÁSZÁR). (Coach: Lázár SZENTES).
FC WIT Georgia Tbilisi: Grigol BEDIASHVILI, Pawel DATUNAISHVILI (YC76), David
LOMAIA (YC60), Alexander KVAKHADZE, David IMEDASHVILI (YC90+4), Luka
RAZMADZE, David DIGMELASHVILI (YC74), Georgi PEIKRISHVILI (40' Georgi
DATUNAISHVILI (YC,YC88)), Oleg GVELESIANI, Vladimer GOCHASHVILI (40' Irakli
EBANOIDZE), Zaza SAKHOKIA (90' David ABSHILAVA). (Coach: Nestor MUMLADZE).
Goals: Lombard-Pápa TFC: 1-0 Tibor SZABÓ (60'), 2-1 Tibor SZABÓ (90'+4' penalty).
FC WIT Georgia Tbilisi: 1-1 Irakli EBANOIDZE (90'+2').
Referee: José Luis MENGUAL PRADES (AND)

19-06-2005   Veritas Stadion, Turku: FC International Turku – Í.A. Akranes   0-0
FC International Turku: Magnus BAHNE, Diego CORPACHE (ARG) (YC63), Jukka
SINISALO, Jermu GUSTAFSSON, Henri LEHTONEN, Aristides PERTOT (ARG), Prince
OTOO, Serge N'GAL (CMR), Miikka ILO, Tomi PETRESCU, Matti HEIMO (69' Martin
MUTUMBA (SWE)). (Coach : Kari VIRTANEN).
Í.A. Akranes: Bjarki GUDMUNDSSON (YC88), Gunnlaugur JÓNSSON, Reynir LEÓSSON,
Gudjón H.SVEINSSON, Igor PESIC (SBM) (YC33), Kári Steinn REYNISSON, Dean
MARTIN (ENG) (YC60), Pálmi HARALDSSON (81' Hafthór VILHJÁLMSSON), Ellert Jón
BJÖRNSSON, Hjörtur J.HJARTARSON, Sigurdur Ragnar EYJÓLFSSON (88' Kristinn
RÖDULSSON). (Coach: Ólafur THÓRDARSON).
Referee: Paulius MALZINSKAS (LIT)

19-06-2005   Shafa Stadium, Baku: FK Karvan Evlakh – KKS Lech Poznán   1-2 (0-1)
FK Karvan Evlakh: Eikhan HASANOV, Ruslan AMIRJANOV, Alexander INTSKIRVELI
(GEO), Samir MUTALLIMOV (87' Timur ANNAMAMEDOV), Pape Samba PA (YC61),
Mekan NASIROV, Yuriy MUZIKA (82' Dzhavid MIRZAYEV), Nazar BAYRAMOV,
Gokhan YAZICI, Jamshid MAHARRAMOV (YC59), Kanan KERIMOV. (Coach: Fuat
YAMAN (TUR)).
KKS Lech Poznán: Waldemar PIATEK, Ariel JAKUBOWSKI, Mariusz MOWLIK, Marcin
KUS, Rafal LASOCKI, Piotr SWIERCZEWSKI, Maciej SCHERFCHEN (YC32), Pawel
BUGALA (67' Marcin WACHOWICZ), Krzysztof GAJTKOWSKI, Pawel SASIN, Zbigniew
ZAKRZEWSKI (83' Lukasz PAULEWICZ). (Coach: Czeslaw MICHNIEWICZ).
Goals: FK Karvan Evlakh: 1-1 Yuriy MUZIKA (63').
KKS Lech Poznán: 0-1 Krzysztof GAJTKOWSKI (25'), 1-2 Mariusz MOWLIK (82' penalty).
Referee: Cem PAPILA (TUR)   Attendance: 4.500

25-06-2005   New Grosvenor Stadium, Ballyskaegh:
Lisburn Distillery FC – FK Zalgiris Vilnius   0-1 (0-0)
Lisburn Distillery FC: Michael DOUGHERTY, Gareth McKEOWN (YC52), Michael
FERGUSON, Wayne BUCHANAN, Paul MUIR, Andy BARRON (USA) (78' Ryan
McCANN), Andrew KILMARTIN, Andrew DICKSON, Johm MARTIN (RC66), Christopher
COFFEY (54' Francis MURPHY), Sean ARMSTRONG (YC12) (59' James WILLIS).
(Coach: Paul KIRK).
FK Zalgiris Vilnius: Mindaugas MALINAUSKAS, Paulius PAKNYS (YC90+1), Tadas
GRAZIUNAS, Tomas MIKUCKIS, Andrejus TERESKINAS, Vadim PETRENKO (87'
Andzey MAKSIMOVIC), Andrei SHYLO (BLS) (70' Karolis JASAITIS), Virmantas
LEMEZIS, Branislav JASUREK (SVK), Andrejus SOROKINAS, Aleksandr OSIPOVITCH
(BLS) (57' Vidas KAUSPADAS). (Coach: Saulius SIRMELIS).
Goal: FK Zalgiris Vilnius: 0-1 Andrei SHYLO (48' penalty).
Referee: Lassin ISAKSEN (FAR)

25-06-2005   Nya Ullevi, Göteborg: I.F.K. Göteborg – FC Victoria Rosport   3-1 (1-1)
I.F.K. Göteborg: John ALVBÅGE, Adam JOHANSSON (74' Gustaf SVENSSON), Mattias
BJÄRSMYR, Dennis JONSSON, Bastian ANDERSSON, Jonathan BERG, Håkan MILD,
Martin SMEDBERG, Andres VASQUES (YC55), Joel GUSTAFSSON (YC47), Marcus
BERG (YC25). (Coach: Arne ERLANDSEN (NOR)).
FC Victoria Rosport: Sascha APITZ, Frank BUSCHMANN, Alexander PAULOS (YC88),
Thomas BERENS, Asmeron HABTE, Denis GIESE (GER) (YC12) (81' Steve TOLLARDO
(YC90+1)), Markus HUWER (YC62), Patrick ZÖLLNER (46' Laurent SCHILTZ), Fabio
MORAIS (YC43) (77' Filipe RAMADA (POR)), Marc GÖRRES (GER), David SCHMIDT.
(Coach: Reiner BRINSA (GER)).
Goals: I.F.K. Göteborg: 1-0 Dennis JONSSON (1'), 2-1 Dennis JONSSON (80'), 3-1 Marcus
BERG (89').
FC Victoria Rosport: 1-1 Fabio MORAIS (19').
Referee: Andriy SHANDOR (UKR)   Attendance: 1.274

25-06-2005   Gradski Stadion, Skopje: FK Sileks Kratova – Beitar Jerusalem FC   1-2 (1-1)
FK Sileks Kratova: Vukmir MIJANOVIC (SBM), Aleksandar KIRKOV (SBM) (YC39) (68'
Igor ARSOVSKI), Gjoksen LIMANOV (61' Nikola TRIPUMOVSKI), Blagoja
TODOROVSKI, Daniel IVANOVSKI (YC59), Marjan MICKOV, Aleksandar
KONJANOVSKI (YC21), Dalibor STOJKOVIC (YC1), Sasko PANDEV (75' Eftim
AKSENTIEV), Stevica RISTIC (SBM), Sinisa JOVANOVSKI. (Coach: Nebojsa
PETROVIC).
Beitar Jerusalem FC: Izhak KORENFIEN, David AMSALEM, Yoni KIM, Eli SASON, Eliav
YONI (YC77), Idan MALACHI, Mor EFRAIM (81' Shal CHDAD), Ophir AZO, Aviram
BROCHYAN, Maor MELIKSON (90'+3' Shemoel KOZOKIN), Amit BEN SHOSHAN (66'
Shlomi MOSHE). (Coach: Azon GUY).
Goals: FK Sileks Kratova: 1-0 Stevica RISTIC (30').
Beitar Jerusalem FC: 1-1 Aviram BROCHYAN (37'), 1-2 Shlomi MOSHE (90'+2')
Referee: Szabolcs SASKOY (HUN)

25-06-2005   Stade de Genève, Genève:
Neuchâtel-Xamax FC – FC Lernagorts Ararat   6-0 (4-0)
Neuchâtel-Xamax FC: Florent DELAY, Kader MANGANE (SEN) (YC29), Eddy BAREA,
Mounir SOUFIANI (FRA), Pascal OPPLIGER (72' Juan MUNOZ JUAN (ESP)), Bastien
GEIGER, Christophe MARANINCHI (FRA) (57' Raphael NUZZOLO), Julien
CORDONNIER (FRA), Patrick BAUMANN, Charles-André DOUDIN (46' Alexandre REY),
Joel GRIFFITHS (AUS). (Coach: Alain GEIGER).
FC Lernagorts Ararat: Slavik SUKIASYAN, Vakhtang HAKOBYAN (GEO) (YC82), Karen
GRIGORYAN, Arkadi CHILINGARYAN, Hayk NARIMANYAN, Karen NAVOYAN, Arsen
DALLAKYAN, Albert NERSISYAN, Vardan ABRAKHAMYAN (YC50), Paul Okwuchkwu
BANNEY (55' Gagik AVAGYAN), Irumenhay Musa IDOVU (NIG). (Coach: Sevada
ARZUMANYAN).
Goals: Neuchâtel-Xamax FC: 1-0 Patrick BAUMANN (14'), 2-0 Pascal OPPLIGER (17'), 3-0
Christophe MARANINCHI (36'), 4-0 Charles-André DOUDIN (39'), 5-0 Joel GRIFFITHS
(64'), 6-0 Julien CORDONNIER (86').
Referee: Hristo RISTOSKOV (BUL)

25-06-2005   Jules Ottenstadion, Gentbrugge: KAA Gent – Bohemians FC   3-1 (2-0)
KAA Gent: Frédéric HERPOEL, Dario SMOJE (CRO), Stephen LAYBUTT (AUS), Nicolas
LOMBAERTS, Steve COOREMAN, Mamar MAMOUNI (ALG), Wouter VRANCKEN
(YC78), Yngvar HÅKONSEN (NOR), Moubarak (Mbark) BOUSSOUFA (HOL) (YC13) (88'
Davy DE BEULE), Nordin JBARI (83' Sandy MARTENS), Tim MATTHIJS (46' Mamadou
DIOP (FRA)). (Coach: Georges LEEKENS).
Bohemians FC: Matthew GREGG (ENG), Stephen RICE, Ken OMAN, Desmond BYRNE,
James KEDDY, John KELLY (66' Fergal HARKIN), Kevin HUNT (ENG) (67' Mark
O'BRIEN), Gareth FARRELLY, Stephen WARD, Anthony GRANT, Dominic FOLEY.
(Coach: Patrick (Pat) CLEARY).
Goals: KAA Gent: 1-0 Nordin JBARI (1'), 2-0 Yngvar HÅKONSEN (11'), 3-0 Wouter
VRANCKEN (60').
Bohemians FC: 3-1 Desmond BYRNE (75').
Referee: Khagani MAMMADOV (AZE)
*(Nordin JBARI scored one of the fastest goals in the history of the Intertoto Cup, a mere
18 seconds after kick-off)*

25-06-2005   Arnold-Schwarzenegger-Stadion, Graz:
SK Sturm Graz – FC Ranger's   5-0 (3-0)
SK Sturm Graz: Grzegorz SZAMOTULSKI (POL), Günther NEUKIRCHNER (YC19), Adam
LEDWON (POL) (YC26), Franck SILVESTRE (FRA), Ronald GERCALIU (YC35),
Johannes ERTL (64' Gerald SÄUMEL), Thomas KRAMMER, Jürgen SÄUMEL (64' Dragan
SARAC (SBM)), Bojan FILIPOVIC (SBM), David MUJIRI (GEO), Amadou RABIHOU
(CMR) (59' Diego ROTTENSTEINER). (Coach: Mihajlo PETROVIC (SRB)).
FC Ranger's: Gregorio RODRIGUEZ (ESP), José PORTA (ESP) (YC9), Francisco Javier
MARTIN SANCHEZ (ESP), Genis GARCÍA, Sergio ALBANELL (ESP), José ALVAREZ
(ARG) (83' Carles BERGUES (ESP)), Toni CAÇADOR (76' Christian CRUZZATE
(ESP)), Justo GONZALEZ (ESP), LEONARDO, Manolo JIMÉNEZ (YC30), Norberto
URBANI (ARG) (YC81) (90'+1' Johnny CASAL (ESP)). (Coach: Vicente MARQUES
Gonzalez).
Goals: SK Sturm Graz: 1-0 Bojan FILIPOVIC (26'), 2-0 Amadou RABIHOU (33'), 3-0 Jürgen
SÄUMEL (43'), 4-0 Dragan SARAC (79'), 5-0 Dragan SARAC (82').
Referee: Adrian McCOURT (NIR)

25-06-2005   Gradski Stadion, Varazdin:
NK Varteks Varazdin – KS Dinamo Tiranë   4-1 (1-1)
NK Varteks Varazdin: Miroslav KOPRIC, Nikola POKRIVAC, Mirko PLANTIC, Goran
MUJANOVIC (46' Enes NOVINIC), Kristijan IPSA, Zoran KASTEL, Dario JERTEC, Nikola
SAFARIC, Leon BENKO (YC89), Nikola MELNJAK (70' Marko BASIC), Nedim
HALILOVIC (BOS) (14' Zedi RAMADANI). (Coach: Zlatko DALIC).
KS Dinamo Tiranë: Elion LIKA, Leandro ESCUDERO (ARG), Erion XHAFA (62' Fjodor
XHAFA), Ibrahim KONI (MLI), Papa DIOP (SEN) (YC82), Artion POÇI, Ilir QORRI, Erald
DELIALLISI, Masseye GAYE (SEN) (84' Enkel ALIKAJ), Paulin DHËMBI (70' Pape FALL
(SEN)), Elhadji GOUDIABY (SEN) (YC90+2). (Coach: Ramón Armando CABRERO
(ARG)).
Goals: NK Varteks Varazdin: 1-1 Leon BENKO (32'), 2-1 Leon BENKO (53'), 3-1 Leon
BENKO (74'), 4-1 Leon BENKO (90'+2 penalty).
KS Dinamo Tiranë: 0-1 Elhadji GOUDIABY (12').
Referee: Asaf KENAN (ISR)

25-06-2005   Stadion Miejski, Poznán: KKS Lech Poznán – FK Karvan Evlakh   2-0 (0-0)
KKS Lech Poznán: Krzysztof KOTOROWSKI, Arkadiusz CZARNECKI (YC72), Mariusz
MOWLIK, Zbigniew WÓJCIK, Pawel SASIN, Piotr SWIERCZEWSKI (YC50) (73' Matias
FAVANO (ARG)), Maciej SCHERFCHEN (YC80), Zbigniew ZAKRZEWSKI (82' Ebrahima
SAWANEH (GAM)), Krzysztof GAJTKOWSKI, Marcin WACHOWICZ (YC53) (69' Artur
MARCINIAK), Piotr REISS. (Coach: Czeslaw MICHNIEWICZ).
FK Karvan Evlakh: Eikhan HASANOV, Ruslan AMIRJANOV, Alexander INTSKIRVELI
(GEO) (YC45), Gocha TRAPAIDZE (GEO), Pape Samba PA, Kanan KERIMOV, Mekan
NASIROV (21' Samir ABBASOV), Yuriy MUZIKA (71' Farrukh ISMAYLOV (YC80)),
Gokhan YAZICI (90' Dzhavid MIRZAYEV), Nazar BAYRAMOV (YC30), Jamshid
MAHARRAMOV (YC48). (Coach: Fuat YAMAN (TUR)).
Goals: KKS Lech Poznán: 1-0 Marcin WACHOWICZ (60'), 2-0 Maciej SCHERFCHEN (78').
Referee: Johannes VALGEIRSSON (ISL)   Attendance: 2.000

25-06-2005   Stadion Pod Goricom, Podgorica:
FK Buducnost Podgorica – Valletta FC   2-2 (1-1)
FK Buducnost Podgorica: Miroslav VUJADINOVIC (RC19), Risto LAKIC, Marko
DZEVERDANOVIC, Nikola VUKCEVIC, Ivan CARAPIC, Mirko RAICEVIC (46' Slobodan
ROVCANIN), Nikola VUJOVIC (68' Goran BURZANOVIC), Aleksandar CADJENOVIC
(20' Mladen BOZOVIC goalkeeper), Radislav SEKULIC, Igor BURZANOVIC, Bojan
USANOVIC (YC49). (Coach: Branislav MILACIC).
Valletta FC: Sean SULLIVAN, Kevin CASSAR, Massimo GRIMA, Branko NISEVIC (SBM)
(YC25), Rennie FORACE, Jonathan BONDIN (77' Stefano GRIMA), Keith FENECH, Milen
Penchev STEFANOV (BUL), Anatole DEBONO (78' Ian ZAMMIT), Gilbert AGIUS, Mark
GALEA (87' Chris CAMILLERI). (Coach: John Joseph AQUILINA).
Goals: FK Buducnost Podgorica: 1-0 Radislav SEKULIC (1'), 2-1 Radislav SEKULIC (62').
Valletta FC: 1-1 Massimo GRIMA (21' penalty), 2-2 Gilbert AGIUS (80').
Referee: Marek MIKOLAJEWSKI (POL)

25-06-2005   Het Kuipje, Westerlo: KSC Lokeren – JK Trans Narva   0-1 (0-1)
KSC Lokeren: Jugoslav LAZIC (SBM), JOÃO CARLOS Pinto Chaves (BRA), Ivan
VUKOMANOVIC (SBM), Runar KRISTINSSON (ISL) (54' Arnar GRETARSSON (ISL)),
Killian OVERMEIRE, Marc HENDRIKX (80' Glen COPPENS), Aboubacar M'BAYE
CAMARA (GUI) (YC30), José Ilson dos Santos "TAILSON" (BRA) (69' Xavier
DESCHACHT), Lezou Hugues DOBA (CIV), Michael VAN HOEY, Frederik DE WINNE.
(Coach: Slavoljub MUSLIN (SRB)).
JK Trans Narva: Sergei USSOLTSEV, Andrei PRUSS, Ilya DJORD (RUS), Sergei
KAZAKOV (54' Sergei POPOV), Irfan AMETOV (UKR) (80' Dmytro DOBROVOLSKIY
(UKR)), Aleksandr TARASSENKOV, Dmitri LIPARTOV (RUS) (YC75), Maksim
GRUZNOV (YC81), Stanislav KITTO, Dmitri SELEHHOV (67' Aleksei GORSKOV),
Aleksandr KULIK. (Coach: Valeri BONDARENKO).
Goal: JK Trans Narva: 0-1 Aleksandr TARASSENKOV (27').
Referee: Sergey TSAREGRADSKIYI (KAZ)   Attendance: 500

25-06-2005   Stadion Miejski, Szczecin: KS Pogon Szczecin – FC Tiligul Tiraspol   6-2 (3-1)
KS Pogon Szczecin: Boris PESKOVIC (SVK) (70' Bartosz FABINIAK), Krzysztof
MICHALSKI, JULCIMAR De Souza (BRA), Pawel MAGDON, Tomasz PARZY, Sergio
BATATA (BRA) (70' Marek KOWAL (CZE)), Lukasz TRALKA, Michal LABEDZKI (78'
Petr KASPRAK (CZE)), Rafal GRZELAK, Roberto Claudio MILAR Decaudra (URU), Artur
BUGAJ. (Coach: Boguslaw PIETRZAK).
FC Tiligul Tiraspol: Eugen IVANOV, Serghei CUZNETOV (YC60), Eduard GROSU, Igor
SOLTANICI, Olexandr DYNDIKOV (UKR), Serghei STROENCO (YC16), Serghei
BUTELSCHI, Vitali PINIASKINE (RUS) (29' Alexei MACASIOR, 86' Alexander
PETROV), Vladimir TARANU, Igor DOBROVOLSKI, Victor COMLEONOC (68' Dumitru
BACAL). (Coach: Igor Ivanovich DOBROVOLSKIY (UKR)).
Goals: KS Pogon Szczecin: 1-0 Sergio BATATA (22'), 2-0 Sergio BATATA (24'), 3-0
Roberto Claudio MILAR Decaudra (27' penalty), 4-1 Artur BUGAJ (52'), 5-2 Serghei
STROENCO (88' own goal), 6-2 Marek KOWAL (90').
FC Tiligul Tiraspol: 3-1 Serghei CUZNETOV (36'), 4-2 Dumitru BACAL (70' penalty).
Referee: Alexandru DEACONU (ROM)   Attendance: 3.000

25-06-2005   Ljudski vrt Stadium, Maribor:
               NK Drava Ptuj – NK Slaven Belupo Koprivnica   0-1 (0-0)
NK Drava Ptuj: Mladen DABANOVIC, Matej MILJATOVIC, Emil STERBAL, Matjaz
LUNDER, Primoz PETEK (64' Ales CEH (YC80)), Robert TEZACKI (CRO), Nedzad
ALIBABIC (13' Andrej PREJAC), Aljaz ZAJC, Majtaz KOREZ (46' Vladimir SLADOJEVIC
(BOS), Viktor TRENEVSKI (MCD), Gorazd GORINSEK. (Coach: Srecko LUSIC (CRO)).
NK Slaven Belupo Koprivnica: Tomislav PELIN, Pavo CRNAC, Sime KURILIC, Igor GAL
(YC23), Petar BOSNJAK (78' Edin SARANOVIC (BOS)), Ognjen VUKOJEVIC (YC15),
Igor MUSA (78' Marijo DODIK), Dejan SOMOCI (90' Tomislav KELEMEN), Dalibor
VISKOVIC, Pero PEJIC, Ivica KARABOGDAN. (Coach: Branko KARACIC).
Goal: NK Slaven Belupo Koprivnica: 0-1 Edin SARANOVIC (90').
Referee: David McKEON (IRL)   Attendance: 800

26-06-2005   Akranesvöllur, Akranes: Í.A. Akranes – FC International Turku 0-4 (0-1)
Í.A. Akranes: Páll Gisli JÓNSSON, Kristinn RÖDULSSON, Gudjón H.SVEINSSON, Heimir
EINARSSON, Ellert Jón BJÖRNSSON (65' Thorsteinn GISLASON), Jón Vilhelm ÁKASON
(73' Arnar Már GUDJÓNSSON), Igor PESIC (SBM), Pálmi HARALDSSON (60' Dean
MARTIN (ENG) (YC88)), Hafthór VILHJÁLMSSON, Sigurdur Ragnar EYJÓLFSSON, Kári
Steinn REYNISSON. (Coach: Ólafur THÓRDARSON).
FC International Turku: Magnus BAHNE, Diego CORPACHE (ARG), Jukka SINISALO,
Jermu GUSTAFSSON, Henri LEHTONEN, Aristides PERTOT (ARG), Prince OTOO, Serge
N'GAL (CMR) (84' Mika MÄKITALO (YC88)), Miikka ILO (88' Matti HEIMO), Tomi
PETRESCU (86' Sami SANEVUORI), Martin MUTUMBA (SWE). (Coach : Kari
VIRTANEN).
Goals: FC International Turku: 0-1 Henri LEHTONEN (24'), 0-2 Miikka ILO (65'), 0-3 Kári
Steinn REYNISSON (75' own goal), 0-4 Tomi PETRESCU (81').
Referee: Radek MATEJEK (CZE)

26-06-2005   Stadionul Gloria, Bistrita:
              FC Gloria Bistrita – Olympiakos FC Nicosia 11-0 (7-0)
FC Gloria Bistrita: Septimiu Calin ALBUT, Alin Valer RUS, Alin CHIBULCUTEAN (46'
Marius DRULE), Daniel PAICA, Dinu Daniel SANMARTEAN, Catalin BUCUR, Adrian
NALATI (57' Andrei Dan BOZESAN), Adrian PREDICA, Adrian Ioan SALAGEAN, Sandu
NEGREAN (38' Szabolocs SZEKELY), Ionut Bogdan PERES. (Coach: Ion BALAUR).
Olympiakos FC Nicosia: Anastasios YIALLOURIS, Nicolas THERAPONTOS, Stelios
CHARALAMBOUS, Christodoulos CHRISTODOULOU (46' Kyriacos LEFAS), Georgios
HADJIKYRIACOU (63' Balli ERBAY), Joseph FRANGISKOS, Theodosis
CHARALAMBOUS, Fidias PANAYIOTOU (46' Odysseas STAVROU), Rodolfos
POURGOURIDIS, Loizos SOLONOS, Angelos SERPETINIS. (Coach: Costas SERAFIM).
Goals: FC Gloria Bistrita: 1-0 Catalin BUCUR (7'), 2-0 Ionut Bogdan PERES (12'), 3-0 Ionut
Bogdan PERES (19'), 4-0 Sandu NEGREAN (27'), 5-0 Sandu NEGREAN (29'), 6-0 Ionut
Bogdan PERES (33'), 7-0 Sandu NEGREAN (35'), 8-0 Catalin BUCUR (64'), 9-0 Szabolocs
SZEKELY (76'), 10-0 Catalin BUCUR (78'), 11-0 Andrei Dan BOZESAN (89' penalty).
Referee: Igor ZAKHAROV (RUS)

26-06-2005   Mestský futbalový stadion, Dubnica Nad Váhom:
              FK ZTS Dubnica – Vasas SC 2-0 (1-0)
FK ZTS Dubnica: Dusan PERNIS (YC76), Peter PEKÁRIK (YC67), Dalibor PLEVA (YC30),
Martin SVESTKA (CZE), Marián ZIMEN, Peter KISKA (55' Juraj DOVICOVIC), Pavol
KOPACKA (YC35), Igor DRZIK, Matej IZVOLT, Lukás TESÁK (88' Erik GRENDEL),
Pavol STRAKA (90' Marián ADAM). (Coach: Lubomir NOSICKY).
Vasas SC: Zsolt POSZA, Zoltán MOLNÁR (YC61), János GYÖRI, Iván JANJIC (SBM)
(YC51) (61' Nobert HEGEDÜS), András TÓTH, Zsolt BALOG (53' Levente SCHULTZ),
Henrik RÓSA, György KISS, László GAÁL, Robert WALTNER, Ádám WEITHER. (Coach:
Sándor EGERVÁRI).
Goals: FK ZTS Dubnica: 1-0 Peter KISKA (21'), 2-0 Lukás TESÁK (49').
Referee: Marijo STRAHONJA (CRO)   Attendance: 3.200

131

26-06-2005   Gradski Stadion, Skopje: FK Pobeda Prilep – FK Sartid Smederevo   2-1 (0-1)
FK Pobeda Prilep: Darko TOFILOVSKI, Aleksandar POPOVSKI, Blagojce DAMEVSKI,
Dejan CVETKOVSKI, Sulaimon OMO (NGR), Toni MEGLENSKI, Dimitar KAPINKOVSKI
(YC64), Vladimir VUJOVIC (SBM) (YC75) (90' Pereira EMERSON (BRA)), Dejan
RISTOVSKI, Borce MANEVSKI (51' Marjan NACEV (YC78)), Saso KRSTEV (80'
Draganco DIMITROVSKI). (Coach: Petar KURCUBIC (SRB)).
FK Sartid Smederevo: Dejan RANKOVIC, Dejan KEKEZOVIC, Nebojsa SAVIC (80' Marko
SOCANAC), Zeljko KOVACEVIC (YC62), Ivan ZIVANOVIC, Sasa KOCIC (YC27), Vladen
CUKIC (80' Aleksandar MILJKOVIC), Milan NIKOLIC, Nicola JEVTIC, Petar DIVIC,
Dragan TADIC (52' Aleksandar JEVTIC). (Coach: Tomislav SIVIC).
Goals: FK Pobeda Prilep: 1-1 Vladimir VUJOVIC (75'), 2-1 Dimitar KAPINKOVSKI (82').
FK Sartid Smederevo: 0-1 Petar DIVIC (16').
Referee: Thomas EINWALLER (AUT)

26-06-2005   Celtnieks Stadion, Daugavpils:
              FC Dinaburg Daugavpils – Bangor City FC   2-0 (1-0)
FC Dinaburg Daugavpils: Vadims FJODOROVS, Deniss SOKOLSKIS, Sergey KHIMICH
(RUS), Andrejs ZUROMSKIS, Edgars BURLAKOVS, Pavels KOLCOVS (49' Jurgis
PUCINSKIS), Nikita CHMYKOV (RUS) (YC65) (85' Dmitri TIMACHEV (RUS)), Jurijs
SOKOLOVS, Mikhails ZIZILEVS, Olexandr KRIKLIVY (UKR), Sergejs VALUSKINS (75'
Vladimir VOLKOVS). (Coach: Roman Yosypovych GRYGORCHUK (UKR)).
Bangor City FC: Andrew Oliver RALPH, Lee Francis ATHERTON (ENG), Kevin SCOTT,
Eifion JONES (YC60), Paul O'NEILL (ENG), Christopher PRIEST (ENG) (83' Benjamin
O'GILVEY), Tony GRAY (ENG), Owain JONES (YC88), Paul ROBERTS (YC38), Carl
LAMB (ENG) (62' Paul FRIEL (IRL)), Leslie DAVIES (62' Gareth WILLIAMS). (Coach:
Peter DAVENPORT (ENG)).
Goals: FC Dinaburg Daugavpils: 1-0 Deniss SOKOLSKIS (13'), 2-0 Lee Francis ATHERTON
(56' own goal).
Referee: Ararat TCHAGHARYAN (ARM)   Attendance: 615

26-06-2005   Letná Stadium, Zlín: FC Tescoma Zlín – FC Neman Grodno   0-0
FK Tescoma Zlín: Ales KORÍNEK, Tomás JANÍCEK (56' Jan JELÍNEK), Jaroslav SVACH,
Zdenik KROCA, Bronislav CERVENKA (YC36), Václav ZAPLETAL (90' Martin BIELIK),
Vít VRTILKA (YC85), Roman DOBES, Josef LUKASTÍK, Tomás KLINKA (61' Martin
BACA), Václav CINCALA. (Coach: Pavel HOFTYCH).
FC Neman Grodno: Andrei ASHYKHMIN, Andrei KORZHUK (YC80), Artur KRYVANOS
(33' Yury MAMIDA), Gennadi MARDAS, Vitali NADZIYENSKI, Dzmitry HINTAU
(YC71) (83' Nikoloz ZEDELASHVILI (GEO) (YC87)), Mikalai YASERSKI, Iouri
LOUKACHOV (YC68), Vyacheslav GRYGORAV, Dzmitry PARFIONAU, Andrei
LIASIUK. (Coach: Siarhei Vytalievych SOLODOVNIKOV).
Referee: Merab MALAGOURADZE (GEO)   Attendance: 1.958

26-06-2005   Vetros Stadionas, Vilnius: FK Vetra Vilnius – CFR Cluj 1-4 (1-2)
FK Vetra Rudiskes Vilnius: Ramunas MERKELIS, Zilvinas ZUDYS (YC86), Julius
RALIUKONIS (RC30), Igoris STESKO, Janis RINKUS (LAT), Gediminas
BUTRIMAVICIUS (YC54) (76' Arturas STESKO), Aidas PREIKSAITIS, Andrius
KOCHANAUSKAS (46' Nerijus VASILIAUSKAS), Darvydas SERNAS, Rolandas
VAINEIKIS (46' Nerijus SASNAUSKAS), Edvinas BLAZYS. (Coach: Siarhei BAROUSKI
(BLS)).
CFR Cluj: Petru TURCAS, Cristian Calin PANIN, Vasile Ilie JULA, Zoran MILOSEVIC
(SBM) (YC34), Dorin TOMA (YC40), Cosmin Marin VASIE, Florin Cristian DAN (66'
Cristian TURCU), Radu Leon MARGINEAN, Stefan Sorin ONCICA (90' Sabin GOIA),
Adrian Gheorghe ANCA (71' Djordje VLAJIC (SBM)), Cosmin TILINCA. (Coach: Aurel
SUNDA).
Goals: FK Vetra Vilnius: 1-2 Gediminas BUTRIMAVICIUS (37').
CFR Cluj: 0-1 Florin DAN (3'), 0-2 Adrian Gheorghe ANCA (31'), 1-3 Vasile Ilie JULA (86'
penalty), 1-4 Cosmin TILINCA (90'+3').
Referee: Pavel OLSIAK (SVK)

26-06-2005   Boris Paichadze Stadium, Tbilisi:
              FC WIT Georgia Tbilisi – Lombard-Pápa TFC   0-1 (0-0)
FC WIT Georgia Tbilisi: Grigol BEDIASHVILI, David ABSHILAVA (40' Parnaoz
KUSHASHVILI (YC75)), David LOMAIA, Alexander KVAKHADZE (YC77), David
IMEDASHVILI, Luka RAZMADZE (75' Lasha MANTSKAVA), Pawel DATUNAISHVILI,
David DIGMELASHVILI (YC86), Otar MARTSVALADZE, Zaza SAKHOKIA (YC56),
Irakli EBANOIDZE (53' Vladimer GOCHASHVILI). (Coach: Nestor MUMLADZE).
Lombard-Pápa TFC: Anoras DOMBAI, Attila FARKAS, Viktor FARKAS, Zoltán LIPTÁK
(YC15) (66' Attila CSÁSZÁR (YC86)), Dorel MUTICA (ROM), Tamas GERI (YC84), Tibor
SZABÓ, Balász LÁSZKA, Ákos KOVRIG (76' Zoltán SZABÓ), Gábor ÚJHEGYI (80'
Kristián SZALAI), Zoltán HERCEGFALVI (YC,YC56). (Coach: Lázár SZENTES).
Goal: Lombard-Pápa TFC: 0-1 Zoltán HERCEGFALVI (50').
Referee: Robert KRAJNC (SLO)

26-06-2005   Ratina Stadium, Tampere: Tampere United FC – Skála ÍF 1-0 (0-0)
Tampere United FC: Mikko KAVÉN, Heikki AHO, Janne RÄSÄNEN, Antti OJANPERÄ,
Jussi KUOPPALA, Jussi KUJALA (84' Sakari SAARINEN), Jarkko WISS, Kari SAINIO
(YC45), Petri HEINÄNEN, Henri SCHEWELEFF, Antti HYNYNEN (56' Mika LAHTINEN).
(Coach: Ari Juhani HJELM).
Skála ÍF: Vlada FILIPOVIC (SBM), Paetur Dam JACOBSEN, Runi RASMUSSEN, Milic
CURCIC (SBM), Iulian FLORESCU (ROM), Bjarni JØRGENSEN, Nenad STANKOVIC
(SBM), Pauli G.HANSEN (YC73), Hanus THORLEIFSON (84' Jenel Christian
GORGONARU (ROM)), Jønhard FREDERIKSBERG (84' Arnhold BERG), Bogi
GREGERSEN (18' Sveinur JUSTINUSSEN). (Coach: Jóhan NIELSEN).
Goal: Tampere United FC: 1-0 Janne RÄSÄNEN (67').
Referee: Andrejs SIPAILO (LAT)   Attendance: 1.803

133

SECOND ROUND

02-07-2005   Volkswagen-Arena, Wolfsburg: VfL Wolfsburg – SK Sturm Graz 2-2 (0-0)
VfL Wolfsburg: Simon JENTZSCH, Thomas RYTTER (DEN) (79' Cedric MAKIADI), Maik
FRANZ, Kevin HOFLAND (HOL) (YC43), Peter VAN DER HEYDEN (BEL), Miroslav
KARHAN (SVK), Karsten FISCHER, Andrés Nicolas D'ALESSANDRO (ARG), Juan Carlos
MENSEGUEZ (ARG) (46' Mike HANKE), Martin PETROV (BUL), Diego Fernando
KLIMOWICZ (ESP) (74' Marko TOPIC (BOS)). (Coach: Holger FACH).
SK Sturm Graz: Grzegorz SZAMOTULSKI (POL), Günther NEUKIRCHNER, Franck
SILVESTRE (FRA), Frank VERLAAT (HOL), Ronald GERCALIU, Bojan FILIPOVIC
(SBM), Adam LEDWON (POL) (RC71), Dragan SARAC (SBM) (69' David MUJIRI (GEO)),
Jürgen SÄUMEL, Oliver NZUZI POLO (CGO) (69' Johannes ERTL), Amadou RABIHOU
(CMR) (YC34) (74' Gerald SÄUMEL). (Coach: Mihajlo PETROVIC (SRB)).
Goals: VfL Wolfsburg: 1-0 Miroslav KARHAN (49'), 2-1 Andrés Nicolas D'ALESSANDRO
(54').
SK Sturm Graz: 1-1 Bojan FILIPOVIC (52'), 2-2 David MUJIRI (80').
Referee: Alfonso PEREZ BURRULL (ESP)   Attendance: 8.376

02-07-2005   Stadionul CFR Gruia, Cluj-Napoca:
              CFR Cluj – Athletic Club Bilbao 1-0 (1-0)
CFR Cluj: Petru TURCAS, Cristian Calin PANIN (YC43), Vasile Ilie JULA, Zoran
MILOSEVIC (SBM), Cosmin Marin VASIE, Stefan Sorin ONCICA, Radu Leon
MARGINEAN (46' Gheorghe GOSA (YC52)), Dorinel Ionel MUNTEANU (YC31), Cristian
TURCU (18' Laur Marian ASTILEAN), Adrian Gheorghe ANCA (90+' Svetozar MIJIN
(SBM)), Cosmin TILINCA (YC90). (Coach: Dorinel Ionel MUNTEANU).
Athletic Club Bilbao: Iñaki LAFUENTE Sánchez, Asier ORMAZÁBAL Larizgoitia (YC83),
EDER MARTÍNEZ Telletxea, Fernando AMOREBIETA Mardaras, Javier CASAS Cuevas,
David DE PAULA Gallardo (83' David LIZOAIN Loizu), Aritz SOLABARRIETA
Aranzamendi (46' Jon Andoni "JONAN" García Arambillet), Julen GUERRERO López,
IBON GUTIÉRREZ Fernández (YC41), Pablo PAREDES Arratia (46' Javier "JAVI"
GONZÁLEZ Gómez), Joseba ARRIAGA Dosantos (YC86). (Coach: José Luis MENDILIBAR
Etxebarria).
Goal: CFR Cluj: 1-0 Cosmin TILINCA (36').
Referee: Milan SEDIVY (CZE)   Attendance: 6.500
(Javier "JAVI" GONZÁLEZ Gómez missed penalty in the 60ᵗʰ minute)

02-07-2005   Gradski Stadion, Koprivnica:
              NK Slaven Belupo Koprivnica – FC Gloria Bistrita 3-2 (1-1)
NK Slaven Belupo Koprivnica: Robert LISJAK, Igor GAL, Sime KURILIC (YC33), Dario
BODRUSIC (RC30), Petar BOSNJAK (82' Pero PEJIC), Dejan SOMOCI, Igor MUSA,
Tomislav KELEMEN (YC79), Dalibor VISKOVIC, Bojan VRUCINA (64' Ivica
KARABOGDAN), Edin SARANOVIC (BOS) (64' Marijo DODIK). (Coach: Branko
KARACIC).
FC Gloria Bistrita: Septimiu Calin ALBUT, Dan MATEI, Alin Valer RUS (YC20), Alin
CHIBULCUTEAN (58' Adrian PREDICA), Daniel PAICA, Dinu Daniel SANMARTEAN,
Marius DRULE (68' Catalin BUCUR), Sergiu Ioan COSTIN, Adrian Ioan SALAGEAN, Ionut
Bogdan PERES (72' Szabolocs SZEKELY), Sandu NEGREAN (YC24). (Coach: Ion
BALAUR).
Goals: NK Slaven Belupo Koprivnica: 1-1 Bojan VRUCINA (45'), 2-1 Edin SARANOVIC
(60'), 3-2 Igor MUSA (81' penalty).
FC Gloria Bistrita: 0-1 Ionut Bogdan PERES (31' penalty), 2-2 Catalin BUCUR (70').
Referee: Johny VER EECKE (BEL)   Attendance: 1.000

02-07-2005   AOL Arena, Hamburg: Hamburger SV – FK Pobeda Prilep   4-1 (0-1)
Hamburger SV: Stefan WÄCHTER, Collin BENJAMIN (NAM) (36' Piotr TROCHOWSKI),
Bastian REINHARDT, René KLINGBEIL, Volker SCHMIDT, David JAROLIM (CZE) (67'
Charles TAKYI), Guy DEMEL (FRA), Stefan BEINLICH, Alexander LAAS, Mustafa
KUCUKOVIC, Naohiro TAKAHARA (JPN) (57' Benjamin LAUTH). (Coach: Thomas
DOLL).
FK Pobeda Prilep: Darko TOFILOVSKI, Aleksandar POPOVSKI, Sulaimon OMO (NGR)
(71' Pereira EMERSON (BRA)), Dejan CVETKOVSKI, Blagojce DAMEVSKI, Borce
MANEVSKI (YC90+1), Toni MEGLENSKI (YC68), Saso ZDRAVEVSKI, Marjan NACEV,
Dejan RISTOVSKI (66' Nikolce ZDRAVEVSKI), Saso KRSTEV (62' Blagoja GESOSKI).
(Coach: Petar KURCUBIC (SRB)).
Goals: Hamburger SV: 1-1 Guy DEMEL (49'), 2-1 Alexander LAAS (67'), 3-1 Charles
TAKYI (71'), 4-1 Piotr TROCHOWSKI (72').
FK Pobeda Prilep: 0-1 Aleksandar POPOVSKI (44').
Referee: Viktor KASSAI (HUN)   Attendance: 27.612

02-07-2005   Jules Ottenstadion, Gentbrugge: KAA Gent – FK Tescoma Zlín   1-0 (0-0)
KAA Gent: Frédéric HERPOEL, Dario SMOJE (CRO), Stephen LAYBUTT (AUS), Nicolas
LOMBAERTS, Mamar MAMOUNI (ALG), Wouter VRANCKEN (YC27), Yngvar
HÅKONSEN (NOR), Moubarak (Mbark) BOUSSOUFA (HOL), Sandy MARTENS, Nordin
JBARI (82' Nenad MLADENOVIC (SBM)), Mohammed Aliyu DATTI (NGR). (Coach:
Georges LEEKENS).
FK Tescoma Zlín: Ales KORÍNEK, Tomás JANÍCEK (YC20), Zdenik KROCA, Jaroslav
SVACH, Jan JELÍNEK, Václav ZAPLETAL (72' Tomás DUJKA), Roman DOBES (YC35),
Martin BACA (90'+1' Radim DITRICH), Václav CINCALA, Josef LUKASTÍK (YC40),
Martin BIELIK (63' Richard KALOD). (Coach: Pavel HOFTYCH).
Goal: KAA Gent: 1-0 Sandy MARTENS (50').
Referee: Egill Mar MARKUSSON (ISL)   Attendance: 3.000

02-07-2005   Andruv stadion, Olomouc:
               SK Sigma Olomouc – KS Pogon Szczecin   1-0 (1-0)
SK Sigma Olomouc: Tomás LOVÁSIK (SVK), Roman HUBNIK, Michal KOVÁR, Martin
HUDEC, Tomás RANDA (YC50), Martin VYSKOCIL (YC59) (61' Jan SCHULMEISTER),
Filip RÝDEL (YC85), Radek SPILÁCEK, Andrej PECNIK (SLO) (66' Radim KOPECKY),
Peter BABNIC (SVK), David ROJKA (79' Michal HUBNIK (YC90+1)). (Coach: Petr
ULICNY).
KS Pogon Szczecin: Boris PESKOVIC (SVK), Krzysztof MICHALSKI, JULCIMAR De
Souza (BRA), Pawel MAGDON, Grzegorz MATLAK (YC88), Lukasz TRALKA (82' Marek
KOWAL (CZE)), Michal LABEDZKI, Przemyslaw KAZMIERCZAK, Rafal GRZELAK,
Sergio BATATA (BRA) (58' Tomasz PARZY), Roberto Claudio MILAR Decaudra (URU).
(Coach: Boguslaw PIETRZAK).
Goal: SK Sigma Olomouc: 1-0 Peter BABNIC (35').
Referee: Adrian D.CASHA (MLT)   Attendance: 3.097

02-07-2005   Stadion u Nisy, Liberec: FC Slovan Liberec – Beitar Jerusalem FC   5-1 (1-0)
FC Slovan Liberec: Petr BOLEK, Peter SINGLÁR (SVK), Milan MATULA, Tomás
ZÁPOTOCNY, Tomás JANU, Ivan HODÚR (SVK), Martin ABRAHÁM, Daniel PUDIL (59'
Filip DORT), Miroslav SLEPICKA, Libor DOSEK (85' Jan BLAZEK), Filip HOLOSKO
(SVK) (74' Jan BROSCHINSKY). (Coach: Vítezslav LAVICKA).
Beitar Jerusalem FC: Izhak KORENFIEN, Eliav YONI, Eli SASON, Yoni KIM, David
AMSALEM, Aviram BROCHYAN, Ophir AZO (YC47) (58' Shlomi MOSHE), Mor
EFRAIM, Maor MELIKSON (YC70) (87' Shal CHDAD), Idan MALACHI, Amit BEN
SHOSHAN. (Coach: Azon GUY).
Goals: FC Slovan Liberec: 1-0 Filip HOLOSKO (28'), 2-0 Tomás ZÁPOTOCNY (48'), 3-0
Miroslav SLEPICKA (55'), 4-1 Libor DOSEK (83'), 5-1 Miroslav SLEPICKA (90').
Beitar Jerusalem FC: 3-1 Amit BEN SHOSHAN (66').
Referee: Pavel SALIY (KAZ)   Attendance: 2.622

02-07-2005   Stade Geoffroy Guichard, Saint-Etienne:
                 AS Saint-Etienne – Neuchâtel-Xamax FC   1-1 (0-0)
AS Saint-Etienne: Jérémy JANOT, Vincent HOGNON, Zoumana CAMARA, Fousseiny
DIAWARA (MLI), Alledine YAHIA (TUN) (59' Herita N'Kongolo ILUNGA (DRC)
(YC79)), David HELLEBUYCK (83' Lamine SAKHO (SEN)), Julien SABLÉ, Loïc PERRIN,
Pascal FEINDOUNO (GUI), Frédéric PIQUIONNE, Frédéric MENDY (SEN) (59' Sébastien
MAZURE). (Coach: Élie BAUP).
Neuchâtel-Xamax FC: Jean-François BEDENIK (FRA), Mounir SOUFIANI (FRA), Henri-
Georges SIQUEIRA-BARRAS, Julien CORDONNIER (FRA) (YC38), Massimo
LOMBARDO (83' Raphael NUZZOLO), Pascal OPPLIGER, Patrick BAUMANN (79' Herve
AKA'A (CMR)), Bastien GEIGER, Alexandre REY, Christophe MARANINCHI (FRA) (68'
Charles-André DOUDIN), Joel GRIFFITHS (AUS). (Coach: Alain GEIGER).
Goals: AS Saint-Etienne: 1-1 Julien SABLÉ (74').
Neuchâtel-Xamax FC: 0-1 Massimo LOMBARDO (57').
Referee: Richard HAVRILLA (SVK)   Attendance: 32.021

02-07-2005   Het Kuipje, Westerlo: KSC Lokeren – BSC Young Boys Bern   1-4 (0-2)
KSC Lokeren: Zvonko MILOJEVIC (SBM), JOÃO CARLOS Pinto Chaves (BRA), Lezou
Hugues DOBA (CIV) (46' Runar KRISTINSSON (ISL) (YC89)), Frederik DE WINNE
(YC39), Ivan VUKOMANOVIC (SBM) (YC86), Arnar GRETARSSON (ISL), Marc
HENDRIKX, Aboubacar M'BAYE CAMARA (GUI), José Ilson dos Santos "TAILSON"
(BRA) (60' Xavier DESCHACHT), Stjepan JUKIC (CRO) (32' Killian OVERMEIRE),
Gunter VAN HANDEN HOVEN. (Coach: Slavoljub MUSLIN (SRB)).
BSC Young Boys Bern: Marco WÖLFLI, TIAGO Coelho Branco Calvano (BRA), Mark
DISLER (YC75), Gretar STEINSSON (ISL) (73' Gabriel José URDANETA Rangel (VEN)),
Gürkan SERMETER, Joël MAGNIN, Thomas HÄBERLI, Mario RAIMONDI, Carlos Vila
VARELA (ESP) (70' Patrick DE NAPOLI), Pirmin SCHWEGLER, Francisco "NERI"
Valmeri Souza (BRA) (79' Marco SCHNEUWLY). (Coach: Hans-Peter ZAÜGG).
Goals: KSC Lokeren: 1-4 Xavier DESCHACHT (70').
BSC Young Boys Bern: 0-1 Gretar STEINSSON (4'), 0-2 Francisco "NERI" Valmeri Souza
(25'), 0-3 Carlos Vila VARELA (49'), 0-4 Thomas HÄBERLI (67').
Referee: Brage SANDMOEN (NOR)

02-07-2005   Gradski Stadion,Varazdin:
NK Varteks Varazdin – FC International Turku   4-3 (1-2)
NK Varteks Varazdin: Miroslav KOPRIC, Nikola POKRIVAC, Mirko PLANTIC, Goran
MUJANOVIC (70' Zedi RAMADANI), Zoran KASTEL, Dario JERTEC, Nikola SAFARIC,
Leon BENKO (YC62), Nikola MELNJAK, Ivan JOLIC (BOS) (46' Enes NOVINIC), Nedim
HALILOVIC (BOS) (72' Mladen JURCEVIC (BOS)). (Coach: Zlatko DALIC).
FC International Turku: Magnus BAHNE, Diego CORPACHE (ARG), Jukka SINISALO,
Mats GUSTAFSSON (YC42), Henri LEHTONEN, Aristides PERTOT (ARG), Prince OTOO
(YC77), Mika MÄKITALO, Serge N'GAL (CMR), Miikka ILO, Tomi PETRESCU (YC52)
(88' Valtter LAAKSONEN). (Coach : Kari VIRTANEN).
Goals: NK Vartkes Varazdin: 1-0 Leon BENKO (4'), 2-2 Nedim HALILOVIC (55'), 3-3
Nikola SAFARIC (85'), 4-3 Leon BENKO (90').
FC International Turku: 1-1 Serge N'GAL (9'), 1-2 Miikka ILO (14'), 2-3 Serge N'GAL (75').
Referee: Costas THEODOTOU (CYP)   Attendance: 2.000

02-07-2005   Ankara 19 Mayis Stadium, Ankara:
BB Ankaraspor Kulübü – FK ZTS Dubnica   0-4 (0-3)
BB Ankaraspor Kulübü: Cihan KAYAALP (YC28), Ramazan TUNC, Savas BAHADIR, Ediz
BAHTIYAROGLU (32' Emrah ÇOLAK), Musa BÜYÜK, Mustafa SARP (YC90), Mustafa
YALÇINKAYA, Hürriyet GÜCER, Özer HURMACI (73' Fatih ÖZECE), Halit KÖPRÜLÜ
(YC27), Hüseyin Kartal (57' Erman OZGUR). (Coach: Samet AYBABA).
FK ZTS Dubnica: Dusan PERNIS, Dalibor PLEVA (YC90), Robert NOVAK, Martin
SVESTKA (CZE), Marián ZIMEN, Igor DRZIK (85' Ján SVIKRUHA), Pavol KOPACKA,
Matej IZVOLT, Juraj DOVICOVIC, Lukás TESÁK (79' Peter AUGUSTÍNI), Marián ADAM
(88' Lukás ZÁPOTOKA). (Coach: Lubomir NOSICKY).
Goals: FK ZTS Dubnica: 0-1 Igor DRZIK (15'), 0-2 Pavol KOPACKA (29' penalty), 0-3
Marián ADAM (34'), 0-4 Matej IZVOLT (90').
Referee: Howard WEBB (ENG)

02-07-2005   Estadio Municipal de Riazor, La Coruña:
RC Deportivo la Coruña – FK Buducnost Podgorica   3-0 (1-0)
RC Deportivo la Coruña: José Francisco MOLINA Jiménez, MANUEL PABLO García Díaz,
CÉSAR Martín Villar (46' HÉCTOR Berenguel del Rio), Enrique Fernández ROMERO, Joan
CAPDEVILA Méndez, VÍCTOR Sánchez Del Amo, SERGIO González Soriano, Julián Bobby
DE GUZMÁN (CAN), Pedro MUNITIS Alvarez, Juan Carlos VALERÓN Santana (66' IVÁN
CARRIL Regueiro), Francisco "XISCO" Jiménez Tejada (82' RUBÉN CASTRO Martín).
(Coach: Joaquín Jesús CAPARRÓS Camino).
FK Buducnost Podgorica: Mladen BOZOVIC, Risto LAKIC, Ivan CARAPIC, Goran
PERISIC, Bracan POPOVIC, Marco MUGOSA, Mirko RAICEVIC, Nenad SOFRANAC,
Petar VUKCEVIC (65' Aleksandar CADJENOVIC, 81' Bojan USANOVIC), Nikola
VUJOVIC, Igor BURZANOVIC (YC75). (Coach: Branislav MILACIC).
Goals: RC Deportivo la Coruña: 1-0 Francisco "XISCO" Jiménez Tejada (5'), 2-0 SERGIO
González Soriano (81'), 3-0 HÉCTOR Berenguel del Rio (86').
Referee: Bruno DERRIEN (FRA)   Attendance: 5.000

03-07-2005   Perutz Stadion, Pápa: Lombard-Pápa TFC – I.F.K. Göteborg   2-3 (1-0)
Lombard-Pápa TFC: Anoras DOMBAI, Attila FARKAS, Viktor FARKAS, Dorel MUTICA
(ROM) (YC65), Tamas GERI, Tibor SZABÓ, Péter KINCSES, Zoltán LIPTÁK, Ákos
KOVRIG (46' Ferenc RÓTH), Miklós HERCZEG, Gábor ÚJHEGYI (60' Balász LÁSZKA).
(Coach: Lázár SZENTES).
I.F.K. Göteborg: John ALVBÅGE, Magnus JOHANSSON (46' Adam JOHANSSON (YC73)),
Dennis JONSSON, Mattias BJÄRSMYR, Oscar WENDT, Jonathan BERG (71' Marcus
BERG), Sebastian JOHANSSON, Andres VASQUES, Samuel WOWOAH (YC32) (79'
Pontus WERNBLOM), Stefan SELAKOVIC, George MOURAD (YC47). (Coach: Arne
ERLANDSEN (NOR)).
Goals: Lombard-Pápa TFC: 1-0 Tibor SZABÓ (18'), 2-0 Miklós HERCZEG (64').
I.F.K. Göteborg: 1-2 Stefan SELAKOVIC (65' penalty), 2-2 Marcus BERG (79'), 2-3 Oscar
WENDT (90'+1').
Referee: Tsvetan GEORGIEV (BUL)   Attendance: 3.000

03-07-2005   Vetros Stadionas, Vilnius:
          FK Zalgiris Vilnius – FC Dinaburg Daugavpils   2-0 (0-0)
FK Zalgiris Vilnius: Mindaugas MALINAUSKAS, Paulius PAKNYS, Tadas GRAZIUNAS,
Tomas MIKUCKIS, Andrejus TERESKINAS (31' Vidas KAUSPADAS), Andrius JOKSAS
(65' Karolis JASAITIS), Andrei SHYLO (BLS), Andrejus SOROKINAS (80' Andzey
MAKSIMOVIC), Branislav JASUREK (SVK), Virmantas LEMEZIS, Aleksandr
OSIPOVITCH (BLS). (Coach: Saulius SIRMELIS).
FC Dinaburg Daugavpils: Vadims FJODOROVS, Deniss SOKOLSKIS, Sergey KHIMICH
(RUS) (YC85), Andrejs ZUROMSKIS (73' Dmitri TIMACHEV (RUS)), Edgars
BURLAKOVS (RC43), Alekjejs BORUNS, Nikita CHMYKOV (RUS) (82' Pavels
KOLCOVS), Jurijs SOKOLOVS, Mikhails ZIZILEVS, Sergejs VALUSKINS (46' Jurgis
PUCINSKIS), Pavel RYZHEUSKI (BLS). (Coach: Roman Yosypovych GRYGORCHUK
(UKR)).
Goals: FK Zalgiris Vilnius: 1-0 Karolis JASAITIS (66'), 2-0 Virmantas LEMEZIS (70').
Referee: Valery VIALICHKA (BLS)

03-07-2005   Stade Félix Bollaert, Lens:
          Racing Club de Lens – KKS Lech Poznán   2-1 (2-0)
Racing Club de Lens: Sébastien CHABBERT, Nicolas GILLET (YC10), Adama
COULIBALY (MLI), Benoît ASSOU-EKOTO, Eric CARRIÈRE (68' Dagui BAKARI (CIV)),
Jérôme LEROY (68' Olivier THOMERT), Yohan DEMONT, Seydou KEITA (MLI), Alou
DIARRA (RC90+2), Daniel COUSIN (GAB), JUSSIÊ Ferreira Vieira (BRA). (Coach: Francis
GILLOT).
KKS Lech Poznán: Krzysztof KOTOROWSKI, Marcin KUS (YC37), Blazej TELICHOWSKI,
Mariusz MOWLIK (YC61), Dawid TOPOLSKI, Piotr SWIERCZEWSKI (YC82) (90'
Arkadiusz CZARNECKI), Pawel SASIN, Marcin WACHOWICZ (88' Artur MARCINIAK),
Piotr REISS, Zbigniew ZAKRZEWSKI, Krzysztof GAJTKOWSKI. (Coach: Czeslaw
MICHNIEWICZ).
Goals: Racing Club de Lens: 1-0 JUSSIÊ Ferreira Vieira (19'), 2-0 Nicolas GILLET (44').
KKS Lech Poznán: 2-1 Krzysztof GAJTKOWSKI (67').
Referee: Charles RICHMOND (SCO)   Attendance: 20.232

03-07-2005   Ratina Stadium, Tampere: Tampere United FC – RSC Charleroi 1-0 (1-0)
Tampere United FC: Mikko KAVÉN, Heikki AHO, Janne RÄSÄNEN, Antti OJANPERÄ, Jussi KUOPPALA, Jussi KUJALA, Jarkko WISS, Sakari SAARINEN, Petri HEINÄNEN (72' Mika LAHTINEN (YC74), Henri SCHEWELEFF (46' Toni JUNNILA), Antti HYNYNEN. (Coach: Ari Juhani HJELM).
RSC Charleroi: Bertrand LAQUAIT (FRA), Frank DEFAYS, Velimir VARGA (SLO), Loris REINA (FRA) (64' Steeve THEOPHILE (FRA)), Mahamoudoi KERE, Thierry SIQUET (YC81), Laurent CIMAN (YC52) (64' Gregory CHRIST (FRA)), Sébastien CHABAUD (FRA), Nasrédine KRAOUCHE (FRA), Toni BROGNO (80' Fabien CAMUS (FRA)), ORLANDO Dossantos Costa (BRA). (Coach: Dante BROGNO).
Goal: Tampere United FC: 1-0 Antti HYNYNEN (25').
Referee: David MALCOLM (NIR)

09-07-2005   Nya Ullevi, Göteborg: I.F.K. Göteborg – Lombard-Pápa TFC 1-0 (0-0)
I.F.K. Göteborg: Bengt ANDERSSON, Magnus JOHANSSON, Karl SVENSSON, Mattias BJÄRSMYR, Oscar WENDT, Jonathan BERG, Sebastian JOHANSSON (87' Andres VASQUES), Mikael SANDKLEF (46' Samuel WOWOAH (YC90)), Nicolas ALEXANDERSSON, George MOURAD, Stefan SELAKOVIC (46' Marcus BERG). (Coach: Arne ERLANDSEN (NOR)).
Lombard-Pápa TFC: Anoras DOMBAI, Attila FARKAS, Viktor FARKAS, Dorel MUTICA (ROM), Tamas GERI, Balász LÁSZKA, Ákos KOVRIG, Zoltán LIPTÁK (YC25), Tibor SZABÓ, Miklós HERCZEG (YC14), Zoltán HERCEGFALVI. (Coach: Lázár SZENTES).
Goal: I.F.K. Göteborg: 1-0 Marcus BERG (90'+3').
Referee: Sten KALDMA (EST)   Attendance: 1.556

09-07-2005   Arnold-Schwarzenegger-Stadion, Graz:
          SK Sturm Graz – VfL Wolfsburg 1-3 (0-1)
SK Sturm Graz: Grzegorz SZAMOTULSKI (POL), Günther NEUKIRCHNER, Franck SILVESTRE (FRA), Frank VERLAAT (HOL), Ronald GERCALIU, Oliver NZUZI POLO (CGO) (46' Cédric TSIMBA (SUI)), Gerald SÄUMEL (83' Diego ROTTENSTEINER), Jürgen SÄUMEL (YC14), Bojan FILIPOVIC (SBM), Dragan SARAC (SBM) (YC19) (74' Thomas KRAMMER), David MUJIRI (GEO). (Coach: Mihajlo PETROVIC (SRB)).
VfL Wolfsburg: Simon JENTZSCH, Hans SARPEI (GHA) (73' Juan Carlos MENSEGUEZ (ARG)), Facundo Hernan QUIROGA (ARG), Kevin HOFLAND (HOL), Peter VAN DER HEYDEN (BEL) (YC30) (90'+1' Stefan SCHNOOR), Miroslav KARHAN (SVK), Pablo THIAM (GUI), Martin PETROV (BUL) (YC70), Andrés Nicolas D'ALESSANDRO (ARG), Diego Fernando KLIMOWICZ (ESP) (63' Karsten FISCHER), Marko TOPIC (BOS) (YC67). (Coach: Holger FACH).
Goals: SK Sturm Graz: 1-1 Günther NEUKIRCHNER (68').
VfL Wolfsburg: 0-1 Martin PETROV (12' penalty), 1-2 Martin PETROV (78'), 1-3 Juan Carlos MENSEGUEZ (90'+2').
Referee: Petteri KARI (FIN)   Attendance: 6.712

139

09-07-2005   Mestský futbalový stadion, Dubnica Nad Váhom:
FK ZTS Dubnica – BB Ankaraspor Kulübü 0-1 (0-0)
FK ZTS Dubnica: Dusan PERNIS, Martin SVESTKA (CZE), Marián ZIMEN (YC71), Igor
DRZIK (YC22), Robert NOVAK, Pavol KOPACKA, Matej IZVOLT, Marián ADAM (90'
Lukás ZÁPOTOKA), Lukás TESÁK (YC76), Peter AUGUSTÍNI (78' Erik GRENDEL), Peter
KISKA (84' Ján SVIKRUHA). (Coach: Lubomir NOSICKY).
BB Ankaraspor Kulübü: Faruk GÜRSOY (GHA), Ramazan TUNC (YC16), Hasan YIGIT
(YC88), Senol YAVAS (66' Ahmet YILDIRIM), Musa BÜYÜK (YC75), Erman OZGUR,
Murat ERDOGAN (57' Silvinho João de Carvalho "JABÁ" (BRA)), Hürriyet GÜCER, Balazs
MOLNÁR (HUN) (87' Mustafa SARP), SIDNEY Cristiano Dos Santos (BRA), WEDERSON
Luiz da Silva Medeiros (BRA). (Coach: Samet AYBABA).
Goal: BB Ankaraspor Kulübü: 0-1 Silvinho João de Carvalho "JABÁ" (74').
Referee: Drazenko KOVACIC (CRO)

09-07-2005   Celtnieks Stadion, Daugavpils:
FC Dinaburg Daugavpils – FK Zalgiris Vilnius 2-1 (2-0)
FC Dinaburg Daugavpils: Vadims FJODOROVS (YC90+3), Dmitrijs CUGUNOVS (YC47),
Andrejs ZUROMSKIS (YC81), Deniss SOKOLSKIS, Alekjejs BORUNS (YC47) (78'
Vladimirs VOLKOVS), Jurijs SOKOLOVS (YC65), Nikita CHMYKOV (RUS) (62' Sergejs
VALUSKINS), Jurgis PUCINSKIS, Mikhails ZIZILEVS, Pavel RYZHEUSKI (BLS) (43'
Pavels KOLCOVS), Olexandr KRIKLIVY (UKR) (YC71). (Coach: Sergejs DIGULEVS).
FK Zalgiris Vilnius: Marius RAPALIS, Paulius PAKNYS, Tadas GRAZIUNAS, Tomas
MIKUCKIS (YC76), Andrejus SOROKINAS, Andrius JOKSAS (46' Andzey
MAKSIMOVIC, 90'+3' Jevgenij DOVKSA), Andrei SHYLO (BLS), Karolis JASAITIS,
Branislav JASUREK (SVK) (YC75), Virmantas LEMEZIS, Aleksandr OSIPOVITCH (BLS)
(63' Vidas KAUSPADAS). (Coach: Saulius SIRMELIS).
Goals: FC Dinaburg Daugavpils: 1-0 Dmitrijs CUGUNOVS (16'), 2-0 Mikhails ZIZILEVS
(18').
FK Zalgiris Vilnius: 2-1 Karolis JASAITIS (47' penalty).
Referee: Dejan STANISIC (SBM)   Attendance: 600

09-07-2005   Stadion Miejski, Szczecin: KS Pogon Szczecin – SK Sigma Olomouc 0-0
KS Pogon Szczecin: Boris PESKOVIC (SVK), Krzysztof MICHALSKI, JULCIMAR De
Souza (BRA), Piotr CELEBAN, Grzegorz MATLAK, Michal LABEDZKI (YC), Przemyslaw
KAZMIERCZAK, Sergio BATATA (BRA) (16' Edi Carlos Dias Marcal "ANDRADINA"
(BRA) (YC)), Rafal GRZELAK, Radek DIVECKY (CZE) (67' Lukasz TRALKA), Roberto
Claudio MILAR Decaudra (URU) (78' Artur BUGAJ). (Coach: Boguslaw PIETRZAK).
SK Sigma Olomouc: Tomás LOVÁSIK (SVK) (YC..), Ales SKERLE, Martin HUDEC (YC),
Michal KOVÁR, Tomás RANDA, Radim KÖNIG (YC), Radek SPILÁCEK (YC), Filip
RÝDEL (YC), Andrej PECNIK (SLO) (46' Jan SCHULMEISTER, 90'+2' Martin
VYSKOCIL), Michal HUBNIK (46' David ROJKA), Peter BABNIC (SVK). (Coach: Petr
ULICNY).
Referee: Albano JANKU (ALB)   Attendance: 5.000

140

09-07-2005   Stade Communal, Charleroi: RSC Charleroi – Tampere United FC   0-0
RSC Charleroi: Bertrand LAQUAIT (FRA), Frank DEFAYS, Velimir VARGA (SLO),
Mahamoudoi KERE, Thierry SIQUET (82' Giovanni CACCIATORE), Sébastien CHABAUD
(FRA), Nasrédine KRAOUCHE (FRA) (YC26), Steeve THEOPHILE (FRA) (75' François
STERCHELE), Gregory CHRIST (FRA) (61' Abdelmajid OULMERS (FRA)), Toni
BROGNO, ORLANDO Dossantos Costa (BRA). (Coach: Jacky MATHIJSSEN).
Tampere United FC: Mikko KAVÉN, Jussi KUOPPALA, Petri HEINÄNEN, Janne
RÄSÄNEN (YC46), Antti OJANPERÄ (YC76), Jussi KUJALA, Jarkko WISS, Kari SAINIO,
Antti HYNYNEN (87' Mika LAHTINEN), Velibor KOPUNOVIC (CRO) (18' Toni
JUNNILA (YC89)), Sakari SAARINEN (YC28). (Coach: Ari Juhani HJELM).
Referee: Stefan JOHANNESSON (SWE)

09-07-2005   Stadion Pod Goricom, Podgorica:
                    FK Buducnost Podgorica – RC Deportivo la Coruña   2-1 (0-0)
FK Buducnost Podgorica: Miroslav VUJADINOVIC, Risto LAKIC, Ivan CARAPIC, Goran
PERISIC, Bracan POPOVIC (YC90), Marco MUGOSA (66' Petar VUKCEVIC), Mirko
RAICEVIC (YC4), Milos LAKIC (73' Milan DJURISIC), Igor BURZANOVIC, Radislav
SEKULIC (78' Ivan BOSKOVIC), Nikola VUJOVIC (YC88). (Coach: Branislav MILACIC).
RC Deportivo la Coruña: José Francisco MOLINA Jiménez, MANUEL PABLO García Díaz,
HÉCTOR Berenguel del Rio, Enrique Fernández ROMERO, Joan CAPDEVILA Méndez,
VÍCTOR Sánchez Del Amo (YC4) (74' Julián Bobby DE GUZMÁN (CAN)), Roberto Miguel
"Toro" ACUÑA (PAR), Lionel Sebastián SCALONI (ARG), IVÁN CARRIL Reguero
(YC42) (65' Jerónimo Figueroa Cabrera "MOMO"), Pedro MUNITIS Alvarez, Francisco
"XISCO" Jiménez Tejada (57' RUBÉN CASTRO Martín). (Coach: Joaquín Jesús
CAPARRÓS Camino).
Goals: FK Buducnost Podgorica: 1-0 Radislav SEKULIC (65'), 2-0 Nikola VUJOVIC (87').
RC Deportivo la Coruña: 2-1 Roberto Miguel "Toro" ACUÑA (90'+3' penalty).
Referee: Ferenc BEDE (HUN)   Attendance: 9.000

09-07-2005   Estadio San Mamés, Bilbao: Athletic Club Bilbao – CFR Cluj   1-0 (1-0)
Athletic Club Bilbao: Iñaki LAFUENTE Sánchez, GONTZAL Rodríguez Díez, USTARITZ
Aldekoatalora Astarloa, Fernando AMOREBIETA Mardaras, Javier CASAS Cuevas (46'
EDER MARTÍNEZ Telletxea), David DE PAULA Gallardo (74' Asier ORMAZÁBAL
Larizgoitia), Jon Andoni "JONAN" García Arambillet, Julen GUERRERO López, IBON
GUTIÉRREZ Fernández, Javier "JAVI" GONZÁLEZ Gómez (YC54) (84' David LIZOAIN
Loizu), Mikel DAÑOBEITIA Martín. (Coach: José Luis MENDILIBAR Etxebarria).
CFR Cluj: Petru TURCAS, Cristian Calin PANIN, Vasile Ilie JULA, Zoran MILOSEVIC
(SBM), Dorin TOMA (YC19), Stefan Sorin ONCICA (YC54), Laur Marian ASTILEAN (90'
Djordje VLAJIC (SBM)), Dorinel Ionel MUNTEANU (93' Svetozar MIJIN (SBM) (YC109)),
Cosmin Marin VASIE (66' Ambrosie Cristian COROIAN (YC110)), Adrian Gheorghe
ANCA, Cosmin TILINCA. (Coach: Dorinel Ionel MUNTEANU).
Goal: Athletic Club Bilbao: 1-0 Javier "JAVI" GONZÁLEZ Gómez (36').
Referee: Joaquim Paulo PARATY DA SILVA (POR) Attendance: 15.000
Penalties: 1 Vasile Ilie JULA   * USTARITZ Aldekoatalora Astarloa
              2 Djordje VLAJIC   1 GONTZAL Rodríguez Diez
              3 Dorin TOMA   2 IBON GUTIÉRREZ Fernández
              4 Adrian Gheorghe ANCA   3 Julen GUERRERO López
              5 Ambrosie Cristian COROIAN

10-07-2005   Stadion Neufeld, Bern: BSC Young Boys Bern – KSC Lokeren   2-1 (0-0)
BSC Young Boys Bern: Marco WÖLFLI, TIAGO Coelho Branco Calvano (BRA), Mark
DISLER, Gretar STEINSSON (ISL), Gürkan SERMETER, Joël MAGNIN (74' Patrick DE
NAPOLI), Thomas HÄBERLI, Mario RAIMONDI, Carlos Vila VARELA (ESP), Pirmin
SCHWEGLER (46' Miguel Alfredo PORTILLO (ARG) (YC53)), Hakan YAKIN (78' Gabriel
José URDANETA Rangel (VEN)). (Coach: Hans-Peter ZAÜGG).
KSC Lokeren: Zvonko MILOJEVIC (SBM), JOÃO CARLOS Pinto Chaves (BRA), Mamadou
DIALLO (GUI), Michael VAN HOEY, Frederik DE WINNE, Arnar VIDARSSON (ISL)
(YC22) (68' Killian OVERMEIRE), Ivan VUKOMANOVIC (SBM), Arnar GRETARSSON
(ISL), Runar KRISTINSSON (ISL) (YC83), Aristide BANCE (BKF) (74' José Ilson dos
Santos "TAILSON" (BRA)), Gunter VAN HANDEN HOVEN (85' Aboubacar M'BAYE
CAMARA (GUI)). (Coach: Slavoljub MUSLIN (SRB)).
Goals: BSC Young Boys Bern: 1-1 Gretar STEINSSON (79'), 2-1 Gürkan SERMETER (82'
penalty).
KSC Lokeren: 0-1 Arnar GRETARSSON (63' penalty).
Referee: Ian STOKES (IRL)

10-07-2005   Bloomfield Stadium, Tel-Aviv:
                    Beitar Jerusalem FC – FC Slovan Liberec   1-2 (0-0)
Beitar Jerusalem FC: Izhak KORENFIEN, Eliav YONI, Eli SASON, Yoni KIM (YC76),
David AMSALEM, Aviram BROCHYAN, Mor EFRAIM, Shlomi MOSHE (YC55) (84'
Eitamar ICHUA), Shal CHDAD (68' Eliran DANIN), Ophir AZO, Amit BEN SHOSHAN.
(Coach: Azon GUY).
FC Slovan Liberec: Marek CECH, Peter SINGLÁR (SVK), Tomás ZÁPOTOCNY, Radek
HOCHMEISTER (YC36) (74' Milan MATULA), Tomás JANU, Josef HAMOUZ, Martin
ABRAHÁM, Ivan HODÚR (SVK) (84' Jan BROSCHINSKY), Daniel PUDIL (YC72), Filip
DORT (64' Jan HOLENDA), Libor DOSEK. (Coach: Vítezslav LAVICKA).
Goals: Beitar Jerusalem FC: 1-1 Amit BEN SHOSHAN (59').
FC Slovan Liberec: 0-1 Filip DORT (52'), 1-2 Jan HOLENDA (87').
Referee: Dietmar DRABEK (AUT)

10-07-2005   Stadionul Gloria, Bistrita:
                    FC Gloria Bistrita – NK Slaven Belupo Koprivnica   0-1 (0-0)
FC Gloria Bistrita: Septimiu Calin ALBUT (YC60), Dan MATEI, Sandu Lucian BORS, Alin
Valer RUS, Dinu Daniel SANMARTEAN, Constantin Marin CONSTANTINESCU, Sergiu
Ioan COSTIN, Romeo PADURET (58' Razvan PADURETU), Adrian Ioan SALAGEAN
(YC45) (73' Cristian Vasile SURU (YC84)), Sandu NEGREAN, Ionut Bogdan PERES (32'
Dan Claudiu GAVRILESCU). (Coach: Ion BALAUR).
NK Slaven Belupo Koprivnica: Tomislav PELIN, Pero PEJIC (67' Petar BOSNJAK (YC68)),
Pavo CRNAC (YC56), Sime KURILIC, Igor GAL, Dalibor VISKOVIC, Dejan SOMOCI (46'
Antonio KOVAC), Igor MUSA, Antun DUNKOVIC, Ivica KARABOGDAN, Edin
SARANOVIC (BOS) (YC54) (76' Jurica KARABATIC). (Coach: Branko KARACIC).
Goal: NK Slaven Belupo Koprivnica: 0-1 Igor MUSA (66' penalty).
Referee: Meir LEVI (ISR)   Attendance: 1.500

10-07-2005   Stade de Genève, Genève: Neuchâtel-Xamax FC – AS Saint-Etienne 1-2 (0-0)
Neuchâtel-Xamax FC: Jean-François BEDENIK (FRA), Mounir SOUFIANI (FRA), Eddy
BAREA, Ansi AGOLLI (ALB) (64' Christophe MARANINCHI (FRA)), Julien
CORDONNIER (FRA) (YC90+2), Massimo LOMBARDO, Pascal OPPLIGER, Kader
MANGANE (SEN), Nebi MUSTAFI (MCD) (YC48) (72' Patrick BAUMANN), Alexandre
REY (YC81), Joel GRIFFITHS (AUS) (77' Charles-André DOUDIN). (Coach: Alain
GEIGER).
AS Saint-Etienne: Jérémy JANOT, Vincent HOGNON, Zoumana CAMARA (RC80),
Fousseiny DIAWARA (MLI) (YC90+1), Herita N'Kongolo ILUNGA (DRC), David
HELLEBUYCK (51' Sébastien MAZURE), Julien SABLÉ, Didier ZOKORA (CIV), Pascal
FEINDOUNO (GUI) (82' Damien PERQUIS), Frédéric PIQUIONNE, Frédéric MENDY
(SEN) (76' Lamine SAKHO (SEN)). (Coach: Élie BAUP).
Goals: Neuchâtel-Xamax FC: 2-1 Christophe MARANINCHI (81').
AS Saint-Etienne: 0-1 Sébastien MAZURE (59'), 0-2 Pascal FEINDOUNO (70').
Referee: Marian Mircea SALOMIR (ROM)   Attendance: 11.273

10-07-2005   Gradski Stadion, Skopje: FK Pobeda Prilep – Hamburger SV 1-4 (1-1)
FK Pobeda Prilep: Darko TOFILOVSKI, Aleksandar POPOVSKI (52' Nikolce
ZDRAVEVSKI), Sulaimon OMO (NGR), Dejan CVETKOVSKI (YC13), Blagojce
DAMEVSKI, Marjan NACEV (YC27) (52' Blagoja GESOSKI), Toni MEGLENSKI, Dimitar
KAPINKOVSKI, Vladimir VUJOVIC (SBM), Saso KRSTEV (60' Draganco
DIMITROVSKI), Dejan RISTOVSKI. (Coach: Petar KURCUBIC (SRB)).
Hamburger SV: Stefan WÄCHTER, René KLINGBEIL (71' Benjamin LAUTH), Khalid
BOULAHROUZ (HOL), Daniel VAN BUYTEN (BEL), Volker SCHMIDT, David JAROLIM
(CZE) (46' Alexander LAAS), Markus KARL, Stefan BEINLICH, Rafael VAN DER VAART
(HOL) (64' Piotr TROCHOWSKI), Emile MPENZA (BEL), Sergej BARBAREZ (BOS).
Goals: FK Pobeda Prilep: 1-0 Dejan RISTOVSKI (32'). (Coach: Thomas DOLL).
Hamburger SV: 1-1 Emile MPENZA (38'), 1-2 Stefan BEINLICH (65'), 1-3 Markus KARL
(76'), 1-4 Benjamin LAUTH (90').
Referee: Pavel Cristian BALAJ (ROM)   Attendance: 2.000

10-07-2005   Stadion Miejski, Poznán: KKS Lech Poznán – Racing Club de Lens 0-1 (0-1)
KKS Lech Poznán: Krzysztof KOTOROWSKI, Marcin KUS, Blazej TELICHOWSKI,
Mariusz MOWLIK (YC58), Arkadiusz CZARNECKI, Pawel SASIN (81' Ebrahima
SAWANEH (GAM)), Marcin WACHOWICZ (46' Dawid TOPOLSKI), Artur MARCINIAK
(59' Jakub WILK), Maciej SCHERFCHEN, Piotr REISS, Krzysztof GAJTKOWSKI. (Coach:
Czeslaw MICHNIEWICZ).
Racing Club de Lens: Charles ITANDJE, Jacek BAK (POL) (YC39), Yoann LACHOR (65'
Seydou KEITA (MLI)), Patrick BARUL, Benoît ASSOU-EKOTO, Vitorino HILTON de Silva
(BRA), Jérôme LEROY, Yohan DEMONT, Dagui BAKARI (CIV) (65' Aruna DINDANE
(CIV)), Olivier THOMERT, JUSSIÊ Ferreira Vieira (BRA) (77' Daniel COUSIN (GAB)).
(Coach: Francis GILLOT).
Goal: Racing Club de Lens: 0-1 JUSSIÊ Ferreira Vieira (11').
Referee: Michael SVENDSEN (DEN)   Attendance: 15.000

143

10-07-2005   Letná Stadium, Zlín: FC Tescoma Zlín – KAA Gent   0-0
FK Tescoma Zlín: Ales KORÍNEK, Vlastimil VIDLICKA, Zdenik KROCA, Jaroslav SVACH (YC64), Bronislav CERVENKA, Tomás JANÍCEK, Vit VRTILKA, Roman DOBES (72' Jan JELÍNEK), Václav ZAPLETAL (84' Martin BIELIK), Jan KRAUS (58' Martin BACA), Václav CINCALA (YC84). (Coach: Pavel HOFTYCH).
KAA Gent: Frédéric HERPOEL (YC90+1), Dario SMOJE (CRO), Stephen LAYBUTT (AUS), Nicolas LOMBAERTS, Steve COOREMAN, Jovica TRAJCEV (MCD), Mamar MAMOUNI (ALG) (YC22), Moubarak (Mbark) BOUSSOUFA (HOL), Yngvar HÅKONSEN (NOR), Sandy MARTENS (36' Mamadou DIOP (FRA)), Nenad MLADENOVIC (SBM) (86' Kenny THOMPSON). (Coach: Georges LEEKENS).
Referee: Kostadin KOSTADINOV (BUL)   Attendance: 3.054

10-07-2005   Veritas Stadion, Turku:
                       FC International Turku – NK Varteks Varazdin   2-2 (1-1)
FC International Turku: Magnus BAHNE, Diego CORPACHE (ARG) (RC89), Jukka SINISALO, Mats GUSTAFSSON, Henri LEHTONEN, Aristides PERTOT (ARG) (YC90+5), Prince OTOO, Touko TUMANTO, Serge N'GAL (CMR) (77' Martin MUTUMBA (SWE)), Miikka ILO (YC27), Tomi PETRESCU (57' Ari NYMAN (YC90+3)). (Coach : Kari VIRTANEN).
NK Varteks Varazdin: Miroslav KOPRIC, Nikola POKRIVAC (YC21), Mirko PLANTIC (72' Enes NOVINIC), Goran MUJANOVIC (81' Dominik MOHOROVIC (YC90+4)), Kristijan IPSA, Zoran KASTEL, Dario JERTEC, Nikola SAFARIC (YC,YC54), Nikola MELNJAK, Neven VUKMAN (75' Gordan GOLIK), Ivan JOLIC (BOS). (Coach: Zlatko DALIC).
Goals: FC International Turku: 1-0 Serge N'GAL (17'), 2-1 Serge N'GAL (58').
NK Varteks Varazdin: 1-1 Ivan JOLIC (27'), 2-2 Dominik MOHOROVIC (90'+4').
Referee: Drago KOS (SLO)

THIRD ROUND

16-07-2005   Westfalenstadion, Dortmund:
                       Borussia Dortmund – SK Sigma Olomouc   1-1 (1-1)
Borussia Dortmund: Roman WEIDENFELLER, Christian WÖRNS (YC71), Christoph METZELDER, Philipp DEGEN (SUI), Florian KRINGE, Tomas ROSICKY (CZE) (YC48) (84' David ODONKOR), Leonardo de Deus Santos "DÉDÉ" (BRA), Marc-André KRUSKA (YC68), Delron BUCKLEY (RSA) (YC30), Jan KOLLER (CZE), Ebi SMOLAREK (POL) (78' Salvatore GAMBINO). (Coach: Lambertus (Bert) VAN MARWIJK (HOL)).
SK Sigma Olomouc: Tomás LOVÁSIK (SVK), Tomás RANDA, Ales SKERLE (11' Andrej PECNIK (SLO) (YC39)), Martin HUDEC, Michal KOVÁR, Tarciso Rogeiro Pereira "MELINHO" (BRA), Ladislav ONOFREJ (SVK), Radek SPILÁCEK (32' Radim KOPECKY), Radim KÖNIG, Ales BEDNÁR (90' Michal HUBNIK), Peter BABNIC (SVK). (Coach: Petr ULICNY).
Goals: Borussia Dortmund: 1-0 Florian KRINGE (8').
SK Sigma Olomouc: 1-1 Radim KÖNIG (43').
Referee: Kevin B.R.BLOM (HOL)   Attendance: 43.000

16-07-2005   Estádio Dr. Magalhães Pessoa, Leiria:
União Desportiva Leiria – Hamburger SV   0-1 (0-0)
União Desportiva Leiria: Paulo Roberto COSTINHA Melo Castro, JOÃO PAULO Andrade
(YC83), Nuno Filipe Rodrigues LARANJEIRO, Jorge Magalhães Dias Assunção "RENATO",
Nuno Miguel Da Cunha "KATA", Adriano Barbosa Miranda "NENE", PAULO Jorge de Sousa
GOMES (59' Josieley FERREIRA Rosa (BRA)), Luís Miguel Assunção Joaquim
"ALHANDRA", Carlos Eduardo Castro da Silva "CADU" (BRA) (49' PAULO CÉSAR Rocha
Rosa (BRA)), MACIEL Lima Barbosa da Cunha (BRA), FÁBIO Alexandre Duarte FELÍCIO
(75' Luís Carlos LOURENÇO da Silva). (Coach: JOSÉ Manuel Martins Teixeira GOMES).
Hamburger SV: Stefan WÄCHTER, Daniel VAN BUYTEN (BEL), René KLINGBEIL,
Khalid BOULAHROUZ (HOL) (YC75), Thimothée ATOUBA (CMR) (64' Volker
SCHMIDT), Piotr TROCHOWSKI, Guy DEMEL (CIV) (YC35), Stefan BEINLICH, Rafael
VAN DER VAART (HOL), Sergej BARBAREZ (BOS) (64' Naohiro TAKAHARA (JPN)),
Emile MPENZA (BEL) (76' Benjamin LAUTH). (Coach: Thomas DOLL).
Goal: Hamburger SV: 0-1 Piotr TROCHOWSKI (57').
Referee: Grzegorz GILEWSKI (POL)   Attendance: 1.500

16-07-2005   Gradski Stadion,Varazdin:
NK Varteks Varazdin – Racing Club de Lens   1-1 (0-0)
NK Varteks Varazdin: Tomislav VRANJIC, Zoran KASTEL, Mirko PLANTIC, Nikola
POKRIVAC, Goran MUJANOVIC (YC39), Kristijan IPSA, Dario JERTEC (66' Nedim
HALILOVIC (BOS)), Leon BENKO, Nikola MELNJAK, Neven VUKMAN (58' Zedi
RAMADANI), Ivan JOLIC (BOS) (63' Enes NOVINIC). (Coach: Zlatko DALIC).
Racing Club de Lens: Charles ITANDJE, Nicolas GILLET (79' Kamil ZAYATTE), Adama
COULIBALY (MLI), Benoît ASSOU-EKOTO, Jérôme LEROY (YC56), Yohan DEMONT,
Seydou KEITA (MLI), Daniel COUSIN (GAB), Olivier THOMERT, JUSSIÊ Ferreira Vieira
(BRA) (YC89), Issam JOMA'A (TUN) (46' Patrick BARUL). (Coach: Francis GILLOT).
Goals: NK Varteks Varazdin: 1-1 Mirko PLANTIC (90'+2').
Racing Club de Lens: 0-1 Daniel COUSIN (60').
Referee: Claudio CIRCHETTA (SUI)   Attendance: 3.500

16-07-2005   Stade de Suisse Wankdorf, Bern:
BSC Young Boys Bern – Olympique Marseille   2-3 (0-2)
BSC Young Boys Bern: Marco WÖLFLI, Adrian EUGSTER (YC33), TIAGO Coelho Branco
Calvano (BRA), Mark DISLER (46' Gabriel José URDANETA Rangel (VEN)), Gretar
STEINSSON (ISL), Gürkan SERMETER (67' Carlos Vila VARELA (ESP)), Hakan YAKIN
(83' Joël MAGNIN), Thomas HÄBERLI, Mario RAIMONDI, Pirmin SCHWEGLER (YC48),
Francisco "NERI" Valmeri Souza (BRA). (Coach: Hans-Peter ZAÜGG).
Olympique Marseille: Cédric CARRASSO, Taye Ismaila TAIWO (NGR), Demétrius
FERREIRA Leite (BRA) (YC84), Abdoulaye MÉÏTÉ (CIV), Wilson ORUMA (NGR),
Frédéric DÉHU, Laurent BATLLES, Mamadou NIANG (SEN) (YC69), Sergio "KOKE"
Contreras Pardo (ESP) (77' Salomon OLEMBÉ (CMR)), Péguy LUYINDULA (70' Habib
BAMOGO), Samir NASRI. (Coach: Jean FERNANDEZ).
Goals: BSC Young Boys Bern: 1-2 Mario RAIMONDI (61'), 2-2 Hakan YAKIN (74').
Olympique Marseille: 0-1 Wilson ORUMA (15'), 0-2 Mamadou NIANG (35'), 2-3 Taye
Ismaila TAIWO (82').
Referee: Craig THOMSON (SCO)   Attendance: 14.000

16-07-2005   Stadio Yiannis Pathiakakis, Athens:
Egaleo FC Athens – FK Zalgiris Vilnius   1-3 (0-1)
Egaleo FC Athens: Alexandros THEODORAKOPOULOS, Alexandros BIRIS (YC42), Ioannis
TABAKIS (46' Alexandros ATHANASOPOULOS), Miltiades GOUGOULAKIS (70'
Theodoros KOUMPAROULIS), Georgios TSIROGIANNIS, Georgios BAKOS, Apostolos
GOUDELITSAS, Sotirios BETHANIS (72' Georgios LABROPOULOS), Efstratios
MICHELIS, Prokopios SAGANAS, Spiridon KONTOPOULOS (YC63). (Coach: Eleftherios
PISTOLIS).
FK Zalgiris Vilnius: Pavel LEUS, Paulius PAKNYS (YC34), Tadas GRAZIUNAS, Andrejus
SOROKINAS (73' Andrejus TERESKINAS), Ramunas STONKUS, Andrei SHYLO (BLS)
(61' Vidas KAUSPADAS (YC79)), Virmantas LEMEZIS, Karolis JASAITIS, Andzey
MAKSIMOVIC, Igoris MORINAS, Branislav JASUREK (SVK) (79' Jevgenij DOVKSA).
Goals: Egaleo FC Athens: 1-3 Prokopios SAGANAS (85'). (Coach: Saulius SIRMELIS).
FK Zalgiris Vilnius: 0-1 Virmantas LEMEZIS (16'), 0-2 Igoris MORINAS (60'), 0-3
Branislav JASUREK (67').
Referee: Miroslaw RYSZKA (POL)

16-07-2005   Parkstad Limburg Stadion, Kerkrade: SV Roda JC – FC Slovan Liberec   0-0
SV Roda JC: Vladan KUJOVIC (SBM), Boldiszár BÖDÖR (HUN) (YC78), Vincent
LACHAMBRE (BEL), László BODNÁR (HUN), Pa-Modou KAH (NOR), Ivan VICELICH
(NZL), SÉRGIO Pacheco de Oliveira (BRA) (87' Charlie VAN DEN OUWELAND), Gregoor
VAN DIJK, Edrissa SONKO (GAM), Arouna KONE (CIV) (82' Dirk Jan DERKSEN), Sekou
CISSÉ (CIV). (Coach: Hubertus Jozef Margaretha (Huub) STEVENS).
FC Slovan Liberec: Zbynek HAUZR, Tomás ZÁPOTOCNY, Pavel KOSTÁL, Peter
SINGLÁR (SVK), Daniel PUDIL (90'+2' Filip HOLOSKO (SVK)), Ivan HODÚR (SVK) (78'
Milan MATULA (YC80)), Tomás JANU, Petr PAPOUSEK (YC40) (67' Josef HAMOUZ),
Martin ABRAHÁM, Libor DOSEK, Jan HOLENDA. (Coach: Vítezslav LAVICKA).
Referee: Bruno Miguel DUARTE PAIXÄO (POR)   Attendance: 3.280

16-07-2005   Estadio Municipal de Riazor, La Coruña:
RC Deportivo la Coruña – NK Slaven Belupo Koprivnica   1-0 (0-0)
RC Deportivo la Coruña: José Francisco MOLINA Jiménez, MANUEL PABLO García Díaz,
Enrique Fernández ROMERO, JORGE Manuel Almeida Gomes ANDRADE (POR), Joan
CAPDEVILA Méndez, SERGIO González Soriano (YC80), Lionel Sebastián SCALONI
(ARG), VÍCTOR Sánchez Del Amo (66' RUBÉN CASTRO Martín), Juan Carlos VALERÓN
Santana (55' IVÁN CARRIL Regueiro), Pedro MUNITIS Alvarez (YC20), Alberto LUQUE
Martos. (Coach: Joaquín Jesús CAPARRÓS Camino).
NK Slaven Belupo Koprivnica: Robert LISJAK, Petar BOSNJAK (73' Pero PEJIC), Pavo
CRNAC, Igor GAL, Sime KURILIC, Dalibor VISKOVIC, Igor MUSA, Antun DUNKOVIC,
Antonio KOVAC (81' Dejan SOMOCI), Ivica KARABOGDAN, Edin SARANOVIC (BOS)
(46' Bojan VRUCINA). (Coach: Branko KARACIC).
Goal: RC Deportivo la Coruña: 1-0 RUBÉN CASTRO Martín (73').
Referee: Bülent DEMIRLEK (TUR)   Attendance: 6.000

17-07-2005   Nya Ullevi, Göteborg: I.F.K. Göteborg – VfL Wolfsburg 0-2 (0-1)
I.F.K. Göteborg: Bengt ANDERSSON, Magnus JOHANSSON (YC45), Karl SVENSSON
(YC7), Mattias BJÄRSMYR, Oscar WENDT, Adam JOHANSSON (46' Pontus
WERNBLOM (YC62)), Sebastian JOHANSSON, Nicolas ALEXANDERSSON, Jonathan
BERG (YC20), Stefan SELAKOVIC (78' Andrés VASQUES), George MOURAD (71'
Marcus BERG). (Coach: Arne ERLANDSEN (NOR)).
VfL Wolfsburg: Simon JENTZSCH, Peter VAN DER HEYDEN (BEL) (79' Patrick
WEISER), Karsten FISCHER (YC48), Kevin HOFLAND (HOL), Maik FRANZ, Pablo
THIAM (GUI), Andrés Nicolas D'ALESSANDRO (ARG), Martin PETROV (BUL) (83'
Cedric MAKIADI), Miroslav KARHAN (SVK), Diego Fernando KLIMOWICZ (ESP) (YC39)
(73' Marko TOPIC (BOS)), Juan Carlos MENSEGUEZ (ARG). (Coach: Holger FACH).
Goals: VfL Wolfsburg: 0-1 Andrés Nicolas D'ALESSANDRO (33'), 0-2 Maik FRANZ (51').
Referee: Darko CEFERIN (SLO)   Attendance: 3.711

17-07-2005   Mestský futbalový stadion, Dubnica Nad Váhom:
               FK ZTS Dubnica – Newcastle United FC 1-3 (1-2)
FK ZTS Dubnica: Dusan PERNIS, Dalibor PLEVA, Martin SVESTKA (CZE), Marián
ZIMEN, Igor DRZIK (85' Michal FILO), Robert NOVAK, Pavol KOPACKA, Matej IZVOLT
(69' Erik GRENDEL), Lukás TESÁK, Peter KISKA (79' Tomas BRUSKO), Marián ADAM.
(Coach: Lubomir NOSICKY).
Newcastle United FC: Stephen HARPER, Robert ELLIOTT, Jean-Alain BOUMSONG (FRA),
Charles N'ZOGBIA (FRA), Steven TAYLOR, Céléstine BABAYARO (NGR), Nicky BUTT,
Amdy FAYE (SEN), James MILNER, Alan SHEARER, Michael CHOPRA (58' Martin
BRITTAIN). (Coach: Graeme James SOUNESS (SCO)).
Goals: FK ZTS Dubnica: 1-2 Lukás TESÁK (42').
Newcastle United FC: 0-1 Michael CHOPRA (4'), 0-2 Charles N'ZOGBIA (6'), 1-3 James
MILNER (70').
Referee: Alon YEFET (ISR)   Attendance: 6.200

17-07-2005   Stadionul CFR Gruia, Cluj-Napoca: CFR Cluj – AS Saint-Etienne 1-1 (1-1)
CFR Cluj: Petru TURCAS, Cristian Calin PANIN (YC86), Vasile Ilie JULA, Dorin TOMA
(57' Cosmin Marin VASIE), Zoran MILOSEVIC (SBM), Stefan Sorin ONCICA (51' Cristian
TURCU), Dorinel Ionel MUNTEANU, Florin Cristian DAN (77' Svetozar MIJIN (SBM)),
Adrian Gheorghe ANCA, Cristian Ambrosie COROIAN, Cosmin TILINCA. (Coach:
Gheorghe MIHALI).
AS Saint-Etienne: Jérémy JANOT, Vincent HOGNON, Fousseiny DIAWARA (MLI), Herita
N'Kongolo ILUNGA (DRC), Alledine YAHIA (TUN), Didier ZOKORA (CIV) (YC79) (90'
Mouhamadou DABO (SEN)), David HELLEBUYCK, Pascal FEINDOUNO (GUI), Julien
SABLÉ, Frédéric PIQUIONNE (65' Sébastien MAZURE), Frédéric MENDY (SEN) (75' Loïc
PERRIN). (Coach: Élie BAUP).
Goals: CFR Cluj: 1-0 Cosmin TILINCA (3').
AS Saint-Etienne: 1-1 Frédéric PIQUIONNE (27').
Referee : Peter VERVECKEN (BEL)   Attendance : 7.000

17-07-2005   Stadio Olimpico, Roma: SS Lazio Roma – Tampere United FC   3-0 (2-0)
SS Lazio Roma: Matteo SERENI, Manuel BELLERI, Sanchez Emilson CRIBARI (BRA) (81'
Simone SANNIBALE), Luciano ZAURI (YC86), Matías Emanuel LEQUI (ARG), Fabio
FIRMANI, CÉSAR Aparecido Rodrigues (BRA), Christian MANFREDINI, Fabio
LIVERANI, Paolo DI CANIO (69' Roberto MUZZI), Tommaso ROCCHI (85' Goran
PANDEV (MCD)). (Coach: Delio ROSSI).
Tampere United FC: Mikko KAVÉN, Jussi KUOPPALA, Petri HEINÄNEN, Janne
RÄSÄNEN, Antti OJANPERÄ, Jussi KUJALA (49' Mika LAHTINEN), Jarkko WISS, Kari
SAINIO (YC90+2), Antti HYNYNEN, Sakari SAARINEN, Henri SCHEWELEFF. (Coach:
Ari Juhani HJELM).
Goals: SS Lazio Roma: 1-0 Manuel BELLERI (28'), 2-0 Tommaso ROCCHI (29'), 3-0 Paolo
DI CANIO (48').
Referee: Hervé PICCIRILLO (FRA)   Attendance: 16.000

17-07-2005   Jules Ottenstadion, Gentbrugge: KAA Gent – Valencia CF   0-0
KAA Gent: Frédéric HERPOEL, Dario SMOJE (CRO), Nicolas LOMBAERTS, Stephen
LAYBUTT (AUS), Yngvar HÅKONSEN (NOR), Mamar MAMOUNI (ALG), Moubarak
(Mbark) BOUSSOUFA (HOL) (86' Davy DE BEULE), Steve COOREMAN, Wouter
VRANCKEN, Mohammed Aliyu DATTI (NGR) (YC81) (86' Mamadou DIOP (FRA)),
Gnahoua Zéphirin ZOKO (CIV) (75' Nenad MLADENOVIC (SBM)). (Coach: Georges
LEEKENS).
Valencia CF: José Santiago CAÑIZARES Ruiz, Manuel RUZ Baños, FÁBIO AURÉLIO
Rodrigues (BRA) (60' VICENTE Rodríguez Guillén), Roberto Fabián AYALA (ARG),
Amadeo CARBONI (ITA), Emiliano MORETTI (ITA), David ALBELDA Aliqués (YC32),
RAÚL ALBIOL Tortajada, Francisco Joaquín Pérez RUFETE (86' Juan Luis "JUANLU" Hens
Lorite), Patrick Stephan KLUIVERT (HOL), Marco DI VAIO (ITA) (66' David VILLA
Sánchez). (Coach: Enrique "QUIQUE" Sánchez FLORES).
Referee: Paolo DONDARINI (ITA)   Attendance: 8.500

23-07-2005   Saint James' Park, Newcastle:
              Newcastle United FC – FK ZTS Dubnica   2-0 (0-0)
Newcastle United FC: Shay GIVEN (IRL), Stephen CARR (IRL), Jean-Alain BOUMSONG
(FRA), Charles N'ZOGBIA (FRA), Steven TAYLOR, Céléstine BABAYARO (NGR),
Jermaine JENAS (46' Michael CHOPRA, 55' Martin BRITTAIN), Amdy FAYE (SEN),
James MILNER, Lee BOWYER, Alan SHEARER. (Coach: Graeme James SOUNESS
(SCO)).
FK ZTS Dubnica: Dusan PERNIS, Dalibor PLEVA, Martin SVESTKA (CZE), Marián
ZIMEN, Igor DRZIK, Robert NOVAK, Pavol KOPACKA (81' Roman SKULTÉTY), Matej
IZVOLT, Lukás TESÁK, Peter KISKA (68' Peter AUGUSTINI), Marián ADAM (85' Ján
SVIKRUHA). (Coach: Lubomir NOSICKY).
Goals: Newcastle United FC: 1-0 Alan SHEARER (70'), 2-0 Alan SHEARER (90'+1').
Referee: Knut KIRCHER (GER)   Attendance: 25.135

148

23-07-2005   Gradski Stadion, Koprivnica:
NK Slaven Belupo Koprivnica – RC Deportivo la Coruña   0-3 (0-1)
NK Slaven Belupo Koprivnica: Tomislav PELIN, Petar BOSNJAK, Pavo CRNAC (YC34),
Igor GAL, Sime KURILIC, Dalibor VISKOVIC, Igor MUSA (65' Dejan SOMOCI), Antun
DUNKOVIC, Antonio KOVAC (46' Jeong-Yong LEE (KOR)), Ivica KARABOGDAN
(YC5), Edin SARANOVIC (BOS) (71' Bojan VRUCINA). (Coach: Branko KARACIC).
RC Deportivo la Coruña: José Francisco MOLINA Jiménez, Enrique Fernández ROMERO,
JORGE Manuel Almeida Gomes ANDRADE (POR), Joan CAPDEVILA Méndez, HÉCTOR
Berenguel del Rio, SERGIO González Soriano, Lionel Sebastián SCALONI (ARG) (71' Julián
Bobby DE GUZMÁN (CAN)), VÍCTOR Sánchez Del Amo (64' Roberto Miguel "Toro"
ACUÑA (PAR)), Juan Carlos VALERÓN Santana (58' DIEGO TRISTÁN Herrera), Pedro
MUNITIS Alvarez, RUBÉN CASTRO Martín. (Coach: Joaquín Jesús CAPARRÓS Camino).
Goals: RC Deportivo la Coruña: 0-1 RUBÉN CASTRO Martín (18'), 0-2 VÍCTOR Sánchez
Del Amo (46' penalty), 0-3 DIEGO TRISTÁN Herrera (80').
Referee: Nicolai VOLLQUARTZ (DEN)   Attendance: 4.000

23-07-2005   AOL Arena, Hamburg: Hamburger SV – União Desportiva Leiria   2-0 (0-0)
Hamburger SV: Stefan WÄCHTER, Thimothée ATOUBA (CMR), Daniel VAN BUYTEN
(BEL), René KLINGBEIL, Khalid BOULAHROUZ (HOL), Piotr TROCHOWSKI (62' David
JAROLIM (CZE)), Guy DEMEL (CIV) (YC39) (46' Raphael WICKY (SUI) (YC60)), Stefan
BEINLICH (YC31), Rafael VAN DER VAART (HOL) (69' Benjamin LAUTH), Sergej
BARBAREZ (BOS) (YC64), Emile MPENZA (BEL). (Coach: Thomas DOLL).
União Desportiva Leiria: Paulo Roberto COSTINHA Melo Castro, Oliveira Bonfim "EDER",
Jorge Magalhães Dias Assunção "RENATO", JOÃO PAULO Andrade (YC64), PAULO Jorge
de Sousa GOMES (YC74), Luís Miguel Assunção Joaquim "ALHANDRA" (YC49), Nuno
Miguel Da Cunha "KATA" (YC18) (50' Josieley FERREIRA Rosa (BRA) (YC60)), Adriano
Barbosa Miranda "NENE", PAULO CÉSAR Rocha Rosa (BRA) (70' Carlos Eduardo Castro
da Silva "CADU" (BRA)), FÁBIO Alexandre Duarte FELÍCIO (64' Luís Carlos LOURENÇO
da Silva), MACIEL Lima Barbosa da Cunha (BRA). (Coach: JOSÉ Manuel Martins Teixeira
GOMES).
Goals: Hamburger SV: 1-0 Sergej BARBAREZ (50' penalty), 2-0 Benjamin LAUTH (76').
Referee: Athanassios BRIAKOS (GRE)   Attendance: 25.164

23-07-2005   Zalgirio Stadionas, Vilnius: FK Zalgiris Vilnius – Egaleo FC Athens   2-3 (2-1)
FK Zalgiris Vilnius: Pavel LEUS, Tomas MIKUCKIS, Tadas GRAZIUNAS, Andrejus
SOROKINAS, Ramunas STONKUS, Andrei SHYLO (BLS) (72' Aleksandr OSIPOVITCH
(BLS)), Virmantas LEMEZIS, Karolis JASAITIS, Andzey MAKSIMOVIC, Igoris MORINAS,
Branislav JASUREK (SVK) (90'+2' Andrejus TERESKINAS). (Coach: Saulius SIRMELIS).
Egaleo FC Athens: Luigi CENNAMO (ITA), Dimitrios TSITSOMITSOS (76' Georgios
BAKOS), Miltiades GOUGOULAKIS, Theodoros KOUMPAROULIS, Georgios
TSIROGIANNIS, Apostolos GOUDELITSAS, Georgios LABROPOULOS, Georgios
BARKOGLOU (28' Efstratios MICHELIS), Prokopios SAGANAS (70' Spiridon
KONTOPOULOS), Ioannis CHLOROS, Thomas MAKRIS. (Coach: Eleftherios PISTOLIS).
Goals: FK Zalgiris Vilnius: 1-0 Virmantas LEMEZIS (3'), 2-0 Igoris MORINAS (32').
Egaleo FC Athens: 1-2 Prokopios SAGANAS (40'), 2-2 Ioannis CHLOROS (46' penalty), 2-3
Ioannis CHLOROS (50' penalty).
Referee: Vitaliy GODULYAN (UKR)

23-07-2005   Stadion u Nisy, Liberec: FC Slovan Liberec – SV Roda JC   1-1 (0-1)
FC Slovan Liberec: Marek CECH, Tomás ZÁPOTOCNY, Pavel KOSTÁL, Peter SINGLÁR
(SVK) (77' Milan MATULA), Ivan HODÚR (SVK), Tomás JANU, Petr PAPOUSEK, Martin
ABRAHÁM, Filip DORT (61' Jan HOLENDA), Libor DOSEK, Filip HOLOSKO (SVK) (67'
Josef HAMOUZ). (Coach: Vítezslav LAVICKA).
SV Roda JC: Vladan KUJOVIC (SBM) (YC80), Ger SENDEN (YC57), Boldiszár BÖDÖR
(HUN), Vincent LACHAMBRE (BEL), László BODNÁR (HUN), Pa-Modou KAH (NOR),
Ivan VICELICH (NZL), SÉRGIO Pacheco de Oliveira (BRA) (85' Kevin VAN DESSEL
(BEL)), Gregoor VAN DIJK, Arouna KONE (CIV) (90' Edrissa SONKO (GAM)), Sekou
CISSÉ (CIV) (71' Dirk Jan DERKSEN). (Coach: Hubertus Jozef Margaretha (Huub)
STEVENS).
Goals: FC Slovan Liberec: 1-1 Libor DOSEK (80').
SV Roda JC: 0-1 SÉRGIO Pacheco de Oliveira (38').
Referee: Franz-Xaver WACK (GER)   Attendance: 5.050

23-07-2005   Ratina Stadium, Tampere: Tampere United FC – SS Lazio Roma   1-1 (0-0)
Tampere United FC: Mikko KAVÉN, Jussi KUOPPALA, Petri HEINÄNEN, Janne
RÄSÄNEN, Antti OJANPERÄ, Jussi KUJALA (61' Antti HYNYNEN), Jarkko WISS, Kari
SAINIO (YC70), Sakari SAARINEN, Henri SCHEWELEFF (75' Mika LAHTINEN), Ville
LEHTINEN. (Coach: Ari Juhani HJELM).
SS Lazio Roma: Matteo SERENI, Manuel BELLERI, Sanchez Emilson CRIBARI (BRA),
Luciano ZAURI, Matías Emanuel LEQUI (ARG), Fabio FIRMANI, CÉSAR Aparecido
Rodrigues (BRA), Christian MANFREDINI (87' Lorenzo DE SILVESTRI), Fabio
LIVERANI, Paolo DI CANIO (75' Goran PANDEV (MCD)), Tommaso ROCCHI (65'
Roberto MUZZI). (Coach: Delio ROSSI).
Goals: Tampere United FC: 1-0 Jarkko WISS (88').
SS Lazio Roma: 1-1 Roberto MUZZI (90'+1').
Referee: Robert STYLES (ENG)   Attendance: 6.000

23-07-2005   Stade Félix Bollaert, Lens:
              Racing Club de Lens – NK Varteks Varazdin   4-1 (0-0)
Racing Club de Lens: Charles ITANDJE, Vitorino HILTON de Silva (BRA), Nicolas GILLET,
Yoann LACHOR, Patrick BARUL (72' Yohan DEMONT), Jérôme LEROY, Alou DIARRA
(YC87), Jonathan LACOURT (YC58) (72' Benoît ASSOU-EKOTO), JUSSIÊ Ferreira Vieira
(BRA) (72' Daniel COUSIN (GAB)), Olivier THOMERT, Aruna DINDANE (CIV). (Coach:
Francis GILLOT).
NK Varteks Varazdin: Tomislav VRANJIC, Nikola POKRIVAC (YC79), Mirko PLANTIC
(61' Dario JERTEC), Kristijan IPSA, Goran MUJANOVIC, Nikola SAFARIC, Neven
VUKMAN, Srebrenko POSAVEC, Leon BENKO (40' Nikola MELNJAK), Ivan JOLIC
(BOS), Nedim HALILOVIC (BOS) (72' Enes NOVINIC). (Coach: Zlatko DALIC).
Goals: Racing Club de Lens: 1-0 Yoann LACHOR (47'), 2-0 Jonathan LACOURT (58'), 3-0
Olivier THOMERT (66'), 4-1 Daniel COUSIN (90'+2').
NK Varteks Varazdin: 3-1 Neven VUKMAN (71').
Referee: Bernardino GONZÁLEZ VÁZQUEZ (ESP)   Attendance: 25.000

23-07-2005   Andruv stadion, Olomouc: SK Sigma Olomouc – Borussia Dortmund   0-0
SK Sigma Olomouc: Tomás LOVÁSIK (SVK) (YC88), Tomás RANDA, Ales SKERLE,
Martin HUDEC, Michal KOVÁR (YC82), Tarciso Rogeiro Pereira "MELINHO" (BRA),
Radek SPILÁCEK, Jaroslav PREKOP (SVK), Radim KÖNIG (41' Kamil VACEK), Ales
BEDNÁR (46' Michal HUBNIK (YC59), 82' Filip RÝDEL), Peter BABNIC (SVK). (Coach:
Petr ULICNY).
Borussia Dortmund: Roman WEIDENFELLER, Christian WÖRNS, Christoph METZELDER,
Philipp DEGEN (SUI) (75' Salvatore GAMBINO), Florian KRINGE, Tomas ROSICKY
(CZE), Leonardo de Deus Santos "DÉDÉ" (BRA), Marc-André KRUSKA (YC62) (67' Nuri
SAHIN (TUR)), Delron BUCKLEY (RSA) (75' David ODONKOR), Jan KOLLER (CZE)
(YC86), Ebi SMOLAREK (POL). (Coach: Lambertus (Bert) VAN MARWIJK (HOL)).
Referee: Daniel STALHAMMAR (SWE)   Attendance: 12.052

23-07-2005   Volkswagen-Arena, Wolfsburg: VfL Wolfsburg – I.F.K. Göteborg   2-0 (1-0)
VfL Wolfsburg: Simon JENTZSCH, Facundo Hernan QUIROGA (ARG), Karsten FISCHER
(61' Hans SARPEI (GHA)), Kevin HOFLAND (HOL), Pablo THIAM (GUI) (YC35), Patrick
WEISER (73' Stefan SCHNOOR), Andrés Nicolas D'ALESSANDRO (ARG) (YC75), Mirko
HRGOVIC (BOS), Miroslav KARHAN (SVK), Diego Fernando KLIMOWICZ (ESP), Mike
HANKE (68' Juan Carlos MENSEGUEZ (ARG)). (Coach: Holger FACH).
I.F.K. Göteborg: Bengt ANDERSSON, Karl SVENSSON, Mattias BJÄRSMYR, Magnus
JOHANSSON, Sebastian JOHANSSON (YC76), Håkan MILD (YC75), Oscar WENDT,
Jonathan BERG (78' Mikael SANDKLEF), Stefan SELAKOVIC (72' George MOURAD),
Samuel WOWOAH (87' Andrés VASQUES). (Coach: Arne ERLANDSEN (NOR)).
Goals: VfL Wolfsburg: 1-0 Andrés Nicolas D'ALESSANDRO (24'), 2-0 Diego Fernando
KLIMOWICZ (76').
Referee: Igor EGOROV (RUS)   Attendance: 6.510

23-07-2005   Stade Vélodrome, Marseille:
                Olympique Marseille – BSC Young Boys Bern   2-1 (0-1)
Olympique Marseille: Cédric CARRASSO, Habib BEYE (SEN), Frédéric DÉHU, Abdoulaye
MÉÏTÉ (CIV), Taye Ismaila TAIWO (NGR), Sergio "KOKE" Contreras Pardo (ESP) (46'
Samir NASRI (YC49)), Laurent BATLLES (89' Sylvain N'DAIYE (SEN)), Wilson ORUMA
(NGR), Franck RIBÉRY, Mamadou NIANG (SEN), Péguy LUYINDULA. (Coach: Jean
FERNANDEZ).
BSC Young Boys Bern: Marco WÖLFLI, Ronny HODEL, Miguel Alfredo PORTILLO (ARG)
(YC27), TIAGO Coelho Branco Calvano (BRA), Gretar STEINSSON (ISL), Pirmin
SCHWEGLER (73' Roman FRIEDLI), Mario RAIMONDI, Yao AZIAWONOU (TOG)
(YC86), Thomas HÄBERLI (85' Gabriel José URDANETA Rangel (VEN)), Carlos Vila
VARELA (ESP), Patrick DE NAPOLI (YC22) (72' Marco SCHNEUWLY). (Coach: Hans-
Peter ZAÜGG).
Goals : Olympique Marseille: 1-1 Péguy LUYINDULA (69' penalty), 2-1 Samir NASRI (83').
BSC Young Boys Bern: 0-1 Mario RAIMONDI (43').
Referee: Ivan BEBEK (CRO)   Attendance: 14.000

151

23-07-2005   Estadio Mestalla, Valencia: Valencia CF – KAA Gent   2-0 (1-0)
Valencia CF: José Santiago CAÑIZARES Ruiz, FÁBIO AURÉLIO Rodrigues (BRA), Roberto
Fabián AYALA (ARG) (YC33), Marco António Simões CANEIRA (POR), Emiliano
MORETTI (ITA), Eduardo César Daude Gaspar "EDU" (BRA), David ALBELDA Aliqués,
VICENTE Rodríguez Guillén (70' Juan Luís "JUANLU" Hens Lorite), Francisco Joaquín
Pérez RUFETE (86' Pedro LÓPEZ Muñoz), Patrick Stephan KLUIVERT (HOL), David
VILLA Sánchez (64' Marco DI VAIO (ITA)). (Coach: Enrique "QUIQUE" Sánchez
FLORES).
KAA Gent: Frédéric HERPOEL, Dario SMOJE (CRO) (YC29), Nicolas LOMBAERTS,
Stephen LAYBUTT (AUS), Yngvar HÅKONSEN (NOR), Mamar MAMOUNI (ALG),
Moubarak (Mbark) BOUSSOUFA (HOL) (73' Jovica TRAJCEV (MCD)), Steve
COOREMAN, Wouter VRANCKEN (YC53) (73' Davy DE BEULE), Mohammed Aliyu
DATTI (NGR), Gnahoua Zéphirin ZOKO (CIV) (68' Nenad MLADENOVIC (SBM)).
(Coach: Georges LEEKENS).
Goals: Valencia CF: 1-0 David VILLA Sánchez (6'), 2-0 Patrick Stephan KLUIVERT (78').
Referee: Ruud BOSSEN (HOL)   Attendance: 17.000

24-07-2005   Stade Geoffroy Guichard, Saint-Etienne:
                 AS Saint-Etienne – CFR Cluj   2-2 (0-1)
AS Saint-Etienne: Jérémy JANOT, Damien PERQUIS, Vincent HOGNON, Alledine YAHIA
(TUN) (46' Mouhamadou DABO (SEN)), Hérita N'Kongolo ILUNGA (DRC) (RC23), David
HELLEBUYCK (77' Sébastien MAZURE), Didier ZOKORA (CIV), Julien SABLÉ (YC90),
Pascal FEINDOUNO (GUI), Frédéric PIQUIONNE, Frédéric MENDY (SEN) (46' Lamine
SAKHO). (Coach: Élie BAUP).
CFR Cluj: Petru TURCAS (YC90+3), György László BALINT (YC25,YC53), Vasile Ilie
JULA, Zoran MILOSEVIC (SBM), Cosmin Marin VASIE (19' Casian Vasile MICLAUS),
Ambrosie Cristian COROIAN (73' Svetozar MIJIN (SBM) (YC82)), Alin Ilie MINTEOAN
(YC42), Dorinel Ionel MUNTEANU, Cristian TURCU (75' Stefan Sorin ONCICA) Adrian
Gheorghe ANCA, Cosmin TILINCA. (Coach: Gheorghe MIHALI).
Goals: AS Saint-Etienne: 1-1 Julien SABLÉ (51'), 2-2 Mouhamadou DABO (88).
CFR Cluj: 0-1 Ambrosie Cristian COROIAN (23' penalty), 1-2 Cosmin TILINCA (66').
Referee: Pasquale RODOMONTI (ITA)   Attendance: 29.516

SEMI-FINALS

27-07-2005   Zalgirio Stadionas, Vilnius: FK Zalgiris Vilnius – CFR Cluj   1-2 (0-1)
FK Zalgiris Vilnius: Mindaugas MALINAUSKAS, Tadas GRAZIUNAS, Tomas MIKUCKIS,
Paulius PAKNYS (YC58), Andrejus SOROKINAS (46' Vidas KAUSPADAS), Andrei
SHYLO (BLS) (YC24), Andzej MAKSIMOVIC, Karolis JASAITIS (46' Andrejus
TERESKINAS), Virmantas LEMEZIS (53' Aleksandr OSIPOVITCH (BLS)), Igoris
MORINAS, Branislav JASUREK (SVK) (YC77). (Coach: Saulius SIRMELIS).
CFR Cluj: Petru TURCAS, Cristian Calin PANIN (YC90+2), Vasile Ilie JULA, Zoran
MILOSEVIC (SBM), Dorin TOMA, Florin Cristian DAN, Ambrosie Cristian COROIAN,
Dorinel Ionel MUNTEANU (YC63) (78' Alin Ilie MINTEOAN), Stefan Sorin ONCICA (78'
Cristian TURCU), Sead BRUNCEVIC (SBM), Cosmin TILINCA (64' Adrian Gheorghe
ANCA). (Coach: Dorinel Ionel MUNTEANU).
Goals: FK Zalgiris Vilnius: 1-1 Aleksandr OSIPOVITCH (74').
CFR Cluj: 0-1 Florin Cristian DAN (37'), 1-2 Adrian Gheorghe ANCA (78').
Referee: Ruud BOSSEN (HOL)   Attendance: 1.000
(Cristian Ambrosie COROIAN missed penalty in the 77ᵗʰ minute)

152

27-07-2005   Andruv stadion, Olomouc: SK Sigma Olomouc – Hamburger SV   0-1 (0-0)
SK Sigma Olomouc: Martin BLAHA, Tomás RANDA, Roman HUBNIK (39' Radim
KOPECKY), Martin HUDEC, Michal KOVÁR, Tarciso Rogeiro Pereira "MELINHO" (BRA),
Ladislav ONOFREJ (SVK), Andrej PECNIK (SLO), Kamil VACEK, David ROJKA (57' Ales
BEDNÁR), Peter BABNIC (SVK). (Coach: Petr ULICNY).
Hamburger SV: Stefan WÄCHTER, Thimothée ATOUBA (CMR) (YC78), Daniel VAN
BUYTEN (BEL), René KLINGBEIL (YC39), Khalid BOULAHROUZ (HOL), Raphael
WICKY (SUI) (89' Markus KARL), David JAROLIM (CZE), Stefan BEINLICH, Rafael
VAN DER VAART (HOL), Sergej BARBAREZ (BOS), Emile MPENZA (BEL) (73'
Benjamin LAUTH). (Coach: Thomas DOLL).
Goal: Hamburger SV: 0-1 Rafael VAN DER VAART (49').
Referee: Paolo BERTINI (ITA)   Attendance: 11.435

27-07-2005   Volkswagen-Arena, Wolfsburg: VfL Wolfsburg – Racing Club de Lens   0-0
VfL Wolfsburg: Simon JENTZSCH, Facundo Hernan QUIROGA (ARG), Karsten FISCHER,
Kevin HOFLAND (HOL), Pablo THIAM (GUI), Patrick WEISER (75' Stefan SCHNOOR),
Andrés Nicolas D'ALESSANDRO (ARG), Mirko HRGOVIC (BOS) (46' Mike HANKE),
Miroslav KARHAN (SVK), Diego Fernando KLIMOWICZ (ESP) (82' Marko TOPIC (BOS)),
Juan Carlos MENSEGUEZ (ARG). (Coach: Holger FACH).
Racing Club de Lens: Charles ITANDJE, Vitorino HILTON de Silva (BRA), Adama
COULIBALY (MLI), Jacek BAK (POL), Benoît ASSOU-EKOTO (YC39), Seydou KEITA
(MLI) (YC72), Eric CARRIÈRE (84' Patrick BARUL), Yohan DEMONT, Daniel COUSIN
(GAB) (68' JUSSIÊ Ferreira Vieira (BRA)), Dagui BAKARI (CIV) (68' Aruna DINDANE
(CIV)), Issam JOMA'A (TUN) (YC70). (Coach: Francis GILLOT).
Referee: Emil BOZINOVSKI (MCD)   Attendance: 10.511

27-07-2005   Estadio Municipal de Riazor, La Coruña:
                RC Deportivo la Coruña – Newcastle United FC   2-1 (1-0)
RC Deportivo la Coruña: José Francisco MOLINA Jiménez, MANUEL PABLO García Díaz,
JORGE Manuel Almeida Gomes ANDRADE (POR), Enrique Fernández ROMERO, Joan
CAPDEVILA Méndez (YC55), Aldo Pedro DUSCHER (ARG) (71' VÍCTOR Sánchez Del
Amo), SERGIO González Soriano, Pedro MUNITIS Alvarez, DIEGO TRISTÁN Herrera (55'
Juan Carlos VALERÓN Santana), RUBÉN CASTRO Martín (YC28), Alberto LUQUE Martos
(62' Lionel Sebastián SCALONI (ARG)). (Coach: Joaquín Jesús CAPARRÓS Camino).
Newcastle United FC: Shay GIVEN (IRL), Stephen CARR (IRL) (YC29), Jean-Alain
BOUMSONG (FRA), Steven TAYLOR (YC51), Céléstine BABAYARO (NGR), James
MILNER (72' Michael CHOPRA), Charles N'ZOGBIA (FRA), Nicky BUTT, Amdy FAYE
(SEN), Lee BOWYER, Alan SHEARER. (Coach: Graeme James SOUNESS (SCO)).
Goals: RC Deportivo la Coruña: 1-0 RUBÉN CASTRO Martín (11'), 2-1 JORGE Manuel
Almeida Gomes ANDRADE (57').
Newcastle United FC: 1-1 Lee BOWYER (47').
Referee: Serge GUMIENNY (BEL)   Attendance: 12.000

27-07-2005   Stadio Olimpico, Roma: SS Lazio Roma – Olympique Marseille 1-1 (1-0)
SS Lazio Roma: Matteo SERENI, Manuel BELLERI, Sanchez Emilson CRIBARI (BRA) (YC10), Luciano ZAURI, Simone SANNIBALE, Fabio FIRMANI (YC40), CÉSAR Aparecido Rodrigues (BRA), Christian MANFREDINI (YC38) (84' Lorenzo DE SILVESTRI), Fabio LIVERANI (YC81), Paolo DI CANIO (YC31) (70' Igli TARE (ALB)), Roberto MUZZI (65' Goran PANDEV (MCD)). (Coach: Delio ROSSI).
Olympique Marseille: Cédric CARRASSO, Habib BEYE (SEN) (YC42), Frédéric DÉHU, Abdoulaye MÉÏTÉ (CIV) (YC63), Taye Ismaila TAIWO (NGR), Franck RIBÉRY (90' Laurent BATLLES), Wilson ORUMA (NGR), Sabri LAMOUCHI, Sergio "KOKE" Contreras Pardo (ESP) (64' Andrés Augusto MENDOZA Azevedo (PER)), Mamadou NIANG (SEN), Samir NASRI (81' Demétrius FERREIRA Leite (BRA)). (Coach: Jean FERNANDEZ).
Goals: SS Lazio Roma: 1-0 Paolo DI CANIO (42').
Olympique Marseille: 1-1 Abdoulaye MÉÏTÉ (69').
Referee: Carlos MEGÍA DÁVILLA (ESP)   Attendance: 5.000

27-07-2005   Estadio Mestalla, Valencia: Valencia CF – SV Roda JC 4-0 (2-0)
Valencia CF: José Santiago CAÑIZARES Ruiz, FÁBIO AURÉLIO Rodrigues (BRA), Roberto Fabian AYALA (ARG), Carlos MARCHENA López, Pedro LÓPEZ Muñoz, Eduardo César Daude Gaspar "EDU" (BRA), David ALBELDA Aliqués, VICENTE Rodríguez Guillén (80' Emiliano MORETTI (ITA)), Francisco Joaquín Pérez RUFETE (84' Juan Luis "JUANLU" Hens Lorite), Patrick Stephan KLUIVERT (HOL) (58' David VILLA Sánchez), Marco DI VAIO (ITA). (Coach: Enrique "QUIQUE" Sánchez FLORES).
SV Roda JC: Vladan KUJOVIC (SBM), Ger SENDEN, Boldiszár BÖDÖR (HUN) (57' Predrag FILIPOVIC (SBM)), Vincent LACHAMBRE (BEL), László BODNÁR (HUN), Pa-Modou KAH (NOR), SÉRGIO Pacheco de Oliveira (BRA) (43' Kevin VAN DESSEL (BEL)), Gregoor VAN DIJK, Edrissa SONKO (GAM) (64' Charlie VAN DEN OUWELAND), Arouna KONÉ (CIV), Sekou CISSÉ (CIV) (YC31). (Coach: Hubertus Jozef Margaretha (Huub) STEVENS).
Goals: Valencia CF: 1-0 Francisco Joaquín Pérez RUFETE (36'), 2-0 Francisco Joaquín Pérez RUFETE (41'), 3-0 Francisco Joaquín Pérez RUFETE (50'), 4-0 Emiliano MORETTI (83').
Referee: Markus NOBS (SUI)   Attendance: 22.000

03-08-2005   Stadionul CFR Gruia, Cluj-Napoca: CFR Cluj – FK Zalgiris Vilnius 5-1 (2-0)
CFR Cluj: Petru TURCAS, Cristian Calin PANIN, Vasile Ilie JULA (68' Dorin TOMA), György László BALINT, Casian Vasile MICLAUS, Florin Cristian DAN, Alin Ilie MINTEOAN, Ambrosie Cristian COROIAN (60' Stefan Sorin ONICICA), Cristian TURCU, Adrian Gheorghe ANCA, Cosmin TILINCA (80' Sead BRUNCEVIC (SBM)). (Coach: Dorinel Ionel MUNTEANU).
FK Zalgiris Vilnius: Mindaugas MALINAUSKAS, Paulius PAKNYS, Tadas GRAZIUNAS, Tomas MIKUCKIS (YC45), Ramunas STONKUS, Andzej MAKSIMOVIC (60' Andrius JOKSAS), Virmantas LEMEZIS (78' Anton NAUMOV), Karolis JASAITIS, Marijanas CHORUZIJUS, Vidas KAUSPADAS (YC23) (52' Jevgenij DOVKSA), Igoris MORINAS. (Coach: Saulius SIRMELIS).
Goals: CFR Cluj: 1-0 Cosmin TILINCA (11'), 2-0 Vasile Ilie JULA (45' penalty), 3-0 Ambrosie Cristian COROIAN (49'), 4-0 Alin Ilie MINTEOAN (57'), 5-0 Adrian Gheorghe ANCA (72').
FK Zalgiris Vilnius: 5-1 Andrius JOKSAS (90').
Referee: Bernhard BRUGGER (AUT)   Attendance: 6.000

154

03-08-2005   Stade Félix Bollaert, Lens: Racing Club de Lens – VfL Wolfsburg 4-0 (1-0)
Racing Club de Lens: Charles ITANDJE, Vitorino HILTON de Silva (BRA), Adama
COULIBALY (MLI), Benoît ASSOU-EKOTO (YC32), Jérôme LEROY, Seydou KEITA
(MLI), Alou DIARRA (YC40), Yohan DEMONT, JUSSIÊ Ferreira Vieira (BRA) (76' Eric
CARRIÈRE), Olivier THOMERT (64' Issam JOMA'A (TUN)), Aruna DINDANE (CIV) (76'
Daniel COUSIN (GAB)). (Coach: Francis GILLOT).
VfL Wolfsburg: Simon JENTZSCH, Peter VAN DER HEYDEN (BEL) (YC30) (76'Maik
FRANZ), Facundo Hernan QUIROGA (ARG) (YC10) (76' Patrick WEISER), Kevin
HOFLAND (HOL), Hans SARPEI (GHA) (57' Cedric MAKIADI), Pablo THIAM (GUI)
(YC72), Andrés Nicolas D'ALESSANDRO (ARG), Miroslav KARHAN (SVK) (YC37),
Diego Fernando KLIMOWICZ (ESP), Mike HANKE, Juan Carlos MENSEGUEZ (ARG)
(RC60). (Coach: Holger FACH).
Goals: Racing Club de Lens: 1-0 Aruna DINDANE (42'), 2-0 Seydou KEITA (48'), 3-0 Issam
JOMA'A (89'), 4-0 Issam JOMA'A (90+').
Referee: Mark HALSEY (ENG)   Attendance: 25.941

03-08-2005   Saint James' Park, Newcastle:
                    Newcastle United FC – RC Deportivo la Coruña   1-2 (1-1)
Newcastle United FC: Shay GIVEN (IRL), Stephen CARR (IRL), Robert ELLIOTT (YC87),
Jean-Alain BOUMSONG (FRA), Steven TAYLOR (YC44), Emre BELÖZOGLU (TUR)
(90'+3' Martin BRITTAIN), Scott PARKER (YC29), Amdy FAYE (SEN) (53' Shola
AMEOBI), James MILNER (72' Charles N'ZOGBIA (FRA)), Lee BOWYER, Alan
SHEARER (YC35). (Coach: Graeme James SOUNESS (SCO)).
RC Deportivo la Coruña: José Francisco MOLINA Jiménez, MANUEL PABLO García Díaz
(YC57), Enrique Fernández ROMERO, JORGE Manuel Almeida Gomes ANDRADE (POR),
Joan CAPDEVILA Méndez (YC85), Aldo Pedro DUSCHER (ARG), SERGIO González
Soriano (73' Juan Carlos VALERÓN Santana), Lionel Sebastián SCALONI (ARG), DIEGO
TRISTÁN Herrera (YC35) (55' Alberto LUQUE Martos), Pedro MUNITIS Alvarez (YC50),
RUBÉN CASTRO Martín (64' Juan Maria "JUANMA" Delgado Moreno (YC78)). (Coach:
Joaquín Jesús CAPARRÓS Camino).
Goals: Newcastle United FC: 1-0 James MILNER (39').
RC Deportivo la Coruña: 1-1 JORGE Manuel Almeida Gomes ANDRADE (45'), 1-2 Pedro
MUNITIS Alvarez (47').
Referee: Helmut FLEISCHER (GER)   Attendance: 34.215

03-08-2005   Parkstad Limburg Stadion, Kerkrade: SV Roda JC – Valencia CF   0-0
SV Roda JC: Vladan KUJOVIC (SBM), Alexander VOIGT (GER), Predrag FILIPOVIC
(SBM) (YC61), László BODNÁR (HUN), Pa-Modou KAH (NOR), SÉRGIO Pacheco de
Oliveira (BRA), Kevin VAN DESSEL (BEL), Charlie VAN DEN OUWELAND, Gregoor
VAN DIJK (68' Ivan VICELICH (NZL)), Edrissa SONKO (GAM), Arouna KONÉ (CIV) (73'
Dirk Jan DERKSEN). (Coach: Hubertus Jozef Margaretha (Huub) STEVENS).
Valencia CF: Juan Luis MORA Palacios, FÁBIO AURÉLIO Rodrigues (BRA), Roberto
Fabián AYALA (ARG), Carlos MARCHENA López, Marco António Simões CANEIRA
(POR), Amadeo CARBONI (ITA), Emiliano MORETTI (ITA), RAÚL ALBIOL Tortajada,
Francisco Joaquín Pérez RUFETE (74' Juan Luis "JUANLU" Hens Lorite), David VILLA
Sánchez (63' Marco DI VAIO (ITA)), Miguel Ángel Ferrer Martínez "MISTA" (66' Eduardo
Cesar Daude Gaspar "EDU" (BRA)). (Coach: Enrique "QUIQUE" Sánchez FLORES).
Referee; Espen BERNTSEN (NOR)   Attendance: 3.300

155

03-08-2005   AOL Arena, Hamburg: Hamburger SV – SK Sigma Olomouc   3-0 (1-0)
Hamburger SV: Stefan WÄCHTER, Thimothée ATOUBA (CMR), Bastian REINHARDT, René KLINGBEIL, Raphael WICKY (SUI) (62' Markus KARL), David JAROLIM (CZE), Piotr TROCHOWSKI, Guy DEMEL (CIV), Rafael VAN DER VAART (HOL) (58' Stefan BEINLICH), Benjamin LAUTH, Naohiro TAKAHARA (JPN) (76' Emile MPENZA (BEL)). (Coach: Thomas DOLL).
SK Sigma Olomouc: Tomás LOVÁSIK (SVK), Tomás RANDA, Radim KOPECKY, Martin HUDEC, Michal KOVÁR, Ladislav ONOFREJ (SVK) (YC40) (78'David ROJKA), Andrej PECNIK (SLO), Kamil VACEK (76' Tomás GLOS), Filip RÝDEL (SVK) (66' Ales BEDNÁR), Jan SCHULMEISTER, Peter BABNIC (SVK) (YC13). (Coach: Petr ULICNY).
Goals: Hamburger SV: 1-0 Benjamin LAUTH (30'), 2-0 Rafael VAN DER VAART (56'), 3-0 Benjamin LAUTH (81').
Referee: Costas KAPITANIS (CYP)   Attendance: 31.358

03-08-2005   Stade Vélodrome, Marseille: Olympique Marseille – SS Lazio Roma   3-0 (0-0)
Olympique Marseille: Cédric CARRASSO, Taye Ismaila TAIWO (NGR), Demétrius FERREIRA Leite (BRA), Frédéric DÉHU, Abdoulaye MÉÏTÉ (CIV) (YC67), Habib BEYE (SEN) (YC56), Franck RIBÉRY, Wilson ORUMA (NGR) (78' Laurent BATLLES), Sabri LAMOUCHI (73' Sylvain N'DIAYE (SEN)), Mamadou NIANG (SEN), Andrés Augusto MENDOZA Azevedo (PER) (81' Péguy LUYINDULA). (Coach: Jean FERNANDEZ).
SS Lazio Roma: Matteo SERENI, Manuel BELLERI (18' Simone SANNIBALE), Luciano ZAURI, Sanchez Emilson CRIBARI (BRA) (YC9), Matías Emanuel LEQUI (ARG) (YC1), Fabio FIRMANI, CÉSAR Aparecido Rodrigues (BRA), Christian MANFREDINI (63' Igli TARE (ALB)), Fabio LIVERANI, Paolo DI CANIO (52' Roberto MUZZI), Tommaso ROCCHI (YC67). (Coach: Delio ROSSI).
Goals: Olympique Marseille: 1-0 Mamadou NIANG (60'), 2-0 Andrés Augusto MENDOZA Azevedo (61'), 3-0 Franck RIBÉRY (65').
Referee: Antonio Manuel ALMEIDA COSTA (POR)   Attendance: 50.000

FINALS

09-08-2005   Stadionul CFR Gruia, Cluj-Napoca:
                        CFR Cluj – Racing Club de Lens   1-1 (0-1)
CFR Cluj: Petru TURCAS, Cristian Calin PANIN, Vasile Ilie JULA, György László BALINT (YC77), Casian Vasile MICLAUS, Florin Cristian DAN (64' Ambrosie Cristian COROIAN), Alin Ilie MINTEOAN, Dorinel Ionel MUNTEANU, Stefan Sorin ONCICA (54' Cristian TURCU), Adrian Gheorghe ANCA (YC88), Cosmin TILINCA (87' Sead BRUNCEVIC (SBM)). (Coach: Gheorghe MIHALI).
Racing Club de Lens: Charles ITANDJE, Vitorino HILTON de Silva (BRA), Adama COULIBALY (MLI) (YC48), Nicolas GILLET, Yohan DEMONT, Seydou KEITA (MLI), Patrick BARUL, Yoann LACHOR, Eric CARRIÈRE (74' Issam JOMA'A (TUN)), Daniel COUSIN (GAB), Olivier THOMERT (65' Jérôme LEROY (RC83)). (Coach: Francis GILLOT).
Goals: CFR Cluj: 1-1 Cristian TURCU (57').
Racing Club de Lens: 0-1 Yoann LACHOR (24').
Referee: Grzegorz GILEWSKI (POL)   Attendance: 9.000

156

09-08-2005   AOL Arena, Hamburg: Hamburger SV – Valencia CF   1-0 (0-0)
Hamburger SV: Stefan WÄCHTER, Thimothée ATOUBA (CMR), Bastian REINHARDT, Khalid BOULAHROUZ (HOL), Raphael WICKY (SUI), David JAROLIM (CZE) (YC83), Guy DEMEL (CIV) (YC47), Stefan BEINLICH (21' Piotr TROCHOWSKI), Rafael VAN DER VAART (HOL) (90+' Markus KARL), Sergej BARBAREZ (BOS) (YC71,YC83), Emile MPENZA (BEL) (77' Benjamin LAUTH). (Coach: Thomas DOLL).
Valencia CF: José Santiago CAÑIZARES Ruiz, FÁBIO AURÉLIO Rodrigues (BRA) (YC83), Roberto Fabián AYALA (ARG), Carlos MARCHENA López, Marco António Simões CANEIRA (POR), David ALBELDA Aliqués, VICENTE Rodríguez Guillén (YC71), Eduardo César Daude Gaspar "EDU" (BRA) (YC83), Francisco Joaquín Pérez RUFETE (37' Pedro LÓPEZ Muñoz), Patrick Stephan KLUIVERT (HOL) (78' Miguel Ángel Ferrer Martínez "MISTA"), Marco DI VAIO (ITA) (46' David VILLA Sánchez (YC74)). (Coach: Enrique "QUIQUE" Sánchez FLORES).
Goal: Hamburger SV: 1-0 Sergej BARBAREZ (51').
Referee: Stuart DOUGAL (SCO)   Attendance: 55.386

09-08-2005   Estadio Municipal de Riazor, La Coruña:
               RC Deportivo la Coruña – Olympique Marseille   2-0 (0-0)
RC Deportivo la Coruña: José Francisco MOLINA Jiménez, MANUEL PABLO García Díaz, Enrique Fernández ROMERO, JORGE Manuel Almeida Gomes ANDRADE (POR), Juan Maria "JUANMA" Delgado Moreno, Aldo Pedro DUSCHER (ARG), SERGIO González Soriano (YC22), VÍCTOR Sánchez Del Amo (72' Lionel Sebastián SCALONI (ARG)), DIEGO TRISTÁN Herrera (68' Juan Carlos VALERÓN Santana), RUBÉN CASTRO Martín, Alberto LUQUE Martos (72' IVÁN CARRIL Regueiro). (Coach: Joaquín Jesús CAPARRÓS Camino).
Olympique Marseille: Cédric CARRASSO, Taye Ismaila TAIWO (NGR), Demétrius FERREIRA Leite (BRA) (YC11), Frédéric DÉHU, Koji NAKATA (JPN), "DELFIM" José Fernandes Rola Teixeira (POR) (75' Laurent BATLLES), Franck RIBÉRY (YC25) (79' Sergio "KOKE" Contreras Pardo (ESP)), Wilson ORUMA (NGR), Sylvain N'DIAYE (SEN), Mamadou NIANG (SEN), Andrés Augusto MENDOZA Azevedo (PER) (46' Samir NASRI). (Coach: Jean FERNANDEZ).
Goals: RC Deportivo la Coruña: 1-0 RUBÉN CASTRO Martín (68'), 2-0 IVÁN CARRIL Regueiro (87').
Referee: Jaroslav JARA (CZE)   Attendance: 19.000

23-08-2005   Stade Félix Bollaert, Lens: Racing Club de Lens – CFR Cluj   3-1 (1-0)
Racing Club de Lens: Charles ITANDJE, Yohan DEMONT, Yoann LACHOR, Adama COULIBALY (MLI), Vitorino HILTON de Silva (BRA) (82' Nicolas GILLET), Benoît ASSOU-EKOTO (82' Eric CARRIÈRE), Alou DIARRA, Seydou KEITA (MLI) (YC29), JUSSIÊ Ferreira Vieira (BRA) (80' Olivier THOMERT (YC90+2)), Daniel COUSIN (GAB), Aruna DINDANE (CIV). (Coach: Francis GILLOT).
CFR Cluj: Martin Gheorghe TUDOR, Cristian Calin PANIN (YC62), György László BALINT, Zoran MILOSEVIC (SBM), Casian Vasile MICLAUS, Alin Ilie MINTEOAN (YC19), Dorinel Ionel MUNTEANU (YC78), Cosmin TILINCA (74' Sead BRUNCEVIC (SBM)), Ambrosie Cristian COROIAN (52' Florin Cristian DAN), Cristian TURCU (YC15) (72' Stefan Sorin ONCICA), Adrian Gheorghe ANCA. (Coach: Gheorghe MIHALI).
Goals: Racing Club de Lens: 1-0 Vitorino HILTON de Silva (38'), 2-0 Adama COULIBALY (76'), 3-0 Daniel COUSIN (78' penalty).
CFR Cluj: 3-1 Dorinel Ionel MUNTEANU (88').
Referee: Alon YEFET (ISR)   Attendance: 37.934

23-08-2005   Stade Vélodrome, Marseille:
Olympique Marseille – RC Deportivo la Coruña 5-1 (1-1)
Olympique Marseille: Cédric CARRASSO, Habib BEYE (SEN) (76' Rachmane BARRY
(SEN)), Abdoulaye MÉÏTÉ (CIV) (YC81), Taye Ismaila TAIWO (NGR), Koji NAKATA
(JPN) (YC32), Sabri LAMOUCHI (YC16) (69' Laurent BATLLES), Wilson ORUMA (NGR),
"DELFIM" José Fernandes Rola Teixeira (POR) (56' Sergio "KOKE" Contreras Pardo (ESP)),
Franck RIBÉRY (RC12), Mamadou NIANG (SEN) (YC87), Andrés Augusto MENDOZA
Azevedo (PER). (Coach: Jean FERNANDEZ).
RC Deportivo la Coruña: José Francisco MOLINA Jiménez, MANUEL PABLO García Díaz
(YC60), JORGE Manuel Almeida Gomes ANDRADE (POR), Juan Maria "JUANMA"
Delgado Moreno (YC39), Joan CAPDEVILA Méndez (YC22,YC71), Julián Bobby DE
GUZMÁN (CAN) (YC48), Lionel Sebastián SCALONI (ARG) (YC16) (63' Roberto Miguel
"Toro" ACUÑA (PAR) (YC87)), Aldo Pedro DUSCHER (ARG) (RC12), Pedro MUNITIS
Alvarez, RUBÉN CASTRO Martín (74' HÉCTOR Berenguel del Rio), DIEGO TRISTÁN
Herrera (58' Enrique Fernández ROMERO). (Coach: Joaquín Jesús CAPARRÓS Camino).
Goals: Olympique Marseille: 1-0 Franck RIBÉRY (5'), 2-1 Abdoulaye MÉÏTÉ (65'), 3-1
Andrés Augusto MENDOZA Azevedo (74'), 4-1 Mamadou NIANG (88'), 5-1 Wilson
ORUMA (90'+3').
RC Deportivo la Coruña: 1-1 JORGE Manuel Almeida Gomes ANDRADE (9').
Referee: Nikolai IVANOV (RUS)   Attendance: 50.000

23-08-2005   Estadio Mestalla, Valencia: Valencia CF – Hamburger SV 0-0
Valencia CF: José Santiago CAÑIZARES Ruiz, RAÚL ALBIOL Tortajada, Emiliano
MORETTI (ITA), Roberto Fabián AYALA (ARG), FÁBIO AURÉLIO Rodrigues (BRA),
Francisco Joaquín Pérez RUFETE (57' Miguel Ángel ANGULO Valderrey), David
ALBELDA Aliqués (YC84), Rubén BARAJA Vegas (72' Marco DI VAIO (ITA)), VICENTE
Rodríguez Guillén, Pablo César AIMAR (ARG) (YC44), Patrick Stephan KLUIVERT (HOL)
(46' David VILLA Sánchez). (Coach: Enrique "QUIQUE" Sánchez FLORES).
Hamburger SV: Stefan WÄCHTER, Guy DEMEL (CIV) (59' Bastian REINHARDT), Khalid
BOULAHROUZ (HOL) (YC60), Daniel VAN BUYTEN (BEL), Thimothée ATOUBA
(CMR), David JAROLIM (CZE) (85' Piotr TROCHOWSKI), Raphael WICKY (SUI), Rafael
VAN DER VAART (HOL), Stefan BEINLICH (46' Mehdi MAHDAVIKIA (IRN)), Benjamin
LAUTH (YC66), Emile MPENZA (BEL). (Coach: Thomas DOLL).
Referee: Laurent DUHAMEL (FRA)   Attendance: 43.000

**Hamburger SV, Olympique Marseille and Racing Club de Lens all qualified for the
UEFA Cup competition.**

2006

17-06-2006   Shakhtyor Stadium,Karagandy:
                  FC Shakhtyor Karaganda – FC MTZ-RIPO Minsk   1-5 (0-0)
FC Shakhtyor Karaganda: Sergey SARANA, Oleg KORNILENKO, Zeljko JOKSIMOVIC (58' Veaceslav RUSNAC (MOL)), Vladica CURCIC (SBM) (68' Rakhman ASUKHANOV), Ruslan KENETAEV, Ilnur MANGUTKIN, Rafael URAZBAKHTIN, NILTON Mendes Pereira (BRA), Andrey FINONCHENKO, Mikhail GLUSHKO, Evgeniy LUNEV. (Coach: Sergey MICHSHENKO).
FC MTZ-RIPO Minsk: Aleksandr SULIMA, Artem FEDORCHENKO (UKR), Aleksandr BYLINA, Aleksandr STASHCHENYUK, Aleksandr GORBACHEV, Vyacheslav HLEB (53' Bojan MAMIC (SBM)), Oleg STRAKANOVICH, Dmitri SHEGRIKOVICH, Vitali TARASHCHIK, Mikhail YEREMCHUK (70' Mikhail AFANASIEV), Artem KONTSEVOI (83' Igor MALTSEV). (Coach: Yuri Iosifovich PUNTUS).
Goals: FC Shakhtyor Karaganda: 1-4 NILTON Mendes Pereira (67').
FC MTZ-RIPO Minsk: 0-1 Dmitri SHEGRIKOVICH (46'), 0-2 Vyacheslav HLEB (52'), 0-3 Bojan MAMIC (62'), 0-4 Oleg STRAKANOVICH (64'), 1-5 Bojan MAMIC (82').
Referee: Johny VER EECKE (BEL)

17-06-2006   Heydar Aliyev Stadium, Imishli: MKT Araz Imishli – FC Tiraspol   1-0 (0-0)
MKT Araz Imishli: Etibar TANRIVERDIEV, Sasha YUNISOGLU, Ceyhun ADISHIRINOV, Valentin VISHTALYUK (YC71), Dmytro PARKHOMENKO (UKR), Victor BARISEV (MOL), Evgeni SHIMAN (UKR) (62' Arif DASHDEMIROV), Zeynal ZEYNALOV (YC58), Murad AGHAKISHIYEV, Marcel RESHITSA (72' Asif MAMMADOV), Ihor MAKOVEY (UKR) (62' Bahruz ZEYNALOV). (Coach: Igor NAKONECHNYY (UKR)).
FC Tiraspol: Stanislav NAMASCO, Andrey NOVICOV, Victor GOLOVATENCO, Valentin Giani NECSULESCU (ROM) (YC89), Kyrylo SYDORENKO (UKR), Serghei NAMASCO, Nicolai RUDAC, Andrey SECRIERU, Igor PICUSCIAC, Serghei ALEXEEV (72' Andrey PORFIREANU), Oleksandr BYCHKOV (UKR) (80' Evgheni GORODETCHIL). (Coach: Yuriy Petrovych KULISH (UKR)).
Goal: MKT Araz Imishli: 1-0 Marcel RESHITSA (65').
Referee: Cüneyt ÇAKIR (TUR)

17-06-2006   Ratina Stadium, Tampere:
                  Tampere United FC – Carmarthen Town AFC   5-0 (3-0)
Tampere United FC: Mikko KAVÉN, Vasile MARCHIS (ROM), Jussi KUOPPALA, Petri HEINÄNEN, Heikki AHO, Jussi-Pekka SAVOLAINEN, Jarkko WISS, Aristides PERTOT (ARG), Antti HYNYNEN (86' Antti OJANPERÄ), Ville LEHTINEN (YC52) (66' Miki SIPILÄINEN (YC85)), Sakari SAARINEN (69' Juska SAVOLAINEN). (Coach: Ari Juhani HJELM).
Carmarthen Town AFC: Mark OVENDALE (ENG), Christopher THOMAS, Luke HARDY (IRL), Martyn GILES, Kaid MOHAMED (63' Matthew DAVIES), Colin LOSS (YC59), Rhodri JONES (63' Sacha WALTERS), Kevin AHERNE-EVANS, Neil SMOTHERS, Nathan COTTERRALL, Mark DODDS (83' Craig LIMA). (Coach: Mark JONES).
Goals: Tampere United FC: 1-0 Antti HYNYNEN (24'), 2-0 Ville LEHTINEN (40'), 3-0 Jussi-Pekka SAVOLAINEN (43'), 4-0 Petri HEINÄNEN (65'), 5-0 Aristides PERTOT (90'+1').
Referee: Nebojsa RABRENOVIC (SBM)

17-06-2006   Dasáki, Áchnas: Ethnikós Áchnas FC – KS Partizani Tiranë   4-2 (2-0)
Ethnikós Áchnas FC: Milos ADAMOVIC (SRB), Dimitris SIMOU, Antonis KEZOS, Marius
Sandu IORDACHE (ROM) (72' Elipidoforos ILIA), Christos KOTSONIS (85' Christos
SHAILIS), Zoran STJEPANOVIC (SRB), Lars SCHLICHTING (GER), Christos
POYIATZIS, Christofis PASHIALIS, Marko KMETEC (SLO), Patrik IPAVEC (SLO) (72'
Milan BELIC (SRB)). (Coach: Toza SAPURIC (MCD)).
KS Partizani Tiranë: Orges SHEHI, Alpin GALLO (71' Mahir HALILI), Arjan SHETA, Ardit
BEQIRI, Dorian BYLYKBASHI (YC52), Abdullahi Salihu ISHAKA (NGR), Igli
ALLMUÇA, Erlind KORESHI (46' Rahman HALLAÇI), Arbër ABILALIAJ (46' Viktor
GJYLA (YC57)), Elis BAKAJ (YC48), Sasa DELAIN (DRC). (Coach: Sulejman STAROVA).
Goals: Ethnikós Áchnas FC: 1-0 Marko KMETEC (21'), 2-0 Zoran STJEPANOVIC (30'), 3-0
Marko KMETEC (48'), 4-0 Marko KMETEC (59').
KS Partizani Tiranë: 4-1 Elis BAKAJ (66'), 4-2 Arjan SHETA (78').
Referee: Aleksandr GONCHAR (RUS)

17-06-2006   A. Le Coq Arena, Tallinn: JK Trans Narva – Kalmar FF   1-6 (1-1)
JK Trans Narva: Martin KAALMA, Andrei PRUSS, Dmitri SELEHHOV, Sergei KAZAKOV,
Oleg GORJATSOV, Stanislav KITTO, Aleksandr TARASSENKOV, Dmitri LIPARTOV
(RUS), Maksim GRUZNOV, Aleksandr KULATSENKO, Alexandr DUBOKIN. (Coach:
Valeri BONDARENKO).
Kalmar FF: Petter WASTÅ, Niklas KALDNER, Tobias CARLSSON, Mikael EKLUND,
Patrik ROSENGREN, Mikael BLOMBERG (70' Fredrik PETERSSON), Henrik
RYDSTRÖM, Viktor ELM (75' Rasmus ELM), Lasse JOHANSSON, CÉSAR Santin (BRA)
(70' Shpetim HASANI (BOS)), ARI da Silva FERREIRA (BRA). (Coach: Nanne
BERGSTRAND).
Goals: JK Trans Narva: 1-0 Aleksandr KULATSENKO (2').
Kalmar FF: 1-1 Lasse JOHANSSON (44'), 1-2 CÉSAR Santin (62'), 1-3 ARI da Silva
FERREIRA (67'), 1-4 Viktor ELM (70'), 1-5 ARI da Silva FERREIRA (86'), 1-6 Fredrik
PETERSSON (90'+3').
Referee: Nicole PETIGNAT (SUI)

17-06-2006   Gradski Stadion, Mostar: HSK Zrinjski Mostar – Marsaxlokk FC   3-0 (3-0)
HSK Zrinjski Mostar: Nicola MARIC (CRO), Vladimir BRANKOVIC (SBM), Velimir
VIDIC, Ivica DZIDIC (CRO), Davor LANDEKA, Bulent BISCEVIC (63' Ilija
PRODANOVIC (SBM)), Lamine DIARRA (SEN), Damir DZIDIC (CRO), Mladen ZIZOVIC
(84' Ante SEMREN), Kresimir KORDIC (CRO) (46' Goran JURIC (CRO)), Velibor DJURIC
(YC32). (Coach: Blaz "Baka" SLISKOVIC).
Marsaxlokk FC: Reuben DEBONO, Carlo MAMO (YC78), Stephen WELLMANN, Carmelo
MAGRO, Andre SCHEMBRI, Gareth SCIBERRAS, Jamie PACE, Shaun BAJADA (60'
David CAMILLERI), Cleaven FRENDO, Daniel BOGDANOVIC, Kevin SAMMUT. (Coach:
Oliver SPITERI).
Goals: HSK Zrinjski Mostar: 1-0 Mladen ZIZOVIC (18' penalty), 2-0 Velibor DJURIC (26'),
3-0 Kresimir KORDIC (44').
Referee: Sebastian COLTESCU (ROM)

17-06-2006   Keflavíkurvöllur, Keflavík: IB Keflavík – Dungannon Swifts FC   4-1 (1-0)
IB Keflavík: Ómar JÓHANNSSON, Gudmundur Vidar METE, Gudjón Ámi ANTONÍUSSON (YC87), Geoff MILES (USA), Jónas Gudni SÆVARSSON, Hólmar Örn RÚNARSSON, Daniel SEVERINO (AUS) (67' Branislav MILICEVIC (SBM)), Símun SAMUELSEN (FAR) (86' Ólafur Jón JÓNSSON), Baldur SIGURDSSON (YC27), Gudmundur STEINARSSON, Magnús THORSTEINSSON (84' Stefán Örn ARNARSON). (Coach: Kristján GUDMUNDSSON).
Dungannon Swifts FC: David WELLS, Jonathan MONTGOMERY (YC71), Thomas WRAY, John GALLAGHER (78' Pedro DELGADO (VEN)), Gary FITZPATRICK, Rodney McAREE (RC73), Shane McCABE (YC21) (83' Andrew HAMILTON), David SCULLION, Darren MURPHY, Michael WARD, Aiden McVEIGH (78' Terence FITZPATRICK).
Goals: IB Keflavík: 1-0 Símun SAMUELSEN (16'), 2-0 Gudmundur STEINARSSON (67'), 3-0 Gudmundur STEINARSSON (73' penalty), 4-0 Magnús THORSTEINSSON (80').
Dungannon Swifts FC: 4-1 Jonathan MONTGOMERY (87').
Referee: Peter RASMUSSEN (DEN)

18-06-2006   Estadi Comunal d'Andorra la Vella, Andorra la Vella:
                UE Sant Julià – NK Maribor   0-3 (0-0)
UE Sant Julià: GUILLERMO José Burgos Viguera (CHI), FELIX Álvarez Blázquez (YC68), CRISTIAN Roig Mauri, Luciano Javier Nastri "LUCHO" (ARG) (YC20), Yael FONTAN (ESP), Christian Xinos "CHINO" (ARG), Laureano Miraglia "PACHA" (ARG) (71' Marc Joval "ANDRES"), Leonardo Miraglia "LEO" (ARG) (75' José GUERRA (PER)), MARIO Neves Pimentel (POR) (YC40), ALEJANDRO Fabián Romero Rectte (ARG) (YC73) (81' Joel MARTINEZ), LUIS Maria De Veriz Lozada (ARG). (Coach: Patricio GONZÁLEZ Fernández).
NK Maribor: Marko RANILOVIC, Erdzan BECIRI (YC13), Zikica VUKSANOVIC, Predrag SIMIC (CRO) (YC73) (79' Dejan KORAT), Milan RAKIC, Leon PANIKVAR (56' Marko POKLEKA (YC89)), David TOMAZIC-SERUGA, Zajko ZEBA (BOS), Marko POPOVIC (SRB) (46' Rene MIHELIC), Dragan JELIC, Gorazd ZAJC. (Coach: Marijan PUSNIK).
Goals: NK Maribor: 0-1 Gorazd ZAJC (56'), 0-2 Zajko ZEBA (83'), 0-3 Zajko ZEBA (90'+2').
Referee: Lasha SILAGAVA (GEO)   Attendance: 800

18-06-2006   Hrazdan Stadium, Yerevan:
                FC Kilikia Yerevan – FC Dinamo Tbilisi   1-5 (1-2)
FC Kilikia Yerevan: Armen KIRAKOSYAN, Valeri ALEKSANYAN (YC16), Artashes BAGHDASARYAN, Edward VARDANYAN (YC61), Karen ZAKARYAN, Artur VOSKANYAN, Vahagn BAGHOYAN (65' Sargis MOVSISYAN), Sergey ERZRUMYAN (76' Aram HAKOBYAN), Rafael NAZARYAN, Nshan ERZRUMYAN, Armen HOVHANNISYAN. (Coach: Sergey AGHABABYAN).
FC Dinamo Tbilisi: Georgi LORIA, Sergi ORBELADZE, David GIGAURI (YC78), Shota KASHIA (YC58), Shota GRIGALASHVILI (69' Irakli CHIRIKASHVILI), Giorgi MEREBASHVILI, Alexander KOBAKHIDZE, AMBROSIO Jozimar Luis Domingos (BRA), Jaba DVALI (76' Zamer JANASHIA), RODRIGO TORNIN Korndoerfer (BRA) (YC20) (57' Mikhail BOBOKHIDZE), Mikheil KHUTSISHVILI (YC28). (Coach: Kakhaber (Khaki) KATCHARAVA).
Goals: FC Kilikia Yerevan: 1-2 Nshan ERZRUMYAN (42').
FC Dinamo Tbilisi: 0-1 RODRIGO TORNIN Korndoerfer (36'), 0-2 Jaba DVALI (37'), 1-3 Jaba DVALI (57'), 1-4 Mikheil KHUTSISHVILI (72'), 1-5 Mikhail BOBOKHIDZE (90').
Referee: Marcin BORSKI (POL)   Attendance: 1.200

161

18-06-2006   Nitra Stadión, Nitra: FC Nitra – CS Grevenmacher   6-2 (3-0)
FC Nitra: Stefan SENECKY, Pavol FARKAS, Adrián CEMAN, Csaba SZÓRÁD, Erik
HRNCÁR, Peter GRAJCIAR, Slavomír BALIS (59' Ján STAJER), Martin BABIC, Michal
FARKAS, Róbert RÁK (85' Roman SLOBODA), Andrej HESEK (75' Martin CIZMÁR).
(Coach: Ivan GALÁD).
CS Grevenmacher: André ORIGER, Volker SCHMITT (GER), Stephan KORDIAN (GER),
Jérôme HENROT (FRA), Paul ENGEL, Sven DI DOMENICO (YC66), Malik BENACHOUR
(FRA), Tom MUNOZ, Christian BRAUN (YC41), Nino HELBIG (GER), Anton BOZIC
(YC55).
Goals: FC Nitra: 1-0 Slavomír BALIS (14'), 2-0 Róbert RÁK (18'), 3-0 Andrej HESEK (40'),
4-1 Róbert RÁK (78'), 5-1 Róbert RÁK (84'), 6-2 Martin BABIC (90+').
CS Grevenmacher: 3-1 Anton BOZIC (55'), 5-2 Anton BOZIC (87').
Referee: Vusal ALIYEV (AZE)   Attendance: 1.084

18-06-2006   Celtnieks Stadion, Daugavpils:
              FC Dinaburg Daugavpils – H.B. Tórshavn   1-1 (1-0)
FC Dinaburg Daugavpils: Vadims FJODOROVS, Mihails POPOVS, Vadims LOGINS, Ivans
RODINS, Andrejs ZUROMSKIS, Edgars BURLAKOVS, Pavel RYZHEUSKI (BLS),
Alexander TORYAN (RUS) (56' Aleksejs BORUNS), Sergejs VALUSKINS (46' Olexandr
KRIKLIVY (UKR) (YC73)), Jurijs SOKOLOVS, Andrejs MARKOVS (68' Nikita
CHMYKOV (RUS) (YC90+3)). (Coach: Sergey Nikolayevich POPKOV (RUS)).
H.B. Tórshav: Tróndur VATNHAMAR (YC51), Mortan úr HØRG, Janus Mouritsarson
JOENSEN, Rasmus NOLSØE, Poul Thomas DAM, Tór-Ingar AKSELSEN (84' Páll Mohr
JOENSEN), Kári NIELSEN, Emil NOLSØE LEIFSSON, Jovan RADINOVIC-PANIC (SBM)
(YC79), Ólavur Sakarisson í ÖLAVSSTOVU (87' Rókur av Fløtum JESPERSEN), Johan
Ejvind Restorff MOURITSEN (90'+3' Høgni Mouritsarson JOENSEN). (Coach: Krzysztof
POPCZYNSKI (POL)).
Goals: FC Dinaburg Daugavpils: 1-0 Vadims LOGINS (13').
H.B. Tórshavn: 1-1 Rasmus NOLSØE (59').
Referee: Aliaksei KULBAKOU (BLS)   Attendance: 500

18-06-2006   Vetros Stadionas, Vilnius: FK Vetra Vilnius – Shelbourne FC   0-1 (0-1)
FK Vetra Vilnius: Mirza MERLANI (GEO), Nerijus SASNAUSKAS, Algis JANKAUSKAS,
Zilvinas ZUDYS (YC40), Andrey USACHEV (RUS) (YC18), Dejan MILOSEVSKI (MCD),
Darvydas SERNAS (80' Andrius KOCANAUSKAS), Robertas VEZEVICIUS (74' Edvinas
BLAZYS), Aidas PREIKSAITIS (YC71), Donatas VENCEVICIUS (46' Bobi BOZINOVSKI
(MCD)), Sergei KUZNETSOV (UKR). (Coach: Vitas JANCIAUSKAS).
Shelbourne FC: Dean DELANEY, Owen HEARY (YC20), David CRAWLEY, Colin
HAWKINS, Sean DILLON, Oliver CAHILL, Stuart BYRNE, Alan MOORE (85' Alan
REYNOLDS), Bobby RYAN (YC76), Joseph Cyrille N'DO (CMR), Jason BYRNE (YC27)
(66' Glen CROWE). (Coach: Patrick (Pat) FENLON).
Goal: Shelbourne FC: 0-1 Sean DILLON (43').
Referee: Svein Oddvar MOEN (NOR)

18-06-2006   Goce Delcev Stadium, Prilep:
                FK Pobeda Prilep – FC Farul Constanta   2-2 (0-1)
FK Pobeda Prilep: Edin NUREDINOVSKI, Aleksandar KRSTEVSKI, Blagojce DAMEVSKI,
Blagoja GESOVSKI, Dimitar KAPINKOVSKI (YC47), Nebojsa STOJKOVIC (SBM)
(YC63), Marjan MICKOV (62' Pance RISTOVSKI), Toni MEGLENSKI, Mirce NATKOV
(YC79) (84' Nove ACESKI), Miodrag JOVANOVIC (SBM), EMERSON de Souza Pereira
(BRA) (57' Nikolce TANCEVSKI). (Coach: Nikolce ZDRAVESKI).
FC Farul Constanta: George CURCA, Stefanel Razvan FARMACHE, Ion BARBU, Decebal
Virgil GHEARA, Laurentiu FLOREA, Adrian SENIN (YC67), Claudiu VOICULET, Ionut
Justinian LARIE (YC81), Liviu Ionut MIHAI (73' Radu Bogdan APOSTU), Mihai GURITA
(87' Vasile PACURARU), Tibor Florian MOLDOVAN (80' Marius Adrian SOARE). (Coach:
Lucian MARINOF).
Goals: FK Pobeda Prilep: 1-1 Nebojsa STOJKOVIC (51'), 2-2 Nikolce TANCEVSKI (72').
FC Farul Constanta: 0-1 Stefanel Razvan FARMACHE (30'), 1-2 Liviu Ionut MIHAI (59').
Referee: Vlado SVILOKOS (CRO)

24-06-2006   Latham Park, Newtown:
                Carmarthen Town AFC – Tampere United FC   1-3 (1-2)
Carmarthen Town AFC: Mark OVENDALE (ENG), Christopher THOMAS (YC27), Luke
HARDY (IRL), Martyn GILES, Craig LIMA (56' John Wayne JONES), Kaid MOHAMED
(61' Matthew DAVIES), Colin LOSS (YC42) (60' Sacha WALTERS), Neil SMOTHERS
(YC90+2), Nathan COTTERRALL, Mark DODDS, Daniel THOMAS. (Coach: Mark JONES).
Tampere United FC: Mikko KAVÉN, Vasile MARCHIS (ROM), Jussi KUOPPALA, Heikki
AHO, Jussi-Pekka SAVOLAINEN (85' Antti OJANPERÄ), Jarkko WISS, Kari SAINIO,
Aristides PERTOT (ARG) (YC32) (60' Risto OJANEN), Antti HYNYNEN, Ville LEHTINEN
(51' Juska SAVOLAINEN (YC90+2)), Sakari SAARINEN. (Coach: Ari Juhani HJELM).
Goals: Carmarthen Town AFC: 1-1 Christopher THOMAS (36').
Tampere United FC: 0-1 Ville LEHTINEN (8'), 1-2 Ville LEHTINEN (38'), 1-3 Ville
LEHTINEN (48').
Referee: Hannes KAASIK (EST)   Attendance: 325

24-06-2006   Windsor Park, Belfast: Dungannon Swifts FC – IB Keflavík   0-0
Dungannon Swifts FC: David WELLS, John GALLAGHER (YC26), Gary FITZPATRICK,
Shane McCABE (YC16), David SCULLION, Terence FITZPATRICK (YC90), Pedro
DELGADO (VEN), Darren MURPHY (RC32), EVERALDO Luiz (BRA) (46' Adam
McMINN), Aiden McVEIGH (62' James SLATER), Niall McGINN (69' Mark SCOTT).
(Coach: Joe McAREE).
IB Keflavík: Ómar JÓHANNSSON (69' Magnús THORMAR), Gudmundur Vidar METE (76'
Magnús THORSTEINSSON), Gudjón Ämi ANTONÍUSSON, Kenneth GUSTAVSSON
(SWE), Geoff MILES (USA), Branislav MILICEVIC (SBM) (YC35), Jónas Gudni
SÆVARSSON, Hólmar Örn RÚNARSSON, Símun SAMUELSEN (FAR) (58' Daniel
SEVERINO (AUS)), Baldur SIGURDSSON, Ólafur Jón JÓNSSON. (Coach: Kristján
GUDMUNDSSON).
Referee: Manuel Jorge NEVES MOREIRA DE SOUSA (POR)   Attendance: 250

24-06-2006   Mikheil Meskhi Stadium, Tbilisi:
FC Dinamo Tbilisi – FC Kilikia Yerevan   3-0 (2-0)
FC Dinamo Tbilisi: Georgi LORIA, David GIGAURI, Shota KASHIA, Gulverd
TOMASHVILI, Shota GRIGALASHVILI, Giorgi MEREBASHVILI (46' Levan
KHMALADZE), Alexander KOBAKHIDZE, AMBROSIO Jozimar Luis Domingos (BRA)
(21' Kakhi MAKHARADZE), Mikhail BOBOKHIDZE (YC44), Jaba DVALI, Mikheil
KHUTSISHVILI (72' Sandro IASHVILI). (Coach: Kakhaber (Khaki) KATCHARAVA).
FC Kilikia Yerevan: Armen KIRAKOSYAN, Aram HAKOBYAN, Karen YAYLOYAN,
Eduard VARDANYAN, Arsen AYVAZYAN, Karen ZAKARYAN, Vahagn BAGHOYAN,
Gagik GHASABYAN (46' Garnik GHASABYAN), Armen HOVHANNISYAN (YC31),
Levon GHASABOGHLYAN (78' Artavazd MKRTCHYAN), Sargis MOVSISYAN. (Coach:
Sergey AGHABABYAN).
Goals: FC Dinamo Tbilisi: 1-0 Shota GRIGALASHVILI (27'), 2-0 David GIGAURI (40'), 3-0
Sandro IASHVILI (87').
Referee: Stanislav TODOROV (BUL)

24-06-2006   Selman Stërmasi Stadium, Tiranë:
KS Partizani Tiranë – Ethnikós Áchnas FC   2-1 (1-1)
KS Partizani Tiranë: Orges SHEHI, Alpin GALLO (76' Arbër ABILALIAJ), Arjan SHETA
(YC,YC90+2), Paulin DHËMBI, Ardit BEQIRI (5' Fatjon TAFAJ), Dorian BYLYKBASHI,
Abdullahi Salihu ISHAKA (NGR), Igli ALLMUÇA, Richard BOKATOLA-LOSSOMBO
(DRC) (YC82), Elis BAKAJ, Mahir HALILI (53' Viktor GJYLA). (Coach: Sulejman
STAROVA).
Ethnikós Áchnas FC: Milos ADAMOVIC (SBM) (YC76), Christos SHAILIS, Dimitris
SIMOU, Marius Sandu IORDACHE (ROM), Christos KOTSONIS, Zoran STJEPANOVIC
(SRB), Lars SCHLICHTING (GER) (YC57), Christos POYIATZIS (YC26), Christofis
PASHIALIS (YC69), Marko KMETEC (SLO) (67' Milan BELIC (SRB) (YC90+3)), Patrik
IPAVEC (SLO) (YC48) (90'+2' Demosthenis DEMOSTHENOUS). (Coach: Toza SAPURIC
(MCD)).
Goals: KS Partizani Tiranë: 1-1 Dorian BYLYKBASHI (29'), 2-1 Arbër ABILALIAJ (90').
Ethnikós Áchnas FC: 0-1 Zoran STJEPANOVIC (3').
Referee: Marijo STRAHONJA (CRO)

24-06-2006   Ljudski vrt Stadium, Maribor: NK Maribor – UE Sant Julià   5-0 (2-0)
NK Maribor: Miha BRATUSEK, Erdzan BECIRI, Zikica VUKSANOVIC, Predrag SIMIC
(CRO) (46' Rene MIHELIC), Milan RAKIC (67' Klemen MEDVED), Leon PANIKVAR (31'
Marko POKLEKA), David TOMAZIC-SERUGA, Zajko ZEBA (BOS), Marko POPOVIC
(SRB), Dragan JELIC, Gorazd ZAJC (YC79). (Coach: Marijan PUSNIK).
UE Sant Julià: Ignacio J.Saiz González "IÑAKI" (85' GUILLERMO José Burgos Viguera
(CHI)), FELIX Álvarez Blázquez, CRISTIAN Roig Mauri, Luciano Javier Nastri "LUCHO"
(ARG) (YC69), Yael FONTAN (ESP), Christian Xinos "CHINO" (ARG) (67' Joel
MARTINEZ), Laureano Miraglia "PACHA" (ARG) (83' Matias MEDINA (ARG)), MARIO
Neves Pimentel (POR) (YC82), Richard IMBERNON Rios, ALEJANDRO Fabián Romero
Rectte (ARG), LUIS Maria De Veriz Lozada (ARG). (Coach: Patricio GONZÁLEZ
Fernández).
Goals: NK Maribor: 1-0 Milan RAKIC (25'), 2-0 Gorazd ZAJC (27'), 3-0 Zikica
VUKSANOVIC (48'), 4-0 Rene MIHELIC (64'), 5-0 Rene MIHELIC (70').
Referee: Igor KISTER (KAZ)   Attendance: 1.200

24-06-2006   Sport Complex Sheriff, Tiraspol: FC Tiraspol – MKT Araz Imishli   2-0 (0-0)
FC Tiraspol: Stanislav NAMASCO (YC81), Victor GOLOVATENCO, Valentin Giani
NECSULESCU (ROM) (YC90+3), Kyrylo SYDORENKO (UKR), Andrey NOVICOV,
Andrey SECRIERU (84' Andrey PORFIREANU), Evgheni GORODETCHIL, Serghei
NAMASCO, Oleksandr BYCHKOV (UKR) (82' Nicolai RUDAC), Igor PICUSCIAC, Serghei
ALEXEEV (90' Mihail DODUL). (Coach: Yuriy Petrovych KULISH (UKR)).
MKT Araz Imishli: Etibar TANRIVERDIEV, Dmytro PARKHOMENKO (UKR), Ceyhun
ADISHIRINOV, Valentin VISHTALYUK, Ruslan GAFITULLIN, Victor BARISEV (MOL),
Evgeni SHIMAN (UKR) (52' Arif DASHDEMIROV), Zeynal ZEYNALOV, Marcel
RESHITSA, Ihor MAKOVEY (UKR) (84' Asif MAMMADOV (YC90+3)), Murad
AGHAKISHIYEV (YC16). (Coach: Igor NAKONECHNYY (UKR)).
Goals: FC Tiraspol: 1-0 Serghei ALEXEEV (71'), 2-0 Serghei ALEXEEV (116').
Referee: Drazenko KOVACIC (CRO)
(After extra time)

24-06-2006   Tórsvøllur, Tórshavn: H.B. Tórshavn – FC Dinaburg Daugavpils   0-1 (0-0)
H.B. Tórshav: Tróndur VATNHAMAR, Mortan úr HØRG (YC69), Rasmus NOLSØE, Poul
Thomas DAM (83' Hendrik RUBEKSEN), Tór-Ingar AKSELSEN (83' Rókur av Fløtum
JESPERSEN), Vagnur Mohr MORTENSEN, Kári NIELSEN, Jovan RADINOVIC-PANIC
(SBM), Ólavur Sakarisson í ÖLAVSSTOVU, Jákup á BORG (YC59), Páll Mohr JOENSEN
(67' Johan Ejvind Restorff MOURITSEN). (Coach: Krzysztof POPCZYNSKI (POL)).
FC Dinaburg Daugavpils: Vadims FJODOROVS (YC85), Mihails POPOVS, Vadims LOGINS
(YC24), Andrejs ZUROMSKIS, Olexandr KRIKLIVY (UKR) (75' Jurgis PUCINSKIS),
Nikita CHMYKOV (RUS), Aleksejs BORUNS (YC32), Edgars BURLAKOVS (58' Sergejs
VALUSKINS (YC69)), Pavel RYZHEUSKI (BLS) (YC44) (88' Dimitrijs CEBOTARJOVS),
Jurijs SOKOLOVS, Andrejs MARKOVS. (Coach: Sergey Nikolayevich POPKOV (RUS)).
Goal: FC Dinaburg Daugavpils: 0-1 Vagnur Mohr MORTENSEN (55' *own goal*).
Referee: Adrian McCOURT (NIR)

24-06-2006   Tolka Park, Dublin: Shelbourne FC – FK Vetra Vilnius   4-0 (1-0)
Shelbourne FC: Dean DELANEY, Owen HEARY (72' Greg O'HALLORAN), David
CRAWLEY (YC19) (53' Jason BYRNE), Colin HAWKINS, Sean DILLON, Oliver CAHILL,
Stuart BYRNE, Bobby RYAN, Joseph Cyrille N'DO (CMR) (72' Gary DEEGAN), Alan
REYNOLDS, Glen CROWE. (Coach: Patrick (Pat) FENLON).
FK Vetra Vilnius: Mirza MERLANI (GEO), Julius RALIUKONIS (RC5), Olegs BAIKOVS
(LAT) (YC59), Andrey USACHEV (RUS), Darvydas SERNAS (90' Andrius
KOCANAUSKAS), Robertas VEZEVICIUS (YC,YC66), Aidas PREIKSAITIS, Donatas
VENCEVICIUS, Sergei KUZNETSOV (UKR) (87' Rolandas VAINEIKIS), Edvinas
BLAZYS (78' Sarunas LITVINAS), Rolandas KARCEMARSKAS (YC,YC48). (Coach: Vitas
JANCIAUSKAS).
Goals: Shelbourne FC: 1-0 Oliver CAHILL (36'), 2-0 Jason BYRNE (66'), 3-0 Glen CROWE
(69'), 4-0 Jason BYRNE (90'+2').
Referee: Markus STRÖMBERGSSON (SWE)

25-06-2006   Hibernians Stadium, Paola: Marsaxlokk FC – HSK Zrinjski Mostar 1-1 (1-0)
Marsaxlokk FC: Reuben GAUCI, Carlo MAMO (YC46), Stephen WELLMANN, Carmelo
MAGRO (86' Shaun TELLUS), Andre SCHEMBRI, Gareth SCIBERRAS (YC70) (82' Kevin
MAMO), David CAMILLERI, Shaun BAJADA (62' Jamie PACE), Cleaven FRENDO
(YC,YC78), Daniel BOGDANOVIC, Kevin SAMMUT. (Coach: Oliver SPITERI).
HSK Zrinjski Mostar: Nicola MARIC (CRO), Velimir VIDIC (35' Ilija PRODANOVIC
(SBM)), Ivica DZIDIC (CRO), Davor LANDEKA, Igor ZURZINOV (22' Vladimir
BRANKOVIC (SBM)), Damir DZIDIC (CRO), Stanisa NIKOLIC, Sulejman SMAJIC
(YC78), Mladen ZIZOVIC, Admir JOLDIC (YC51) (80' Goran JURIC (CRO)), Velibor
DJURIC. (Coach: Blaz "Baka" SLISKOVIC).
Goals: Marsaxlokk FC: 1-0 Andre SCHEMBRI (34').
HSK Zrinjski Mostar: 1-1 Sulejman SMAJIC (81').
Referee: Ghennadi SIDENCO (MOL)
(Cleaven FRENDO missed a penalty in the 26th minute)

25-06-2006   Fredriksskans Idrottsplats, Kalmar: Kalmar FF – JK Trans Narva 2-0 (2-0)
Kalmar FF: Petter WASTÅ, Joachim LANTZ, Tobias CARLSSON, Mikael EKLUND, Mikael
BLOMBERG (72' Viktor ELM), Henrik RYDSTRÖM, Daniel PETTERSON, Rasmus ELM,
Fredrik PETERSSON, CÉSAR Santin (BRA) (72' Brima KOROMA (SLE)), ARI da Silva
FERREIRA (BRA) (65' Lasse JOHANSSON). (Coach: Nanne BERGSTRAND).
JK Trans Narva: Martin KAALMA, Andrei PRUSS (55' Vladislav IVANOV), Dmitri
SELEHHOV, Sergei KAZAKOV (75' Irfan AMETOV (UKR)), Oleg GORJATSOV, Stanislav
KITTO, Sergei POPOV, Dmitri LIPARTOV (RUS) (69' Aleksei GORSKOV), Maksim
GRUZNOV, Aleksandr KULATSENKO, Alexandr DUBOKIN. (Coach: Valeri
BONDARENKO).
Goals: Kalmar FF: 1-0 Rasmus ELM (7'), 2-0 ARI da Silva FERREIRA (27').
Referee: William COLLUM (SCO)   Attendance: 678

25-06-2006   Traktor Stadium, Minsk:
                    FC MTZ-RIPO Minsk – FC Shakhtyor Karaganda 1-3 (0-2)
FC MTZ-RIPO Minsk: Aleksandr SULIMA, Tajia Adam SORO (CIV) (YC90+4), Artem
FEDORCHENKO (UKR), Aleksandr BYLINA, Aleksandr STASHCHENYUK (YC80),
Dmitri SHEGRIKOVICH, Vitali TARASHCHIK, Hamlet MKHITARYAN (ARM) (74'
Mikhail YEREMCHUK), Bojan MAMIC (SBM), Sergiu JAPALAU (MOL) (20' Mikhail
AFANASIEV), Artem KONTSEVOI (YC16) (46' Oleg STRAKANOVICH). (Coach: Yuri
Iosifovich PUNTUS).
FC Shakhtyor Karaganda: Sergey SARANA (YC58), Veaceslav RUSNAC (MOL) (YC30)
(87' Rakhman ASUKHANOV), Oleg KORNILENKO, Zeljko JOKSIMOVIC (YC44), Vladica
CURCIC (SBM), Vladimir KASHTANOV, Ilnur MANGUTKIN, Rafael URAZBAKHTIN
(YC48), Andrey FINONCHENKO (YC66), Mikhail GLUSHKO (76' NILTON Mendes
Pereira (BRA)), Evgeniy LUNEV. (Coach: Sergey MICHSHENKO).
Goals: FC MTZ-RIPO Minsk: 1-3 Oleg STRAKANOVICH (59' penalty).
FC Shakhtyor Karaganda: 0-1 Veaceslav RUSNAC (14'), 0-2 Rafael URAZBAKHTIN (37'),
0-3 Mikhail GLUSHKO (54').
Referee: Leontios TRATTOU (CYP)

25-06-2006   Stade Op Flohr, Grevenmacher: CS Grevenmacher – FC Nitra   0-6 (0-2)
CS Grevenmacher: André ORIGER, Volker SCHMITT (GER) (YC65), Stephan KORDIAN (GER), Jérôme HENROT (FRA) (88' Ben RUPPERT), Christian ALBRECHT (GER), Paul ENGEL, Tim HEINZ (15' NELSON Filipe Jesus da Silva), Sven DI DOMENICO (YC72), Tom MUNOZ, Christian BRAUN, Anton BOZIC.
FC Nitra: Tomás TUJVEL, Pavol FARKAS (46' Ján STAJER), Adrián CEMAN, Csaba SZÓRÁD (YC74), Erik HRNCÁR, Peter GRAJCIAR, Slavomír BALIS, Martin BABIC (71' Lukás HNILICA), Michal FARKAS (56' Martin CIZMÁR), Róbert RÁK, Andrej HESEK. (Coach: Ivan GALÁD).
Goals: FC Nitra: 0-1 Róbert RÁK (5'), 0-2 Martin BABIC (12'), 0-3 Slavomír BALIS (51'), 0-4 Martin CIZMÁR (57'), 0-5 Andrej HESEK (60'), 0-6 Peter GRAJCIAR (63').
Referee: Goran SPIRKOSKI (MCD)

25-06-2006   Stadionul Farul, Constanta: FC Farul Constanta – FK Pobeda Prilep   2-0 (1-0)
FC Farul Constanta: George CURCA, Stefanel Razvan FARMACHE, Ion BARBU, Decebal Virgil GHEARA, Laurentiu FLOREA, Adrian SENIN (46' Dinu Marius TODORAN), Claudiu VOICULET, Ionut Justinian LARIE (YC5), Liviu Ionut MIHAI (46' Marius Adrian SOARE), Mihai GURITA (YC48), Tibor Florian MOLDOVAN (YC45) (78' Radu Bogdan APOSTU). (Coach: Lucian MARINOF).
FK Pobeda Prilep: Edin NUREDINOVSKI, Aleksandar KRSTEVSKI, Blagojce DAMEVSKI, Zeljko DZOKIC (SBM), Dimitar KAPINKOVSKI, Marjan MICKOV (46' Mirce NATKOV), Toni MEGLENSKI, Pance RISTOVSKI, Miodrag JOVANOVIC (SBM) (YC49), EMERSON de Souza Pereira (BRA) (39' Blagoja GESOVSKI (YC85)), Nikolce TANCEVSKI (YC90). (Coach: Nikolce ZDRAVESKI).
Goals: FC Farul Constanta: 1-0 Tibor Florian MOLDOVAN (22'), 2-0 Mihai GURITA (65').
Referee: Libor KOVARIK (CZE)   Attendance: 1.500

SECOND ROUND

01-07-2006   Eduard Streltsov Stadion, Moskva:
               FK Moskva – FC MTZ-RIPO Minsk   2-0 (0-0)
FK Moskva: Yuriy ZHEVNOV (BLS), Dmitriy GODUNOK, Radu REBEJA (MOL), Oleg KUZMIN, Isaac OKORONKWO (NGR), Jerry-Christian TCHUISSE (CMR), Pyotr BYSTROV, Sergey SEMAK (46' Pavel GOLISHEV), Tomás CÍZEK (CZE), Héctor Andrés BRACAMONTE (ARG) (72' Roman ADAMOV), Dmitriy GOLUBOV (46' Dmitriy KIRICHENKO (YC71)). (Coach: Leonid Viktorovich SLUTSKY).
FC MTZ-RIPO Minsk: Aleksandr SULIMA, Tajia Adam SORO (CIV) (72' Vyacheslav HLEB), Yanko VALKANOV (BUL) (YC33), Aleksandr BYLINA, Aleksandr STASHCHENYUK, Aleksandr GORBACHEV, Oleg STRAKANOVICH (YC17), Dmitri SHEGRIKOVICH, Hamlet MKHITARYAN (ARM) (YC40) (46' Mikhail YEREMCHUK), Vitali TARASHCHIK, Artem KONTSEVOI. (Coach: Yuri Iosifovich PUNTUS).
Goals: FK Moskva: 1-0 Pyotr BYSTROV (56'), 2-0 Roman ADAMOV (83').
Referee: Michalis GERMANAKOS (GRE)

167

01-07-2006   Åråsen Stadion, Lillestrøm: Lillestrøm SK – IB Keflavík 4-1 (2-1)
Lillestrøm SK: Heinz MÜLLER (GER), Shane STEFANUTTO (AUS), Cyril KALI (FRA),
Pål Steffen ANDRESEN, Anders RAMBEKK, Pål STRAND (80' Espen SØGÅRD), Robert
KOREN (SLO), Bjørn Helge RIISE, Kasey WEHRMAN (AUS) (85' Khaled MOUELHI
(TUN)), Arild SUNDGOT, Michael MIFSUD (MLT) (77' Magnus MYKLEBUST). (Coach:
Uwe RÖSLER (GER)).
IB Keflavík: Ómar JÓHANNSSON, Gudmundur Vidar METE, Gudjón Ámi
ANTONÍUSSON, Kenneth GUSTAVSSON (SWE), Jónas Gudni SÆVARSSON, Hallgrímur
JÓNASSON (74' Branislav MILICEVIC (SBM)), Hólmar Örn RÚNARSSON, Símun
SAMUELSEN (FAR), Baldur SIGURDSSON, Gudmundur STEINARSSON (88' Thórarinn
KRISTJÁNSSON), Stefán Örn ARNARSON (74' Magnús THORSTEINSSON). (Coach:
Kristján GUDMUNDSSON).
Goals: Lillestrøm SK: 1-0 Bjørn Helge RIISE (26'), 2-0 Kasey WEHRMAN (35'), 3-1 Kasey
WEHRMAN (52'), 4-1 Magnus MYKLEBUST (90'+1').
IB Keflavík: 2-1 Stefán Örn ARNARSON (38').
Referee: Igor ISHCHENKO (UKR)   Attendance: 608

01-07-2006   Municipal Stadium, Hertzliya:
              Maccabi Petach Tikva FC – HSK Zrinjski Mostar 1-1 (0-0)
Maccabi Petach Tikva FC: Ohad COHEN, Ismael AMAR, Murad MAGOMEDOV, Shay
BANAY (54' Dovev GABBAY), Naor PESER, Nitzan DAMARI, Roy BAKEL (YC80), Ori
LUZON, Banny GHANAH (46' Emmanuel EBIEDE (NGR) (YC85)), Ohad KADUSI, Rubel
SARSOUR (79' Daniel UNGER). (Coach: Guy LUZON).
HSK Zrinjski Mostar: Nicola MARIC (CRO), Ivica DZIDIC (CRO), Davor LANDEKA,
Vladimir BRANKOVIC (SBM), Stanisa NIKOLIC, Damir DZIDIC (CRO), Bulend
BISCEVIC (69' Goran JURIC (CRO)), Sulejman SMAJIC, Ilija PRODANOVIC (SBM),
Mladen ZIZOVIC (69' Admir JOLDIC), Velibor DJURIC (90' Vladimir SLISKOVIC).
(Coach: Blaz "Baka" SLISKOVIC).
Goals: Maccabi Petach Tikva FC: 1-1 Emmanuel EBIEDE (67').
HSK Zrinjski Mostar: 0-1 Shay BANAY (54' own goal).
Referee: Luc WILMES (LUX)   Attendance: 150

01-07-2006   Stadion Városi, Sopron: FC Sopron – Kayserispor Kulübü 3-3 (0-2)
FC Sopron: Balász RABÓCZKI (YC37), Marius Adrian RADU (ROM), Ion IBRIC (ROM)
(81' István SIRA), Sergiu Victor HOMEI (ROM), Gábor BAGOLY (YC28), András
HORVÁTH (YC67), Tamás SIFTER (YC29), Gábor DEMJÉN, Róbert FECZESIN, Cristian
Lucian CIGAN (ROM) (62' Gellért IVÁNCSICS), Sebastian Florin IANC (ROM) (46' Georgi
KORUDZHIEV (BUL)). (Coach: László VASS).
Kayserispor Kulübü: Dimitar Ivanov IVANKOV (BUL), Rashad F.SADIKHOV (AZE),
Bülent BÖLÜKBASI (89' Kemal OKYAY), Hamed KAVIANPOUR (IRN) (79' Kamber
ARSLAN), Ragip BASDAG (YC32), Samuel JOHNSON (GHA), Aydin TOSCALI, Mehmet
TOPUZ, Fatih CEYLAN (YC71), Gökhan ÜNAL, Muhammet Hanifi AKAGÜNDÜZ (AUT)
(90' İlhan PARLAK). (Coach: Ertugrul SAGLAM).
Goals: FC Sopron: 1-2 Róbert FECZESIN (47'), 2-3 Georgi KORUDZHIEV (66'), 3-3 Ion
IBRIC (71').
Kayserispor Kulübü: 0-1 Gökhan ÜNAL (37' penalty), 0-2 Gökhan ÜNAL (45'), 1-3 Mehmet
TOPUZ (59').
Referee: Igor ZAKHAROV (RUS)

01-07-2006   Fill-Metallbau-Stadion, Ried im Innkreis:
SV Ried – FC Dinamo Tbilisi   3-1 (1-1)
SV Ried: Hans-Peter BERGER, Christoph JANK, Dario DABAC (CRO), Oliver GLASNER, Thomas Günther EDER (68' Michael ANGERSCHMID), Sebastian MARTÍNEZ, Jung-Won SEO (KOR) (86' Patrick WOLF), Herwig DRECHSEL, Ewald BRENNER, Daniel KASTNER (YC63) (68' Ronald BRUNMAYR), Emin SULIMANI. (Coach: Helmut KRAFT).
FC Dinamo Tbilisi: Soso GRISHIKASHVILI, David GIGAURI (YC47), Shota KASHIA, Gulverd TOMASHVILI, Shota GRIGALASHVILI (88' Zamir JANASHIA), Alexander KOBAKHIDZE (YC77), Irakli CHIRIKASHVILI, AMBROSIO Jozimar Luis Domingos (BRA) (YC5), Sandro IASHVILI, Mikhail BOBOKHIDZE (67' Jaba DVALI), Mikheil KHUTSISHVILI (52' Kakhi MAKHARADZE). (Coach: Kakhaber (Khaki) KATCHARAVA).
Goals: SV Ried: 1-0 Oliver GLASNER (7'), 2-1 Herwig DRECHSEL (47' penalty), 3-1 Jung-Won SEO (80').
FC Dinamo Tbilisi: 1-1 Shota GRIGALASHVILI (37').
Referee: Dejan STANISIC (SBM)   Attendance: 3.500

01-07-2006   Sport Complex Sheriff, Tiraspol: FC Tiraspol – KKS Lech Poznán   1-0 (1-0)
FC Tiraspol: Stanislav NAMASCO, Victor GOLOVATENCO (YC57), Kennedy Chimezie CHINWO (NGR), Andrey NOVICOV, Kyrylo SYDORENKO (UKR), Evgheni GORODETCHIL (75' Nicolai RUDAC), Andrey SECRIERU, Serghei NAMASCO, Serghei ALEXEEV (77' Andrey PORFIREANU), Oleksandr BYCHKOV (UKR), Igor PICUSCIAC (90'+1' Vadim CEMIRTAN). (Coach: Yuriy Petrovych KULISH (UKR)).
KKS Lech Poznán: Pawel LINKA, Dawid KUCHARSKI, Grzegorz WOJTKOWIAK, Rafal MURAWSKI, Arkadiusz BAK (46' Artur MARCINIAK (YC62)), Marcin KIKUT (YC90), Maciej SCHERFCHEN, Jacek DEMBINSKI, Karol GREGOREK (YC32) (62' Marcin WACHOWICZ), Przemyslaw PITRY (80' Iliyan MITSANSKI (BUL)), Zbigniew ZAKRZEWSKI (YC66). (Coach: Franciszek SMUDA).
Goal: FC Tiraspol: 1-0 Igor PICUSCIAC (18').
Referee: David McKEON (IRL)   Attendance: 1.500

01-07-2006   Stadionul Farul, Constanta:
FC Farul Constanta – PFC Lokomotiv Plovdiv   2-1 (1-1)
FC Farul Constanta: George CURCA, Stefanel Razvan FARMACHE, Ion BARBU, Decebal Virgil GHEARA, Laurentiu FLOREA, Iulian Catalin APOSTOL (61' Radu Bogdan APOSTU (YC88)), Claudiu VOICULET, Dinu Marius TODORAN (YC38), Marius Adrian SOARE (67' Ionel BOGHITOI), Mihai GURITA (YC85), Tibor Florian MOLDOVAN (84' Viorel GHEORGHE). (Coach: Momcilo "Moca" VUKOTIC (SRB)).
PFC Lokomotiv Plovdiv: Stoyan KOLEV (YC5), Georgi SAMOKISHEV, Dobrin ORLOVSKI (30' Danail BACHKOV), Yordan MILIEV, Velko HRISTEV, Ilami HALIMI (MCD), Hristo ZLATINSKI (YC65), Krasimir DIMITROV, Radoslav ANEV (59' Marko ILIC (SBM)), Zoran ZLATKOVSKI (MCD) (74' Zoran ZLATINOV), Yavor VANDEV (YC50). (Coach: Ayan Faikov SADAKOV).
Goals: FC Farul Constanta: 1-0 Tibor Florian MOLDOVAN (20'), 2-1 Radu Bogdan APOSTU (88').
PFC Lokomotiv Plovdiv: 1-1 Yavor VANDEV (33').
Referee: János MEGYEBÍRÓ (HUN)   Attendance: 200

02-07-2006   Fionia Park, Odense: Odense BK – Shelbourne FC   3-0 (2-0)
Odense BK: Arek ONYSZKO (POL), Ulrik LAURSEN, Anders Møller CHRISTENSEN (84'
Jan Tore OPHAUG (NOR)), Alexander AAS, Chris SØRENSEN, Morten FEVANG (NOR)
(79' Søren JENSEN), Esben HANSEN, Martin BORRE, Magne STURØD (NOR), Jonas
BORRING, Mads TIMM (46' Tobias GRAHN (SWE)). (Coach: Bruce David RIOCH (ENG)).
Shelbourne FC: Dean DELANEY, Owen HEARY, David ROGERS (ENG) (YC66), Colin
HAWKINS (46' Jamie HARRIS (WAL)), Sean DILLON, Oliver CAHILL, Stuart BYRNE,
Alan MOORE (59' Greg O'HALLORAN (YC63)), Joseph Cyrille N'DO (CMR) (YC75),
Glen CROWE, Jason BYRNE (YC55) (81' Bobby RYAN). (Coach: Patrick (Pat) FENLON).
Goals: Odense BK: 1-0 Morten FEVANG (28'), 2-0 Morten FEVANG (42'), 3-0 Morten
FEVANG (58').
Referee: Tsvetan GEORGIEV (BUL)   Attendance: 1.903

02-07-2006   Easter Road, Edinburgh:
             Hibernian FC Edinburgh – FC Dinaburg Daugavpils 5-0 (1-0)
Hibernian FC Edinburgh: Simon BROWN (ENG), Steven WHITTAKER, David MURPHY
(ENG), Robert Marc JONES (ENG), Chris HOGG (ENG), Michael STEWART (60' Dean
SHIELS (NIR)), Kevin THOMSON, Steven FLETCHER, Scott BROWN (YC10), Paul
DALGLISH (46' Ivan SPROULE (NIR)), Chris KILLEN (NZL) (76' Amadou KONTE
(MLI)). (Coach: Anthony Mark (Tony) MOWBRAY (ENG)).
FC Dinaburg Daugavpils: Vadims FJODOROVS, Vadims LOGINS (70' Jurgis PUCINSKIS),
Mihails POPOVS (YC78), Ivans RODINS, Andrejs ZUROMSKIS, Olexandr KRIKLIVY
(UKR) (YC19), Nikita CHMYKOV (RUS), Edgars BURLAKOVS (46' Sergejs
VALUSKINS), Pavel RYZHEUSKI (BLS) (73' Dimitrijs CEBOTARJOVS), Jurijs
SOKOLOVS, Andrejs MARKOVS (YC56). (Coach: Sergey Nikolayevich POPKOV (RUS)).
Goals: Hibernian FC Edinburgh: 1-0 Chris KILLEN (38'), 2-0 Scott BROWN (49'), 3-0 Ivan
SPROULE (73'), 4-0 David MURPHY (76'), 5-0 Steven FLETCHER (85').
Referee: Sinisa ZRNIC (BOS)   Attendance: 11.731

02-07-2006   Nitra Stadión, Nitra: FC Nitra – FC Dnipro Dnipropetrovsk 2-1 (2-1)
FC Nitra: Tomás TUJVEL, Adrián CEMAN (YC47), Csaba SZÓRÁD, Peter GUNDA, Erik
HRNCÁR, Peter GRAJCIAR (84' Roman SLOBODA), Slavomír BALIS (60' Andrej
HESEK), Martin BABIC (80' Pavol FARKAS), Ján STAJER, Michal FARKAS, Róbert RÁK.
(Coach: Ivan GALÁD).
FC Dnipro Dnipropetrovsk: Artem KUSLIY, Olexandr GRYTSAY (YC89), Olexandr
RADCHENKO (YC28), Serhiy MATIUKHIN, Bohdan SHERSHUN, Mladen BARTULOVIC
(CRO), Ruslan BIDNENKO (70' Vitaliy LYSYTSKIY), Konstyantyn KRAVCHENKO (21'
Konstyantyn BALABANOV), Maksym PASHAYEV, Sergei KORNILENKO (BLS) (83'
Olexandr MELASHCHENKO), Ruslan KOSTYSHIN. (Coach: Oleh Valeriyovych
PROTASOV).
Goals: FC Nitra: 1-1 Róbert RÁK (16'), 2-1 Erik HRNCÁR (32').
FC Dnipro Dnipropetrovsk: 0-1 Sergei KORNILENKO (8').
Referee: Paulius MALZINSKAS (LIT)   Attendance: 1.780

02-07-2006   Stadion Partizana, Beograd: FK Zeta Golubovci – NK Maribor   1-2 (0-0)
FK Zeta Golubovci: Sasa IVANOVIC, Blazo IGUMANOVIC, Miroslav KALUDJEROVIC,
Milan RADULOVIC, Ivan TODOROVIC, Bojan IVANOVIC (YC21), Ivan VUKOVIC,
Branislav VUKOMANOVIC, Marko CETKOVIC (YC90), Janko TUMBASEVIC (65' Zarko
KORAC), Drazen MILIC (62' Slaven STJEPANOVIC (BOS)). (Coach: Dejan VUKICEVIC
(MNE)).
NK Maribor: Marko RANILOVIC, Fabijan CIPOT, Zikica VUKSANOVIC, Predrag SIMIC
(CRO) (55' Rene MIHELIC), Milan RAKIC, Leon PANIKVAR (YC39), David TOMAZIC-
SERUGA (YC72), Zajko ZEBA (BOS), Marko POPOVIC (SRB), Dragan JELIC (90' Marko
POKLEKA), Gorazd ZAJC (83' Klemen MEDVED). (Coach: Marijan PUSNIK).
Goals: FK Zeta Golubovci: 1-2 Slaven STJEPANOVIC (83').
NK Maribor: 0-1 Zajko ZEBA (75'), 0-2 Blazo IGUMANOVIC (81' *own goal*).
Referee: Radek MATEJEK (CZE)   Attendance: 200

02-07-2006   Ratina Stadium, Tampere: Tampere United FC – Kalmar FF   1-2 (0-1)
Tampere United FC: Mikko KAVÉN, Vasile MARCHIS (ROM) (YC90+2), Jussi
KUOPPALA, Heikki AHO, Jussi-Pekka SAVOLAINEN (63' Jussi KUJALA), Jarkko WISS,
Juska SAVOLAINEN, Aristides PERTOT (ARG), Antti HYNYNEN (YC14) (20' Miki
SIPILÄINEN), Ville LEHTINEN, Sakari SAARINEN. (Coach: Ari Juhani HJELM).
Kalmar FF: Petter WASTÅ, Niklas KALDNER, Tobias CARLSSON, Mikael EKLUND,
Patrik ROSENGREN, Mikael BLOMBERG, Henrik RYDSTRÖM, Viktor ELM (YC79),
Lasse JOHANSSON (81' Rasmus ELM), Sphetim HASANI (BOS) (69' Fredrik
PETERSSON), CÉSAR Santin (BRA) (69' Brima KOROMA (SLE)). (Coach: Nanne
BERGSTRAND).
Goals: Tampere United FC: 1-2 Miki SIPILÄINEN (75').
Kalmar FF: 0-1 Sphetim HASANI (7'), 0-2 Sphetim HASANI (69').
Referee: Johannes VALGEIRSSON (ISL)

02-07-2006   Gradski vrt, Osijek: NK Osijek – Ethnikós Áchnas FC   2-2 (0-1)
NK Osijek: Filip SUSNJARA, Damir VUICA, Josip MILARDOVIC, Ivo SMOJE (YC52),
Mijo NADJ (46' Mario VRATOVIC), Anton DEDAJ (YC75), Dejan PRIJIC (56' Aljosa
VOJNOVIC), Ante VITAJIC (YC85), Marko DINJAR, Karlo PRIMORAC (80' Josip
BARISIC), Igor MOSTARLIC. (Coach: Ivan SUSAK).
Ethnikós Áchnas FC: Milos ADAMOVIC (SBM), Christos SHAILIS (YC26), Dimitris
SIMOU, Marius Sandu IORDACHE (ROM) (86' Demosthenis DEMOSTHENOUS), Christos
KOTSONIS (64' Goran GRKINIC (SRB)), Zoran STJEPANOVIC (SRB) (YC90+2), Lars
SCHLICHTING (GER) (YC46), Christos POYIATZIS, Christofis PASHIALIS (YC90),
Marko KMETEC (SLO) (77' Milan BELIC (SRB)), Patrik IPAVEC (SLO). (Coach: Toza
SAPURIC (MCD)).
Goals: NK Osijek: 1-1 Christofis PASHIALIS (55' *own goal*), 2-1 Aljosa VOJNOVIC (61').
Ethnikós Áchnas FC: 0-1 Marko KMETEC (2'), 2-2 Christos POYIATZIS (70').
Referee: Ian STOKES (IRL)

02-07-2006   Stadion Letzigrund, Zürich: Grasshopper-Club – FK Teplice 2-0 (0-0)
Grasshopper-Club: Fabio COLTORTI, Matthias LANGKAMP (GER), Luca DENICOLA (60'
Roland SCHWEGLER), Kim JAGGY, Scott SUTTER, Gerardo SEOANE (77' Veroljub
SALATIC (SRB)), Michel RENGGLI, Roberto PINTO (POR) (33' Demba TOURÉ (SEN)),
ANTONIO Carlos DOS SANTOS (BRA), BISCOTTE MBALA Mbuta (DRC), Sreto RISTIC
(SRB). (Coach: Krassimir Guenchev BALAKOV).
FK Teplice: Tomás POSTULKA, Jiri PIMPARA, Josef KAUFMAN, Martin KLEIN, Michal
VALENTA, Tomás HUNAL, Antonin ROSA, Tomás JIRSÁK (86' Jan STOHANZL), Michal
DOLEZAL (75' Martin FENIN), Pavel VERBIR (YC57) (65' Emil RILKE), Edin DZEKO
(BOS). (Coach: Vlastislav MARECEK).
Goals: Grasshopper-Club: 1-0 Demba TOURÉ (48'), 2-0 BISCOTTE MBALA Mbuta (68').
Referee: Charles RICHMOND (SCO)   Attendance: 1.700

08-07-2006   Dasáki, Áchnas: Ethnikós Áchnas FC – NK Osijek 0-0
Ethnikós Áchnas FC: Milos ADAMOVIC (SRB) (YC80), Demosthenis DEMOSTHENOUS,
Christos SHAILIS, Goran GRKINIC (SRB) (YC90+2), Dimitris SIMOU (YC90), Marius
Sandu IORDACHE (ROM) (YC64), Christos KOTSONIS, Zoran STJEPANOVIC (SRB),
Christos POYIATZIS, Marko KMETEC (SLO), Patrik IPAVEC (SLO) (51' Levan KEBADZE
(GEO)). (Coach: Toza SAPURIC (MCD)).
NK Osijek: Filip SUSNJARA, Josip MILARDOVIC (YC90+3), Mario VRATOVIC (73'
Dejan PRIJIC (YC76)), Ivo SMOJE, DAVID JUNIOR Lopes (BRA), Anton DEDAJ (YC31)
(55' Ante MILAS), Ante VITAJIC (YC25), Marko DINJAR, Karlo PRIMORAC, Igor
MOSTARLIC (55' Stipe BULJAN), Aljosa VOJNOVIC (YC78). (Coach: Ivan SUSAK).
Referee: Adrian D.CASHA (MLT)

08-07-2006   Celtnieks Stadion, Daugavpils:
              FC Dinaburg Daugavpils – Hibernian FC Edinburgh 0-3 (0-1)
FC Dinaburg Daugavpils: Vadims FJODOROVS, Mihails POPOVS, Vadims LOGINS
(YC37), Ivans RODINS, Andrejs ZUROMSKIS, Nikita CHMYKOV (RUS), Edgars
BURLAKOVS (46' Aleksejs KOSTENKO), Pavel RYZHEUSKI (BLS), Sergejs
VALUSKINS, Jurijs SOKOLOVS, Andrejs MARKOVS (51' Dimitrijs CEBOTARJOVS).
Hibernian FC Edinburgh: Simon BROWN (ENG), Steven WHITTAKER (YC89), David
MURPHY (ENG), Robert Marc JONES (ENG), Chris HOGG (ENG), Michael STEWART
(71' Dean SHIELS (NIR)), Kevin THOMSON (46' Stephen GLASS), Ivan SPROULE (NIR),
James McCLUSKEY, Steven FLETCHER (60' Paul DALGLISH), Amadou KONTÉ (MLI).
(Coach: Anthony Mark (Tony) MOWBRAY (ENG)).
Goals: Hibernian FC Edinburgh: 0-1 Amadou KONTÉ (21'), 0-2 Amadou KONTÉ (56'), 0-3
Ivan SPROULE (77').
Referee: Petteri KARI (FIN)   Attendance: 350

08-07-2006   Fredriksskans Idrottsplats, Kalmar: Kalmar FF – Tampere United FC   3-2 (1-1)
Kalmar FF: Petter WASTÅ, Niklas KALDNER, Joachim LANTZ, Tobias CARLSSON, Patrik
ROSENGREN, Mikael BLOMBERG (YC49), Henrik RYDSTRÖM, Viktor ELM, Lasse
JOHANSSON, Sphetim HASANI (BOS) (YC45) (75' Brima KOROMA (SLE)), CÉSAR
Santin (BRA) (76' Rasmus ELM). (Coach: Nanne BERGSTRAND).
Tampere United FC: Mikko KAVÉN, Vasile MARCHIS (ROM), Jussi KUOPPALA (YC15),
Heikki AHO, Jussi KUJALA, Jarkko WISS, Juska SAVOLAINEN (73' Risto OJANEN),
Aristides PERTOT (ARG), Ville LEHTINEN, Sakari SAARINEN (59' Antti OJANPERÄ),
Miki SIPILÄINEN (65' Jussi-Pekka SAVOLAINEN). (Coach: Ari Juhani HJELM).
Goals: Kalmar FF: 1-1 Tobias CARLSSON (38'), 2-1 Sphetim HASANI (67'), 3-2 Brima
KOROMA (90'+2').
Tampere United FC: 0-1 Ville LEHTINEN (31'), 2-2 Jarkko WISS (86').
Referee: David MALCOLM (NIR)

08-07-2006   Ljudski vrt Stadium, Maribor: NK Maribor – FK Zeta Golubovci 2-0 (0-0)
NK Maribor: Marko RANILOVIC, Fabijan CIPOT, Zikica VUKSANOVIC (YC73), Vladislav
LUNGU (MOL), Milan RAKIC (46' Predrag SIMIC (CRO)), Leon PANIKVAR (YC50),
Zajko ZEBA (BOS) (46' David TOMAZIC-SERUGA), Marko POPOVIC (SRB) (YC35),
Rene MIHELIC, Dragan JELIC, Gorazd ZAJC (YC14) (82' Klemen MEDVED). (Coach:
Marijan PUSNIK).
FK Zeta Golubovci: Sasa IVANOVIC, Milan RADULOVIC (YC61), Aleksandar
KALUDJEROVIC (46' Miroslav KALUDJEROVIC), Ivan TODOROVIC, Bojan IVANOVIC
(YC79), Darko MARKOVIC (YC13) (51' Zarko KORAC), Ivan VUKOVIC, Branislav
VUKOMANOVIC, Marko CETKOVIC, Janko TUMBASEVIC, Slaven STJEPANOVIC
(BOS) (66' Srdjan NIKIC (YC67)). (Coach: Dejan VUKICEVIC (MNE)).
Goals: NK Maribor: 1-0 Gorazd ZAJC (53'), 2-0 David TOMAZIC-SERUGA (90'+3').
Referee: Michael SVENDSEN (DEN)   Attendance: 2.500

08-07-2006   Meteor Stadium, Dnipropetrovsk:
              FC Dnipro Dnipropetrovsk – FC Nitra 2-0 (1-0)
FC Dnipro Dnipropetrovsk: Vyacheslav KERNOZENKO (YC85), Olexandr GRYTSAY,
Olexandr RADCHENKO, Serhiy MATIUKHIN, Bohdan SHERSHUN, Mladen
BARTULOVIC (CRO) (YC80) (90' Vyacheslav SERDYUK), Ruslan BIDNENKO (YC43)
(61' Vitaliy LYSYTSKIY), Denis ANDRIENKO, Sergei KORNILENKO (BLS), Konstyantyn
BALABANOV (73' Denis GLAVINA (CRO)), Ruslan KOSTYSHIN. (Coach: Oleh
Valeriyovych PROTASOV).
FC Nitra: Tomás TUJVEL, Adrián CEMAN, Csaba SZÓRÁD, Peter GUNDA (YC66), Erik
HRNCÁR, Peter GRAJCIAR, Slavomír BALIS (YC33) (63' Andrej HESEK), Martin BABIC,
Ján STAJER, Michal FARKAS (68' Pavol FARKAS), Róbert RÁK (82' Roman SLOBODA).
(Coach: Ivan GALÁD).
Goals: FC Dnipro Dnipropetrovsk: 1-0 Sergei KORNILENKO (31'), 2-0 Ruslan BIDNENKO
(57').
Referee: Per Ivar STABERG (NOR)   Attendance: 5.800

08-07-2006   Stadion Miejski, Poznán: KKS Lech Poznán – FC Tiraspol 1-3 (0-1)
KKS Lech Poznán: Radoslaw CIERZNIAK, Dawid KUCHARSKI, Grzegorz
WOJTKOWIAK, Marcin WASILEWSKI, Rafal MURAWSKI, Maciej SCHERFCHEN,
Marcin WACHOWICZ (YC45) (71' Artur MARCINIAK), Przemyslaw PITRY (57' Iliyan
MITSANSKI (BUL)), Jacek DEMBINSKI (64' Karol GREGOREK), Piotr REISS, Zbigniew
ZAKRZEWSKI. (Coach: Franciszek SMUDA).
FC Tiraspol: Stanislav NAMASCO, Andrey NOVICOV, Kyrylo SYDORENKO (UKR),
Kennedy Chimezie CHINWO (NGR) (85' Valter KHORGUASHVILI (GEO)), Victor
GOLOVATENCO, Evgheni GORODETCHIL (78' Andrey PORFIREANU), Andrey
SECRIERU (YC1) (75' Nicolai RUDAC), Serghei NAMASCO, Oleksandr BYCHKOV
(UKR), Igor PICUSCIAC (YC27), Serghei ALEXEEV. (Coach: Yuriy Petrovych KULISH
(UKR)).
Goals: KKS Lech Poznán: 1-3 Zbigniew ZAKRZEWSKI (73').
FC Tiraspol: 0-1 Igor PICUSCIAC (27'), 0-2 Kyrylo SYDORENKO (63'), 0-3 Serghei
NAMASCO (69').
Referee: Robert KRAJNC (SLO)   Attendance: 8.000

08-07-2006   Kayseri Atatürk Stadyumu, Kayseri:
              Kayserispor Kulübü – FC Sopron 1-0 (0-0)
Kayserispor Kulübü: Dimitar Ivanov IVANKOV (BUL), Rashad F.SADIKHOV (AZE),
Bülent BÖLÜKBASI, Hamed KAVIANPOUR (IRN) (54' Kamber ARSLAN), Ragip
BASDAG, Samuel JOHNSON (GHA), Aydin TOSCALI, Mehmet TOPUZ (90' Tayfun
CORA), Fatih CEYLAN, Gökhan ÜNAL, Muhammet Hanifi AKAGÜNDÜZ (AUT) (74'
İlhan PARLAK). (Coach: Ertugrul SAGLAM).
FC Sopron: Balász RABÓCZKI, Marius Adrian RADU (ROM) (YC81), Ion IBRIC (ROM),
Sergiu Victor HOMEI (ROM) (YC77), Gábor BAGOLY (YC73), András HORVÁTH,
Cristian Lucian MUNTEANU (ROM) (YC16) (65' István SIRA), Jozsef MAGASFÖLDI,
Gábor DEMJÉN (79' Georgi KORUDZHIEV (BUL)), Róbert FECZESIN, Sebastian Florin
IANC (ROM) (46' Gellért IVÁNCSICS). (Coach: László VASS).
Goal: Kayserispor Kulübü: 1-0 Fatih CEYLAN (88').
Referee: Pavel OLSIAK (SVK)

08-07-2006   Gradski Stadion, Mostar:
              HSK Zrinjski Mostar – Maccabi Petach Tikva FC 1-3 (1-1)
HSK Zrinjski Mostar: Nicola MARIC (CRO), Ivica DZIDIC (CRO) (YC73), Davor
LANDEKA (72' Kresimir KORDIC (CRO)), Nenad GAGRO (64' Bulend BISCEVIC),
Stanisa NIKOLIC, Damir DZIDIC (CRO) (YC45), Sulejman SMAJIC, Ilija PRODANOVIC
(SBM) (RC50), Mladen ZIZOVIC (YC13) (62' Admir JOLDIC), Lamine DIARRA (SEN),
Velibor DJURIC. (Coach: Blaz "Baka" SLISKOVIC).
Maccabi Petach Tikva FC: Ohad COHEN, Ismael AMAR, Murad MAGOMEDOV, Naor
PESER, Nitzan DAMARI, Emmanuel EBIEDE (NGR) (YC69) (69' Blessing KAKU (NGR)),
André JEFISLEY Caldeira (BRA), Roy BAKEL (YC74) (76' Daniel UNGER), Ori LUZON,
Dovev GABBAY (64' Omer GOLAN), Rubel SARSOUR. (Coach: Guy LUZON).
Goals: HSK Zrinjski Mostar: 1-0 Lamine DIARRA (17').
Maccabi Petach Tikva FC: 1-1 Rubel SARSOUR (19'), 1-2 Dovev GABBAY (57' penalty),
1-3 Naor PESER (73').
Referee: Veaceslav BANARI (MOL)

174

08-07-2006   Vasil Levski National Stadium, Sofia:
PFC Lokomotiv Plovdiv – FC Farul Constanta 1-1 (1-0)
PFC Lokomotiv Plovdiv: Stoyan KOLEV, Danail BACHKOV, Georgi SAMOKISHEV
(YC58) (66' Jason Marcel ELAME (CMR)), Yordan MILIEV, Velko HRISTEV (YC31),
Ilami HALIMI (MCD), Hristo ZLATINSKI, Krasimir DIMITROV, Radoslav ANEV (77'
Dimitar ILIEV), Zoran ZLATKOVSKI (MCD) (65' Zoran ZLATINOV), Yavor VANDEV.
(Coach: Ayan Faikov SADAKOV).
FC Farul Constanta: George CURCA, Stefanel Razvan FARMACHE, Ion BARBU, Decebal
Virgil GHEARA, Laurentiu FLOREA, Cosmin Nicolae BACILA (YC43), Iulian Catalin
APOSTOL (84' Florin Ioan NEAGA), Claudiu VOICULET, Ionut LARIE, Dinu Marius
TODORAN (90' Ionel BOGHITOI), Armel Disney MAMOUNA-OSSILA (80' Daniel
Constantin FLOREA). (Coach: Momcilo "Moca" VUKOTIC (SRB)).
Goals: PFC Lokomotiv Plovdiv: 1-0 Ilami HALIMI (35').
FC Farul Constanta: 1-1 Decebal Virgil GHEARA (55')
Referee: Meir LEVI (ISR)   Attendance: 5.200

08-07-2006   Traktor Stadium, Minsk: FC MTZ-RIPO Minsk – FK Moskva 0-1 (0-0)
FC MTZ-RIPO Minsk: Pavel CHESNOVSKI, Artem FEDORCHENKO (UKR) (YC46),
Yanko VALKANOV (BUL), Tajia Adam SORO (CIV), Aleksandr BYLINA, Aleksandr
STASHCHENYUK (46' Vyacheslav HLEB), Oleg STRAKANOVICH (73' Mikhail
AFANASIEV), Dmitri SHEGRIKOVICH (83' Igor MALTSEV), Vitali TARASHCHIK
(YC,YC90+1), Mikhail YEREMCHUK, Artem KONTSEVOI. (Coach: Yuri Iosifovich
PUNTUS).
FK Moskva: Yuriy ZHEVNOV (BLS), Dmitriy GODUNOK, Oleg KUZMIN, Isaac
OKORONKWO (NGR), Mariusz JOP (POL), Pyotr BYSTROV, Sergey SEMAK, Tomás
CÍZEK (CZE) (67' Damian GORAWSKI (POL)), Stanislav IVANOV (MOL) (58' Radu
REBEJA (MOL)), Dmitriy KIRICHENKO (63' Roman ADAMOV), Héctor Andrés
BRACAMONTE (ARG). (Coach: Leonid Viktorovich SLUTSKY).
Goal: FK Moskva: 0-1 Roman ADAMOV (81' penalty).
Referee: Marek MIKOLAJEWSKI (POL)

09-07-2006   Tolka Park, Dublin: Shelbourne FC – Odense BK 1-0 (1-0)
Shelbourne FC: Dean DELANEY, Owen HEARY, David ROGERS (ENG), Colin
HAWKINS, Sean DILLON (73' Jamie HARRIS (WAL)), Oliver CAHILL (YC41), Stuart
BYRNE, Alan MOORE (35' Greg O'HALLORAN), Bobby RYAN (73' Richard BAKER),
Joseph Cyrille N'DO (CMR), Glen CROWE. (Coach: Patrick (Pat) FENLON).
Odense BK: Arek ONYSZKO (POL), Ulrik LAURSEN, Anders Møller CHRISTENSEN,
Alexander AAS, Chris SØRENSEN, Morten FEVANG (NOR) (87' Jan Tore OPHAUG
(NOR)), Esben HANSEN, Martin BORRE (82' Michael LARSEN), Magne STURØD (NOR)
(68' Mads TIMM), Jonas BORRING, Tobias GRAHN (SWE). (Coach: Bruce David RIOCH
(ENG)).
Goal: Shelbourne FC: 1-0 Joseph Cyrille N'DO (33').
Referee: Dietmar DRABEK (AUT)   Attendance: 800

175

09-07-2006   Keflavíkurvöllur, Keflavík: IB Keflavík – Lillestrøm SK   2-2 (0-2)
IB Keflavík: Ómar JÓHANNSSON, Gudmundur Vidar METE (46' Thórarinn
KRISTJÁNSSON), Gudjón Ámi ANTONÍUSSON, Kenneth GUSTAVSSON (SWE), Jónas
Gudni SÆVARSSON, Hallgrímur JÓNASSON, Hólmar Örn RÚNARSSON, Símun
SAMUELSEN (FAR) (67' Magnús THORSTEINSSON), Baldur SIGURDSSON, Gudmundur
STEINARSSON, Stefán Öm ARNARSON (82' Einar Orri EINARSSON). (Coach: Kristján
GUDMUNDSSON).
Lillestrøm SK: Heinz MÜLLER (GER), Shane STEFANUTTO (AUS), Pål Steffen
ANDRESEN, Anders RAMBEKK, Pål STRAND, Johan Petter WINSNES, Robert KOREN
(SLO) (46' Espen SØGÅRD), Bjørn Helge RIISE (57' Cyril KALI (FRA)), Kasey
WEHRMAN (AUS), Magnus MYKLEBUST (64' Olivier OCCEAN (CAN)), Arild
SUNDGOT. (Coach: Uwe RÖSLER (GER)).
Goals: IB Keflavík: 1-2 Thórarinn KRISTJÁNSSON (58'), 2-2 Hólmar Örn RÚNARSSON
(67').
Lillestrøm SK: 0-1 Magnus MYKLEBUST (10'), 0-2 Robert KOREN (19').
Referee: Andrejs SIPAILO (LAT)   Attendance: 300

09-07-2006   Mestský Stadion na Stínadlech, Teplice:
              FK Teplice – Grasshopper-Club   0-2 (0-0)
FK Teplice: Tomás POSTULKA, Josef KAUFMAN, Martin KLEIN, Michal VALENTA,
Tomás HUNAL (61' Vlastimil STOZICKY), Tomás JIRSÁK (YC21), Petr BENAT, Vitezslav
BROZIK (76' Jan STOHANZL), Martin FENIN (54' Michal DOLEZAL), Emil RILKE, Edin
DZEKO (BOS). (Coach: Vlastislav MARECEK).
Grasshopper-Club: Dragan DJUKIC, Matthias LANGKAMP (GER), Roland SCHWEGLER,
Kim JAGGY, Scott SUTTER, Gerardo SEOANE, Michel RENGGLI (64' Veroljub SALATIC
(SRB)), ANTONIO Carlos DOS SANTOS (BRA) (73' EDUARDO Ribeiro (BRA)), Demba
TOURÉ (SEN), BISCOTTE MBALA Mbuta (DRC) (46' Dusan PAVLOVIC), Sreto RISTIC
(SRB). (Coach: Krassimir Guenchev BALAKOV).
Goals: Grasshopper-Club: 0-1 Dusan PAVLOVIC (52'), 0-2 EDUARDO Ribeiro (85').
Referee: Sergiy BEREZKA (UKR)   Attendance: 3.050

09-07-2006   Mikheil Meskhi Stadium, Tbilisi: FC Dinamo Tbilisi – SV Ried   0-1 (0-0)
FC Dinamo Tbilisi: Soso GRISHIKASHVILI, Shota KASHIA (YC84), Gulverd
TOMASHVILI, Shota GRIGALASHVILI (69' Zamir JANASHIA), Levan KHMALADZE
(51' Irakli CHIRIKASHVILI (YC57)), Alexander KOBAKHIDZE, Giorgi NAVALOVSKY
(YC37) (63' Mikhail BOBOKHIDZE), AMBROSIO Jozimar Luis Domingos (BRA), Sandro
IASHVILI, Jaba DVALI, Mikheil KHUTSISHVILI. (Coach: Kakhaber (Khaki)
KATCHARAVA).
SV Ried: Hans-Peter BERGER, Christoph JANK, Dario DABAC (CRO), Oliver GLASNER,
Thomas Günther EDER, Sebastian MARTÍNEZ, Jung-Won SEO (KOR) (81' Markus
BERGER), Herwig DRECHSEL, Ewald BRENNER (YC13), Ronald BRUNMAYR (64'
Daniel KASTNER), Emin SULIMANI (46' Michael MEHLEM). (Coach: Helmut KRAFT).
Goal: SV Ried: 0-1 Herwig DRECHSEL (66').
Referee: Mark Steven WHITBY (WAL)   Attendance: 2.000

THIRD ROUND

15-07-2006   Fredriksskans Idrottsplats, Kalmar:
Kalmar FF – FC Twente Enschede   1-0 (0-0)
Kalmar FF: Petter WASTÅ, Niklas KALDNER, Tobias CARLSSON, Mikael EKLUND, Patrik ROSENGREN, Mikael BLOMBERG, Henrik RYDSTRÖM, Viktor ELM (46' Rasmus ELM), Lasse JOHANSSON, Sphetim HASANI (BOS) (81' Brima KOROMA (SLE)), CÉSAR Santin (BRA) (YC66) (85' THIAGO Silva MATOS (BRA)). (Coach: Nanne BERGSTRAND).
FC Twente Enschede: Sander BOSCHKER, Rob WIELAERT (YC22), Ramon ZOMER (RC50), Jeroen HEUBACH, Peter NIEMEYER (GER), Wout BRAMA, Sharbel TOUMA (SWE) (74' Guilherme AFONSO (SUI)), Kennedy BAKIRCIOGLÜ (SWE), Blaise N'KUFO (SUI), Dmitri SHOUKOV (RUS) (54' Rahim OUÉDRAOGO (BKF)), Patrick GERRITSEN (79' Otman BAKKAL). (Coach: Fredericus Jacobus (Fred) RUTTEN).
Goal: Kalmar FF: 1-0 Mikael BLOMBERG (51' penalty).
Referee: Martin ATKINSON (ENG)   Attendance: 2.684

15-07-2006   Municipal Stadium, Hertzliya:
Maccabi Petach Tikva FC – Ethnikós Áchnas FC   0-2 (0-0)
Maccabi Petach Tikva FC: Ohad COHEN, Ismael AMAR (56' Shay DAVID), Murad MAGOMEDOV, Kobi GANON (78' Ohad KADUSI), Naor PESER (YC84), Nitzan DAMARI, André JEFISLEY Caldeira (BRA), Shlomo TZEMAH (YC47), Opir AZU (63' Omar DAMARI), Dovev GABBAY, Rubel SARSOUR. (Coach: Guy LUZON).
Ethnikós Áchnas FC: Panagiotis CHARALAMBOUS, Christos SHAILIS, Goran GRKINIC (SRB) (YC86), Christos KOTSONIS, Zoran STJEPANOVIC (SRB) (87' Marius Sandu IORDACHE (ROM)), Lars SCHLICHTING (GER), Christos POYIATZIS, Christos PASHIALIS (58' Panayiotis ENGOMITIS (YC79)), Gábor VINCZE (HUN), Marko KMETEC (SLO) (82' Milan BELIC (SRB)), Levan KEBADZE (GEO). (Coach: Toza SAPURIC (MCD)).
Goals: Ethnikós Áchnas FC: 0-1 Lars SCHLICHTING (65'), 0-2 Levan KEBADZE (77').
Referee: Claudio CIRCHETTA (SUI)

15-07-2006   Saint James' Park, Newcastle: Newcastle United FC – Lillestrøm SK   1-1 (0-1)
Newcastle United FC: Shay GIVEN (IRL), Stephen CARR (IRL), Charles N'ZOGBIA (FRA), Titus BRAMBLE, Steven TAYLOR, Celestine BABAYARO (NGR), James MILNER (65' Foluwashola AMEOBI (NGR)), Nolberto SOLANO Todco (PER), Emre BELÖZOGLU (TUR), Scott PARKER, Albert LUQUE Martos (ESP) (81' Alan O'BRIEN (IRL)). (Coach: Glenn Victor ROEDER).
Lillestrøm SK: Heinz MÜLLER (GER), Shane STEFANUTTO (AUS), Pål Steffen ANDRESEN, Anders RAMBEKK, Espen SØGÅRD, Johan Petter WINSNES (5' Cyril KALI (FRA)), Robert KOREN (SLO) (61' Pål STRAND), Bjørn Helge RIISE (68' Kasey WEHRMAN (AUS)), Khaled MOUELHI (TUN), Michael MIFSUD (MLT), Olivier OCCEAN (CAN) (YC54). (Coach: Uwe RÖSLER (GER)).
Goals: Newcastle United FC: 1-1 Albert LUQUE Martos (50').
Lillestrøm SK: 0-1 Robert KOREN (21').
Referee: Joeri VAN DE VELDE (BEL)   Attendance: 31.059

15-07-2006   Fionia Park, Odense: Odense BK – Hibernian FC Edinburgh   1-0 (1-0)
Odense BK: Arek ONYSZKO (POL), Ulrik LAURSEN, Anders Møller CHRISTENSEN
(YC90+2), Alexander AAS, Chris SØRENSEN, Morten FEVANG (NOR) (YC42) (90'+3'
Michael LARSEN), Esben HANSEN, Martin BORRE, Jonas BORRING, Mads TIMM (86'
Jan Tore OPHAUG (NOR)), Tobias GRAHN (SWE). (Coach: Bruce David RIOCH (ENG)).
Hibernian FC Edinburgh: Simon BROWN (ENG), Steven WHITTAKER, David MURPHY
(ENG) (YC32), Robert Marc JONES (ENG), Chris HOGG (ENG) (46' Oumar KONDÉ
(SUI)), Michael STEWART, Kevin THOMSON (YC62), Ivan SPROULE (NIR) (83' Paul
DALGLISH), Steven FLETCHER (72' Dean SHIELS (NIR)), Scott BROWN (YC79), Chris
KILLEN (NZL) (YC55). (Coach: Anthony Mark (Tony) MOWBRAY (ENG)).
Goal: Odense BK: 1-0 Chris SØRENSEN (32' penalty).
Referee: Philippe KALT (FRA)   Attendance: 2.341

15-07-2006   Hardturm, Zürich: Grasshopper-Club – KAA Gent   2-1 (0-1)
Grasshopper-Club: Fabio COLTORTI, Matthias LANGKAMP (GER), Roland SCHWEGLER,
Kim JAGGY, Scott SUTTER (YC46), Gerardo SEOANE (46' Veroljub SALATIC (SRB)),
Michel RENGGLI, ANTONIO Carlos DOS SANTOS (BRA), Demba TOURÉ (SEN),
BISCOTTE MBALA Mbuta (DRC) (64' EDUARDO Ribeiro (BRA)), Sreto RISTIC (SRB)
(89' Dusan PAVLOVIC). (Coach: Krassimir Guenchev BALAKOV).
KAA Gent: Frédéric HERPOEL, Dario SMOJE (CRO) (YC52), Nicolas LOMBAERTS, Steve
LAYBUTT (AUS), Nebojsa PAVLOVIC (SRB), Randall AZOFEIFA Corrales (CRC) (YC56)
(68' Kenny THOMPSON), Christophe GRÉGOIRE (82' Guillaume GILLET), Davy DE
BEULE, Marcin ZEWLAKOW (POL), Sandy MARTENS (70' Damir MIRVIC (BOS)),
Dominic FOLEY (IRL). (Coach: Georges LEEKENS).
Goals: Grasshopper-Club: 1-1 Sreto RISTIC (50'), 2-1 Veroljub SALATIC (57').
KAA Gent: 0-1 Marcin ZEWLAKOW (2').
Referee: Sorin CORPODEAN (ROM)   Attendance: 2.500

15-07-2006   Fill-Metallbau-Stadion, Ried im Innkreis: SV Ried – FC Tiraspol   3-1 (1-0)
SV Ried: Hans-Peter BERGER, Christoph JANK, Dario DABAC (CRO), Oliver GLASNER
(YC85), Thomas Günther EDER (YC38), Sebastian MARTÍNEZ, Jung-Won SEO (KOR),
Herwig DRECHSEL (YC9) (55' Michael MEHLEM), Ewald BRENNER, Ronald
BRUNMAYR (61' Daniel KASTNER), Emin SULIMANI (77' Patrick WOLF). (Coach:
Helmut KRAFT).
FC Tiraspol: Stanislav NAMASCO, Andrey NOVICOV (YC40), Kennedy Chimezie
CHINWO (NGR), Kyrylo SYDORENKO (UKR), Victor GOLOVATENCO, Andrey
SECRIERU, Evgheni GORODETCHIL (81' Valter KHORGUASHVILI (GEO)), Serghei
NAMASCO (YC57) (64' Nicolai RUDAC), Igor PICUSCIAC, Serghei ALEXEEV, Oleksandr
BYCHKOV (UKR) (65' Andrey PORFIREANU). (Coach: Yuriy Petrovych KULISH (UKR)).
Goals: SV Ried: 1-0 Herwig DRECHSEL (26'), 2-0 Sebastian MARTÍNEZ (52'), 3-1 Jung-
Won SEO (80').
FC Tiraspol: 2-1 Serghei ALEXEEV (69').
Referee: Cem PAPILA (TUR)   Attendance: 2.315

178

15-07-2006   Panthessalikó Stádio, Vólos: AE Larissa – Kayserispor Kulübü 0-0
AE Larissa: Spyridon CHRISTOPOULOS, Nikolaos DABIZAS, Spiros VALLAS, Panagiotis
KATSIAROS (YC22), Dimitrios GIKAS (YC32) (46' Angelos DIGKOZIS), Georgios
GALITSIOS (73' Thomas KYPARISSIS), Zisis ZIAGKAS (61' Ioannis CHLOROS),
Nektarios ALEXANDROU (CYP) (YC78), Christos KALANTZIS (YC40), Efstathios
ALONEFTIS (CYP), Alexis GAVRILOPOULOS. (Coach: Georgios DONIS).
Kayserispor Kulübü: Dimitar Ivanov IVANKOV (BUL), Rashad F.SADIKHOV (AZE) (83'
Tayfun CORA), Bülent BÖLÜKBASI (YC15), Ragip BASDAG, Samuel JOHNSON (GHA)
(YC27), Aydin TOSCALI, Mehmet TOPUZ, Fatih CEYLAN, Gökhan ÜNAL (YC38) (90'+3'
Hamed KAVIANPOUR (IRN)), Muhammet Hanifi AKAGÜNDÜZ (AUT) (YC8) (68'
Leonardo Andres IGLESIAS (ARG)), Kamber ARSLAN. (Coach: Ertugrul SAGLAM).
Referee: Tiziano PIERI (ITA)   Attendance: 5.917

15-07-2006   Stade Parsemain, Istres:
            Olympique de Marseille – FC Dnipro Dnipropetrovsk 0-0
Olympique de Marseille: Sébastien HAMEL, Ronald ZUBAR,Taye Ismaila TAIWO (NGR),
Renato CIVELLI (ARG), Habib BEYE (SEN), Wilson ORUMA (NGR), Lorik CANA (ALB),
Samir NASRI (71' Thomas DERUDA), Toifilou MAOULIDA, Mamadou NIANG (SEN),
Mickaël PAGIS (67' Habib BAMOGO). (Coach: Albert EMON).
FC Dnipro Dnipropetrovsk: Vyacheslav KERNOZENKO, Olexandr GRYTSAY, Olexandr
RADCHENKO, Serhiy MATIUKHIN, Bohdan SHERSHUN (YC88), Oleh SHELAYEV,
Mladen BARTULOVIC (CRO) (64' Denis GLAVINA (CRO)), Denis ANDRIENKO, Sergey
NAZARENKO (YC51), Sergei KORNILENKO (BLS) (90'+3' Konstyantyn BALABANOV),
Ruslan KOSTYSHIN (87' Ruslan BIDNENKO). (Coach: Oleh Valeriyovych PROTASOV).
Referee: Bernardino GONZÁLEZ VÁZQUEZ (ESP)   Attendance: 6.895

15-07-2006   Stade de l'Abbé Deschamps, Auxerre:
            AJ Auxerre – FC Farul Constanta 4-1 (2-1)
AJ Auxerre: Fabien COOL, Johan RADET, Younes KABOUL (YC63), Bakari SAGNA
(YC90), Frédéric THOMAS, Benoît CHEYROU, Thomas KAHLENBERG (DEN) (83' Alain
GOMA), Jean-Pascal MIGNOT, Lionel MATHIS, Daniel George NICULAE (ROM) (68'
Alain TRAORÉ (BKF)), Luigi PIERONI (BEL) (81' Issa BA (SEN)). (Coach: Jean
FERNANDEZ).
FC Farul Constanta: George CURCA, Cristian SCHIOPU (YC19), Decebal Virgil GHEARA
(YC53), Vasile PACURANU (YC19), Laurentiu FLOREA (YC59), Cosmin Nicolae BACILA,
Iulian Catalin APOSTOL, Claudiu VOICULET, Dinu Marius TODORAN, Armel Disney
MAMOUNA-OSSILA, Mihai GURITA. (Coach: Momcilo "Moca" VUKOTIC (SRB)).
Goals: AJ Auxerre: 1-0 Lionel MATHIS (7'), 2-0 Luigi PIERONI (9'), 3-1 Thomas
KAHLENBERG (53'), 4-1 Alain TRAORÉ (77').
FC Farul Constanta: 2-1 Mihai GURITA (17').
Referee: Thorsten KINHÖFER (GER)   Attendance: 4.000

15-07-2006   Estadio El Madrigal, Villarreal: Villarreal CF – NK Maribor 1-2 (0-1)
Villarreal CF: Mariano Damián BARBOSA (ARG), Gonzalo Javier RODRÍGUEZ (ARG),
Enrique "QUIQUE" ÁLVAREZ Sanjuan (YC39), José Miguel González Rey "JOSEMI"
(RC47), Carlos ALCÁNTARA Cuevas, José Joaquín Moreno Verdu "JOSICO" (73' BRUNO
SORIANO Llido), Robert PIRÈS (FRA) (60' José María Romero Poyón "JOSÉ MARI"),
Rubén Garcia Calmache "CANI", Alessio TACCHINARDI (ITA) (YC40), Diego Martín
FORLÁN Corazo (URU) (YC44), Nihat KAHVECI (TUR). (Coach: Manuel Luis
PELLEGRINI Ripamonti (CHI)).
NK Maribor: Marko RANILOVIC (YC79), Fabijan CIPOT, Zikica VUKSANOVIC, Vladislav
LUNGU (MOL) (73' Klemen MEDVED), Predrag SIMIC (CRO) (YC35), Milan RAKIC
(YC33) (58' Martin PREGELJ (YC87)), David TOMAZIC-SERUGA, Marko POKLEKA (48'
Armel MUJKANOVIC (YC52)), Marko POPOVIC (SRB), Rene MIHELIC (YC84), Dragan
JELIC. (Coach: Marijan PUSNIK).
Goals: Villarreal CF: 1-1 Diego Martín FORLÁN Corazo (71').
NK Maribor: 0-1 Milan RAKIC (41'), 1-2 Rene MIHELIC (84').
Referee: Kevin BLOM (HOL)   Attendance: 12.000

16-07-2006   Friedrich-Ludwig-Jahn-Sportpark, Berlin:
              Hertha BSC Berlin – FK Moskva 0-0
Hertha BSC Berlin: Christian FIEDLER, Dick VAN BURIK (HOL), Sofian CHAHED, Malik
FATHI (YC49), Christopher SAMBA Veijeany (CGO) (YC32), Yildiray BASTÜRK (TUR),
Pál DÁRDAI (HUN), Andreas NEUENDORF (81' Patrick EBERT), Marko PANTELIC
(SRB) (85' Chinedu EDE), Ellery CAIRO (HOL), Ashkan DEJAGAH (63' Solomon Ndubisi
OKORONKWO (NGR)). (Coach: Falko GÖTZ).
FK Moskva: Yuriy ZHEVNOV (BLS), Dmitriy GODUNOK, Radu REBEJA (MOL), Oleg
KUZMIN, Isaac OKORONKWO (NGR), Jerry-Christian TCHUISSE (CMR), Pyotr
BYSTROV (72' Tomás CÍZEK (CZE)), Damian GORAWSKI (POL), Sergey SEMAK
(YC60), Dmitriy KIRICHENKO (83' Dmitriy GOLUBOV), Roman ADAMOV (61' Héctor
Andrés BRACAMONTE (ARG)). (Coach: Leonid Viktorovich SLUTSKY).
Referee: Mark CLATTENBURG (ENG)   Attendance: 8.404

22-07-2006   Arke Stadion, Enschede: FC Twente Enschede – Kalmar FF 3-1 (0-0)
FC Twente Enschede: Sander BOSCHKER, Rob WIELAERT, Jeroen HEUBACH (YC64),
Rahim OUÉDRAOGO (BKF) (73' Otman BAKKAL), Peter NIEMEYER (GER), Wout
BRAMA, Sharbel TOUMA (SWE), Kennedy BAKIRCIOGLÜ (SWE), Blaise N'KUFO (SUI),
Dmitri SHOUKOV (RUS) (63' Karim EL AHMADI), Patrick GERRITSEN (85' Niels
WELLENBERG). (Coach: Fredericus Jacobus (Fred) RUTTEN).
Kalmar FF: Petter WASTÅ, Niklas KALDNER, Tobias CARLSSON, Mikael EKLUND,
Patrik ROSENGREN, Mikael BLOMBERG (88' Rasmus ELM), Henrik RYDSTRÖM, Viktor
ELM (81' Brima KOROMA (SLE)), Lasse JOHANSSON, Sphetim HASANI (BOS) (46' ARI
da Silva Ferreira (BRA), CÉSAR Santin (BRA). (Coach: Nanne BERGSTRAND).
Goals: FC Twente Enschede: 1-0 Sharbel TOUMA (49'), 2-1 Sharbel TOUMA (73'), 3-1
Sharbel TOUMA (79').
Kalmar FF: 1-1 Lasse JOHANSSON (67').
Referee: Alfonso PÉREZ BURRULL (ESP)

22-07-2006   Åråsen Stadion, Lillestrøm: Lillestrøm SK – Newcastle United FC   0-3 (0-2)
Lillestrøm SK: Otto FREDRIKSON (FIN), Shane STEFANUTTO (AUS), Frode KIPPE, Anders RAMBEKK, Espen SØGÅRD (46' Pål STRAND), Johan Petter WINSNES, Robert KOREN (SLO), Bjørn Helge RIISE, Khaled MOUELHI (TUN) (46' Kasey WEHRMAN (AUS)), Michael MIFSUD (MLT) (60' Arild SUNDGOT), Olivier OCCEAN (CAN). (Coach: Uwe RÖSLER (GER)).
Newcastle United FC: Shay GIVEN (IRL), Stephen CARR (IRL), Charles N'ZOGBIA (FRA) (86' Matthew PATTISON (RSA)), Titus BRAMBLE, Steven TAYLOR, Celestine BABAYARO (NGR) (69' Craig MOORE (AUS)), James MILNER, Nolberto SOLANO Todco (PER), Emre BELÖZOGLU (TUR), Scott PARKER (YC60), Foluwashola AMEOBI (NGR) (79' Nicky BUTT). (Coach: Glenn Victor ROEDER).
Goals: Newcastle United FC: 0-1 Foluwashola AMEOBI (29'), 0-2 Foluwashola AMEOBI (36'), 0-3 Emre BELÖZOGLU (90').
Referee: Stanislav SUHKINA (RUS)   Attendance: 8.742

22-07-2006   Easter Road, Edinburgh: Hibernian FC Edinburgh – Odense BK   2-1 (0-0)
Hibernian FC Edinburgh: Simon BROWN (ENG), Steven WHITTAKER, David MURPHY (ENG), Robert Marc JONES (ENG), Chris HOGG (ENG), Michael STEWART (66' Dean SHIELS (NIR) (YC82)), Kevin THOMSON (YC18), Stephen GLASS (YC55), Ivan SPROULE (NIR) (70' Lewis STEVENSON (YC88)), Chris KILLEN (NZL) (32' Paul DALGLISH (YC71)), Abdessalam BENJELLOUN (MAR). (Coach: Anthony Mark (Tony) MOWBRAY (ENG)).
Odense BK: Arek ONYSZKO (POL), Jan Tore OPHAUG (NOR), Ulrik LAURSEN, Alexander AAS, Chris SØRENSEN, Morten FEVANG (NOR), Esben HANSEN (YC53), Martin BORRE, Jonas BORRING, Mads TIMM (74' Michael LARSEN), Tobias GRAHN (SWE) (82' Magne STURØD (NOR)). (Coach: Bruce David RIOCH (ENG)).
Goals: Hibernian FC Edinburgh: 1-1 Robert Marc JONES (53'), 2-1 Paul DALGLISH (79').
Odense BK: 0-1 Tobias GRAHN (50').
Referee: Matteo TREFOLONI (ITA)   Attendance: 10.641

22-07-2006   Eduard Streltsov Stadion, Moskva: FK Moskva – Hertha BSC Berlin   0-2 (0-1)
FK Moskva: Yuriy ZHEVNOV (BLS), Dmitriy GODUNOK, Radu REBEJA (MOL) (67' Héctor Andrés BRACAMONTE (ARG)), Oleg KUZMIN, Isaac OKORONKWO (NGR), Jerry-Christian TCHUISSE (CMR) (46' Sergey SEMAK), Pyotr BYSTROV, Damian GORAWSKI (POL), Stanislav IVANOV (MOL), Roman ADAMOV, Dmitriy GOLUBOV (46' Dmitriy KIRICHENKO). (Coach: Leonid Viktorovich SLUTSKY).
Hertha BSC Berlin: Christian FIEDLER, Dick VAN BURIK (HOL), Sofian CHAHED, Josip SIMUNIC (CRO), Malik FATHI, Yildiray BASTÜRK (TUR) (90' Christopher SAMBA Veijeany (CGO)), Pál DÁRDAI (HUN), Andreas SCHMIDT, Andreas NEUENDORF (79' Chinedu EDE), Marko PANTELIC (SRB), Ellery CAIRO (HOL) (88' Patrick EBERT). (Coach: Falko GÖTZ).
Goals: Hertha BSC Berlin: 0-1 Marko PANTELIC (25'), 0-2 Yildiray BASTÜRK (88').
Referee: Bülent DEMIRLEK (TUR)   Attendance: 3.500

22-07-2006   Kayseri Atatürk Stadyumu, Kayseri:
Kayserispor Kulübü – AE Larissa   2-0 (1-0)
Kayserispor Kulübü: Dimitar Ivanov IVANKOV (BUL), Delio César TOLEDO (PAR),
Tayfun CORA (YC34) (62' Rashad F.SADIKHOV (AZE)), Bülent BÖLÜKBASI (YC47) (84'
Kamber ARSLAN), Leonardo Andres IGLESIAS (ARG), Ragip BASDAG, Samuel
JOHNSON (GHA), Aydin TOSCALI, Mehmet TOPUZ, Fatih CEYLAN, Gökhan ÜNAL
(90'+1' Muhammet Hanifi AKAGÜNDÜZ (AUT)). (Coach: Ertugrul SAGLAM).
AE Larissa: Spyridon CHRISTOPOULOS, Nikolaos DABIZAS, Spiros VALLAS, Panagiotis
KATSIAROS, Dimitrios GIKAS (72' Zisis ZIAGKAS), Georgios GALITSIOS (46' Panagiotis
BACHRAMIS), Angelos DIGKOZIS, Nektarios ALEXANDROU (CYP) (YC23) (55' Alexis
GAVRILOPOULOS), Christos KALANTZIS, Efstathios ALONEFTIS (CYP), Ioannis
CHLOROS. (Coach: Georgios DONIS).
Goals: Kayserispor Kulübü: 1-0 Gökhan ÜNAL (32'), 2-0 Gökhan ÜNAL (82').
Referee: Thomas EINWALLER (AUT)

22-07-2006   Meteor Stadium, Dnipropetrovsk:
FC Dnipro Dnipropetrovsk – Olympique de Marseille   2-2 (0-0)
FC Dnipro Dnipropetrovsk: Vyacheslav KERNOZENKO, Olexandr GRYTSAY, Volodymyr
YEZERSKIY (46' Andriy RUSOL), Olexandr RADCHENKO, Serhiy MATIUKHIN, Bohdan
SHERSHUN, Oleh SHELAYEV, Serhiy NAZARENKO (YC45), Sergei KORNILENKO
(BLS) (81' Konstyantyn BALABANOV), Ruslan KOSTYSHIN (70' Konstyantyn
KRAVCHENKO), Denis GLAVINA (CRO). (Coach: Oleh Valeriyovych PROTASOV).
Olympique de Marseille: Cédric CARRASSO, Ronald ZUBAR (YC15), Taye Ismaila TAIWO
(NGR), Habib BEYE (SEN), Bostjan CESAR (SLO), Sabri LAMOUCHI, Lorik CANA (ALB)
(YC49), Samir NASRI (62' Wilson ORUMA (NGR)), Toifilou MAOULIDA, Mamadou
NIANG (SEN) (88' Thomas DERUDA), Mickaël PAGIS (83' Habib BAMOGO). (Coach:
Albert EMON).
Goals: FC Dnipro Dnipropetrovsk: 1-2 Serhiy NAZARENKO (78'), 2-2 Andriy RUSOL (87').
Olympique de Marseille: 0-1 Mamadou NIANG (72'), 0-2 Wilson ORUMA (76').
Referee: Howard WEBB (ENG)   Attendance: 19.000

22-07-2006   Dasáki, Áchnas: Ethnikós Áchnas FC – Maccabi Petach Tikva FC   2-3 (0-2)
Ethnikós Áchnas FC: Milos ADAMOVIC (SRB), Christos SHAILIS, Dimitris SIMOU
(YC21), Christos KOTSONIS (YC30), Zoran STJEPANOVIC (SRB), Lars SCHLICHTING
(GER), Christos POYIATZIS, Christos PASHIALIS, Gábor VINCZE (HUN) (YC59), Marko
KMETEC (SLO) (YC65), Levan KEBADZE (GEO). (Coach: Toza SAPURIC (MCD)). (Used
sub: Milan BELIC (SRB)).
Maccabi Petach Tikva FC: Ohad COHEN, Ismael AMAR, Murad MAGOMEDOV, Kobi
GANON, Nitzan DAMARI, Emmanuel EBIEDE (NGR), André JEFISLEY Caldeira (BRA)
(80' Herve Patrick SUFFO Kenge (CMR) (YC90)), Shlomo TZEMAH, Opir AZU (YC32),
Omer GOLAN (60' Naor PESER), Rubel SARSOUR (YC17). (Coach: Guy LUZON).
Goals: Ethnikós Áchnas FC: 1-2 Milan BELIC (72'), 2-2 Christos POYIATZIS (80').
Maccabi Petach Tikva FC: 0-1 Rubel SARSOUR (30'), 0-2 André JEFISLEY Caldeira (43'),
2-3 Herve Patrick SUFFO Kenge (86').
Referee: Duarte Nuno PEREIRA GOMES (POR)

22-07-2006   Stadionul Farul, Constanta: FC Farul Constanta – AJ Auxerre 1-0 (0-0)
FC Farul Constanta: Adrian VLAS, Stefanel Razvan FARMACHE, Cristian SCHIOPU,
Decebal Virgil GHEARA, Vasile PACURANU (72' Ionut LARIE), Laurentiu FLOREA,
Florin LUNGU (YC43) (79' Marius SOARE), Iulian Catalin APOSTOL (67' Tibor Florian
MOLDOVAN), Dinu Marius TODORAN, Armel Disney MAMOUNA-OSSILA, Mihai
GURITA. (Coach: Momcilo "Moca" VUKOTIC (SRB)).
AJ Auxerre: Fabien COOL, Johan RADET, Younes KABOUL, Bakari SAGNA, Frédéric
THOMAS, Benoît CHEYROU (YC52), Thomas KAHLENBERG (DEN) (82' Jean-Sébastien
JAURÈS), Jean-Pascal MIGNOT, Daniel George NICULAE (ROM) (46' Alain TRAORÉ
(BKF)), Ireneusz JELEN (POL), Luigi PIERONI (BEL) (46' Lionel MATHIS (YC72)).
Goal: FC Farul Constanta: 1-0 Dinu Marius TODORAN (46' penalty). (Coach: Jean
FERNANDEZ).
Referee: Bruno Miguel DUARTE PAIXÃO (POR)   Attendance: 5.000

22-07-2006   Sport Complex Sheriff, Tiraspol: FC Tiraspol – SV Ried 1-1 (0-1)
FC Tiraspol: Stanislav NAMASCO (YC66), Andrey NOVICOV (RC90+2), Kennedy
Chimezie CHINWO (NGR) (YC20), Kyrylo SYDORENKO (UKR), Victor
GOLOVATENCO, Andrey SECRIERU, Evgheni GORODETCHIL (84' Andrey
PORFIREANU), Serghei NAMASCO (83' Nicolai RUDAC), Igor PICUSCIAC (87' Vadim
CEMIRTAN), Serghei ALEXEEV, Oleksandr BYCHKOV (UKR). (Coach: Yuriy Petrovych
KULISH (UKR)).
SV Ried: Hans-Peter BERGER, Christoph JANK (YC50), Oliver GLASNER, Michael
MEHLEM, Thomas Günther EDER, Sebastian MARTÍNEZ (82' Ronald BRUNMAYR),
Jung-Won SEO (KOR) (68' Dubravko TESEVIC), Michael ANGERSCHMID (YC18) (54'
Markus BERGER), Ewald BRENNER, Patrick WOLF, Jovan DAMJANOVIC (SRB). (Coach:
Helmut KRAFT).
Goals: FC Tiraspol: 1-1 Nicolai RUDAC (83').
SV Reid: 0-1 Jovan DAMJANOVIC (30').
Referee: Christoforos ZOGRAFOS (GRE)   Attendance: 3.000

22-07-2006   Jules Ottenstadion, Gentbrugge: KAA Gent – Grasshopper-Club 1-1 (0-0)
KAA Gent: Frédéric HERPOEL, Dario SMOJE (CRO), Nicolas LOMBAERTS, Steve
LAYBUTT (AUS), Nebojsa PAVLOVIC (SRB), Randall AZOFEIFA Corrales (CRC) (72'
Bryan RUIZ González (CRC)), Christophe GRÉGOIRE (70' Guillaume GILLET), Davy DE
BEULE (88' Nfor Ernest WEBNJE (CMR)), Marcin ZEWLAKOW (POL), Sandy
MARTENS, Dominic FOLEY (IRL). (Coach: Georges LEEKENS).
Grasshopper-Club: Fabio COLTORTI (YC90+3), Matthias LANGKAMP (GER), Robson
Pena de Oliveira "WELLINGTON" (BRA), Kim JAGGY, Scott SUTTER, Gerardo SEOANE
(YC23) (43' Veroljub SALATIC (SRB)), Michel RENGGLI, ANTONIO Carlos DOS
SANTOS (BRA), Diego LEÓN Ayarza (ESP) (66' Roland SCHWEGLER), BISCOTTE
MBALA Mbuta (DRC), Sreto RISTIC (SRB) (46' EDUARDO Ribeiro (BRA) (YC90+3)).
(Coach: Krassimir Guenchev BALAKOV).
Goals: KAA Gent: 1-1 Dominic FOLEY (67').
Grasshopper-Club: 0-1 Dario SMOJE (64' own goal).
Referee: Daniel STALHAMMAR (SWE)   Attendance: 4.675

22-07-2006   Ljudski vrt Stadium, Maribor: NK Maribor – Villarreal CF   1-1 (0-0)
NK Maribor: Marko RANILOVIC, Fabijan CIPOT, Zikica VUKSANOVIC, Vladislav
LUNGU (MOL), Milan RAKIC (80' Martin PREGELJ (YC90+1)), David TOMAZIC-
SERUGA (46' Zajko ZEBA (BOS)), Marko POKLEKA (YC52), Marko POPOVIC (SRB),
Rene MIHELIC (70' Armel MUJKANOVIC (YC77)), Dragan JELIC, Gorazd ZAJC (YC85).
(Coach: Marijan PUSNIK).
Villarreal CF: Mario Sebastián VIERA (URU), Enrique "QUIQUE" ÁLVAREZ Sanjuan,
Javier Rodriguez "JAVI" VENTA (68' MARCOS GARCÍA Barreño), JUAN Manuel PEÑA
Montaño (BOL), Carlos ALCÁNTARA Cuevas (68' Gonzalo Javier RODRÍGUEZ (ARG)
(RC88)), José Joaquim Moreno Verdu "JOSICO", Robert PIRÈS (FRA), Ruben Garcia
Calmache "CANI" (YC52) (83' JONATHAN Pereira Rodríguez), Alessio TACCHINARDI
(ITA) (YC,YC80), Diego Martín FORLÁN Corazo (URU) (YC,YC90+1), Nihat KAHVECI
(TUR). (Coach: Manuel Luis PELLEGRINI Ripamonti (CHI)).
Goals: NK Maribor: 1-1 Gorazd ZAJC (89').
Villarreal CF: 0-1 Nihat KAHVECI (85').
Referee: Carlo BERTOLINI (SUI)   Attendance: 9.000

**AJ Auxerre, Ethnikós Áchnas FC, Grasshopper-Club, Hertha BSC Berlin, Kayserispor
Kulübü, NK Maribor, Newcastle United FC, Odense BK, Olympique de Marseille, SV
Ried and FC Twente Enschede all qualified for the UEFA Cup competition.**

184

2007

23-06-2007   Stadion Centralny, Kostanay: FK Tobol Kostanay – FC Zestaponi 3-0 (0-0)
FK Tobol Kostanay: Kirill PRYADKIN, Farkhadbek IRISMETOV, Daniyar MUKANOV (88'
Sergey OSTAPENKO), Stanimir DIMITROV (BUL), Kairat NURDAULETOV, Nurbol
ZHUMASKALIEV, Andrey KHARABARA (RUS) (YC65) (82' Yevgeniy MESHKOV),
Sergey SKORIKH, Igor YURIN (53' Azat NURGALIEV), Ruslan BALTIEV, Ulugbek
BAKAEV (UZB). (Coach: Dmitriy Alekseevich OGAI).
FC Zestaponi: Grigol CHANTURIA, Roin ONIANI (YC66), Sevasti TODUA, EDSON
Oliveira dos SANTOS (BRA) (35' Kakhaber CHKHETIANI), Edik SADJAIA (YC17), Gilvan
Gomes Vieira "ESQUERDINHA" (BRA) (70' Amiran SANAIA), JONATAS Oliveira
TORRES (BRA) (46' Nikoloz KVAKHVADZE), Paul KESSANY (GAB), Gaga
CHKHETIANI, Gogi PIPIA, Giorgi CHELIDZE. (Coach: Teimuraz MAKHARADZE).
Goals: FK Tobol Kostanay: 1-0 Nurbol ZHUMASKALIEV (61'), 2-0 Ruslan BALTIEV (63'),
3-0 Ulugbek BAKAEV (73').
Referee: Matej JUG (SLO)   Attendance: 6.500

23-06-2007   Windsor Park, Belfast: Cliftonville FC – FC Dinaburg Daugavpils 1-1 (1-1)
Cliftonville FC: John CONNOLLY, Ronan SCANNELL (YC44), David McALINDEN
(YC72) (87' Vincent SWEENEY (IRL)), Declan O'HARA, Liam FLEMING, Francis
MURPHY (82' Sean FRIARS (IRL)), Kieran O'CONNOR, George McMULLAN (YC60)
(70' Gary KENNEDY), Barry JOHNSTON (YC28), Mark HOLLAND, Chris SCANNELL
(YC47). (Coach: Samuel Eddie PATTERSON).
FC Dinaburg Daugavpils: Vadims FJODOROVS (YC79), Ivan RODIN (RUS) (67' Pavel
RYZHEVSKI (BLS)), Vadims LOGINS, Ritus KRJAUKLIS, Andrejs ZUROMSKIS (37'
Sergejs VALUSKINS), Artem YASHKIN (UKR), Zaur KAZIEV (RUS) (81' Mihail POPOV
(RUS) (YC86)), Pavel KOLCOVS (YC31), Aleksei KOSTENKO (RUS) (RC60), Dmitrijs
CUGUNOVS, Jurijs SOKOLOVS. (Coach: Tamaz PERTIA (GEO)).
Goals: Cliftonville FC: 1-1 Kieran O'CONNOR (40').
FC Dinaburg Daugavpils: 0-1 Jurijs SOKOLOVS (20').
Referee: Aleksandar STAVREV (MCD)

23-06-2007   Tofiq Bahramov Stadium, Baku: FK Baki – FC Dacia Chisinau 1-1 (0-1)
FK Baki: Khalidu SISSOKHO (SEN), Rafael AMIRBEKOV, Ilkhar ABDURAKHMANOV
(YC10), Vugar GULIYEV, Asif ABBASOV, Amiran Omar MUJIRI (GEO) (YC77), Tarlan
KHALILOV (46' Jamshid MAHARRAMOV), Romal HUSEYNOV, Elnur ABDULLAYEV
(89' Emin AMIRASLANOV), Samir MUSAEV (61' Farid GULIYEV), Ahmad TIJANI
(NIG). (Coach: Boyukaga HAJIYEV).
FC Dacia Chisinau: Mihail MORARU, Vitalie MARDARI, Nicolai MINCEV, Vadim
BOLOHAN, Maxim ANDRONIC, Ghenadie PUSCA, Valeriu ONILA, Ghenadie ORBU (87'
Dumitru GUSILA), Alexandru ONICA (65' Dumitru Alin LIPA), Andrei MARTIN (73'
Eugeniu BOICENCO), Iurie SOIMU. (Coach: Emilian (Emil) CARAS).
Goals: FK Baki: 1-1 Maxim ANDRONIC (80' *own goal*).
FC Dacia Chisinau: 0-1 Valeriu ONILA (45').
Referee: Ferenc BEDE (HUN)   Attendance: 3.000

23-06-2007   Råsunda Fotbollstadion, Solna: Hammarby IF – KÍ Klaksvik 1-0 (1-0)
Hammarby IF: Erland HELLSTRÖM, David JOHANSSON, José Monteiro de MACEDO,
Gunnar Thor GUNNARSSON (ISL) (55' Emil JOHANSSON), Christian TRAORÉ (DEN),
Louay CHANKO, Sebastián EGUREN (URU), Haris LAITINEN, Charlie DAVIES (USA),
Heidar Geir JULIUSSON (ISL) (57' Erkan ZENGIN), Nkosinathi "Toni" NHLEKO (RSA)
(75' Paulo Roberto Chamon de Castilho "PAULINHO GUARÁ" (BRA)). (Coach: Tony
GUSTAVSSON).
KÍ Klaksvik: Meinhardt JOENSEN, Sigmund JACOBSEN, Jan ANDREASEN, Kristian á
LAKJUNI (78' John HAMMER), Harley BERTHOLDSEN, Högni MADSEN, Símun
JOENSEN, Gunnar G.NIELSEN (ARG) (83' Erling FLES), Hedin á LAKJUNI, Stefan
KALSØ (46' Kaj ENNIGARD), Paul CLAPSON (ENG). (Coach: Eydun KLAKSTEIN).
Goal: Hammarby IF: 1-0 Charlie DAVIES (3').
Referee: Valery VIALICHKA (BLS)   Attendance: 1.633

23-06-2007   Dasáki, Áchnas: Ethnikós Áchnas FC – FK Makedonija Skopje 1-0 (1-0)
Ethnikós Áchnas FC: Milos ADAMOVIC (SRB), Christos SHAILIS (YC62), Goran
GRKINIC (SRB), Christos KOTSONIS (YC34), Zoran STJEPANOVIC (SRB) (72' Lucas
Ariel COMINELLI (ARG)), Lars SCHLICHTING (GER), Christos POYIATZIS, Christofis
PASHIALIS, Panayiotis EGOMITIS (75' Branislav JOVANOVIC (SRB)), Patrik IPAVEC
(SLO), Damir SULJANOVIC (BOS) (60' George GEBRO (LBR)). (Coach: Toza SAPURIC
(MCD)).
FK Makedonija Skopje: Ljupco KOLEV, Daniel MOJSOV, Borce RISTOVSKI (32' Blagoja
LJANCEVSKI), Vladimir DESPOTOVSKI (YC66), Milan KRIVOKAPIC (MNE), Toni
BRNJACEVSKI (72' Dusan SIMOVSKI), Vladan MILOSAVLJEVIC (SRB) (YC26), Daniel
JOVANOVSKI, Vasko MITREV (YC39), Miroslav MILOSEVIC (SRB), Aleksandar
STOJANOVSKI (83' Adis JAHOVIK). (Coach: Milan KRIVOKAPIC (SRB)).
Goal: Ethnikós Áchnas FC: 1-0 Christos POYIATZIS (6' penalty).
Referee: Mark Steven WHITBY (WAL)

23-06-2007   Estadi Comunal d'Andorra la Vella, Andorra la Vella:
                UE Sant Julià – FK Slavija Sarajevo 2-3 (0-1)
UE Sant Julià: Daniel TREMONTI (CHI), Walter WAGNER (ARG), Diego Matias ABDIAN
Massimino (ARG), Sebastian VARELA (URU) (YC25), Yael FONTAN (ESP), Christian
XINOS (ARG) (85' Marc JOVAL), Laureano MIRAGLIA Pacha (ARG) (66' Emanuel
GOLDSCHMIDT (ARG)), Carlos PEPPE Guerra (URU), Mario SPANO (ARG), Alejandro
Fabián ROMERO Recette (ARG) (81' Ariel LOBO (ARG)), Luis Maria de VERIZ Lozada
(ARG). (Coach: Patricio GONZÁLEZ Fernández).
FK Slavija Sarajevo: Ratko DUJKOVIC, Zoran BELOSEVIC (SRB), Bojan REGOJE, Dragan
BJELICA, Ivan STANKOVIC (SRB), Goran SIMIC (84' Novo PAPAZ), Sretko
VUKSANOVIC (SRB), Vlastimir JOVANOVIC (78' Nemanja SESLIJA (YC89)), Srdjan
STANIC (66' Bojan JAMINA), Milan MUMINOVIC (YC45+2), Darko SPALEVIC (SRB).
(Coach: Zoran ERBEZ).
Goals: UE Sant Julià: 1-2 Carlos PEPPE Guerra (64'), 2-2 Luis Maria de VERIZ Lozada (67').
FK Slavija Sarajevo: 0-1 Sebastian VARELA (23' *own goal*), 0-2 Vlastimir JOVANOVIC
(62'), 2-3 Darko SPALEVIC (87').
Referee: Christopher LAUTIER (MLT)

23-06-2007   Stroitel Stadion,Soligorsk:
FC Shakhter Soligorsk – FC Ararat Yerevan   4-1 (1-1)
FC Shakhter Soligorsk: Mikhail BARANOVSKIY (RUS), Aleksandr YUREVICH, Vadim
LASOVSKIY, Aleksandr KHRAPKOVSKIY, Pavel Sergeevich PLASKONNY, Maksim
GUKAYLO, Aleksandr NOVIK (72' Siarhei KOVALCHUK), Alexei RIOS (56' Mikhail
MARTINOVICH), Aleksandr BYCHENOK (56' Artem GONCHARIK), Aleksandr
KLIMENKO (YC20), Sergei NIKIFORENKO. (Coach: Yuri Vasilevich VERGEICHIK).
FC Ararat Yerevan: Nikolay SARGSYAN, Hovhannes HARUTYUNYAN, Vahagn
MINASYAN, Marcos Pineiro PIZZELI (BRA), Hrayr MKOYAN (YC22), Artur
MINASYAN, Artur VOSKANYAN, Gagik SIMONYAN (77' Sargis MOVSISYAN), Artur
PETROSYAN, RENATO Gabriel de Melo (BRA), Gevorg NRANYAN (62' Harutyun
HOVHANNISYAN). (Coach: Varuzhan SUKIASYAN).
Goals: FC Shakhter Soligorsk: 1-0 Alexei RIOS (22'), 2-1 Maksim GUKAYLO (58'), 3-1
Aleksandr KLIMENKO (69'), 4-1 Sergei NIKIFORENKO (80').
FC Ararat Yerevan: 1-1 Marcos Pineiro PIZZELI (41').
Referee: Akmalkhan KHOLMATOV (KAZ)   Attendance: 2.500

23-06-2007   Stadion u Kranjcevicevoj ulici, Zagreb:
NK Zagreb – KS Vllaznia Shkodër   2-1 (1-1)
NK Zagreb: Goran BASIC, Tomislav LABUDOVIC, Safet NADAREVIC (BOS), Mario
CUTURA (YC23), Ivan LAJTMAN (YC43) (87' Josip JURENDIC), Miroslav PEJIC, Senijad
IBRICIC (BOS) (59' Marko GRGIC (BOS)), Krunoslav LOVREK (RC88), Ivan PARLOV
(YC48), Mensur MUJDZA, Mario MANDZUKIC. (Coach: Miroslav "Ciro" BLAZEVIC).
KS Vllaznia Shkodër: Armir GRIMA, Admir TELI, Safet OSJA, Franc AHI (YC70,YC73),
Suad LICI, Uliks KOTRRI, Albert KAÇI (75' Erjon HOTI), Gilman LIKA (YC50), Klevis
DALIPI (71' Nevian CANI), Arlind NORRA (90'+2' Arsid TAFILI), Ghislain Rostand SIMO
TAVIKO (CMR). (Coach: Mirel JOSA).
Goals: NK Zagreb: 1-1 Safet NADAREVIC (19'), 2-1 Tomislav LABUDOVIC (63').
KS Vllaznia Shkodër: 0-1 Arlind NORRA (3').
Referee: Kuddusi MÜFTÜOGLU (TUR)

23-06-2007   Stade de la Frontière, Esch-sur-Alzette:
FC Differdange 03 – SK Slovan Bratislava   0-2 (0-1)
FC Differdange 03: Yannick SCHLENTZ, Jean WAGNER, André Filipe RODRIGUES de
ALMEIDA, Ante BUKVIC (CRO), Ibrahim DIOP (FRA), Karim GROUNE (FRA) (70' Kim
KINTZIGER), Paolo AMODIO (80' PEDRO Daneil Ribeiro ALVES), Phillipe Michel
LEBRESNE (FRA) (80' Bruno RIBEIRO), Dario SORAIRE (ARG), Jérémie PEIFFER, Pierre
Olivier PISKOR (FRA) (YC90+3). (Coach: Maurice SPITONI).
SK Slovan Bratislava: Daniel KISS, Michal HANEK, Peter STRUHAR, Aziz IBRAHIMOV
(UZB), Samuel SLOVAK, Michal KUBALA, Jaroslav CHLEBEK (YC80), Daniel KOSMEL,
Ottó SZABÓ, Miroslav POLIACEK (58' Pavol SEDLÁK), Pavol MASARYK (86' Lubomir
MESZAROS). (Coach: Boris KITKA).
Goals: SK Slovan Bratislava: 0-1 Miroslav POLIACEK (32'), 0-2 Pavol SEDLÁK (86').
Referee: Drazenko KOVACIC (CRO)   Attendance: 637

23-06-2007   Laugardalsvöllur, Reykjavik: Valur FC – Cork City FC   0-2 (0-1)
Valur FC: Kjartan STURLUSON, Birkir Már SÆVARSSON, Atli Sveinn THÓRARINSSON,
Barry SMITH (SCO), René Skovgaard CARLSEN (DEN), Baldur Ingimar
ADALSTEINSSON, Baldur BETT, Pálmi Rafn PÁLMASON (77' Sigurbjörn Örn
HREIDARSSON), Daníel HJALTASON (64' Gunnar EINARSSON), Dennis Bo
MORTENSEN (DEN), Helgi SIGURDSSON (77' Gudmundur BENEDIKTSSON). (Coach:
Willum Thór THÓRSSON).
Cork City FC: Michael DEVINE, Neal HORGAN, Daniel MURRAY, Sean KELLY (90'+1'
Denis BEHAN), Colin T.O'BRIEN, Joe GAMBLE (YC56), Roy O'DONOVAN, Billy
WOODS, Darren MURPHY (78' Cillian LORDAN), Liam KEARNEY, John O'FLYNN (74'
Admir SOFTIC (BOS)). (Coach: Damien John RICHARDSON).
Goals: Cork City FC: 0-1 Colin T.O'BRIEN (7'), 0-2 Liam KEARNEY (66').
Referee: Aleksandr GONCHAR (RUS)

24-06-2007   Hibernians Stadium, Paola: Birkirkara FC – NK Maribor   0-3 (0-1)
Birkirkara FC: Bernard PARIS, Angelo "Lino" GALEA, Roderick SAMMUT (63' Martin
ANASTASI), Kenneth SCICLUNA, Thomas PARIS (82' Andrew SPITERI), Roderick
BRIFFA, Jonathan HOLLAND (YC31), Joseph ZERAFA (71' Ryan MIFSUD), George
MALLIA, Michael GALEA, Alan TABONE. (Coach: John BUTTIGIEG).
NK Maribor: Marko PRIDIGAR, Fabijan CIPOT, Andrej PECNIK, Miral SAMARDZIC,
Vladislav LUNGU (MOL), Martin PREGELJ (YC1) (41' Dejan MEZGA (CRO)), Dimitar
Ivanov MAKRIEV (BUL) (66' Abdoulaye DIARRA (CIV)), David TOMAZIC-SERUGA,
Marko POPOVIC (SRB), Rene MIHELIC (58' Arnel MUJKANOVIC), Damir PEKIC.
(Coach: Marijan PUSNIK).
Goals: NK Maribor: 0-1 Dimitar Ivanov MAKRIEV (40'), 0-2 Dimitar Ivanov MAKRIEV
(47'), 0-3 Damir PEKIC (87').
Referee: Marcin BORSKI (POL)

24-06-2007   Stadionul Gloria, Bistrita:
              FC Gloria Bistrita – OFK Grbalj Radanovici   2-1 (1-1)
FC Gloria Bistrita: Ciprian Anton TATARUSANU, Razvan DAMIAN, Laur Marian
ASTILEAN, Dorin TOMA, László SEPSI, Enache CÂJU, Ion DUMITRA, Mirel Sorin
SOARE (46' Levente Joszef PERES), Razvan DOBRE (71' Voicu Razvan FLOREA), Catalin
Valentin BUCUR (YC20) (46' Flavius BAD), Dorel ZAHARIA. (Coach: Ioan Ovidiu
SABAU).
OFK Grbalj Radanovici: Srdan Komnen KLJAJEVIC (SRB), Dalibor RODIC, Luka
PEJOVIC, Milan IVANOVIC (80' Sasa POPOVIC), Dusan SADZAKOV, Goran GRUJIC
(YC27), Sasa RADENOVIC (YC22), Branimir IVANISEVIC (SRB) (YC31) (85' Predrag
VIDEKANIC (YC89)), Milos DJALAC, Denis TONKOVIC (SRB) (61' Milan SRECO
(SRB)), Aleksandar NEDOVIC (SRB). (Coach: Dragan PICAN).
Goals: FC Gloria Bistrita: 1-0 Dorel ZAHARIA (3'), 2-1 Flavius BAD (88').
OFK Grbalj Radanovici: 1-1 Milos DJALAC (14').
Referee: Thomas VEJLGAARD (DEN)   Attendance: 1.000

24-06-2007   Pohjola Stadion, Vantaa: FC Honka Espoo – FC T.V.M.K. Tallinn   0-0
FC Honka Espoo: Tuomas PELTONEN, Ville JALASTO, Janne SAARINEN, Rami
HAKANPÄÄ (86' Joel PEROVUO), Hannu PATRONEN, John WECKSTRÖM (71' Nicholas
OTARU), Tero KOSKELA, Tuomo TURUNEN, Peke HUUHTANEN, Jami PUUSTINEN,
Roni POROKARA. (Coach: Mika "Bana" LEHKOSUO).
FC T.V.M.K. Tallinn: Vitali TELESH, Aleksandr VOLODIN, Tomas RIMAS (LIT), Jevgenijs
KACANOVS (LAT), Erko SAVIAUK, Eduard SARAJEV, Andrei BORISOV, Artur
OSSIPOV (90'+2' Nikolai MASITSEV), Viktors DOBRECOVS (LAT) (78' Sergei
ZENJOV), Oliver KONSA (82' Vladislav GUSSEV), Sergei TEREHHOV. (Coach: Vjatseslav
SMIRNOV).
Referee: Tsvetan GEORGIEV (BUL)

24-06-2007   Vetros Stadionas, Vilnius: FK Vetra Vilnius – Llanelli AFC   3-1 (0-0)
FK Vetra Vilnius: Stanislav KOZYREV (RUS), Marijan BUDIMIR (CRO), Andrey
USACHEV (RUS), Andrius SKERLA, Pedro Henrique BOTELHO (BRA), Bobi
BOZINOVSKI (MCD), Darvydas SERNAS (YC76,RC90+6), Mindaugas PANKA, Vitalijus
STANKEVICIUS (84' Denis TSELYUK (RUS)), SEVERINO Lima de Moura (BRA) (58'
Evaldas GRIGAITIS), Egidijus JUSKA (58' Dejan MILOSEVSKI (MCD)). (Coach: Vitas
JANCIAUSKAS).
Llanelli AFC: Ryan HARRISON, Antonio CORBISIERO, Craig WILLIAMS (65' Jordan
Nicholas FOLLOWS), Dale Richard GRIFFITHS (YC75), Gary LLOYD, Darren GRIFFITHS
(89' Daniel CLARE), David THOMAS (YC70), Sam Alexander SMALL, Andrew
MUMFORD, Matthew Ian THOMPSON, Rhys GRIFFITHS. (Coach: Peter NICHOLAS).
Goals: FK Vetra Vilnius: 1-1 Darvydas SERNAS (57'), 2-1 Vitalijus STANKEVICIUS (72'
penalty), 3-1 Dejan MILOSEVSKI (89').
Llanelli AFC: 0-1 Andrew MUMFORD (53').
Referee: Petur REINERT (FAR)

30-06-2007   Gradski Stadion, Skopje:
             FK Makedonija Skopje – Ethnikós Áchnas FC   2-0 (1-0)
FK Makedonija Skopje: Ljupco KOLEV (YC90), Daniel MOJSOV (YC80), Blagoja
LJANCEVSKI (60' Ismail ISMAILI), Vladimir DESPOTOVSKI (YC68), Milan
KRIVOKAPIC (MNE), Toni BRNJACEVSKI, Vladan MILOSAVLJEVIC (SRB), Daniel
JOVANOVSKI, Vasko MITREV (60' Borce RISTOVSKI), Miroslav MILOSEVIC (SRB),
Aleksandar STOJANOVSKI (82' Goran DIMOVSKI). (Coach: Radmilo IVANCEVIC
(SRB)).
Ethnikós Áchnas FC: Milos ADAMOVIC (SRB), Christos SHAILIS, Goran GRKINIC (SRB),
Daniel BLANCO (ESP) (63' NILTON Rogério Cardoso Fernandes (CVI)), Christos
KOTSONIS, Zoran STJEPANOVIC (SRB) (79' George GEBRO (LBR)), Lars
SCHLICHTING (GER) (YC72), Christos POYIATZIS, Christofis PASHIALIS, Patrik
IPAVEC (SLO), Damir SULJANOVIC (BOS). (Coach: Toza SAPURIC (MCD)).
Goals: FK Makedonija Skopje: 1-0 Aleksandar STOJANOVSKI (13'), 2-0 Aleksandar
STOJANOVSKI (65').
Referee: Meir LEVI (ISR)

30-06-2007   Ljudski vrt Stadium, Maribor: NK Maribor – Birkirkara FC   2-1 (0-0)
NK Maribor: Marko RANILOVIC, Fabijan CIPOT (21' Klemen MEDVED (YC65)), Andrej
PECNIK, Zikica VUKSANOVIC (YC29) (50' Matej VRACKO), Vladislav LUNGU (MOL)
(69' Abdoulaye DIARRA (CIV)), Dejan MEZGA (CRO), Dimitar Ivanov MAKRIEV (BUL),
David TOMAZIC-SERUGA, Marko POPOVIC (SRB), Rene MIHELIC, Damir PEKIC.
(Coach: Marijan PUSNIK).
Birkirkara FC: Bernard PARIS, Angelo "Lino" GALEA (86' Joseph ZERAFA), Roderick
SAMMUT, Kenneth SCICLUNA, Thomas PARIS (RC35), Roderick BRIFFA, Martin
ANASTASI, Jonathan HOLLAND (YC32), George MALLIA, Michael GALEA, Alan
TABONE (90' Ryan MIFSUD). (Coach: John BUTTIGIEG).
Goals: NK Maribor: 1-0 Dejan MEZGA (55'), 2-1 Matej VRACKO (78').
Birkirkara FC: 1-1 Michael GALEA (57').
Referee: Sokol JARECI (ALB)   Attendance: 1.000

30-06-2007   Mikheil Meskhi Stadium, Tbilisi:
                FC Zestaponi – FK Tobol Kostanay   2-0 (2-0)
FC Zestaponi: Grigol CHANTURIA, Roin ONIANI, EDSON Oliveira dos SANTOS (BRA),
Sevasti TODUA, Edik SADJAIA (YC55), Nikoloz KVAKHVADZE, Aleks BENASHVILI
(60' JONATAS Oliveira TORRES (BRA)), Paul KESSANY (GAB), Gilvan Gomes Vieira
"ESQUERDINHA" (BRA) (90' Shalva GONGADZE), Gogi PIPIA (YC80), Gaga
CHKHETIANI. (Coach: Teimuraz MAKHARADZE).
FK Tobol Kostanay: Kirill PRYADKIN (72' Alexandr PETUKHOV), Farkhadbek
IRISMETOV, Daniyar MUKANOV, Stanimir DIMITROV (BUL), Kairat NURDAULETOV,
Azat NURGALIEV (46' Igor YURIN), Nurbol ZHUMASKALIEV, Andrey KHARABARA
(RUS), Sergey SKORIKH, Ruslan BALTIEV (YC17), Sergey OSTAPENKO (YC55) (90'
Oleg LOTOV). (Coach: Dmitriy Alekseevich OGAI).
Goals: FC Zestaponi: 1-0 Edik SADJAIA (3'), 2-0 Gaga CHKHETIANI (37').
Referee: Vlado SVILOKOS (CRO)   Attendance: 1.200

30-06-2007   Svangaskard, Toftír: KÍ Klaksvík – Hammarby IF   1-2 (1-1)
KÍ Klaksvik: Meinhardt JOENSEN, Jan ANDREASEN, Kaj ENNIGARD, Harley
BERTHOLDSEN (70' John HAMMER), Högni MADSEN, Símun JOENSEN, Gunnar
G.NIELSEN (ARG), Kristian á LAKJUNI (70' Erling FLES), Hedin á LAKJUNI, Kristoffur
JAKOBSEN (78' Leon BJARTALID), Paul CLAPSON (ENG). (Coach: Eydun
KLAKSTEIN).
Hammarby IF: Erland HELLSTRÖM, José Monteiro de MACEDO, Isak DAHLIN, Gunnar
Thor GUNNARSSON (ISL), Joakim JENSEN, Fadi MALKE, Christian TRAORÉ (DEN),
Sebastián EGUREN (URU) (73' Nkosinathi "Toni" NHLEKO (RSA)), Haris LAITINEN,
Heidar Geir JULIUSSON (ISL), Paulo Roberto Chamon de Castilho "PAULINHO GUARÁ"
(BRA) (83' Alagie SOSSEH). (Coach: Tony GUSTAVSSON).
Goals: KÍ Klaksvík: 1-1 Kaj ENNIGARD (38').
Hammarby IF: 0-1 Kristoffur JAKOBSEN (34' own goal), 1-2 Paulo Roberto Chamon de
Castilho "PAULINHO GUARÁ" (58' penalty).
Referee: Audrius ZUTA (LIT)   Attendance: 690

30-06-2007   Stadion Pod Goricom, Podgorica:
OFK Grbalj Radanovici – FC Gloria Bistrita   1-1 (1-1)
OFK Grbalj Radanovici: Srdan Komnen KLJAJEVIC (SRB), Dusan SADZAKOV, Milan
IVANOVIC (81' Victor AGBOH (NIG)), Luka PEJOVIC, Bozo MILIC (65' Dragan
BOSKOVIC), Branimir IVANISEVIC (SRB), Aleksandar NEDOVIC (SRB) (YC62), Sasa
RADENOVIC, Dalibor RODIC (76' Dusan IVANOVIC), Goran GRUJIC, Milos DJALAC.
(Coach: Dragan PICAN).
FC Gloria Bistrita: Ciprian Anton TATARUSANU, Octavian ABRUDAN, Vasile Mircea
RUS, László SEPSI, Dorin TOMA (YC81), Cristian Ambrozie COROIAN, Adrian NALATI,
Ion DUMITRA (YC69), Cosmin TILINCA (82' Luvius Marius DEMIAN), Dorel ZAHARIA
(90' Flavius BAD), Razvan DOBRE. (Coach: Ioan Ovidiu SABAU).
Goals: OFK Grbalj Radanovici: 1-1 Milos DJALAC (44').
FC Gloria Bistrita: 0-1 Cristian Ambrozie COROIAN (42').
Referee: Peter VERVECKEN (BEL)

30-06-2007   Stadionul Zimbru, Chisinau: FC Dacia Chisinau – FK Baki   1-1 (1-0)
FC Dacia Chisinau: Mihail MORARU, Vitalie MARDARI, Nicolai MINCEV, Vadim
BOLOHAN, Maxim ANDRONIC, Ghenadie PUSCA (YC42) (81' Eugeniu BOICENCO),
Valeriu ONILA (66' Dumitru GUSILA), Ghenadie ORBU, Alexandru ONICA (66' Dumitru
Alin LIPA), Andrei MARTIN, Iurie SOIMU. (Coach: Emilian (Emil) CARAS).
FK Baki: Khalidu SISSOKHO (SEN), Rafael AMIRBEKOV, Vugar GULIYEV (YC10), Asif
ABBASOV, Bojan ILICH (SRB), Amiran Omar MUJIRI (GEO), Tarlan KHALILOV (46'
Asen NIKOLOV (BUL)), Romal HUSEYNOV, Elnur ABDULLAYEV, Farid GULIYEV (74'
Jamshid MAHARRAMOV (YC83)), Ahmad TIJANI (NIG) (46' Samir MUSAEV). (Coach:
Boyukaga HAJIYEV).
Goals: FC Dacia Chisinau: 1-0 Valeriu ONILA (7').
FK Baki: 1-1 Amiran Omar MUJIRI (65').
Referee: Leontios TRATTOU (CYP)   Attendance: 3.000

Penalties:	1 Dumitru Alin LIPA	* Asen NIKOLOV
	* Ghenadie ORBU	1 Samir MUSAEV
	* Vadim BOLOHAN	* Romal HUSEYNOV
	2 Dumitru GUSILA	* Rafael AMIRBEKOV
	3 Maxim ANDRONIC	

30-06-2007   Loro Boriçi Stadium, Shkodër: KS Vllaznia Shkodër – NK Zagreb   1-0 (1-0)
KS Vllaznia Shkodër: Armir GRIMA, Admir TELI, Safet OSJA, Suad LICI, Uliks KOTRRI
(YC48), Albert KAÇI (90'+2' Arsid TAFILI), Gjilman LIKA, Xhevahir SUKAJ (69' Vioresin
SINANI), Erjon HOTI, Arlind NORRA (89' Arsen BEQIRI), Ghislain Rostand SIMO
TAVIKO (CMR) (YC66). (Coach: Mirel JOSA).
NK Zagreb: Dragan STOKIC, Tomislav LABUDOVIC (80' Josip MIKULIC), Safet
NADAREVIC (BOS), Mario CUTURA, Ivan LAJTMAN, Miroslav PEJIC, Senijad IBRICIC
(BOS) (59' Marko GRGIC (BOS)), Ivan PARLOV, Mensur MUJDZA, Josip JURENDIC (85'
Marin ORSULIC), Mario MANDZUKIC. (Coach: Miroslav "Ciro" BLAZEVIC).
Goal: KS Vllaznia Shkodër: 1-0 Arlind NORRA (26').
Referee: Joseph R.ATTARD (MLT)

30-06-2007   Turners Cross, Cork: Cork City FC – Valur FC   0-1 (0-1)
Cork City FC: Michael DEVINE (YC66), Neal HORGAN, Daniel MURRAY, Sean KELLY
(YC82), Colin T.O'BRIEN (90' Admir SOFTIC (BOS)), Joe GAMBLE, Roy O'DONOVAN
(YC87), Billy WOODS, Darren MURPHY (82' Cillian LORDAN), Liam KEARNEY
(YC90+2), John O'FLYNN (73' Denis BEHAN). (Coach: Damien John RICHARDSON).
Valur FC: Kjartan STURLUSON, Barry SMITH (SCO), Atli Sveinn THÓRARINSSON,
Birkir Már SÆVARSSON (YC13), Baldur BETT, Hafthór Aegir VILHJÁLMSSON, Pálmi
Rafn PÁLMASON, Baldur Ingimar ADALSTEINSSON (85' Gudmundur Steinn
HAFSTEINSSON), René Skovgaard CARLSEN (DEN) (45'+1' Gunnar EINARSSON),
Gudmundur BENEDIKTSSON (85' Sigurbjörn Örn HREIDARSSON (RC89)), Helgi
SIGURDSSON. (Coach: Willum Thór THÓRSSON).
Goal: Valur FC: 0-1 Helgi SIGURDSSON (22').
Referee: Andriy SHANDOR (UKR)

30-06-2007   Asim Ferhatovic Hase Stadium, Sarajevo:
              FK Slavija Sarajevo – UE Sant Julià 3-2 (1-0)
FK Slavija Sarajevo: Ratko DUJKOVIC, Dragan BJELICA, Bojan REGOJE, Ivan
STANKOVIC (SRB), Bojan JAMINA (YC87) (88' Srdjan STANIC), Vlastimir
JOVANOVIC, Milan MUMINOVIC, Sretko VUKSANOVIC (SRB), Goran SIMIC (90'+4'
Nemanja SESLIJA), Ognjen DAMJANOVIC (84' Predrag PADAZ), Darko SPALEVIC
(SRB) (YC36). (Coach: Zoran ERBEZ).
UE Sant Julià: Daniel TREMONTI (CHI), Walter WAGNER (ARG), Diego Matias ABDIAN
Massimino (ARG) (69' Ariel LOBO (ARG)), Cristian Roig MAURI (YC77) (89' Rayco
RODRIGUEZ Barceló (ESP)), Sebastian VARELA (URU) (YC33), Yael FONTAN (ESP)
(YC42) (79' Luciano Javier NASTRI (ARG)), Christian XINOS (ARG), Carlos PEPPE Guerra
(URU), Mario SPANO (ARG) (YC63), Alejandro Fabián ROMERO Recette (ARG) (YC17),
Luis Maria de VERIZ Lozada (ARG). (Coach: Patricio GONZÁLEZ Fernández).
Goals: FK Slavija Sarajevo: 1-0 Bojan JAMINA (22'), 2-0 Yael FONTAN (65' own goal), 3-2
Sretko VUKSANOVIC (90'+4').
UE Sant Julià: 2-1 Sebastian VARELA (71'), 2-2 Alejandro Fabián ROMERO Recette (88'
penalty).
Referee: Lasha SILAGAVA (GEO)

30-06-2007   Tehelné Pole Stadium, Bratislava:
              SK Slovan Bratislava – FC Differdange 03   3-0 (1-0)
SK Slovan Bratislava: Daniel KISS, Michal HANEK, Peter STRUHAR, Pavol SEDLÁK,
Samuel SLOVAK, Jaroslav CHLEBEK (YC17) (64' Michal KUBALA), Daniel KOSMEL,
Ottó SZABÓ, Lubomir MESZAROS (74' Jakub SYLVESTR), Miroslav POLIACEK (58'
Michal BREZNANIK), Pavol MASARYK. (Coach: Boris KITKA).
FC Differdange 03: Yannick SCHLENTZ, Ante BUKVIC (CRO), Kim KINTZIGER (YC4),
Jean WAGNER, André Filipe RODRIGUES de ALMEIDA, Phillipe Michel LEBRESNE
(FRA), PEDRO Daneil Ribeiro ALVES (72' Mirko ALBANESE), Dario SORAIRE (ARG),
Ibrahim DIOP (FRA) (87' David CHALMANDRIER), Jérémie PEIFFER (76' Michel
KETTENMEYER), Pierre Olivier PISKOR (FRA) (YC6). (Coach: Maurice SPITONI).
Goals: SK Slovan Bratislava: 1-0 Lubomir MESZAROS (4'), 2-0 Pavol MASARYK (56'), 3-0
Jakub SYLVESTR (78').
Referee: Arman AMIRKCHANIAN (ARM)   Attendance: 2.400

01-07-2007   Republican Stadium, Yerevan:
FC Ararat Yerevan – FC Shakhter Soligorsk   2-0 (1-0)
FC Ararat Yerevan: Garnik HOVHANNISYAN, Hovhannes HARUTYUNYAN (72' Sargis
MOVSISYAN), Vahagn MINASYAN, Marcos Pineiro PIZZELI (BRA), Hrayr MKOYAN,
Artur MINASYAN, Artur VOSKANYAN, Gagik SIMONYAN, Artur PETROSYAN (85'
Mkhitar GRIGORYAN), RENATO Gabriel de Melo (BRA), Nshan ERZRUMYAN. (Coach:
Varuzhan SUKIASYAN).
FC Shakhter Soligorsk: Mikhail BARANOVSKIY (RUS), Aleksandr YUREVICH, Vadim
LASOVSKIY, Aleksandr KHRAPKOVSKIY, Pavel Sergeevich PLASKONNY, Andrey Ivan
LEONCHIK, Aleksandr NOVIK (50' Artem GONCHARIK, 88' Ishrev MAGOMEDOV
(RUS)), Siarhei KOVALCHUK, Aleksandr BYCHENOK (57' Maksim GUKAYLO (YC75)),
Aleksandr KLIMENKO (YC61,YC78), Sergei NIKIFORENKO. (Coach: Yuri Vasilevich
VERGEICHIK).
Goals: FC Ararat Yerevan: 1-0 Nshan ERZRUMYAN (32'), 2-0 Marcos Pineiro PIZZELI
(54').
Referee: Dragomir STANKOVIC (SRB)

01-07-2007   Celtnieks Stadion, Daugavpils:
FC Dinaburg Daugavpils – Cliftonville FC   0-1 (0-1)
FC Dinaburg Daugavpils: Jevgenijs LAIZANS, Ivan RODIN (RUS) (YC41) (46' Levan
KORGALIDZE (GEO), Vadims LOGINS (YC45+1), Ritus KRJAUKLIS, Mihail POPOV
(RUS) (32' Pavel RYZHEVSKI (BLS)), Artem YASHKIN (UKR) (YC73,YC90+4), Zaur
KAZIEV (RUS), Pavel KOLCOVS (YC57), Dmitrijs CUGUNOVS, Jurijs SOKOLOVS
(YC73), Sergejs VALUSKINS (60' Vladimir KULESHOV (RUS) (YC75)). (Coach: Tamaz
PERTIA (GEO)).
Cliftonville FC: John CONNOLLY, David McALINDEN, Declan O'HARA, Liam FLEMING
(YC37), Ronan SCANNELL, Kieran O'CONNOR, Sean FRIARS (IRL) (71' Barry
HOLLAND), Barry JOHNSTON (YC57), George McMULLAN (66' Gary KENNEDY), Mark
HOLLAND (83' Vincent SWEENEY (IRL) (YC90+1)), Chris SCANNELL. (Coach: Samuel
Eddie PATTERSON).
Goal: Cliftonville FC: 0-1 Mark HOLLAND (7').
Referee: Luc WILMES (LUX)   Attendance: 1.000

01-07-2007   A. Le Coq Arena, Tallinn: FC T.V.M.K. Tallinn – FC Honka Espoo   2-4 (0-1)
FC T.V.M.K. Tallinn: Vitali TELESH, Aleksandr VOLODIN, Tomas RIMAS (LIT), Jevgenijs
KACANOVS (LAT) (75' Vladislavs GABOVS (LAT)), Erko SAVIAUK, Eduard SARAJEV
(46' Sergei ZENJOV), Andrei BORISOV, Artur OSSIPOV, Markus JÜRGENSON (62'
Nikolai MASITSEV (YC90+2)), Oliver KONSA, Sergei TEREHHOV. (Coach: Vjatseslav
SMIRNOV).
FC Honka Espoo: Tuomas PELTONEN, Ville JALASTO, Janne SAARINEN (YC35), Rami
HAKANPÄÄ (YC16), Hannu PATRONEN, John WECKSTRÖM (64' Nicholas OTARU),
Tero KOSKELA (73' Joel PEROVUO), Tuomo TURUNEN, Peke HUUHTANEN (82'
Aleksandr KOKKO), Jami PUUSTINEN, Roni POROKARA. (Coach: Mika "Bana"
LEHKOSUO).
Goals: FC T.V.M.K. Tallinn: 1-1 Sergei TEREHHOV (68'), 2-4 Oliver KONSA (88').
FC Honka Espoo: 0-1 Peke HUUHTANEN (6'), 1-2 Jami PUUSTINEN (69'), 1-3 Rami
HAKANPÄÄ (74'), 1-4 Jami PUUSTINEN (84').
Referee: Rusmir MRKOVIC (BOS)

01-07-2007   Richmond Park, Carmarthen: Llanelli AFC – FK Vetra Vilnius 5-3 (2-3)
Llanelli AFC: Ryan HARRISON, Antonio CORBISIERO, Stuart JONES, Craig WILLIAMS,
Gary LLOYD (YC90+3), David THOMAS, Sam Alexander SMALL, Andrew MUMFORD
(68' Paul WANLESS (ENG)), Andrew LEGG, Rhys GRIFFITHS, Lloyd Jason BLACKMAN
(ENG) (75' Jordan Nicholas FOLLOWS). (Coach: Peter NICHOLAS).
FK Vetra Vilnius: Stanislav KOZYREV (RUS) (YC90), Marijan BUDIMIR (CRO), Andrey
USACHEV (RUS), Andrius SKERLA (YC90+2), Pedro Henrique BOTELHO (BRA), Dejan
MILOSEVSKI (MCD) (YC41) (57' Rolandas KARCEMARSKAS), Bobi BOZINOVSKI
(MCD), Mindaugas PANKA (77' Gediminas BUTRIMAVICIUS), Vitalijus
STANKEVICIUS, SEVERINO Lima de Moura (BRA), Egidijus JUSKA (72' Maksut AZIZI
(SLO) (YC89)). (Coach: Vitas JANCIAUSKAS).
Goals: Llanelli AFC: 1-1 Dejan MILOSEVSKI (17' own goal), 2-1 David THOMAS (38'), 3-3
Rhys GRIFFITHS (54'), 4-3 Rhys GRIFFITHS (88'), 5-3 Rhys GRIFFITHS (90'+3' penalty).
FK Vetra Vilnius: 0-1 SEVERINO Lima de Moura (4'), 2-2 Vitalijus STANKEVICIUS (43'
penalty), 2-3 Egidijus JUSKA (45'+3').
Referee: Magnus THORISSON (ISL)

SECOND ROUND

07-07-2007   Stadion Centralny, Kostanay:
                   FK Tobol Kostanay – FC Slovan Liberec 1-1 (1-1)
FK Tobol Kostanay: Alexandr PETUKHOV, Farkhadbek IRISMETOV, Daniyar MUKANOV
(YC46), Stanimir DIMITROV (BUL) (88' Oleg LOTOV), Kairat NURDAULETOV, Nurbol
ZHUMASKALIEV, Andrey KHARABARA (RUS), Sergey SKORIKH, Igor YURIN (68'
Azat NURGALIEV), Ruslan BALTIEV (YC28), Sergey OSTAPENKO (70' Didarklych
URAZOV (TMS)). (Coach: Dmitriy Alekseevich OGAI).
FC Slovan Liberec: Zbynek HAUZR, Milan MATULA, Jan POLÁK, Petr KRÁTKY, Jirí
BÍLEK, Jirí LISKA (YC52), Ivan HODÚR (SVK), Petr PAPOUSEK (62' HUDSON Fernando
Tobias de Carvalho (BRA)), Daniel PUDIL, Martin JIROUS (56' Tomas RADZINEVICIUS
(LIT)), Jan NEZMAR (84' Radek HOCHMEISTER). (Coach: Michal ZACH).
Goals: FK Tobol Kostanay: 1-1 Ruslan BALTIEV (40').
FC Slovan Liberec: 0-1 Jan NEZMAR (34').
Referee: Bernhard BRUGGER (AUT)   Attendence: 5.000

07-07-2007   Ljudski vrt Stadium, Maribor: NK Maribor – NK Hajduk Kula 2-0 (1-0)
NK Maribor: Marko PRIDIGAR, Andrej PECNIK (YC49), Miral SAMARDZIC (YC88),
Zikica VUKSANOVIC, Vladislav LUNGU (MOL), Dejan MEZGA (CRO) (61' Klemen
MEDVED), David TOMAZIC-SERUGA (YC56), Marko POPOVIC (SRB), Rene MIHELIC
(76' Armin BACINOVIC), Dimitar Ivanov MAKRIEV (BUL) (YC90+3), Mitja BRULC (65'
Matej VRACKO). (Coach: Marijan PUSNIK).
NK Hajduk Kula: Andjelko DJURICIC, Savo PAVICEVIC (MNE) (YC72) (85' Bojan
DOJKIC), Darko FEJSA, Sinisa RADANOVIC, Rados BULATOVIC, Goran HABENSUS,
Jovan RADIVOJEVIC (YC1), Nikola BOGIC, Aleksandar DAVIDOV (62' Nikola
KOMAZEC), Miodrag VASILJEVIC, Igor KOZOS (68' Milan PERIC). (Coach: Zarko
SOLDO).
Goals: NK Maribor: 1-0 Dimitar Ivanov MAKRIEV (29'), 2-0 Miral SAMARDZIC (51').
Referee: Istvan VAD (HUN)   Attendence: 3.000

194

07-07-2007   Gradski Stadion, Skopje:
FK Makedonija Skopje – PFC Cherno More Varna   0-4 (0-0)
FK Makedonija Skopje: Ljupco KOLEV, Daniel MOJSOV, Blagoja LJAMCEVSKI (YC41)
(75' Borce RISTOVSKI), Goran DIMOVSKI, Milan KRIVOKAPIC (MNE), Toni
BRNJACEVSKI (65' Genc ISEINI), Vladan MILOSAVLJEVIC (SRB), Daniel
JOVANOVSKI, Vasko MITREV (57' Ismail ISMAILI), Miroslav MILOSEVIC (SRB),
Aleksandar STOJANOVSKI (YC83). (Coach: Radmilo IVANCEVIC (SRB)).
PFC Cherno More Varna: Karamfil ILCHEV, Radoslav BACHEV (87' Nikolai
DOMAKINOV), Aleksandar TOMASH, MARCOS da Silva (BRA) (77' Miroslav
MANOLOV), Daniel DIMOV, Kiril DZHOROV, RICARDO ANDRÉ Duarte Pires (POR),
Georgi ANDONOV, Petar KOSTADINOV, Daniel Atanasov GEORGIEV (79' Stanislav
STOYANOV), Aleksandar ALEKSANDROV. (Coach: Nikola Asenov SPASOV).
Goals: PFC Cherno More Varna: 0-1 Radoslav BACHEV (53'), 0-2 MARCOS da Silva (72'),
0-3 MARCOS da Silva (73'), 0-4 Stanislav STOYANOV (82').
Referee: Alfonso PÉREZ BURRULL (ESP)   Attendance: 2.000

07-07-2007   Chernomorets Stadium, Odessa:
FK Chornomorets Odessa – FC Shakhter Soligorsk   4-2 (2-1)
FK Chornomorets Odessa: Vitaliy RUDENKO, Gennadi Aleksandrovich NIZHEGORODOV
(RUS), Oleg SHANDRUK (YC63), Valentin POLTAVETS, Vladimir KORYTKO (BLS) (61'
Konstantin YAKOSHENKO), Oleksandr ZOTOV, Sergiy DANILOVSKIY, Andriy KORNEV
(YC39) (90'+3' Dmitro GRISHKO), Sergiy SHISHCHENKO (72' Ruslan VALEEV), Oleg
VENHLINSKIY, Igor BUGAEV (MOL). (Coach: Vitaliy Viktorovich SHEVCHENKO
(RUS)).
FC Shakhter Soligorsk: Vitaliy MAKAVCHIK (YC36), Vadim LASOVSKIY, Aleksandr
KHRAPKOVSKIY, Pavel Sergeevich PLASKONNY, Andrey Ivan LEONCHIK, Maksim
GUKAYLO, Aleksandr NOVIK (64' Mikhail MARTINOVICH), Aleksey RIOS (76' Nikita
BUKATKIN), Siarhei KOVALCHUK, Artem GONCHARIK (62' Aleksandr BYCHENOK),
Sergei NIKIFORENKO. (Coach: Yuri Vasilevich VERGEICHIK).
Goals: FK Chornomorets Odessa: 1-0 Igor BUGAEV (13'), 2-1 Oleg VENHLINSKIY (18'),
3-1 Igor BUGAEV (67'), 4-2 Igor BUGAEV (88').
FC Shakhter Soligorsk: 1-1 Aleksey RIOS (14'), 3-2 Mikhail MARTINOVICH (79').
Referee: Richard HAVRILLA (SVK)   Attendance: 7.000

07-07-2007   Kiryat Eliezer Stadium, Haifa:
Maccabi Haifa FC – FC Gloria Bistrita   0-2 (0-2)
Maccabi Haifa FC: Tom ALMADON, Mohamad SHAKHBARI (YC74), Mor MAMAM,
Islam KANAN (YC70), Shai MAIMON (46' Shlomi HANAKA), Abbass SWAN (YC50) (65'
Tomer HEMAD), Alain MASUDI (DRC), Baram KAYAL (YC46), Lior RAFAELOV, Maor
Bar BUZAGLO (53' Asher GITA), Yero BELLO (NGR). (Coach: Ronny LEVY).
FC Gloria Bistrita: Septimiu Calin ALBUT, Mircea Vasile RUS (YC16) (82' Cosmin Vali
FRASINESCU), Dorin TOMA, László SEPSI, Octavian ABRUDAN, Cristian Ambrozie
COROIAN (60' Enache CÂJU), Sergiu Vasile COSTEA (74' Andrei Dan BOZESAN), Adrian
NALATI (YC88), Razvan Gabriel DOBRE (YC63), Cosmin TILINCA, Dorel ZAHARIA.
(Coach: Ioan Ovidiu SABAU).
Goals: FC Gloria Bistrita: 0-1 Cosmin TILINCA (12'), 0-2 Dorel ZAHARIA (41').
Referee: Oleh ORIEKHOV (UKR)   Attendance: 15.000

07-07-2007   Stadionul Zimbru, Chisinau: FC Dacia Chisinau – FC St.Gallen   0-1 (0-1)
FC Dacia Chisinau: Mihail MORARU, Vitalie MARDARI, Nicolai MINCEV, Vadim
BOLOHAN, Maxim ANDRONIC, Ghenadie PUSCA, Valeriu ONILA (RC81), Ghenadie
ORBU (73' Dumitru GUSILA), Alexandru ONICA (61' Dumitru Alin LIPA), Andrei
MARTIN (46' Eugeniu BOICENCO), Iurie SOIMU. (Coach: Emilian (Emil) CARAS).
FC St.Gallen: Stefano RAZZETTI (ITA), Bernt HAAS (YC88), Juan Pablo GARAT (ARG),
Serdal KÜL (TUR), Marc ZELLWEGER, Marcos Agustín GELABERT (ARG) (YC81),
Jürgen GJASULA (GER), David MARAZZI, Jesús David José MÉNDEZ (ARG) (79' Diego
CICCONE (ITA)), Francisco AGUIRRE (ARG) (63' Guy Armand FEUTCHINE (CMR)),
Alexander TACHIE-MENSAH (GHA). (Coach: Rolf FRINGER (AUT)).
Goal: FC St.Gallen: 0-1 Juan Pablo GARAT (7').
Referee: Jiri JECH (CZE)   Attendance: 2.156

07-07-2007   ZTE-Arena, Zalaegerszeg: Zalaegerszegi TE – FC Rubin Kazan   0-3 (0-1)
Zalaegerszegi TE: Martin LIPCÁK (SVK) (RC78), Tamás KÁDÁR, Sorin BOTIS (ROM)
(YC21), Péter POLGÁR (SVK) (YC33), Balász MOLNÁR (YC45+1) (46' Norbert TÓTH),
Béla KOPLÁROVICS, Péter MÁTÉ, Zoltán TÓTH (69' Zsolt BALÁZS), Gábor
SIMONFALVI, Róbert WALTNER, Mahamadou DIAWARA (FRA) (76' Tihamér
LUKÁCS). (Coach: Slavko PETROVIC (SRB)).
FC Rubin Kazan: Aleksandrs KOLINKO (LAT), JEAN Ferreira Narde (BRA), Lasha
SALUKVADZE (GEO), Mikhail SINEV, GABRIEL Fernando Atz (BRA), Macbeth SIBAYA
(RSA), Vitaliy VOLKOV (86' FÁBIO Alexandre Duarte FELÍCIO (POR)), Aleksandr
RYAZANTSEV, Dmitriy VASILEV, Aleksandr GATSKAN (52' Christiano Fernando
NOBOA Tello (ECU)), Vladimir BAYRAMOV (TMS) (78' Petr GITSELOV). (Coach:
Kurban Bekiyevich BERDYEV (TMS)).
Goals: FC Rubin Kazan: 0-1 Vitaliy VOLKOV (21'), 0-2 Vitaliy VOLKOV (66'), 0-3 Vitaliy
VOLKOV (80' penalty).
Referee: Robert SCHÖRGENHOFER (AUT)   Attendance: 4.000

07-07-2007   Gerhard-Hanappi-Stadion, Wien:
                SK Rapid Wien – SK Slovan Bratislava   3-1 (2-0)
SK Rapid Wien: Helge PAYER, Jürgen PATOCKA (YC66), Martin HIDEN, Christian
THONHOFER (YC42), Markus HEIKKINEN (FIN) (YC50) (79' Stefan KULOVITS), Steffen
HOFMANN (GER) (YC75) (79' Hannes EDER), Ümit KORKMAZ (84' George HARDING
(YC90)), Mario SARA, Branko BOSKOVIC (MNE), Mate BILIC (CRO), Mario BAZINA
(CRO). (Coach: Peter PACULT).
SK Slovan Bratislava: Daniel KISS, Michal HANEK (YC45), Martin DOBROTKA (YC35),
Peter STRUHAR, Matej IZVOLT (73' Miroslav POLIACEK), Pavol SEDLÁK (46' Michal
BREZNANIK (YC70)), Samuel SLOVÁK, Michal KUBALA (85' Lubomir MESZAROS),
Daniel KOSMEL (YC22), Ottó SZABÓ, Pavol MASARYK. (Coach: Boris KITKA).
Goals: SK Rapid Wien: 1-0 Steffen HOFMANN (31'), 2-0 Mario BAZINA (38'), 3-0 Steffen
HOFMANN (53').
SK Slovan Bratislava: 3-1 Samuel SLOVÁK (88').
Referee: Veaceslav BANARI (MOL)   Attendance: 12.600

07-07-2007   Jules Ottenstadion, Gentbrugge: KAA Gent – Cliftonville FC   2-0 (1-0)
KAA Gent: Alexandre MARTINOVIC (FRA), Djordje SVETLICIC (SRB), Boban
GRNCAROV (MCD), Christophe GRONDIN (FRA), Guillaume GILLET (YC90+2),
Christophe GRÉGOIRE (RC90+1), Alin STOICA (ROM) (90' Admir HAZNADAR (BOS)),
Davy DE BEULE, Aleksandar MUTAVDZIC (SRB) (79' Massimo MOIA), Adekanmi
OLUFADE (TOG) (70' Marcin ZEWLAKOW (POL)), Dominic FOLEY (IRL). (Coach:
Trond Johan SOLLIED (NOR)).
Cliftonville FC: John CONNOLLY, David McALINDEN, Declan O'HARA (RC90+1), Liam
FLEMING, Ronan SCANNELL, Barry HOLLAND, George McMULLAN (YC57) (74'
Vincent SWEENEY (IRL)), Kieran O'CONNOR, Sean FRIARS (IRL) (74' Gary
KENNEDY), Chris SCANNELL (YC20) (87' Daniel LYONS (IRL)), Mark HOLLAND.
(Coach: Samuel Eddie PATTERSON).
Goals: KAA Gent: 1-0 Dominic FOLEY (8'), 2-0 Dominic FOLEY (63').
Referee: Joaquim Paulo GOMES Ferreira PARATY DA SILVA (POR)

07-07-2007   Asim Ferhatovic Hase Stadium, Sarajevo:
              FK Slavija Sarajevo – FC Otelul Galati   0-0
FK Slavija Sarajevo: Ratko DUJKOVIC, Dragan BJELICA, Bojan REGOJE (YC90+1), Ivan
STANKOVIC (SRB), Bojan JAMINA (86' Nemanja SESLIJA), Vlastimir JOVANOVIC,
Milan MUMINOVIC, Goran SIMIC (81' Dragisa LAZIC), Sretko VUKSANOVIC (SRB),
Vukasin BENOVIC (YC46), Darko SPALEVIC (SRB). (Coach: Zoran ERBEZ).
FC Otelul Galati: Paulius GRYBAUSKAS (LIT), Salif NOGO (BKF) (YC41,YC78), Cristian
SARGHI, Constantin Dorin SEMEGHIN, Gabriel Nicu GIURGIU, Gabriel Ioan
PARASCHIV, Ramses GADO (59' Marian CARJA (YC72)), Emil Gabriel JULA (81' Silviu
ILIE), Daniel Dorin STAN, Janos Jozsef SZEKELY,Tadas LABUKAS (LIT) (55' Gil-Sik
KIM (KOR)). (Coach: Petre GRIGORAS).
Referee: Sascha KEVER (SUI)   Attendance: 7.000

07-07-2007   Turners Cross, Cork: Cork City FC – Hammarby IF   1-1 (1-0)
Cork City FC: Michael DEVINE, Neal HORGAN, Daniel (Dan) MURRAY, Sean KELLY
(79' Cillian LORDAN), Gareth FARRELLY (70' Darren MURPHY), Joe GAMBLE, Roy
O'DONOVAN, Billy WOODS, Colin HEALY (YC56), Liam KEARNEY, John O'FLYNN
(61' Leon McSWEENEY (YC88)). (Coach: Damien John RICHARDSON).
Hammarby IF: Erland HELLSTRÖM, David JOHANSSON, José Monteiro de MACEDO,
Emil JOHANSSON, Suleyman "Sulan" SLEYMAN (YC40), Louay CHANKO, Sebastián
EGUREN (URU), Haris LAITINEN, Sebastian CASTRO-TELLO (73' Gunnar Thor
GUNNARSSON (ISL) (YC89)), Charlie DAVIES (USA) (90'+1' Joakim JENSEN), Paulo
Roberto Chamon de Castilho "PAULINHO GUARÁ" (BRA) (85' Heidar Geir JULIUSSON
(ISL)). (Coach: Tony GUSTAVSSON). (Not used sub: Isak DAHLIN (YC74)).
Goals: Cork City FC: 1-0 Roy O'DONOVAN (10').
Hammarby IF: 1-1 Daniel (Dan) MURRAY (57' own goal).
Referee: Romans LAJUKS (LAT)

08-07-2007   Pohjola Stadion, Vantaa: FC Honka Espoo – Aalborg BK   2-2 (2-2)
FC Honka Espoo: Tuomas PELTONEN, Ville JALASTO, Janne SAARINEN, Rami
HAKANPÄÄ, Hannu PATRONEN (46' Joel PEROVUO), Tero KOSKELA (YC43), Nicholas
OTARU, Tuomo TURUNEN, Peke HUUHTANEN, Jami PUUSTINEN, Roni POROKARA.
(Coach: Mika "Bana" LEHKOSUO).
Aalborg BK: Kenneth Stenhild NIELSEN, Michael JAKOBSEN (YC32), Martin PEDERSEN
(YC66), Daniel Benjamin CALIFF (USA) (27' Kasper RISGÅRD), Allan OLESEN (46' Jón
Roi JACOBSEN (FAR)), Mattias LINDSTRÖM (SWE) (YC77), Súni OLSEN (FAR) (YC76),
Jens Kristian SØRENSEN (83' Thomas ENEVOLDSEN), Rade PRICA (SWE) (YC74), Jeppe
CURTH, Siyabonga NOMVETHE (RSA). (Coach: Erik HAMRÉN (SWE)).
Goals: FC Honka Espoo: 1-1 Roni POROKARA (8' penalty), 2-2 Jami PUUSTINEN (30').
Aalborg BK: 0-1 Mattias LINDSTRÖM (1'), 1-2 Rade PRICA (23').
Referee: William COLLUM (SCO)   Attendance: 3.723

08-07-2007   Hüseyin Avni Aker Stadyumu, Trabzon:
               Trabzonspor Kulübü – KS Vllaznia Shkodër   6-0 (3-0)
Trabzonspor Kulübü: Ahmet SAHIN, Çagdas ATAN, Tayfun CORA, Ferhat ÇÖKMÜS (SUI),
Hüseyin ÇIMSIR (59' Yusuf KURTULUS), Ayman Mohamad ABDELAZIZ (EGY) (54'
Hasan ÜÇÜNCÜ), Ceyhun ERIS (74' Adnan GÜNGÖR), Serkan BALCI, Celaleddin
KOÇAK, Ömer RIZA, Ersen MARTIN. (Coach: Ziyaettin (Ziya) DOGAN).
KS Vllaznia Shkodër: Armir GRIMA (46' Bishani OLSI), Admir TELI, Safet OSJA, Suad
LICI, Uliks KOTRRI (46' Franc AHI), Albert KAÇI, Gilman LIKA, Xhevahir SUKAJ, Erjon
HOTI (70' Arsen BEQIRI), Arlind NORRA, Ghislain Rostand SIMO TAVIKO (CMR).
(Coach: Mirel JOSA).
Goals: Trabzonspor Kulübü: 1-0 Ersen MARTIN (12'), 2-0 Ceyhun ERIS (32'), 3-0 Çagdas
ATAN (39'), 4-0 Ersen MARTIN (51'), 5-0 Ersen MARTIN (58'), 6-0 Ömer RIZA (89').
Referee: Bas NIJHUIS (HOL)

08-07-2007   Vetros Stadionas, Vilnius: FK Vetra Vilnius – WKS Legia Warszawa   2-0
FK Vetra Vilnius: Stanislav KOZYREV (RUS), Marijan BUDIMIR (CRO), Andrey
USACHEV (RUS), Andrius SKERLA, Pedro Henrique BOTELHO (BRA), Dejan
MILOSEVSKI (MCD), Bobi BOZINOVSKI (MCD), Mindaugas PANKA, Maksut AZIZI
(SLO), SEVERINO Lima de Moura (BRA), Egidijus JUSKA. (Coach: Vitas
JANCIAUSKAS).
WKS Legia Waszawa: Ján MUCHA (SVK), Jakub WAWRZYNIAK, Iñaki ASTIZ Ventura
(ESP), Dickson CHOTO (ZIM), Grzegorz BRONOWICKI, Marcin SMOLINSKI, ROGER
GUERREIRO (BRA), Aleksandar VUKOVIC (SRB), Miroslav RADOVIC (SRB), Bartlomiej
GRZELAK, Maciej KORZYM.
Goals: FK Vetra Vilnius: 1-0 SEVERINO Lima de Moura (8'), 2-0 Dejan MILOSEVSKI
(45').
Referee: Mario VLK (SVK)

*The match was abandoned after the first half due to rioting by the supporters of WKS Legia
Warszawa. UEFA awarded the game to FK Vetra Vilnius with a 3-0 scoreline and WKS Legia
Warszawa was suspended from all UEFA competitions for a season as further punishment.*

14-07-2007   Windsor Park, Belfast: Cliftonville FC – KAA Gent   0-4 (0-3)
Cliftonville FC: John CONNOLLY, Declan O'HARA (YC22), Liam FLEMING, Barry
HOLLAND (YC27), David McALINDEN (50' Aaron SMYTH), Francis MURPHY (54' Sean
FRIARS (IRL)), Kieran O'CONNOR, Barry JOHNSTON, Vincent SWEENEY (IRL) (70'
Ciaran McMULLAN), Mark HOLLAND, Gary KENNEDY. (Coach: Samuel Eddie
PATTERSON).
KAA Gent: Alexandre MARTINOVIC (FRA), Djordje SVETLICIC (SRB) (RC77), Boban
GRNCAROV (MCD), Christophe GRONDIN (FRA) (54' Nebojsa PAVLOVIC (SRB)),
Guillaume GILLET, Alin STOICA (ROM) (70' Roberto ROSALES (VEN)), Davy DE
BEULE, Massimo MOIA (YC34), Marcin ZEWLAKOW (POL) (80' Damir MIRVIC (BOS)),
Adekanmi OLUFADE (TOG) (YC67), Dominic FOLEY (IRL). (Coach: Trond Johan
SOLLIED (NOR)).
Goals: KAA Gent: 0-1 Dominic FOLEY (12'), 0-2 Adekanmi OLUFADE (44'), 0-3 Davy DE
BEULE (45'+1'), 0-4 Adekanmi OLUFADE (87').
Referee: Tomasz MIKULSKI (POL)   Attendance: 907

14-07-2007   Råsunda Fotbollstadion, Solna: Hammarby IF – Cork City FC   1-0 (0-0)
Hammarby IF: Benny LEKSTRÖM, David JOHANSSON, Suleyman "Sulan" SLEYMAN,
Christian TRAORÉ (DEN), José Monteiro de MACEDO, Sebastian CASTRO-TELLO (62'
Sebastián EGUREN (URU)), Louay CHANKO, Haris LAITINEN (78' Joakim JENSEN),
Erkan ZENGIN, Petter ANDERSSON, Paulo Roberto Chamon de Castilho "PAULINHO
GUARÁ" (BRA) (90' Heidar Geir JULIUSSON (ISL)). (Coach: Tony GUSTAVSSON).
Cork City FC: Michael DEVINE, Neal HORGAN (88' Cillian LORDAN), Sean KELLY,
Daniel MURRAY (YC40), Billy WOODS, Joe GAMBLE (YC47), Colin HEALY, Gareth
FARRELLY, Liam KEARNEY (83' Denis BEHAN (YC90)), Roy O'DONOVAN (YC33),
John O'FLYNN. (Coach: Damien John RICHARDSON).
Goal: Hammarby IF: 1-0 Petter ANDERSSON (53').
Referee: Radek MATEJEK (CZE)   Attendance: 4.045

14-07-2007   Stadionul Otelul, Galati: FC Otelul Galati – FK Slavija Sarajevo   3-0 (2-0)
FC Otelul Galati: Paulius GRYBAUSKAS (LIT), Constantin Dorin SEMEGHIN, Cristian
SARGHI, Gabriel Nicu GIURGIU, Gabriel Ioan PARASCHIV, Gil-Sik KIM (KOR), Emil
Gabriel JULA (83' Robert ELEK), Silviu ILIE, Janos Jozsef SZEKELY (YC44), Daniel Dorin
STAN (77' George CARJAN), Tadas LABUKAS (LIT) (73' Gheorghe "Jara" BOGHIU
(YC90)). (Coach: Petre GRIGORAS).
FK Slavija Sarajevo: Ratko DUJKOVIC, Dragan BJELICA (70' Branislav ARSENIEVIC
(MCD)), Bojan REGOJE, Ivan STANKOVIC (SRB), Milan MUMINOVIC, Goran SIMIC
(71' Nemanja SESLIJA), Sretko VUKSANOVIC (SRB), Vukasin BENOVIC (YC44,YC73),
Bojan JAMINA (46' Dragisa LAZIC), Vlastimir JOVANOVIC, Darko SPALEVIC (SRB).
(Coach: Zoran ERBEZ).
Goals: FC Otelul Galati: 1-0 Emil Gabriel JULA (31'), 2-0 Emil Gabriel JULA (42'), 3-0
Gabriel Ioan PARASCHIV (70').
Referee: Mihaly FABIAN (HUN)

199

14-07-2007   Stadion Crvena Zvezda, Beograd: NK Hajduk Kula – NK Maribor 5-0 (4-0)
NK Hajduk Kula: Andjelko DJURICIC, Darko FEJSA, Sinisa RADANOVIC (YC86), Rados
BULATOVIC (84' Srdjan DJUKANOVIC), Jovan RADIVOJEVIC, Nikola BOGIC, Ljubomir
FEJSA (19' Goran HABENSUS), Miodrag VASILJEVIC, Igor KOZOS, Milan PERIC (YC7)
(53' Bojan DOJKIC), Nikola KOMAZEC. (Coach: Zarko SOLDO).
NK Maribor: Marko PRIDIGAR, Andrej PECNIK (YC35), Miral SAMARDZIC, Zikica
VUKSANOVIC (65' Gorazd ZAJC), Vladislav LUNGU (MOL), Dejan MEZGA (CRO),
David TOMAZIC-SERUGA, Marko POPOVIC (SRB), Rene MIHELIC (YC75), Dimitar
Ivanov MAKRIEV (BUL), Mitja BRULC (YC58). (Coach: Marijan PUSNIK).
Goals: NK Hajduk Kula: 1-0 Miodrag VASILJEVIC (15'), 2-0 Nikola KOMAZEC (30'), 3-0
Milan PERIC (38'), 4-0 Sinisa RADANOVIC (45'+1'), 5-0 Nikola KOMAZEC (67' penalty).
Referee: David MALCOLM (NIR)

14-07-2007   Stadionul Gloria, Bistrita: FC Gloria Bistrita – Maccabi Haifa FC   0-2 (0-1)
FC Gloria Bistrita: Septimiu Calin ALBUT (YC58), Dorin TOMA (YC7), László SEPSI,
Cosmin Vali FRASINESCU, Octavian ABRUDAN, Cristian Ambrozie COROIAN, Sergiu
Vasile COSTEA (64' Razvan DAMIAN), Adrian NALATI (62' Ion DUMITRA), Razvan
Gabriel DOBRE, Cosmin TILINCA (96' Flavius BAD (YC98)), Dorel ZAHARIA. (Coach:
Ioan Ovidiu SABAU).
Maccabi Haifa FC: Nir DAVIDOVITZ, Mohamad SHAKHBARI (YC47), Ronny GAFNEY,
Dekil KEINAN, Shai MAIMON, Abbass SWAN (YC21,YC111), Baram KAYAL (YC23)
(62' Tomer HEMAD), Lior RAFAELOV, Asher GITA, Maor Bar BUZAGLO, Yero BELLO
(NGR) (111' Shlomi HANAKA). (Coach: Ronny LEVY).
Goals: Maccabi Haifa FC: 0-1 Shai MAIMON (6'), 0-2 Tomer HEMAD (65').
Referee: Novo PANIC (BOS)

Penalties: * Maor Bar BUZAGLO   * Cristian Ambrozie COROIAN
                 1 Dekil KEINAN   1 László SEPSI
                 * Ronny GAFNEY   2 Dorin TOMA
                 2 Asher GITA   3 Flavius BAD
                 * Lior RAFAELOV

14-07-2007   Central Stadium, Kazan: FC Rubin Kazan – Zalaegerszegi TE   2-0 (1-0)
FC Rubin Kazan: Aleksandrs KOLINKO (LAT), JEAN Ferreira Narde (BRA), Andrey
Vitalevich FEDOROV, Mikhail SINEV, GABRIEL Fernando Atz (BRA), Macbeth SIBAYA
(RSA) (YC45) (46' Andrey Igorevich KIREEV), Vitaliy VOLKOV, Aleksandr
RYAZANTSEV (69' Sergey NESTERENKO), Christiano Fernando NOBOA Tello (ECU),
Dmitriy VASILEV, Vladimir BAYRAMOV (TMS) (46' Aleksandr Vladislavovich YARKIN).
(Coach: Kurban Bekiyevich BERDYEV (TMS)).
Zalaegerszegi TE: Krisztián POGACSICS, Tamás KÁDÁR (35' Tihamér LUKÁCS), Sorin
BOTIS (ROM), Péter POLGÁR (SVK) (YC61), Jozsef BOZSIK (85' András HORVÁTH),
Béla KOPLÁROVICS, Péter MÁTÉ (YC51), Zoltán TÓTH (YC28), Gábor SIMONFALVI,
Róbert WALTNER, Zsolt BALÁZS (63' Mahamadou DIAWARA (FRA)). (Coach: Slavko
PETROVIC (SRB)).
Goals: FC Rubin Kazan: 1-0 Vitaliy VOLKOV (37' penalty), 2-0 JEAN Ferreira Narde (67').
Referee: Augustus Viorel CONSTANTIN (ROM)   Attendance: 14.000

200

14-07-2007   Espenmoos stadium, St.Gallen: FC St.Gallen – FC Dacia Chisinau   0-1 (0-0)
FC St.Gallen: Stefano RAZZETTI (ITA), Bernt HAAS, Juan Pablo GARAT (ARG), Serdal
KÜL (TUR) (YC62), Marc ZELLWEGER, Marcos Agustín GELABERT (ARG), Jürgen
GJASULA (GER) (105' Philipp MUNTWILER), David MARAZZI, Jesús David José
MÉNDEZ (ARG) (YC78) (81' Diego CICCONE (ITA)), Francisco AGUIRRE (ARG),
Alexander TACHIE-MENSAH (GHA) (YC81) (86' Kwabena AGOUDA (GHA)). (Coach:
Rolf FRINGER (AUT)).
FC Dacia Chisinau: Mihail MORARU, Vitalie MARDARI, Nicolai MINCEV, Vadim
BOLOHAN (YC66), Maxim ANDRONIC, Ghenadie PUSCA (100' Andrei MARTIN),
Eugeniu BOICENCO, Ghenadie ORBU (23' Dumitru Alin LIPA, 105' Marius CALIN
(ROM)), Alexandru ONICA, Iurie SOIMU, Dumitru GUSILA (YC109). (Coach: Emilian
(Emil) CARAS).
Goal: FC Dacia Chisinau: 0-1 Dumitru Alin LIPA (56').
Referee: Marek MIKOLAJEWSKI (POL)   Attendance: 1.976

Penalties: 1 Alexandru ONICA   * Francisco AGUIRRE
              2 Marius CALIN   * Marcos Agustín GELABERT
              3 Andrei MARTIN   * Juan Pablo GARAT

14-07-2007   Naftex Stadion, Burgas:
              PFC Cherno More Varna – FK Makedonija Skopje   3-0 (1-0)
PFC Cherno More Varna: Karamfil ILCHEV, Nikolai DOMAKINOV, Radoslav BACHEV,
Aleksandar TOMASH, MARCOS da Silva (BRA) (69' Stanislav STOYANOV), Daniel
DIMOV, Kiril DZHOROV, RICARDO ANDRÉ Duarte Pires (POR), Petar KOSTADINOV
(52' Valdimir KOSTADINOV), Daniel Atanasov GEORGIEV (81' Konstantin SETLINOV),
Miroslav MANOLOV. (Coach: Nikola Asenov SPASOV).
FK Makedonija Skopje: Ljupco KOLEV, Borce RISTOVSKI, Vladimir DESPOTOVSKI
(YC7), Saban REPZEP (YC10), Milan KRIVOKAPIC (MNE), Toni BRNJACEVSKI (YC37)
(85' Blagoja LJAMCEVSKI), Vladan MILOSAVLJEVIC (SRB), Daniel JOVANOVSKI,
Vasko MITREV (60' Dusan SIMOVSKI), Miroslav MILOSEVIC (SRB), Aleksandar
STOJANOVSKI (66' Adis JAHOVIK (YC69)). (Coach: Radmilo IVANCEVIC (SRB)).
Goals: PFC Cherno More Varna: 1-0 Daniel Atanasov GEORGIEV (12'), 2-0 Miroslav
MANOLOV (46'), 3-0 Daniel DIMOV (80').
Referee: Joeri VAN DE VELDE (BEL)   Attendance: 1.500

14-07-2007   Aalborg Stadion, Aalborg: Aalborg BK – FC Honka Espoo   1-1 (0-0)
Aalborg BK: Kenneth Stenhild NIELSEN, Michael JAKOBSEN, Martin PEDERSEN (YC69),
Jón Roi JACOBSEN (FAR) (YC62) (85' José Roberto Rodrigues MOTA Junior (BRA)),
Mattias LINDSTRÖM (SWE) (YC22) (65' Patrick KRISTENSEN), "CACÁ" Lucas de Deus
Santos (BRA) (53' Thomas ENEVOLDSEN), Súni OLSEN (FAR), Kasper RISGÅRD, Rade
PRICA (SWE), Jeppe CURTH, Siyabonga NOMVETHE (RSA) (YC90+1). (Coach: Erik
HAMRÉN (SWE)).
FC Honka Espoo: Tuomas PELTONEN, Ville JALASTO, Janne SAARINEN, Rami
HAKANPÄÄ (YC23), Tero KOSKELA, Nicholas OTARU (76' Hannu HAARALA), Joel
PEROVUO, Tuomo TURUNEN (YC55), Peke HUUHTANEN (84' Aleksandr KOKKO),
Jami PUUSTINEN, Roni POROKARA. (Coach: Mika "Bana" LEHKOSUO).
Goals: Aalborg BK: 1-1 Siyabonga NOMVETHE (61').
FC Honka Espoo: 0-1 Roni POROKARA (50').
Referee: Dejan FILIPOVIC (SRB)   Attendance: 2.114

201

14-07-2007   Loro Boriçi Stadium, Shkodër:
KS Vllaznia Shkodër – Trabzonspor Kulübü   0-4 (0-0)
KS Vllaznia Shkodër: Bishani OLSI, Admir TELI, Safet OSJA (58' Klevis DALIPI), Suad
LICI, Uliks KOTRRI, Albert KAÇI, Gilman LIKA, Erjon HOTI (69' Alsid TAFILI), Vioresin
SINANI (58' Franc AHI), Arlind NORRA (YC58), Ghislain Rostand SIMO TAVIKO (CMR).
(Coach: Mirel JOSA).
Trabzonspor Kulübü: Ahmet SAHIN, Çagdas ATAN, Tayfun CORA, Ferhat ÇÖKMÜS (SUI)
(49' Adnan GÜNGÖR), Hasan ÜÇÜNCÜ, Ayman Mohamad ABDELAZIZ (EGY), Serkan
BALCI (YC69), Celaleddin KOÇAK (54' Eyüp KADRI ATAOGLU), Ömer RIZA (46' Yusuf
KURTULUS), Umut BULUT, Ibrahima YATTARA (GUI). (Coach: Ziyaettin (Ziya)
DOGAN).
Goals: Trabzonspor Kulübü: 0-1 Umut BULUT (47'), 0-2 Ibrahima YATTARA (49'), 0-3
Yusuf KURTULUS (52'), 0-4 Umut BULUT (89').
Referee: Alan KELLY (IRL)

14-07-2007   Tehelné Pole Stadium, Bratislava:
SK Slovan Bratislava – SK Rapid Wien   1-0 (1-0)
SK Slovan Bratislava: Daniel KISS, Martin SVESTKA (CZE) (YC60), Michal HANEK,
Martin DOBROTKA, Matej IZVOLT (65' Daniel KOSMEL), Samuel SLOVAK, Michal
BREZNANIK (65' Miroslav POLIACEK), Michal KUBALA, Ottó SZABÓ (YC15), Jakub
SYLVESTR (YC35), Pavol MASARYK (79' Lubomir MESZAROS). (Coach: Boris KITKA).
SK Rapid Wien: Helge PAYER (YC90+3), Jürgen PATOCKA (YC54), Andreas DOBER,
Stefan KULOVITS (YC19,YC75), Markus HEIKKINEN (FIN), Steffen HOFMANN (GER),
Ümit KORKMAZ, Mario SARA, Branko BOSKOVIC (MNE) (YC80), Mate BILIC (CRO),
Mario BAZINA (CRO) (76' Hannes EDER). (Coach: Peter PACULT).
Goal: SK Slovan Bratislava: 1-0 Martin DOBROTKA (18').
Referee: Stanislav TODOROV (BUL)   Attendance: 6.100

15-07-2007   Stroitel Stadion,Soligorsk:
FC Shakhter Soligorsk – FK Chornomorets Odessa   0-2 (0-1)
FC Shakhter Soligorsk: Mikhail BARANOVSKIY (YC62), Pavel Sergeevich PLASKONNY,
Andrey Ivan LEONCHIK, Mikhail MARTINOVICH, Maksim GUKAYLO, Aleksandr
NOVIK (YC27) (60' Aleksandr BYCHENOK), Aleksey RIOS, Siarhei KOVALCHUK, Artem
GONCHARIK (46' Nikita BUKATKIN), Aleksandr KLIMENKO, Sergei NIKIFORENKO.
(Coach: Yuri Vasilevich VERGEICHIK).
FK Chornomorets Odessa: Vitaliy RUDENKO, Gennadi Aleksandrovich NIZHEGORODOV
(RUS), Oleg SHANDRUK, Dmitro GRISHKO, Valentin POLTAVETS (83' Rinar VALEEV),
Maksim Andreevich BILETSKIY, Vladimir KORYTKO (BLS) (YC61), Sergiy
DANILOVSKIY (79' Andriy KIRLIK), Andriy KORNEV (YC44), Sergiy SHISHCHENKO
(YC30) (72' Konstantin YAKOSHENKO), Igor BUGAEV (MOL) (YC60). (Coach: Vitaliy
Viktorovich SHEVCHENKO (RUS)).
Goals: FK Chornomorets Odessa: 0-1 Valentin POLTAVETS (27' penalty), 0-2 Dmitro
GRISHKO (64').
Referee: Emil LAURSEN (DEN)   Attendance: 4.200

202

15-07-2007   Stadion u Nisy, Liberec: FC Slovan Liberec – FK Tobol Kostanay   0-2 (0-2)
FC Slovan Liberec: Petr BOLEK, Jan POLÁK (78' Milos BREZINSKY (SVK)), Pavel
KOSTÁL, HUDSON Fernando Tobias de Carvalho (BRA), Petr KRÁTKY (46' Jan
BLAZEK), Jirí BÍLEK, Ivan HODÚR (SVK), Petr PAPOUSEK, Daniel PUDIL (35' Jirí
LISKA), Jan NEZMAR, Robin DEJMEK. (Coach: Michal ZACH).
FK Tobol Kostanay: Alexandr PETUKHOV, Farkhadbek IRISMETOV (YC55), Oleg
LOTOV, Daniyar MUKANOV, Stanimir DIMITROV (BUL), Kairat NURDAULETOV, Azat
NURGALIEV (YC67) (79' Talgat SABALAKOV), Nurbol ZHUMASKALIEV, Sergey
SKORIKH, Igor YURIN (YC57) (83' Yevgeniy MESHKOV), Sergey OSTAPENKO (YC70)
(89' Valeri GARKUSHA). (Coach: Dmitriy Alekseevich OGAI).
Goals: FK Tobol Kostanay: 0-1 Nurbol ZHUMASKALIEV (16'), 0-2 Sergey OSTAPENKO
(35').
Referee: MikkoVUORELA (FIN)   Attendance: 5.125

THIRD ROUND

21-07-2007   Stadionul Gloria, Bistrita:
              FC Gloria Bistrita – Club Atlético de Madrid   2-1 (2-0)
FC Gloria Bistrita: Septimiu Calin ALBUT, Vasile Mircea RUS, László SEPSI, Cosmin Vali
FRASINESCU (YC29), Octavian ABRUDAN, Cristian Ambrozie COROIAN (68' Enache
CAJU), Adrian NALATI (89' Ion DUMITRA), Kenan RAGIPOVIC (SRB) (76' Luvius
Razvan DAMIAN), Razvan Gabriel DOBRE, Cosmin TILINCA, Dorel ZAHARIA. (Coach:
Ioan Ovidiu SABAU).
Club Atlético de Madrid: Leonardo Neoren "LEO" FRANCO (ARG), Georgios Dimitrios
SEITARIDIS (GRE), ANTONIO LÓPEZ Guerrero, Fabiano ELLER dos Santos (BRA), Luis
Amarando PEREA Mosquera (COL), RAÚL GARCÍA Escudero, Peter Bernard LUCCIN
(FRA) (YC62) (76' Francisco José da Costa "COSTINHA" (POR)), Maximiliano Rubén
"MAXI" RODRÍGUEZ (ARG), Martin PETROV (BUL) (57' José Manuel JURADO Marín),
Nuno Ricardo de Oliveira Ribeiro "MANICHE" (POR), Miguel Ángel Ferrer Martínez
"MISTA" (70' BRAULIO Nóbrega Rodríguez). (Coach: Javier "El Vasco" AGUIRRE
Onaindía (MEX)).
Goals: FC Gloria Bistrita: 1-0 Dorel ZAHARIA (8'), 2-0 Cosmin TILINCA (39').
Club Atlético de Madrid: 2-1 Georgios Dimitrios SEITARIDIS (55').
Referee: Nicola RIZZOLI (ITA)   Attendance: 8.000

21-07-2007   Stadionul Otelul, Galati: FC Otelul Galati – Trabzonspor Kulübü   2-1 (1-0)
FC Otelul Galati: Paulius GRYBAUSKAS (LIT), Zhivko ZHELEV (BUL) (YC66), Constantin
Dorin SEMEGHIN (80' Eduard RATNIKOV (EST)), Salif NOGO (BKF), Cristian SARGHI,
Gabriel Nicu GIURGIU (YC88), Gil-Sik KIM (KOR), Gabriel Ioan PARASCHIV (YC64),
Emil Gabriel JULA (88' Silviu ILIE), Janos Jozsef SZEKELY, Daniel Dorin STAN (YC62)
(69' Tadas LABUKAS (LIT) (YC90+3)). (Coach: Petre GRIGORAS).
Trabzonspor Kulübü: Ahmet SAHIN, Çagdas ATAN (YC66,YC90+3), Ferhat ÇÖKMÜS
(SUI), Hüseyin ÇIMSIR, Hasan ÜÇÜNCÜ (46' Ceyhun ERIS), Ayman Mohamad
ABDELAZIZ (EGY), Serkan BALCI (82' Adnan GÜNGÖR), Gökdeniz KARADENIZ (82'
Ersen MARTIN), Celaleddin KOÇAK, Umut BULUT, Ibrahima YATTARA (GUI) (RC28).
(Coach: Ziyaettin (Ziya) DOGAN).
Goals: FC Otelul Galati: 1-0 Daniel Dorin STAN (27'), 2-1 Gabriel Ioan PARASCHIV (86').
Trabzonspor Kulübü: 1-1 Ersen MARTIN (83').
Referee: César MUÑIZ FERNÁNDEZ (ESP)   Attendance: 5.000

203

21-07-2007   Naftex Stadion, Burgas: PFC Cherno More Varna – UC Sampdoria 0-1 (0-1)
PFC Cherno More Varna: Karamfil ILCHEV, Jovaldir PERIS Ferreira (BRA) (YC25) (70'
Georgi ANDONOV (YC80)), Nikolai DOMAKINOV, Radoslav BACHEV, Aleksandar
TOMASH, Daniel DIMOV, Kiril DZHOROV (YC55), RICARDO ANDRÉ Duarte Pires
(POR) (72' Petar KOSTADINOV), DJALMA Henrique da Silva (BRA), Daniel Atanasov
GEORGIEV (84' Miroslav MANOLOV), FABINHO Aigar Laurentino (BRA). (Coach:
Nikola Asenov SPASOV).
UC Sampdoria: Luca CASTELLAZZI, Pietro ACCARDI (YC41), Stefano LUCCHINI (45'+4'
Hugo Armando CAMPAGNARO (ARG)), Christian MAGGIO, Luigi SALA, Mirko PIERI,
Sergio VOLPI, Angelo PALOMBO (YC57), Vladimir KOMAN (UKR) (YC10) (60' Reto
ZIEGLER (SUI) (YC87)), Claudio BELLUCCI (YC45+1), Andrea CARACCIOLO (90'
Salvatore FOTI). (Coach: Walter MAZZARRI).
Goal: UC Sampdoria: 0-1 Stefano LUCCHINI (43').
Referee: Brage SANDMOEN (NOR)   Attendance: 5.000

21-07-2007   Chernomorets Stadium, Odessa:
               FK Chernomorets Odessa – Racing Club de Lens   0-0
FK Chornomorets Odessa: Vitaliy RUDENKO, Gennadi Aleksandrovich NIZHEGORODOV
(RUS) (YC80), Oleg SHANDRUK, Igor LOZO (CRO), Dmitro GRISHKO, Valentin
POLTAVETS (65' Sergiy SHISHCHENKO), Maksim Areevich BILETSKIY (87' Rinar
VALEEV), Vladimir KORYTKO (BLS), Konstantin YAKOSHENKO (YC90+2), Sergiy
DANILOVSKIY, Oleg VENHLINSKIY. (Coach: Vitaliy Viktorovich SHEVCHENKO
(RUS)).
Racing Club de Lens: Vedran RUNJE (CRO), MARCO Miguel Gonçalves RAMOS (POR)
(YC37) (46' Lucien AUBEY), Vitorino HILTON de Silva (BRA), Adama COULIBALY
(MLI), Eric CARRIÈRE, Kanga Gauthier AKALÉ (CIV), Nenad KOVACEVIC (SRB), Yohan
DEMONT, Julien SABLÉ Fourtassou, Daniel COUSIN (GAB), Olivier MONTERRUBIO.
(Coach: Guy ROUX).
Referee: Tommy SKJERVEN (NOR)   Attendance: 13.000

21-07-2007   Stadionul Zimbru, Chisinau: FC Dacia Chisinau – Hamburger SV 1-1 (1-0)
FC Dacia Chisinau: Mihail MORARU, Vitalie MARDARI (80' Dimitar I.BELCHEV (BUL)),
Nicolai MINCEV, Vadim BOLOHAN, Maxim ANDRONIC (YC69), Ghenadie PUSCA
(YC44), Eugeniu BOICENCO (YC75), Alexandru ONICA (45'+1' Andrei MARTIN),
Dumitru Alin LIPA, Iurie SOIMU, Dumitru GUSILA (40' Miguel NIMES Lopes de PINA
(POR)). (Coach: Emilian (Emil) CARAS).
Hamburger SV: Frank Peter ROST, Joris MATHIJSEN (HOL), Vincent KOMPANY (BEL),
Nigel DE JONG (HOL) (YC22) (65' Collin BENJAMIN (NAM)), David JAROLIM (CZE),
Piotr TROCHOWSKI (65' Mohamed ZIDAN (EGY)), Guy Roland DEMEL (CIV), Rafael
VAN DER VAART (HOL), Alexander LAAS, Ivica OLIC (CRO), Boubacar SANOGO
(CIV). (Coach: Hubertus Jozef Margaretha (Huub) STEVENS (HOL)).
Goals: FC Dacia Chisinau: 1-0 Eugeniu BOICENCO (7').
Hamburger SV: 1-1 Rafael VAN DER VAART (70' penalty).
Referee: Bruno Miguel DUARTE PAIXÄO (POR)   Attendance: 8.000

21-07-2007   Jules Ottenstadion, Gentbrugge: KAA Gent – Aalborg BK   1-1 (0-0)
KAA Gent: Alexandre MARTINOVIC (FRA), Boban GRNCAROV (MCD), Christophe
GRONDIN (FRA), Rándall AZOFEIFA Corrales (CRC) (86' Admir HAZNADAR (BOS),
Guillaume GILLET, Davy DE BEULE (YC88), Massimo MOIA (75' Gil VERMOUTH
(ISR)), Aleksandar MUTAVDZIC (SRB), Marcin ZEWLAKOW (POL), Adekanmi
OLUFADE (TOG), Dominic FOLEY (IRL). (Coach: Trond Johan SOLLIED (NOR)).
Aalborg BK: Martin JENSEN, Michael JAKOBSEN, Daniel Benjamin CALIFF (USA), Jón
Roi JACOBSEN (FAR), Allan OLESEN (YC26), Andreas JOHANSSON (66' Patrick
KRISTENSEN), Kasper RISGÅRD, Thomas ENEVOLDSEN (81' Súni OLSEN (FAR)), Rade
PRICA (SWE), Jeppe CURTH, Siyabonga NOMVETHE (RSA) (YC31,YC55). (Coach: Erik
HAMRÉN (SWE)).
Goals: KAA Gent: 1-0 Adekanmi OLUFADE (47' penalty).
Aalborg BK: 1-1 Siyabonga NOMVETHE (55').
Referee: Jérôme LAPERRIÈRE (SUI)   Attendance: 5.135

21-07-2007   Gerhard-Hanappi-Stadion, Wien :
              SK Rapid Wien – FC Rubin Kazan   3-1 (0-1)
SK Rapid Wien: Helge PAYER, Mario TOKIC (CRO), Martin HIDEN, Andreas DOBER (56'
Christian THONHOFER), Markus HEIKKINEN (FIN), Steffen HOFMANN (GER), Ümit
KORKMAZ (84' FABIANO de Lima Campos Maria (BRA)), Mario SARA (56' Markus
KATZER), Branko BOSKOVIC (MNE), Mate BILIC (CRO), Mario BAZINA (CRO). (Coach:
Peter PACULT).
FC Rubin Kazan: Aleksandrs KOLINKO (LAT), JEAN Ferreira Narde (BRA) (YC28),
Mikhail SINEV, GABRIEL Fernando Atz (BRA) (RC73), Macbeth SIBAYA (RSA), Vitaliy
VOLKOV (YC81) (82' Andrey Vitalevich FEDOROV), Aleksandr RYAZANTSEV,
Christiano Fernando NOBOA Tello (ECU), Sergey BUDYLIN, Dmitriy VASILEV (YC53)
(90'+1' Ansar AYUPOV), Vladimir BAYRAMOV (TMS) (YC31) (76' Lasha
SALUKVADZE (GEO) (RC78)). (Coach: Kurban Bekiyevich BERDYEV (TMS)).
Goals: SK Rapid Wien: 1-1 Steffen HOFMANN (69'), 2-1 Mate BILIC (80' penalty), 3-1
Steffen HOFMANN (90'+3').
FC Rubin Kazan: 0-1 Aleksandr RYAZANTSEV (29').
Referee: David McKEON (IRL)   Attendance: 10.200

22-07-2007   Stadion Centralny, Kostanay: FK Tobol Kostanay – FC O.F.I. Crete   1-0 (1-0)
FK Tobol Kostanay: Alexandr PETUKHOV, Farkhadbek IRISMETOV, Daniyar MUKANOV,
Stanimir DIMITROV (BUL), Kairat NURDAULETOV, Azat NURGALIEV, Nurbol
ZHUMASKALIEV (82' Talgat SABALAKOV), Sergey SKORIKH, Igor YURIN (65'
Yevgeniy MESHKOV), Ruslan BALTIEV, Didarklych URAZOV (TMS) (53' Vyacheslav
NURMAGOMBETOV). (Coach: Dmitriy Alekseevich OGAI).
FC O.F.I. Crete: Tristan PEERSMAN (BEL), Cosmin BARCAUAN (ROM) (YC68), Dimitris
ARVANITIS, Pierre Sanitarib ISSA (RSA), Giannis TARALIDIS, Aleksandar SIMIC (SRB)
(88' Emmanouil Stylianos ROUMBAKIS), Minas Konstantinos PITSOS, Vasileios-Aris
Chronis PLOUSIS (67' Dimitrios PLIAGAS), Fabian GERBER (GER), Zdravko POPOVIC
(CRO), Joseph NWAFOR (NGR). (Coach: Reiner MAURER (GER)).
Goal: FK Tobol Kostanay: 1-0 Ruslan BALTIEV (29').
Referee: Damien LEDENTU (FRA)   Attendance: 457

22-07-2007   Råsunda Fotbollstadion, Solna: Hammarby IF – FC Utrecht   0-0
Hammarby IF: Benny LEKSTRÖM, David JOHANSSON, José Monteiro de MACEDO,
Suleyman "Sulan" SLEYMAN (YC74), Christian TRAORÉ (DEN), Louay CHANKO,
Sebastián EGUREN (URU) (YC65), Petter ANDERSSON, Haris LAITINEN (71' Charlie
DAVIES (USA)), Sebastian CASTRO-TELLO (57' Erkan ZENGIN), Paulo Roberto Chamon
de Castilho "PAULINHO GUARÁ" (BRA) (YC86). (Coach: Tony GUSTAVSSON).
FC Utrecht: Frank GRANDEL (GDL) (YC70), Tim CORNELISSE, Étienne SHEW-ATJON
(88' Erik PIETERS), Sander KELLER, Francis DICKOH (GHA), Tom CALUWÉ (BEL),
Gregoor VAN DIJK, Rick KRUYS (YC41) (84' Leroy GEORGE), Hans SOMERS (BEL),
Loïc LOVAL-LANDRÉ (GDL), Robin NELISSE (69' Giuseppe ROSSINI (ITA) (YC86)).
(Coach: Willem VAN HANEGEM).
Referee: Philippe KALT (FRA)   Attendance: 5.361

22-07-2007   Vetros Stadionas, Vilnius: FK Vetra Vilnius – Blackburn Rovers FC   0-2 (0-1)
FK Vetra Vilnius: Vaidotas ZUTAUTAS, Andrey USACHEV (RUS) (YC50), Nerijus
SASNAUSKAS, Andrius SKERLA, Pedro Henrique BOTELHO (BRA), Bobi BOZINOVSKI
(MCD), Mindaugas PANKA, Gediminas BUTRIMAVICIUS (63' Rolandas
KARCEMARSKAS), Vitalis STANKEVICIUS (63' Maksut AZIZI (SLO)), SEVERINO Lima
de Moura (BRA) (74' Robertas VEZEVICIUS), Egidijus JUSKA (YC90+2). (Coach: Vitas
JANCIAUSKAS).
Blackburn Rovers FC: Bradley Howard FRIEDEL (USA), André OOIJER (HOL), Ran
NELSEN (NZL), Christopher SAMBA Veijeany (CGO), Stephen WARNOCK, Tugay
KERIMOGLU (TUR) (46' Aaron MOKOENA (RSA)), Robert SAVAGE (WAL), Morten
Gamst PEDERSEN (NOR), Benedict Saul McCARTHY (RSA) (65' Maceo RIGTERS
(HOL)), David BENTLEY (65' Matthew DERBYSHIRE), Jason ROBERTS (GRN). (Coach:
Leslie Mark HUGHES (WAL)).
Goals: Blackburn Rovers FC: 0-1 Benedict Saul McCARTHY (30'), 0-2 Matthew
DERBYSHIRE (81').
Referee: Tony ASUMAA (FIN)   Attendance: 5.200

22-07-2007   Stadion Crvena Zvezda, Beograd:
                    NK Hajduk Kula – União Desportiva de Leiria   1-0 (1-0)
NK Hajduk Kula: Andjelko DJURICIC (YC83), Sinisa RADANOVIC, Rados BULATOVIC
(YC82), Bojan DOJKIC, Goran HABENSUS (YC32), Nebojsa SODIC, Nikola BOGIC
(YC18), Miodrag VASILJEVIC (90'+3' Dusan ZELIC), Igor KOZOS, Milan PERIC (89'
Aleksandar JOVANOVIC (BOS)), Nikola KOMAZEC. (Coach: Zarko SOLDO).
União Desportiva de Leiria: FERNANDO Büttenbender Prass (BRA), ÉDER José de Oliveira
Bonfim (BRA), RENATO Jorge Magalhães Dias Assunção, Nuno Filipe Rodrigues
LARANJEIRO, ÉDER GAÚCHO Guterres Silveira (BRA), "ALHANDRA" Luís Miguel
Assunção Joaquim (YC59) (68' Modou SOUGOU (SEN)), HUGO Miguel da Encarnação
Pires FARIA (YC87), TIAGO César Moreira Pereira, PAULO CÉSAR Rocha Rosa (BRA)
(53' MACIEL Lima Barbosa da Cunha (BRA)), "CADU" Carlos Eduardo Castro da Silva
(BRA) (56' "TOÑITO" António Jesus García González (ESP)), JOÃO PAULO Pinto Ribeiro
(YC82). (Coach: PAULO Jorge Rebelo DUARTE).
Goal: NK Hajduk Kula: 1-0 Milan PERIC (42').
Referee: Bülent YILDIRIM (TUR)

28-07-2007   Ewood Park, Blackburn: Blackburn Rovers FC – FK Vetra Vilnius   4-0 (1-0)
Blackburn Rovers FC: Bradley Howard FRIEDEL (USA), André OOIJER (HOL), Ran
NELSEN (NZL), Aaron MOKOENA (RSA) (53' Davin DUNN), Christopher SAMBA
Veijeany (CGO), Stephen WARNOCK, Robert SAVAGE (WAL), Morten Gamst PEDERSEN
(NOR), Benedict Saul McCARTHY (RSA) (57' Matthew DERBYSHIRE), David BENTLEY,
Jason ROBERTS (GRN) (57' Maceo RIGTERS (HOL)). (Coach: Leslie Mark HUGHES
(WAL)).
FK Vetra Vilnius: Vaidotas ZUTAUTAS, Romanas JUSKA (58' Robertas VEZEVICIUS),
Andrey USACHEV (RUS), Nerijus SASNAUSKAS, Andrius SKERLA, Pedro Henrique
BOTELHO (BRA), Dejan MILOSEVSKI (MCD) (RC40), Bobi BOZINOVSKI (MCD),
Mindaugas PANKA (82' Julius RALIUKONIS), Maksut AZIZI (SLO) (74' Rolandas
KARCEMARSKAS), SEVERINO Lima de Moura (BRA). (Coach: Vitas JANCIAUSKAS).
Goals: Blackburn Rovers FC: 1-0 Morten Gamst PEDERSEN (26'), 2-0 Jason ROBERTS
(48'), 3-0 Benedict Saul McCARTHY (50'), 4-0 Christopher SAMBA Veijeany (56').
Referee: Michael WEINER (GER)   Attendance: 11.854

28-07-2007   Hüseyin Avni Aker Stadyumu, Trabzon:
              Trabzonspor Kulübü – FC Otelul Galati   1-2 (1-1)
Trabzonspor Kulübü: Tolga ZENGIN, Tayfun CORA, Erdinç YAVUZ, Hüseyin ÇIMSIR,
Ayman Mohamad ABDELAZIZ (EGY) (85' Adnan GÜNGÖR), Ceyhun ERIS (YC56),
Serkan BALCI, Gökdeniz KARADENIZ, Celaleddin KOÇAK, Umut BULUT (76' Yusuf
KURTULUS), Ersen MARTIN. (Coach: Ziyaettin (Ziya) DOGAN).
FC Otelul Galati: Paulius GRYBAUSKAS (LIT), Salif NOGO (BKF), Cristian SARGHI,
Zhivko ZHELEV (BUL) (YC63), Constantin Dorin SEMEGHIN, Gil-Sik KIM (KOR) (71'
Eduard RATNIKOV (EST)), Gabriel Ioan PARASCHIV, Gabriel Nicu GIURGIU, Emil
Gabriel JULA, Janos Jozsef SZEKELY (YC52) (90' Silviu ILIE), Daniel Dorin STAN (15'
Tadas LABUKAS (LIT)). (Coach: Petre GRIGORAS).
Goals: Trabzonspor Kulübü: 1-0 Ceyhun ERIS (8').
FC Otelul Galati: 1-1 Janos Jozsef SZEKELY (13'), 1-2 Emil Gabriel JULA (89' penalty).
Referee: Stanislav SUKHINA (RUS)   Attendance: 22.000

28-07-2007   Stade Félix Bollaert, Lens:
              Racing Club de Lens – FK Chornomorets Odessa   3-1 (2-1)
Racing Club de Lens: Vedran RUNJE (CRO) (YC80), Lucien AUBEY (89' MARCO Miguel
Gonçalves RAMOS (POR)), Vitorino HILTON de Silva (BRA), Adama COULIBALY (MLI),
Eric CARRIÈRE (71' Sidi Yaya KEITA (MLI)), Kanga Gauthier AKALÉ (CIV) (86'
Abdoulrazak BOUKARI), Nenad KOVACEVIC (SRB), Yohan DEMONT, Julien SABLÉ
Fourtassou, Bonaventura KALOU (CIV) (YC88), Olivier MONTERRUBIO (YC27). (Coach:
Guy ROUX).
FK Chornomorets Odessa: Vitaliy RUDENKO, Gennadi Aleksandrovich NIZHEGORODOV
(RUS), Oleg SHANDRUK, Igor LOZO (CRO), Pavel KIRILCHIK (BLS) (46' Valentin
POLTAVETS (YC49)), Dmitro GRISHKO, Vladimir KORYTKO (BLS), Andriy KIRLIK
(46' Maksim Andreevich BILETSKIY), Sergiy DANILOVSKIY, Sergiy SHISHCHENKO
(71' Konstantin YAKOSHENKO), Oleg VENHLINSKIY. (Coach: Vitaliy Viktorovich
SHEVCHENKO (RUS)).
Goals: Racing Club de Lens: 1-1 Adama COULIBALY (19'), 2-1 Kanga Gauthier AKALÉ
(39'), 3-1 Kanga Gauthier AKALÉ (72').
FK Chornomorets Odessa: 0-1 Oleg VENHLINSKIY (10').
Referee: Manuel GRÄFE (GER)   Atendance: 25.570

28-07-2007   Stadio Luigi Ferraris, Genoa:
UC Sampdoria – PFC Cherno More Varna   1-0 (0-0)
UC Sampdoria: Luca CASTELLAZZI, Pietro ACCARDI, Luigi SALA, Hugo Armando
CAMPAGNARO (ARG), Mirko PIERI, Cristian ZENONI, Sergio VOLPI (YC67) (86' Paolo
SAMMARCO), Angelo PALOMBO (YC49), Vladimir KOMAN (UKR) (61' Christian
MAGGIO), Claudio BELLUCCI, Andrea CARACCIOLO (67' Vincenzo MONTELLA).
(Coach: Walter MAZZARRI).
PFC Cherno More Varna: Karamfil ILCHEV, Nikolai DOMAKINOV, Radoslav BACHEV
(YC71), Aleksandar TOMASH, Daniel DIMOV (89' Konstantin SETLINOV), Kiril
DZHOROV, RICARDO ANDRÉ Duarte Pires (POR) (YC32), Georgi ANDONOV (86'
MARCOS da Silva (BRA)), DJALMA Henrique da Silva (BRA), Daniel Atanasov
GEORGIEV (89' Miroslav MANOLOV), FABINHO Aigar Laurentino (BRA) (YC38).
(Coach: Nikola Asenov SPASOV).
Goal: UC Sampdoria: 1-0 Christian MAGGIO (90'+1').
Referee: Bjorn KUIPERS (HOL)   Attendance: 20.000

28-07-2007   Estadio Vicente Calderón, Madrid:
Club Atlético de Madrid – FC Gloria Bistrita   1-0 (1-0)
Club Atlético de Madrid: Leonardo Neoren "LEO" FRANCO (ARG), Georgios Dimitrios
SEITARIDIS (GRE) (88' Fabiano ELLER dos Santos (BRA)), Mariano Andrés PERNÍA
(ARG), Luis Amarando PEREA Mosquera (COL), PABLO Ibáñez Tébar, Peter Bernard
LUCCIN (FRA), Maximiliano Rubén "MAXI" RODRÍGUEZ (ARG), José Manuel JURADO
Marín (YC8), Nuno Ricardo de Oliveira Ribeiro "MANICHE" (POR) (77' RAÚL GARCÍA
Escudero), Diego Martín FORLÁN Corazo (URU), Sergio Leonel AGÜERO (ARG) (89'
BRAULIO Nóbrega Rodríguez). (Coach: Javier "El Vasco" AGUIRRE Onaindía (MEX)).
FC Gloria Bistrita: Ciprian Anton TATARUSANU, Vasile Mircea RUS (46' Lucian Dan
TURCU), Octavian ABRUDAN, Laszlo SEPSI (YC21) (73' Ion DUMITRA), Razvan Gabriel
DOBRE, Adrian NALATI, Cristian Ambrozie COROIAN, Dorin TOMA, Cosmin Vali
FRASINESCU, Sergiu Vasile COSTEA (YC51) (78' Luvius Razvan DAMIAN), Cosmin
TILINCA (YC81). (Coach: Ioan Ovidiu SABAU).
Goal: Club Atlético de Madrid: 1-0 Diego Martín FORLÁN Corazo (11').
Referee: Charles Joseph RICHMOND (SCO)   Attendance: 22.000

29-07-2007   AOL Arena, Hamburg: Hamburger SV – FC Dacia Chisinau   4-0 (0-0)
Hamburger SV: Frank Peter ROST, Joris MATHIJSEN (HOL) (78' Bastian REINHARDT),
Vincent KOMPANY (BEL), Collin BENJAMIN (NAM), Nigel DE JONG (HOL), David
JAROLÍM (CZE), Piotr TROCHOWSKI, Guy Roland DEMEL (CIV) (77' Miso BRECKO
(SLO)), Rafael VAN DER VAART (HOL), Mohamed ZIDAN (EGY) (80' Eric-Maxim
CHOUPO-MOTING), Ivica OLIC (CRO). (Coach: Hubertus Jozef Margaretha (Huub)
STEVENS (HOL)).
FC Dacia Chisinau: Mihail MORARU, Vitalie MARDARI, Nicolai MINCEV (YC22),
Dumitru Alin LIPA (73' Marius CALIN (ROM)), Vadim BOLOHAN, Maxim ANDRONIC,
Ghenadie ORBU, Alexandru ONICA (YC30), Andrei MARTIN, Iurie SOIMU (88' Marcel
RESHITSA), Dumitru GUSILA (63' Miguel NIMES Lopes de PINA (POR)). (Coach: Emilian
(Emil) CARAS).
Goals: Hamburger SV: 1-0 Vincent KOMPANY (50'), 2-0 Rafael VAN DER VAART (71'),
3-0 Collin BENJAMIN (76'), 4-0 David JAROLÍM (89').
Referee: Ivan BEBEK (CRO)   Attendance: 50.800

208

29-07-2007   Stadion Galgenwaard, Utrecht: FC Utrecht – Hammarby IF 1-1 (0-0)
FC Utrecht: Frank GRANDEL (GDL), Tim CORNELISSE, Étienne SHEW-ATJON (69' Erik
PIETERS), Sander KELLER (RC67), Francis DICKOH (GHA), Tom CALUWÉ (BEL)
(YC90+3), Gregoor VAN DIJK (YC53), Rick KRUYS (84' Kees VAN BUUREN), Hans
SOMERS (BEL) (46' Leroy GEORGE), Robin NELISSE, Giuseppe ROSSINI (ITA) (YC42).
(Coach: Willem VAN HANEGEM).
Hammarby IF: Benny LEKSTRÖM, David JOHANSSON, José Monteiro de MACEDO,
Gunnar Thor GUNNARSSON (ISL) (46' Joakim JENSEN), Christian TRAORÉ (DEN),
Louay CHANKO (YC89), Sebastián EGUREN (URU), Petter ANDERSSON, Erkan ZENGIN
(87' Sebastian CASTRO-TELLO), Haris LAITINEN (YC62), Paulo Roberto Chamon de
Castilho "PAULINHO GUARÁ" (BRA) (80' Charlie DAVIES (USA) (YC85)). (Coach: Tony
GUSTAVSSON).
Goals: FC Utrecht: 1-0 Robin NELISSE (64').
Hammarby IF: 1-1 David JOHANSSON (66').
Referee: Michael Leslie DEAN (ENG)   Attendance: 10.200

29-07-2007   Central Stadium, Kazan: FC Rubin Kazan – SK Rapid Wien 0-0
FC Rubin Kazan: Aleksandrs KOLINKO (LAT), JEAN Ferreira Narde (BRA), Andrey
Vitalevich FEDOROV, Mikhail SINEV, Macbeth SIBAYA (RSA) (RC66), Vitaliy VOLKOV,
Aleksandr RYAZANTSEV, Sergey BUDYLIN, Dmitriy VASILEV (59' Aleksandr
Vladislavovich YARKIN), Aleksandr GATSKAN (YC25) (77' Ansar AYUPOV), Vladimir
BAYRAMOV (TMS) (76' Andrey Igorevich KIREEV). (Coach: Kurban Bekiyevich
BERDYEV (TMS)).
SK Rapid Wien: Helge PAYER, Mario TOKIC (CRO), Jürgen PATOCKA (YC90+1), Martin
HIDEN, Markus KATZER, Andreas DOBER (YC27), Markus HEIKKINEN (FIN), Steffen
HOFMANN (GER), Branko BOSKOVIC (MNE), Mate BILIC (CRO), Mario BAZINA (CRO)
(61' Ümit KORKMAZ). (Coach: Peter PACULT).
Referee: Stefan JOHANNESSON (SWE)   Attendance: 15.000

29-07-2007   Estádio Dr. Magalhães Pessoa, Leiria:
              União Desportiva de Leiria – NK Hajduk Kula 4-1 (0-0)
União Desportiva de Leiria: FERNANDO Büttenbender Prass (BRA), ÉDER José de Oliveira
Bonfim (BRA), RENATO Jorge Magalhães Dias Assunção (YC54), Nuno Filipe Rodrigues
LARANJEIRO, ÉDER GAÚCHO Guterres Silveira (BRA) (YC106), HUGO Miguel da
Encarnação Pires FARIA, Modou SOUGOU (SEN) (YC118), TIAGO César Moreira Pereira,
"CADU" Carlos Eduardo Castro da Silva (BRA) (54' PAÚLO CÉSAR Rocha Rosa (BRA)),
"TOÑITO" António Jesus García González (ESP) (67'"ALHANDRA" Luís Miguel Assunção
Joaquim), JOÃO PAULO Pinto Ribeiro (66' JESSUI Silva do Nascimento (BRA)). (Coach:
PAULO Jorge Rebelo DUARTE).
NK Hajduk Kula: Andjelko DJURICIC, Savo PAVICEVIC (MNE), Darko FEJSA, Rados
BULATOVIC, Goran HABENSUS (101' Bojan DOJKIC), Nebojsa SODIC (YC94,RC120),
Jovan RADIVOJEVIC, Nikola BOGIC, Ljubomir FEJSA (91' Miodrag VASILJEVIC
(YC96)), Igor KOZOS, Milan PERIC (90' Dusan ZELIC). (Coach: Zarko SOLDO).
Goals: União Desportiva de Leiria: 1-0 ÉDER GAÚCHO Guterres Silveira (90'+3'), 2-0 Nuno
Filipe Rodrigues LARANJEIRO (97' penalty), 3-1 Modou SOUGOU (112'), 4-1 Nuno Filipe
Rodrigues LARANJEIRO (120' penalty).
NK Hajduk Kula: 2-1 Nikola BOGIC (107' penalty).
Referee: Fritz STUCHLIK (AUT)   Attendance: 1.097
(After extra time)

209

29-07-2007   Aalborg Stadion, Aalborg: Aalborg BK – KAA Gent   2-1 (1-1)
Aalborg BK: Martin JENSEN, Michael JAKOBSEN, Martin PEDERSEN (YC70), Daniel
Benjamin CALIFF (USA), Allan OLESEN, Mattias LINDSTRÖM (SWE), Andreas
JOHANSSON (90'+1' Patrick KRISTENSEN), Kasper RISGÅRD, Thomas ENEVOLDSEN,
Rade PRICA (SWE) (YC50), Jeppe CURTH. (Coach: Erik HAMRÉN (SWE)).
KAA Gent: Alexandre MARTINOVIC (FRA), Djordje SVETLICIC (SRB) (21' Massimo
MOIA), Boban GRNCAROV (MCD), Christophe GRONDIN (FRA), Guillaume GILLET
(YC60) (83' Gil VERMOUTH (ISR)), Alin STOICA (ROM) (YC79) (83' Bryan RUIZ
González (CRC)), Davy DE BEULE, Aleksandar MUTAVDZIC (SRB), Marcin
ZEWLAKOW (POL) (YC75), Adekanmi OLUFADE (TOG), Dominic FOLEY (IRL). (Coach:
Trond Johan SOLLIED (NOR)).
Goals: Aalborg BK: 1-1 Daniel Benjamin CALIFF (31'), 2-1 Andreas JOHANSSON (78').
KAA Gent: 0-1 Adekanmi OLUFADE (27').
Referee: Sorin CORPODEAN (ROM)   Attendance: 3.725

29-07-2007   Pankrítio Stádio, Heraklion: FC O.F.I. Crete – FK Tobol Kostanay   0-1 (0-0)
FC O.F.I. Crete: Tristan PEERSMAN (BEL), Cosmin BARCAUAN (ROM) (YC73), Dimitris
ARVANITIS (68' Vasileios-Aris Chronis PLOUSIS), Pierre Sanitarib ISSA (RSA),
Emmanouil Stylianos ROUMBAKIS (56' Dimitrios PLIAGAS), Giannis TARALIDIS
(YC64), Aleksandar SIMIC (SRB), Minas Konstantinos PITSOS (82' Kostas
MICHELAKAKIS (YC85)), Nikolaos KOUNENAKIS, Fabian GERBER (GER), Joseph
NWAFOR (NGR). (Coach: Reiner MAURER (GER)).
FK Tobol Kostanay: Alexandr PETUKHOV, Farkhadbek IRISMETOV, Daniyar MUKANOV,
Stanimir DIMITROV (BUL), Kairat NURDAULETOV (YC60), Azat NURGALIEV (69'
Yevgeniy MESHKOV), Sergey SKORIKH, Igor YURIN (61' Andrei KHARABARA (RUS)
(YC74)), Ruslan BALTIEV, Vyacheslav NURMAGOMBETOV (YC75), Sergey
OSTAPENKO (YC27) (42' Ulugbek BAKAEV (UZB) (YC83)). (Coach: Dmitriy Alekseevich
OGAI).
Goal: FK Tobol Kostanay: 0-1 Andrei KHARABARA (86').
Referee: Pavel Cristian BALAJ (ROM)   Attendance: 46

**Aalborg BK, Club Atlético de Madrid, Blackburn Rovers FC, Hamburger SV,
Hammarby IF, FC Otelul Galati, Racing Club de Lens, SK Rapid Wien, UC Sampdoria,
FK Tobol Kostanay and União Desportiva de Leiria all qualified for the UEFA Cup
competition.**

2008

21-06-2008   Mika Stadium, Yerevan: FC MIKA Ashtarak – FC Tiraspol   2-2 (2-0)
FC MIKA Ashtarak: Feliks HAKOBYAN, Armen PETROSYAN, Gevorg POGHOSYAN,
Rafael SAFARYAN (YC60), Zaza SAKHOKIA (GEO) (59' Hrachya MIKAELYAN), David
GRIGORYAN (74' Maksim FEDOROV (RUS)), Stepan HAKOBYAN, Arkadi
CHILINGARYAN, THIAGO Manoel De Souza (BRA), Khoren VERANYAN (71'
MODESTO Danilo Da Silva (BRA)), Narek BEGLARYAN. (Coach: Arkadi
ANDRIASYAN).
FC Tiraspol: Serghei JURIC, Kyrylo SYDORENKO (UKR), Mihail DODUL, Stanislav
SOLODYAK (YC67), Igor KARPOVICH (BUL), Sergey REVA (UKR) (60' Vitalie
BULAT), Andrey SECRIERU (87' Andrei VERBETCHI), Serghei NAMASCO, Nicolai
RUDAC, Andrey PORFIREANU, Alexandru SUVOROV (73' Anatoli CHEPTINE). (Coach:
Volodymyr REVA (UKR)).
Goals: FC MIKA Ashtarak: 1-0 Khoren VERANYAN (18'), 2-0 Stepan HAKOBYAN (41').
FC Tiraspol: 2-1 Kyrylo SYDORENKO (61' penalty), 2-2 Serghei NAMASCO (79').
Referee: Ninoslav SPASIC (SRB)   Attendance: 2.110

21-06-2008   The Showgrounds, Ballymena: Lisburn Distillery FC – T.P.S. Turku   2-3 (1-0)
Lisburn Distillery FC: Alexander SPACKMAN, Wayne BUCHANAN (YC28), Patrick
McSHANE, Jonathan MAGEE, Ryan McCANN (SCO), Christopher KINGSBERRY (84'
Neal GAWLEY), Andrew KILMARTIN (IRL), Mark COOLING (84' Peter MUIR), Darren
ARMOUR, Curtis ALLEN (86' Nathan McCONNELL), Peter McCANN (IRL). (Coach: Paul
KIRK).
T.P.S. Turku: Henrik MOISANDER, Urmas ROOBA (EST), Ville LEHTONEN, Christian
Atta GYAN (GHA), Sami RÄHMÖNEN, Jarno HEINIKANGAS, Aristides PERTOT (ARG),
Kasper HÄMÄLÄINEN, Mika ÄÄRITALO (YC89), Armand ONE (FRA), Mikko
PAATELAINEN (90'+2' Antti HAKALA). (Coach: Martti KUUSELA).
Goals: Lisburn Distillery FC: 1-0 Darren ARMOUR (42'), 2-3 Darren ARMOUR (90'+2'
penalty).
T.P.S. Turku: 1-1 Aristides PERTOT (68'), 1-2 Mika ÄÄRITALO (76'), 1-3 Aristides
PERTOT (88').
Referee: Luc WOUTERS (BEL)

21-06-2008   Stade am Deich, Ettelbruck:
              FC Etzella Ettelbruck – FC Lokomotivi Tbilisi   0-0
FC Etzella Ettelbruck: Joé FLICK, Gauthier REMACLE (BEL), Eric HOFFMANN, Jacques
PLEIN, Gilles ENGELDINGER, Charles LEWECK (YC73) (88' SIDNEY Do Rosario),
NILTON Jorge Rocha (BRA), Ben FEDERSPIEL, Daniel DA MOTA, João Carlos
FERREIRA Capela, Alphonse LEWECK (YC88). (Coach: Florim ALIJAJ (ALB)).
FC Lokomotivi Tbilisi: Zurab BATIASHVILI, Nika GUSHARASHVILI, Georgi
GULORDAVA, Levan SARALIDZE, Dachi POPKHADZE, Zviadi CHKHETIANI, Irakli
CHIRIKASHVILI, Vitali DARASELIA (YC87), Rati ALEKSIDZE, Teimuraz
PHARULAVA, Irakli SAMKHARADZE. (Coach: Zaza ZAMTARADZE).
Referee: Gediminas MAZEIKA (LIT)

21-06-2008   Daugavas stadions, Liepaja: FK Riga – IF Fylkir 1-2 (0-1)
FK Riga: Sergey Andreevich CHEPCHUGOV (RUS), Roberts MEZECKIS, Igors
KORABLOVS (YC78), Grigory Alexandrovich CHIRKIN (RUS), Valeriy Viktorovich
LEONOV (RUS), Mindaugas KALONAS (LIT) (71' Gints FREIMANIS), Maksims
RAFALSKIS (61' Evgeniy NOVIKOV (EST)), Pavels MIHADJUKS, Vladimirs
ZAVORONKOVS, Mihails MIHOLAPS, Ivan Vladimirovich SHPAKOV (RUS). (Coach:
Genadijs MOROZOVS).
IF Fylkir: Fjalar THORGEIRSSON, Kristján VALDIMARSSON, Thórir HANNESSON, Peter
GRAVESEN (DEN) (YC41), Valur Fannar GÍSLASON, Björn Orri HERMANNSSON (80'
Vidar GUDJONSSON), Gudni Rúnar HELGASON, Hermann ADALGEIRSSON, Kjartan
Ágúst BREIDDAL, Halldór Arnar HILMISSON, Allan DYRING (DEN) (77' Kjartan Andri
BALDVINSSON). (Coach: Leifur Sigfinnur GARDARSSON).
Goals: FK Riga: 1-2 Evgeniy NOVIKOV (76').
IF Fylkir: 0-1 Valur Fannar GÍSLASON (26'), 0-2 Peter GRAVESEN (70' penalty).
Referee: Svein Erik EDVARTSEN (NOR)

21-06-2008   Hibernians Stadium, Paola: Hibernians FC Paola – ND Gorica 0-3 (0-1)
Hibernians FC Paola: Mario MUSCAT, Jonathan CARUANA, Jonathan XERRI (79' Tristan
CARUANA), Jonathan PEARSON (55' Mauro BONNICI), Timothy Fleri SOLER, Aaron
XUEREB, Adrian PULIS, Edafe UZEH (NGR) (YC80), Clayton FAILLA (YC72) (88' Adrian
MIFSUD), Andrew COHEN, Terence SCERRI. (Coach: Robert GATT).
ND Gorica: Vasja SIMCIC, Bojan DUKIC (CRO), Aris ZARIFOVIC, Nebosja KOVACEVIC,
Admir KRSIC (74' Dario SMITRAN), Sebastjan KOMEL (YC64), Simon ZIVEC, Enes
DEMIROVIC (BOS), Goran CVIJANOVIC, Etien VELIKONJA (65' Goran GALESIC),
Milan OSTERC (61' Mladen KOVACEVIC). (Coach: Primoz GLIHA).
Goals: ND Gorica: 0-1 Aaron XUEREB (34' own goal), 0-2 Goran CVIJANOVIC (56'), 0-3
Etien VELIKONJA (58').
Referee: Ovidia Alin HATEGAN (ROM)

21-06-2008   Tofiq Bahramov Stadium, Baku: Neftchi Baku PFK – FC Nitra 2-0 (2-0)
Neftchi Baku PFK: Vladimir MICOVIC (SRB), Rail MELIKOV (YC90), Elnur
ALLAHVERDIEV (80' Ruslan ABBASOV), Volodimr OLEFIR (UKR), Rashad
A.SADIKHOV, Olexandr CHERTOGANOV, Rashad Ferhad SADIKHOV, Oleg
GERASIMYUK (UKR), Nazar BAYRAMOV (TMS) (76' Ruslan ABUSHEV), Georgi
CHELIDZE (GEO) (67' Samir ALIYEV), Georgi ADAMIA (GEO). (Coach: Anatoliy
Vasiliyovich DEMYANENKO (UKR)).
FC Nitra: Tomas TUJVEL, Marián DATKO (YC90+2), Martin TÓTH, Adrián CEMAN, Karol
KARLÍK (YC34), Jan GRUBER (CZE), Lubos KOLAR (63' Róbert GLENDA), Peter
GRAJCIAR (83' Marek KOSTOLÁNI (YC89)), Ján STAJER, Robert SEMENIK, Martin
BACA (CZE) (65' Irakli LILUASHVILI (GEO)). (Coach: Pavel MALURA (CZE)).
Goals: Neftchi Baku PFK: 1-0 Rashad Ferhad SADIKHOV (7'), 2-0 Rashad A.SADIKHOV
(10').
Referee: Marcin BORSKI (POL)   Attendance: 4.000

21-06-2008   Stadion Cracovii, Kraków:
KS Cracovia Kraków – FC Shakhter Soligorsk   1-2 (1-0)
KS Cracovia Kraków: Marcin CABAJ, Przemyslaw KULIG, Marek WASILUK, Piotr
POLCZAK (YC11), Lukasz TUPALSKI, Arkadiusz BARAN (61' Michal KARWAN),
Dariusz PAWLUSINSKI (72' Árpád MAJOROS (HUN)), Dariusz KLUS (75' Karol
KOSTRUBALA), Pawel NOWAK, Kamil WITKOWSKI (YC14,YC29), Marcin
KRZYWICKI. (Coach: Stefan MAJEWSKI).
FC Shakhter Soligorsk: Vitaliy MAKAVCHIK, Mikalai BRANFILOV, Valeriy
ZHUKOVSKIY (YC51), Dmitriy CHALEY, Andrey LEONCHIK, Nikita BUKATKIN (57'
Aleksandr BYCHENOK), Maksim GUKAYLO, Aleksey RIOS (40' Sergey NIKIFORENKO),
Sergey KOVALCHUK, Sergey BALANOVICH, Igor ZYULEV (58' Mikhail
MARTINOVICH). (Coach: Yuri Vasilevich VERGEICHIK).
Goals: KS Cracovia Kraków: 1-0 Pawel NOWAK (25').
FC Shakhter Soligorsk: 1-1 Andrey LEONCHIK (68'), 1-2 Aleksandr BYCHENOK (72').
Referee: Joseph R.ATTARD (MLT)   Attendance: 5.000

21-06-2008   Stadion Kantrida, Rijeka: HNK Rijeka – FK Renova   0-0
HNK Rijeka: Velimir RADMAN, Luka VUCKO, Fausto BUDICIN, Sandi KRIZMAN (68'
Alen SKORO (BOS)), Dario BODRUSIC, Anas SHARBINI, Hrvoje STROK (68' Alen
PAMIC), Nikola SAFARIC, Georgi Aleksandrov IVANOV (BUL) (YC77) (80' Damir
KREILACH), Radomir DJALOVIC (MNE), Nedim HALILOVIC (BOS). (Coach: Zlatko
DALIC).
FK Renova: Armend ELEZI, Zvonimir STANKOVIC (SRB) (YC47), Agron MEMEDI,
Vladimir DESPOTOVSKI (YC62), Besart IBRAIMI (62' Vulnet EMINI), Igorce
STOJANOV, Fisnik NUHIU, Pance STOJANOV (83' Sakir REDZEPI), Vance TRAJCOV,
Aleksandar ANGELOVSKI, Ismail ISMAILI (72' Genc ISEINI). (Coach: Vlatko KOSTOV).
Referee: Hubert SIEJEWICZ (POL)   Attendance: 700

21-06-2008   Bilino Polje, Zenica: NK Celik Zenica – OFK Grbalj Radanovici 3-2 (1-1)
NK Celik Zenica: Jasmin BURIC, Bojan MARKOVIC, Mladen JURCEVIC (YC69), Almir
HASANOVIC, Fenan SALCINOVIC (86' Zlatan GAFUROVIC), Armin KAPETAN (CRO),
Nermin SABIC (70' Serif HASIC), Bojan PUPCEVIC, Jasmin MORANJKIC, Mahir KARIC
(59' Zoran NOVAKOVIC), Emir HADZIC. (Coach: Ivo ISTUK).
OFK Grbalj Radanovici: Srdjan KLJAJEVIC (SRB), Gavrilo PETROVIC, Ivica
FRANCISKOVIC (SRB), Igor DRAGICEVIC (SRB) (73' Miljan RADOVIC), Darko
BOJOVIC (YC40), Slobodan MAZIC (SRB), Predrag VIDEKANIC (SRB), Goran GRUJIC,
Marko KASALICA (80' Sasa POPOVIC), Darko PAVICEVIC, Dragan BOSKOVIC (YC58).
(Coach: Nebojsa VIGNJEVIC (SRB)).
Goals: NK Celik Zenica: 1-1 Mahir KARIC (30'), 2-1 Emir HADZIC (59' penalty), 3-1 Zoran
NOVAKOVIC (77').
OFK Grbalj Radanovici: 0-1 Marko KASALICA (7'), 3-2 Darko PAVICEVIC (90'+2').
Referee: Michael KOUKOULAKIS (GRE)

213

21-06-2008   Dalymount Park, Dublin: Bohemians FC – Rhyl FC   5-1 (0-1)
Bohemians FC: Brian MURPHY, Liam BURNS (NIR), Owen HEARY, Kenneth OMAN, Kevin HUNT (ENG) (83' Chris TURNER (NIR)), Kilian BRENNAN (YC48), John Paul KELLY (YC34), Stephen O'DONNELL, Mark ROSSITER, Neale FENN (72' Glen CROWE), Jason BYRNE (77' Darren MANSARAM (ENG)). (Coach: Patrick (Pat) FENLON).
Rhyl FC: Lee Mark KENDALL (YC63), Carl James RUFFER (ENG), George HORAN, Paul O'NEILL (ENG), Chris ROBERTS (74' Gary POWELL (ENG)), James BREWERTON (YC12), Mark CONNOLLY, Craig Steven JONES (90'+2' Matthew HOLT (ENG)), Gareth WILSON, Craig GARSIDE (ENG) (72' James KELLY (ENG)), Marc Lloyd WILLIAMS. (Coach: Osian ROBERTS).
Goals: Bohemians FC: 1-1 Jason BYRNE (51'), 2-1 Thomas HEARY (59'), 3-1 Kilian BRENNAN (63' penalty), 4-1 Neale FENN (71'), 5-1 Glen CROWE (80').
Rhyl FC: 0-1 Mark CONNOLLY (25').
Referee: Jouni HIETALA (FIN)

21-06-2008   Qemal Stafa Stadium, Tirana : KS Besa Kavajë – Ethnikós Áchnas FC   0-0
KS Besa Kavajë: Suat ZENDELI (MCD), Artan SAKAJ (73' Emiliano VELIAJ), Artim SHAKIRI (MCD), Erand HOXHA, Dritan KRASNIQI, Zekirija RAMADAN (MCD), Ilirjan MERTIRI, Herby FORTUNAT (CGO), Gerhard PROGNI (77' Meglid MIHANI), Enkeleid ALIKAJ, Bledar MANÇAKU (YC57) (58' Liridon LECI (KOS)). (Coach: Iljaz HAXHIRAJ).
Ethnikós Áchnas FC: Panagiotis CHARALAMBOUS, António Pedro De Brito Lopes "TONI" (POR), Christos SHAILIS, Daniel EDUSEI (GHA), Eduardo Angeli "EDU" (BRA), Zoran STJEPANOVIC (SRB), Lars SCHLICHTING (GER), Eleftherakis ELEFTHERIOU, Ivan PETROVIC (SRB), Panayiotis EGOMITIS (75' Elipidoforos ILIA (YC77)), Constantinos GEORGIADES (58' Christos KOTSONIS). (Coach: Stéphane August DEMOL (BEL)).
Referee: Alan BLACK (NIR)

22-06-2008   Zhetysu Stadium,Taldykorgan:
               FC Zhetysu Taldykorgan – Budapest Honvéd FC   1-2 (0-0)
FC Zhetysu Taldykorgan: Kirill PRYADKIN, Maksim ZABELIN, Aydar KUMISBEKOV, Dmitriy TURENKO (YC43), Evgeniy OVSHINOV, Sergey KUTSOV (56' Vyacheslav NURMAGAMBETOV), Konstantin MUNTEANU (ROM) (YC64), Dmitriy MAMONOV, Ion Ionut LUTU (ROM) (75' Konstantin PANIN (UKR)), Guvanchmuhamed OVEKOV (TMS), Anton SIDELNIKOV (RUS) (46' Ruslan MIKHAYLOV (RUS) (YC73)). (Coach: Eduard GLAZUNOV).
Budapest Honvéd FC: Balázs RABÓCZKI, András DEBRECENI, Zoltan VINCZE, Ákos TAKÁCS, Tamás FILÓ, Gellért IVÁNCSICS (YC47), Laszlo HORVATH (YC78), DIEGO Rigonato Rodrigues (BRA), Dieng Cheikh ABASS (SEN) (63' László BOJTOR), Abraham Gneki GUIÉ-GUIÉ (CIV) (71' Edouard NDJODO (CMR)), Zoltán HERCEGFALVI (83' Róbert ZSOLNAI). (Coach: Gábor PÖLÖSKEI).
Goals: FC Zhetysu Taldykorgan: 1-0 Ruslan MIKHAYLOV (60').
Budapest Honvéd FC: 1-1 Zoltán HERCEGFALVI (66'), 1-2 László BOJTOR (75').
Referee: Vlado SVILOKOS (CRO)

22-06-2008   Aukstaitija Stadium, Panevezys:
FK Ekranas Panevezys – JK Trans Narva   1-0 (0-0)
FK Ekranas Panevezys: Bogdan STEFANOVIC (SRB), Taavi RÄHN (EST), Alfredas
SKROBLAS (YC49), Nerijus SASNAUSKAS (80' Deividas PADAIGIS), Laurynas
RIMAVICIUS, Dusan MATOVIC (SRB), Zilvinas BANYS, Andrius ARLAUSKAS (46'
Deimantas BICKA), Vitalijus KAVALIAUSKAS (YC45), Giedrius TOMKEVICIUS, Egidijus
VARNAS. (Coach: Valdas URBONAS).
JK Trans Narva: Sergei USOLTSEV, Oleg LEPIK, Aleksei GORSKOV, Aleksandrs
ABRAMENKO (LIT), Sergei KAZAKOV, Oleg MAKSIMOV, Vladislav IVANOV, Stanislav
KITTO, Dmitri LIPARTOV (RUS), Maksim GRUZNOV (87' Ivan SELEZNJOV), Nikolai
LOSANOV. (Coach: Alexei YAGUDIN (RUS)).
Goal: FK Ekranas Panevezys: 1-0 Deimantas BICKA (88' penalty).
Referee: Gabriele ROSSI (SMR)

22-06-2008   Gundadalur, Tórshavn: HB Tórshavn – IF Elfsborg   1-4 (1-2)
HB Tórshavn: Tróndur VATNHAMAR, Poul Thomas DAM (62' Rasmus NOLSØE), Ólafur
Sakarisson í ÓLAVSSTOVU (46' Milan KULJIC (SRB) (YC89)), Fródi BENJAMINSEN,
Kári NIELSEN, Vagnur Mohr MORTENSEN (YC54), Jákup á BORG (72' Rógvi
POULSEN), Andrew av FLØTUM, Christian Högni JACOBSEN, Petur Tórstein
JORGENSEN, Páll Mohr JOENSEN. (Coach: Rúni NOLSØE).
IF Elfsborg: Abbas HASSAN, Johan KARLSSON, Teddy LUCIC, Andreas AUGUSTSSON,
Mathias FLORÉN, Helgi Valur DANÍELSSON (ISL), Elmin KURBEGOVIC (BOS), Stefan
ISHIZAKI, Emir BAJRAMI (68' Daniel NORDMARK), Daniel MOBÄCK, Joakim
SJÖHAGE (85' Henrik SVEDBERG). (Coach: Magnus HAGLUND).
Goals: HB Tórshav: 1-1 Christian Högni JACOBSEN (16').
IF Elfsborg: 0-1 Elmin KURBEGOVIC (12'), 1-2 Daniel MOBÄCK (26'), 1-3 Joakim
SJÖHAGE (50'), 1-4 Daniel MOBÄCK (55').
Referee: Calum MURRAY (SCO)   Attendance: 600

28-06-2008   Borås Arena, Borås: IF Elfsborg – HB Tórshavn   0-0
IF Elfsborg: Abbas HASSAN (YC65), Martin ANDERSSON, Johan SJÖBERG, Andreas
AUGUSTSSON, Mathias FLORÉN (YC68), Emir BAJRAMI, Jari ILOLA (FIN) (46' Helgi
Valur DANÍELSSON (ISL)), Elmin KURBEGOVIC (BOS), Daniel NORDMARK, Stefan
ISHIZAKI (YC65) (68' Henrik SVEDBERG), Fredrik BERGLUND (76' Joakim SJÖHAGE).
(Coach: Magnus HAGLUND).
HB Tórshavn: Marcin DAWID (POL), Milan KULJIC (SRB) (YC45+1) (85' Petur Tórstein
JORGENSEN), Mortan úr HØRG, Rasmus NOLSØE, Fródi BENJAMINSEN, Kári NIELSEN
(YC73,YC75), Vagnur Mohr MORTENSEN, Andrew av FLØTUM (90' Poul Thomas DAM),
Christian Högni JACOBSEN, Jákup á BORG, Páll Mohr JOENSEN (62' Rógvi POULSEN).
(Coach: Rúni NOLSØE).
Referee: Anthony BUTTIMER (IRL)   Attendance: 2.135

28-06-2008   Belle Vue, Rhyl: Rhyl FC – Bohemians FC   2-4 (2-4)
Rhyl FC: John GANN (ENG) (YC31), Carl James RUFFER (ENG), George HORAN, Paul
O'NEILL (ENG), Chris ROBERTS (63' James KELLY (ENG)), James BREWERTON, Mark
CONNOLLY (YC33) (81' Craig GARSIDE (ENG)), Craig Steven JONES, Gareth WILSON,
Gary POWELL (ENG), Marc Lloyd WILLIAMS. (Coach: Osian ROBERTS).
Bohemians FC: Brian MURPHY, Owen HEARY (63' Thomas HEARY), Jason
McGUINNESS, Kenneth OMAN, Kevin HUNT (ENG), John Paul KELLY (43' Michael
McGINLAY (ENG)), Harpal SINGH (ENG), Stephen O'DONNELL, Mark ROSSITER, Glen
CROWE (77' Darren MANSARAM (ENG)), Jason BYRNE. (Coach: Patrick (Pat) FENLON).
Goals: Rhyl FC: 1-3 Mark CONNOLLY (37'), 2-3 Mark CONNOLLY (41').
Bohemians FC: 0-1 Stephen O'DONNELL (29'), 0-2 Jason BYRNE (32' penalty), 0-3 Jason
McGUINNESS (34'), 2-4 Harpal SINGH (42').
Referee: Aliaksei KULBAKOV (BLS)

28-06-2008   A. Le Coq Arena, Tallinn: JK Trans Narva – FK Ekranas Panevezys   0-3 (0-2)
JK Trans Narva: Sergei USOLTSEV, Oleg LEPIK, Aleksei GORSKOV, Aleksandrs
ABRAMENKO (LIT) (YC43), Sergei KAZAKOV, Oleg MAKSIMOV, Vladislav IVANOV,
Stanislav KITTO, Dmitri LIPARTOV (RUS) (80' Dmitri SMIRNOV), Maksim GRUZNOV,
Nikolai LOSANOV. (Coach: Alexei YAGUDIN (RUS)).
FK Ekranas Panevezys: Bogdan STEFANOVIC (SRB), Taavi RÄHN (EST), Alfredas
SKROBLAS (YC27), Nerijus SASNAUSKAS, Laurynas RIMAVICIUS, Dusan MATOVIC
(SRB), Vitalijus KAVALIAUSKAS, Deimantas BICKA, Giedrius TOMKEVICIUS (58'
Andrius ARLAUSKAS), Valdas TRAKYS, Egidijus VARNAS (46' Zilvinas BANYS).
(Coach: Valdas URBONAS).
Goals: FK Ekranas Panevezys: 0-1 Deimantas BICKA (35' penalty), 0-2 Valdas TRAKYS
(37'), 0-3 Dusan MATOVIC (79').
Referee: Pavel OLSIAK (SVK)   Attendance: 100

28-06-2008   Dasáki, Áchnas: Ethnikós Áchnas FC – KS Besa Kavajë   1-1 (0-0)
Ethnikós Áchnas FC: Panagiotis CHARALAMBOUS, António Pedro De Brito Lopes "TONI"
(POR), Christos SHAILIS, Daniel EDUSEI (GHA), Eduardo Angeli "EDU" (BRA), Zoran
STJEPANOVIC (SRB) (81' Christos KOTSONIS), Lars SCHLICHTING (GER) (YC11),
Eleftherakis ELEFTHERIOU, Ivan PETROVIC (SRB), Panayiotis EGOMITIS (64' Zoran
JANKOVIC (BUL)), Dimosthenis MANOUSAKIS (GRE) (86' Christofis PASHIALIS).
(Coach: Stéphane August DEMOL (BEL)).
KS Besa Kavajë: Suat ZENDELI (MCD), Artan SAKAJ (YC69), Artim SHAKIRI (MCD),
Erand HOXHA, Dritan KRASNIQI (46' Meglid MIHANI), Zekirija RAMADAN (MCD)
(YC20), Ilirjan MERTIRI, Herby FORTUNAT (CGO), Gerhard PROGNI, Enkeleid ALIKAJ
(82' Liridon LECI (KOS)), Bledar MANÇAKU (58' Emiliano VELIAJ). (Coach: Iljaz
HAXHIRAJ).
Goals: Ethnikós Áchnas FC: 1-0 Dimosthenis MANOUSAKIS (57').
KS Besa Kavajë: 1-1 Liridon LECI (90'+1').
Referee: Karen NALBANDYAN (ARM)

28-06-2008   Gradski Stadion, Skopje: FK Renova – HNK Rijeka 2-0 (1-0)
FK Renova: Armend ELEZI, Zvonimir STANKOVIC (SRB), Agron MEMEDI, Vladimir
DESPOTOVSKI, Besart IBRAIMI (78' Ilber ALIJU), Igorce STOJANOV, Sakir REDZEPI,
Fisnik NUHIU (90' Armend GAFURI), Vance TRAJCOV, Genc ISEINI (67' Vulnet EMINI),
Aleksandar ANGELOVSKI (YC8). (Coach: Vlatko KOSTOV).
HNK Rijeka: Velimir RADMAN, Luka VUCKO, Fausto BUDICIN, Sandi KRIZMAN (78'
Vedran TURKALJ), Dario BODRUSIC, Mario TADEJEVIC (46' Alen SKORO (BOS)),
Hrvoje STROK, Damir KREILACH, Alen PAMIC (75' Igor CAGALJ), Radomir DJALOVIC
(MNE), Nedim HALILOVIC (BOS). (Coach: Zlatko DALIC).
Goals: FK Renova: 1-0 Genc ISEINI (5'), 2-0 Genc ISEINI (46').
Referee: Simon Lee EVANS (WAL)   Attendance: 2.000

28-06-2008   Sport Complex Sheriff, Tiraspol: FC Tiraspol – FC MIKA Ashtarak   0-0
FC Tiraspol: Serghei JURIC, Andrey NOVICOV, Kyrylo SYDORENKO (UKR) (YC70),
Stanislav SOLODYAK, Igor KARPOVICH (BUL), Sergey REVA (UKR) (46' Anatoli
CHEPTINE (YC89)), Andrey SECRIERU (YC69) (76' Andrei VERBETCHI), Serghei
NAMASCO, Nicolai RUDAC (YC30) (46' Alexandru SUVOROV), Andrey PORFIREANU,
Dmitri GLIGA. (Coach: Volodymyr REVA (UKR)).
FC MIKA Ashtarak: Feliks HAKOBYAN, Armen PETROSYAN (52' Dilshod VASIEV (TJK)
(YC87)), Gevorg POGHOSYAN, ALEX Henrique da Silva (BRA), David GRIGORYAN,
Stepan HAKOBYAN, Arkadi CHILINGARYAN, THIAGO Manoel De Souza (BRA) (79'
Maksim FEDOROV (RUS)), Khoren VERANYAN, Karen AVOYAN (YC69) (75' Zaza
SAKHOKIA (GEO)), Narek BEGLARYAN. (Coach: Arkadi ANDRIASYAN).
Referee: Dimitrios KALOPOULOS (GRE)

28-06-2008   Nitra Stadión, Nitra: FC Nitra – Neftchi Baku PFK   3-1 (1-0)
FC Nitra: Lukás HROSSO, Marián DATKO, Martin TÓTH (56' Karol KARLÍK), Adrián
CEMAN, Jan GRUBER (CZE), Peter GRAJCIAR (YC16), Marek KOSTOLÁNI (YC73), Ján
STAJER, Michal FARKAS (73' Róbert GLENDA), Irakli LILUASHVILI (GEO) (68' Martin
BACA (CZE)), Robert SEMENIK. (Coach: Pavel MALURA (CZE)).
Neftchi Baku PFK: Vladimir MICOVIC (SRB), Rail MELIKOV, Dmitriy KRUGLOV (EST)
(YC54), Ruslan ABBASOV (56' Elnur ALLAHVERDIEV), Volodimr OLEFIR (UKR),
Rashad A.SADIKHOV, Olexandr CHERTOGANOV, Rashad Ferhad SADIKHOV, Oleg
GERASIMYUK (UKR) (YC89) (90' Ruslan ABUSHEV), Nazar BAYRAMOV (TMS)
(YC21) (67' JOSE KARLOS dos Reyes (BRA)), Georgi ADAMIA (GEO). (Coach: Anatoliy
Vasiliyovich DEMYANENKO (UKR)).
Goals: FC Nitra: 1-0 Robert SEMENIK (21'), 2-0 Adrián CEMAN (46'), 3-0 Robert
SEMENIK (83').
Neftchi Baku PFK: 3-1 JOSE KARLOS dos Reyes (84').
Referee: Novo PANIC (BOS)   Attendance: 2.860

217

28-06-2008   Mikheil Meskhi Stadium, Tbilisi:
FC Lokomotivi Tbilisi – FC Etzella Ettelbruck   2-2 (2-1)
FC Lokomotivi Tbilisi: Zurab BATIASHVILI (YC81), Nika GUSHARASHVILI (YC60),
Levan SARALIDZE, Dachi POPKHADZE, Teimuraz PHARULAVA (YC75), Vitali
DARASELIA (71' Davit CHAGELISHVILI), Zviadi CHKHETIANI (YC52), Irakli
CHIRIKASHVILI, Giorgi BARBAKADZE (YC6), Rati ALEKSIDZE, Irakli
SAMKHARADZE (YC42). (Coach: Zaza ZAMTARADZE).
FC Etzella Ettelbruck: Joé FLICK, Eric HOFFMANN, Jacques PLEIN, Gauthier REMACLE
(BEL), Gilles ENGELDINGER (YC33), Charles LEWECK (61' Daniel PEREIRA), NILTON
Jorge Rocha (BRA) (68' Cleudir JOSÉ Lopez Montero PIRES (POR)), Jorge FERNANDES
(75' Daniel BERNARD (YC85)), Ben FEDERSPIEL, Claudio DA LUZ, Alphonse LEWECK
(YC84). (Coach: Florim ALIJAJ (ALB)).
Goals: FC Lokomotivi Tbilisi: 1-1 Irakli CHIRIKASHVILI (28'), 2-1 Rati ALEKSIDZE (30').
FC Etzella Ettelbruck: 0-1 Claudio DA LUZ (21'), 2-2 Alphonse LEWECK (81' penalty).
Referee: Pavle RADOVANOVIC (MNE)

28-06-2008   Stadion Gradski, Niksic: OFK Grbalj Radanovici – NK Celik Zenica   2-1 (0-1)
OFK Grbalj Radanovici: Srdjan KLJAJEVIC (SRB), Gavrilo PETROVIC, Predrag
VIDEKANIC (SRB) (76' Miljan RADOVIC), Slobodan MAZIC (SRB), Goran GRUJIC, Ivica
FRANCISKOVIC (SRB), Igor DRAGICEVIC (SRB) (62' Sasa RADENOVIC), Darko
BOJOVIC, Darko PAVICEVIC, Marko KASALICA (90'+2' Rade ZEC), Dragan
BOSKOVIC. (Coach: Nebojsa VIGNJEVIC (SRB)).
NK Celik Zenica: Bojan TRIPIC, Bojan MARKOVIC, Mladen JURCEVIC, Almir
HASANOVIC, Fenan SALCINOVIC, Bojan PUPCEVIC, Zoran NOVAKOVIC (79' Serif
HASIC), Jasmin MORANJKIC, Armin KAPETAN (CRO), Zlatan GAFUROVIC, Emir
HADZIC. (Coach: Ivo ISTUK).
Goals: OFK Grbalj Radanovici: 1-1 Darko PAVICEVIC (51'), 2-1 Marko KASALICA (75').
NK Celik Zenica: 0-1 Emir HADZIC (18').
Referee: Sandor SZABO (HUN)   Attendance: 1.500

28-06-2008   József Bozsik Stadium, Budapest:
Budapest Honvéd FC – FC Zhetysu Taldykorgan   4-2 (2-0)
Budapest Honvéd FC: Balázs RABÓCZKI, Mico SMILJANIC (SRB), Zoltan VINCZE, Ákos
TAKÁCS, Tamás FILÓ, Gellért IVÁNCSICS (YC81), Attila DOBOS (64' Dieng Cheikh
ABASS (SEN)), DIEGO Rigonato Rodrigues (BRA) (YC56) (88' László BOJTOR), Eugenio
Fernando Bila "GENITO" (MOZ) (YC38), Abraham Gneki GUIÉ-GUIÉ (CIV) (82' Laszlo
HORVATH), Zoltán HERCEGFALVI. (Coach: Gábor PÖLÖSKEI).
FC Zhetysu Taldykorgan: Kirill PRYADKIN, Maksim ZABELIN, Aydar KUMISBEKOV
(45' Sergey KUTSOV), Evgeniy OVSHINOV (82' Aleksandr KRUTSKEVICH) (YC85),
Konstantin MUNTEANU (ROM), Dmitriy MAMONOV (YC64), Chingiz ABUGALIEV (41'
Vladislav KISELEV (YC70)), Konstantin PANIN (UKR), Ion Ionut LUTU (ROM),
Guvanchmuhamed OVEKOV (TMS), Vyacheslav NURMAGAMBETOV. (Coach: Eduard
GLAZUNOV).
Goals: Budapest Honvéd FC: 1-0 Eugenio Fernando Bila "GENITO" (26'), 2-0 Mico
SMILJANIC (45'+1'), 3-1 Abraham Gneki GUIÉ-GUIÉ (53'), 4-2 László BOJTOR (90'+2').
FC Zhetysu Taldykorgan: 2-1 Vladislav KISELEV (52'), 3-2 Vladislav KISELEV (74').
Referee: Veaceslav BANARI (MOL)

218

28-06-2008   Stadion Sportni Park, Nova Gorica: ND Gorica – Hibernians FC Paola   0-0
ND Gorica: Vasja SIMCIC, Bojan DUKIC (CRO), Aris ZARIFOVIC, Nebosja KOVACEVIC,
Admir KRSIC (58' Dario SMITRAN), Sebastjan KOMEL, Simon ZIVEC (71' Gregor
BALAZIC), Enes DEMIROVIC (BOS), Goran CVIJANOVIC, Etien VELIKONJA (YC26)
(59' Mladen KOVACEVIC), Milan OSTERC. (Coach: Primoz GLIHA).
Hibernians FC Paola: Mario MUSCAT, Aaron XUEREB, Jonathan XERRI, Adrian PULIS,
Timothy Fleri SOLER (YC53), Jonathan CARUANA, Edafe UZEH (NGR), Terence SCERRI,
Adrian MIFSUD (YC51) (62' Jonathan PEARSON), Clayton FAILLA, Andrew COHEN (90'
Tristan CARUANA). (Coach: Robert GATT).
Referee: Siarghei SHMOLIK (BLS)   Attendance: 500

29-06-2008   Stroitel Stadion,Soligorsk:
              FC Shakhter Soligorsk – KS Cracovia Kraków   3-0 (0-0)
FC Shakhter Soligorsk: Vitaliy MAKAVCHIK (YC56), Mikalai BRANFILOV, Valeriy
ZHUKOVSKIY (60' Mikhail MARTINOVICH), Dmitriy CHALEY, Andrey LEONCHIK,
Nikita BUKATKIN (YC7), Maksim GUKAYLO, Aleksey RIOS (YC59) (89' Sergey KROT),
Sergey KOVALCHUK, Sergey BALANOVICH (67' Aleksandr BYCHENOK), Sergey
NIKIFORENKO. (Coach: Yuri Vasilevich VERGEICHIK).
KS Cracovia Kraków: Marcin CABAJ (YC70,YC90+3), Przemyslaw KULIG (YC81),
Krzysztof RADWANSKI, Piotr POLCZAK, Lukasz TUPALSKI (YC55) (77' Michal
KARWAN), Arkadiusz BARAN (YC60) (76' Karol KOSTRUBALA), Dariusz
PAWLUSINSKI (YC22) (76' Árpád MAJOROS (HUN)), Dariusz KLUS, Pawel NOWAK
(YC85), Tomasz MOSKALA, Marcin KRZYWICKI. (Coach: Stefan MAJEWSKI).
Goals: FC Shakhter Soligorsk: 1-0 Sergey KOVALCHUK (71' penalty), 2-0 Sergey KROT
(90'+2'), 3-0 Sergey NIKIFORENKO (90'+3').
Referee: Akmalkhan KHOLMATOV (KAZ)   Attendance: 4.000

29-06-2008   Veritas Stadion, Turku: T.P.S. Turku – Lisburn Distillery FC   3-1 (1-0)
T.P.S. Turku: Jukka LEHTOVAARA, Urmas ROOBA (EST), Christian Atta GYAN (GHA),
Sami RÄHMÖNEN, Kheireddine ZARABI (ALG), Jarno HEINIKANGAS (65' Ville
LEHTONEN), Aristides PERTOT (ARG) (70' Riku RISKI), Kasper HÄMÄLÄINEN, Mika
ÄÄRITALO, Armand ONE (FRA), Mikko PAATELAINEN (YC19) (76' Patrik LOMSKI).
(Coach: Martti KUUSELA).
Lisburn Distillery FC: Alexander SPACKMAN, Stuart THOMPSON, Paul MUIR, Patrick
McSHANE, Jonathan MAGEE, Wayne BUCHANAN, Andrew KILMARTIN (IRL), Mark
COOLING (70' Ryan EVANS), Peter McCANN (IRL), Darren ARMOUR (YC20) (56' Gary
BROWNE), Curtis ALLEN (76' Christopher KINGSBERRY). (Coach: Paul KIRK).
Goals: T.P.S. Turku: 1-0 Mika ÄÄRITALO (42'), 2-0 Mikko PAATELAINEN (75'), 3-1
Armand ONE (86').
Lisburn Distillery FC: 2-1 Gary BROWNE (84' penalty).
Referee: Paulius MALZINSKAS (LIT)

29-06-2008   Laugardalsvöllur, Reykjavik: IF Fylkir – FK Riga   0-2 (0-1)
IF Fylkir: Fjalar THORGEIRSSON, Kristján VALDIMARSSON (43' Andrés Már
JÓHANNESSON (YC71)), Thórir HANNESSON, Peter GRAVESEN (DEN), Valur Fannar
GISLASON, Gudni Rúnar HELGASON, Ólafur Ingi STÍGSSON, Hermann
ADALGEIRSSON (78' Kjartan Andri BALDVINSSON), Kjartan Ágúst BREIDDAL, Halldór
Arnar HILMISSON (84' Allan DYRING (DEN)), Jóhann THÓRHALLSSON. (Coach: Leifur
Sigfinnur GARDARSSON).
FK Riga: Sergey Andreevich CHEPCHUGOV (RUS), Roberts MEZECKIS (YC76), Igors
KORABLOVS (70' Andrei Valentinovich AGAFONOV (YC89) (RUS)), Evgeniy NOVIKOV
(EST), Grigory Alexandrovich CHIRKIN (RUS), Valeriy Viktorovich LEONOV (RUS),
Mindaugas KALONAS (LIT), Pavels MIHADJUKS, Vladimirs ZAVORONKOVS, Mihails
MIHOLAPS (90'+2' Gints FREIMANIS), Ivan Vladimirovich SHPAKOV (RUS) (YC40) (87'
Maksims RAFALSKIS). (Coach: Genadijs MOROZOVS).
Goals: FK Riga: 0-1 Mindaugas KALONAS (7'), 0-2 Mindaugas KALONAS (73').
Referee: Pol P.H.M.VAN BOEKEL (HOL)

SECOND ROUND

05-07-2008   Stadion Saturn, Ramenskoje:
              FK Saturn Ramenskoje – FC Etzella Ettelbruck   7-0 (4-0)
FK Saturn Ramenskoje: Antonin KINSKY (CZE), Vadim Valentinovich EVSEEV, Luiz
Ricardo da Silva "ZELÃO" (BRA), Benoît Christian ANGBWA Ossoemeyang (CMR), Petr
NEMOV, Alexei EREMENKO Jr. (FIN), Andrey KARYAKA, Andrei GUSIN (UKR) (69'
Aleksey IGONIN), Roman VOROBIEV (62' Aleksey IVANOV), Marko TOPIC (BOS) (76'
Vladimir YURCHENKO (BLS)), Dmitriy Sergeevich KIRICHENKO. (Coach: Gadzhi
Muslimovich GADZHIEV).
FC Etzella Ettelbruck: Joé FLICK, Eric HOFFMANN, Gauthier REMACLE (BEL), Daniel
PEREIRA, Gilles ENGELDINGER, Claude REITER (YC18), Daniel BERNARD (83' Sidney
DO ROSARIO), NILTON Jorge Rocha (BRA) (90' François PAPIER (BEL)), Jorge
FERNANDES (67' David Alves DA MOTA), Ben FEDERSPIEL, Claudio DA LUZ. (Coach:
Florim ALIJAJ (ALB)).
Goals: FK Saturn Ramenskoje: 1-0 Dmitriy Sergeevich KIRICHENKO (1'), 2-0 Claudio DA
LUZ (12' own goal), 3-0 Marko TOPIC (18'), 4-0 Dmitriy Sergeevich KIRICHENKO (34'),
5-0 Aleksey IVANOV (65'), 6-0 Dmitriy Sergeevich KIRICHENKO (70'), 7-0 Dmitriy
Sergeevich KIRICHENKO (71').
Referee: Stelios TRIFONOS (CYP)   Attendance: 8.750

05-07-2008   Stadion Niedermatten, Wohlen:
              Grasshopper-Club Zürich – KS Besa Kavajë   2-1 (0-0)
Grasshopper-Club Zürich: Massimo COLOMBA, Guillermo VALLORI (ESP), Josip COLINA
(CRO), Boris SMILJANIC, Yassin MIKARI (TUN), Rolf FELTSCHER, Senad LULIC
(BOS), Veroljub SALATIC (SRB), Demba TOURÉ (SEN), Gonzalo Eulogio ZARATE (ARG)
(55' Davide CALLÀ), Samel SABANOVIC (MNE) (70 Raúl Marcelo BOBADILLA (ARG)).
(Coach: Hanspeter LATOUR).
KS Besa Kavajë: Suat ZENDELI (MCD), Artan SAKAJ, Liridon LECI (KOS), Erand
HOXHA, Emiliano VELIAJ (63' Agim METO (YC87)), Zekirija RAMADAN (MCD), Herby
FORTUNAT (CGO) (YC70) (90'+2' Vangjel MILE), Gerhard PROGNI, Enkeleid ALIKAJ,
Bledar MANÇAKU, Maringlen SHOSHI (YC32) (55' Sokol ISHKA). (Coach: Iljaz
HAXHIRAJ).
Goals: Grasshopper-Club Zürich: 1-0 Senad LULIC (66'), 2-0 Senad LULIC (79').
KS Besa Kavajë: 2-1 Herby FORTUNAT (83').
Referee: Jiri JECH (CZE)   Attendance: 624

220

05-07-2008   Stadion Gradski, Niksic:
OFK Grbalj Radanovici – Sivasspor Kulübü   2-2 (2-2)
OFK Grbalj Radanovici: Srdjan KLJAJEVIC (SRB), Gavrilo PETROVIC (YC17), Igor
RADUSCINOVIC (SRB) (YC59), Igor DRAGICEVIC (SRB) (62' Miljan RADOVIC), Goran
GRUJIC (RC38), Darko BOJOVIC (75' Veselin BOJIC (SRB)), Predrag VIDEKANIC (SRB),
Ivica FRANCISKOVIC (SRB) (YC60), Slobodan MAZIC (SRB), Dragan BOSKOVIC (75'
Kristijan KRSTOVIC (MNE), Marko KASALICA. (Coach: Nebojsa VIGNJEVIC (SRB)).
Sivasspor Kulübü: Akin VARDAR (RC30), Aytac AK, Alimou Mamadou DIALLO (GUI)
(56' Kanfory SYLLA (GUI)), Hayrettin YERLIKAYA, Onur TUNCER (YC60), Murat
SÖZGELMER, Ibrahim DAGASAN (YC83), Ilhan UMMAK (79' Musa AYDIN), Emre EFE
(32' Volkan ÜNLÜ goalkeeper), Mehmet YILDIZ (YC31), Pini Felix BALILI (ISR). (Coach:
Bülent UYGUN).
Goals: OFK Grbalj Radanovici: 1-1 Ivica FRANCISKOVIC (23'), 2-1 Ivica FRANCISKOVIC
(34').
Sivasspor Kulübü: 0-1 Mehmet YILDIZ (14'), 2-2 Mehmet YILDIZ (39' penalty).
Referee: Manuel Jorge NEVES MOREIRA DE SOUSA (POR)

05-07-2008   UPC-Arena, Graz: SK Sturm Graz – FC Shakhter Soligorsk   2-0 (1-0)
SK Sturm Graz: Josef SCHICKLGRUBER, Mario SONNLEITNER, Ferdinand FELDHOFER,
Georgi SHASHIASHVILI (YC76) (GEO), Ilia KANDELAKI (GEO), Petr HLINKA (SVK),
Samir MURATOVIC (BOS), Andreas HÖLZL (82' Patrick SCHERRER), Marko
STANKOVIC (87' Daniel BEICHLER), Mario HAAS (67' Jakob JANTSCHER), Mario
KIENZL. (Coach: Franco FODA (GER)).
FC Shakhter Soligorsk: Vitaliy MAKAVCHIK, Denis ANELIKOV (UKR) (46' Mikhail
MARTINOVICH), Mikalai BRANFILOV, Valeriy ZHUKOVSKIY, Andrey LEONCHIK,
Nikita BUKATKIN, Maksim GUKAYLO (YC51), Sergey KOVALCHUK, Aleksandr
BYCHENOK (58' Aleksandr KLIMENKO), Dmitriy CHALEY, Sergey NIKIFORENKO (76'
Aleksandr BYLINA). (Coach: Yuri Vasilevich VERGEICHIK).
Goals: SK Sturm Graz: 1-0 Ferdinand FELDHOFER (38'), 2-0 Mario KIENZL (55').
Referee: Libor KOVARIK (CZE)   Attendance: 5.680

05-07-2008   Mestský Stadion na Stínadlech, Teplice:
FK Teplice – Budapest Honvéd FC   1-3 (0-1)
FK Teplice: Martin SLAVIK, Martin KLEIN, Vlastimil VIDLICKA, Petr LUKÁS (YC90+2),
Antonín ROSA, Stepán VACHOUSEK (55' Michal GASPARÍK (SVK)), Jirí SABOU, Michal
DOLEZAL, Pavel VERBÍR, Tomás JUN (80' Andrej HESEK (SVK)), Tomás VONDRASEK
(61' Ajdin MAHMUTOVIC (BOS)). (Coach: Petr RADA).
Budapest Honvéd FC: Balázs RABÓCZKI, Benjamin Angoua BROU (CIV) (YC90+1), Mico
SMILJANIC (SRB), Zoltan VINCZE (YC10), Ákos TAKÁCS, Béla MAROTI, Attila DOBOS
(66' Dieng Cheikh ABASS (SEN)), Eugenio Fernando Bila "GENITO" (MOZ), Abraham
Gneki GUIÉ-GUIÉ (CIV) (83' Edouard NDJODO (CMR)), Zoltán HERCEGFALVI (YC90),
László BOJTOR (74' Tamás FILÓ). (Coach: Gábor PÖLÖSKEI).
Goals: FK Teplice: 1-1 Petr LUKÁS (58').
Budapest Honvéd FC: 0-1 Zoltán HERCEGFALVI (35'), 1-2 Abraham Gneki GUIÉ-GUIÉ
(81'), 1-3 Dieng Cheikh ABASS (90'+4').
Referee: Hannes KAASIK (EST)   Attendance: 3.050

05-07-2008   Sport Complex Sheriff, Tiraspol: FC Tiraspol – SK Tavriya Simferopol   0-0
FC Tiraspol: Serghei JURIC, Andrey NOVICOV, Kyrylo SYDORENKO (UKR), Stanislav
SOLODYAK, Igor KARPOVICH (BUL), Andrei VERBETCHI, Serghei NAMASCO, Nicolai
RUDAC (80' Dmitri GLIGA), Andrey PORFIREANU, Anatoli CHEPTINE (73' Vitalie
BULAT), Yuri BONDARCHUK (YC63) (64' Alexandru SUVOROV). (Coach: Volodymyr
REVA (UKR)).
SK Tavriya Simferopol: Andrey DIKAN (RUS), Andriy BOYKO, Pawel HAJDUCZEK
(POL), Dmitro NAZAROV, Taras ILNITSKIY, Slobodan MARKOVIC (SRB) (75' Vasil
GIGIADZE (GEO)), Illya GALYUZA, Zeljko LJUBENOVIC (SRB), Denis GOLAYDO,
Lucky Isi IDAHOR (NGR) (82' Andriy ZBOROVSKIY), Volodimir HOMENYUK. (Coach:
Mykhailo FOMENKO).
Referee: Tsvetan GEORGIEV (BUL)   Attendance: 2.000

05-07-2008   Vasil Levski National Stadium, Sofia:
               FK Chernomorets Burgas – ND Gorica   1-1 (0-0)
FK Chernomorets Burgas: Vladislav STOJANOV, Trayan DYANKOV, Nikolai KRASTEV,
Stefan TRAYKOV, Martin KOVACHEV, Vanco TRAJANOV (MCD) (YC81) (84' Georgi
KARAKANOV), Tsvetomir TSONKOV (YC40) (57' Ljubomir BOZHINOV), Shener
HYUSEIN Remzi (73' Lyubomir LYUBENOV), ADALTON Luis Juvenal (BRA),
LEANDRO Mesias Dos Santos (BRA) (YC74), MICHEL Platini Ferreira Mesquita (BRA)
(YC77). (Coach: Dimitar "Héro" DIMITROV).
ND Gorica: Vasja SIMCIC (RC67), Bojan DUKIC (CRO), Aris ZARIFOVIC (YC8), Nebosja
KOVACEVIC (46' Gzim REXHAY (YC58)), Admir KRSIC, Matija SKARABOT, Sebastjan
KOMEL, Simon ZIVEC, Enes DEMIROVIC (BOS) (63' Etien VELIKONJA (YC78)), Goran
CVIJANOVIC (68' Jan ZIBELNIK goalkeeper), Milan OSTERC. (Coach: Primoz GLIHA).
Goals: FK Chernomorets Burgas: 1-1 MICHEL Platini Ferreira Mesquita (63').
ND Gorica: 0-1 Milan OSTERC (57').
Referee: Asaf KENAN (ISR)

05-07-2008   Olympisch Stadion, Antwerpen:
               KFC Germinal Beerschot – Neftchi Baku PFK   1-1 (1-1)
KFC Germinal Beerschot: Kristof MAES, Martijn MONTEYNE, Didier DHEEDENE, Kurt
VAN DOOREN, Pieter-Jan MONTEYNE, Justice WAMFOR (CMR), KING Gyan Osei
(GHA) (YC54), Daniel CRUZ (COL), Paul KPAKA (SLE) (46' Khalilou FADIGA (SEN)),
Henri MUNYANEZA (RWA) (79' Tosin DOSUNMU (NGR)), Sanharib MALKI Sabah
(SYR). (Coach: Harm VAN VELDHOVEN).
Neftchi Baku PFK: Vladimir MICOVIC (SRB) (YC89), Rail MELIKOV, Rashad Ferhad
SADIKHOV, Volodimr OLEFIR (UKR) (YC62), Elnur ALLAHVERDIEV (88' Ruslan
ABUSHEV), Olexandr CHERTOGANOV (YC61), Rashad A.SADIKHOV (YC42), Dmitriy
KRUGLOV (EST) (70' Zaur TAGIZADE), Oleg GERASIMYUK (UKR), Martcho
DAVTCHEV (BUL) (79' Nazar BAYRAMOV (TMS)), Georgi ADAMIA (GEO). (Coach:
Anatoliy Vasiliyovich DEMYANENKO (UKR)).
Goals: KFC Germinal Beerschot: 1-0 Sanharib MALKI Sabah (18').
Neftchi Baku PFK: 1-1 Georgi ADAMIA (27').
Referee: Dejan FILIPOVIC (SRB)   Attendance: 4.411

06-07-2008   Easter Road, Edinburgh: Hibernian FC Edinburgh – IF Elfsborg   0-2 (0-1)
Hibernian FC Edinburgh: Yves MAKABA-MAKALAMBY (BEL), David VAN ZANTEN
(IRL), Paul HANLON, Chris HOGG (ENG), Robert JONES (ENG) (46' Martin CANNING),
Ian MURRAY, Brian KERR (55' Ross Stephen CHISHOLM), John RANKIN, Dean SHIELS
(NIR), FILIPE Alexandre MORAIS (POR) (71' Colin John NISH), Steven FLETCHER.
(Coach: Mika-Matti Petteri "Mixu" PAATELAINEN (FIN)).
IF Elfsborg: Johan WILAND, Mathias FLORÉN, Johan KARLSSON, Martin ANDERSSON,
Daniel MOBÄCK, Teddy LUCIC, Andreas AUGUSTSSON, Helgi Valur DANÍELSSON
(ISL), Anders SVENSSON, Denni AVDIC, Emir BAJRAMI (74' Stefan ISHIZAKI). (Coach:
Magnus HAGLUND).
Goals: IF Elfsborg: 0-1 Emir BAJRAMI (17'), 0-2 Andreas AUGUSTSSON (65').
Referee: Albert TOUSSAINT (LUX)   Attendance: 7.809

06-07-2008   Aukstaitija Stadium, Panevezys:
               FK Ekranas Panevezys – Rosenborg BK   1-3 (1-2)
FK Ekranas Panevezys: Bogdan STEFANOVIC (SRB), Taavi RÄHN (EST), Laurynas
RIMAVICIUS (YC44), Dusan MATOVIC (SRB), Zilvinas BANYS (67' Paulius
JANUSAUSKAS), Vitalijus KAVALIAUSKAS, Deimantas BICKA (78' Andrius
ARLAUSKAS), Giedrius TOMKEVICIUS, Valdas TRAKYS (YC21) (57' Nerijus
SASNAUSKAS), Andrius SIDLAUSKAS, Egidijus VARNAS. (Coach: Valdas URBONAS).
Rosenborg BK: Rune Almenning JARSTEIN (YC39), Fredrik STOOR (SWE) (YC63), Vadim
DEMIDOV, Eduardo Alejandro LAGO Correa (URU), Roy MILLER (CRC), Roar STRAND
(75' Andreas Kristoffer NORDVIK), Alexander Banor TETTEY, Per Ciljan SKJELBRED,
Abdoulrazak TRAORÉ (CIV), Didier KONAN Ya (CIV) (46' Jo Sondre AAS), Steffen
IVERSEN (46' Yssouf KONÉ (BKF) (YC66)). (Coach: Erik HAMRÉN (SWE)).
Goals: FK Ekranas Panevezys: 1-1 Egidijus VARNAS (14').
Rosenborg BK: 0-1 Roar STRAND (12'), 1-2 Laurynas RIMAVICIUS (33' own goal), 1-3
Yssouf KONÉ (67').
Referee: Adrian McCOURT (NIR)

06-07-2008   Omladinski stadion, Beograd:
               O.F.K. Beograd – PAE Panionios FC Athens   1-0 (0-0)
O.F.K. Beograd: Radisa ILIC, Branko LAZAREVIC (YC90+3), Bojan MARKOSKI (MCD),
Novica MILENOVIC (YC90+2), Milos ADAMOVIC, Predrag LAZIC (67' Nemanja MILIC),
WILLIAM Artur De Oliveira (BRA), Nicola BELJIC, Nenad KRSTICIC (YC13) (83' Emir
LOTINAC), Igor MISAN (62' Zoran MILOVAC), Andrija KALUDJEROVIC. (Coach:
Mihajlo IVANOVIC).
PAE Panionios FC Athens: Dario KRESIC (CRO), Ioannis Georgios MANIATIS, Fousseni
DIAWARA (MLI), Evangelos KOUTSOPOULOS, Ivica MAJSTORIVIC (GER) (YC45+1),
Euripidis-Grigorios Vasileios MAKOS (YC90+4), Bennard Yao KUMORDZI (GHA) (YC33),
Fanourios Apostolos GOUNDOULAKIS (67' Alexandre Joaquim D'ACOL (BRA)), Manolis
Konstantinos SKOUFALIS (67' Marios NICOLAOU (CYP)), Dimitris SIALMAS, Lampros
CHOUTOS (75' Georgios BARKOGLOU). (Coach: Ewald LIENEN (GER)).
Goal: O.F.K. Beograd: 1-0 Andrija KALUDJEROVIC (69').
Referee: Manuel GRÄFE (GER)

223

06-07-2008   Daugavas stadions, Liepaja: FK Riga – Bohemians FC   1-0 (1-0)
FK Riga: Sergey Andreevich CHEPCHUGOV (RUS), Roberts MEZECKIS, Dimitrijs
HALVITOVS, Igors KORABLOVS, Evgeniy NOVIKOV (EST), Grigory Alexandrovich
CHIRKIN (RUS), Andrei Valentinovich AGAFONOV (RUS), Valeriy Viktorovich LEONOV
(RUS), Mindaugas KALONAS (LIT), Vladimirs ZAVORONKOVS, Ivan Vladimirovich
SHPAKOV (RUS) (90'+1' Maksims RAFALSKIS). (Coach: Genadijs MOROZOVS).
Bohemians FC: Brian MURPHY, Liam BURNS (NIR) (YC47), Thomas HEARY, Jason
McGUINNESS, Connor POWELL, Glenn CRONIN, Kevin HUNT (ENG) (76' Neale FENN),
Kilian BRENNAN, Stephen O'DONNELL, Glen CROWE, Jason BYRNE (29' John Paul
KELLY). (Coach: Patrick (Pat) FENLON).
Goal: FK Riga: 1-0 Valeriy Viktorovich LEONOV (45').
Referee: Robert KRAJNC (SLO)

06-07-2008   Veritas Stadion, Turku: T.P.S. Turku – Odense BK   1-2 (1-1)
T.P.S. Turku: Jukka LEHTOVAARA, Urmas ROOBA (EST) (YC84), Christian Atta GYAN
(GHA), Sami RÄHMÖNEN, Kheireddine ZARABI (ALG), Jarno HEINIKANGAS (YC68),
Aristides PERTOT (ARG), Riku RISKI (67' Patrik LOMSKI), Mika ÄÄRITALO, Armand
ONE (FRA) (YC81), Mikko PAATELAINEN. (Coach: Martti KUUSELA).
Odense BK: Arkadiusz ONYSZKO (POL), Atle Roar HÅLAND, Anders MØLLER
CHRISTENSEN, Thomas HELVEG, Chris SØRENSEN, Hans Henrik ANDREASEN, Morten
BISGAARD, Christián BOLAÑOS Navarro (CRC), Djiby Baye FALL (SEN), Björn Sandro
RUNSTRÖM (SWE), Johan ABSALONSEN. (Coach: Lars Christian OLSEN).
Goals: T.P.S. Turku: 1-1 Armand ONE (37').
Odense BK: 0-1 Djiby Baye FALL (5'), 1-2 Chris SØRENSEN (84').
Referee: Andrejs SIPAILO (LAT)   Attendance: 2.400

06-07-2008   Gradski Stadion, Skopje: FK Renova – Ihoud Bnei Sakhnin FC   1-2 (0-1)
FK Renova: Armend ELEZI, Zvonimir STANKOVIC (SRB), Agron MEMEDI (YC47),
Vladimir DESPOTOVSKI (YC61), Besart IBRAIMI (YC90+2), Igorce STOJANOV, Fisnik
NUHIU (46' Pance STOJANOV), Vance TRAJCOV, Genc ISEINI (YC13) (67' Ilber ALIJU),
Aleksandar ANGELOVSKI, Ismail ISMAILI (46' Vulnet EMINI). (Coach: Vlatko KOSTOV).
Ihoud Bnei Sakhnin FC: Meir COHEN, Abed RABAH, Allah Abu SALAH, Basem GENAIM,
Halal KHALEILA (YC80), Yaniv LUZON (86' Muhammad SHALAATA), Haim BENON,
Khaled KHALAILA (YC37) (72' Muhammad RAIYA), Hamed GENAIM, Ali OTHMAN,
Musa SHAABAN (90'+2' Tarik GANAEIM). (Coach: Freddy DAVID).
Goals: FK Renova: 1-2 Besart IBRAIMI (65').
Ihoud Bnei Sakhnin FC: 0-1 Khaled KHALAILA (41' penalty), 0-2 Abed RABAH (64').
Referee: Markus STRÖMBERGSSON (SWE)

12-07-2008   Borås Arena, Borås: IF Elfsborg – Hibernians FC Edinburgh   2-0 (1-0)
IF Elfsborg: Johan WILAND, Mathias FLORÉN, Johan KARLSSON, Martin ANDERSSON,
Daniel MOBÄCK (41' Fredrik BERGLUND), Teddy LUCIC, Helgi Valur DANÍELSSON
(ISL), Anders SVENSSON, Denni AVDIC (82' Elmin KURBEGOVIC (BOS)), Emir
BAJRAMI, Stefan ISHIZAKI (65' Jesper FLORÉN). (Coach: Magnus HAGLUND).
Hibernian FC Edinburgh: Andrew McNEIL, David VAN ZANTEN (IRL), Paul HANLON,
Chris HOGG (ENG), Robert JONES (ENG), Ian MURRAY, Dean SHIELS (NIR) (84' Lewis
STEVENSON), Ross Stephen CHISHOLM (63' John RANKIN), Alan O'BRIEN (IRL),
Steven FLETCHER, Colin John NISH (84' Ross CAMPBELL). (Coach: Mika-Matti Petteri
"Mixu" PAATELAINEN (FIN)).
Goals: IF Elfsborg: 1-0 Mathias FLORÉN (20'), 2-0 Emir BAJRAMI (80').
Referee: Marijo STRAHONJA (CRO)   Attendance: 3.523

224

12-07-2008   Niko Dovana Stadium, Durrës:
KS Besa Kavajë – Grasshopper-Club Zürich   0-3 (0-0)
KS Besa Kavajë: Suat ZENDELI (MCD), Artan SAKAJ (YC38), Andi LILA (YC34) (57'
Sokol ISHKA), Agim METO (64' Vangjel MILE), Liridon LECI (KOS) (YC45+1) (62'
Emiliano VELIAJ), Zekirija RAMADAN (MCD), Herby FORTUNAT (CGO), Gerhard
PROGNI, Enkeleid ALIKAJ (YC76), Bledar MANÇAKU, Maringlen SHOSHI. (Coach: Iljaz
HAXHIRAJ).
Grasshopper-Club Zürich: Eldin JAKUPOVIC, Kay VOSER (YC45+1), Guillermo VALLORI
(ESP), Josip COLINA (CRO), Boris SMILJANIC, Yassin MIKARI (TUN), Senad LULIC
(BOS), Ricardo CABANAS (63' Paulo Rinaldo CRUZADO Durand (PER)), Veroljub
SALATIC (SRB) (YC28), Gonzalo Eulogio ZARATE (ARG) (46' Demba TOURÉ (SEN)),
Samel SABANOVIC (MNE) (83' Steven ZUBER). (Coach: Hanspeter LATOUR).
Goals: Grasshopper-Club Zürich: 0-1 Samel SABANOVIC (54'), 0-2 Samel SABANOVIC
(68'), 0-3 Steven ZUBER (86').
Referee: Augustus Viorel CONSTANTIN (ROM)   Attendance: 1.900

12-07-2008   Tofiq Bahramov Stadium, Baku:
Neftchi Baku PFK – KFC Germinal Beerschot   1-0 (0-0)
Neftchi Baku PFK: Vladimir MICOVIC (SRB), Rail MELIKOV (YC81), Dmitriy KRUGLOV
(EST) (79' Zaur TAGIZADE), Elnur ALLAHVERDIEV, Volodimr OLEFIR (UKR), Rashad
A.SADIKHOV (90' Ruslan ABUSHEV), Olexandr CHERTOGANOV, Martcho DAVTCHEV
(BUL) (80' Nazar BAYRAMOV (TMS)), Rashad Ferhad SADIKHOV, Oleg GERASIMYUK
(UKR), Georgi ADAMIA (GEO). (Coach: Anatoliy Vasiliyovich DEMYANENKO (UKR)).
KFC Germinal Beerschot: Kristof MAES, Kurt VAN DOOREN, Pieter-Jan MONTEYNE,
Martijn MONTEYNE, Daniel CRUZ (COL), KING Gyan Osei (GHA), Justice WAMFOR
(CMR) (87' Rocky PEETERS), Didier DHEEDENE, Khalilou FADIGA (SEN) (YC81), Henri
MUNYANEZA (RWA) (64' Tosin DOSUNMU (NGR)), Sanharib MALKI Sabah (YC90+2).
(Coach: Harm VAN VELDHOVEN).
Goal: Neftchi Baku PFK: 1-0 Elnur ALLAHVERDIEV (57').
Referee: Mark CLATTENBURG (ENG)   Attendance: 24.000

12-07-2008   József Bozsik Stadium, Budapest:
Budapest Honvéd FC – FK Teplice   0-2 (0-0)
Budapest Honvéd FC: Balázs RABÓCZKI, Benjamin Angoua BROU (CIV) (YC69), Mico
SMILJANIC (SRB), Zoltan VINCZE (YC90+2), Ákos TAKÁCS, Béla MAROTI, Gellért
IVÁNCSICS (79' Tamás FILÓ), Attila DOBOS (63' Dieng Cheikh ABASS (SEN)), Eugenio
Fernando Bila "GENITO" (MOZ), Abraham Gneki GUIÉ-GUIÉ (CIV) (84' Edouard
NDJODO (CMR)), Zoltán HERCEGFALVI. (Coach: Gábor PÖLÖSKEI).
FK Teplice: Tomas BELIC (SVK), Martin KLEIN, Vlastimil VIDLICKA, Petr LUKÁS,
Antonín ROSA, Admir LJEVAKOVIC (BOS), Stepán VACHOUSEK (64' Michal
GASPARÍK (SVK)), Michal DOLEZAL (85' Michal SMEJKAL), Jakub MARES (77' Pavel
VERBÍR), Tomás JUN, Ajdin MAHMUTOVIC (BOS). (Coach: Petr RADA).
Goals: FK Teplice: 0-1 Tomás JUN (66'), 0-2 Antonín ROSA (71').
Referee: Gardar Örn HINRIKSSON (ISL)   Attendance: 1.500

225

12-07-2008   Kiryat Eliezer Stadium, Haifa: Ihoud Bnei Sakhnin FC – FK Renova   1-0 (1-0)
Ihoud Bnei Sakhnin FC: Omri ALON, Paty Yeye LENKEBE (CGO) (85' Muhammad
RAIYA), Abed RABAH, Allah Abu SALAH, Basem GENAIM, Yaniv LUZON (82' Halal
KHALEILA), Haim BENON, Khaled KHALAILA (YC59) (90'+1' Imad BADARNE),
Hamed GENAIM, Ali OTHMAN, Musa SHAABAN. (Coach: Freddy DAVID).
FK Renova: Armend ELEZI, Zvonimir STANKOVIC (SRB) (YC49), Agron MEMEDI, Besart
IBRAIMI, Igorce STOJANOV (YC66), Vulnet EMINI (YC74) (81' Armend GAFURI), Fisnik
NUHIU (68' Festim ADEMI), Pance STOJANOV, Vance TRAJCOV, Genc ISEINI (46' Ilber
ALIJU (YC89)), Aleksandar ANGELOVSKI. (Coach: Vlatko KOSTOV).
Goal: Ihoud Bnei Sakhnin FC: 1-0 Hamed GENAIM (17').
Referee: Istvan VAD (HUN)

12-07-2008   Stadion Sportni Park, Nova Gorica:
               ND Gorica – FK Chernomorets Burgas   0-2 (0-0)
ND Gorica: Mitja PIRIH, Gregor BALAZIC, Bojan DUKIC (CRO), Aris ZARIFOVIC, Admir
KRSIC, Matija SKARABOT (49' Gzim REXHAY), Sebastjan KOMEL, Simon ZIVEC (60'
Nebosja KOVACEVIC), Enes DEMIROVIC (BOS) (YC78), Goran CVIJANOVIC (YC15)
(57' Mladen KOVACEVIC), Milan OSTERC. (Coach: Primoz GLIHA (RC79)).
FK Chernomorets Burgas: Vladislav STOJANOV, Trayan DYANKOV (YC78), Nikolai
KRASTEV, Stefan TRAYKOV (YC62), Martin KOVACHEV, Georgi KARAKANOV
(YC18), Vanco TRAJANOV (MCD), Shener HYUSEIN Remzi (90'+1' Ljubomir
BOZHINOV), ADALTON Luis Juvenal (BRA) (81' Tsvetomir TSONKOV), LEANDRO
Mesias Dos Santos (BRA), MICHEL Platini Ferreira Mesquita (BRA) (90'+4' Lyubomir
LYUBENOV). (Coach: Dimitar "Héro" DIMITROV).
Goals: FK Chernomorets Burgas: 0-1 Shener HYUSEIN Remzi (55' penalty), 0-2 MICHEL
Platini Ferreira Mesquita (86').
Referee: Marcin BORSKI (POL)

12-07-2008   Dalymount Park, Dublin: Bohemians FC – FK Riga   2-1 (1-0)
Bohemians FC: Brian MURPHY, Owen HEARY (RC90+3), Liam BURNS (NIR) (YC81),
Jason McGUINNESS, Connor POWELL, Kilian BRENNAN, John Paul KELLY, Stephen
O'DONNELL (YC90+4), Glenn CRONIN (21' Kevin HUNT (ENG)), Neale FENN, Glen
CROWE. (Coach: Patrick (Pat) FENLON).
FK Riga: Sergey Andreevich CHEPCHUGOV (RUS), Roberts MEZECKIS, Dimitrijs
HALVITOVS (YC33), Igors KORABLOVS, Evgeniy NOVIKOV (EST), Grigory
Alexandrovich CHIRKIN (RUS) (YC63), Andrei Valentinovich AGAFONOV (RUS) (55'
Gints FREIMANIS (YC81)), Valeriy Viktorovich LEONOV (RUS) (YC18) (75' Maksims
RAFALSKIS), Mindaugas KALONAS (LIT), Vladimirs ZAVORONKOVS, Ivan
Vladimirovich SHPAKOV (RUS). (Coach: Genadijs MOROZOVS).
Goals: Bohemians FC: 1-0 Jason McGUINNESS (20'), 2-1 Kilian BRENNAN (90' penalty).
FK Riga: 1-1 Grigory Alexandrovich CHIRKIN (65').
Referee: Brage SANDMOEN (NOR)

226

13-07-2008   Lerkendal Stadion, Trondheim:
Rosenborg BK – FK Ekranas Panevezys   4-0 (1-0)
Rosenborg BK: Alexander Lund HANSEN, Fredrik STOOR (SWE), Eduardo Alejandro
LAGO Correa (URU), Andreas Kristoffer NORDVIK, Roy MILLER (CRC), Alexander Banor
TETTEY (78' Albert BERBATOVCI), Per Ciljan SKJELBRED (68' Øyvind STORFLOR),
Marek SAPARA (SVK), Yssouf KONÉ (BKF), Didier KONAN Ya (CIV), Steffen IVERSEN
(65' Jo Sondre AAS). (Coach: Erik HAMRÉN (SWE)).
FK Ekranas Panevezys: Vytautas Gadiminas CERNIAUSKAS, Taavi RÄHN (EST) (YC14),
Laurynas RIMAVICIUS, Dusan MATOVIC (SRB), Zilvinas BANYS (73' Andrius
ARLAUSKAS), Dominykas GALKEVICIUS (46' Deimantas BICKA), Vitalijus
KAVALIAUSKAS, Giedrius TOMKEVICIUS, Andrius SIDLAUSKAS, Egidijus VARNAS,
Serghei POGREBAN (MOL) (58' Alfredas SKROBLAS). (Coach: Valdas URBONAS).
Goals: Rosenborg BK: 1-0 Didier KONAN Ya (16'), 2-0 Steffen IVERSEN (48'), 3-0 Yssouf
KONÉ (52'), 4-0 Yssouf KONÉ (90'+2').
Referee: Babak GULIYEV (AZE)   Attendance: 4.986

13-07-2008   Stroitel Stadion,Soligorsk: FC Shakhter Soligorsk – SK Sturm Graz   0-0
FC Shakhter Soligorsk: Vitaliy MAKAVCHIK, Mikalai BRANFILOV, Valeriy
ZHUKOVSKIY (60' Aleksandr BYCHENOK), Andrey LEONCHIK, Nikita BUKATKIN (65'
Aleksandr BYLINA), Mikhail MARTINOVICH, Maksim GUKAYLO, Sergey
KOVALCHUK (61' Sergey KROT), Dmitriy CHALEY, Aleksandr KLIMENKO, Sergey
NIKIFORENKO (YC24). (Coach: Yuri Vasilevich VERGEICHIK).
SK Sturm Graz: Josef SCHICKLGRUBER, Mario SONNLEITNER (RC2), Ferdinand
FELDHOFER, Georgi SHASHIASHVILI (GEO), Ilia KANDELAKI (GEO), Petr HLINKA
(SVK), Samir MURATOVIC (BOS), Sandro FODA (GER), Andreas HÖLZL, Marko
STANKOVIC (18' Mattias SEREINIG), Mario HAAS (60' Patrick SCHERRER). (Coach:
Franco FODA (GER)).
Referee: Martin ATKINSON (ENG)   Attendance: 2.500

13-07-2008   Stádio Néas Smýrnis, Néa Smýrni:
PAE Panionios FC Athens – O.F.K. Beograd   3-1 (2-0)
PAE Panionios FC Athens: Dario KRESIC (CRO), Ioannis Georgios MANIATIS, Fousseni
DIAWARA (MLI) (YC41), Evangelos KOUTSOPOULOS (YC80), Ivica MAJSTORIVIC
(GER), Euripidis-Grigorios Vasileios MAKOS, Bennard Yao KUMORDZI (GHA), Georgios
BARKOGLOU (85' Mehmet HETEMAJ (FIN)), Marios NICOLAOU (CYP), Manolis
Konstantinos SKOUFALIS (YC57), Lampros CHOUTOS (70' Dimitris SIALMAS). (Coach:
Ewald LIENEN (GER)).
O.F.K. Beograd: Radisa ILIC, Nebojsa SKOPLJAK, Branko LAZAREVIC (YC41), Bojan
MARKOSKI (MCD), Novica MILENOVIC, Milos ADAMOVIC, Zoran MILOVAC (46'
Nicola BELJIC (YC47)), WILLIAM Artur De Oliveira (BRA), Nenad KRSTICIC, Andrija
KALUDJEROVIC (77' Petar JELIC (BOS)), Nemanja MILIC (46' Roboljub
MARJANOVIC). (Coach: Mihajlo IVANOVIC).
Goals: PAE Panionios FC Athens: 1-0 Georgios BARKOGLOU (27'), 2-0 Lampros
CHOUTOS (44'), 3-1 Lampros CHOUTOS (63' penalty).
O.F.K. Beograd: 2-1 WILLIAM Artur De Oliveira (54').
Referee: Sascha KEVER (SUI)

13-07-2008   Stade Josy Barthel, Luxembourg:
                FC Etzella Ettelbruck – FK Saturn Ramenskoje   1-1 (0-0)
FC Etzella Ettelbruck: Christophe DIEDERICH, Eric HOFFMANN, Jacques PLEIN, Gauthier
REMACLE (BEL) (90'+2' Daniel PEREIRA), Gilles ENGELDINGER, Charles LEWECK
(YC27), Ben FEDERSPIEL, Claudio DA LUZ, Joao Carlos FERREIRA Capela (YC76),
Alphonse LEWECK (83' Daniel BERNARD), Cleudir JOSÉ Lopez Montero PIRES (POR)
(YC88) (90' Jorge FERNANDES). (Coach: Florim ALIJAJ (ALB)).
FK Saturn Ramenskoje: Aleksandr MAKAROV, Benoît Christian ANGBWA Ossoemeyang
(CMR) (45' Petr NEMOV), Dmitriy POLOVINCHUK (17' Roman RAZDELKIN), Aleksey
IGONIN, Ruslan NAKHUSHEV, Vladimir YURCHENKO (BLS), Roman VOROBIEV (78'
Mikhail KUZYAEV), Aleksandr SAPETA (YC76), Anton KOZLOV, Aleksey IVANOV,
Leonid KOVEL (BLS). (Coach: Boris Petrovich IGNATIEV).
Goals: FC Etzella Ettelbruck: 1-0 Claudio DA LUZ (70').
FK Saturn Ramenskoje: 1-1 Leonid KOVEL (77').
Referee: René ROGALLA (SUI)

13-07-2008   Lokomotiv Stadion, Simferopol:
                SK Tavriya Simferopol – FC Tiraspol   3-1 (2-0)
SK Tavriya Simferopol: Andrey DIKAN (RUS), Andriy BOYKO (64' Andriy DONETS),
Pawel HAJDUCZEK (POL), Dmitro NAZAROV, Taras ILNITSKIY, Illya GALYUZA,
Zeljko LJUBENOVIC (SRB) (81' Oleksandr KOVPAK), Denis GOLAYDO, Lucky Isi
IDAHOR (NGR), Volodimir HOMENYUK (67' Andriy ZBOROVSKIY), Vasil GIGIADZE
(GEO). (Coach: Mykhailo FOMENKO).
FC Tiraspol: Serghei JURIC, Andrey NOVICOV, Kyrylo SYDORENKO (UKR), Stanislav
SOLODYAK (YC55), Igor KARPOVICH (BUL), Andrei VERBETCHI, Sergey REVA
(UKR) (57' Vitalie BULAT), Serghei NAMASCO (65' Andrey SECRIERU), Nicolai
RUDAC, Alexandru SUVOROV, Yuri BONDARCHUK (46' Andrey PORFIREANU).
(Coach: Volodymyr REVA (UKR)).
Goals: SK Tavriya Simferopol: 1-0 Zeljko LJUBENOVIC (10'), 2-0 Volodimir HOMENYUK
(45'+1'), 3-0 Vasil GIGIADZE (51').
FC Tiraspol: 3-1 Vitalie BULAT (90'+2').
Referee: Anders HERMANSEN (DEN)   Attendance: 10.000

13-07-2008   Sivas 4 Eylül Stadi, Sivas:
                Sivasspor Kulübü – OFK Grbalj Radanovici   1-0 (0-0)
Sivasspor Kulübü: Volkan ÜNLÜ, Aytac AK (YC31), Alimou Mamadou DIALLO (GUI),
Hayrettin YERLIKAYA, Musa AYDIN (86' Ilgar GURBANOV (AZE)), Kanfory SYLLA
(GUI), Ibrahim DAGASAN (89' Tayfur EMRE YILMAZ), Ilhan UMMAK, Abdurrahman
DERELI, Mehmet YILDIZ, Pini Felix BALILI (ISR) (81' SERGIO Pacheco de Oliveira
(BRA)). (Coach: Bülent UYGUN).
OFK Grbalj Radanovici: Srdjan KLJAJEVIC (SRB), Gavrilo PETROVIC, Igor
RADUSCINOVIC (SRB) (YC30), Veselin BOJIC (SRB), Igor DRAGICEVIC (SRB) (64'
Miljan RADOVIC), Darko BOJOVIC (76' Kristijan KRSTOVIC (MNE) (YC90)), Predrag
VIDEKANIC (SRB), Ivica FRANCISKOVIC (SRB), Slobodan MAZIC (SRB), Dragan
BOSKOVIC (YC54), Marko KASALICA (YC40). (Coach: Nebojsa VIGNJEVIC (SRB)).
Goal: Sivasspor Kulübü: 1-0 Alimou Mamadou DIALLO (83').
Referee: Igorj ISHCHENKO (UKR)

13-07-2008   Fionia Park, Odense: Odense BK – T.P.S. Turku   2-0 (1-0)
Odense BK: Arkadiusz ONYSZKO (POL), Atle Roar HÅLAND, Anders MØLLER
CHRISTENSEN, Thomas HELVEG, Chris SØRENSEN, Hans Henrik ANDREASEN, Morten
BISGAARD, Matti Lund NIELSEN (78' Peter NYMANN Mikkelsen), Djiby Baye FALL
(SEN) (YC43) (85' Srdjan RADONJIC (MNE)), Björn Sandro RUNSTRÖM (SWE), Johan
ABSALONSEN. (Coach: Lars Christian OLSEN).
T.P.S. Turku: Jukka LEHTOVAARA, Urmas ROOBA (EST), Ville LEHTONEN, Sami
RÄHMÖNEN, Jarno HEINIKANGAS (70' Jesse SAARINEN), Aristides PERTOT (ARG)
(YC40), Kasper HÄMÄLÄINEN (63' Patrik LOMSKI), Riku RISKI, Mika ÄÄRITALO,
Armand ONE (FRA), Mikko PAATELAINEN. (Coach: Martti KUUSELA).
Goals: Odense BK: 1-0 Djiby Baye FALL (21'), 2-0 Djiby Baye FALL (52').
Referee: Igor ZAKHAROV (RUS)   Attendance: 4.034

THIRD ROUND

19-07-2008   Borås Arena, Borås: IF Elfsborg – FK Riga   1-0 (1-0)
IF Elfsborg: Johan WILAND, Mathias FLORÉN, Johan KARLSSON, Martin ANDERSSON,
Daniel MOBÄCK, Teddy LUCIC, Helgi Valur DANÍELSSON (ISL), Anders SVENSSON,
Denni AVDIC (87' Daniel NORDMARK), Emir BAJRAMI (64' Lasse NILSSON), Fredrik
BERGLUND (71' Elmin KURBEGOVIC (BOS)). (Coach: Magnus HAGLUND).
FK Riga: Sergey Andreevich CHEPCHUGOV (RUS), Dimitrijs HALVITOVS, Igors
KORABLOVS, Evgeniy NOVIKOV (EST), Grigory Alexandrovich CHIRKIN (RUS), Andrei
Valentinovich AGAFONOV (RUS) (77' Gints FREIMANIS), Valeriy Viktorovich LEONOV
(RUS), Mindaugas KALONAS (LIT), Maksims RAFALSKIS, Vladimirs ZAVORONKOVS,
Ivan Vladimirovich SHPAKOV (RUS) (64' Guntars SILAGAILIS). (Coach: Genadijs
MOROZOVS).
Goal: IF Elfsborg: 1-0 Denni AVDIC (18').
Referee: Oleh ORIEKHOV (UKR)   Attendance: 3.351

19-07-2008   Stadion Saturn, Ramenskoje: FK Saturn Ramenskoje – VfB Stuttgart   1-0 (1-0)
FK Saturn Ramenskoje: Antonin KINSKY (CZE), Vadim Valentinovich EVSEEV, "ZELÃO"
Luiz Ricardo da Silva (BRA), Benoît Christian ANGBWA Ossoemeyang (CMR), Aleksey
IGONIN (45' Petr NEMOV), Alexei EREMENKO Jr. (FIN) (59' Roman VOROBIEV),
Andrey KARYAKA, Andrei GUSIN (UKR), Aleksey IVANOV, Marko TOPIC (BOS) (78'
Leonid KOVEL (BLS)), Dmitriy Sergeevich KIRICHENKO. (Coach: Gadzhi Muslimovich
GADZHIEV).
VfB Stuttgart: Alexander STOLZ, Serdar TASCI (YC89), Etienne Arthur BOKA (CIV),
Matthieu DELPIERRE (FRA), Jan SIMAK (CZE), Yildiray BASTÜRK (TUR) (66' Martin
LANIG), Pável PARDO Segura (MEX), Roberto HILBERT, Sami KHEDIRA, "CACAU"
Jeronimo Barreto Claudimir (BRA) (76' Manuel FISCHER), Danijel LJUBOJA (SRB) (YC24)
(46' Ciprian Andrei MARICA (ROM)). (Coach: Armin VEH).
Goal: FK Saturn Ramenskoje: 1-0 Dmitriy Sergeevich KIRICHENKO (4').
Referee: Peter RASMUSSEN (DEN)   Attendance: 9.500

229

19-07-2008   Stadion Letzigrund, Zürich:
Grasshopper-Club Zürich – FK Chernomorets Burgas   3-0 (2-0)
Grasshopper-Club Zürich: Eldin JAKUPOVIC, Kay VOSER, Guillermo VALLORI (ESP),
Josip COLINA (CRO), Boris SMILJANIC, Yassin MIKARI (TUN), Senad LULIC (BOS),
Veroljub SALATIC (SRB), Demba TOURÉ (SEN) (84' Steven ZUBER), Gonzalo Eulogio
ZÁRATE (ARG) (46' Paulo Rinaldo CRUZADO Durand (PER)), Raúl Marcelo BOBADILLA
(ARG) (63' Samel SABANOVIC (MNE)). (Coach: Hanspeter LATOUR).
FK Chernomorets Burgas: Vladislav STOJANOV, Trayan DYANKOV, Nikolai KRASTEV,
Stefan TRAYKOV, Martin KOVACHEV, Georgi KARAKANOV (46' Tsvetomir
TSONKOV), Vanco TRAJANOV (MCD), Shener HYUSEIN Remzi (52' Marin PETROV),
ADALTON Luis Juvenal (BRA) (YC6), LEANDRO Mesias Dos Santos (BRA) (77' Lyubomir
LYUBENOV), MICHEL Platini Ferreira Mesquita (BRA). (Coach: Dimitar "Héro"
DIMITROV).
Goals: Grasshopper-Club Zürich: 1-0 Veroljub SALATIC (21'), 2-0 Gonzalo Eulogio
ZÁRATE (41'), 3-0 Samel SABANOVIC (80').
Referee: Damien LEDENTU (FRA)   Attendance: 1.200

19-07-2008   Tofiq Bahramov Stadium, Baku: Neftchi Baku PFK – FC Vaslui   2-1 (1-1)
Neftchi Baku PFK: Vladimir MICOVIC (SRB), Dmitriy KRUGLOV (EST), Elnur
ALLAHVERDIEV, Volodimr OLEFIR (UKR) (YC41), Rashad A.SADIKHOV (YC51),
Olexandr CHERTOGANOV (YC59) (81' Ruslan ABUSHEV (YC88)), Martcho DAVTCHEV
(BUL) (71' Georgi CHELIDZE (GEO)), Rashad Ferhad SADIKHOV, Oleg GERASIMYUK
(UKR), Nazar BAYRAMOV (TMS) (69' Zaur TAGIZADE), Georgi ADAMIA (GEO).
(Coach: Anatoliy Vasiliyovich DEMYANENKO (UKR)).
FC Vaslui: Dusam KUCIAK (SVK), Bogdan Constantin BUHUS (YC9), Silviu Constantin
BALACE (YC22,YC68), Gabriel CANU, Daniel MUNTEANU, Stanislav GENCHEV (BUL),
Marian ALIUTA (65' Adrian GHEORGHIU (YC82)), Marko LJUBINKOVIC (SRB),
Ousmane N'DOYE (SEN), Lucian BURDUJAN (70' Neven MARKOVIC (SRB)), Mike
TEMWANJIRA (ZIM) (85' Nemanja JOVANOVIC (SRB)). (Coach: Viorel Doru HIZO).
Goals: Neftchi Baku PFK: 1-0 Oleg GERASIMYUK (27'), 2-1 Rashad A.SADIKHOV (87').
FC Vaslui: 1-1 Stanislav GENCHEV (29').
Referee: Igor EGOROV (RUS)   Attendance: 30.000

19-07-2008   UPC-Arena, Graz: SK Sturm Graz – Budapest Honvéd FC   0-0
SK Sturm Graz: Josef SCHICKLGRUBER, Fabian LAMOTTE (GER), Ferdinand
FELDHOFER, Ilia KANDELAKI (GEO), Petr HLINKA (SVK), Samir MURATOVIC (BOS)
(35' Jakob JANTSCHER), Mattias SEREINIG, Andreas HÖLZL (85' Patrick SCHERRER),
Marko STANKOVIC, Mario HAAS, Mario KIENZL (80' Daniel BEICHLER). (Coach:
Franco FODA (GER)).
Budapest Honvéd FC: Balázs RABÓCZKI, Mico SMILJANIC (SRB), Ákos TAKÁCS, Tamás
FILÓ, Béla MAROTI, Gellért IVÁNCSICS, Attila DOBOS (66' Dieng Cheikh ABASS
(SEN)), George GEBRO (LBR), Eugenio Fernando Bila "GENITO" (MOZ), Abraham Gneki
GUIÉ-GUIÉ (CIV) (84' Edouard NDJODO (CMR)), Zoltán HERCEGFALVI (78' Laszlo
BOJTOR). (Coach: Gábor PÖLÖSKEI).
Referee: Bjorn KUIPERS (HOL)   Attendance: 5.830

19-07-2008   Kiryat Eliezer Stadium, Haifa:
Ihoud Bnei Sakhnin FC – RC Deportivo la Coruña 1-2 (0-0)
Ihoud Bnei Sakhnin FC: Omri ALON, Paty Yeye LENKEBE (CGO) (YC59), Abed RABAH
(87' Halal KHALEILA), Allah Abu SALAH, Basem GENAIM, Yaniv LUZON (83' Imad
BADARNE), Haim BENON, Hamed GENAIM, Ali OTHMAN, Musa SHAABAN (66'
Muhammad RAIYA), Bernard DONG-BORTEY (GHA). (Coach: Freddy DAVID).
RC Deportivo la Coruña: Fabricio Agosto Ramírez "FABRI", MANUEL PABLO García Díaz,
ADRIÁN López Rodríguez "PISCU", FILIPE Luís Kasmirski (BRA), Alberto LOPO García,
Juan Antonio González Fernández "JUANAN", Ángel LAFITA Castillo, SERGIO González
Soriano (74' Joan VERDÚ Fernández), Juan Carlos VALERÓN Santana (82' PABLO
ÁLVAREZ Núñez), JUAN Antonio RODRÍGUEZ Villanueva (YC50), Iván Sánchez-Rico
Soto "RIKI" (66' Francisco Jiménez Tejada "XISCO" (YC82)). (Coach: Miguel Ángel
LOTINA Oruechebarría).
Goals: Ihoud Bnei Sakhnin FC: 1-2 Basem GENAIM (59').
RC Deportivo la Coruña: 0-1 Ángel LAFITA Castillo (54'), 0-2 Iván Sánchez-Rico Soto
"RIKI" (57').
Referee: Fredy FAUTREL (FRA)   Attendance: 3.000

19-07-2008   Stade de la Route de Lorient, Rennes:
Stade Rennais FC – SK Tavriya Simferopol 1-0 (0-0)
Stade Rennais FC: Nicolas DOUCHEZ, Guillaume BORNE, Petter HANSSON (SWE), Bira
DEMBÉLÉ, Jérôme LEROY, Bruno CHEYROU, Fabien LEMOINE, Romain DANZÉ,
Mickaël PAGIS (85' Sylvain MARVEAUX), Olivier THOMERT (78' Rod FANNI (YC88)),
Moussa SOW (78' Jirès KEMBO Ekoko (DRC)). (Coach: Guy LACOMBE).
SK Tavriya Simferopol: Andrey DIKAN (RUS), Vidas ALUNDERIS (LIT) (YC83), Pawel
HAJDUCZEK (POL), Dmitro NAZAROV, Taras ILNITSKIY, Illya GALYUZA, Zeljko
LJUBENOVIC (SRB), Denis GOLAYDO, Lucky Isi IDAHOR (NGR) (90' Andriy
ZBOROVSKIY), Volodimir HOMENYUK, Vasil GIGIADZE (GEO) (43' Oleksandr
KOVPAK). (Coach: Mykhailo FOMENKO).
Goal: Stade Rennais FC: 1-0 Rod FANNI (90'+2').
Referee: Nicola RIZZOLI (ITA)   Attendance: 12.500

19-07-2008   Rat Verlegh Stadion, Breda: N.A.C. Breda – Rosenborg BK 1-0 (1-0)
N.A.C. Breda: Jelle TEN ROUWELAAR, Rob PENDERS (YC87), Patrick ZWAANSWIJK
(74' Donny GORTER (BEL)), Ahmed AMMI (MAR), Tyrone Gabriel LORAN (AHO), Kees
KWAKMAN, Joonas KOLKKA (FIN) (79' Ellery CAIRO), Patrick MTILIGA (DEN), Ronnie
STAM, Anthony LURLING, Matthew AMOAH (GHA) (90'+1' Fouad IDABDELHAY).
(Coach: Robert Patrick MAASKANT).
Rosenborg BK: Rune Almenning JARSTEIN, Fredrik STOOR (SWE), Eduardo Alejandro
LAGO Correa (URU), Andreas Kristoffer NORDVIK, Roy MILLER (CRC), Roar STRAND
(78' Øyvind STORFLOR), Alexander Banor TETTEY (YC89), Per Ciljan SKJELBRED (84'
John PELU (SWE)), Marek SAPARA (SVK), Yssouf KONÉ (BKF) (44' Jo Sondre AAS),
Steffen IVERSEN. (Coach: Erik HAMRÉN (SWE)).
Goal: N.A.C. Breda: 1-0 Matthew AMOAH (19').
Referee: Levan PANIASHVILI (GEO)

231

19-07-2008   Fionia Park, Odense: Odense BK – Aston Villa FC   2-2 (1-1)
Odense BK: Arkadiusz ONYSZKO (POL), Atle Roar HÅLAND, Anders MØLLER
CHRISTENSEN (YC86), Thomas HELVEG, Chris SØRENSEN, Hans Henrik
ANDREASEN, Henrik HANSEN, Ebsen HANSEN (28' Eric DJEMBA-DJEMBA (CMR)),
Djiby Baye FALL (SEN), Björn Sandro RUNSTRÖM (SWE) (79' Christián BOLAÑOS
Navarro (CRC)), Johan ABSALONSEN. (Coach: Lars Christian OLSEN).
Aston Villa FC: Stuart TAYLOR, Wilfred BOUMA (HOL), Martin LAURSEN (DEN),
Zatyiah KNIGHT, Steven SIDWELL (82' Wayne Neville ROUTLEGDE), Ashley Simon
YOUNG (YC32), Stilian PETROV (BUL), Nigel REO-COKER, Craig GARDNER, John
Alieu CAREW (NOR) (YC29), Gabriel AGBONLAHOR. (Coach: Martin Hugh Michael
O'NEILL (NIR)).
Goals: Odense BK: 1-1 Steven SIDWELL (25' own goal), 2-2 Anders MØLLER
CHRISTENSEN (90').
Aston Villa FC: 0-1 John Alieu CAREW (7'), 1-2 Martin LAURSEN (76').
Referee: Andrea DE MARCO (ITA)   Attendance: 11.393

20-07-2008   Stádio Néas Smýrnis, Néa Smýrni:
              PAE Panionios FC Athens – SSC Napoli   0-1 (0-1)
PAE Panionios FC Athens: Dario KRESIC (CRO), Ioannis Georgios MANIATIS, Evangelos
KOUTSOPOULOS, Ivica MAJSTORIVIC (GER), Matthias LANGKAMP (GER), Dimitris
KILIARAS (YC55) (73' WAGNER RIBEIRO (BRA)), Euripidis-Grigorios Vasileios MAKOS
(YC90+1), Bennard Yao KUMORDZI (GHA), Marios NICOLAOU (CYP) (57' Dimitris
SIALMAS), Manolis Konstantinos SKOUFALIS (YC32) (79' Michael DELURA), Lampros
CHOUTOS. (Coach: Ewald LIENEN (GER)).
SSC Napoli: Gennaro IEZZO, Paolo CANNAVARO, Matteo CONTINI, Leandro RINAUDO
(YC65,YC77), Luigi VITALE (YC69), Manuele BLASI, Christian MAGGIO, Marek
HAMSÍK (SVK) (83' Michele PAZIENZA), Mariano Adrian BOGLIACINO (URU) (74' João
Batista INÁCIO "PIÁ" (BRA)), Walter Alejandro GARGANO Guevara (URU), Germán
Gustavo DENIS (ARG). (Coach: Edoardo "Edy" REJA).
Goals: SSC Napoli: 0-1 Mariano Adrian BOGLIACINO (31').
Referee: Duarte Nuno PEREIRA GOMES (POR)

20-07-2008   Sivas 4 Eylül Stadi, Sivas:
              Sivasspor Kulübü – Sporting Clube de Braga   0-2 (0-1)
Sivasspor Kulübü: Volkan ÜNLÜ, FÁBIO BILICA Alves da Silva (BRA), Alimou Mamadou
DIALLO (GUI) (YC74), Hayrettin YERLIKAYA (YC13), Onur TUNCER (YC81), Musa
AYDIN (52' Hervé TUM (CMR)), Kanfory SYLLA (GUI) (YC31) (62' SERGIO Pacheco de
Oliveira (BRA)), Ibrahim DAGASAN, Abdurrahman DERELI, Mehmet YILDIZ (YC55), Pini
Felix BALILI (ISR) (73' Faruk BAYAR (YC81)). (Coach: Bülent UYGUN).
Sporting Clube de Braga: EDUARDO dos Reis Carvalho, MOISÉS Moura Pinheuro (ANG),
EVALDO dos Santos Fabiano (BRA), Nuno Miguel FRECHAUT Barreto, ANDRÉ Augusto
LEONE (BRA), JOÃO Pedro da Silva PEREIRA, Luís Bernardo AGUIAR Burgos (URU)
(73' MATHEUS Leite Nascimento (BRA)), Vanderson Valter De Almeida "VANDINHO"
(BRA), PAULO CÉSAR Rocha Rosa (BRA) (46' STÉLVIO Rosa da Cruz), Wenderson
Arruda Said "WENDER" (BRA) (90'+2' FILIPE Vilaça de OLIVEIRA), Roland LINZ (AUT).
(Coach: JORGE Fernando Pinheiro de JESUS).
Goals: Sporting Clube de Braga: 0-1 Roland LINZ (45'+1'), 0-2 MOISÉS Moura Pinheuro
(78').
Referee: Douglas George McDONALD (SCO)

232

26-07-2008   Lokomotiv Stadion, Simferopol:
SK Tavriya Simferopol – Stade Rennais FC   1-0 (0-0)
SK Tavriya Simferopol: Andrey DIKAN (RUS), Vidas ALUNDERIS (LIT), Pawel HAJDUCZEK (POL) (YC63), Taras ILNITSKIY, Slobodan MARKOVIC (SRB) (98' Andriy DONETS), Illya GALYUZA, Zeljko LJUBENOVIC (SRB), Denis GOLAYDO (YC75), Lucky Isi IDAHOR (NGR) (106' Oleksandr KOVPAK), Volodimir HOMENYUK (112' Andriy ZBOROVSKIY), Vasil GIGIADZE (GEO). (Coach: Mykhailo FOMENKO).
Stade Rennais FC: Nicolas DOUCHEZ, Guillaume BORNE (90'+1' Elderson Uwa ECHIÉJILÉ (NGR)), Rod FANNI, Petter HANSSON (SWE), Bira DEMBÉLÉ, Sylvain MARVEAUX (82' Jérôme LEROY), Fabien LEMOINE (YC90+3), Olivier SORLIN, Romain DANZÉ (YC101), Olivier THOMERT, Daniel MOREIRA (YC41) (70' Mickaël PAGIS (YC113)). (Coach: Guy LACOMBE).
Goal: SK Tavriya Simferopol: 1-0 Vasil GIGIADZE (71').
Referee: Stefan JOHANNESSON (SWE)

Penalties:	1 Jérôme LEROY	1 Illya GALYUZA
	2 Mickaël PAGIS	2 Denis GOLAYDO
	* Olivier THOMERT	* Andriy DONETS
	* Fabien LEMOINE	3 Vasil GIGIADZE
	3 Petter HANSSON	* Zeljko LJUBENOVIC
	4 Olivier SORLIN	4 Andriy ZBOROVSKIY
	5 Rod FANNI	5 Taras ILNITSKIY
	6 Romain DANZÉ	6 Vidas ALUNDERIS
	7 Elderson Uwa ECHIÉJILÉ	7 Pawel HAJDUCZEK
	8 Bira DEMBÉLÉ	8 Oleksandr KOVPAK
	9 Nicolas DOUCHEZ	9 Andrey DIKAN
	10 Jérôme LEROY	* Illya GALYUZA

26-07-2008   Villa Park, Birmingham: Aston Villa FC – Odense BK   1-0 (0-0)
Aston Villa FC: Stuart TAYLOR, Wilfred BOUMA (HOL) (15' Gareth BARRY), Martin LAURSEN (DEN), Zatyiah KNIGHT, Steven SIDWELL, Ashley Simon YOUNG, Stilian PETROV (BUL), Nigel REO-COKER, Craig GARDNER, John Alieu CAREW (NOR), Gabriel AGBONLAHOR. (Coach: Martin Hugh Michael O'NEILL (NIR)).
Odense BK: Arkadiusz ONYSZKO (POL), Atle Roar HÅLAND, Thomas HELVEG (46' Espen RUUD (NOR)), Chris SØRENSEN, Jonas TROEST, Hans Henrik ANDREASEN (74' Christián BOLAÑOS Navarro (CRC)), Henrik HANSEN, Eric DJEMBA-DJEMBA (CMR), Djiby Baye FALL (SEN), Björn Sandro RUNSTRÖM (SWE) (81' Anders K.JACOBSEN), Johan ABSALONSEN (YC58). (Coach: Lars Christian OLSEN).
Goal: Aston Villa FC: 1-0 Ashley Simon YOUNG (50').
Referee: Cüneyt ÇAKIR (TUR)   Attendance: 31.423

26-07-2008   Stadionul Municipal, Vaslui: FC Vaslui – Neftchi Baku PFK   2-0 (2-0)
FC Vaslui: Dusam KUCIAK (SVK), Bogdan Constantin BUHUS, HUGO Duarte de Sousa
LUZ (POR), Gabriel CANU (YC80), Daniel MUNTEANU, Stanislav GENCHEV (BUL),
Marian ALIUTA (YC44) (73' Adrian GHEORGHIU), Marko LJUBINKOVIC (SRB) (63'
Petar JOVANOVIC (BOS)), Ousmane N'DOYE (SEN), Lucian BURDUJAN (90'+2' Vasile
Bogdan PANAIT), Mike TEMWANJIRA (ZIM). (Coach: Viorel Doru HIZO).
Neftchi Baku PFK: Vladimir MICOVIC (SRB), Rail MELIKOV, Dmitriy KRUGLOV (EST)
(87' Eshgin GULIYEV), Elnur ALLAHVERDIEV (YC75), Martcho DAVTCHEV (BUL),
Rashad Ferhad SADIKHOV (YC52), Ruslan ABUSHEV (73' Georgi CHELIDZE (GEO)),
Oleg GERASIMYUK (UKR) (YC81), Nazar BAYRAMOV (TMS) (YC87), Georgi ADAMIA
(GEO), Zaur TAGIZADE. (Coach: Anatoliy Vasiliyovich DEMYANENKO (UKR)).
Goals: FC Vaslui: 1-0 Lucian BURDUJAN (30'), 2-0 Mike TEMWANJIRA (38').
Referee: Robert SCHÖRGENHOFER (AUT)   Attendance: 5.000

26-07-2008   Georgi Asparukhov Stadium, Sofia:
                    FK Chernomorets Burgas – Grasshopper-Club Zürich   0-1 (0-0)
FK Chernomorets Burgas: Vladislav STOJANOV, Trayan DYANKOV (YC22), Nikolai
KRASTEV (YC57), Stefan TRAYKOV (YC84), Martin KOVACHEV (YC71), Vanco
TRAJANOV (MCD), Tsvetomir TSONKOV (YC45), Marin PETROV, ADALTON Luis
Juvenal (BRA) (67' Ivan CVOROVIC (SRB)), LEANDRO Mesias Dos Santos (BRA) (46'
Ljubomir BOZHINOV), MICHEL Platini Ferreira Mesquita (BRA) (19' Lyubomir
LYUBENOV). (Coach: Dimitar "Héro" DIMITROV).
Grasshopper-Club Zürich: Eldin JAKUPOVIC, Kay VOSER, Guillermo VALLORI (ESP)
(YC75), Josip COLINA (CRO), Boris SMILJANIC, Pasquale SBARRA (ITA), Senad LULIC
(BOS) (82' Demba TOURÉ (SEN)), Ricardo CABANAS (64' Leonel ROMERO), Veroljub
SALATIC (SRB), Samel SABANOVIC (MNE) (46' Raúl Marcelo BOBADILLA (ARG)
(YC57)), Steven ZUBER. (Coach: Hanspeter LATOUR).
Goal: Grasshopper-Club Zürich: 0-1 Raúl Marcelo BOBADILLA (53').
Referee: Brage SANDMOEN (NOR)

26-07-2008   Estádio Municipal de Braga, Braga:
                    Sporting Clube de Braga – Sivasspor Kulübü   3-0 (1-0)
Sporting Clube de Braga: EDUARDO dos Reis Carvalho, MOISÉS Moura Pinheiro (ANG),
EVALDO dos Santos Fabiano (BRA), Nuno Miguel FRECHAUT Barreto (YC46), ANDRÉ
Augusto LEONE (BRA), JOÃO Pedro da Silva PEREIRA, Luís Bernardo AGUIAR Burgos
(URU), Vanderson Valter De Almeida "VANDINHO" (BRA), Wenderson Arruda Said
"WENDER" (BRA) (YC28) (84' JorgeLuíz Pereira de Sousa "JORGINHO" (BRA)), Roland
LINZ (AUT) (84' ORLANDO Carlos Braga de SÀ), MATHEUS Leite Nascimento (BRA)
(71' STÉLVIO Rosa da Cruz). (Coach: JORGE Fernando Pinheiro de JESUS).
Sivasspor Kulübü: Akin VARDAR, FÁBIO BILICA Alves da Silva (BRA) (60' Murat
SÖZGELMEZ (YC81)), Alimou Mamadou DIALLO (GUI) (YC65), Musa AYDIN, Kanfory
SYLLA (GUI) (YC26), SERGIO Pacheco de Oliveira (BRA), Ibrahim DAGASAN (54' Hervé
TUM (CMR) (YC72)), Ilhan UMMAK, Abdurrahman DERELI (36' Faruk BAYAR), Devran
AYHAN, Pini Felix BALILI (ISR) (YC39). (Coach: Bülent UYGUN).
Goals: Sporting Clube de Braga: 1-0 MATHEUS Leite Nascimento (45'), 2-0 Roland LINZ
(57'), 3-0 Luís Bernardo AGUIAR Burgos (70' penalty).
Referee: Dr. Felix BRYCH (GER)

26-07-2008   József Bozsik Stadium, Budapest:
Budapest Honvéd FC – SK Sturm Graz   1-2 (1-0)
Budapest Honvéd FC: Balázs RABÓCZKI (YC63), Mico SMILJANIC (SRB), Zoltan
VINCZE (YC90+2), Ákos TAKÁCS (YC73), Tamás FILÓ (YC38), Béla MAROTI (YC45)
(78' Róbert ZSOLNAI), Gellért IVÁNCSICS (60' George GEBRO (LBR)), Attila DOBOS
(66' Dieng Cheikh ABASS (SEN)), Eugenio Fernando Bila "GENITO" (MOZ), Edouard
NDJODO (CMR) (YC12), Zoltán HERCEGFALVI. (Coach: Gábor PÖLÖSKEI).
SK Sturm Graz: Josef SCHICKLGRUBER, Fabian LAMOTTE (GER), Mario
SONNLEITNER, Ferdinand FELDHOFER (63' Andreas HÖLZL), Georgi SHASHIASHVILI
(GEO), Ilia KANDELAKI (GEO), Petr HLINKA (SVK) (66' Samir MURATOVIC (BOS)),
Daniel BEICHLER, Mario HAAS (83' Mattias SEREINIG), Jakob JANTSCHER, Mario
KIENZL. (Coach: Franco FODA (GER)).
Goals: Budapest Honvéd FC: 1-0 Mico SMILJANIC (8').
SK Sturm Graz: 1-1 Daniel BEICHLER (72'), 1-2 Mario HAAS (77').
Referee: Alan KELLY (IRL)

26-07-2008   Estadio Municipal de Riazor, La Coruña:
RC Deportivo la Coruña – Ihoud Bnei Sakhnin FC   1-0 (1-0)
RC Deportivo la Coruña: Fabricio Agosto Ramírez "FABRI", MANUEL PABLO García Díaz,
FILIPE Luís Kasmirski (BRA) (YC), ADRÍAN López Rodríguez "PISCU", Alberto LOPO
García (46' José Eduardo Rosa Vale de "ZÉ" CASTRO (POR)), Juan Antonio González
Fernández "JUANAN", Ángel LAFITA Castillo, ANTONIO TOMÁS González, Juan Carlos
VALERÓN Santana (61' Miguel Ángel Ferrer Martínez "MISTA"), JUAN Antonio
RODRÍGUEZ Villanueva, Iván Sánchez-Rico Soto "RIKI" (72' Omar BRAVO Tordecillas
(MEX)). (Coach: Miguel Ángel LOTINA Oruechebarría).
Ihoud Bnei Sakhnin FC: Omri ALON, Paty Yeye LENKEBE (CGO), Abed RABAH, Allah
Abu SALAH (46' Emmanuel Mazuwa NSUMBU (DRC)), Basem GENAIM, Halal
KHALEILA, Yaniv LUZON, Haim BENON, Hamed GENAIM, Ali OTHMAN, Musa
SHAABAN (60' Bernard DONG-BORTEY (GHA)). (Coach: Freddy DAVID).
Goal: RC Deportivo la Coruña: 1-0 Juan Carlos VALERÓN Santana (40').
Referee: Bas NIJHUIS (HOL)   Attendance: 6.000

26-07-2008   Stadio San Paolo, Napoli: SSC Napoli – PAE Panionios FC Athens   1-0 (0-0)
SSC Napoli: Gennaro IEZZO, Gianluca GRAVA, Paolo CANNAVARO, Matteo CONTINI,
Luigi VITALE, Manuele BLASI (YC44), Christian MAGGIO, Marek HAMSÍK (SVK)
(YC74) (75' Michele PAZIENZA), Mariano Adrian BOGLIACINO (URU) (59' João Batista
INÁCIO "PIÁ" (BRA)), Walter Alejandro GARGANO Guevara (URU), Germán Gustavo
DENIS (ARG) (83' Roberto DE ZERBI). (Coach: Edoardo "Edy" REJA).
PAE Panionios FC Athens: Dario KRESIC (CRO), Ioannis Georgios MANIATIS, Evangelos
KOUTSOPOULOS (80' Kostantinos Ioannis KAPETANOS), Ivica MAJSTORIVIC (GER),
Matthias LANGKAMP (GER) (YC60), Giorgios TZAVELLAS (YC67), Dimitris KILIARAS,
Bennard Yao KUMORDZI (GHA) (YC36), Marios NICOLAOU (CYP), Alexandre Joaquim
D'ACOL (BRA) (72' Giannis KONTOES), Lampros CHOUTOS (55' Michael DELURA).
(Coach: Ewald LIENEN (GER)).
Goal: SSC Napoli: 1-0 Marek HAMSÍK (65').
Referee: César MUÑIZ FERNÁNDEZ (ESP)

27-07-2008   Lerkendal Stadion, Trondheim: Rosenborg BK – N.A.C. Breda   2-0 (1-0)
Rosenborg BK: Alexander Lund HANSEN, Fredrik STOOR (SWE) (90'+3' Christer
BASMA), Vadim DEMIDOV (YC90+1,YC90+3), Eduardo Alejandro LAGO Correa (URU),
Andreas Kristoffer NORDVIK, Roy MILLER (CRC), Alexander Banor TETTEY, Per Ciljan
SKJELBRED (81' Roar STRAND), Marek SAPARA (SVK), Didier KONAN Ya (CIV),
Steffen IVERSEN (70' John PELU (SWE)). (Coach: Erik HAMRÉN (SWE)).
N.A.C. Breda: Jim VAN FESSEM, Rob PENDERS, Patrick ZWAANSWIJK (YC51), Ahmed
AMMI (MAR) (YC64), Kees KWAKMAN (87' Fouad IDABDELHAY), Joonas KOLKKA
(FIN) (79' Csaba FEHÉR (HUN)), Patrick MTILIGA (DEN), Ronnie STAM (YC72), Anthony
LURLING (YC37), Matthew AMOAH (GHA), Donny GORTER (BEL) (69' Gerardus
Johannes Paulus TAMERUS). (Coach: Robert Patrick MAASKANT).
Goals: Rosenborg BK: 1-0 Fredrik STOOR (34'), 2-0 Steffen IVERSEN (50' penalty).
Referee: Pavel Cristian BALAJ (ROM)   Attendance: 5.815

27-07-2008   Daugavas stadions, Liepaja: FK Riga – IF Elfsborg   0-0
FK Riga: Sergey Andreevich CHEPCHUGOV (RUS), Aleksanders LASKO, Dimitrijs
HALVITOVS (YC45,YC84), Igors KORABLOVS, Gints FREIMANIS, Evgeniy NOVIKOV
(EST), Grigory Alexandrovich CHIRKIN (RUS) (YC34), Andrei Valentinovich AGAFONOV
(RUS), Valeriy Viktorovich LEONOV (RUS) (79' Olegs ZATKINS), Mindaugas KALONAS
(LIT), Vladimirs ZAVORONKOVS. (Coach: Andrei Ivanovich MANANNIKOV (TJK)).
IF Elfsborg: Johan WILAND, Mathias FLORÉN, Johan KARLSSON, Martin ANDERSSON
(YC54), Daniel MOBÄCK (YC84), Andreas AUGUSTSSON, Helgi Valur DANÍELSSON
(ISL) (20' Elmin KURBEGOVIC (BOS)), Anders SVENSSON (43' Emir BAJRAMI), Denni
AVDIC, Stefan ISHIZAKI, Lasse NILSSON (78' Joakim SJÖHAGE). (Coach: Magnus
HAGLUND).
Referee: Alexey NIKOLAEV (RUS)

27-07-2008   Gottlieb-Daimler-Stadion, Stuttgart:
             VfB Stuttgart – FK Saturn Ramenskoje   3-0 (0-0)
VfB Stuttgart: Alexander STOLZ, Ricardo OSORIO Mendoza (MEX) (51' Sami KHEDIRA),
Serdar TASCI, Etienne Arthur BOKA (CIV) (52' Manuel FISCHER), Matthieu DELPIERRE
(FRA) (YC65), Ludovic MAGNIN (SUI), Jan SIMAK (CZE) (YC80), Yildiray BASTÜRK
(TUR) (74' Martin LANIG), Pável PARDO Segura (MEX), Roberto HILBERT, Ciprian
Andrei MARICA (ROM). (Coach: Armin VEH).
FK Saturn Ramenskoje: Antonin KINSKY (CZE), Vadim Valentinovich EVSEEV (YC102),
"ZELÃO" Luiz Ricardo da Silva (BRA) (YC32), Benoît Christian ANGBWA Ossoemeyang
(CMR), Aleksey IGONIN (YC49), Petr NEMOV, Andrey KARYAKA (YC70) (88' Dmitriy
Vyacheslavovich LOSKOV), Andrei GUSIN (UKR), Roman VOROBIEV (53' Alexei
EREMENKO Jr. (FIN)), Aleksey IVANOV, Marko TOPIC (BOS) (78' Dmitriy Sergeevich
KIRICHENKO). (Coach: Gadzhi Muslimovich GADZHIEV).
Goals: VfB Stuttgart: 1-0 Jan SIMAK (82'), 2-0 Ciprian Andrei MARICA (107'), 3-0 Ciprian
Andrei MARICA (110').
Referee: Bernardino GONZÁLEZ VÁZQUEZ (ESP)   Attendance: 12.600
(After extra time)

Aston Villa FC, RC Deportivo la Coruña, IF Elfsborg, Grasshopper-Club Zürich, SSC
Napoli, Rosenborg BK, Sporting Clube de Braga, Stade Rennais FC, SK Sturm Graz,
VfB Stuttgart and FC Vaslui all qualified for the UEFA Cup competition.

Intertoto Cup Participating clubs between 2002 and 2008

Club	Country	2002	2003	2004	2005	2006	2007	2008
Aalborg BK	DEN						X	
Aberystwyth Town FC	WAL			X				
Akademisk BK	DEN	X						
Akratitos FC	GRE		X					
AC Allianssi	FIN		X					
BB Ankaraspor Kulübü	TUR				X			
FC Ararat Yerevan	ARM						X	
FC MKT Araz Imishli	AZE					X		
FC Ashdod	ISR	X						
Aston Villa FC	ENG	X						X
Athletic Club Bilbao	ESP				X			
FK Atlantas Klaipeda	LIT			X				
Club Atlético de Madrid	ESP			X			X	
AJ Auxerre	FRA					X		
B68 Toftír	FAR	X						
FK Baki	AZE						X	
Ballymena United FC	NIR			X				
Bangor City FC	WAL		X		X			
FC BATE Borisov	BLS	X						
Beitar Jerusalem FC	ISR				X			
CF OS Belenenses	POR	X						
KS Besa Kavajë	ALB							X
Birkirkara FC	MLT						X	
Blackburn Rovers FC	ENG						X	
Bohemians FC	IRL				X			X
FC Bologna	ITA	X						
Borussia Dortmund	GER			X	X			
SW Bregenz	AUT	X		X				
Brescia Calcio SpA	ITA		X					
1.FC Brno	CZE		X					
NK Brotnjo Citluk	BOS	X						

Club	Country	2002	2003	2004	2005	2006	2007	2008
Budapest Honvéd FC	HUN							X
FK Buducnost Podgorica	SBM			X				
Caersws FC	WAL	X						
Carmarthen Town AFC	WAL				X			
FC Ceahlaul Piatra Neamt	ROM		X					
NK Celik Zenica	BOS							X
FK Cementarnica 55	MCD	X						
RSC Charleroi	BEL				X			
PFC Cherno More Varna	BUL						X	
FK Chernomorets Burgas	BUL							X
FK Chornomorets Odessa	UKR						X	
HNK Cibalia Vinkovci	CRO			X				
Cliftonville FC	NIR						X	
CFR Cluj	ROM				X			
Coleraine FC	NIR	X						
FC Constructorul Cioburci	MOL	X						
Cork City FC	IRL			X			X	
KS Cracovia Kraków	POL							X
FC Dacia Chisinau	MOL			X			X	
Debreceni VSC	HUN			X				
RC Deportivo la Coruña	ESP				X			X
FC Differdange 03	LUX						X	
FC Dila Gori	GEO			X				
FC Dinaburg Daugavpils	LAT	X	X	X	X	X	X	
FC Dinamo Minsk	BLS				X			
FC Dinamo Tbilisi	GEO					X		
KS Dinamo Tiranë	ALB				X			
FC Dnipro Dnipropetrovsk	UKR					X		
NK Drava Ptuj	SLO				X			
Dungannon Swifts FC	NIR					X		
Egaleo FC Athens	GRE	X	X		X			
FK Ekranas Panevezys	LIT							X

Club	Country	2002	2003	2004	2005	2006	2007	2008
IF Elfsborg	SWE							X
En Avant Guingamp	FRA		X					
FC Encamp Dicoansa	AND		X					
Enosis Neon Paralimni FC	CYP	X						
Esbjerg FB	DEN			X				
Ethnikós Áchnas FC	CYP		X	X		X	X	X
FC Etzella Ettelbruck	LUX							X
FC Farul Constanta	ROM					X		
F.H. Hafnarfjördur	ISL	X						
Fulham FC	ENG	X						
IF Fylkir	ISL			X				X
KRC Genk	BEL			X				
KAA Gent	BEL	X		X	X	X		
KFC Germinal Beerschot	BEL							X
GI Gøtu	FAR		X					
FC Gloria Bistrita	ROM	X	X	X	X		X	
ND Gorica	SLO							X
Grasshopper-Club	SUI					X		X
OFK Grbalj Radanovici	MNE						X	X
CS Grevenmacher	LUX				X		X	
Györi ETO FC	HUN		X					
NK Hajduk Kula	SRB						X	
FC Haka Valkeakosken	FIN	X						
Hamburger SV	GER				X	X		X
Hammarby IF	SWE						X	
Hapoel Beer Sheva FC	ISR			X				
H.B. Tórshavn	FAR						X	X
SC Heerenveen	HOL		X					
Helsingborgs IF	SWE	X						
Hertha BSC Berlin	GER					X		
Hibernian FC Edinburgh	SCO			X		X		X
Hibernians FC Malta	MLT		X	X				X

Club	Country	2002	2003	2004	2005	2006	2007	2008
FC Honka Espoo	FIN						X	
Í.A. Akranes	ISL			X				
I.F.K. Göteborg	SWE			X				
Ihoud Bnei Sakhnin FC	ISR							X
FC International Turku	FIN				X			
K.A. Akureyri	ISL		X					
1.FC Kaiserslautern	GER	X						
Kalmar FF	SWE					X		
NK Kamen Ingrad Velika	CRO			X				
FK Karvan Evlakh	AZE				X			
Kayserispor Kulübü	TUR					X		
IB Keflavík	ISL					X		
FK Khazar Universiteti	AZE			X				
KÍ Klaksvík	FAR						X	
FC Kilikia Yerevan	ARM					X		
Kispest Honvéd FC	HUN	X						
NK Koper	SLO	X	X					
FC Kotayk Abovyan	ARM		X					
FC Krylya Sovetov Samara	RUS	X						
AE Larisa	GRE					X		
SS Lazio Roma	ITA				X			
KKS Lech Poznán	POL					X	X	
WKS Legia Warszawa	POL						X	
FC Lernagorts Ararat	ARM					X		
FC Levadia Maardu	EST	X						
K.Lierse SK	BEL			X				
Lille Olympique SC	FRA	X		X				
Lillestrøm SK	NOR					X		
Lisburn Distillery FC	NIR				X			X
Llanelli AFC	WAL						X	
KSC Lokeren	BEL	X			X			
PFC Lokomotiv Plovdiv	BUL					X		

Club	Country	2002	2003	2004	2005	2006	2007	2008
FC Lokomotivi Tbilisi	GEO							X
Lombard-Pápa TFC	HUN				X			
Maccabi Haifa FC	ISR						X	
Maccabi Nethanya FC	ISR		X					
Maccabi Petach Tikva FC	ISR					X		
FK Makedonija Skopje	MCD						X	
Málaga CF	ESP	X						
Malmö FF	SWE				X			
FC Marek Dupnitsa	BUL	X	X	X				
NK Maribor	SLO					X	X	
Marsaxlokk FC	MLT					X		
Matáv FC Sopron	HUN				X			
FC MIKA Ashtarak	ARM							X
FK Moskva	RUS					X		
FC MTZ-RIPO Minsk	BLS					X		
TSV 1860 München	GER	X						
Myllykosken Pallo-47	FIN				X			
N.A.C. Breda	HOL	X						X
FC Nantes	FRA		X	X				
SSC Napoli	ITA							X
N.E.C. Nijmegen	HOL				X			
Neftchi Baku PFK	AZE							X
FC Neman Grodno	BLS					X		
Neuchâtel-Xamax FC	SUI					X		
Newcastle United FC	ENG					X	X	
FC Nitra	SVK						X	X
NSÍ Runavík	FAR				X			
FK Obilic Beograd	YUG	X						
Odense BK	DEN			X		X		X
MKS Odra Wodzislaw Slaski	POL			X	X			
FC O.F.I. Crete	GRE						X	
O.F.K. Beograd	SBM		X	X				X

Club	Country	2002	2003	2004	2005	2006	2007	2008
O.G.C. Nice	FRA		X	X				
FC Otelul Galati	ROM						X	
Olympiakos FC Nicosia	CYP		X		X			
Olympique de Marseille	FRA			X	X			
Omagh Town FC	NIR		X					
Örgryte IS	SWE		X					
NK Osijek	CRO					X		
FK Ozeta Dukla Trencin	SVK	X						
PAE Panionios FC Athens	GRE							X
KS Partizani Tiranë	ALB		X		X			
SV Pasching	AUT		X					
AC Perugia	ITA	X	X					
FK Pobeda Prilep	MCD		X		X	X		
KS Pogon Szczecin	POL				X			
KP Polonia Warszawa	POL		X					
NK Publikum Celje	SLO			X				
Racing Club de Lens	FRA				X		X	
FC Ranger's	AND				X			
SK Rapid Wien	AUT						X	
Real Racing Club Santander	ESP		X					
FK Renova	MCD							X
Rhyl FC	WAL							X
SV Ried	AUT					X		
FK Riga	LAT							X
HNK Rijeka	CRO	X						X
SV Roda JC	HOL			X	X			
Rosenborg BK	NOR							X
FC Rubin Kazan	RUS						X	
AS Saint-Etienne	FRA			X				
UC Sampdoria	ITA						X	
CD Santa Clara	POR	X						
UE Sant Julià	AND	X		X		X	X	

Club	Country	2002	2003	2004	2005	2006	2007	2008
FK Sartid Smederevo	SBM			X	X			
FK Saturn Ramenskoje	RUS							X
FC Schalke 04	GER		X	X				
FC Shakhter Soligorsk	BLS		X			X	X	
FC Shakhtyor Karaganda	KAZ					X		
Shamrock Rovers FC	IRL		X					
Shelbourne FC	IRL						X	
FC Shinnik Yaroslavl	RUS				X			
FC Shirak Gyumri	ARM	X						
SK Sigma Olomouc	CZE				X			
FK Sileks Kratovo	MCD				X			
K.Sint Truidense VV	BEL			X				
Sivasspor Kulübü	TUR							X
Skála ÍF	FAR				X			
NK Slaven Belupo	CRO	X		X	X			
FK Slavija Sarajevo	BOS						X	
FK Sloboda Tuzla	BOS		X	X				
SK Slovan Bratislava	SVK						X	
FC Slovan Liberec	CZE		X	X	X		X	
FC Sochaux Montbéliard	FRA	X						
FC Sopron	HUN					X		
FC Spartak Moskva	RUS				X			
FC Spartak Trnava	SVK		X	X				
Sporting Clube de Braga	POR							X
FC St.Gallen	SUI	X					X	
St.Patrick's Athletic FC	IRL	X						
Stade Rennais FC	FRA							X
FC Stavo Artikel Brno	CZE	X						
SK Sturm Graz	AUT				X			X
VfB Stuttgart	GER	X						X
FK Sutjeska Niksic	SBM		X					
1.FC Synot Staré Mêsto	CZE	X	X					

Club	Country	2002	2003	2004	2005	2006	2007	2008
Tampere United FC	FIN		X	X	X	X		
SK Tavriya Simferopol	UKR							X
FK Teplice	CZE	X		X		X		X
FK Tescoma Zlín	CZE			X	X			
KS Teuta Durrës	ALB	X		X				
FC Thun	SUI			X	X			
FC Tiligul Tiraspol	MOL					X		
FC Tiraspol	MOL					X		X
FK Tobol Kostanay	KAZ			X			X	
AC Torino	ITA	X						
T.P.S. Turku	FIN							X
Trabzonspor Kulübü	TUR						X	
JK Trans Narva	EST		X	X	X	X		X
ES Troyes AC	FRA	X						
FC T.V.M.K. Tallinn	EST						X	
FC Twente Enschede	HOL					X		
União Desportiva Leiria	POR	X		X	X		X	
U.S. Luxembourg	LUX	X	X					
FC Utrecht	HOL						X	
Valencia CF	ESP				X			
Valletta FC	MLT	X			X			
Valur FC	ISL						X	
FK Vardar Skopje	MCD			X				
NK Varteks Varazdin	CRO					X		
Vasas SC	HUN					X		
FC Vaslui	ROM							X
FK Vetra (Rudiskes) Vilnius	LIT			X	X	X	X	
FC Victoria Rosport	LUX					X		
Videoton FC	HUN		X					
Villarreal CF	ESP	X	X	X			X	
KS Vllaznia Shkodër	ALB			X			X	
SV Werder Bremen	GER		X					

Club	Country	2002	2003	2004	2005	2006	2007	2008
KVC Westerlo	BEL			X				
FC Wil 1900	SUI		X					
Willem II Tilburg	HOL	X	X					
FC WIT Georgia Tbilisi	GEO	X	X		X			
VfL Wolfsburg	GER		X	X	X			
BSC Young Boys Bern	SUI				X			
MKS Zaglebie Lubin	POL	X						
NK Zagreb	CRO		X				X	
Zalaegerszegi TE	HUN						X	
FK Zalgiris Vilnius	LIT	X	X		X			
FC Zestaponi	GEO						X	
FK Zeta Golubovci	SBM					X		
FC Zhetysu Taldykorgan	KAZ							X
HSK Zrinjski Mostar	BOS					X		
FK ZTS Dubnica	SVK		X	X	X			
FC Zürich	SUI	X						